Lowe's Transport Manager's & Operator's Handbook 2020

50TH EDITION

Lowe's Transport Manager's & Operator's Handbook 2020

David Lowe and Clive Pidgeon

KoganPage

The masculine pronoun has been used in this book. This stems from a desire to avoid ugly and cumbersome language, and no discrimination, prejudice or bias is intended.

First published in Great Britain as *The Transport Manager's Handbook* in 1970 by Kogan Page Limited
Nineteenth edition published as *The Transport Manager's and Operator's Handbook* in 1989
Forty-first edition published as *Lowe's Transport Manager's and Operator's Handbook* in 2010
Fiftieth edition published in Great Britain and the United States in 2020

2nd Floor, 45 Gee Street
London
EC1V 3RS
United Kingdom

122 W 27th St, 10th Floor
New York, NY 10001
USA

4737/23 Ansari Road
Daryaganj
New Delhi 110002
India

www.koganpage.com

ISBNs
Hardback 978 1 78966 315 0
Paperback 978 1 78966 313 6
Ebook 978 1 78966 314 3
ISSN 2399-5114

British Library Cataloguing-in-Publication Data

A CIP record for this book is available from the British Library.

Typeset by Hong Kong FIVE Workshop
Print production managed by Jellyfish
Printed and bound by CPI Group (UK) Ltd, Croydon CR0 4YY

BRIEF CONTENTS

Appendices

CONTENTS

*Where reference is made to the EU, at the time of writing the rules and regulations referred to remain in force.

Appendices

BIOGRAPHICAL NOTES

David Lowe FCILT

David Lowe is a freelance writer and lecturer who has been actively involved with the road transport industry for many years.

He is the original author of *Lowe's Transport Manager's and Operator's Handbook*, now in its celebratory and noted 50th year of annual publication. His many other works include two best-selling titles for CPC students: *A Study Manual of Professional Competence in Road Haulage* (12 editions), *1001 Typical CPC Questions and Answers* (three editions), *Goods Vehicle Costing and Pricing Handbook* (four editions), *The Tachograph Manual* (two editions) and *The European Road Freighting Handbook* (1994), all published by Kogan Page. Two other works, *The Dictionary of Transport and Logistics* and *The Pocket Guide to LGV Drivers' Hours and Tachograph Law*, were published by Kogan Page in 2002 and 2006 (third edition) respectively.

He has written extensively for the transport press, including *Commercial Motor*, and also wrote a number of successful operator and driver handbooks for *Headlight* magazine. He was the author of the Chartered Institute of Purchasing and Supply (CIPS) graduate diploma study guides *Distribution* and *Storage and Distribution in Supply Chains* published in 2000 and 2003 respectively. Another of his works, *Intermodal Freight Transport*, was published by Elsevier in 2005.

With his detailed practical knowledge of UK and European transport law, David Lowe is well qualified to explain complex legal issues in layman's terms. He understands what the transport manager and small fleet operator need to know, and he tells them in no uncertain terms what they must and must not do to stay on the right side of the law.

He is a Chartered Fellow of the Chartered Institute of Logistics and Transport, a Freeman of the City of London and a Freeman of the Worshipful Company of Carmen. He is also a past winner of the Carmen's prestigious Herbert Crow silver medal award for 'consistent achievement for over thirty years as an outstanding freelance writer specializing in transport and logistics'.

Clive Pidgeon FCILT

Clive Pidgeon is a freelance writer, lecturer and examiner who has been actively involved with the road transport industry for many years. He has been co-author of *Lowe's Transport Manager's and Operator's Handbook*, now in its 50th year, since 2013. He recently wrote *A Study Guide for the Operator Certificate of Professional Competence (CPC) in Road Freight*, which is a self-study book published by Kogan Page for anybody interested in studying for the Operator CPC qualification but unable to attend a formal training course for whatever reason.

He has also written examinations for UK-based, European and Chinese transport and logistics qualification awarding bodies and writes technical text books relating to transport and logistics, including the current Operator Road Freight CPC qualification notes, offered by the CILT (UK). He has written the examination questions used by an accredited examination awarding body in the People's Republic of China where he has also lectured in several subjects and has worked on training and development projects in Central Asia.

He has worked in many other different countries, teaching transport studies, quality assuring examination delivery and awarding organizations and working on UN, EU and World Bank transport related projects and supports a host of domestic and international students undergoing distance learning courses relating to transport and logistics.

As an ex-practitioner, he is able to use years of experience and understanding to help clarify many of the more complicated facets of fleet management and control. He has also represented companies at public inquiries using his detailed knowledge of legal compliance standards to good advantage.

He is also a Chartered Fellow of the Chartered Institute of Logistics and Transport.

ACKNOWLEDGEMENTS

I am particularly grateful to my co-author Clive Pidgeon and all the many individuals and organizations that have provided helpful information for inclusion in this *Handbook*. During 50 years of writing the *Handbook* I have approached so many individuals, firms and industry-related organizations for information, guidance and assistance that it really is impossible to thank them all individually. Some are consulted regularly year after year; some have been newly sought out for guidance. There is no doubt that without such help the *Handbook* would not have achieved its prominence as the so-called 'bible' for transport managers and others. To all concerned, once again, I express my sincere thanks for their help.

Reference for information has been made to many sources – the legislation itself, both British and EU; published guides and notes; the Department for Transport (D*f*T) and its forebears; many D*f*T executive agencies, especially the Driver and Vehicle Standards Agency (DVSA) and the Driver and Vehicle Licensing Agency (DVLA); the Traffic Commissioners and their Traffic Area Office staff; and the enforcement authorities. Many other relevant bodies have been consulted and both the national press and the transport trade press have provided a continuous reminder of changing legislation and developments in the industry. Similarly, a constant flow of comments and questions from consultancy clients and seminar delegates has provided the source of many leads for inclusion of information and the inspiration to continue revising the contents of the *Handbook* to include more and more legislative detail. To all these publications, organizations and nameless individuals I am greatly indebted.

I would like to thank especially my wife Patricia and the many friends in the industry who are a constant source of encouragement and, as always, the editorial staff of Kogan Page whose help ensures yet another edition of the *Handbook*.

PREFACE TO THE 50TH EDITION

In the 50-year history of this *Handbook*, I have never yet been able to tell readers that they can look forward to less legislation in future rather than more, and this year will certainly be no different, not least because of the extended Brexit process. In fact it's the delay to Brexit that makes writing this year's Handbook such a problem because so much future legislation is somewhat unknown or at least only available in less than detailed format at the time of writing.

However, the content in this *Handbook* that relates to planned and future changes through 2020, as in 2019, has been researched and, as far as is reasonably possible, is accurate; which in itself is something of a coup given the lack of a crystal ball.

Clearly our leaving the EU will need international and national operations and regulations to be extensively revised and, one suspects, extensively rewritten, but as always we must view change as an opportunity for the British transport industry to seek out new markets, new ways of working, gain competitive advantage and to embrace innovative solutions.

Throughout the book many references are made relating to EU rules and regulations, etc and these will remain in force until the UK Government decides otherwise. As has always been believed, the UK Government has declared that it will adopt many of the EU's standards as 'best practice' and continue to apply those standards, albeit perhaps re-branded to suit UK operations but, by doing so, it will also ensure that our standards align with those of our closest trading partners. What is perhaps less certain is how the individual EU member states will accept our adoption of their rules and practices insofar that failure by them to do so could make UK international road freight transport excessively complex and difficult.

Other more readily identifiable changes last year included a new Secretary of State for Transport, the continuing rise of 'Clean Air Zones', 'Low Emission Zones' and the Ultra-Low Emission Zone (ULEZ) in the nation's capital, the introduction of fourth generation smart tachographs, new International Driving Permits, Direct Vision Standards consultation, the completion of the whole set of online services for operating licence purposes, the introduction of rules permitting more over-length vehicles in order to fit aerodynamic kits and legislation allowing some overweight vehicles powered by electricity. There were also, of course, many initiatives requiring comment and opinion from vehicle operators in relation to proposed changes for the future and, as always and where possible, readers are asked to participate in order to be a part of solutions and not problems. This is particularly important as the UK faces new challenges.

In addition, as noted above, the Office of the Traffic Commissioners is now fully accessible online, saving time and cost to apply for operator licences and to make changes and updates, etc. Operators who have not as yet used this facility are strongly advised to contact the Central Licensing Office (CLO) to apply for a password and PIN.

However, as noted almost year on year, the D*f*T is still promising to look for ways to improve and broaden the way we raise awareness of the rules covering British domestic and EU drivers' hours laws while developing simplified longer-term solutions to take us into our non-EU future, which is yet another reason for operators to work with them and their agencies to have input at this most important time of change.

Longer term, there are still overarching efforts to switch more long-distance road freight on to rail and waterways (the aim is a 50 per cent switch by 2050) and to cut transport greenhouse gas emissions by 60 per cent by 2050, which will continue and no doubt be added to, not least by the announcement that 'motor vehicles' could be a thing of the past by the same sort of date, although this seems something more like 'hope' by some 'extremists' than reality but, as always, time will tell.

As I mentioned last year, many haulage firms are still struggling, others have already gone under and many others continue to be unable to see a secure long-term and sustainable future, not least because of the changes to cabotage operations, individual country-specific requirements in Europe and a largely unknown future for our industry. However, as I always state, 'our industry is nothing if not resilient; and although many other industries are suffering too, in order for a true recovery to be realized, a thriving and efficient road haulage industry is an integral element for successful home markets and for export and import'. I am convinced that the UK haulage industry will meet the new challenges and overcome them with a will and a professionalism that many of those EU countries can only marvel at and, if I'm honest, actually envy. However, as usual there is still much to do if the road freight and road passenger industries are to be able to function efficiently and effectively and counter any potentially threatening initiatives that may be brought against us as a newly independent country. I said this last year but it does still amaze me that several EU member states have already declared that UK freight traffic will be subject to additional bureaucracy and delays and that we must expect shortages and additional legislation in spite of the fact that we are one of their largest markets and trade travels both ways across and under the Channel. I also still firmly believe that both EU and GB politicians and the general public actually need to recognize the role that road freight transport plays in maintaining and growing national economics and sustaining national populations. Whilst it is relatively easy for politicians and campaigners to criticize the industry that they have formed and use it is something more of a challenge for them to map out a future industry that is cost effective, sustainable and would actually 'deliver the goods'. The critics need to remember that we are a service industry and nobody drives and operates vehicles for a hobby – everything on the road is there serving a demand and that demand, and meeting it, has probably never been more important than at this time of massive change. This new 50th edition of the *Handbook* has been updated with many snippets of new information – too numerous to specify here, but nevertheless indicating just what a constantly moving picture the whole business of transport law compliance really is and, as we know, this year may be something of a 'super-year' in relation to change.

My annual statement that keeping up to date with the latest legislation is reputed to be the biggest challenge facing the road haulage industry, is still my belief and as usual I refer to the statement made some years ago that 'there is so much legislation coming through these days that your eyes glaze over', according to Bob Durward, Director of the British Aggregates Association, who sadly passed away in January

2018. This statement may be dated but it does seem to continue to be true and is something many of us can empathize with, not least those of us who have tried to follow the Brexit negotiations!

On a positive note, however, readers of this *Handbook* should have no such problems comprehending the law or recognizing their statutory responsibilities, since, as always, its purpose is to help goods vehicle operators, transport managers and the many other individuals responsible for road transport operations to know and understand their legal obligations. More particularly, it should help them avoid the risks of prosecution, along with the heavy financial penalties imposed these days on conviction and, even more worrying, the imposition of punitive action against their operator's licence – these being the almost certain consequences of illegal activities that the transport trade press continues to report week by week with unfailing regularity. I hope this 50th edition of this *Handbook* will, as ever, help to steer readers clear of such problems and provide both interesting and intelligible reading as well as a useful and ready source of reference to the many and complex legal requirements relating to goods vehicle ownership and use and I apologise for any inaccuracies which this edition may contain due to it having been written at a time of much uncertainty, proposals, counter-proposals, arguments, political unrest and a general tiredness at the lack of political action to deliver a decision made by the British people which the politicians seem to ignore, which together combine to place us in our current position where we have little agreed future direction and strategy.

Previous Editions of *Lowe's Transport Manager's and Operator's Handbook*

Readers may be interested to note that a full set of all previous editions of the *Handbook* (ie 49 editions to date from the first in 1970) are held by the Chartered Institute of Logistics and Transport in its Corby Knowledge Centre, where they may be accessed by anybody researching the progress of transport legislation over this period.

David Lowe

Introduction

Firstly, please let me say how grateful I am to present this 50th edition of the *Handbook*. It is truly gratifying to think that my work has, even in some small way, been used and valued for over half a century and to think that I have been able to play at least some sort of role in the evolution of the industry to which I belong and seek to serve.

As a transport professional, I am keenly aware that the road transport industry in Great Britain has had to contend with changing trading patterns and such a mass of legislation, often EU driven, that have imposed considerable restrictions on operations and investment, to say nothing of the burdens of high cost and considerable worry for the owners, operators and managers of goods and passenger vehicle fleets. However, this year must surely be the year when this statement may begin to require change as we once again become an independent trading nation. This statement is something of a 'prediction' as it is likely to take several years before our true direction is fully forged but it is spoken with hope for a dynamic and economically successful future.

Clearly, at the time of writing the actual direction the UK will take is still dependent upon our agreeing (or not) final terms of departure from the EU and, whilst politicians do not appear too concerned about the exceptionally lengthy and politically charged exit process, it is our industry which will undoubtedly have to make the most of whatever our elected leaders finally leave us with and maintain services and essential supplies to both industry and the British public. I have no doubt that our industry will overcome the obstacles but how different it could have been if decisions (however hard) had been made earlier. Indeed, what a luxury it must be to not need to comply with deadlines and key dates.

As in the past, the picture will become a lot clearer as an independent UK becomes a more accepted concept and our politicians and legislators are given a clearer strategic direction enabling them to forge ahead with changes and amendments aimed at promoting the UK's transport sector which has, for many years, suffered from EU competition and distortions. Whilst I am not criticizing competition it is a fact that our international road freight fleet has shrunk markedly in recent history and that some EU member states have introduced measures aimed at giving their domestic carriers some degree of commercial advantage.

In addition to Brexit, I'm sure our normal high pace of change will continue with changes and legislative re-drafting following the announcements such as the intention to ban all new petrol, diesel and hybrid cars in the UK from 2040 and that many producers are committed to ceasing production of the more pollutive models. This must surely rank as one of the largest steps taken in relation to a fundamental change but we must not forget that environmental issues and protection are also driving 'clean air' and 'low emission' requirements and alternative fuel analysis and that our industry must move with required change and not simply try to resist change unless, I suppose, it's really only change for change's sake. The main point is that, as an industry, we must act responsibly and accept that some change is going to be required and embraced in order to sustain our dominant position within the market overall.

Historically, many changes have had varying degrees of impact, as respective chapters in past issues of this *Handbook* show, not least in 1984, again in 1996, 2006 and 2009 and, more recently, in 2015 and 2016. Clearly, the current EU hours regulations have become those of Europe, although AETR regulations, which mirror those of the EU, are the set of rules we will need to follow when we adopt non-EU status. As the two sets are identical this is, in reality, nothing more than a change of title and this transition should not really impact on scheduling vehicles or drivers' driving and duty limits, etc at the current time.

The records requirements also changed to meet European law late in 1976 and subsequently have been largely replaced by tachographs on a mandatory basis from 1981. The introduction of fourth generation smart tachographs in new vehicles last year sees them now fitted to new vehicles with retro-fit requirements declared as not becoming a requirement in the UK until 2034 although by that date the fifth generation generation tachographs will have entered service and so it is unlikely that the date of 2034 will actually hold.

Between 1986 and 2009 further changes were made to amend the drivers' hours rules (Regulation EC561/2006), introduce the Working Time Directive 2005, harmonize professional competence requirements, harmonize the carriage of different types of goods, introduce additional elements to vocational driver training and introduce the concept of vocational Driver Certificate of Professional Competence (DCPC). It is to be remembered that the DCPC was heralded as a major road safety initiative and the cost of uploads has certainly brought HM Government considerable revenue. However, there does not appear to be any formal statistics that can actually show the improvement in road safety related to this revenue stream, in spite of Clive Pidgeon requesting this data on two separate occasions. One DCPC change that was welcomed was the fact that Fleet Operator Recognition Scheme (FORS) elements can now be delivered as part of DCPC training. This list of changes is not exhaustive but it does indicate an ongoing theme of change and the need for transport operators and managers to manage change and perhaps to consider the value of some changes.

What is certain is that the EU has agreed that the UK's DCPC will be recognized (at least for the time being) within the member states and that the Operator Certificate of Professional Competence (Operator CPC) will also be accepted. However, UK national driving licences and other previously accepted documentation may well be rejected by individual EU member states acting unilaterally. In addition, there are still uncertainties relating to minimum wage requirements and weekly rest options for UK drivers operating within the EU, whilst the need for one of the two new style International Driving Permits (IDPs) and permits, etc, will be discussed, along with what changes we know about to date, throughout the various chapters.

At the end of 2011, the European Commission launched new regulations which have had a significant impact on road transport operators and professional transport managers (Regulations 1071 & 1072/2009/EC) and published its 2011 White Paper on transport, *Road Map to a Single European Transport Area*, which takes a futuristic look at how the industry will be conducted in the years ahead – particularly up to 2020. With our leaving the EU it is not clear how much of the White Paper will now be valid.

2015 also saw new legislation relating to Vehicle Excise Duty discs, paper counterpart driving licences, speed limits, operator licensing, record keeping and the DCPC, as well as Regulation EU 165/2014 being introduced to replace the old EEC Regulation 3821/85, amongst other things, clearly evidencing the continuing evolution of transport regulations and control mechanisms.

The pace did not reduce and in 2016 we had to learn to cope with a National Minimum Wage and 'Living Wage', changes to some Special Types General Order (STGO) movements (also continued into 2017), changes resulting from a change of London mayor, notifiable medical conditions, a raft of new statutory documents being published and the need to have many ISO containers weighed before being loaded onto ships, changes to the Eurovignette system and the increasing need for foreign drivers to prove levels of earnings when operating in some EU member states, which is now something of a serious issue in countries such as France and Germany and one which the EU has declared it will examine with a view to introducing an EU-wide minimum wage requirement. Even 2019 saw major changes with the DVLA online trailer registration service, a complete online 'O' licence service, new International Driving Permits being founded and available only through the Post Office, electrically powered vans being allowed to operate at 4,250 kg instead of 3,500 kg, Direct Vision Standards being finalized and a date of 26 October 2020 being decided for operators operating vehicles over 12,000 kg entering Greater London to obtain a Safety Permit and fourth generation tachographs entering service. At the same time the EU continued to deliberate on more formal drivers' hours regulations for goods vehicles exceeding 2,400 kg but not exceeding 3,500 kg and whether or not to more strictly enforce the 'flawed rule' that drivers should take no more than two weekly rests in vehicle cabs, providing the vehicle is in a safe and secure site/location, with the third weekly rest to be taken at their place of residence or in a hotel, etc; and so it goes on.

In spite of the changes it does appear that some earlier proposals may have been put on hold, not least the proposed introduction of large goods vehicle (LGV) 'platoons' where it was planned that a lead vehicle would control acceleration and braking of the accompanying vehicles but each of the accompanying vehicles would still require a driver to steer their vehicles and, of course, there is the continued evaluation of the use of longer vehicles and the ever-evolving low-emission technology.

The purpose of this *Handbook* is to gather as much of this legislative material together as can be reasonably squeezed between the covers, to explain what it is all about in lay terms which are both easy to read and to understand and apply, and thereby to provide the hard-pressed (and, it could be argued, often underpaid) vehicle operator or transport manager with one accessible, intelligible source of information on the responsibilities laid on him by law emanating from the British Government, UK regional governments and legislative bodies, the UN and UNECE. The EU is also included as much of our current legislation is based on EU regulations and directives.

The *Handbook* is intended for the fleet operator (whatever the size of his fleet – large or very small), the transport manager, the owner-driver haulier or anybody else, whatever their title, whose responsibilities include the day-to-day control, administration or operation of goods vehicles, and the small operator who has found that there is a lot more to running a goods vehicle besides just taxing and insuring it. In addition to its function as a ready source of reference for the main legal requirements affecting goods vehicle operation and other useful information, the book may also be found, by those studying for transport examinations such as the Operator CPC, or any of the freight transport focused qualifications offered by the Chartered Institute of Logistics and Transport and/or the Trade Associations such as the Road Haulage Association (RHA) and Freight Transport Association (FTA), to be an additional means of acquiring a detailed knowledge of the relevant legislation currently applicable to the UK road freight industry.

Apart from these general issues, there is still a great deal more information that the operator and manager should have at his fingertips. Some of it concerns particular branches of the transport industry; international movements, the carriage of dangerous goods, abnormal loads, food or livestock, for example. The person responsible for these specialized traffics should have acquired, through experience, some knowledge of the regulations concerning his particular field.

The newcomer to such operations will need to obtain the appropriate regulations, which are available as 'free to download' guides, such as the DVSA *Rules on Drivers' Hours and Tachographs* (GV262), the DVSA *Guide to Goods Vehicle Operator Licensing* (GV74), the new DVSA guide *Load Securing – Vehicle Operator Guidance*, the 2018 edition of the DVSA *Guide to Maintaining Roadworthiness* or any of the following: the DVSA *Categorisation of Defects*, the DVSA *Road Side Checks: Fines and Financial Deposits, Operator Compliance Risk Score* (GOV.UK), the DfT *Safety of Loads on Vehicles: Code of Practice* (2015), *Driving Dangerous Goods and Special Loads*, the DVSA *Guide to ATP, Managing Vehicle Safety in the Workplace, Working with ADR* and *Illegal Immigrants and Lorry Crime Prevention* – many of which can be downloaded direct from the internet (www.legislation.gov.uk (archived at https://perma.cc/EEX3-LM7D)) or by visiting the GOV.UK website and typing in the details. Other sources of information include trade associations such as the FTA and RHA, the Stationery Office (TSO) – address at the end of this Introduction – or booksellers who stock TSO publications. Once obtained, this information and the guides need to be studied carefully.

The principal Acts of Parliament which form the basis of much of the legislation explained in this book are supported by, and their provisions brought into effect by, a much larger number of regulations, orders and amendments. These are the means by which the Secretary of State for Transport puts into effect the legal requirements laid down in principle in an Act of Parliament. Legislation contained in an Act is not of itself effective until brought into force by regulations or orders made by the Secretary of State, for which purpose he is given the necessary powers in the Act. Many provisions contained in such Acts may, in fact, never be brought into use, but they do not automatically become extinct by lack of use. They remain dormant on the statute book unless repealed by a further Act. This year in particular we might reasonably expect to see new or previously unused legislation come into force as the UK re-positions itself within Europe.

European Commission legislation, of which we now have a great deal (some of which we will retain) arises as the result of draft proposals, similar to British Government White Papers, which are circulated among interested parties (the trade unions, trade associations, and so on) for comment prior to legislative action being taken, and are then enforced by means of directives and regulations of the Council of the European Union. The impact of EU legislation on the UK in the future will, of course, depend on our final position upon leaving the EU and the terms, or not, under which we actually leave.

It is most important for transport people to be aware of the regulations affecting both their own special type of operations and transport in general. To keep up with all the individual acts, regulations, amendments and modifications which TSO publishes on behalf of the Government in connection with transport, and the statutory publications of the European Communities, is no mean task. A more convenient method of keeping up to date on many of the new measures affecting the industry is to use the GOV.UK website and to read the trade press regularly.

The principal journals covering the road goods transport field are *Motor Transport* and *Commercial Motor*, published weekly, and *Truck and Driver* and *Trucking*, published monthly. Contents include the latest industry news, new regulations with simple explanations and articles on subjects of special interest such as legislative updates, evolving vehicle technology, insurance, vehicle maintenance, road tests of new vehicles, costing, education and training, and management topics. In particular, these journals are of special interest because of their extensive reporting of court and tribunal cases, which give the reader a good indication of how the law is applied, how the enforcement agencies, and subsequently the courts, interpret legal provisions and the levels of penalties imposed on offenders and those who lose out in tribunal cases.

It must be emphasized that the fleet operator and transport manager should keep abreast of what is happening in the industry if they want to be efficient, progressive and stay on the right side of the law. This is particularly relevant to operator licensing where a nominated person must be able to demonstrate 'effective' control of the fleet. To concentrate on the job in hand to the exclusion of all that is happening in the industry at large is an attitude adopted by many operators and many of them have already suffered the consequences of not being prepared to meet some of the drastic changes that have taken place in recent years.

A valuable aid to the operator is membership of one or other of the trade associations. The Freight Transport Association, which represents the own-account operator, and the Road Haulage Association, looking after the interests of the hire and reward professional haulier, provide a number of services to their members as well as keeping them informed about what is happening in the industry through their respective journals, *Freight Transport* and *Roadway*. Both organizations hold open meetings and training sessions, addressed by specialists on various topics of importance, at which members can hear first-hand details of current and new legislation, ask questions and air their views.

It should also be noted that the Chartered Institute of Logistics and Transport (CILT) also provides a journal to its members entitled *Logistics and Transport Focus* which includes news of legislative change, articles on new initiatives, case studies from the logistics and transport sector, employment opportunities, information on training courses and information on the extensive range of training offered.

Additionally, for the operator or manager who wants to keep abreast of current legislation and practices in the industry there are commercial seminars and training sessions ranging from one day to over a week in duration. These provide an excellent means of keeping up to date with what is going on, and of meeting and talking to other people in the industry with similar interests and problems.

Many larger organizations do try to keep their staff informed of changes on a fairly regular basis, but smaller businesses and owner-drivers, etc, may do well to use some of the websites offering updates – although care must be taken to ensure the legality and authenticity of any items posted.

The road transport industry plays an important part in the life of Great Britain and is facing some serious challenges. Its safe operation is essential for the well-being of the people and its efficient operation is vital to the economy. Higher standards of management and control within the industry with a far greater awareness and understanding of the legal requirements, the operational demands and the economic considerations are necessary if these essential criteria of safety and efficient operation are to be achieved and upheld.

Special Note

It should be noted that this *Handbook* is intended purely as a practical interpretation of legal matters for the lay reader and is only a *guide* to matters current at the time of writing. This is particularly true this year given that these notes had to be produced before many of the required Brexit details had either been decided or published. It is not a definitive legal work of reference and should not be used as such. Readers are advised to check the legislation itself before committing time or expenditure to any particular course of action and any operator needing detailed legal advice is recommended to acquire it through normal legal channels. The authors and publishers accept no responsibility whatsoever for decisions taken or other irrevocable actions based on the contents herein.

Bookshops

Official publications, including Statutory Instruments, may be obtained from TSO bookshops and at a number of TSO agency bookshops in major UK cities. TSO also offers an online system for the purchase of these publications.

The Stationery Office

TSO Head Office and Shop
St Clements House
2-16 Colgate
Norwich
NR3 1BQ
Telephone: +44 (0)1603 621000 (telephone orders, general enquiries, subscriptions and standing orders)
Email: book.orders@tso.co.uk
Website: www.tso.co.uk/bookshop (archived at https://perma.cc/77TL-BS87)

The Stationery Office also has a network of UK based agents authorized to supply materials. These are located in:

Aberdeen	Glasgow	Manchester
Bristol	Hull	Newcastle
Cambridge	Leeds	Norwich
Cardiff	Liverpool	Oxford
Edinburgh	London	Sheffield

Parliamentary publications may be obtained from:

The Houses of Parliament Shop
12 Bridge Street
Parliament Square
London SW1A 2JX
Telephone orders: 020 7219 3890
General enquiries: 020 7219 3890
Email orders: shop@parliament.uk

Transport Ministers 1970 to Date

The author has been asked many times about the names and dates in office of successive Transport Ministers. The following list of such Ministers in post during the life of this *Handbook* from 1970 shows what a potentially vulnerable position this is, with some incumbents lasting only a matter of months. The very first Minister of Transport was Sir Eric Geddes, who served from 19 May 1919 to 7 November 1921.

Minister for Transport Industries

- John Peyton (15 October 1970 to 4 March 1974)

Minister for Transport

- Fred Mulley (7 March 1974 to 12 June 1975)
- John Gilbert (12 June 1975 to 10 September 1976)

Secretary of State for Transport

- William (Bill) Rodgers (10 September 1976 to 4 May 1979)

Minister of Transport

- Norman Fowler (11 May 1979 to 5 January 1981)

Secretary of State for Transport

- Norman Fowler (5 January 1981 to 14 September 1981)
- David Howell (14 September 1981 to 11 June 1983)

- Tom King (11 June 1983 to 16 October 1983)
- Nicholas Ridley (16 October 1983 to 21 May 1986)
- John Moore (21 May 1986 to 13 June 1987)
- Paul Channon (13 June 1987 to 24 July 1989)
- Cecil Parkinson (24 July 1989 to 28 November 1990)
- Malcolm Rifkind (28 November 1990 to 10 April 1992)
- John MacGregor (10 April 1992 to 5 July 1995)
- Sir George Young, Bt (5 July 1995 to 2 May 1997)

Secretary of State for Environment, Transport and the Regions

- John Prescott (2 May 1997 to 8 June 2001)

From 1997 to 2001, the Ministers of State with responsibility for Transport were:

- Gavin Strang (3 May 1997 to 27 July 1998)
- John Reid (27 July 1998 to 17 May 1999)
- Helen Liddell (17 May 1999 to 29 July 1999)
- Lord Macdonald of Tradeston (29 July 1999 to 8 June 2001)

Gavin Strang and John Reid attended Cabinet meetings, but were not formally members of the Cabinet.

Secretary of State for Transport, Local Government and the Regions

- Stephen Byers (8 June 2001 to 29 May 2002) (Resigned)

Secretary of State for Transport

- Alistair Darling (29 May 2002 to 5 May 2006)
- Douglas Alexander (5 May 2006 to 28 June 2007)
- Ruth Kelly (28 June 2007 to 3 October 2008)
- Geoff Hoon (3 October 2008 to 6 October 2008)
- Lord Andrew Adonis (6 October 2008 to 11 May 2010)
- Philip Hammond (12 May 2010 to 13 October 2011)
- Justine Greening (14 October 2011 to 4 September 2012)
- Patrick McLoughlin (4 September 2012 to 14 July 2016)
- Chris Grayling (14 July 2016 to 24 July 2019)
- Grant Shapps (24 July 2019 to present)

Goods Vehicle Operator Licensing

01

Operator ('O') licensing is the regulatory 'quality' control system imposed by the UK Government. Similar systems operate throughout the EU, all established to ensure the safe and legal operation of most goods and passenger vehicles in Great Britain and Europe. In spite of our leaving the EU it has been decided that the current 'O' licensing system will remain in force. It should also be noted that the whole system is now available to operators online providing they have obtained a PIN and password from the Central Licensing Office (CLO). This online service seriously reduces the time it takes to process applications and changes and it is also able to process electronic signatures. Applicants may also use the online facility when applying for a licence, providing that they contact the CLO in order to register and obtain a PIN and password.

While other individual aspects of legislation in the UK also apply to road vehicles, the 'O' licensing system provides the overriding control of road freight transport operations. Failure to observe the requirements and conditions under which 'O' licences are granted will lead to increasingly severe penalties; likewise, breaches of other legislation can result in appropriate penalties as set out in respective statutes and, subsequently, will involve penalties against the operators' licence itself and, in some cases, nominated individuals within the transport operation. Similar licensing controls apply to goods vehicle operations in Northern Ireland under the NI operator licensing scheme, operated by the Department of the Environment (Northern Ireland) (see later).

Under the current UK licensing schemes, trade or business users of most goods vehicles and vehicle combinations (vehicles with trailers) over 3,500 kg maximum permissible weight must hold an 'O' licence for such vehicles, whether they are used for carrying goods in connection with the operator's main trade or business as an own-account operator (ie a trade or business other than that of carrying goods for hire or reward) or are used for hire or reward road haulage operations. Certain goods vehicles, including those used exclusively for private purposes, are exempt from the licensing requirements. Details of the exempt vehicles to which 'O' licensing does not apply are given on pp 13–16.

Note: Current exemptions are always under review and there has been pressure from Europe for the UK to introduce 'O' licensing for goods vehicles from 2,400 kg to 3,500 kg being used for international hire and reward operations. If adopted they would also need to be fitted with tachographs if used for international work. The likelihood is that smaller vans, vehicles only used domestically and vehicles used for own-account carriage of goods will be exempted. This proposal is a part of the EU's Mobility Package and should have been implemented but it has been put back and no set date for implementation has been agreed. Also note that new electrically powered vans are now able to operate at weights up to 4,250 kg without coming into the operator licensing scheme.

The original UK system of operator licensing was established by the Transport Act 1968, the relevant provisions of which are now consolidated into the Goods Vehicle (Licensing of Operators) Act 1995 (as amended). This Act states that no person may use a goods vehicle on a road for hire or reward or in connection with any trade or business carried on by him except under an operator's licence.

Important EU rules concerning the conditions to be complied with to pursue the occupation of road transport operator and accompanying UK rules giving effect to the EU rules in the UK were introduced with effect from 4 December 2011 as follows:

- EC Regulation 1071/2009/EC
- The Road Transport Operator Regulations 2011 (SI 2632/2011/EC)

As stated earlier, the EU regulations in force at the time of writing continue to apply until the UK Government decides to retain them or not. However, the UK Government has indicated that any future UK operator licensing regime will be very similar to the one used by the EU, although it is unclear whether or not different EU member states will recognize the UK's qualification, post-Brexit.

While much of the pre-existing operator ('O') licensing scheme described in this chapter remains unchanged, there are certain new provisions which are noted in the following text.

List of Relevant Legislation

Copies of the legislation can be freely downloaded from http://www.legislation.gov.uk (archived at https://perma.cc/4MRL-2DS7).

- The Goods Vehicles (Licensing of Operators) Act 1995
- The Goods Vehicles (Licensing of Operators) Regulations 1995 (SI 1995/2869) (as amended)
- The Goods Vehicle Operators (Qualifications) Regulations 1999 (SI 1999/2430) (as amended)
- The Road Transport Operator Regulations 2011 (SI 2011/2632)
- The Road Transport Act 2013
- The Road Transport (Vehicle Registration) Regulation 2017
- The Road Transport (Driver Licensing) Regulation 2017
- The Road Vehicles (Authorised Weights) and (Construction & Use) Regulations 2017

- EU Regulation 1071/2009 establishing common rules concerning conditions to be complied with to pursue the occupation of road transport operator
- EU Regulation 1072/2009 on common rules for access to the international road haulage market
- The Goods Vehicles (Community Licences) Regulations 2011 (SI 2011/2633)

There are also guides and advice available from the website above, and the GV74, which is the official guide to operator licensing, is on the GOV.UK website. In addition there are a series of 13 separate statutory documents written and updated by the Senior Traffic Commissioner covering, in great detail, all aspects of operator licensing, which are also free to download from the GOV.UK website.

For those of us who want to see what the EU has as an intended way forward they also have a publication entitled 'A Road Transport Strategy for Europe', which may be of interest to many readers. It's available through the European Commission website.

Administration of Licensing System

The 'O' licensing system, which is based on the concept of ensuring legal and safe operation and thus is a system of 'quality' as opposed to 'quantity' licensing, which was in force prior to 1968, is administered on a regional (ie Traffic Area) basis throughout Great Britain. (Northern Ireland's Road Freight Vehicle Operator Licensing system is dealt with separately by the Driver and Vehicle Agency – part of the Department of the Environment in Belfast.)

The Traffic Areas each have their own Traffic Commissioner (TC) and Traffic Area Offices (TAOs), to form the network (see Appendix I for a list).

There is also a 'Senior' TC and 'Lead' TCs are appointed where operators hold operating licences in more than one Traffic Area. Where this is the case, the Lead TC will be the person that the operator in question will need to deal with and it will be the Lead TC who will make final decisions. Lead TCs also have a team working for them to deal with operators who hold licences in more than one Traffic Area, known as the Multi Licence Holder (MLH) team.

Operator licence application administration is now centralized at the address below where the staff either deal with the issue or forward it for consideration by the TC concerned:

Central Licensing Office
Hillcrest House
386 Harehills Lane
Leeds LS9 6NF

In spite of much of the administration being centred in Leeds, post and correspondence for the public inquiry and regional intelligence units, and personal post for the Traffic Commissioners, should continue to be sent to local offices.

The Central Licensing Office (CLO) supports the existing Traffic Commissioners, and their roles as independent licensing authorities are not affected. Traffic area boundaries remain unchanged and public inquiries will continue to be held in the area of each TC. These TCs are appointed by the Secretary of State for Transport and are 'independent quasijudicial authorities', who have the statutory power to grant or refuse operators' licences, to place road safety and environmental conditions or restrictions on such licences where necessary, and subsequently to impose penalties against licences in the event of the holder being convicted for goods vehicle-related and what are deemed to be 'other serious' offences, including offences related to health and safety, environmental issues, commercial law, insolvency law and people and drugs trafficking, etc. The team of TCs are further supported by a team of Deputy TCs.

NB: The male gender is used throughout this Handbook when referring to TCs although at the time of writing there are two female TCs. No discrimination, prejudice or bias is intended by such use. (Note: Beverley Bell used to be the Senior Traffic Commissioner but she stood down and was replaced by Richard Turfitt in April 2017.)

Figures published in March 2018 showed that there were 370,606 goods vehicles specified in 72,547 'O' licences in Great Britain, of which 37,514 were restricted licences, 26,682 were standard national licences and 8,351 were standard international licences. These numbers show mostly falling of figures year on year with an increase since the 2015 figures were released, but are still well below the high 1989/90 figure of 132,236 valid 'O' licences in issue, covering 441,656 goods vehicles. Currently, 32,433 certified copies of European Community Authorisations are in issue.

Source: Annual reports of the TCs (covering Goods Vehicle Operator Licensing) for the period 2017 to 2018. These are the latest figures released as at September 2019.

The Vehicle Operator Licensing System (VOL)

The old Traffic Area Network (TAN) 'self-service' computer system has now been largely superseded by the new Vehicle Operator Licensing system (VOL) (see below) which has a totally online capability for those who register although all 'paper' driven functions and processes are still available. Principally, the current system significantly reduces the time taken to process 'O' licence applications, changes and amendments as operators are now, more and more, expected to transact such business online using VOL, where they must use a pre-registered user ID and a case-sensitive password. It is expected that this will eventually become the single point of access for all routine processes although no date has been announced for this as yet. Additionally, VOL provides enforcement agencies with 'real-time' data to help them catch illegal operators which with the introduction of fourth generation tachographs will make a significant change to enforcement 'out on the road'.

This online Government service enables the application process to be reduced from 9 weeks to 7 weeks and goods vehicle operators to add and remove vehicles from their operator's licence at any time of the day or night without the need to complete an application form and without any intervention by DVSA staff. It also reduces the time taken to add a vehicle to a licence from 14 days to within a couple of minutes. Operators can register online to check their own licence details held on the DVSA's operator licence computer system; transfer vehicles between licences they hold in different areas; track the progress of licence applications; and set up access for other members of their staff, allowing greater access to records and transactions for larger companies. The system allows operators to pay their licence invoices and renew licences online. The site also contains a template for use by operators advertising changes to their licences in local newspapers.

VOL is aimed at allowing operators to complete an increasing number of tasks online and is simply designed to reduce the time taken using the old paper-based systems, to enable operators to make changes much more quickly and easily and to reduce bureaucracy.

To access the VOL system operators with access to the old 'self-service' system should log in using their old PIN and password. Operators are advised at this time to check the details held on the VOL system to ensure that everything is up to date. If an operator does not have an existing account then they need to create a new VOL account. Operators can still use hard copy but it is in decline and the move is towards the electronic system and operators are strongly advised to contact the Central Licensing Office (details above) or their trade association to find out how to obtain their PIN and password to log into the new VOL system. (As mentioned above, the VOL system is also available to 'O' licence applicants providing they register with the Central Licensing Office.)

'O' Licences Not for Sale

Operator's licences are issued only to applicants who meet strict criteria as set out in the regulations and as described in this chapter. As such, 'O' licences are *not* transferable between operators and may *not* be borrowed, used on loan or sold, with or without the vehicles to which they relate, by any person other than the authorized holder.

Exemptions from 'O' Licensing

There are a number of categories of vehicle which are exempt from 'O' licensing requirements as described below.

Small Vehicles

The principal exemption applies to 'small' vehicles identified as follows.
Rigid vehicles are 'small' if:

- they are plated and the gross plated (ie maximum permissible) weight is not more than 3.5 tonnes;
- they are unplated and have an unladen weight of not more than 1,525 kg.

A combination of a rigid vehicle and a drawbar trailer is 'small' if:

- both the vehicle and the trailer are plated, and the total of the gross *plated* weights is not more than 3.5 tonnes (this is increased to 4.25 tonnes for vans which are fuelled using totally alternative fuel systems);
- either the vehicle or the trailer is not plated, and the total of the *unladen* weights is not more than 1,525 kg.

NB: The text throughout this Handbook *will refer to 3.5 tonnes as the relevant total gross plated weight, as these sized vehicles make up over 95 per cent of these types of vehicles.*

The old exemption from 'O' licensing for rigid vehicles not weighing more than 3.5 tonnes gross plated weight, used in combination with trailers with an unladen weight of not more than 1,020 kg, has been withdrawn for operators engaged in hire and reward work. Combinations of vehicles and trailers exceeding the 3.5 tonne gross plated weight, or the 1,525 kg unladen weight threshold, are likely to be subject to the 'O' licensing regulation unless exempt for some other reason.

However, operators engaged in 'own-account' work with vehicles that do not exceed 3.5 tonnes gross plated weight used in combination with trailers that have an unladen weight that does not exceed 1,020 kg remain out of scope of the 'O' licence regulations.

It should be noted that consultations are taking place to ascertain whether or not the 3,500 kg threshold for operator licensing should be lowered in order to bring some smaller goods under the operator licensing regime. To date no decisions have been made or released but there is pressure from Europe for smaller vehicles on international hire and reward operations to come into the operator licensing scheme.

Articulated vehicles are 'small' if:

- the semi-trailer is plated, and the total of the *unladen* weight of the tractive unit and the plated weight of the semi-trailer is not more than 3.5 tonnes;
- the semi-trailer is not plated, and the total of the *unladen* weights of the tractive unit and the semi-trailer is not more than 1,525 kg. However, this exemption does not apply if other people's goods are carried for hire or reward.

Older Vehicles

Also included in the exemptions are pre-1 January 1977 vehicles which have an unladen weight not exceeding 1,525 kg and a gross weight greater than 3.5 tonnes.

Other Exemptions

Regulations list the following further specific exemptions from 'O' licensing requirements:

1. Vehicles licensed as agricultural tractors used solely for handling specified goods, and any trailer drawn by them.

2 Dual-purpose vehicles and any trailer drawn by them.

3 Vehicles used on roads only for the purpose of passing between private premises in the immediate neighbourhood and belonging to the same person (except in the case of a vehicle used only in connection with excavation or demolition) provided that the distance travelled on the road in any one week does not exceed in aggregate 9.654 km (ie 6 miles).

4 Motor vehicles constructed or adapted primarily for the carriage of passengers and their effects and any trailer drawn by them while being so used.

5 Vehicles being used for funerals.

6 Vehicles being used for police, fire brigade and ambulance service purposes.

7 Vehicles being used for fire-fighting or rescue work at mines.

8 Vehicles on which a permanent body has not yet been built carrying goods for trial or for use in building the body.

9 Vehicles being used under a trade licence.

10 Vehicles used in the service of a visiting force or headquarters.

11 Vehicles used by or under the control of HM Armed Forces.

12 Trailers not constructed for the carriage of goods but which are used incidentally for that purpose in connection with the construction, maintenance or repair of roads.

13 Road rollers or any trailer drawn by them.*

14 Vehicles used by the Maritime and Coastguard Agency (MCA) or the Royal National Lifeboat Institution (RNLI) for the carriage of lifeboats, life-saving appliances or crew.

15 Vehicles fitted with permanent equipment (ie machines or appliances) so that the only goods carried are:

- **(a)** for use in connection with the equipment;
- **(b)** for threshing, grading, cleaning or chemically treating grain or for mixing by the equipment with other goods not carried on the vehicle to make animal fodder; or
- **(c)** mud or other matter swept up from the road by the equipment.

16 Vehicles while being used by a local authority for the purpose of enactments relating to weights and measures or the sale of food or drugs.

17 Vehicles used by a local authority under the Civil Defence Act 1948.

18 Steam-propelled vehicles.

19 Tower wagons or any trailer drawn by them provided that any goods carried on the trailer are required for use in connection with the work on which the tower wagon is used.

20 Vehicles used on airports under the Civil Aviation Act 1982.

21 Electrically propelled vehicles*.

22 Showmen's goods vehicles and any trailer drawn by such vehicles.

23 Vehicles first registered prior to 1 January 1977 which are not over 1,525 kg unladen weight and are plated for more than 3,500 kg but not more than 3,556.21 kg (3.5 tonnes).

24 Vehicles used by a highway authority in connection with weigh-bridges.

25 Vehicles used for emergency operations by the water, electricity, gas and telephone services.

26 Recovery vehicles*.

27 Incomplete vehicles (with no fixed body).

28 Vehicles used for snow clearing or the distribution of grit, salt or other materials on frosted, ice-bound or snow-covered roads and for any other purpose connected with such activities.
NB: This exemption is not restricted solely to local authority-owned vehicles.

29 Vehicles going to or coming from a test station and carrying a load which is required for the test at the request of the Secretary of State for Transport (ie by the test station).

**At the time of writing, vehicles such as road rollers, recovery vehicles and electrically powered vehicles are still under review as to whether or not they should lose their exemptions.*

Exemption for Private Vehicles

Exemptions also apply to vehicles used privately (ie for carrying goods for solely private purposes and not in any way connected with a business activity) and by voluntary organizations.

Non-Exempt Vehicles

All other conventionally powered goods-carrying vehicles over 3.5 tonnes gross weight not specifically shown as exempt in the list above must be covered by an 'O' licence. This includes such vehicles that are only temporarily in the operator's possession, or are hired from another operator without a driver, or borrowed on a short-term basis, if they are used in connection with a business (even a part-time business).

No Exemption for Fast Agricultural Tractors

Fastrac-type agricultural tractors capable of pulling substantial loads at speeds of up to 40 mph on public roads must be specified on an 'O' licence if used for hire or reward haulage work. The agricultural exemption mentioned above applies only when such machines are used by farmers in connection with their own agricultural business.

These vehicles provide unfair competition to licensed road hauliers by using red diesel and underage drivers, by paying a reduced rate Vehicle Excise Duty and by not having any requirements to observe the law on goods vehicle plating and testing, drivers' hours, breaks and rest periods, and tachographs.

The Vehicle User

An 'O' licence must be obtained by the 'user' of the vehicle for all the vehicles he operates to which the regulations apply. The 'user' may be the operating company or the owner or hirer of the vehicle. If the vehicle was hired without a driver, the hirer is the 'user'. There is considerable importance attached to the word 'user', and its exact meaning, both for the purposes of 'O' licensing and in other regulations. It may be explained simply as follows:

- A company or organization that is responsible for the operation of a vehicle that is either owned, leased or hired to it.
- An owner-driver who uses his vehicle in connection with his own business is the 'user' of his own vehicle as long as he is also responsible for the success or failure of the business.
- If the owner of a vehicle employs a driver to drive it for him and he pays the driver's wages then the owner is the 'user' because he is the employer of the driver.
- If a vehicle is borrowed, leased or hired without a driver and the borrower or hirer drives it himself or pays the wages of a driver he employs to drive it then the borrower or hirer is the 'user'.

From this it can be seen that, in general, the person or company who pays the driver's wages is the 'user' of a vehicle, and it is this person (or company) or the nominated 'competent person' (usually a transport manager) who is responsible for holding an 'O' licence and for the safe condition of the vehicle on the road and for ensuring that it is operated in accordance with the law. However, it must be remembered that the driver, although an employee, is still also the user of the vehicle in the context of certain legislation (eg the Road Vehicles (Construction and Use) Regulations 1986, as amended) and he, too, is responsible for its safe condition on the road and is liable to prosecution if it is not in a safe and legal condition.

Agency Drivers

Dependence on agencies for the supply of temporary drivers to provide relief manpower when regular drivers are not available has caused difficulty in interpretation of the term 'user' and in deciding who should hold the 'O' licence: the vehicle owner or the agency which employs the driver. It can be seen from the items above that the person who pays the driver's wages is the 'user', and is therefore the person who should hold the 'O' licence.

However, the status of the vehicle 'user' in these circumstances has been determined by the agencies getting operators to sign agreements whereby the vehicle operator technically becomes the employer of the driver rather than the agency being the employer and consequently the operator remains the legal 'user' of the vehicle. Usually the agency asks the hirer to sign an agreement whereby the agency becomes the 'agent' of the operator for these purposes in paying the driver's wages. This practice has been proved in court to be legally acceptable on the grounds that the

Transport Act 1968 section 92(2) states that 'the person whose servant or agent the driver is, shall be deemed to be the person using the vehicle'. The driver is considered to be the servant of the hirer because the hirer gives instructions and directs the activities of the driver who is temporarily in his employ. The key issue here is who controls how the drivers do their job. This must be the 'user' of the vehicle and the holder of the 'O' licence. However, there can be difficulties when a court interprets it such that because the agency actually 'pays' the driver then the driver is a servant of the agency and not the hirer. As can be seen, operators employing agency drivers need to take extreme care to ensure the true 'status' of any agency drivers used and are advised to discuss this matter with the supplying agency in order to agree an acceptable position.

The great danger with agency drivers is that the operator has no sound means of establishing whether the driver is legally qualified to drive or whether he has already exceeded his permitted driving hours on previous days and whether he has had adequate rest periods, other than to be able to download information held on the driver's 'digi' tacho card. Reputable agencies usually go to considerable lengths to ensure that drivers provided by them for their clients are properly licensed and have complied with the driving hours rules in all respects. It is worth also remembering that the use of casually hired or temporary drivers (whose backgrounds and previous experiences may not be fully known) can result in jeopardy of the contract of insurance covering the use of vehicles and there could also be serious security risks as well as possible 'O' licence penalties for infringements of the law. For this reason the operator should confine himself to obtaining drivers from reputable agencies who are known to have vetted drivers satisfactorily and always ask agency drivers coming 'on-fleet' to have their licences, DCPC card and tacho card with them ready for inspection.

Operators who use agency drivers should be aware that they may be held liable for negligence or driving offences committed by such drivers. They are also liable for ensuring the health and safety of hired drivers, and must inform them of the legal requirements of vehicle operations, such as the 'hours' law, tachographs, safe loading and vehicle checks. Operators also need to ensure that they obtain copies of agency drivers' records for duties performed whilst under their control.

A Code of Practice for the employment of agency drivers is available from offices of the Freight Transport Association (FTA), the Road Haulage Association (RHA) and the Recruitment and Employment Confederation (REC). The Code sets out the respective duties and responsibilities of the haulier on the one hand and the supplying agency on the other, with a checklist for each to ensure that full and correct information is exchanged as to the requirement for the driver (eg the skills and personal attributes required) and the particular job to be done. It also contains a model set of instructions and procedures which should be given to drivers.

Copies of the Code can be obtained from local FTA and RHA offices or from the REC at Dorset House, First Floor, 27–45 Stamford Street, London SE1 9NT (tel: 020 7009 2100, email: info@rec.uk.com).

Rental of Vehicles

Rental of vehicles on a short-term basis of a few days or a few weeks, which is the usual arrangement, does not impose onerous contractual obligations on the hirer. It should be noted that whilst under the control of the hirer, the mechanical condition of the vehicle is the hirer's responsibility (see below).

'O' Licensing Provisions

Hiring does involve other legal obligations in respect of the vehicle itself and its use. For a start, much depends on the gross weight of the vehicle. If it is over 3.5 tonnes permissible maximum weight and has been rented for use in connection with a trade or business, then the person or firm renting it must hold an 'O' licence and there must be a margin on that licence to cover the renting of one or more additional vehicles.

There is no need to advise the TC of details of the vehicle unless it is to be retained on hire for more than one month, after which time the TC must be notified so an 'O' licence windscreen disc can be issued for the vehicle. If the vehicle is rented for a shorter period and then returned to the rental company to be replaced by another vehicle, the TC does not have to be notified if the combined total of the two rental periods exceeds one month unless both are part of the same rental agreement.

If the over-3.5-tonne vehicle is rented by a firm for use in another traffic area different from the one in which the 'O' licence is held, then an 'O' licence must be obtained in that other traffic area before a vehicle is permitted to operate from a base there.

Whether or not the rented vehicle comes within the scope of 'O' licensing, the person or firm renting it carries the user responsibility for its safe mechanical condition when it is on the road. Consequently, if vehicle faults result in prosecution the user will have to pay any fines imposed (not the rental company) and the user's 'O' licence will be put in jeopardy (even if the vehicle is not specified on his 'O' licence). Therefore, careful selection of a reputable rental company with high maintenance standards is essential.

Hire and Contract Hire

Hiring of vehicles (or more specifically contract hire), as opposed to rental, implies a longer-term arrangement with a more rigid agreement as to the obligations of the parties involved. Hiring arrangements vary considerably since the vehicle provider and the customer draw up a contract to incorporate the services required. There are two principal forms of contract hire: vehicles supplied with drivers and vehicles supplied without drivers.

The important difference is that in the former case the contract hire company, as the employer of the driver, is the 'user' of the vehicles in law and therefore holds the 'O' licence and shoulders the legal responsibilities previously described, while the hirer merely operates the vehicles exclusively to suit his requirements. However, in the latter case the hirer is the 'user' and 'O' licence holder and, as with vehicles purchased and leased with his own employee drivers at the wheel, he carries the full legal responsibilities.

Advantages of Contract Hire

This method of vehicle acquisition offers a number of advantages. Principally, there is no investment of capital (generally not even an initial deposit to be found) and cash flow for transport services is predictable throughout the year, thus allowing easy budgeting. One regular monthly invoice covers all capital and operating costs. The hire charges are fully allowable against tax.

Overall, full contract hire with driver is advantageous to the operator, because it relieves him of the burdens of capital expenditure on an ancillary activity and of a welter of legal responsibilities and yet provides him with the right vehicles for his exclusive use to fulfil his delivery requirements as he wishes. He thus has the best of both worlds – all his transport needs met without the major burdens usually encountered by own-fleet operators.

A further financial advantage can arise for a firm operating its own fleet but wishing to switch to contract hire to gain the benefits outlined. Contract hire companies will usually purchase a whole existing fleet and then contract-hire it back to the operator, thus still giving him resources to meet his transport needs and yet providing him with an immediate refund of the capital tied up in vehicles. This proposition can be used to advantage in relieving cash-flow pressure.

Leasing

Leasing is a totally different concept from outright purchase or hire purchase in that the operator (ie the lessee) never actually owns the vehicle (and usually pays the VAT throughout the term of the lease as opposed to 'up front' when a purchase is made) but he has the full use of it as though it were his own. It is also a different concept from rental and hiring arrangements in that it is purely a financial means of acquiring vehicles. In other words, those putting up the money are not transport or vehicle operators, they are finance houses.

Several different forms of leasing are available (basically divided by the assumption of risk, with the lessee taking the risk with a pure finance lease and the lessor retaining the risk with an operating lease) and legislation governing leasing arrangements is subject to change. Also, the way in which the accountancy profession treats leasing is subject to variation, so it is important to discuss any proposed leasing arrangement with a professional accountant before commitment to an agreement.

The general concept of leasing is that a finance house (ie the lessor) purchases a vehicle, for which the operator has specified his requirements and negotiated the price and any available discount from the supplier, and then it spreads the capital cost, interest charges, overhead costs and its profit margin over a period of time to determine the amount of the periodic repayments.

Where leasing is purely a financial arrangement, the advantages and disadvantages from an operational viewpoint are the same as for outright purchase. Because in principle the lessee operates the vehicle as though he owns it and he employs the driver, the full weight of legal responsibility, as already outlined, applies to him so he needs to have a full transport back-up of administration and operational staff, maintenance facilities and policies for selection of the correct vehicles and for replacement at the most economic intervals. Where maintenance is included in the leasing package this allows the operator to more accurately forecast expenditure, develop quotations and form operating budgets.

Clearly, whilst both contract hire and leasing enable operators to avoid major capital expenditure there are costs involved with both options. Whilst these costs may mean additional expenditure for the operator, they are usually fixed costs, or largely fixed costs, and this often enables operators to more accurately produce charge out rates and operating cost tables.

Restricted and Standard 'O' Licences

There are three main types of 'O' licence as described below and, in exceptional circumstances, a temporary licence known as an interim licence or interim authorization may be granted (see p 39).

1. **Restricted licences:** available only to own-account operators who carry nothing other than goods in connection with their own trade or business, which is a business other than that of carrying goods for hire or reward. These licences cover both national and international transport operations with own-account goods. Restricted 'O' licence holders must not use their vehicles to carry goods for hire or reward or on behalf of customers' businesses – even if it is done only as a favour or is seen as being part of the service provided to a customer and even if no charges are raised (see below). Such activities are illegal and could result in penalties.
2. **Standard licences (national transport operations):** for hire or reward (ie professional) hauliers, or own-account operators who also engage in hire or reward operations, but restricted solely to national transport operations (ie operations exclusively within the UK). Own-account holders of such licences may also carry their own goods (but not goods for hire or reward) on international journeys.
3. **Standard licences (national and international transport operations):** for hire or reward (ie professional) hauliers, or own-account operators who also engage in hire or reward carrying, on both national and international transport operations.

Standard Licences for Own-Account Operators

Own-account operators may voluntarily choose to hold a standard 'O' licence for national or both national and international transport operations instead of a restricted licence provided they are prepared to meet the necessary additional qualifying requirements (principally the professional competence qualification – see Chapter 2 – and the need for a status of 'good repute'). Among the reasons which may influence them to take this step is the desire to carry goods for hire or reward to utilize spare capacity on their vehicles, especially on return trips. Such a requirement may also arise because a firm is involved in carrying goods for associate companies on a reciprocal or integrated working basis which does not come within the scope of activities which are permitted under 'O' licensing between subsidiary companies and holding companies (see pp 55–56) or firms may find themselves in the position where they carry goods in connection with their customers', as opposed to their own, businesses.

Firms holding restricted 'O' licences may not carry goods on behalf of customers (ie in connection with the trade or business of the customer rather than in connection with their own business) or other firms even if such operations are described as being a 'favour' or 'part of the service' to the customer and involve no payment whatsoever. This may occur, for example, when a vehicle delivers goods to a customer and the customer then asks the driver to drop off items on his return journey because he is 'going past the door' and their own vehicle is not available. Such activities would be illegal under the terms of a restricted 'O' licence and if two convictions for such an offence are made within five years, the licence must be revoked by the TC.

Requirements for 'O' Licensing

In order to obtain an 'O' licence, applicants must satisfy certain conditions specified in regulations.

Restricted Licences

Applicants must be:

- fit and proper persons;
- of appropriate financial standing.

Standard Licences (National Transport Operations)

Applicants must be:

- of good repute;
- of appropriate financial standing;
- professionally competent, or must employ a person who is professionally competent.

Standard Licences (National and International Transport Operations)

Applicants must be:

- of good repute;
- of appropriate financial standing;
- professionally competent, or must employ a person who is professionally competent.

Other Legal Requirements

Besides the specific requirements mentioned above, licence applicants need to declare any 'relevant convictions' (usually related to previous vehicle operation), whilst both applicants and holders have to satisfy further legal requirements relating to the suitability and environmental acceptability of their vehicle operating centres, the suitability of their vehicle maintenance facilities or arrangements and, overall, their ability and willingness to comply with the law in regard to vehicle operating as demonstrated by signing the undertakings on the 'O' licence application form. These matters are dealt with in detail in this chapter.

NB: Since 2014 applicants, and any person named on the application as a controlling figure, now also need to declare 'any previous bankruptcy or financial failures' when applying for an 'O' licence.

Good Repute

For a TC to be able to grant a 'Standard' 'O' licence, he must determine that the applicant is of 'good repute'. Without this particular requirement being well established, the fact that the applicant may meet all other relevant criteria is of no account; no licence will be granted.

With the introduction of new provisions from EU Regulation 1071/2009/EC (still in force), much tougher good repute standards are imposed on both new and existing operators.

The term 'good repute' is defined on the basis that an individual is not of good repute if he has been convicted of more than one serious offence or of road transport offences concerning:

- pay and employment conditions in the profession (ie of road haulier);
- drivers' hours and rest periods;
- operator licensing;
- weights and dimensions of goods vehicles;
- vehicle maintenance;

- road and vehicle safety;
- protection of the environment;
- rules concerning professional liability;
- rules relating to the contravention of provisions contained within traffic orders.

For the purposes of the standard 'O' licensing scheme this means that the applicant for a licence (ie an individual) must not have a past record which includes more than one conviction for serious offences or conviction for road transport offences during the previous five years (excluding convictions that are 'spent' – see below) relating to the above issues. Similarly, to be a fit and proper person in order to obtain a restricted 'O' licence means that there should not be a past record of such offences.

If it is a limited liability company applying for a licence and the company, or any director, has relevant convictions on their record (ie for serious offences; the term used is 'relevant' offences and these may include prosecutions for issues such as breaches of Health and Safety Regulations, etc, as listed below), then the TC may use his discretion in deciding whether the firm, or director, is of good repute.

It should be noted that the TC will not necessarily refuse to grant a licence to an applicant who has had 'relevant' or transport-related convictions – but he must if they are for more than one serious offence, which affects the applicant's good repute – but he will consider the number and seriousness of the convictions before making a grant. He may, for example, issue a licence for a shorter period to see if the applicant has 'mended his ways', or grant a licence for fewer vehicles than the number requested. If, during the currency of a licence, an 'O' licence holder is convicted of offences related to goods vehicle operations, the TC may call the operator to a public inquiry and determine whether he is still a fit and proper person or of good repute and whether he should be allowed to continue holding an 'O' licence (see also pp 84–86).

In the case of partnership applications for licences, if one of the partners is considered not to be of good repute, then the TC will be bound to conclude that the partnership firm is not of good repute and, on that basis, he may also refuse to grant a licence.

The relevant offences for which conviction damages a person's good repute are those specified in Regulation 1071/2009/EC Article 6(1)(2) and Annex IV as follows:

- commercial law;
- insolvency law (see note above);
- pay and employment conditions in the profession;
- road traffic;
- professional liability;
- trafficking in human beings or drugs;
- the driving time and rest periods of drivers, working time and the installation and use of recording equipment;
- the maximum weights and dimensions of commercial vehicles used in international traffic;

- the initial qualification and continuous training of drivers;
- the roadworthiness of commercial vehicles, including the compulsory technical inspection of motor vehicles;
- access to the market in international road haulage or, as appropriate, access to the market in road passenger transport;
- safety in the carriage of dangerous goods by road;
- the installation and use of speed-limiting devices in certain categories of vehicle;
- driving licences;
- admission to the occupation of road transport operator;
- live animal transport.

Under Regulation 1071/2009/EC the most serious infringements for the purposes of Article 6(2) (see first six points above) are as follows:

1 **(a)** Exceeding the maximum six-day or fortnightly driving time limits by margins of 25 per cent or more.

  (b) Exceeding, during a daily working period, the maximum daily driving time limit by a margin of 50 per cent or more without taking a break or without an uninterrupted rest period of at least 4.5 hours.

2 Not having a tachograph and/or speed limiter, or using a fraudulent device able to modify the records of the recording equipment and/or the speed limiter or falsifying record sheets or data downloaded from the tachograph and/or the driver card.

3 Driving without a valid roadworthiness certificate if such a document is required under Community law and/or driving with a very serious deficiency of, among other things, the braking system, the steering linkages, the wheels/tyres, the suspension or chassis that would create such an immediate risk to road safety that it leads to a decision to immobilize the vehicle.

4 Transporting dangerous goods that are prohibited for transport or transporting such goods in a prohibited or non-approved means of containment or without identifying them on the vehicle as dangerous goods, thus endangering lives or the environment to such extent that it leads to a decision to immobilize the vehicle.

5 Carrying passengers or goods without holding a valid driving licence or carrying by an undertaking not holding a valid Community licence.

6 Driving with a driver card that has been falsified, or with a card of which the driver is not the holder, or which has been obtained on the basis of false declarations and/or forged documents.

7 Carrying goods exceeding the maximum permissible laden mass by 20 per cent or more for vehicles the permissible laden weight of which exceeds 12 tonnes, and by 25 per cent or more for vehicles the permissible laden weight of which does not exceed 12 tonnes.

The seven main categorized offences above are now normally referred to as the 'Seven Deadly Sins'.

Commission of any of the seven offences listed above, besides any fines imposed by the Courts, may result in:

- the operator's Operator Compliance Risk Score (OCRS) score being seriously affected (see p 448);
- loss of good repute for the operator and/or transport manager;
- if appropriate, a premises check of the undertaking;
- a record of the offence(s) being made in the National Electronic Register (see p 61);
- revocation, suspension, curtailment or loss of the 'O' Licence.

Serious Offences

A serious offence, by an individual or by a company or its management, as referred to above, is defined as one where, if committed in the UK, a sentence of more than three months' imprisonment, or a community service order of more than 60 hours was ordered, or a fine exceeding level four on the standard scale (currently £2,500) was imposed. If committed abroad the seriousness of the offence would be determined by assessing the punishment relative to UK standards.

Criminal Offences

Convictions for offences such as falsifying records (eg tachograph charts or records), forgery (eg of insurance documents or a driving licence) and fraudulent use or display of an official document (eg an 'O' licence disc), including aiding and abetting these offences, brand the offender a criminal. These convictions will be recorded and can be accessed by the police and, if required, by the TCs in determining a person's good repute for 'O' licensing purposes.

Spent Convictions

Spent convictions, which are referred to above in the context of good repute, are those which *do not* have to be declared on the licence application form, because they were incurred sufficiently long ago to be considered legally invalid for determining a person's past record. Under the Legal Aid, Sentencing and Punishment of Offenders Act 2012, the rehabilitation period (the length of time before a caution or conviction becomes spent) is determined by the type of disposal administered or the length of the sentence imposed. Rehabilitation periods that run beyond the end of a sentence are made up of the total sentence length plus an additional period that runs from the end of the sentence, which are commonly called the 'buffer periods'. Other rehabilitation periods start from the date of conviction or the date the penalty was imposed. The 'buffer periods' are halved for those who are under 18 at date of conviction (save for custodial sentences of six months or less where the 'buffer period' is 18 months). The rehabilitation periods for sentences with additional 'buffer periods' which run from the end date of the sentence are shown in the table below:

Sentence/disposal	Buffer period for adults (18 and over at the time of conviction or the time the disposal is administered). This applies from the end date of the sentence (including the licence period)	Buffer period for young people (under 18 at the time of conviction or the time the disposal is administered). This applies from the end date of the sentence (including the licence period)
Custodial sentence* of over 4 years, or a public protection sentence	Never spent	Never spent
Custodial sentence of over 30 months (2½ years) and up to and including 48 months (4 years)	7 years	3½ years
Custodial sentence of over 6 months and up to and including 30 months (2½ years)	4 years	2 years
Custodial sentence of 6 months or less	2 years	18 months
Community order or youth rehabilitation order**	1 year	6 months

*Custodial sentence includes a sentence of imprisonment (both an immediate custodial sentence and a suspended sentence), a sentence of detention in a young offender institution, a sentence of detention under section 91 of the Powers of Criminal Courts (Sentencing) Act 2000, a detention and training order, a sentence of youth custody, a sentence of corrective training and a sentence of Borstal training.**In relation to any community or youth rehabilitation order which has no specified end date, the rehabilitation period is 2 years from the date of conviction.

The following table sets out the rehabilitation period for sentences which do not have 'buffer periods' and for which the rehabilitation period runs from the date of conviction:

Sentence/disposal	Rehabilitation period for adults (18 and over at the time of conviction or the time the disposal is administered)	Rehabilitation period for young people (under 18 at the time of conviction or the time the disposal is administered)
Fine	1 year	6 months
Conditional discharge	Period of the order	Period of the order
Absolute discharge	None	None
Conditional caution and youth conditional caution	3 months or when the caution ceases to have effect if earlier	3 months
Simple caution, youth caution	Spent immediately	Spent immediately
Compensation order	On the discharge of the order (ie when it is paid in full)	On the discharge of the order (ie when it is paid in full)
Binding over order	Period of the order	Period of the order
Attendance centre order	Period of the order	Period of the order
Hospital order (with or without a restriction order)	Period of the order	Period of the order
Referral order	Not available for adults	Period of the order
Reparation order	Not available for adults	None

Financial Standing

The requirement for financial standing means the applicant being able to prove to, or assure, the TC that sufficient funds (ie money) are readily available to maintain the vehicles authorized to be covered by the licence to the standards of fitness and safety required by law. (The requirement to have sufficient funds to cover authorized vehicles means that an operator with five vehicles, with an operator licence authorizing 10 vehicles, will need to be able to prove sufficient financial reserves for all 10 authorized vehicles).

The actual levels of financial reserves are quoted in euros as €9,000 for the first authorized vehicle and €5,000 for each additional authorized vehicle.

However, in recent years, due to the fluctuations of the value of the euro, the UK TCs review this provision annually and, at the time of writing (November 2019), the financial resources required for UK operators in support of an 'O' licence application changed as follows.

For a standard national or standard international 'O' licence the relevant amounts for 2019 are:

- First authorized vehicle £8,000
- Each additional authorized vehicle £4,450

For a restricted 'O' licence the relevant amounts are:

- First authorized vehicle £3,100
- Each additional vehicle £1,700

The financial resources figure for Standard Licences is higher than it was in 2018 due to the fluctuating value of the British pound against the euro following the Brexit decision. The financial resources for Restricted Licences remain the same as previously.

These resources comprising both capital and reserves must be available to the operator at all times and must be demonstrated on the basis of annual accounts certified by an auditor or duly accredited person.

The above values are converted from euros, which vary daily in line with exchange rate fluctuations. For the purposes of the Directive its value against national currencies is fixed annually based on its value on the first working day of October each year to take effect from 1 January of the following calendar year (the rate is published in the *Official Journal of the European Communities*).

It is important to realize that the requirement for minimum levels of capital and reserves applies to the total number of vehicles authorized on an 'O' licence, not just to the vehicles currently specified. In the case where an operator has a significant margin between the number of authorized vehicles and those actually specified, he may wish to consider decreasing this margin to reduce the amount of financial resources he has to prove to the Traffic Commissioner. The number of authorized vehicles on an 'O' licence can be reduced by application to the TC using form GV81 (see p 55).

The EU Directive allows for the financial standards described above to be established by means of confirmation or assurance from a bank or from other properly qualified institutions that such funds are available, in the form of a bank guarantee, pledge or security, or by similar means. The operator does not need to actually hold the reserves but must have agreed access to them.

A key point that has been reiterated recently is that proof of sufficient finances to meet the legal requirement should not relate to a single day when a bank balance may have been artificially boosted by a temporary injection of funds that are, in effect, moved away again the next day, but rather should relate to an average balance over the life of the licence. The TC has to be certain that the licence applicant or operator has sufficient funds 'available'* to establish and properly administer the business on a daily basis, not just to meet a target balance on a particular day.

** 'Available' in this context means, according to the Transport Tribunal: 'capable of being used'; 'at one's disposal'; 'within one's reach'; 'easy to get at'. (These definitions cover agreed access to a sufficient overdraft.)*

Failure to pay fines, other penalties and business debts as well as non-payment of vehicle excise duties will suggest to the TC that an operator has cash-flow problems and is therefore unlikely to meet the legal requirement for financial standing. This could lead to a licence not being granted or the loss of an existing 'O' licence.

Assessment of Financial Standing

On the fifth anniversary of the grant of a licence, the TC may carry out a 'wealth' check to determine whether the required reserves have been available during the previous five years. If they have *not*, the licence holder will be deemed to be no longer of the required financial standing and the licence can be revoked.

The TC has considerable powers to inquire into the finances of applicants, including the new requirement that applicants need to declare any past bankruptcy or financial failures, and the right to ask for the production of proof of financial standing by means of audited accounts and bank statements or bank references, savings or deposit account books or other evidence of funds stated to be available for the maintenance of vehicles. He will particularly look at the firm's balance sheet within the audited accounts and determine its liquidity (ie its capability of paying its debts as they fall due). He will examine the relevant financial ratios such as current assets to current liabilities, which should exceed 0.5 (meaning that the applicant can only pay half their creditors). However, any ratio between 0.5 and 1.0 may indicate a problem and must be referred to the TC to ensure that there are arrangements in place to cover any deficit.

Where an operator becomes unable to meet the financial standing requirements, perhaps because of a loss of business or some sort of major financial expenditure, the TC can allow a 'period of grace' of up to six months for the operator to resolve the issue and to prove that they can, once again, meet the requirements.

NB: Road hauliers who make a practice of factoring their debts (ie selling their unpaid invoices at less than face value to secure a quick cash return) may find the TC questioning their financial standing on the grounds that such practices are an indicator that all is not well within a firm and that it might not meet the required financial standards for holding an 'O' licence.

In complex cases, usually involving companies where, perhaps, funds are moved between one subsidiary and another, and there is cross-accounting and suchlike, the TCs can call on financial experts (assessors) to help determine the true position of an applicant.

Operating Centres

The vehicle operating centre is defined as the place where the vehicle is 'normally kept'. This is commonly taken to mean the place where the vehicle is regularly parked when it is not in use and sufficient space must be available to park all the vehicles and trailers on the 'O' licence. However, places where vehicles are parked occasionally, even if on a regular basis, in circumstances that are exceptional to the normal conduct of the business, are not considered to be operating centres.

Where operators regularly permit drivers to take vehicles home with them at night and at weekends in circumstances that are not 'exceptional' to the normal conduct of the business, then the place where the drivers park vehicles near to their home becomes the vehicle operating centre. This place must be declared on the 'O' licence application form.

In these circumstances an operator could have to declare a number of separate operating centres in addition to his normal depot or base and he could face environmental representation against each of these places and have restrictive environmental conditions placed on his licence in respect of their use. Alternatively, he could lose his licence if he fails to declare such places as operating centres. Failure to notify the TC of new or additional operating centres is an offence. Similarly, the practice of allowing drivers to take vehicles home regularly or, for other reasons, park away from the operating centre regularly (except when on genuine journeys away from base) puts the 'O' licence in jeopardy, as well as risking prosecution.

What is abundantly clear is that Traffic Commissioners expect licence applicants to be able to show that their proposed operating centre is both suitable in environmental terms and sufficiently large to accommodate all the vehicles authorized to be based there. Should this not be the case a licence may be refused or a grant made authorizing fewer vehicles (ie only as many, possibly, as can be parked at the centre).

Where an operating centre may be overcrowded at times leading to vehicles (including staff cars, etc) having to park outside on a road or roads in the area, or wait for periods outside in order to enter, this may also affect the suitability in relation to residents making representations about the centre affecting their use and enjoyment of their land, or vehicles causing an obstruction.

It is useful to stress again that the use of an unauthorized operating centre or failure to notify the TC of a change of operating centre is an offence which can result in a fine of up to £2,500 on conviction and penalty against the 'O' licence.

Operating centres are subject to review as to their continued suitability at five-yearly intervals – at the TC's discretion. In other words, the TC may call an operator for review once every five years, but should he decide not to do so the centre remains 'suitable' for another five years.

A recent consideration for some international operators is whether or not to move their operating centres/operations from the UK and into the EU. This is being considered due to the expected shortage of permits available to UK-based operators hoping to move goods from a non-EU country to EU countries, once we no longer belong to the EU. Relocation would mean that the operation would become an EU operation and they are not currently subject to the UK's harsh permit restrictions.

Licence Application

Applications for 'O' licences are based on where the operator keeps his vehicles. In the first instance the completed application form (GV79) must be sent to the DVSA Central Licensing Office in Leeds (see Appendix I). After initial processing the application will be forwarded to the TC for each Traffic Area in which the operator has vehicles based. These bases will be the operating centres (see above for definition) for the vehicles. One 'O' licence will be sufficient to cover any number of vehicles operating at one centre and any number of operating centres in any one Traffic Area. If operating centres are required in different Traffic Areas then separate 'O' licences will be required for each Traffic Area. (A list of Traffic Area Office addresses is to be found in Appendix I.)

Form GV79

Application for a licence has to be made on the appropriate form – form GV79. Copies of the form and the official guidance notes – GV79 (G) – can be requested in hard copy from the CLO or downloaded by going to GOV.UK and typing in 'Goods Vehicle Operator'. Applications can also be made online, using an electronic version of the GV79, through the GOV.UK website. The GV79 form incorporates questions relating to vehicle operating centres, the previous history of licence applicants during the past five years and the type of licence required. DVSA also publish a Guide to Operator Licensing (GV74) which is free to download from the DVSA website.

There are questions to be answered on the form relating to the name and address of the business, its partners or directors; information regarding vehicles currently owned and those which it is planned to acquire is also required and the address of their respective operating centres. Questions ask if the applicant company or individual or any partners of the business have convictions which are not 'spent' (see above). Details are required of any such convictions including the date of the conviction, the nature of the offence, the name of the court and the penalty imposed.

Further questions require information about vehicle maintenance – who is to do it, when and where is it to be done, and what facilities there are at that place. Questions are asked about the financial status of the business proprietor, his partners or the directors of the business, in particular asking whether during the past three years any of them have been made bankrupt, been involved with a company which has gone into insolvent liquidation, or been disqualified from acting as a director or taking part in the management of a company. Details about the professionally competent person supporting the application for a standard licence are also required using a form TM1. This is a declaration evidencing their personal details, details of the agreed hours of work, any relevant, or transport-specific convictions, previous employment covered by operator licensing, the actual place of work and the address of the operating centre(s) for which he is responsible.

Accompanying the TM1, an original version of their Certificate of Professional Competence and proof of their appointment must also be submitted.

Undertakings

When the applicant signs the form he is not only declaring that the statements of fact made on the form are true but also, in effect, he is making legally binding promises – undertakings – that statements of what he intends to do will be fulfilled. The undertakings relate to the observation of certain aspects of the law concerned with goods vehicle operation and the maintenance of vehicles included in the licence application. If at some time during the currency of the licence the TC finds that these undertakings have not been fulfilled, as evidenced by any convictions for relevant offences, he may use his powers to revoke, suspend or curtail the licence. The basis on which the applicant makes the undertakings is that he promises the following:

I, or the licensed operator, undertake to make proper arrangements so that:

- the laws relating to the driving and operation of vehicles used under this licence are observed;
- the rules on drivers' hours and tachographs are observed, proper records are kept and these are made available on request;
- vehicles and trailers are not overloaded;
- vehicles operate within speed limits;
- vehicles and trailers, including hired vehicles and trailers, are kept in a fit and serviceable condition;
- drivers report promptly any defects or symptoms of defects that could prevent the safe operation of vehicles and/or trailers, and that any defects are recorded in writing;
- records are kept (for 15 months) of all driver reports which record defects, all safety inspections, routine maintenance and repairs to vehicles, and that these are made available on request;
- in respect of each operating centre specified, the number of vehicles and the number of trailers kept there will not exceed the maximum numbers authorized at each operating centre (which will be noted on the licence);
- an unauthorized operating centre is not used in any Traffic Area;
- furthermore, I will notify the TC of any convictions against myself, or the company, business partner(s), the company directors, nominated transport manager/s named in this application, or employees or agents of the applicant for this licence and, if the licence is issued, convictions against the licence holder or employees or agents of the licence holder;
- I will ensure that the TC is notified within 28 days of any other changes, for example a change to the proposed maintenance arrangements*; a change in the financial status of the licence holder (eg if placed in liquidation or receivership), or a change to limited company status or partnership, that might affect the licence, if issued.

For Standard Licence holders only:

- I must be able to prove that I have a formal arrangement for access at all times to at least one vehicle registered or in circulation in GB. This could be by specifying a vehicle for use under an 'O' licence or by demonstrating on request that I (the licence holder) have a vehicle available – so vehicles may be either wholly owned or held under a hire purchase, hire/leasing arrangement or other type of formal arrangement.
- I have an establishment in GB with premises in which I keep core business documents. These include (as a minimum) accounting and personnel management documents and data on driving time and rest. I understand that the use of a PO box or third-party address is not permitted.

** In 2016, the Senior TC re-issued Statutory Document No 2 which states that, whilst 28 days will normally be acceptable, in cases such as a change of maintenance provider, the TC should be notified 'as soon as possible'*

The application form is straightforward and simple to answer and extensive explanatory notes are provided for guidance. The Traffic Area Office also sends applicants a free booklet, *Goods Vehicle Operator Licensing – Guide for Operators* (GV74), to provide further help. Further information is also available at the DVSA website: http://www.dvsa.gov.uk (archived at https://perma.cc/M4FM-5N7D). This does not, however, mean that the form should not be carefully studied or that any answer will do in an attempt to gain a licence. While it is obvious that to get an 'O' licence the undertakings must be signed, it should be remembered that the consequences of not fulfilling the stated undertakings can lead to penalties so severe as to put a small operator out of business and even to cause hardship to a large one. A warning about this in the following terms is included in the explanatory notes just before the space for the applicant's signature on the form so that applicants are left in no doubt as to the consequences of making false statements or not fulfilling statements:

> 'I declare that the statements made in this application are true and that all supporting evidence supplied with regard to my application is correct. I understand that it is an offence to make a false declaration.'

The GV79 also has a section used for supplying details of vehicles, for example, registration number, maximum gross weight, body type – flat or sided including skeletals, box body or van, tanker or other type such as cement mixer or livestock carrier – and whether the vehicle is articulated, a tipper or refrigerated. Certain designation letters and numbers are used to indicate body and vehicle type as follows:

1. flat or sided including skeletals;
2. box body or van;
3. tanker;
4. other type (such as cement mixer, livestock carrier).

After using one of the numbers above a letter will follow as below:

If it is a tipper then put a T after the number.
If it is a refrigerated vehicle put an R after the number.
If it is an articulated vehicle put an A after the number.

Where a vehicle falls into more than one category multiple letters may need to be used. (For example an articulated, refrigerated box body will be listed as 2AR.)

Form TM1

When completing the GV79 application form the operator must list all of the nominated transport managers they propose to name on the licence. In addition, using form TM1, each named manager must provide their personal details, and give information of other employments and particulars of previous convictions. They should also submit a signed contract of employment in order to confirm their stature. The manager is also required to sign a 'Declaration' contained within the TM1, in which he undertakes to ensure vehicles are operated in a safe and legal manner. This means that the transport manager will be responsible for drivers' hours and records, speed limits, driver licensing, DCPC, road traffic rules, vehicle maintenance, vehicle weights, operating centres and notifying the TC as and when required, including upon resignation from the company. The manager's original certificate which provides proof of their professional competence must accompany the application. Guidance on completing form TM1 is available on a document, TM1(G).

The TCs have now also re-issued guidelines on the number of hours that need to be spent by a nominated transport manager in order for them to be able to satisfy the TCs that they have actual control over the fleet(s) under their charge. These are as follows:

Vehicles	Guideline hours (per week)
2 or less	2–4
3–5	4–8
6–10	8–12
11–14	12–20
15–29	20–30
30 and above	30 Full-time*
More than 50	Full-time and additional assistance is required

Additional hours may be required for fleets with trailers.
*When a single person is in control of 30 or more vehicles the TCs expect the operator to provide details on how the person will administer 'effective and continuous' control of the fleet

Additional Application Forms

Supplementary application forms are used in connection with licence applications. These forms are used as Annexes to the application form GV79 and are:

Annex A – the advertisement (Form GV79A)
Annex B – current financial levels (Form GV79B)
Annex C – scale of fees (Form GV79C)
Annex D – maintenance contract (Form GV79D)
Annex E – supplementary environmental information (Form GV79E)

Annexes A–D are all part of the initial application process and further financial information may be called for in the form of bank guarantees, bank references, credit ratings, etc, should the TC have any concerns about the contents of Annex B. The final Annex, Annex E, is a supplementary form in its own right and is explained below.

Environmental Information

Form GV79E is sent to a licence applicant if the TC receives representations from local residents following publication of details of the applicant's proposals regarding his vehicle operating centre in the local newspaper. The form must be completed and returned to the TC, who will then consider the application in the light of this further information, the information given by those making the environmental representations and as a result of making his own enquiries.

The form requires details of the applicant's name and address, and the address of his proposed operating centre (see p 30 for definition). It then requires information about the vehicles to be normally kept at the centre and the number and types of trailer to be kept there. Information must be given about any other parking place in the vicinity of the operating centre which is to be used for parking authorized vehicles (ie those authorized on the licence). If the applicant is not the owner of the premises he must send evidence to show that he has permission or authority to use the place for parking vehicles.

A number of further questions must be answered on the form about the operating times of authorized vehicles – in particular, what time lorries will arrive at and leave the centre, whether they will use the centre on Saturdays or Sundays, what times they will arrive and leave on these days, whether maintenance work will be carried out there and between what hours, and whether any of this work will take place on Saturdays or Sundays and, if so, between what hours. The TC also wants to know whether there are any covered buildings at the centre in which this work is carried out.

A plan showing the parking positions for authorized vehicles must be sent when returning the completed form. This should show entry and exit points, main buildings, surrounding roads with names and the normal parking area for the vehicles. The scale of the plan must be indicated and this is suggested as being 1:500, which is 1 centimetre to 5 metres or, roughly, 1 inch to 40 feet. A larger scale of 1 inch to 100 feet can be used if this is more convenient when the operating centre is large. If the proposed operating centre has not previously been used as such the TC must be given information about any application for or planning permission granted for the proposed use of the site as a goods vehicle operating centre.

Date for Applications

Application for an 'O' licence should be made at least nine weeks (seven weeks if using VOL) before the day on which it is desired to take effect. In some Traffic Areas the time taken to process applications is much longer than nine weeks so new operators should be aware of the fact that it is illegal to start operating vehicles until their licence has actually been granted. Where there is an urgent need to start operations before a licence is granted through the normal processes, application can be made to the TC for an interim licence (see p 39), although the granting of an interim licence is unlikely if the applicant is unable to show any previous experience of having held, or holding, an 'O' licence.

Offences while Applications are Pending

Applicants for licences have a duty to advise the TC if, in the period of time between the application being submitted and it being dealt with by the TC, they are convicted of a relevant offence or declared bankrupt, etc which they would have had to include on the application form had the conviction, etc been made before the application was made. Failure to notify the TC is an offence and it could jeopardize any licence subsequently granted.

Advertising of Applications

Applicants for 'O' licences who are seeking a new licence, or variation of an existing licence, are required to arrange for publication of an advertisement (following a specified format to contain the necessary information for potential environmental representors – see Figure 1.1) in a local newspaper (or newspapers) circulating in the area where the operating centre is located. If more than one operating centre is specified in the application separate advertisements must be placed for each such centre in the respective local newspapers serving those locations. The sole purpose of the advertisement is to give local residents an opportunity (given to them under the regulations) to make representations against proposals to use a particular place as a goods vehicle operating centre.

The advertisement needs appear only once but it must be published during a period extending from not more than 21 days before and not more than 21 days after the licence application is made. There is no specified minimum or maximum size requirement for the advertisement but the TCs advise that it 'should not be too small and should be easy to read'. Most adverts appear in single-column format extending to a few inches of text and at an average cost estimated to be in the region of £100–200. Normally the advertisement will appear in the public or official notices section of the newspaper. (Because the TC can refuse a licence if the advertisement is not in the correct format, a sample blank advertisement proforma is included in the GV79 as Annex A).

Proof that the advertisement has appeared – and is published correctly (which many are not) – must be given to the TC before he considers the application and failure to produce this proof (achieved by sending in the appropriate page from the newspaper showing the advertisement itself and the name and date of the paper) will mean that the TC, by law, must refuse to consider the application. Normally this would mean making a fresh application, which, of course, delays the whole matter, adds to the costs by requiring another advertisement and could mean vehicles having to stand until the licence or variation is granted.

FIGURE 1.1 Format which must be used for 'O' licence newspaper advertisements

Advertisement	**Goods Vehicle Operator's Licence**
Your name (name of operator) ►	______________________
Your trading name (if any) ►	trading as ______________________
Your full correspondence address (as stated in Section 1) ►	of ______________________ ______________________ ______________________
Full address of first operating centre including postcode. If there is a unit number you must also include this. This must be the same as the address given in Section 10. ►	is applying for a licence to use ______________________ ______________________ ______________________
Enter the total number of vehicles and trailers to be kept at this address. These must match the numbers given in Section 10. ►	as an operating centre for ______ goods vehicles and ______ trailers
If you are applying for two operating centres and the same newspaper can be used for both, you should enter the details here. If you are only putting one operating centre in this advert then you should strike through this section. ►	and to use ______________________ ______________________ ______________________ as an operating centre for _____ goods vehicles and _____ trailers
All advertisements must finish with this section and you must not amend any of the wording otherwise you will have to place a fresh advertisement. ►	Owners or occupiers of land (including buildings) near the operating centre(s) who believe that their use or enjoyment of that land would be affected, should make written representations to the Traffic Commissioner at Hillcrest House, 386 Harehills Lane, Leeds, LS9 6NF, stating their reasons, within 21 days of this notice. Representors must at the same time send a copy of their representations to the applicant at the address given at the top of this notice. A Guide to Making Representations is available from the Traffic Commissioner's office.

Schedule 4 Application Procedure

This procedure can be used by a TC to allow an operating centre to be accepted without the need to put an advert in a local paper, as is normally required. This would apply, for example, when transferring an operating centre currently on one operator's licence to another operator, perhaps when the other operator takes over an existing operation.

However, there are particular circumstances that must be taken into consideration. These include:

- The operating centre is an existing, properly authorized centre being given up by the original operator.
- The new operator must use it on the same terms as the original licence holder.
- The applicant may specify only up to the total number of vehicles already specified at the operating centre of the original operator.
- Any conditions that apply to the operating centre concerned are transferred with it.

Such approval of the Schedule 4 Procedure is allowed at the discretion of the TC. Applications for the Schedule 4 Procedure need to be made using forms GV79, GV81 and the supplementary form GV72. These are all available from the GOV.UK website.

Interim Licences

In certain circumstances the TC may grant an interim licence pending his decision on the full licence application. The circumstances under which such a licence may be granted are not precisely specified but they may be connected with some urgent need to move goods quickly because they are perishable or for some other urgent reason. A grant of an interim licence should not be taken as a guarantee that a full-term licence will be granted by the TC. An interim licence will not be granted in any case where the main requirements for 'O' licensing appear not to be met. For example, such a licence would not be granted to an applicant for a standard 'O' licence if he has not yet passed the CPC examination nor, indeed, while examination results are being awaited, nor on the assumption that the candidate will have passed. Neither will a grant of an interim licence normally be considered before the statutory 21-day waiting period for environmental representations and objections has expired.

Interim licences are not granted for any fixed period. Normally they remain in force until the TC has made his decision on the grant of a full licence or, alternatively, until they are revoked. Applications are made using form INT 1.

Duration of Licences

Operators' licences, since 1 January 1996, are valid indefinitely and will remain so unless the operator contravenes the terms under which his licence was granted or fails to renew or pay the necessary fees by the due dates. Under normal circumstances the only reason for making a new application, and thus being subject to the risk of objection or environmental representation, is when a major variation of a licence is necessary in order to add to the number of authorized vehicles or to change an existing, or to add a new, operating centre to the licence. Despite being valid indefinitely, licences are still liable to penalty or total revocation should the operator be found to have contravened the law or breached the conditions placed on his licence. Additionally, operating centres are subject to 'review' (normally at five-yearly intervals, but not exclusively so) to determine whether they remain environmentally suitable – see p 40.

Licence Fees, Refunds and Discs

Operator licensing fees have been simplified and revised in order to part-fund enforcement and compliance activities.

Application fees and administrative charges:

Application fee for a licence (GV79) or for a major (publishable) variation (GV81)	£257 (Payment to accompany application)
Fee payable for the issue of a licence	£401 (Payment within 15 working days of issue)
Charge for the continuation of an existing licence	£401 (Payment before the end of the month preceding the end of the five-year period)
Fee payable for the issue of an interim licence or direction	£68 (Payment within 15 working days of issue)

It should be noted that all fees paid are *non-refundable.*

Termination of Licences for Unpaid Fees

It is important to note that failure to pay any of the fees described above by the due date will result in a licence being automatically terminated from the date on which the fee was due. In this event, the vehicle operation will have to cease and a new licence will have to be applied for before recommencing is permitted, if indeed it is permitted at all.

Licence Discs

'O' licence discs, issued on the grant (or variation) of a licence, must be displayed on the vehicle (normally in the windscreen) in a clearly visible position and in a waterproof container. Licence discs are coloured as follows to differentiate between restricted and standard licences and between standard national and standard international licences:

- restricted licence – orange;
- standard licence, national – blue;
- standard licence, international – green;
- interim licence – issued in the colour appropriate to the type of licence applied for with the word 'INTERIM' across the face of the disc;
- copy discs – with the word 'COPY' in red across face of disc.

Goods vehicles' licence discs are not interchangeable between vehicles or between operators. They are valid only when displayed on the vehicle whose registration number is shown on the disc (even if it is faded almost beyond recognition) and when that vehicle is being 'used' by the named operator to whom it was issued. Heavy fines are imposed on offenders who loan and borrow discs (this is fraudulent use and is a serious offence); their own 'O' licence may be jeopardized and the vehicle insurance could be invalidated.

Licence Surrender/Termination

The 'O' licence itself and all vehicle windscreen discs must be returned to the TC on the change of type, surrender or termination of an 'O' licence.

Issue of EU Community Licences/UK Licences for the Community

The title of this licence is dependent upon whether the international licence is new or existing. Older EU Community Licences continue to be valid but will eventually all be replaced with UK Licences for the Community as time passes and the UK has left the EU.

All UK holders of standard 'O' licences covering international operations are currently issued (automatically) with a UK Licence for the Community document to be kept at their main place of business together with certified copies equalling the total number of vehicles authorized on their operator's licence (a certified copy must be carried on each vehicle when undertaking journeys from the UK to the EU and/or cross-border journeys within the EU) – more information on Community Licensing is to be found in Chapter 26. Our position following Brexit (deal or no deal) will affect whether the EU continues to accept our Community Licensing status or whether we need to adopt a wholly new permit procedure for vehicles entering some countries of the EU. In either case the EU has declared that it is prepared to accept a transition period upon the UK initially leaving the EU.

The TC's Considerations

When an application for an 'O' licence is made, the TC will have certain points to take into consideration before deciding whether or not to grant any licence. Mainly he has to ensure that the basic legal requirements as described previously have been met and particularly that those relating to vehicle operation and maintenance will be complied with. These points are dealt with here.

Fit Persons and Good Repute

The first point, and one of the fundamental requirements for 'O' licensing (as already described on pp 23–26, but a repeat here is useful), is whether the applicant, and any nominated person, is a fit person or is of good repute and is therefore fit to hold a licence. Basically, being a fit person and being of good repute are the same but the former relates to restricted 'O' licences over which the EU has/had no influence while the latter is the term used by the EU in setting its requirements for the holding of a licence to carry goods for hire or reward (ie the UK system of standard 'O' licences which has been agreed as equivalent to that of the EU).

The TC, when deciding this, will take into account any previous record which the applicant (or the partners, directors or transport manager of the applicant's business) might have had as an operator in terms of his ability or willingness to comply with the law in respect of vehicle operations and particularly maintenance, drivers' hours and records, overloading and the like, also any previous convictions they may have for offences relating to the roadworthiness of vehicles and for other 'relevant' offences. The regulations require that a TC take account of 'serious offences' besides just road transport offences when determining the good repute of an individual, or of company management for a corporate 'O' licence application. (It should be noted that the terms 'relevant offences' and 'serious offences' may apply to many different types of offences including offences related to fraud or forgery, breaches of health and safety regulations, insolvency and many other offences which, whilst related to business, may not be directly related to the operation of a transport fleet.)

Maintenance Facilities/Arrangements

The next point that the TC will consider, and one of the most important since it is at the very foundation of the 'O' licensing system, is whether the applicant has suitable facilities or has made satisfactory arrangements for the maintenance of vehicles which are to be specified on the licence in a safe and legal condition and for keeping suitable maintenance records (this is dealt with in more detail in Chapter 16). In particular the TC will be concerned to know that vehicles are being subjected to safety inspections at regular intervals of time or mileage and that any person carrying out the safety inspections is capable of doing so to a professional standard.

Currently applicants for an 'O' licence need to give details of their proposed periods between safety inspections and submit the forms that will be used for the inspections, although the final decision will be made by the TC. In general terms, inspections should be based on a time interval only but high mileage vehicles, older vehicles or vehicles undertaking arduous operations may also be considerations for the TC. However, TCs generally accept that, under normal conditions, a period of six weeks between inspections is the maximum that they find acceptable. This 'acceptable' six-week period is now mandatory for trailers which are more than 12 years old, irrespective of either light work or low annual mileage. The TCs also seek assurances that operators are using a *written* driver defect reporting system and wall charts, or electronic planners, for planning inspection and maintenance schedules. Applicants will also be expected to prove that they have a planning system in place that is capable of planning inspections for at least the next six months.

Drivers' Hours and Records

The TC will consider whether there are satisfactory arrangements for ensuring that the law relating to drivers' hours and records (including tachographs) will be complied with.

Overloading

Similarly, the TC will want to be sure that arrangements are made to prevent the overloading of vehicles and that vehicle weight limits in general will be observed.

Professional Competence Requirements

When a standard licence is applied for, the TC will want to know details of the nominated professionally competent person, who may be the applicant himself or an employee who holds a Certificate of Professional Competence. Form TM1 is used to provide most of the required details. The named professionally competent person in respect of a standard 'O' licence must be an active employee carrying out the functions of a transport manager in an adequate manner who must be able to prove that they have effective control over the vehicles under their charge and be able to 'exercise continuous and effective management of the vehicles on a day-to-day basis'.

This point is reiterated in Regulation 1071/2009/EC (Article 4 (1)(b)) which states that the 'transport manager' must have a genuine link to the undertaking (ie the operator's firm) such as, for example, being an employee, a director or a shareholder or must be engaged under contract as a freelance manager to carry out the duties of transport manager for the undertaking (eg as an 'external transport manager'). The key points that the TC will take account of are as follows:

- whether the nominated transport manager is an 'internal' manager (ie a direct employee of the undertaking) or an 'external' manager (ie a freelance manager engaged under contract);
- the number of operator licences for which that transport manager will be responsible – maximum four since 4 December 2011;
- the amount of time that the external transport manager will spend in carrying out his duties for the operator;

- the number of operating centres and authorized vehicles for which the external transport manager is responsible both on that licence and any other operator's licences;
- the geographical location of the transport manager in relation to the operator's licence and the operating centres on that licence;
- any other employment or activities in which the proposed transport manager is engaged which may restrict his ability to devote sufficient time to the duties of a transport manager on that operator's licence;
- the terms upon which the proposed transport manager is to be employed.

In order to further ensure that nominated transport managers carry out their duties effectively and in accordance with the law, a proposed transport manager's contract of employment form has been devised (see Figure 1.2 on p 46), which must be completed by the 'O' licence holder and the appointed transport manager as it may be required to produce it 'upon request'.

NB: Again the EU has declared a transition period of acceptance of the UK CPC to reflect the decision by HM Government that the UK will continue to accept CPCs issued in EU member states. Whether or not this acceptance of our CPC status will become permanent is yet to be decided and may depend upon individual member states making unilateral decisions.

Number of Qualified Persons

There is no restriction under the regulations (see Chapter 2) on the number of people in a transport department or organization who may be professionally competent and consequently hold certificates of competence although not necessarily nominated on an 'O' licence. Further, although restricted 'O' licence holders have no need to specify the name of a professionally competent person in order to obtain a licence, there is no restriction on such licence holders or their employees being professionally competent if they qualify personally.

In determining how many qualified persons must be named on a standard 'O' licence the TC will take account of the management structure of applicant firms and the size of the fleet (see above), but generally there will need to be a minimum of one qualified person per 'O' licence. The TC may require the names of more qualified persons to be specified if he considers it appropriate in view of a division of responsibilities for the operation of vehicles under the licence or if vehicles specified on the licence are located at different operating centres within the Traffic Area.

Part-Time (ie 'External') Managers

Increasingly, TCs are questioning the role of part-time and agency-provided professionally competent transport managers. There is concern that such managers are not in a position to meet the statutory requirement for managers whereby they should have 'continuous and effective responsibility' for the fleet for which they are named. In particular, in addition to only being allowed to manage a total of 50 goods vehicles, the question arises of the number of clients for whom many such agency managers are acting (now set in regulations at a maximum of four) and the remoteness from the operating bases for which they are supposedly responsible, with some such named managers being in contact only by telephone or via a fleeting visit and thus having, as one TC put it, 'little physical contact with the drivers, the vehicles and the documentation'. The TCs have stated that they intend to scrutinize closely any future applications involving agency-provided transport managers.

NB: Rules affecting part-time transport managers were introduced from 4 December 2011 under EU Regulation 1071/2009/EC – see Chapter 2.

Travel

The distance that a part-time transport manager needs to travel to each site they may be responsible for is also a factor as the TC needs to ensure that they are able to attend each centre within a reasonable time, if required.

A sample contract of employment is overleaf.

Financial Standing

In addition to these points, the TC is required under the regulations (as already stated) to establish details of the applicant's financial standing (a bank statement, a bank manager's letter of reference or an accountant's certificate of solvency may be requested, for example, or other evidence of the availability of funds) because this has a bearing on the applicant's ability to operate and maintain vehicles in a safe condition and in compliance with the law (see also p 30). While considering an applicant's financial status for this purpose, the TC also has the authority to call for the services of an assessor from a panel of persons appointed by the Secretary of State for Transport, if appropriate, due to the complexity of the financial structure of the applicant's business or affairs.

Suitability of Operating Centres

An operating centre is defined as 'a place where a vehicle is usually kept'. TCs must inquire into and be satisfied that the place or places to be used as vehicle operating centres are suitable, cause no danger to the public, are environmentally acceptable and sufficiently large to accommodate all the vehicles authorized on the licence (or requested in the application). Local residents have rights (as described below) to make representations about the environmental consequences of the use of places for transport depots or vehicle operating centres and the TCs are bound to listen to these representations and make appropriate decisions about the application depending on the weight of the argument on either side – residents or operator. In particular, the TC, when considering the suitability of premises, will take account of the following:

- whether danger to the public may be caused where vehicles first join (or last leave) a public road;
- whether danger to the public may be caused on roads (other than public roads) along which vehicles are driven between the operating centre and a public road;

FIGURE 1.2 Transport manager – contract of employment

TRANSPORT MANAGER – CONTRACT OF EMPLOYMENT

Surname	First name(s)	Date of birth

Home address

(Postcode)

Address of place of work (if not the same as operating centre)

(Postcode)

Which operating centres will the nominated TM be responsible for?
All? Yes ☐ No ☐

If no, please list individual operating centres (by first address line only)

How many hours a week is the TM contracted to work?

Will the TM be responsible for vehicles on any other licences (in *any* Traffic Area)?
Yes ☐ No ☐

If yes, please list details below

Licence number	Vehicles/trailers authorized	Hours worked per week

Declaration: In accordance with the requirements of the Goods Vehicles (Licensing of Operators) Act 1995, we declare that .... will carry out all necessary checks on the operation of the licence holder's business. We also confirm that we understand the requirements placed on both of us by the above Act.

We understand that these responsibilities include:

- the method of control of drivers' hours;
- the maintenance of the licence holder's vehicles, including the inspection of vehicles at the appropriate time, the action taken to remedy defects found and the recording of these events;
- the reporting and recording of vehicle defects by drivers;
- the method of compilation and the accuracy of all records kept;
- the making of arrangements to ensure that the licence holder's vehicle/s are not overloaded.

Signature (Licence Holder) **date**

Signature (Transport Manager) **date**

- the nature or use of any other land in the vicinity of the operating centre and the effect which the granting of the licence would be likely to have on the environment of that land;
- how much granting a licence which is to materially change the use of an existing (or previously used) operating centre would harm the environment of the land in the vicinity of the operating centre;
- for a new operating centre, any planning permission (or planning application) relating to the operating centre or the land in its vicinity;
- the number, type and size of the authorized vehicles (including trailers) which will use the operating centre;
- the parking arrangements for authorized vehicles within and near to the operating centre;
- nature and times of use of the operating centre;
- nature and times of use of equipment at the operating centre;
- how many vehicles would be entering or leaving the operating centre, and how often.

Reviews of Operating Centres

TCs are given powers to review all operating centres, normally at five-yearly intervals counting from the date when the licence was first issued – in certain circumstances more frequent reviews may be carried out. Where the TC decides to review an operating centre he must give two months' notice in writing. Once the period has passed for the TC making a decision to review an operating centre, the licence holder can rest assured that he is safe for another five years, unless he operates outside the terms of his licence, fails to pay fees or applies for a major variation of the licence.

When carrying out the review of a centre, which will most likely be as a result of written complaints by local residents (who may now write in at any time rather than just when a licence application/variation advertisement appears), the TC will be concerned to ensure that it remains environmentally suitable, meets road safety considerations and can accommodate all the vehicles authorized on the licence, or that their parking causes no adverse effect on the local environment.

When carrying out the review the TC may decide that no action is required, but he has powers to act if necessary. For example, if an operating centre is found to be unsuitable he may attach conditions or vary any existing conditions for road safety or environmental reasons. However, the licence holder is given the opportunity to make representations about the effect that such conditions would have on his business before they are attached. The TC also has the power to remove an operating centre from a licence for non-environmental reasons (eg on the basis of road safety considerations), or because the operating centre is environmentally unsuitable by reason (only) of the parking of vehicles used under the licence at or near the centre.

Applications and Decisions

When an application for a new 'O' licence or a variation of an existing licence is received by the TC, details of the application (ie the name of the applicant and the number of vehicles and trailers included in the application) will be published in a Traffic Area notice called *Applications and Decisions (As and Ds)*. As its name implies, this notice will also contain details of licences granted by the TC and details of public inquiries to be held. The notice is published either weekly or fortnightly by all Traffic Areas and may be inspected at Traffic Area Offices or purchased as an individual copy or on a regular basis. It is by means of this notice that statutory objectors (see below) are able to know when applications have been made, against which they may wish to object. They can do this within 21 days of publication of the relevant As and Ds notice. As and Ds are also available for download from the GOV.UK website by typing in 'Applications and Decisions'.

Objections to the Application

Applications for 'O' licences are open to statutory objection by certain bodies listed below (and only by the listed bodies – no other individual or organization has this statutory right). Potential objectors to 'O' licences become aware of pending applications for new licences or variations to existing licences through the publication *Applications and Decisions* mentioned above.

Objections to applications can only be made by the bodies mentioned on the grounds that the applicant does not meet the essential qualifying criteria for the grant of a licence: namely that the applicant is not a fit person or is not of good repute; is not of adequate financial standing or does not meet the professional competence requirements (where appropriate); that the law in respect of those matters which the TC will be considering when he is deciding whether or not to grant a licence is not likely to be complied with, namely that the drivers' hours and records regulations will not be observed; that vehicles will be overloaded and that there are not satisfactory arrangements or facilities for maintaining the vehicles. The bodies may also object on environmental grounds (for example that the operating centre is environmentally unsuitable).

The bodies who may make statutory objection to an 'O' licence application are as follows:

- the police;
- a local authority (but not a parish council or community council);
- a planning authority;
- the British Association of Removers (BAR);
- the Freight Transport Association (FTA);
- the Road Haulage Association (RHA);
- the General and Municipal Workers' Union (GMWU);
- the Rail, Maritime and Transport Union (RMTU);
- the Transport and General Workers' Union (TGWU);
- the Union of Shop, Distributive and Allied Workers (USDAW);
- the United Road Transport Union (URTU).

These are the only sources of objection (not to be confused with an environmental representation) to an application for an 'O' licence. If any of these bodies do make a statutory objection they are required to send a copy of their objection to the applicant at his published address at the same time as sending one to the TC and this must be within 21 days of the publication of details of the application in *Applications and Decisions*. Failure to send a copy to the applicant renders the objection invalid.

Representations by Local Residents

Opportunities are given to local residents individually to make representations against 'O' licence applications and variations on environmental grounds. Local residents are more precisely defined in the regulations as 'owners or occupiers of land within the vicinity' (ie of the operating centre). Those residents who wish to make representation must do so individually because group action is not permitted (although a group of individual representors may appoint a joint spokesperson or legal representative to put forward their case), nor is representation by any environmental pressure group, political or other campaigning body. Similarly, parish councils, which regularly feature in such matters, have no right of objection per se unless they own/occupy land in the vicinity of an operating centre featuring in an 'O' licence application, in which case they may make representation as the owner/occupier of the land.

The grounds on which such owners or occupiers can make their representations are confined purely to environmental matters such as noise, vibration, fumes and visual intrusion but could include obstruction. They do not include road safety matters, which are not an environmental issue. The grounds must be stated precisely in the written representation; to state that the representation is made for 'environmental reasons' is not sufficient. The exact wording which forms the basis of representations is specified in the legislation in the following terms: 'that place (ie the operating centre) is unsuitable on environmental grounds for (such use and) any adverse effects on environmental conditions arising from that use would be capable of prejudicially affecting the use or enjoyment of the land' (ie the land owned or occupied by the person making the representation).

One of the facts that has been difficult to establish in connection with this is a definition of the term 'within the vicinity'. It has been shown that residents living along an access road to a vehicle operating centre can be considered to be in the vicinity and adverse environmental effects of vehicles travelling along the road could be taken account of by the TC in his consideration of any environmental representations against a licence application. Each TC is left to make his own determination of whether a representor lives 'within the vicinity', but as a general rule if a representor can see, hear or smell a vehicle operating centre from his property then he will be considered to be 'in the vicinity' for the purposes of making an environmental representation. That said, representations from relatives of elderly people living 'in the vicinity', on behalf of the elderly person, have been accepted by the TC in spite of the actual representor living some distance away.

There is no opportunity for people living near an operating centre to make representations on grounds other than environmental matters or to use the opportunity to vent long-standing grudges against the vehicle operator. The TCs will not consider any representation which falls outside the terms described above or which is considered to be vexatious, frivolous or irrelevant or which is not signed.

Local residents will normally become aware of their opportunity to make representations against the grant of a licence or licence variation through the local newspaper advertisement placed by the applicant (see p 38). Those people wishing to make a representation must do so in writing (or have their solicitor do so on their behalf), within a period of 21 days from the date of publication of the advertisement, to the TC at the Traffic Area Office address given in the advertisement. They must also send an exact copy of their representation (ie their letter to the TC) to the licence applicant at his address, which is also given in the advertisement. Their letter must clearly state the 'particulars' of the matters forming the basis of their representation so that both the TC and the licence applicant may be fully aware of the specific grounds on which the representation is made. Failure to be specific as to the facts in this letter, failure to send a copy to the licence applicant or failure to submit the representation within the specified timescale will render the representation invalid.

Where the TC receives a representation based on environmental issues the normal action is for the TC to call a public inquiry (PI) to give all parties an opportunity to make their cases. The PI takes the form of a quasi-judicial case where both sides submit evidence and make statements to the presiding TC. The TC will often make a ruling at the time but, in some cases, may need time to clarify details or consider wider issues and not give a ruling until some time later.

Whilst representors have no direct right of appeal should their case against use of the operating centre fail, they are able to join together with any statutory objectors in making an appeal. Operators do have a right of appeal through the Transport Tribunal (see later). The rights of 'representation' are not to be confused with the rights of objection described later.

Grant or Refusal of a Licence

The TC has power to grant an 'O' licence to an applicant if he considers that all the necessary requirements are met. Alternatively, he may refuse to grant a licence or he may grant a licence for fewer vehicles or operating centres than the number applied for if he doubts the ability of the applicant to be able to comply with the law with more vehicles, to be able to properly maintain more vehicles or to be able to adequately finance the operation of more vehicles. He can impose environmental conditions on any licence granted and can also refuse to accept the name put forward for the professionally competent person (in the case of standard licence applications) if he believes that the person is not of good repute. The TC may be influenced in his decision by the points made by any statutory objectors or environmental representors.

Licence Grant with Conditions

The case made by those raising valid environmental representations may influence the TC either to refuse the application altogether on the grounds that the operating centre is not environmentally suitable or alternatively to grant the licence but with environmental conditions attached. Thus to prevent or minimize any adverse effects on the environment he may place conditions or restrictions on the licence granted under the following headings:

- the number, type and size of authorized vehicles (including trailers) at any operating centre for maintenance or parking;
- parking arrangements for authorized vehicles (including trailers) at or in the vicinity of the centre(s);
- the times when the centre(s) may be used for maintenance or movement of any authorized vehicle; and
- how authorized vehicles enter and leave the operating centre(s) (including routes used).

As an alternative to imposing environmental conditions on the licence, the TC may seek undertakings from the operator that he will or will not follow certain practices in order to reduce environmental disturbance of local residents (eg control the number of vehicle movements into and out of the centre, times of operation, etc). The licence holder should be aware that any such undertakings he may voluntarily give to the TC become legally binding upon him and could result in a penalty against his licence if he subsequently fails to observe them.

Licence holders who find they have breached environmental conditions on their licence through unforeseen circumstances must notify the TC. Failure to comply with any of these conditions during the currency of a licence may result in the TC imposing penalties on the licence such as suspension or curtailment. In serious cases the licence may be totally revoked.

Where operators find that environmental conditions placed on their licence prove too onerous to allow them to run their businesses effectively they should apply to the TC to vary the conditions rather than ignore the conditions and become liable to a licence penalty.

Additional Vehicles

Seeking a Margin

At the time of making an application for an 'O' licence the applicant is given the opportunity to request authorization for any additional vehicles which he may need to acquire or hire during the currency of the licence. By taking this opportunity the operator saves the problems of making a fresh application when wanting to add or hire-in vehicles on a temporary basis to meet trading peaks. It also saves facing any further environmental representations or statutory objections because once the original application is granted with additional vehicles specified, extra vehicles can be added within the number authorized by completing and submitting form GV80 to the TC when they are acquired. There will be no need for the details to be advertised in a local newspaper or published in *Applications and Decisions*. They will however need to prove at the time of initial application that they have financial reserves for the total number of authorized vehicles.

If additional vehicles were requested and the request was granted at the time of making the original application, the operator will have a 'margin' for extra vehicles on the licence. As described above, the TC will need to be notified (by submitting form GV80) from the date of actually *acquiring* the additional vehicles – *not* the date of putting them into service – so that a windscreen disc can be issued for the vehicle. From the effective date of the issue by the VOL computer system (see p 12) no goods vehicle subject to operator's licensing should be on the road without a current 'O' licence windscreen disc. That said, many small operators who are not yet registered to use VOL are allowed up to 28 days to obtain a disc. Vehicles found without a current disc may be subject to impounding (see p 70).

It is useful here to clarify the terms used in connection with the numbers of vehicles for 'O' licensing purposes:

Authorized vehicles	– the maximum number of vehicles/trailers that the licence is actually granted to cover (it is illegal to operate* more than this number of vehicles at any time).
Specified vehicles	– the actual vehicles which the operator has in possession and which are specified on the licence by registration number.
Margin	– the difference between the numbers of authorized and specified vehicles on the licence, in other words the vehicles still to be acquired by the operator whether on a permanent or a temporary basis.

** 'Operate' in this context means 'use' and this applies to vehicles hired without drivers. Conversely, if they are hired with drivers, then they are operated under the hire firm's 'O' licence and not within the margin of the operator's 'O' licence (see below).*

Hired Vehicles

If an operator plans to hire extra vehicles without drivers (ie where he intends to have his own or hired agency drivers to drive the vehicle/s) during the currency of his licence, whether for a short period (a day, a few days or even one or two weeks) or on a long-term contract, they must be covered by his 'O' licence and he will need to have applied for a sufficient margin of additional vehicles on his licence to cover these. If vehicles are hired within the margin the TC must be notified, and an 'O' licence disc obtained for display on the vehicle.

It is illegal to operate (ie to have employed drivers to drive) more vehicles (ie of over 3.5 tonnes gross weight) than are authorized on the 'O' licence even for a temporary period or reason (eg when an authorized vehicle is off the road for service or repairs or to cover additional delivery requirements).

Number of Extra Vehicles

When making the request for additional vehicles on the initial application for an 'O' licence, the number which may be requested is not limited in any way but it is recommended that it should be in reasonable proportion to the number of vehicles already operated (or initially required) and, most important, it should only be of a number which the applicant can maintain, and prove he can maintain (both physically and financially), on the same basis as the remainder of his fleet. If the request for additional vehicles relates to vehicles that are to be hired rather than owned it must be remembered that the person who hires a self-drive vehicle is fully responsible for the mechanical condition of the vehicle in so far as safety and legal requirements are concerned.

An applicant specifying additional vehicles on the original application should give some careful thought to the exact number of vehicles which may be needed and the reasons for needing them because the TC will ask questions about this if he calls the applicant to a public inquiry. Evidence in the form of business forecasts and trends in trade would be most useful as would figures to indicate past growth of the business; evidence also to show the financial prospects of the applicant during the currency of the licence period will help towards convincing the TC that he would be justified in granting a licence for the additional vehicles requested.

Replacement Vehicles

If for some reason an authorized vehicle ceases to be used the TC must be advised of the fact, but if at that time or later another vehicle is acquired to replace it the operator must either use VOL to make the change or advise the TC on form GV80 within one month of *acquiring* the replacement vehicle. This means within one month from the date of the vehicle coming into the operator's possession, not one month from the date he starts to use it. Vehicles which are not removed from the licence (even when standing in a yard or workshop smashed or cannibalized) are still counted as specified vehicles and cannot be replaced by others within the authorized number on the licence until they are removed by notifying the TC. In any event, the windscreen discs from the vehicle(s) being replaced need to be physically returned to the Central Licensing Office (CLO) in Leeds.

Surrender of Licence

Form SUR1 is used when an operator wishes to surrender the whole of his licence. This form requires the operator surrendering the licence to make a declaration to that effect and, once completed, the form is also required to be sent to the CLO in Leeds. Forms GV80 and SUR1 are both available from the GOV.UK website.

Licence Variation

If the holder of an 'O' licence wishes to change the type of licence he holds – for example from restricted to standard national or from standard national to standard international – or to notify a change of transport manager, an application must be made either through VOL or on form GV80A. It is, of course, necessary to satisfy the legal requirements for standard licences, national or international, where the application is to upgrade from a restricted 'O' licence, particularly in regard to the professional competence requirement. Similarly, a standard national licence holder who wishes to change to a licence covering international operations must satisfy the TC that he or an employee is professionally competent in international transport operations.

Where, during the currency of a licence, the licence holder needs to add extra vehicles to the fleet that were not specified on the original application then an application must be made to the TC by using VOL or completing an application for major changes on form GV81 and submitting this well in advance (minimum nine weeks, but only seven weeks with VOL). This will necessitate placing an advertisement in a local newspaper as with the original application (see p 38).

Unless the variation is only of a trivial nature the TC will publish details of it in *Applications and Decisions* and it may attract objectors in the same way as a new application, and the public inquiry procedure will be the same as that already described.

The licence holder must never operate more vehicles or trailers than the total number specified on his licence. When extra vehicles are required he must wait until the application for an increase in the licence is granted before actually putting the vehicles on the road.

Form GV81

Form GV81 is a document called *Application for Major Changes* and must be used by applicants who wish to:

- change the total number of vehicles/trailers authorized;
- change operating centres (ie by adding another centre or stopping the use of a centre);
- change or remove a condition or undertaking recorded on the licence (including conditions on the use of operating centres).

These changes all involve the need to advertise the application in local newspapers as previously described (see p 38) and a copy of the published advertisement must be sent with the form. The usual information regarding name and address, addresses of operating centres and the number of vehicles to be based there which are in possession now or to be acquired has to be given. Also required is similar information about vehicle maintenance arrangements to that supplied on the original GV79 application (see p 32), but in relation to any additional vehicles applied for and any changed operating centres along with any request to change any of the environmental conditions or undertakings attached to the use of the operating centres. Reasons must be given as to why this change or removal is wanted.

The form has to be signed and the applicant is warned that failure to comply with conditions or undertakings recorded on a licence can result in disciplinary action being taken against the licence holder and that failure to comply with conditions is a criminal offence.

Transfer of Vehicles

If a vehicle is transferred from the Traffic Area in which it is licensed to a base in another Traffic Area for a period of more than three months, it must be removed from the original licence and specified on a licence in the new Traffic Area. Transfers for periods of less than three months are permitted with no need for notification to the TC provided an 'O' licence with a sufficient margin to cover the transferred vehicles is already held for that Traffic Area.

If the operator does not hold an 'O' licence in the other Traffic Area, or holds a licence in the area but it does not have a sufficient margin to accommodate the transferred vehicles, then an application for a new licence or a variation of the existing licence must be made to the TC for that Traffic Area. It is illegal to operate vehicles (ie over 3.5 tonnes gvw) from a base in a Traffic Area unless a licence is held in that area.

Notification of Changes

Licence holders should notify the TC in writing, within *28 days*, or use VOL, to notify of any changes in the legal entity of their business such as a change of name, address, ownership, if a new partnership has been formed, a limited company formed or the constitution of the partnership has been changed, as this makes a material difference to the information given in answer to questions on the original GV79 licence application. The TC must also be informed if the proprietor or persons concerned in the business die or if the business becomes bankrupt or goes into liquidation.

A change of business address as given in the original licence application must be notified to the TC within *28 days*. A change of operating centre (or the use of an additional operating centre) also requires a variation application using form GV81 and the need to follow the newspaper advertisement procedure before any change actually takes place – it is illegal to change or add an operating centre without first seeking the TC's approval by the GV81 application procedure (ie to be submitted at least nine weeks prior to any change being required).

Other changes which must be notified in writing are those in maintenance facilities or arrangements and any breach of environmental conditions which the TC placed on the licence. Failure to notify the TC of such changes can have the same result as making false statements or failing to fulfil intentions stated in the original application, namely the risk of licence suspension, curtailment or revocation. The offender could also be prosecuted with the consequent penalties which can be imposed by the courts.

As mentioned earlier, the TC expects to be notified of some changes 'as soon as possible', other changes may be subject to a 28-day notification period and others may require the use of a specific form. Operators are advised to seek clarification on timescales for any change they intend to make, or have just made, from their local Traffic Area Office or by contacting the CLO.

Subsidiary Companies

A holding company can include in its application for an 'O' licence vehicles belonging to any subsidiary company in which it owns more than a 50 per cent shareholding. But associate companies (ie where the shareholding arrangement is less than 50 per cent), owned by the same holding company, cannot have vehicles specified on each other's licences and separate divisions of a company are not permitted to hold separate licences unless they are separate entities in law.

The vehicles of any subsidiary company acquired during the currency of the holding company's 'O' licence can, if desired, be included in the holding company's licence either within its existing licence margin or by making application to the TC, on form GV81, to vary the licence. It is not generally likely that an application to include a subsidiary company's vehicles on the holding company's licence would be published in *Applications and Decisions* or that it would attract any objections.

Under the regulations, for the purposes of determining whether goods are carried for hire or reward in order to choose between a restricted or a standard 'O' licence, goods belonging to, or in the possession of, a subsidiary company are considered to belong to, or be in the possession of, the holding company and vice versa, so that in such cases a restricted 'O' licence would be adequate even if charges for the movement of the goods were made between the holding company and its subsidiary.

Temporary Derogation

There are provisions in the latest Senior Traffic Commissioner's Statutory Document No 3 to enable a standard 'O' licence to remain in force for up to six months initially and a further three months if the TC feels it is appropriate, should the specified professionally competent person named on the licence die or become legally incapacitated (ie unable to carry out his duties due to reasons of mental disorder), in order to allow a replacement person to be found and specified.

The regulations enable the TC to defer revocation of, or refusal to grant, a standard 'O' licence in the event of the death or incapacity of the holder of the licence, a transport manager or a partner whose professional competence is relied upon. Further, in the event of the death or incapacity of the licence holder the TC is empowered to authorize another person to carry on the business during the changeover period as though that person was the licence holder. Also, the TC may allow time for a transport business to be transferred to another person licensed to carry it on or for a transport manager or new partner to be appointed.

Where a person who was carrying on a business as a licence holder dies, becomes mentally incapacitated, becomes bankrupt or goes into liquidation, or where a partnership is dissolved, the TC must be notified 'as soon as possible'. The person carrying on the business will be considered by the TC to be the holder of the licence while the required changes are made.

Production of 'O' Licences

Operator's licence holders must produce their 'O' licence (form OL 1 plus vehicle disc form OL 2*) for examination when required to do so by the police, DVSA examiners (ie certifying officers) or by the TC or a person with his authority. The holder has 14 days in which to present the licence either at one of the operating centres authorized on the licence or at his principal place of business in the Traffic Area. In the case of production to the police this can be at a police station of the holder's choice, also within 14 days.

** It is an offence to have a vehicle disc that cannot be read (faded by sunlight, etc) and faded or damaged discs need to be replaced before they become unreadable.*

TCs' Powers of Review

TCs have statutory powers (under the Goods Vehicles (Licensing of Operators) Act 1995, section 36) to review and, if they see fit, to vary or revoke any decision they have previously made to grant or refuse:

- an application for an operator's licence; or
- an application for the variation of an operator's licence requiring publication.

These powers to review a previous decision apply only in the following circumstances:

- if, within two months, the TC has given notice to the applicant or the licence holder that he intends to review the decision;
- if, within two months, a person who appears to the TC to have an interest in the decision has requested him to review it;
- where neither of the above situations apply, if the TC considers that there are exceptional circumstances to justify a review.

Variation or revocation of any previous decision by the TC does not make unlawful any actions relying on that decision before the variation or revocation imposed at the review comes into force.

Normally the TC will only decide to review his previous decisions where he is satisfied that a procedural requirement was not complied with in making the decision; for example, where an environmental representation or statutory objection was overlooked, or a decision was made under the wrong section of the Act.

This facility for the TCs to review their own decisions eliminates many of the situations which, hitherto, would have required appeal to the Transport Tribunal.

Current Situation

In 2016, the triannual review of the TCs concluded that, although changes are to be made to the administration and control of operator licensing in the future, which has already led to the appointment of new/additional TCs and Deputy TCs, the current roles of the TCs will continue in their current form. The D*f*T will, however, seek to work more closely with the TCs and the DVSA to standardize policy and improve service delivery. Some future decisions will not require any changes to current legislation and are expected to be brought in over the coming months and years. These include changes to the staffing and roles within the TCs organization, a review of the current Traffic Area boundaries and the combining of the documents 'Applications and Decisions' and 'Notices and Proceedings' (Notices and Proceedings are used for passenger operator licensing).

Changes requiring legislation to be altered or amended were planned to be introduced in 2018. These included having a single 'National' Traffic Area, removing environmental responsibilities from the offices of the TCs and the setting of formal rules for tribunals and public inquiries but Brexit has somewhat 'overtaken' these issues and they appear to be largely on hold.

Penalties against 'O' Licences

Warning

In recent years, largely because of increased levels of non-compliance by operators, the TCs are taking a harder line than before against 'O' licence offenders. In particular, operators are warned to pay more attention to their licence applications and what they are undertaking to do as operators, to ensure that there is sufficient monitoring and control of drivers and vehicles and to act against drivers who continually offend. When dealing with licences the TCs are primarily concerned with legal compliance, road safety, fair competition and the environment.

Penalties

The maximum fine which may currently be imposed by a court for running vehicles without an 'O' licence where one is required by law is £5,000 (ie level 5). Failure to notify the TC of certain information about relevant convictions incurred by the licence holder or by his professionally competent transport manager can result in fines of up to £2,500 on summary conviction.

The TCs, as the issuing authorities for goods vehicle licences, are also given considerable legal powers to revoke, suspend or curtail an 'O' licence for a large number of reasons, of which the following are a few of the important examples:

- contravention by the licence holder of the provision, in the case of standard 'O' licences, regarding professional competence requirements;
- failure to notify the TC of changes in the business;
- convictions for failure to maintain vehicles in a fit and serviceable condition;
- contravention of speed limits, overloading or offences in connection with loading or unloading vehicles in restricted parking or waiting areas;
- failure to ensure that drivers are correctly licensed;
- convictions relating to the use of rebated (duty-free) fuel oil in vehicles (see Chapter 8);

- failure to keep records relating to vehicle inspections and repairs and driver defect reports;
- falsely stating facts on applications for 'O' licences and not fulfilling statements of intent or environmental conditions placed on the licence;
- if the licence holder becomes bankrupt or, in the case of a company, goes into liquidation;
- if a place not listed on the licence is used as a vehicle operating centre.

Offences are committed, for which prosecution and a court appearance may follow, if a:

- windscreen licence disc is not displayed;
- change of address is not notified;
- licence is not produced for examination on request;
- duplicate windscreen disc is not returned if the original is found;
- disc is not returned when a vehicle is disposed of;
- subsidiary company featured on a holding company licence is disposed of and the TC is not advised.

Furthermore, the TCs are active in preventing speeding by LGV drivers, first by imposing a penalty of suspension on the LGV driving licences of offending drivers and then by penalizing the 'O' licences of firms whose drivers persistently and wilfully exceed speed limits. Evidence of such matters is mainly obtained during routine enforcement checking of tachograph records, where recordings showing frequent instances of driving above 100 kph are clear evidence of breach of the 60 mph maximum speed limit for vehicles exceeding 7.5 tonnes maximum laden weight. There are also implications for the Operator Compliance Risk Score (see later) and the power to take historic offences (up to a maximum of 28 days) into account if a driver is stopped and a prosecution is proposed for the offence at the time of that stoppage.

Note: In September 2017 the DVSA started a pilot scheme called 'Earned Recognition for Vehicle Operators'. It is a 'partnership scheme' covering both the freight and the passenger sectors and is a voluntary scheme where every four weeks established operators submit monthly performance information on how well they have met key performance standards set by the DVSA. Under-performing operators will be helped by the DVSA to improve whilst operations where compliance is good will benefit insofar that the operator's vehicles will not be stopped and checked at the roadside as often as would otherwise be the case. Further information is available on the GOV.UK website.

Usually, the offending licence holder will be called to public inquiry by the TC and be required to explain why the offences occurred and what action is being taken to put matters right or to ensure they will not happen again. Depending on his reaction to such explanations, the TC may initially give a warning about future conduct and the likely consequences if there is any repetition of the contraventions of the law or he will decide that an appropriate penalty should be imposed. This will be suspension, curtailment or premature termination of the licence, or even revocation.

If the licence holder is found to no longer comply with the basic requirements for 'O' licensing, namely good repute, financial standing or professional competence, then the TC must revoke the licence (except where a period of temporary derogation is permitted – see above). If a restricted 'O' licence holder is convicted twice in a period of five years of operating outside the terms of the licence his licence must be revoked.

Curtailment (vehicles removed from a licence) is the most commonly imposed penalty and this implies removal of one or more authorized vehicles from the licence for any period up to the expiry of the licence. Suspension involves suspension of the whole licence and this may be combined with premature termination so the TC can review the whole operation under the provisions for consideration of a new licence application. As with premature termination of an existing licence, the need to apply for a new licence places the operator at risk of objection and environmental representation. The TC can direct that a vehicle on a licence which has been suspended or limited may not be used by another operator for a maximum of six months during the period of suspension. The increasing trend by TCs to impose short, sharp two-week 'O' licence periods of suspensions is showing itself to be effective against errant operators, and is generally approved by the Transport Tribunal.

When the TC revokes an 'O' licence – which is not done lightly – he may order the holder to be disqualified, for a certain period or indefinitely, from holding or obtaining an 'O' licence and the order may be limited to one or may apply to more Traffic Areas. When intending to disqualify a person from holding an 'O' licence the TC should warn him of the likelihood, explain the circumstances leading to this decision and allow the person the opportunity of making submissions against disqualification. Following an order to revoke a licence, the TC may allow the licence holder to request a 'stay' to enable the operation to continue until an appeal to the Transport Tribunal is heard.

Revocation of Licences for Smuggling and People Trafficking

Licence holders who are convicted of smuggling and related offences such as people trafficking – mainly resulting from the illegal importation of excessive quantities of tobacco and alcohol products or illegal immigration – risk losing their 'O' licences in addition to facing the standard penalties such as substantial fines, imprisonment in more serious cases and confiscation of vehicles. Where 'O'-licensed vehicles are involved in cross-Channel smuggling or people trafficking activities, HM Revenue & Customs pass details of the operators involved to the TCs for action which could include revocation of licences.

Tough new measures to combat smuggling include financial penalties levied in order for an operator to recover confiscated vehicles, and permanent confiscation in the case of repeated smuggling offences. Drivers caught smuggling or people trafficking may also lose their driving licences and in serious cases individuals risk a prison sentence on conviction.

NB: An HM Revenue & Customs hotline is available for reporting excise duty, fraud and smuggling: 0800 788 887. Alternatively, it is possible to call Crimestoppers on 0800 555111.

Advice on 'best practice' to prevent inadvertent people trafficking is available from HMRC, the UK Border Force and trade associations (FTA and RHA).

Revocation of Licences for Using Unlicensed Sub-contractors

It is essential for 'O'-licensed hauliers to check carefully that any sub-contractor used is correctly licensed (as well as determining that he is using roadworthy vehicles and complies with the law on such matters as drivers' hours and tachographs). The use of an unlicensed operator may result in prosecution for aiding, abetting, counselling or procuring that operator to use a vehicle for hire or reward without an 'O' licence. This is a criminal offence carrying a maximum fine of £5,000 on conviction and could result in loss of the principal contractor's 'O' licence.

National Electronic Registers

One of the key provisions in Regulation 1072/2009/EC (Article 16) was the requirement for all EU member states to establish a National Electronic Register of data relating to road transport undertakings. In the UK this was undertaken by the DVSA. The essential data in the register is as follows:

(a) the name and legal form of the undertaking (ie whether sole trader, partnership or limited company);

(b) the address of the business;

(c) the names of the transport managers designated to meet the conditions of good repute and professional competence or, as appropriate, the name of a legal representative;

(d) the type of authorization (ie 'O' licence), the number of vehicles it covers and, where appropriate, the serial number of the Community licence and of the certified copies;

(e) the number, category and type of serious infringements, as referred to in Article 6(1)(2) – see p 25 – which have resulted in a conviction or penalty during the last two years;

(f) the name of any person declared to be unfit to manage the transport activities of an undertaking, as long as the good repute of that person has not been re-established and the rehabilitation measures applicable (eg additional training).

Since 2012, and currently, the relevant data above must be available upon request or directly accessible to all competent authorities of EU member states and the requested information must be provided within 30 working days of receipt of the request. The data referred to in points (a) to (d) above must be publicly accessible, in accordance with the relevant provisions on personal data protection. (Note: whether or not the UK retains the ability to provide and receive 'relevant data' after we leave the EU is, as yet, not clear.)

In any case, the data referred to in points (e) and (f) may only be made accessible to authorities other than the competent authorities where they are duly endowed with powers relating to supervision and the imposition of penalties in the road transport sector and their officials are sworn to, or otherwise are under a formal obligation of secrecy.

Data concerning an undertaking whose authorization (ie 'O' licence) has been suspended or withdrawn must remain in the National Electronic Register for two years from the expiry of the suspension or the withdrawal of the licence, and must thereafter be removed immediately.

Data concerning any individual person declared to be unfit for the occupation of road transport operator must remain in the National Electronic Register as long as the good repute of that person has not been re-established. Where such a rehabilitation measure or any other measure having an equivalent effect is taken, the data must be immediately removed.

The data referred to above must specify the reasons for the suspension or withdrawal of the 'O' licence or the declaration of unfitness, as appropriate, and the corresponding duration of the suspension.

The future of the UK's Register and whether or not the UK will continue to operate in partnership with the EU, following our departure from it, is as yet unknown.

Protection of Personal Data

The General Data Protection Regulation 2018 (GDPR) and the Data Protection Act 2018 (DPA) both act to protect data and both need to be read and adhered to in order to protect data both internationally and nationally. They both replaced existing data protection legislation and were introduced in 2018.

The GDPR covers the data protection for the EU and consists of 99 separate articles. There are eight which affect individuals. These include allowing people to have easier access to the data held on them, and new responsibilities for organizations to obtain the consent of people they collect information about.

In relation to organizations, the GDPR makes them accountable for their handling of personal data through data protection and secure data processing. It also demands organizations report any data breaches or loss and that some companies appoint data protection officers, monitor compliance and gain consent for data to be gathered.

In addition, companies that have more than 250 employees must document why they need people's data, what it is and how it's kept secure.

The DPA 2018 deals with issues that do not fall within EU law, for example, where it is related to immigration. It certainly applies the same standards as GDPR but applies them to the UK. It also transposes some of the EU Data Protection Directive 2016/680 into domestic UK law and aligns standards of data protection. Finally, it clarifies and lays out the powers, role and duties of the Information Commissioner's Office (ICO).

The Upper Transport Tribunal

Inquiries and Appeals

TCs regularly hold public inquiries (PIs) to which 'O' licence applicants are called to explain the basis of their operations. A PI enables a TC to seek more information prior to determining whether he should grant a licence or not. In the event of a representation on environmental grounds or an objection being made to a licence application the TC will hold a public inquiry at which the parties (applicant, objectors or those making representations) will have an opportunity to state their case further. If the application is refused in whole or in part or if environmental conditions are attached to a licence the applicant has rights of appeal against the TC's decision to the Administrative Appeals Chamber of the Upper Tribunal, using form UT12, within 28 days of the decision being made (see below). (Form UT12 is available from Traffic Area Offices or the GOV.UK website.)

If the appellant is not made aware of the TC's decision within 21 days because the decision is not published for some reason, the appeal must be received by the Upper Tribunal within 49 days after the actual date the appellant receives the decision.

Normally an existing licence will remain in force while an appeal is being heard and the TC may allow a revoked or suspended licence to continue during this time. If the TC refuses this the Tribunal can be asked to allow it to do so.

Statutory objectors also have a right of appeal to the Tribunal if an application for a licence is granted and they still feel that their objection is valid. Those individuals making representations on environmental grounds have *no* similar right of appeal if their case fails.

It should be noted that the Tribunal is the *only* source of appeal in regard to 'O' licensing matters.

Besides public inquiries conducted for the purposes of determining 'O' licence applications, such inquiries are also held at the TC's behest where it is necessary for him to examine the conduct of a licence holder for disciplinary purposes under the powers given him by the Goods Vehicles (Licensing of Operators) Act 1995. Section 26(1) of this Act empowers him to conduct such inquiries and impose penalties of suspension, curtailment or revocation of a licence (further details of this matter are given on pp 58–62).

Appeals are heard only in London and Edinburgh whereas public inquiries are usually held in the town or city in which the TC's office (ie the Traffic Area Office – see Appendix I for addresses) is situated.

Public Inquiries

It is useful here to mention in more detail the way in which a PI is conducted. It is presided over by the TC or his deputy and is open to members of the general public, other operators and interested persons, who may sit in and listen, and to the press, who may report all that is said.

TCs may restrict general attendance at a PI to protect an operator's business, particularly in regard to personal matters, commercially sensitive information and other information obtained in confidence. Hitherto the TC could only close a PI to hear financial information. Further, TCs must disclose at a PI any information or evidence received in writing prior to the inquiry if it is intended that such information is to be taken into account in reaching a decision.

Verbal evidence is given to the TC by the applicant or by his legal representative if he has one – and this is strongly advised in most cases due to the complexities of making legal presentations and arguing points of law in a courtroom situation and possibly the need to cross-examine witnesses such as a vehicle examiner or an environmental representor, even though it is an inquiry, not a court. In fact, the 'call-up' letter to operators facing public inquiries, in which the TC states his reasons for calling the PI and states his powers to curtail, suspend or revoke 'O' licences, as well as giving details of the time and location for the inquiry, advises this. Such advice, if it is required, should be sought from an experienced transport lawyer who fully understands the legal basis of the whole licensing system as well as the intricacies of the PI system.

Most evidence at PIs will be given in response to the TC's questions – the TC effectively playing the role of 'prosecutor' – by the licence holder/applicant, the objectors and those making representations. The evidence, unlike in criminal or civil courts, is not given under oath and statements made at a public inquiry that are defamatory or libellous of other people do not have protection by privilege. The offended person can take civil action if such statements or comments come to his notice. Similarly, if an applicant or witness lies, he will not be prosecuted for perjury, but, where this is an applicant, anything he says in support of his application may be taken by the TC to be a statement of intent to which he will be bound for the duration of any licence granted.

Evidence in some instances may be provided in writing and the TC may ask for certain supporting documents, in which case the applicant should have these to hand with extra copies for the objectors to examine. When he has heard all the evidence the TC will normally make a decision without conferring with anybody else. He may announce this at the time or defer his decision to be given later in writing. The entire proceedings of the inquiry will be recorded and transcripts can be obtained by interested parties.

TCs must now give at least 21 days' written notice of public inquiries both to operators and other parties entitled to attend, and similar notice if they intend to vary the time or place of the inquiry. However, given the consent of all parties, this requirement can be varied.

From time to time the CILT and the Trade Associations provide awareness sessions and information relating to public inquiries and these can be extremely useful to any operator facing a PI or anyone planning to represent an operator at a PI.

Appeals to the Administrative Appeals Chamber of the Upper Tribunal

The Tribunal is a completely independent judicial body supported administratively by the Ministry of Justice. The Tribunal is made up of legally qualified legal members and non-legal members, who have experience in transport operations and its law and procedure.

An appeal on form UT12 for England and Wales should be sent to:

Upper Tribunal
Administrative Appeals Chamber
5th Floor,
7 Rolls Building,

Fetter Lane,
London
EC4A 1NL
Telephone: 020 7071 5662
Email: adminappeals@hmcts.gsi.gov.uk

An appeal on form UT12 for Scotland should be sent to:

Upper Tribunal
Administrative Appeals Chamber
George House,
126 George Street,
Edinburgh
EH2 4HH
Telephone: 0131 271 4310
Email: UTAACmailbox@scotland.gsi.gov.uk

For Northern Ireland the details are:

Tribunal Hearing Centre
2nd Floor,
Royal Courts of Justice,
Chichester Street,
Belfast
BT1 3JF
Telephone: 028 9072 4823
Email: tribunalsunit@courtsni.gov.uk

Appeals may be made against a TC's decision to refuse to grant an 'O' licence if he attaches environmental conditions to an 'O' licence; if a licence is granted authorizing fewer vehicles than the number applied for; if a licence is granted for a shorter period than that applied for; or if an existing licence is withdrawn, suspended or prematurely terminated by the TC.

A time limit of 28 days is allowed in which to make an appeal to the Tribunal following a TC's decision, counting from the date of publication of the issue of *Applications and Decisions* in which the decision is published.

Should the decision not be published, or not be released to the appellant, after a period of 21 days following the date the decision was made, the appellant has a further 49 days to lodge an appeal.

Where a TC makes a disciplinary decision against an 'O' licence (ie suspension, curtailment or revocation) and the licence holder wishes to appeal, he can apply for a 'stay' of the decision until the appeal is heard, in order to keep his vehicles operating. Otherwise he would have to observe the decision irrespective of the consequences (financial and operational) on his business. An initial request for a 'stay' of the decision is made direct to the TC, but failing this an application must be made immediately to the Tribunal giving details of the decision and the reason for requesting the 'stay'. Application for a 'stay' of the decision cannot be made if there is no intention to appeal.

Appeals to the Tribunal must be in writing and should be sent to the Tribunal stating the decision against which the appeal is made, the grounds for the appeal, and the names and addresses of every person to whom a copy of the appeal has been sent. Advice and relevant forms can be obtained by contacting the Tribunal at the address above or by downloading them from the HM Courts & Tribunals Service website.

Copies of the appeal must be sent to the TC and to all objectors if the appeal is being made by a licence applicant, or to the applicant if the appeal is being made by an objector to the decision.

Although the Tribunal has the powers and status of a High Court, its proceedings are conducted informally and appellants may represent themselves or be represented by any person they choose (there are no wigs and gowns even for barristers present). However, in the best interests of the applicant, he should be legally represented at an appeal by a solicitor or barrister experienced in transport law to ensure that his case is fully and correctly made.

When an appeal is heard, the Tribunal examines the transcript of the public inquiry or the TC's statement of his reasons for the decision against which the appeal is lodged and then may ask further questions of the applicant or his advocate. No oath has to be taken and there is no protection by privilege. The proceedings are open to the public and the press. Tribunal appeal decisions may be announced at the hearing or later. All parties will be sent a full statement of the decision usually within three weeks of the hearing.

Generally, Tribunal decisions will fall into one of three categories: either to uphold the TC's decision, to change the decision or to refer the matter back to the TC with a direction that he should reconsider his decision but taking account of legal guidance from the Tribunal. In exceptional circumstances the Tribunal may review its decision subject to a request to do so made within 14 days of the appeal hearing. Decisions of the Tribunal are binding from the date they are given; in other words they have immediate effect.

Further appeals against decisions of the Tribunal may be made to the Court of Appeal or the Court of Sessions in Scotland but only on points of law, not on the original decision of the TC or the subsequent ruling of the Tribunal. The address is:

The Civil Appeals Office
Room E307,
3rd floor East Block,
The Royal Courts of Justice,
Strand,
London WC2A 2LL.
Monday to Friday, 10am to 4:30pm
Telephone: 020 7947 6000

Information on applying to the Court of Session in Scotland is available under the Rules of the Court of Session, which can be found at: http://www.scotcourts.gov.uk (archived at https://perma.cc/T28F-9QNB).

No fees are payable in respect of appeals but costs may be awarded against frivolous, vexatious, improper or unreasonable appeals.

Further details of the appeals procedure can be found in a free publication giving guidance on appeals to the Tribunal, and can be downloaded from its website at http://www.justice.gov.uk/about/hmcts (archived at https://perma.cc/MLU7-VYZZ).

Northern Ireland Licensing

Northern Ireland commenced its own UK-style 'O' licensing system in July 2012 under provisions contained in the Goods Vehicle (Licensing of Operators) Act (Northern Ireland) 2010. The Northern Ireland 'O' licensing scheme mirrors the UK scheme as described in this chapter.

Goods vehicle operators in the Province do not need to obtain a short-term 'O' licence prior to entry into Great Britain. Similarly, there is no need for Great Britain operators to obtain a short-term licence prior to entry into Northern Ireland. A goods vehicle operating on a current 'O' licence issued in Great Britain or a Road Freight 'O' licence issued in Northern Ireland is permitted to carry goods throughout the UK.

Goods vehicles from Northern Ireland engaging in own-account operations for which a Road Freight Operator's licence is required in the Province must, while operating in Great Britain, carry a document showing details of their load and route in Great Britain.

Vehicles based and registered in England, Wales and Scotland must comply with all the normal legal requirements (eg vehicle condition, excise duty, insurance and observance of traffic rules) set out in this *Handbook* when operating in Northern Ireland, but particularly so in regard to 'O' licensing (Chapter 1), professional competence (Chapter 2), drivers' hours and record-keeping regulations (Chapters 3 and 4), tachographs (Chapter 5), driver licensing and testing (Chapters 6 and 7) and plating and testing (Chapter 14). It should be noted that in regard to road traffic and road traffic offences there are differences between the Northern Ireland requirements and those on the British mainland. A separate edition of the *Highway Code* (new edition and e-edition, 2019) is published for Northern Ireland and is free to download at the nidirect.gov.uk (archived at https://perma.cc/S76V-98FJ) website.

Vehicles based and operated in Northern Ireland now also benefit from the Vehicle Operator Licensing System (VOL) and are under the supervision of the Central Licensing Office in Leeds but must comply with the law as it applies in the Province, which is substantially similar to that applicable in the rest of the United Kingdom. Further information may be obtained from:

DfI Central Licensing Office
PO Box 180
Leeds,
LS9 1BU
Telephone: 0300 200 7831 (NI Direct)
Email: niclo@dvsa.gov.uk

Conditions for Grant of 'O' Licence

Under the statutory requirements for the grant of a standard road freight operator's licence, an operator has to have premises in Northern Ireland where he keeps business documents and satisfies the issuing authority that he is:

- of good repute;
- of appropriate financial standing;
- professionally competent or that he employs a full-time manager who is professionally competent and of good repute;
- declaring all previous convictions and penalties.

The requirements of good repute and appropriate financial standing are as stated in detail in this chapter of this *Handbook*. The professional competence requirement in Northern Ireland is as explained in Chapter 2.

For a restricted licence in Northern Ireland the applicant only has to show evidence of good financial standing and declare all previous convictions and penalties.

Since 2012 the criteria relating to the holding of a licence, the validity of a licence (continuous) and most of the exemptions from licensing in Northern Ireland now align with those in the rest of the UK. The main difference is that the licensing regime is controlled and administered by the DoI and not the DVSA.

Note: This 'coming together' is seen by some professionals as preliminary alignment prior to Northern Ireland becoming either a Traffic Area in its own right or an extension of the Scottish Traffic Area controlled by the DVSA. However, this too seems to have been somewhat delayed by our leaving the EU.

Northern Ireland Penalties for Illegal Use

Making a false statement to obtain the grant of a road freight operator's licence or a road freight vehicle licence is an offence punishable on conviction by a fine or imprisonment for up to six months, or both. The 'O' licence could also be suspended or revoked. Use of a motor vehicle on a road for the carriage of goods for reward without a road freight vehicle licence can result in a fine which increases for subsequent convictions. Since February 2011 enforcement officers of the Northern Ireland Driver and Vehicle Agency (NIDVA) have been empowered to issue fixed penalty notices, some of which attract penalty points on driver licences, for certain driver and vehicle offences (see http://www.dvani.gov.uk).

Northern Ireland Powers to Stop

Under new regulations applicable both in Northern Ireland and Great Britain (ie The Road Vehicles (Powers to Stop) Regulations 2011 – SI 2011 No 996) from 30 March 2011 appointed 'stopping' officers (eg enforcement officers of the NIDVA and DVSA, certain police officers and now some police community support officers (PCSOs)) are given the power to require the driver of a commercial vehicle to stop for the purposes of examining the vehicle, the drivers' documents and records or for offences such as non-seat belt use – see also p 91 and 453–4.

Use of Light Goods Vehicles

Many existing transport operators and new entrants to the industry have sought to avoid the problems and pitfalls of 'O' licensing by using vehicles defined as 'small' vehicles – those vehicles not exceeding 3.5 tonnes maximum permissible weight. With such vehicles there is currently no need to obtain an 'O' licence and consequently no need to face the TC and satisfy all the conditions previously explained, but please note the consultations regarding vehicles 2,400 kg–3,500 kg used for hire and reward internationally, and the exemption up to 4.25 tonnes for alternatively fuelled vehicles, mentioned earlier. The operator is also free from the legal requirements under other legislation for his drivers to operate tachographs or to keep other written records of their hours of work, and to hold vocational driving licences.

Despite this apparent freedom the operator of such vehicles does have certain obligations and responsibilities. First, if he tows a trailer for hire and reward only with such a vehicle the combined weight of both vehicle and trailer (if over 1,020 kg unladen) could exceed the 3.5 tonne weight threshold above which an 'O' licence would be needed and the provisions of the EU or British drivers' hours rules and the relevant record-keeping or tachograph requirements may apply (see Chapters 3, 4 and 5). Second, if he also operates, or plans to operate in the future, larger vehicles which are within the scope of 'O' licensing, his conduct as an operator of small vehicles will be taken into account by the TC when deciding whether to grant or renew his 'O' licence.

The TCs have made the point that when an operator applies to renew an 'O' licence they (the TCs) would take notice of any relevant convictions in respect of smaller vehicles belonging to the operator and could call the operator to public inquiry to show cause why the 'O' licence should not be revoked or curtailed. The operator of small vehicles still has to ensure that vehicles are not overloaded and that they are kept in a safe mechanical order under other regulations; they must be tested annually after they become three years old (four years old in Northern Ireland). Drivers of these vehicles are required to observe the drivers' hours regulations with certain exceptions. All these individual legal exemptions and requirements are discussed in later chapters.

Foreign Vehicles in the UK

The picture post-Brexit will certainly bring some changes but currently, vehicles entering Great Britain from EU member states under valid Community Licences do not need a UK 'O' licence although cabotage authorization to operate in this country may well be withdrawn depending upon the decisions made by the EU member states regarding permitting UK registered vehicles to carry out cabotage operations within the EU area. Vehicles from certain non-EU countries where a bilateral agreement exists are exempt from the requirement to hold an 'O' licence under the Goods Vehicles (Licensing of Operators) (Temporary Use in Great Britain) Regulations 1996 and this is likely to be the preferred option for all EU vehicles post-Brexit providing we negotiate further bilateral agreements.

Other foreign vehicles entering Great Britain under an ECMT permit do not need an 'O' licence provided the permit is being carried on the vehicle.

Note 1: ECMT permits are the ones required by UK vehicles entering the EU post-Brexit in the event of a 'no-deal' decision.

Note 2: It is expected that cabotage that is currently carried out by EU vehicles when in the UK will not be allowed following a 'no-deal' decision unless reciprocal arrangements are put in place for UK registered vehicles operating in the EU.

Impounding of Trucks

Principally, impounding applies to vehicles used for hire or reward carriage without an 'O' licence in force. Such vehicles are fitted with an immobilization device (ie a clamp) either on the spot or after removal to a more suitable site, and will be marked by an immobilization notice warning against any attempt to remove the device or move the vehicle except under proper authorization. Impounded vehicles may be returned to their owner in due course provided specified conditions are met, and loads returned to their owner where title is established. Ultimately, however, without satisfactory compliance with requirements for the release of a vehicle and its load, they will be disposed of by sale or by destruction. Obstruction of authorized examiners in the course of vehicle impounding will lead to a fine at level 3 (maximum £1,000) on conviction.

An appeals procedure via the TCs initially and the Transport Tribunal subsequently allows operators to apply for the return of an impounded vehicle, although this may be unsuccessful depending on the circumstances.

Impounding of Rental/Hired Vehicles

The impounding legislation described above has caused concern for vehicle rental, hiring and leasing companies. However, the law is clear in that the regulations permit the seizing of vehicles hired out by such firms to unlicensed operators. The TCs too have made it clear that such firms have a duty to ensure that any hiring arrangement they enter into in relation to relevant (ie over 3.5 tonne) vehicles is with an 'O' licensed operator. The situation becomes more complex where a vehicle leased to an unlicensed operator by a vehicle leasing company is subject to a finance arrangement with a third party (such as a bank or loan company), which is therefore the statutory owner of the vehicle. In such cases, it becomes necessary for the legal owner to make application to the TC for the return of the vehicle on the basis that it, the legal owner, did not know that the vehicle had been, or was being, used without an 'O' licence in accordance with the Goods Vehicles (Licensing of Operators) Act 1995 (section 2). An application for the return of a vehicle in these circumstances has to be made within 21 days of the notification of the impounding being published in the *London Gazette* or *Edinburgh Gazette* (in which all vehicle impoundings are published).

Professional Competence

02

Professional competence qualifications now apply to both transport managers (the Operator Certificate of Professional Competence, or Operator CPC) and to LGV and passenger-carrying vehicle (PCV) drivers (the Driver Certificate of Professional Competence, also referred to as the Driver CPC or the DCPC). However, these are two totally different schemes with very different qualifying requirements for each of them, as described in this chapter – they should not be confused.

Professional Competence for Transport Managers

The current Operator CPC scheme is designed to make individuals more responsible for the safe operation of vehicle fleets in their charge and better qualified to understand the legal, economic and operational requirements for safe and efficient goods vehicle operation in both national and international hire and reward operations. As a result of EU influence via EC Directive 74/561 (as amended by Directives 89/438/EC, 96/26/EC, 98/76/EC and Regulation EC 1071/2009), 'On Admission to the Occupation of Road Haulage Operator in National and International Operations', the current scheme provides all those people who qualify, not just those fulfilling the role of transport manager, with either a Certificate of Professional Competence or a professional competence qualification by exemption or by examination.

One of the principal outcomes of Regulation 1071/2009 was the merging of the hitherto separate national and international CPC qualifications and the consequent merging of the two examinations. Thus, candidates seeking to qualify purely for managing domestic (ie solely within the UK) road haulage operations will nevertheless still have to study the whole international syllabus and answer examination questions on matters relating to both national and international road haulage, including specific questions on different sectors of the transport industry such as dangerous goods, temperature controlled goods and even livestock movements. This could change depending upon the position taken by the EU as the UK's independence becomes stabilized. What is sure that the CPC international questions will have to be amended and many replaced to reflect the UK's non-EU position.

Under the Goods Vehicles (Licensing of Operators) Act 1995 (section 13 and schedule 3), road haulage operators (including own-account operators who wish to carry goods for hire or reward or in connection with a business which is not their own) are required to meet the professional competence requirement in order to obtain a standard operator's licence.

Own-account transport operators who have no desire to or intention of carrying goods for hire or reward or for any purpose which is not in connection with their own trade or business can apply for a restricted 'O' licence, for which there is no need to meet the professional competence requirement. The important point for road hauliers and others who carry goods for hire or reward is that in order to obtain an operator's licence they must request a standard 'O' licence covering either national or both national and international operations and specify in their application the name of a person who is professionally competent and who is responsible for the operation and control of the vehicles authorized on the licence – the law requires the person to have 'continuous and effective responsibility' for the management of the transport operation and a direct link to the application. This person may be the applicant, if suitably qualified, or it may be a person holding the title of transport manager (or some other person – the law is not concerned as to the person's actual job-title, only that he should be the person who is responsible for the vehicle operations on a day-to-day basis) who is professionally competent and who is employed by the applicant.

As mentioned in the previous section, employment in this context does not necessarily mean full-time employment with the licence holder. Part-time or casual employment of a professionally competent person is permitted as a result of a regulation change in November 1991 under which a part-time qualified employee may be nominated in support of a licence application. Also, with this change in the law, a professionally competent person in one firm may be specified in support of the licence held by another, non-related, firm or firms.

The TCs later decided that a self-employed (ie freelance) transport manager is also acceptable as the professionally competent person specified on an 'O' licence. The employment requirement does not necessarily mean that the person concerned must devote all of their working time to the transport management function; they may have other duties and responsibilities in the firm (such as administration manager, works manager, company secretary, etc).

However, concern over the matter of part-time (ie so-called 'proxy') transport managers led the EU to bring into force Article 4(c) of EU Regulation 1071/2009 (ie the rules on access to the profession – professional competence) which stipulates that from 4 December 2011 a nominated transport manager may not manage more than four operations with a total number of 50 vehicles and must declare a minimum number of hours dedicated to transport management depending upon the size of the fleet(s). Additionally, that person must be able to show that they can 'effectively and continuously manage the transport activities of the undertaking on a day-to-day basis'. If applicable, the person must also hold a CPC in their own member state.

More recently, where the fleet is 30 vehicles, or more, the applicant is expected to explain how the fleet will be managed by describing the roles and responsibilities of the competent person.

The new rules also set out the conditions which an operator must meet to be admitted to the profession and the criteria on which good repute will be withdrawn, including drug and human trafficking.

These requirements are other factors it is felt the UK will maintain post-Brexit.

Who May Become Professionally Competent?

Professional competence is available and applicable only to individuals. Under the regulations, a firm or a corporate body cannot be classed as being professionally competent. Any individual, whether employed with the title of 'transport manager' or not, may become professionally competent if he or she meets the necessary qualifying conditions or otherwise passes the official examinations. There is no pre-qualifying standard and no requirement that the person should have any previous experience of or be working, have been working, or plan to work in the transport industry in any capacity whatsoever. It is open to absolutely anybody to become professionally competent if they so wish.

However, only those who are actually responsible for the operation of goods vehicles on a day-to-day basis will need to be 'nominated' as the professionally competent 'transport manager' in support of an application for a standard 'O' licence. Such individuals must themselves be of good repute and of appropriate financial standing. In this case this refers to previous or current bankruptcy or any offences relating to financial problems (These criteria also apply to the 'O' licence applicant – see Chapter 1). They must also be engaged in 'effectively and continuously' managing the transport activities of the undertaking otherwise their name may not be acceptable to the TC despite the fact that they are qualified as being professionally competent (see below).

Proof of Professional Competence

Proof that a person is professionally competent and is therefore able to satisfy the requirements of the 'O' licence system is dependent on holding one (or more) of the following:

- a 'grandfather rights' Certificate of Professional Competence (CPC) issued by a TC (form GV203) with acquired rights from 2013;
- an official CILT(UK) CPC examination pass certificate;
- an official OCR CPC examination pass certificate;
- an official City and Guilds pass examination certificate;
- a membership (or exemption) certificate from one of the recognized professional institutes, which confers exemption (see p 74);
- a certificate issued by an EU member state which fulfils the 'mutual recognition' requirements of EC Directive 77/796 as amended by EC Directive 89/438 that the UK has decided to recognize.

No other document provides evidence of professional competence for these purposes.

For more information on the CPC, please visit www.ciltuk.org.uk/TrainingCPD/Training/DriverCPC (archived at https://perma.cc/WZQ3-MTZL), email: pd@cilt.org.uk or call 01536 740166.

Note: As the CPC evolves, new awarding bodies are planned to come on stream in the future.

Classes of Competence

All certificates of professional competence (CPCs – form GV203) granted under the original 'grandfather rights' scheme (see below) cover both national and international operations (although it does not specifically say so on them).

Candidates who achieve professional competence by examination will obtain appropriate documentary evidence (ie a CILT, OCR or City and Guilds examination pass certificate) indicating that they have passed the examinations.

Holders of certificates of professional competence (form GV203) or those qualified for professional competence in both national and international operations, by exemption or examination, are permitted to engage in or be responsible for the operation of goods vehicles on standard 'O' licences covering national operations within the UK and international operations outside the UK.

Note: Following legal decisions made over many years the definition of what constitutes an international journey has been changed in Britain. So, for example, where loaded trailers are taken to a port for onward movement outside the UK providing the load is not being moved under the terms of CMR, and the tractive unit and driver do not leave the UK, such journeys constitute national operations (previously, these were international operations), and a standard 'O' licence covering national transport operations only is needed for such operations. This is another scenario where a no-deal Brexit will mean change is required.

Qualification by Exemption

New entrants to the industry may obtain the professional competence qualification if they satisfy certain exemption criteria.

The exemption qualifications are normally based on holding current and valid membership of one or more of a number of professional bodies at certain levels, as mentioned above.

For All Hire and Reward Operations

- Fellow or Member of the CILT by examination and/or formal accreditation in Road Freight Transport.
- Fellow, Member or Associate Member of the Society of Operations Engineers.
- Fellow or Associate of the Institute of the Furniture Warehousing and Removing Industry (IFWRI), or, from 13 May 1995, Fellow or Associate of the Movers Institute.
- Associate of the Institute of Transport Administration by examination.

There are no grounds for obtaining professional competence by exemption other than those detailed above. Valid membership of the relevant body (ie subscription paid, etc) is sufficient to confirm professional competence but, if required, the institutes will issue a confirmatory certificate or statement (ie not a certificate of competence of the type issued under grandfather rights).

NB: Above mentioned qualifications remain valid as proof of professional competence indefinitely, but only after 4 December 2011 for those who held the qualification on or before 4 December 2011.

Examinations (from March 2012)

A system of examinations enables new entrants to the transport (ie road freight and road passenger) industry and those people who do not qualify under the previously mentioned grandfather rights or exemption arrangements to study for and obtain professional competence by examination. The examination scheme is organized and conducted on behalf of the D*f*T by the OCR (Oxford and Cambridge Royal Society of Arts), the Chartered Institute of Logistics and Transport (CILT) and City & Guilds. Examinations for both goods and passenger vehicle operations are held at main centres throughout the country four times each year by OCR and six, or more, times a year by the CILT, who are also able to offer ad hoc examinations upon request by a sufficient number of applicants.

Examination Dates

Potential candidates are advised to check dates and locations for forthcoming examinations with OCR or the CILT. Potential candidates studying with the FTA will currently be examined under the City & Guilds system.

OCR Examination System (from March 2012)

OCR's examinations for CPCs in Road Haulage both comprise a single multiple choice assessment of 60 questions and a single case study assessment. Both of these elements test national and international knowledge and application. So, to achieve a new full CPC, candidates only need to pass the two units.

The OCR 60 question, two-hour, multiple-choice assessment (part one) has been available as a quarterly, paper-based test since March 2012. From June 2012, it has also been available on screen and on demand, allowing candidates to sit or re-sit an assessment at a convenient time. The pass mark is 70 per cent (ie 42 correct answers). The RHA offer the OCR version and, whilst the FTA awarding body is City and Guilds, on-screen part one questions are also available through the FTA courses.

Case Study Examination

The new OCR post-March 2012 'open-book' case study examination is no longer preceded by a pre-release scenario. Instead, a shorter, more relevant scenario is issued with the papers at the start of a two-hour examination/assessment. It contains no distractions and only information which enables the candidate to demonstrate the knowledge they have acquired. It now only assesses the syllabus core areas. To pass, candidates will need to achieve 50 per cent over the whole paper (ie 30 correct answers).

CILT Examination System

The CILT CPC is a Level 3 qualification which can be used to progress towards Level 5 qualifications as it 'dovetails' into many other potential units of study. It entails taking two papers. Each paper has 20 short answer questions to complete and three out of four long answer, essay style, questions. There is no requirement to take a multi-choice examination and the two papers are 'open book' examinations.

Certification

When an examination candidate achieves the required examination successes at one sitting, a full Certificate of Professional Competence will be issued.

Examination Fees

Details may be obtained from OCR or the CILT as follows: OCR 01223 553998 or CILT 01536 740100; email: vocationalqualifications@ocr.org.uk; website: www.ocr.org.uk (archived at https://perma.cc/FM5R-NWJH), www.ciltuk.org.uk/training (archived at https://perma.cc/8HNE-FBEK), or through the FTA or RHA (usually for members only) at www.fta.co.uk (archived at https://perma.cc/DZ77-FVJ5) or www.rhaonline.co.uk (archived at https://perma.cc/ET7E-G7BE).

Examination Method

The OCR examinations conducted for the purpose of providing the qualification for professional competence are based partly on the 'objective testing' or multiple-choice method. In the multiple-choice examinations the candidate is faced with either a number of questions, each of which is provided with a choice of possible answers (usually four), only one of which is correct, or alternatively statements to which a 'true' or 'false' answer must be indicated. The candidate must select and mark the correct answer to each question or statement. For the OCR case study, examination candidates will be presented with a scenario (storyboard) followed by a number of questions. They will be required to write a short-response answer applying their knowledge to the situation in the scenario and accompanying questions. There are between six and eight questions in the OCR case study and all are to be attempted.

The CILT examinations require short written explanations or descriptions, etc for the short questions and longer written explanations, etc for the essay-style questions. This balance is set to enable candidates to demonstrate both knowledge and understanding. In the 'essay style' part of the papers the candidate needs to attempt three out of the four relatively short 'essay style' questions and is mostly allowed to answer using their own words and descriptions.

The examinations are designed to be within the grasp of candidates whose educational standard corresponds to the level normally reached in compulsory schooling supplemented either by vocational training and supplementary technical training or by secondary-level school technical training.

Examination Syllabus

Study Facilities

Study for the CPC examinations may be undertaken at courses organized by the CILT or group training associations, trade associations or commercial organizations. Some local technical colleges and other teaching establishments also offer part-time, usually evening, classes on the subject and many private training providers also supply this training either at their own premises, at local centres or on-site.

The study may involve full-time or part-time attendance and, in the case of the CILT, supported distance learning or it may be by correspondence course or by training or home learning package (ie notes and video) or with the aid of teaching manuals.

There are also 'self-study' books available for those who may not be able to commit to formal study. These self-study books can be very useful to give any potential CPC student an insight into the syllabus and level of knowledge and understanding that will be required in order to pass the examinations.

The Council Directive Syllabus

The syllabus for road haulage operations published in Regulation 1071/2009/EC and effective since 4 December 2011 is detailed below. It is still in force within the UK and it shows the assessment objectives and (in brackets) the depth of knowledge required for the examination.

A. Civil Law

Candidates must:

1. be familiar with the main types of contract used in road transport and with the rights and obligations arising therefrom (*Contracts: legal obligations; sub-contracting; legal duties of agents, employers and employees and the elements comprising a contract*);
2. be capable of negotiating a legally valid transport contract, notably with regard to conditions of carriage (*Legal obligations: capacity to contract; specific performance; liability; lien; laws of agency*);
3. be able to consider a claim by his principal regarding compensation for loss of or damage to goods during transportation or for their late delivery, and to understand how such claims affect his contractual responsibility (*Performance: general and specific liabilities of principal, sub-contractors and agents for the performance of a contract. Compensation: for losses relating to damage. Settlements: interim and full payments*);
4. be familiar with the rules and obligations arising from the CMR convention on the contract for the international carriage of goods by road (*CMR liability and unwitting CMR: CMR notes to CMR convention. Successive carriers. Limits of liability. Relevance of insurance*);

5 be familiar with the different categories of transport auxiliaries (*freight forwarders, warehousing and distribution services, groupage services, clearing houses*), their role, their functions and, where appropriate, their status.

B. Commercial Law

Candidates must:

1 be familiar with the conditions and formalities laid down for plying the trade, the general obligations incumbent upon transport operators (registration, keeping records) and the consequences of bankruptcy (*Trading law relating to: sole traders and partnerships; partnership agreements; rights and duties of partners; powers of partners; partners as agents; dissolution of partnerships. Company law: registered companies (private and public); AGMs; liquidation. Documentation: prospectus, memorandum of association; articles of association; certificate of incorporation*);

2 have appropriate knowledge of the various forms of commercial company and the rules governing their constitution and operation (*Types of business organization: sole traders; partnerships; private and public limited companies*).

C. Social Law

Candidates must be familiar with:

1 the role and function of the various social institutions that are concerned with road transport (trade unions, works councils, shop stewards, labour inspectors) (*Role of: employment tribunals; trade unions; ACAS; CAC; HSE; arbitrators. Employees' rights: trade union membership and activities*);

2 the employers' social security obligations (*Relevant parts of current legislation relating to: health and safety; discrimination; employment protection; employment rights*);

3 the rules governing work contracts for the various categories of worker employed by road transport undertakings (form of the contracts, obligations of the parties, working conditions and working hours, paid leave, remuneration, breach of contract) (*Contracts of employment: content of written statement; time limits for the issue of contracts. Employment rights: of full- and part-time employees; of self-employed; of agency staff; transfer of undertakings; remuneration and itemized pay statements; holiday entitlement; statutory payments; agency staff; dismissal and unfair dismissal; notice to terminate employment; working time regulations*);

4 the rules applicable to driving time, rest periods and working time, and in particular the provisions of EU Regulation, Regulation (EC) 165/2014 (this Regulation replaced the old EEC Regulation 3821/85 in March 2015) No 561/2006, Directive 2002/15/EC and Directive 2006/22/EC, and the practical measures for applying those provisions; practical arrangements for

implementing these regulations (*Community regulations: the working week; driving time; breaks; daily and weekly rest periods; emergencies. Domestic hours' law: the working week; driving time; rest periods; emergencies, working time. Tachograph legislation and operation: points of law; the records; driver and employer responsibilities; enforcement and inspection; calibration and sealing; malfunctions*);

5 the rules applicable to the initial qualification and continuous training of drivers (ie the Driver CPC), and in particular those deriving from Directive 2003/59/EC.

D. Fiscal Law

Candidates must be familiar with the rules governing:

1 VAT on transport services (*VAT – national operations: income threshold and registration; zero-rated goods and services; VAT returns; reclaiming VAT. Turnover tax – international operations: registration for VAT; applying VAT; submitting returns; reclaiming VAT*);

2 motor vehicle tax (*Calculation of VED: basis for calculating motor vehicle taxation on general vehicles and vehicles used in special operations and conditions applied to them*);

3 taxes on certain road haulage vehicles and tolls and infrastructure user charges (*Domestic operation: HGV Road User Levy, toll roads and bridges and the basis on which calculation is made. International operation: rules governing tolls and taxation of vehicles on international journeys*);

4 Income Tax (*Corporate taxation. Status: rules governing the status of employees and the self-employed and the imposition of income tax regulations. Employers' responsibilities: deduction and collection of income tax and National Insurance from employees; payment of income tax and National Insurance to HM Revenue & Customs*).

E. Business and Financial Management of the Undertaking

Candidates must:

1 be familiar with the laws and practices regarding the use of cheques, bills of exchange, promissory notes, credit cards and other means or methods of payment (*National operation – payment methods: cash; cheques; credit cards; promissory notes; bills of exchange; debit systems and credit transfer. International operation: banking and payment systems, including the electronic transfer of funds*);

2 be familiar with the various forms of credit (bank credit, documentary credit, guarantee deposits, mortgages, leasing, renting, factoring) and with the charges and obligations arising from them (*Different forms of credit: overdrafts; loans; documentary credit; guarantee deposits; mortgages; leases; rents; factoring*);

3 know what a balance sheet is, how it is set out and how to interpret it (*Determine: fixed assets; net current assets; current assets; long-term liabilities; current liabilities. Interpretation: calculate and interpret*);

4 be able to read and interpret a profit and loss account (*Determine: direct and indirect costs; gross (or operating or trading) profit; net profit*);

5 be able to assess the company's profitability and financial position, in particular on the basis of financial ratios (*Determine: capital employed and return on capital employed; return on sales and assets turnover; working capital; cash flow. Use of ratios: current ratio (working capital ratio); quick ratio (liquidity ratio or acid test ratio)*);

6 be able to prepare a budget (*Construct budgets from data supplied. Use of budgets: to monitor and control performance, budgetary control, variance analysis*);

7 be familiar with their company's cost elements (fixed costs, variable costs, working capital, depreciation, etc), and be able to calculate costs per vehicle, per kilometre, per journey or per tonne (*From data supplied: identify and/or calculate fixed costs, variable costs, overhead costs, depreciation. Determine: time and distance costs*);

8 be able to draw up an organization chart relating to the undertaking's personnel as a whole and to organize work plans (*Prepare an organization chart for an: organization, department, function, unit or depot. Organizing, planning and measuring work*);

9 be familiar with the principles of marketing, publicity and public relations, including transport services, sales promotion and the preparation of customer files (*Market research (primary and secondary); segmentation; product promotion, sales and publicity. Customer: relations; research files*);

10 be familiar with the different types of insurance relating to road transport (liability, accidental injury/life insurance) and with the guarantees and obligations arising therefrom (*EHIC; insurance: risk assessment; cover; claims, risk management and improvement of risk. Types of insurance: fidelity; goods in transit; employers' liability; public liability; professional negligence; motor; plant; travel; health; property; consequential loss; cash in transit. Risks: guarantees; obligations; liability and role of trustees*);

11 be familiar with the applications of electronic data transmission in road transport (*Legislation: Data Protection Act. Hardware and software: electronic vehicle status monitoring; electronic data transmission; real-time information systems; customer information systems; depot readers; GPS; route and load planning systems; vehicle and staff scheduling; data analysis; data information systems*);

12 be able to apply the rules governing the invoicing of road haulage services and know the meaning of Incoterms (agreed trading terms with legal definitions, eg EXW, DAP, DAT, DDP, etc).

NB: Incoterm stands for International Commercial Terms, which are overseen by the International Chamber of Commerce (ICC). The ICC produces several books and guides on the latest Incoterms being used (Incoterms 2010, which were last updated in February 2018).

F. Access to the Market

Candidates must be familiar with:

1 the occupational regulations governing road transport for hire or reward, industrial vehicle rental and sub-contracting, and in particular the rules governing the official organization of the occupation, admission to the occupation, authorizations for intra- and extra-Community road transport operations, inspections and sanctions (*National operation: role of TCs and enforcement agencies; statutory procedures concerning operator licensing; requirements for vehicle maintenance; regulations governing domestic operation. International operation: statutory procedures concerning operator licensing; regulations governing international operations*);

2 the rules for setting up a road transport undertaking (*Rules for setting up a road transport undertaking: statutory procedures and rules concerning operator licensing*);

3 the various documents required for operating road transport services and be able to introduce checking procedures for ensuring that the approved documents relating to each transport operation, and in particular those relating to the vehicle, the driver and the goods or luggage, are kept both in the vehicle and on the premises of the undertaking, permit procedures and types of permits (*Documents and their administration: operator licences and vehicle discs; vehicle authorizations; tachograph records; waybills/consignment notes; driving entitlement; maintenance documents; insurance documents; systems for document checking and control procedures*);

4 the rules on the organization of the market in road haulage services, on freight handling and logistics (*Quality regulation and its role in competitive markets; third country traffic, cabotage; through traffic and own-account operations*);

5 planning international journeys; common transit; community transit; TIR, ATA carnets; carnets de passage en douane; border crossing formalities; Schengen agreement passports and visa controls (*anti-smuggling, immigration controls; restricted goods; required documents for certain goods*).

G. Technical Standards and Aspects of Operation

Candidates must:

1 be familiar with the rules concerning the weights and dimensions of vehicles in the member states of the European Union and the procedures to be followed in the case of abnormal loads that constitute an exception to these rules (*Terms used to identify the differing weight conditions. Statutory limits: weights and dimensions. Formulas used for various calculations*

concerned in weights and dimensions of vehicles. Main rules and most common weights and dimensions used internationally);

2 be able to choose vehicles and their components (chassis, engine, transmission system, braking system, etc) in accordance with the needs of the undertaking (*Vehicle specifications that will improve road safety and economy, and reduce impact on the environment. Vehicle specifications to be taken into account for international operations*);

3 be familiar with the formalities relating to the type approval, registration and technical inspection of these vehicles (Main provisions within current legislation relating to C&U, type approval, plating and testing and safety. Powers of enforcement agencies);

4 understand what measures must be taken to reduce noise and to combat air pollution by motor vehicle exhaust emissions (*Main provisions of the C&U Regulations; EU directives and environmental legislation, EGR, hush kits, low-noise tyres*);

5 be able to draw up periodic maintenance plans for the vehicles and their equipment (*Maintenance programmes: planned preventative; methods of maintenance; operator's obligations and liabilities to maintain vehicles and equipment in a safe, roadworthy condition; responsibility for vehicles whose maintenance is contracted out; record keeping*);

6 be familiar with the different types of cargo-handling and cargo-loading devices (tailboards, containers, pallets, etc) and be able to introduce procedures and issue instructions for loading and unloading goods (load distribution, stacking, stowing, blocking and chocking) (*Risk analysis and safe operations: requirements for various loads and procedures to ensure safe operations*);

7 be familiar with the various techniques of 'piggy-back' and roll-on/roll-off combined transport (*Safety requirements; vehicle specifications charging methods*);

8 be able to implement procedures for complying with the rules on the carriage of dangerous goods and waste, notably those arising from:

- Directive 2008/68/EC with regard to the transport of dangerous goods by road;
- Regulation (EC) 2006/1013/EC on the supervision and control of shipments of waste within, into and out of the European Community, including IMDG requirements;

9 be able to implement procedures for complying with the rules on the carriage of perishable foodstuffs, notably those arising from the agreement on the international carriage of perishable foodstuffs and on the special equipment to be used for such carriage (ATP) (*Procedures to ensure correct compliance with legislation and best practice*);

10 be able to implement procedures for complying with the rules on the transport of live animals (*National and international: procedures to ensure correct compliance with legislation and best practice*).

H. Road Safety

Candidates must:

1 know what qualifications are required for drivers – driving licences, medical certificates, certificates of fitness (*Vocational entitlements: different categories, types and qualifications for driving licences and entitlements. Procedures: relating to the issue, renewal, revocation and production of licences and removal of entitlements. Disciplinary matters: procedures and appeals. Driving tests: scope and conduct and sequence of theory and driving tests. International Driving Permits: issue and validation*);

2 be able to take the necessary steps to ensure that drivers comply with the traffic rules, prohibitions and restrictions in force in the different member states of the European Union – speed limits, priorities, waiting and parking restrictions, use of lights, road signs (*Traffic regulations: signs and signals; variation in weights, dimensions and speed of road haulage vehicles in EU member states and non-member countries. Restrictions: imposed on the movement and speeds of road haulage vehicles*);

3 be able to draw up drivers' instructions for checking their compliance with the safety requirements concerning the condition of the vehicles, their equipment and cargo, and concerning preventive measures to be taken (*Write instructions for inspection, defect reporting and the safe use of vehicles and equipment, including cargo*);

4 be able to lay down procedures to be followed in the event of an accident and to implement appropriate procedures for preventing the recurrence of accidents or serious traffic offences (*Accident procedures: introduce measures to inform appropriate authorities and personnel of accidents; take appropriate action to minimize further dangers and to relieve suffering. The use of European Accident Statements*);

5 be able to implement procedures to properly secure goods;

6 have elementary knowledge of the layout of the road network in the EU member states.

Both awarding bodies state that new legislative measures will not be included in the examination for at least three months from the date of implementation.

Those wishing to study for the examinations should ensure that they have an up-to-date syllabus, covering either road haulage or passenger transport operations, from the CILT or OCR using the contact details above.

From the above syllabus it is clear that there will be some major amendments required to the details within this syllabus, not least in relation to UK vehicles operating abroad and the multiple references to the UK as an EU member state.

Transfer of Qualifications

Currently, provisions are made to allow an interchange of professional competence qualifications and recognition of professional competence qualification certificates between the United Kingdom, Northern Ireland and EU member states. Thus the UK Traffic Commissioners are required, under the 'mutual recognition' requirements of EU Directive 796/77/EEC, to take into account any Certificate of Professional Competence or any alternative to such a certificate showing relevant experience in the road haulage industry issued either in the UK, Northern Ireland or in any EU member state when considering an application for an 'O' licence. Normally, an OCR, CILT or City & Guilds full professional competence certificate issued to UK nationals will be sufficient evidence of professional competence.

However, the TCs in the UK will issue a Certificate of Qualification form confirming the good repute, professional competence and, where relevant, the financial standing of persons or companies from the UK who wish to be admitted to the occupation of road haulage operator, or to be employed to manage the transport operations of a goods haulage undertaking in Northern Ireland or in any EU member state.

Where a person seeking a Certificate of Qualification is not, or has not been, an 'O' licence holder in the UK, the TCs will, of course, have no knowledge of their experience, good repute or financial standing and thus will be unable to issue a certificate. In these cases, application can be made to the Secretary of State (ie for the D*f*T), who is empowered to issue a certificate to such a person on payment of the requisite fee.

NB: In the case of a no-deal it is most likely that the UK will continue to recognize EU CPC holders but it will be left to individual EU member states to decide whether or not to recognize the UK CPC. In cases where they do not recognize the UK qualification the holder may have to sit an EU CPC should they wish to manage or operate goods vehicles based in the EU. As mentioned in the previous section there is a planned period of transition post-Brexit in order to allow these types of details to be finalized and announced.

Also note that it is a declared intention by HM Government to adopt the majority of pre-Brexit existing EU legislation that applied to the UK to remain as domestic legislation wherever possible.

Good Repute

The subject of good repute has been dealt with in detail in Chapter 1 (see pp 23–26) where it is more properly located since it is an issue which arises only when an application for an 'O' licence is made by an individual, by a partnership business or by a company. However, a great deal of attention has been focused on the 'good repute' aspect of professionally competent persons. For this reason, and to catch the attention of those who may read only this chapter rather than the 'O' licensing chapter (Chapter 1), some of the salient facts are repeated here.

As stated above, the good repute of such persons is only called into question when their names are put forward in support of a standard 'O' licence application. At that time the TC will want to know if the person has previous convictions for serious 'relevant' offences and offences relating to the operation of goods vehicles (see below).

Following on from the previous explanation of the interchange of qualifications between the UK and EU member states, the TCs, in considering an application for an 'O' licence and the good repute of the nominated professionally competent person, are required to take into account any convictions incurred by the person in Northern Ireland or in a country or territory outside the UK.

The term 'relevant convictions' means convictions for offences that are relevant to the transport sector under British regulations, namely offences relating to vehicle roadworthiness, speeding, overloading, safe loading, drivers' hours and record keeping, drivers' licensing, maintenance, illegal use of rebated fuel, human trafficking, drugs trafficking, Driver CPC, certain traffic offences and to the International Road Haulage Permits Act 1975.

Further, the Transport Tribunal has ruled that the TC can consider other criminal convictions when considering a professionally competent person's good repute. The Tribunal ruled that the TC does not have to regard only those convictions mentioned above (as identified in the 1968 Transport Act) in deciding good repute.

In another instance a TC has said that a nominated professionally competent person must be clear of past financial difficulties. This followed a case where a nominated person was shown to be an adjudged bankrupt and the TC refused to accept the person's name on this account.

It is also to be noted that the TC can consider any previous bankruptcy or financial difficulty of any applicant, business partner, company director or proposed or in-post transport manager.

Also to be taken into account when considering the transport manager's good repute are convictions for offences listed in Article 6 of Regulation 1072/2009/EC and those infringements listed in Annex IV of that Regulation as being the 'most serious', as follows:

1. **(a)** Exceeding the maximum six-day or fortnightly driving time limits by margins of 25 per cent or more.

   (b) Exceeding, during a daily working period, the maximum daily driving time limit by a margin of 50 per cent or more without taking a break or without an uninterrupted rest period of at least 4.5 hours.
2. Not having a tachograph and/or speed limiter, or using a fraudulent device able to modify the records of the recording equipment and/or the speed limiter or falsifying record sheets or data downloaded from the tachograph and/or the driver card.
3. Driving without a valid roadworthiness certificate if such a document is required under Community law and/or driving with a very serious deficiency of, among other things, the braking system, the steering linkages, the wheels/tyres, the suspension or chassis that would create such an immediate risk to road safety that it leads to a decision to immobilize the vehicle.

4. Transporting dangerous goods that are prohibited for transport or transporting such goods in a prohibited or non-approved means of containment or without identifying them on the vehicle as dangerous goods, thus endangering lives or the environment to such extent that it leads to a decision to immobilize the vehicle.
5. Carrying passengers or goods without holding a valid driving licence or carrying by an undertaking not holding a valid Community licence.
6. Driving with a driver card that has been falsified, or with a card of which the driver is not the holder, or which has been obtained on the basis of false declarations and/or forged documents.
7. Carrying goods exceeding the maximum permissible laden mass by 20 per cent or more for vehicles the permissible laden weight of which exceeds 12 tonnes, and by 25 per cent or more for vehicles the permissible laden weight of which does not exceed 12 tonnes.

The above offences are among those which may be recorded against the transport manager in the National Electronic Register (see p 61) and are commonly referred to as the 'Seven Deadly Sins'.

Rights of Transport Managers

In order to protect the rights of individuals, TCs are not permitted to examine and rule upon a transport manager's good repute or professional competence unless the individual has been notified at least 28 days in advance that this is to happen (and for what reason) and has had an opportunity to make personal representation to the TC (at a public inquiry if necessary and represented by a solicitor if he so wishes) concerning any allegations made about him.

Duties of Transport Managers

TCs have been increasingly tightening up on the role and duties of transport managers nominated in support of 'O' licence applications. New guidance notes have been issued to the TCs and a newly devised, purpose-designed contract of employment form has been brought into use in an effort to eliminate the practice whereby transport managers are put forward in name only, with no concept of their statutory duties or any intention that they should perform this role as required by law (see also pp 43–45).

In an attempt to improve the standard of fleet operation, and because some transport managers are external professionals and/or part time, the Senior Traffic Commissioner has recommended that, in relation to the nominated person carrying out their duties, and being able to demonstrate actual control over the vehicles, the guidelines in the table opposite should be applied.

In addition to the hours in the table opposite, no external transport manager should be nominated on more than four different 'O' licences.

Note: If the professionally competent transport manager or nominated person leaves unexpectedly, or loses their good repute, etc, the Senior Traffic Commissioner has stated that the Traffic Commissioners should be notified 'as soon as possible' and in any case within 28 days of the event.

Vehicles	Guideline hours (per week)
2 or less	2–4
3–5	4–8
6–10	8–12
11–14	12–20
15–29	20–30
30 and above	Full-time*
More than 50	Full-time and additional assistance required

Additional hours may be required for fleets with trailers
* When a single person is in control of 30 or more vehicles the TCs expect the operator to provide details on how the person will administer 'effective and continuous' control of the fleet.

The Driver CPC

This CPC (referred to as a DCPC) is another qualification that some, or all, EU member states may choose not to recognize after the UK leaves the EU. Should it not be recognized then UK drivers will be treated as 'third country drivers' in the countries concerned, the outcome of which will depend upon the country.

An EU Directive on the qualification and training requirements for most LGV drivers (Directive 2003/59/EC of July 2003) became effective in regard to LGV drivers from 10 September 2009 (passenger vehicle drivers had to comply from one year earlier – ie 10 September 2008) in accordance with UK regulations (The Vehicle Drivers (Certificate of Professional Competence) Regulations 2007 – SI2007/605). The objectives are namely to improve road safety and the safety of the driver, and additionally to 'arouse young people's interest in the profession, contributing to the recruitment of new drivers at a time of shortage'.

The drive behind this view was that, with no more than 5–10 per cent of professional lorry drivers in Europe having undertaken any training other than what was needed to pass the relevant driving test, better-trained drivers would lead to fewer road accidents and a better quality of service being offered to customers, and harmonized training standards (which the Directive aims to achieve) would help promote growth and competition in the European transport market. Road accidents in Great Britain for the year ending June 2019 resulted in 1,782 people being killed and a total of 25,484 people seriously injured (KSI). Overall, in addition to the deaths there were 160,378 injured in one way or another on the roads in Great Britain.

These figures show a general decrease in all accidents and are actually the lowest on record (source: *DfT Transport Statistics Bulletin 2018*).

The Directive's aim is for a system of certification of professional competence for drivers who satisfy the training requirements for 'initial' or 'accelerated initial' training and 'periodic' training. However, it is not the intention that the need to obtain an initial qualification should apply to existing drivers who have held a category C1, C1+E, C or C+E licence (or a licence recognized as being equivalent) that was issued no later than three years after the final date for this Directive coming into force (10 September 2009). They nevertheless have to undergo the periodic training amounting to 35 hours every five years (which may be spread over the period by taking one seven-hour training session each year).

Exemptions also apply to drivers of the following vehicles:

- vehicles with a maximum authorized speed not exceeding 45 kph;
- vehicles used by, or under the control of, the armed forces, civil defence, the prison service, the fire service and forces responsible for maintaining public order;
- vehicles undergoing road tests for technical development, repair or maintenance purposes, or of new or rebuilt vehicles which have not yet been put into service;
- vehicles used in states of emergency or assigned to rescue missions;
- vehicles used in the course of driving lessons for any person wishing to obtain a driving licence or a CPC;
- vehicles used for non-commercial carriage of passengers or goods for personal use;
- vehicles carrying material or equipment to be used by the driver in the course of his work, within 100 km of the driver's base, provided that driving the vehicle is not the driver's principal activity;
- vehicles going to, and returning from, a pre-booked test at a DVSA test centre or an Approved Test Facility (ATF).

NB: It was confirmed in 2014 that drivers who only drive in order to take vehicles to, and from, test stations (fitters) for their annual test are now exempted. This followed some confusion in relation to the extent of the term 'vehicle test'.

Initial Training

The Driver and Vehicle Standards Agency (DVSA) is responsible, overall, on behalf of the UK Government, for implementing the EU Driver Training Directive (2003/59/EC) and has established the regime for CPC training to comply with the Directive. Two levels of training requirement must be met by professional LGV drivers, namely:

- initial training (set at the level of NVQ 2) for newcomers to LGV driving since 10 September 2009;
- periodic training, to be undertaken by pre-existing LGV drivers who held their vocational entitlement prior to 10 September 2009.

Initial training applies to drivers who acquire their entitlement to drive vehicles in categories C1, C1+E, C or C+E from 10 September 2009. These drivers need to complete the initial training *in addition to* obtaining their vocational licence before they are allowed to drive LGVs on the public highway.

This initial training involves additional theory and practical testing beyond that required to obtain the LGV vocational licence as follows:

- basic licence theory test of 1½ hours plus 2½ hours of extra theory testing for CPC – making four hours in total;
- basic driving test of 1½ hours plus half an hour of extra practical testing for CPC – making two hours in total.

The basic theory test mentioned above is in two parts comprising:

- 100 multiple choice questions (85 per cent pass mark required) and a 20-video-clip hazard perception test (67/100 pass mark).

Where appropriate, the test presentation should be screen-based and undertaken at existing DVSA driving theory test centres (see Further Information).

Fees for Theory and Practical Tests

Module 1a Theory Test MPC* = £26
Module 1b Theory Test HPT** = £11
Module 2 Theory Test Case Studies = £23
Module 3 Practical Test = £115
Module 4 Practical Demonstration Test = £55

* Multiple choice test

** Hazard perception test

NB: The Module 3 practical test rises to £141.00 if taken at the weekend, in the evening or on a Bank Holiday, and the Module 4 practical test rises to £63.00 if taken during these times.

Initial Training for Young Drivers

The pre-existing Young LGV Driver scheme has been superseded by the new Driver CPC scheme. In consequence of this the standard minimum age for professional LGV drivers is reduced to 18 years and, on gaining an ‘accelerated initial qualification’, such drivers will be allowed to drive goods vehicles in licence categories C1 and C1+E.

This ‘accelerated’ qualification must include the teaching of all subjects in the syllabus over a minimum study period, including a specified number of hours driving in a relevant approved test vehicle, followed by tests as described above.

Periodic Training

All existing LGV driving licence holders as at the date of commencement of the new scheme (10 September 2009) were required to undergo approved periodic training sessions amounting to 35 hours in total within the five years to September 2014.

From that time they need to complete 35 hours of training in each subsequent five-year period. The training periods must be organized by an approved training centre, and each individual period must be of at least seven hours duration (this can be split into two 3.5 hour sessions but these must both be completed within a 24-hour period) – this means seven hours of actual direct contact with the trainer within a 24-hour period. The seven hour periods are recorded and need to be uploaded to the DVSA by the training provider who also needs to send a £1.25 an hour upload fee for each candidate completing the seven hour session (£8.75 per seven-hour session).

In practice, to achieve this training requirement, drivers normally undertake one day of training each year or a week's training once every fifth year, either way amounting to 35 hours in total within the five years. The training objective can be to provide 'up-skilling' in general to improve overall driver performance and safety awareness, or specific training, to account for new technological developments in vehicle design for example, or operating 'best practices' as and when they occur.

Training, Testing and Certification

The whole of the new Driver CPC scheme is based on a system of approved methods of training and certification provided by approved trainers and working within approved training centres. Approval for trainers, training centres and training courses is given only by the Joint Approvals Unit for Periodic Training (JAUPT) – see Appendix II for contact details.

Minimum Age for Driving LGVs

Under the Driver CPC scheme, from 10 September 2009 the minimum age for driving LGVs is reduced to 18 years, but this applies only to drivers holding a Driver Qualification Card who have completed the requisite period of initial training or young drivers being trained to acquire a Driver Qualification Card.

Availability of Training

A current list of approved training centres can be found on the JAUPT website at: http://www.jaupt.org.uk (archived at https://perma.cc/M44D-GAPV).

Testing and Certification

Pre-existing LGV driving licence holders as at the date when the new scheme came into operation (10 September 2009 for LGV licence holders) were not required to undertake any tests to acquire a Driver CPC; they had what are known as 'acquired rights' and therefore were deemed to be 'professionally competent' drivers, albeit without an actual CPC document (known as a 'Driver Qualification Card' – DQC) to prove the fact. Their CPC qualification was evidenced, if such proof was required, by the date on their driving licence that shows when their entitlement to drive LGVs came into effect. Since 10 September 2014 these drivers must now have a DQC, which is to be carried in order that it may be 'produced upon request'. Failure to produce a DQC to the authorities can lead to a fixed penalty fine or even the driver being prosecuted, fined and having their licence endorsed (see below).

In an attempt to reduce the shortage of vocational drivers, in April 2015 it was agreed that where a vocational driver has held a licence but has not undertaken the 35 hours of training in order to obtain their *first* Driver Qualification Card (DQC), they may now either undergo the 35 hours of training or sit Modules 2 and 4 of the driving test. It is important to note that this is only available to drivers requiring their first DQC and that the driver must have acquired their vocational entitlements prior to September 2009.

New drivers who have not held an LGV driving entitlement prior to 10 September 2009 will need to complete the Driver CPC initial training, as described above, at the time of undertaking their LGV driving test. Without this extra qualification it will be illegal for them to drive goods vehicles professionally (ie for payment) unless the vehicle is one that falls into an exempt category (see pp 13–16).

As discussed above, certification of the fact that a new driver holds the CPC qualification is by holding a DQC. These cards are issued by the DVLA on meeting the necessary qualification by passing the various tests outlined above and are sent to the address stated on the driving licence of the driver concerned. They also use a copy photograph of the driver which is the same photograph used on the photocard driving licence and a driver's digital tachograph card.

As a record of all driver training undertaken at approved centres is held on a central database by the DVSA, it is on the basis of this record of training hours achieved that the DVSA will notify the DVLA when to send the candidate his or her DQC. Drivers themselves may also check up on their own personal accumulated training hours by enquiry to the DVSA, and employers will have the same facility provided they have the individual's permission to make such enquiries.

Enforcement, Offences and Penalties

Strict enforcement of the Driver CPC scheme is carried out by the authorities, with offenders receiving tough penalties for failure to comply with the legal requirements relating to acquiring a DQC and for failing to produce a DQC upon request by an authorized officer. Approved centres delivering the training are also regularly audited and 'surprise' visits to centres are a common method of enforcing the required standards.

Enforcing Authorities

In this case the enforcing authorities are the police and the DVSA, both of which will have direct access to the centrally held data at the DVLA, enabling them to instantly check any dubious claims or records.

Offences and Penalties

From 10 September 2014 all vocational (goods vehicles exceeding 3,500 kg MAM) and LGV drivers must carry evidence of their Driver CPC qualification and may be asked to produce this at the time of a roadside check.

Failure by drivers to produce their DQC or their driving licence with date evidence on request by a DVSA enforcement officer or police officer carries a fixed penalty fine of £50.

The more serious offence that drivers are at risk of committing is failure to have undergone the mandatory 35 hours of periodic training within the preceding five years. Whether this occurs through forgetfulness or deliberate avoidance of the training regime matters not; an offending driver could be fined up to £1,000 on conviction.

Since the Driver CPC scheme applies throughout the whole EU community, British drivers must, when driving abroad, carry with them their driving licence (showing evidence of their pre-September 2009 driving qualification) and their DVQ. They risk an on-the-spot penalty if caught out in breach of this requirement. Similarly, foreign LGV drivers operating within the UK face the prospect of a fixed penalty fine if found not to have the requisite documentation with them, but there is an anomaly in the case of the more serious offence mentioned above. Due to the current inadequacy of the DVLA database, which does not carry training records for non-UK drivers, such drivers will avoid the £1,000 fine for having either failed to complete, or totally avoided, the periodic training requirement. (As noted above, due to the Brexit issue, the status and recognition of the DQC remains unclear in all cases.)

Originally, there were issues relating to the fact that some EU member states set later dates for completion of the DCPC periodic training than the date set by the UK Government. This meant that some foreign drivers could have been driving in the UK without having completed their training and would therefore have been unable to provide evidence by the use of a DQC. At the time, DVSA stated that this would be permitted in spite of it possibly being open to an accusation of 'discrimination' against UK vocational drivers who had a shorter timescale in which to gain the qualification.

Minimum Training and Qualification Requirements

List of Subjects

The knowledge to be taken into account when establishing the driver's qualification and training must include at least the subjects in this syllabus.

Trainee drivers must reach the level of knowledge and practical competence necessary to drive the relevant categories of vehicle with safety.

The minimum level of a driver's knowledge must not be less than the level reached during compulsory education, supplemented by professional training.

Syllabus

1 Advanced training in rational driving based on safety regulations

1.1 Objective: to learn the characteristics of the vehicle transmission system in order to use it to the best possible effect:

- curves relating to engine torque and power;
- specific consumption of an engine;
- area of optimum use of revolution counter;
- gearbox-ratio cover diagrams.

1.2 Objective: to learn the technical characteristics and operation of the safety controls in order to control the vehicle, minimize wear and tear, and prevent dysfunctioning:

- specific features of hydraulic, vacuum and servobrake circuits;
- limits to the use of brakes and retarder;
- combined use of brakes and retarder;
- making better use of speed and gear ratios;
- making use of vehicle inertia;
- using ways of slowing down and braking on downhill stretches;
- action in the event of failure.

1.3 Objective: to learn how to optimize fuel consumption:

- optimization of fuel consumption by applying know-how as regards the above-mentioned points in 1.1 and 1.2.

1.4 Objective: to acquire the ability to load a vehicle with due regard for safety rules and proper vehicle use:

- forces affecting vehicles in motion;
- use of gearbox ratios according to vehicle load and road profile;
- calculation of payload of vehicle or assembly;
- calculation of total volume and load distribution;
- consequences of overloading the axle;
- vehicle stability and centre of gravity;
- types of packaging and pallets;
- main categories of goods needing securing;
- damping and securing techniques;
- use of securing straps;
- checking of securing devices;
- use of handling equipment;
- placing and removal of tarpaulins.

2 Application of regulations

2.1 Objective: to understand the social environment of road transport and the rules governing it:

- maximum working periods specific to the transport industry;
- principles, application and consequences of Regulations (EEC) Nos 3820/85 and 3821/85 (now replaced by Regulation EC 165/2014);

- penalties for failure to use, improper use of and tampering with the tachograph;
- knowledge of the social environment of road transport;
- rights and duties of drivers as regards initial qualification and periodic training.

2.2 Objective: to learn the regulations governing the carriage of goods:

- transport operating licences;
- obligations under standard contracts for the carriage of goods;
- drafting of documents which form the transport contract;
- international transport permits;
- obligations under the Convention on the Contract for the International Carriage of Goods by Road (ie CMR);
- dangerous goods and ADR;
- drafting of the international consignment note;
- crossing borders;
- freight forwarders;
- special documents accompanying goods.

3 Health, road safety and environmental safety, service, logistics

3.1 Objective: to make drivers aware of the risks of the road and of accidents at work:

- types of accidents at work in the transport sector;
- road accident statistics;
- involvement of lorries;
- human, material and financial consequences;
- Fleet Operator Recognition Scheme (FORS) training.

3.2 Objective: to learn how to prevent trafficking in illegal immigrants:

- trafficking in illegal immigrants and illegal immigration;
- general information;
- implications for drivers;
- preventive measures: checklist;
- legislation on transport operator liability.

3.3 Objective: to learn how to prevent physical risks:

- ergonomic principles;
- movements and postures that pose a risk;
- physical fitness;
- handling exercises;
- personal protection.

3.4 Objective: to understand the importance of physical and mental ability:
- principles of healthy, balanced eating;
- effects of alcohol, drugs or any other substance likely to affect behaviour;
- symptoms, causes and effects of fatigue and stress;
- fundamental role of the basic work/rest cycle.

3.5 Objective: to learn how to assess emergency situations:
- behaviour in an emergency situation;
- assessment of the situation;
- avoiding complications of an accident;
- summoning assistance;
- assisting casualties and giving first aid;
- reaction in the event of fire;
- evacuation of occupants of a lorry;
- ensuring the safety of all passengers;
- reaction in the event of aggression;
- basic principles for the drafting of an accident report.

3.6 Objective: to learn how to adopt behaviour to help enhance the image of a service undertaking:
- behaviour of the driver and company image;
- importance for the company of the standard of service provided by the driver;
- the roles of the driver and people with whom the driver will be dealing;
- vehicle maintenance;
- work organization;
- commercial and financial effects of a dispute.

3.7 Objective: to understand the economic environment of road haulage and the organization of the market:
- road transport in relation to other modes of transport (competition, shippers);
- different road transport activities (transport for hire or reward, own-account, auxiliary transport activities);
- organization of the main types of transport company and auxiliary transport activities;
- different transport specializations (road tanker, controlled temperature, etc);
- changes in the industry (diversification of services provided, rail–road, sub-contracting, etc).

The lists above are the general lists and FORS training has only recently been accepted by JAUPT but if there is a special or different training need then a request can be made to JAUPT who will consider it as a subject and is able to approve, if it meets the training standard requirements.

NB: In 2015 JAUPT informed all registered training centres that the training must now also (where appropriate) make reference to 'vulnerable' road users.

Further to the 2015 changes to training, in 2018 JAUPT further decided that, following a review of the qualification, the training must be relevant to the driver concerned, and candidates should not be allowed to attend repeated training courses during a periodic training cycle. It also decided that road safety should be included in at least one training session every five year period. These issues were in addition to the earlier decision to allow disability awareness, dangerous goods transportation and animal transport to be included as modules. Clearly, these proposals throw up all sorts of questions especially for drivers needing repeat training in order to fully understand a topic or drivers who plan to change jobs/sectors and will need training not currently appropriate for them in their old job, etc.

The date for the latest changes to be implemented is 2020, which is after Brexit and so once again things may, or may not, change depending upon whether or not EU member states accept the UK DCPC as valid.

Finally, as the existing DCPC is an EU-derived qualification, it has been decided that existing UK DCPCs, and those completed before the date that we leave the EU, will be valid within the EU until their expiry date irrespective of whether or not there is a deal or no deal.

Goods Vehicle Drivers' Hours and Working Time

03

This chapter incorporates both the EU driving hours rules and the legal provisions relating to working time for vocational drivers. With the EU's Directive on Working Time including mobile workers (most predominantly vocational drivers), it was thought to be more appropriate to deal with the subject here along with the long-established driving hours rules as they do impact upon one another. It has been agreed that these rules will remain in force following Brexit although the EU rules will be replaced in the UK by Accord Européen sur les Transports Routier (AETR) rules which exactly mirror those of the EU but apply to certain non-EU countries.

EU and AETR Driving and Rest Time Rules

Any person who uses a vehicle for the carriage of goods for commercial or business purposes (ie not including those used for purely private purposes and other vehicles specifically exempted – see pp 13–16) irrespective of the vehicle weight must conform to strict rules on the amount of time he may spend driving. For most goods vehicle drivers the rules also include requirements relating to minimum breaks to be taken during the driving day and to both daily and weekly rest periods.

Enforcement and Penalties

The driving hours rules are applied solely to protect public safety, especially to protect road users from the dangers of overworked and tired drivers of heavy vehicles. In the UK, enforcement is vigorously undertaken by both the police and the DVSA enforcement officers, and convicted offenders are dealt with severely by the courts, and even the Traffic Commissioners, to emphasize the importance of these road safety measures.

Drivers who are convicted for contravening the rules risk heavy fines, while the most serious of offences can result in imprisonment. LGV and other vocational driving entitlements may be revoked in consequence, losing a driver his job, and the operator may also be prosecuted and/or have action taken against them, particularly in relation to their Operator Compliance Risk Score (OCRS) (see later).

Besides prosecution for infringements and its consequent penalties, provisions brought in by the Transport Act 2000 authorize enforcement officers of the DVSA to detain drivers found to be in breach of the drivers' hours rules.

Where it is determined during a roadside check that a UK, or foreign, driver has not taken sufficient break or rest periods prior to that time, he will be prohibited from continuing his journey. In the case of break period infringements the delay at the roadside will be until a full 45-minute break period has been taken. Where breaches of the daily or weekly rest period requirements are detected, the driver and his vehicle will be escorted by the police to a suitable parking area (eg service area or truck stop) where he will have to remain until he has taken a full 11-hour daily rest or at least a minimum 24-hour weekly rest, if he is entitled to take a reduced weekly rest. Otherwise he will have to take a full 45-hour weekly rest.

Where the infringement results in the driver being notified of a prosecution the enforcement officers may now look at 'historic' evidence of earlier infringements recorded on the tachograph going back for a period not exceeding 28 days and these offences may also be taken into account in relation to the intended prosecution.

The vehicle operator may send a relief driver to take over the vehicle and continue its journey, but this driver will be subject to scrutiny by the DVSA to ensure that he has sufficient time available within legal limits to drive the vehicle. In any case, the first driver will not be able to take a daily, or weekly, rest in a moving vehicle should the relief driver take over the vehicle.

UK-based employers of convicted drivers also risk prosecution and heavy fines for similar offences. Additionally, they may have penalties imposed against their 'O' licences by the Traffic Commissioners (TCs) since they promised in the declaration of intent at the time of their 'O' licence application that they would make arrangements to ensure the drivers' hours law would be observed.

It is also a specific requirement within the rules that employers must make periodic checks to ensure the rules are observed (normally by tachograph analysis) and must take appropriate action if they discover breaches of the law to ensure there is no repetition of offences.

In both mainland Europe and the UK 'historic offences' are also often allowed to be taken into account and breaches of the rules detected in roadside checks may result in drivers incurring heavy on-the-spot fines which must be paid immediately, otherwise the vehicle may be impounded and the driver held until the fine is paid.

Reporting of Illegal Operations

Under the Public Interest Disclosure Act 1998 employees are protected if they report corruption, wrongdoing or danger at work, or if they are unduly pressured by an unscrupulous employer to break the law.

For example, in the context of the drivers' hours law, where drivers are encouraged or pressured to breach the driving hours or tachograph rules, they would have protection under the Act if they reported such matters either to the DVSA or to the TC.

The Act came into force in July 1999. This so-called 'whistle-blowing' charter entitles workers to unlimited compensation if their employer penalizes them for exposing breaches of the law or unsafe practices. Besides this legal protection, the United Road Transport Union (URTU) provides a confidential hotline service for drivers on helplines accessed through their website www.urtu.com (archived at https://perma.cc/49TN-ASY8).

Which Rules Apply?

Goods vehicle driver employers and drivers themselves need to understand the hours rules clearly, and especially which particular set of rules applies to them depending on the vehicle being driven or the nature of the transport operation on which they are engaged. In Statutory Document No 6, produced by the Senior Traffic Commissioner, it specifically states that 'drivers are expected to fully acquaint themselves with the relevant legislation before undertaking employment as a professional driver'. Four main sets of rules apply, the EU rules, the EU's Working Time rules (ie the Road Transport Directive – see p 115), the British domestic rules and what are known as the AETR rules for some international journeys outside the EU (the AETR rules are fully aligned with the EU rules, which is why the UK has decided to adopt them as a post-Brexit action). The specific requirements under each of these sets of rules are explained in the following pages.

European Union and AETR Rules

The drivers' hours EU rules, formerly contained in Regulation 3820/85/EEC, which came into effect in the UK on 29 September 1986, were repealed and replaced by similar provisions contained in EU Regulation 561/2006/EC which took effect from 11 April 2007 apart from the digital tachograph provisions (ie in Articles 10(5), 26(3) and (4), and 27) described in Chapter 5, which became effective from 1 May 2006. These rules are now also used by the European Economic Area (EEA) countries (Iceland, Liechtenstein, and Norway) and also Switzerland. Together these four countries form the European Free Trade Association (EFTA).

Vehicles Covered

EU and AETR rules currently always take precedence over national rules within the EU and AETR countries. Therefore, since all goods vehicles and other vehicles used for the carriage of goods in connection with business activities as stated above are covered by one or other of the sets of drivers' hours rules (ie EU, AETR, British domestic and the Working Time rules), the requirements of specific EU/AETR legislation must be considered first. Mainly, this involves examination of the list of EU/AETR rules exemptions to determine whether the vehicle or the transport operation falls within scope of the rules or outside.

Where a vehicle has a maximum permissible weight not exceeding 3.5 tonnes it is exempt from the EU/AETR rules* or if it is one identified on the EU/AETR exemption list or is used for a purpose which is shown in the list as exempt as mentioned previously (eg vehicles used by the public utilities and local authorities, etc) it automatically comes within the scope of the British domestic rules set out in the 1968 Transport Act as described in detail on pp 110–13.

* *At the time of writing, the EU is considering lowering the 3,500 kg threshold to vehicles exceeding 2,400 kg engaged on international hire and reward operations and it appears to be only a matter of time before this becomes reality and these vehicles too become subject to EU/AETR drivers' hours, at least in some, or all, EU countries.*

Where vehicles are over 3.5 tonnes permissible maximum weight, including the weight of any trailer drawn, and are not exempt as shown by the list or are not used for an exempt purpose, the EU or AETR hours laws apply.

Where vehicles are over 3.5 tonnes permissible maximum weight, including the weight of any trailer drawn, and are not exempt as shown by the list or are not used for an exempt purpose, the EU or AETR hours law applies. Similarly, the law applies to vehicles 'used for the carriage of goods', such as 'off-road' vehicles and so-called 4 × 4s towing trailers, and where the combined weight of the towing vehicle and the trailer exceeds 3.5 tonnes.

Exemptions from EU and AETR rules

EU Regulation 561/2006/EC (in Article 3) lists a number of exemptions and national governments (eg the British Government) are permitted to make certain other exemptions (derogations) if they so wish, as shown below.

International Exemptions (Under EU/AETR regulations)

1. Vehicles used for the carriage of passengers on regular services where the route covered by the service in question does not exceed 50 km.
2. Vehicles with a maximum authorized speed not exceeding 40 km per hour.
3. Vehicles owned or hired without a driver by the armed services, civil defence services, fire services, and forces responsible for maintaining public order when the carriage is undertaken as a consequence of the tasks assigned to these services and is under their control.
4. Vehicles, including vehicles used in the non-commercial transport of humanitarian aid, used in emergencies or by road rescue operations.
5. Specialized vehicles used for medical purposes.
6. Specialized breakdown vehicles operating within a 100 km radius of their base.
7. Vehicles undergoing road tests for technical development, repair or maintenance purposes, and new or rebuilt vehicles which have not yet been put into service.

8 Vehicles or combinations of vehicles with a maximum permissible mass not exceeding 7.5 tonnes used for the non-commercial carriage of goods.

9 Commercial vehicles which have an historic status according to the legislation of the member state in the countries in which they are being driven, and which are used for the non-commercial carriage of passengers or goods.

National Exemptions (Under UK Derogations)

1 Passenger vehicles constructed to carry not more than 17 persons including the driver.

2 Vehicles used by public authorities to provide public services which are not in competition with professional road hauliers.

3 Vehicles used by agricultural, horticultural, forestry or fishery* undertakings, for carrying goods within a 100 km radius of the place where the vehicle is normally based, including local administrative areas the centres of which are situated within that radius.

**To gain this exemption the vehicle must be used to carry live fish or to carry a catch of fish which has not been subjected to any process or treatment (other than freezing) from the place of landing to a place where it is to be processed or treated.*

4 Vehicles used for carrying animal waste or carcasses not intended for human consumption.

5 Vehicles used for carrying live animals no more than 100 km from farms to local markets and vice versa, or from markets to local slaughterhouses.

6 Vehicles specially fitted for and used:

- as shops at local markets and for door-to-door selling;
- for mobile banking, exchange or savings transactions;
- for worship;
- for the lending of books, records or CDs;
- for cultural events or exhibitions.

7 Vehicles (not exceeding 7.5 tonnes gvw) operated by 'universal service providers' (currently only Royal Mail).

8 Vehicles (not exceeding 7.5 tonnes gvw) carrying materials or equipment for the driver's use in the course of his work within a 100 km radius of base provided the driving does not constitute the driver's main activity and does not prejudice the objectives of the regulations.

9 Vehicles operating exclusively on islands not exceeding 2,300 sq km not linked to the mainland by bridge, ford or tunnel for use by motor vehicles (this includes the Isle of Wight, Arran and Bute).

10 Vehicles (not exceeding 7.5 tonnes gvw) used within a 100 km radius of base for the carriage of goods propelled by natural or liquefied gas or by electricity.

11 Vehicles used for driving instruction (but not if carrying goods for hire or reward).

12 Vehicles used for milk collections from farms, for the return of milk containers to farms or for the delivery of milk products which are to be used for animal feed.

13 Vehicles used in connection with sewerage, flood protection, water, gas, electricity maintenance* services, road maintenance and control, door to door household refuse collection or disposal, telegraph or telephone services, radio and television broadcasting and the detection of radio or television transmitters or receivers.

** The DVSA was concerned about abuse of this derogation in relation to the interpretation of 'maintenance' and have concluded that for a vehicle to be exempt it must be directly involved with the maintenance work, where part of an existing utility infrastructure is being repaired or replaced. In effect this means that this derogation would not apply to installation of any new infrastructure such as a new gas supply, only the maintenance of existing gas supplies. Operators should clarify the position with the DVSA if in doubt.*

14 Agricultural and forestry tractors used exclusively for agricultural and forestry work within 100 km radius of base.

15 Vehicles used by the RNLI for hauling lifeboats.

16 Vehicles manufactured before 1 January 1947.

17 Steam-propelled vehicles.

18 Specialized vehicles used for transporting circus and funfair equipment.

19 Vehicles used exclusively on roads inside hub facilities such as ports, airports, interports and railway terminals.

20 Vintage vehicles (ie over 25 years old) not carrying more than nine persons including the driver, not being used for profit, and being driven to or from a vintage rally, museum, public display or a place where it has been or is to be repaired, maintained or tested.

NB: In exemption 2 above relating to vehicles used by public authorities, the exemption applies only if the vehicle is being used by:

a *a health authority in England and Wales, a health board in Scotland or a National Health Service (NHS) Trust:*
- *to provide ambulance services in pursuance of its duty under the NHS Act 1977 or NHS (Scotland) Act 1978; or*
- *to carry staff, patients, medical supplies or equipment in pursuance of its general duties under the Act;*

b *a local authority to fulfil social services functions, such as services for old persons or for physically and mentally handicapped persons;*

c *HM Coastguard or lighthouse authorities;*

d *harbour authorities within harbour limits;*

e *airports authority within airport perimeters;*

f *the British Railways Board, any holder of a rail network licence that is wholly owned by the crown, Transport for London, and a Passenger Transport Executive or local authority for maintaining railways;*

g *the British Waterways Board for maintaining navigable waterways.*

Exemption for Military Reservists

An exemption from EU/AETR drivers' hours rules is now available to military reservists who drive trucks or buses for a living which enables them to take part in weekend military training without breaching the rules on weekly rest requirements. It allows a driver who finishes his normal driving duties on a Friday to complete a 34-hour period of military training, and then resume his normal driving duties again on a Monday morning – providing specified safeguards are met. The exemption applies to volunteer reservists in the Territorial Army, the Royal Naval Reserve, the Royal Marine Reserve and the Royal Auxiliary Air Force, as well as cadet instructors.

The following safeguards are imposed to ensure that road safety is not jeopardized: the exemption applies to 15 days' annual camp and 10 weekend training sessions per annum – a total of 35 days; and weekend training is not allowed to take place on consecutive weeks (other than during the 15-day annual camp). Also:

- A regular daily rest period of 11 hours must be taken between the end of weekend training and start of work for the primary employer.
- A 45-hour weekly rest period must be taken no later than at the end of the sixth day following a period of weekend training.

The Ministry of Defence has issued guidelines as to how drivers can manage their volunteer reserve service in accordance with the exemption.

Regulation 561/2006/EC and AETR rules

To apply the rules as required and appreciate their implications it is necessary to understand the definitions of certain words and phrases used as follows:

- 'Vehicle' means a motor vehicle, tractor, trailer or semi-trailer or a combination of these vehicles, defined as:
  - a 'motor vehicle' is any self-propelled vehicle travelling on the road, other than a vehicle permanently on rails, and normally used for carrying passengers or goods;
  - a 'tractor' is any self-propelled vehicle travelling on the road, other than a vehicle permanently running on rails and specially designed to pull, push or move trailers, semi-trailers, implements or machines;
  - a 'trailer' is any vehicle designed to be coupled to a motor vehicle or tractor;
  - a 'semi-trailer' is a trailer without a front axle coupled in such a way that a substantial part of its weight and the weight of its load is borne by the tractor or motor vehicle.

- 'Driver' means any person who drives the vehicle, even for a short period, or someone who is carried in a vehicle as part of his duties to be available for driving if necessary.
- 'Break' means any period during which a driver may not carry out any driving or any other work and which is used exclusively for recuperation.
- 'Other work' means all activities which are defined as working time in Article 3(a) of Directive 2002/15/EC except 'driving', including any work for the same or another employer, within or outside of the transport sector.
- 'Rest' means any uninterrupted period during which a driver may freely dispose of his time.
- 'Daily rest' means the daily period during which a driver may freely dispose of his time and covers a 'regular daily rest period' and a 'reduced daily rest period':
  - 'Regular daily rest period' means any period of rest of at least 11 hours. Alternatively, this regular daily rest period may be taken in two periods, the first of which must be an uninterrupted period of at least three hours and the second an uninterrupted period of at least nine hours.
  - 'Reduced daily rest period' means any period of rest of at least nine hours but less than 11 hours.
- 'Weekly rest period' means the weekly period during which a driver may freely dispose of his time and covers a 'regular weekly rest period' and a 'reduced weekly rest period':
  - 'regular weekly rest period' means any period of rest of at least 45 hours;
  - 'reduced weekly rest period' means any period of rest of less than 45 hours, which may, subject to the conditions laid down in Article 8(6) (ie relating to compensated rest), be shortened to a minimum of 24 consecutive hours.
- 'A week' means the period of time between 0000 hrs on Monday and 2400 hrs on Sunday.
- 'Driving time' means the duration of driving activity recorded automatically or semi-automatically by the recording equipment.
- 'Daily driving time' means the total accumulated driving time between the end of one daily rest period and the beginning of the following daily rest period or between a daily rest period and a weekly rest period.
- 'Weekly driving time' means the total accumulated driving time during a week.
- 'Maximum permissible mass' means the maximum authorized operating mass (ie weight) of a vehicle when fully laden.
- 'Multi-manning' means the situation where, during each period of driving between any two consecutive daily rest periods, or between a daily rest period and a weekly rest period, there are at least two drivers in the vehicle to do the driving. For the first hour of multi-manning the presence of another driver or drivers is optional but for the remainder of the period it is compulsory.

- 'Driving period' means the accumulated driving time from when a driver commences driving following a rest period or a break. The driving period may be continuous or broken.

Employers' Responsibilities

Under the EU/AETR rules employers have specific responsibilities as follows:

- They must organize drivers' work in such a way that the requirements of the regulations are not broken (ie on driving times, breaks and rest periods, etc).
- They must make regular checks (ie of tachograph records – see Chapter 5) to ensure the regulations are complied with.
- Where they find any breaches of the law by drivers, they must take appropriate steps to prevent any repetition.

Additionally, of course, it goes without saying that employers should ensure their drivers do understand how the law in this respect applies to them and how to comply with its detailed provisions. Although it is no excuse in court for a driver to say he did not know the law, as mentioned earlier, the court would still expect the employer to have instructed the driver in its requirements and might well convict the employer for 'failing to cause' the driver to conform to the law (or for permitting offences) if it felt that insufficient attention had been given to this matter. One way of trying to avoid this is for operators to give drivers copies of the drivers' hours regulations and to get their drivers to sign to confirm that they do actually understand the rules and to place this signed declaration in their work file. In the case of tachographs the employer actually has a duty to ensure that the driver can operate the tachograph correctly. Both these issues are also relevant when agency drivers are used by an operator.

Driving Limits

Goods vehicle drivers are restricted in the amount of time they can spend driving before taking a break and the amount of driving they can do between any two daily rest periods (or a daily and a weekly rest period), in a week and in a fortnight. The maximum limits are as follows:

- Maximum driving before a break: 4½ hours
- Maximum daily driving normally: 9 hours
- Extended driving on 2 days in week only: 10 hours
- Maximum weekly driving: 56 hours (6 daily driving shifts*)
- Maximum fortnightly driving: 90 hours

** The High Court ruled in 1988 that drivers can exceed the maximum of six daily driving shifts within six days as specified in the then EU-only rules, provided they did not exceed the maximum number of hours permitted in six consecutive driving periods. It should be noted that where a driver spends the maximum amount of driving time behind the wheel in one week (ie 4 × 9 hours plus 2 × 10 hours = 56 hours),* *during the following fixed week he may drive for a maximum of only 34 hours. However, he must only have driven for 34 hours during the previous week.*

NB: It should also be noted here that the so-called '12-day rule' reintroduced for coach drivers on international journeys from June 2010 (under article 29 of regulation 1073/2009/EC) which allows such drivers to postpone their weekly rest period for up to 12 consecutive 24-hour periods does not *apply to goods vehicle drivers.*

Break Periods

Drivers are required by law to take a break or breaks if in a day the aggregate of their driving time amounts to 4½ hours or more. If the driver does not drive for periods amounting in aggregate to 4½ hours in the day there is no legal requirement for him to take a break during that day under these regulations but the driver may be required to take a break under the rules of the Road Transport Directive (RTD) (see below).

Break periods must not be regarded as parts of a daily rest period and during breaks the driver must not carry out any 'other work'. However, periods of time driving to or from a vehicle when the vehicle is neither at the driver's home or the employer's operating centre, known periods of waiting time, time spent riding as a passenger in a vehicle or time spent on a ferry or train are either counted as 'other work' for these purposes or they may be recorded as 'periods of availability' (POA) if POA criteria apply (see later).

The requirement for taking a break is that immediately the 4½-hour driving limit is reached a break of 45 minutes must be taken, unless the driver commences a rest period at that time (see below). This 45-minute break may be replaced by a break of at least 15 minutes followed by a break of at least 30 minutes each distributed over the driving period or taken during and immediately after this period, so as to equal at least 45 minutes and taken in such a way that the 4½-hour limit is not exceeded. To re-emphasize the point, once the 45 minutes' break requirement has been met, the slate is effectively wiped clean and the next 4½-hour period can begin.

A break period which was otherwise due in accordance with this requirement does not have to be taken if immediately following the driving period the driver commences a daily or weekly rest period, so long as the 4½ hours' aggregated driving is not exceeded.

NB: It is important to note that break periods (ie especially the 45-minute period as well as the alternative minimum 15- and 30-minute periods) should not be curtailed even by a minute or two. Prosecutions have been brought for offences relating to break periods which are alleged not to conform to the law even though they have been only a matter of minutes below the minimum specified in the regulations. Such matters are, of course, shown clearly on tachograph recordings, which provide ample evidence for the prosecution case.

Rest Periods

Rest periods are defined as uninterrupted time during which the driver 'may freely dispose of his time'. Daily rest periods, and particularly rest periods which are compensating for previously reduced rest periods, should not be confused with, or combined with, statutory break periods required to be taken during the driving day as described above.

It has been held that time spent by drivers on weekend training courses (eg DCPC, Hazchem courses and suchlike), even where there is no direct payment of wages by the employer, breaches the requirements under EU rules for drivers to have a period of weekly rest during which they may freely dispose of their time.

Daily Rest Periods

Once each day drivers are required to observe either a regular, a reduced or a split daily rest period during which time they must be free to dispose of their time. These daily rests are to be taken once in each 24 hours commencing at the time when the driver activates the tachograph following a weekly or daily rest period. Where the daily rest is taken in two separate periods (see below), the calculation must commence at the end of a rest period of not less than nine hours. Thus in each 24-hour period as defined here one or other of the following daily rest periods must be taken:

- Regular daily rest: 11 hours
  or alternatively,
- Reduced rest: nine hours – may be taken no more than three times between any two weekly rest periods;
- Split rest: where the daily rest period is not reduced (as above), the rest may be split and taken in two separate periods during the 24 hours, provided:
  - the first period must be at least three hours;
  - the last period must be at least nine hours.

Split Daily Rest

When a regular daily rest period is split into two or three separate periods (shown above to be permitted under the rules) it should be noted, as a result of a European Court of Justice ruling, that the minimum nine-hour period must be the last portion of the rest.

Multi-Manned Vehicles

Where a vehicle is operated by a two-man crew, the daily rest period requirement is that each man must have had a minimum of nine hours' rest in each period of 30 hours counting from the end of a daily or weekly rest period.

NB: In the case of multi-manning, it should be noted that the hours law applies to the crew members from the commencement of the journey (or their day's work if that commenced earlier) but for the first hour the presence of another driver is optional. This allows the first driver to pick up the second driver up to one hour after leaving base.

Daily Rest on Vehicles

Daily rest periods may be taken on a vehicle provided:

- the vehicle has a bunk so the driver (but not necessarily a mate or attendant) can lie down; and
- the vehicle is stationary for the whole of the rest period.

It follows from this that a driver on a multi-manned vehicle cannot be taking part of his *daily rest period* on the bunk while a co-driver continues to drive the vehicle. He could, however, be taking a *break* at this time while the vehicle is moving or he could merely spend his time lying on the bunk, with his tachograph chart recording other work. It is permissible for the co-driver to book a POA when not driving, instead of a break or other work. This can only be applied when all the POA qualifying conditions exist for him to do so.

Daily Rest on Ferries/Trains

Normal 11-hour daily rest periods which are taken when a vehicle is carried for part of its journey on a ferry crossing or by rail may be interrupted, not more than twice, by other activities (such as embarkation or disembarkation) provided:

- the interruption must be 'as short as possible' and in any event must not be more than one hour;
- during both parts of the rest (ie in the terminal and on board the ferry/train) the driver must have access to a bunk or couchette.

NB: For vehicles arriving at, or departing from, ports, driving within port areas within the UK is now classed as driving and not duty. Embarkation and disembarkation driving times need to be recorded using the 'ferry flag' option in the rest mode and reset to straight rest once embarkation or disembarkation has been completed. On an analogue tachograph these activities need to be recorded manually.

Weekly Rest Period

After six successive 24-hour periods a regular weekly rest period totalling 45 hours must be taken. A weekly rest period which begins in one fixed week and continues into the following week may be attached to either of these weeks but not to both.

While the normal weekly rest period is 45 hours as described above, this may be reduced to a rest period of at least 24 hours whether at base or away from base.

Reduced weekly rest periods must be compensated (ie made up) by an equivalent amount of rest period time taken *en bloc* and added to another rest period of at least nine hours' duration before the end of the third week following the week in which the reduced weekly rest period is taken.

Currently within the UK, DVSA traffic examiners are able to fine drivers who fail to take a full 45 hour weekly rest at least every fortnight. They are also able to fine drivers who spend their weekly rest in a vehicle where the presence of the vehicle may 'cause a problem'.

It is also worth noting that within the EU some member states insist that weekly rests taken in a vehicle must be taken at a safe and secure site, and that only two weekly rests may be taken 'back to back' by a driver, with the third weekly rest needing to be taken either at home or in a hotel, etc. However, reduced weekly rests will always be allowed to be taken in the vehicle cab.

EU member states such as France, the Netherlands, Germany, Austria and Sweden are also 'tightening' their interpretations of the rules in an attempt to reduce what is termed 'social dumping' which is deemed to be where foreign operators are able to undercut national operators because their interpretation of the rules is less onerous and because of lower minimum wage levels in other countries. It is the minimum wage issue that is the increasing problem and the EU is currently proposing that it adopts a single minimum wage right across all member states.

The advice is to seek clarification from the DVSA, RHA or FTA before sending vehicles to these countries if a normal weekly rest will be required en-route, and to keep up to date with this changing scenario.

Compensated Rest Periods

When reduced weekly rest periods are taken, the compensated time must be attached to another rest period of at least nine hours' duration and must be granted, at the request of the driver, at the vehicle parking place or at the driver's base. Compensation in this respect *does not* mean compensation by means of payment; it means the provision of an equivalent amount of rest time taken on a later occasion but by the end of the third following week in the case of compensated weekly rest periods.

Summary of EU Rules

The following summarizes the EU rules applicable to both national and international goods vehicle operations:

- Maximum daily driving: Nine hours, 10 hours on two days in week
- Maximum weekly driving: 56 hours
- Maximum fortnightly driving: 90 hours
- Maximum driving before a break: Four and a half hours
- Minimum breaks after driving: 45 minutes or one break of at least 15 minutes and one of at least 30 minutes each to equal 45 minutes
- Minimum daily rest (normally): 11 hours
- Reduced daily rest: Nine hours on up to three days per week between any two weekly rest periods
- Split daily rest: A regular daily rest period may be split into two periods – the first at least three hours, the other at least nine hours. This gives a minimum total rest of 12 hours
- Minimum weekly rest (normally): 45 hours once each fixed week
- Reduced weekly rest: 24 hours (any reduction must be made up *en bloc* by the end of the third following week)

- Rest on ferries/trains: Normal daily rest (11 hours) may be interrupted not more than twice:
  - no more than one hour between parts
  - drivers must have access to a bunk or couchette for both parts of rest

Unforeseen Circumstances (Previously Known as Emergencies)

It is permitted for the driver to depart from the EU/AETR rules as specified above to the extent necessary to enable him to reach a suitable stopping place when an unforeseen circumstance, such as an emergency, arises where he needs to ensure the safety of persons, the vehicle or its load, providing road safety is not jeopardized. The nature of and reasons for departing from the rules in these circumstances must be shown on the tachograph chart or on a printout from a digital tachograph. The driver should note the reasons when he reaches a suitable stopping place.

Prohibition on Certain Payments

The EU/AETR rules prohibit any payment to wage-earning drivers in the form of bonuses or wage supplements related to distances travelled and/or the amount of goods carried unless such payments do not endanger road safety.

British Domestic Rules

The current British drivers' hours rules contained in the 1968 Transport Act (as amended) came into effect on 29 September 1986. They apply to goods vehicle drivers whose activities are outside the scope of the EU requirements as described above (ie which are specified as exempt from the EU rules) and comprise only limits on daily driving and daily duty.

NB: Detailed provisions which previously applied in regard to daily and weekly duty, daily spreadover, and daily and weekly rest period limits were completely abolished when these rule changes were introduced.

It is important to emphasize that drivers who are exempt from the EU/AETR rules either because their vehicle does not exceed 3.5 tonnes permissible maximum weight or because the activity in which they are engaged falls within the scope of the EU/AETR exemptions list (see pp 100–03), must observe the British domestic rules. The issue of whether or not vehicles exceeding 2,400 kg on international hire and reward operations will still be allowed to use British Domestic Regulations whilst on an international journey whilst within the UK following Brexit is still unclear until full details are released.

NB: It should be noted that:

- *Although no records of driving or working times are required to be kept, drivers of light goods vehicles (ie not exceeding 3.5 tonnes permissible maximum weight, but note the 2,400 kg problem above) must still conform to the legal limits on maximum daily driving and maximum daily duty. In addition, the concession that allows drivers of cleaner/alternative fuelled vans to drive vehicles in the UK up to 4,250 kg on a Category B licence may not be valid in some or all EU member states post-Brexit and operators of these vehicles are advised to monitor this situation closely, especially if intending to drive to or through Germany, which was the country that originally proposed this increase.*

- *If a trailer is attached to a vehicle not exceeding 3.5 tonnes permissible maximum weight (which itself is exempt from the EU/AETR rules on account of its weight) thereby taking the combined weight to over 3.5 tonnes then the EU/AETR rules must be followed as described in the foregoing text (unless it is exempt for other reasons, namely the nature of the operations on which it is engaged) and a tachograph must be fitted to the vehicle and used by the driver for record-keeping purposes (see Chapter 5).*

Exemptions and Concessions

The British domestic rules apply to drivers of all goods vehicles which are exempt from the EU regulations as described earlier but with the following further exceptions which are totally exempt from all hours rules control:

- the armed forces;
- police and fire brigade services;
- driving off the public road system;
- driving for purely private purposes (ie not in connection with any trade or business).

The British domestic rules do not apply:

- to a driver who on any day does not drive a relevant vehicle; or
- to a driver who on each day of the week does not drive a vehicle within the rules for more than four hours (note: this exemption *does not* apply to a driver whose activities fall within the scope of the EU/AETR rules within that fixed week).

Driving and Duty Definitions

For the purposes of the British domestic rules:

- Driving means time spent behind the wheel actually driving a goods vehicle and the specified maximum limit applies to such time spent driving on public roads. Driving on off-road sites and premises such as quarries, civil engineering and building sites and on agricultural and forestry land is counted as duty time, not driving time. If unsure about whether or not a particular road is classed as 'off-road', drivers should be advised to comply with the British domestic rules.

- Duty time is the time a driver spends working for his employer and includes any work undertaken including the driving of private motor cars, for example, and non-driving work which is not driving time for the purposes of the regulations. The daily duty limit does not apply on any day when a driver does not drive a goods vehicle.

Summary of British Domestic Rules

- Maximum daily driving: 10 hours
- Maximum daily duty: 11 hours
- Continuous duty: no specified limit
- Daily spreadover: no specified limit
- Weekly duty: no specified limit
- Breaks during day: no requirement specified
- Daily rest: no specified requirement (but obviously a minimum of 13 hours so as not to exceed the daily 11-hour duty limit)
- Weekly rest: no specified requirement

Again, it should be noted that under these specific rules the driver may be required to take a break under the rules of the Road Transport Directive (RTD) (see below).

It must also be noted that drivers who drive for less than four hours a day for an entire 'fixed week' (midnight Sun/Mon – midnight Sun/Mon) are exempt from the daily duty limit but if on any one day of the fixed week they do drive for more than four hours then the 11-hour daily duty limit will apply for every day of that fixed week.

Emergencies (This Term is Still Used for the Domestic Rules)

The daily driving and duty limits specified above may be suspended when an emergency situation arises. This is defined as an event requiring immediate action to avoid danger to life or health of one or more individuals or animals, serious interruption in the maintenance of essential public services for the supply of gas, water, electricity, drainage, or of telecommunications and postal services, or in the use of roads, railways, ports or airports, or damage to property. Details of the emergency should be entered by the driver on his record sheet when the limits are exceeded. Where a British domestic driver uses a tachograph instead of a record sheet, these details should be added to the tachograph record.

Light Vehicle Driving

As explained above, drivers of light goods vehicles not exceeding 3.5 tonnes permissible maximum weight – as with drivers of other goods vehicles which fall within the scope of these rules – must observe the daily limits on driving (10 hours) and duty (11 hours). However, only the 10-hour daily driving limit applies when such vehicles are used:

- by doctors, dentists, nurses, midwives or vets;
- for any service of inspection, cleaning, maintenance, repair, installation or fitting;
- by a commercial traveller, and carrying only goods used for soliciting orders;
- by an employee of the AA, the RAC or the RSAC;
- for the business of cinematography or of radio or television broadcasting.

Mixed EU/AETR and British Driving

It is possible that a goods vehicle driver may be engaged in transport operations which come within the scope of both the EU/AETR drivers' hours rules and the British domestic hours rules on the same day or within the same week. When such a situation arises he may conform strictly to the EU/AETR rules throughout the whole of the driving/working period or he may take advantage of the more liberal British domestic rules where appropriate. If he decides on this course of action and thereby combines both British and EU/AETR rules he must beware of the following points:

- time spent driving under the EU/AETR rules cannot count as an off-duty period for the British rules;
- time spent driving or on duty under the British rules cannot count as a break or rest period under the EU/AETR rules;
- driving under the EU/AETR rules counts towards the driving and duty limits for the British rules;
- if any EU/AETR rules driving is done in a week the driver must observe the EU/AETR daily and weekly rest period requirements for the whole of that week.
- It needs to be noted here that, where a driver drives under both EU/AETR rules and British rules on the same day, both sets of rules must be complied with. The important point here is that it would limit the total duty time to the 11-hour limit under British rules and not allow the driver to take advantage of the longer duty time available under the EU/AETR rules.

AETR Rules

Throughout the section we have referred to EU/AETR rules as they are exactly the same and the set which the UK finally adopts will depend upon the terms of our exit from the EU. IF we leave with no deal we will adopt the title AETR for our driving rules, but if we have a deal it 'might' be that we are allowed to continue to use the title EU rules. Either way, for most operators it is only a change in title, nothing else; although international operators may be required to use EU titled rules in some EU member states if they decide that is what they want to happen. More details on AETR rules are below.

AETR Countries

Albania	Monaco
Andorra	Montenegro
Armenia	Russia
Azerbaijan	San Marino
Belarus	Serbia
Bosnia and Herzegovina	Turkey
Kazakhstan	Turkmenistan
Liechtenstein	Ukraine
Macedonia	*United Kingdom
Moldova	Uzbekistan

When undertaking journeys to AETR signatory countries EU drivers must follow the AETR rules for the whole journey, including any EU countries where the journey may begin, or any that may be passed through, if permitted to do so by the EU country concerned. Importantly, since September 2010, the AETR rules not only align with the EU Drivers' Hours Regulations 561/2006 they also recognize the digital tachograph.

As the whole journey requires a single set of rules to be followed then the AETR rules for a UK operator operating within the EU would apply. This 'should' also mean that EU vehicles operating within the UK will also need to operate under AETR rules, but, as stated earlier, these scenarios could change depending on the terms under which the UK leaves the EU.

Working Time

Among all the strict regulation that the road transport industry has had to contend with in recent years, there is no doubt that the imposition of the EU's Road Transport Directive (Directive 2002/15/EC – the RTD), which took effect from 4 April 2005, has had a significant impact on transport operators, vocational drivers and LGV drivers alike.

The first step in this particular legislative process started with the European Council Directive 93/104/EC of November 1993 commonly referred to as the Working Time Directive (WTD). This Directive introduced a number of provisions to control working time for most employees in the interest of improving work environments and ensuring better protection for workers by limiting maximum weekly working hours, setting minimum daily and weekly rest periods and minimum in-work breaks, setting minimum annual holidays and requiring regular health checks for night workers. In particular, the Directive specified a maximum 48-hour working week and limited night working in any 24-hour period. These requirements are enforced in the UK by our own domestic working time regulations (see below).

However, while this Directive originally excluded the transport sector, further proposals originally published in 1997 were intended to bring road haulage (and other previously excepted worker categories) into the scope of the working time principles. From 1 August 2003 came the Horizontal Amending Directive (Directive 2000/34/EC – abbreviated to HAD), which amended the original WTD by setting rules for those employment sectors that were expressly excluded from the WTD, such as non-mobile transport workers and mobile workers not covered by the EU drivers' hours rules (for example, light vehicle drivers).

These two EU Directives are given the force of law in Great Britain by the Working Time Regulations 1998 (SI 1998 No 1833).

In the following section, the working times rules are explained in order of their relevance to the road transport industry; namely, first the RTD that applies to vocational drivers operating under EU drivers' hours rules, second the HAD that applies to all road transport personnel not covered by EU regulations and finally the WTD itself, which is applicable to most other workers, classed as 'non-mobile' workers.

The Road Transport Directive

LGV drivers who fall within scope of the drivers' hours law contained in EU Regulation 561/2006/EC, namely most drivers of goods vehicles exceeding 3.5 tonnes gross weight, are covered by the RTD (Directive 2002/15/EC), which deals specifically with working time for those persons performing mobile transport activities within the scope of the EU/AETR drivers' hours rules (mainly LGV drivers), but with the exception of self-employed mobile workers.

This Directive was implemented in the UK from 4 April 2005, following publication of Statutory Instrument SI 2005 No 639.

NB: It is important to note that the RTD does not replace the EU/AETR drivers' hours rules. Instead, it supplements both the current Regulation (ie 561/2006/EC) and the AETR Agreement, so drivers who fall within the scope of these regulations when driving a goods vehicle must also take note of and comply with the provisions of the RTD. The UK Government has expressed a desire to retain WTD and RTD rules post-Brexit.

Definitions

It is useful to consider the definitions for certain terms used and the specific provisions set out in the RTD as follows.

Mobile Transport Activities

Any activity carried out by workers in the course of their employment within a road transport operation.

Mobile Worker

Any worker who forms part of the travelling staff of an undertaking that operates goods or passenger transport for hire or reward or on its own account – obviously this means drivers, but also includes other crew members, trainees and apprentices.

Occasional Mobile Worker

An occasional mobile worker is a worker who is mobile, operating under EU/AETR regulations on no more than 10 days in a 26-week reference period or 15 days if the reference period is more than 26 weeks. In this case, if these limits are exceeded then the worker is treated as a mobile worker.

Self-Employed Drivers

These are similarly categorized as mobile workers (ie driving in a road transport operation) except that such workers are not tied to an employer by an employment contract (see below).

Working Time

This is time spent at work and at the employer's disposal carrying out his activities or duties. This includes travelling as part of job- and work-related training, but not commuting between home and work in a private vehicle, or rest breaks where no work is done, or 'on-call' time when at home.

Periods of Availability

These periods are not working time and do not count as such, nor are they breaks or daily or weekly rest periods. They could include a known period of waiting time (for example, to load or unload or while waiting for a ferry) if the driver is free to dispose of his time during that period of waiting, but not, for example, if he has to remain with his vehicle in a queue – this would be working time. The key to this is whether the waiting period could have been foreseen in advance: if it could, it counts as non-working time; if it could not be foreseen, it is working time.

Working Week

The working week is 48 hours' work (with a maximum of 60 hours in a week) averaged over a four-month (ie 17- or 18-week) reference period, which may be extended by agreement to six months (26 weeks). The total working time is calculated excluding breaks during the working day and any periods of availability (see above). It should be noted that there is *NO* opt-out from the working time limits under this Directive as there is with the other Directives (ie the WTD and the HAD).

Breaks

Breaks taken during the working period must amount to a minimum of 30 minutes if working between six and nine hours; or 45 minutes if working over nine hours. Breaks should be of at least 15 minutes' duration.

Night Work

This is defined as a four-hour period between midnight and 4.00 am. Night working will be limited to 10 hours in any 24-hour period although a collective or workforce agreement will allow this to be extended. This agreement may not apply to agency drivers as they are employed by the agency in question. Operators are advised to check the position of any workforce agreement with the agency supplying the drivers.

NB: This night work definition should not be confused with the night work definition contained in either the HAD or the WTD (see later).

Holidays

Holidays are to comprise a minimum of 5.6 weeks (ie 28 days). It is to be an important provision of new regulations that mobile workers must tell their employer, in writing, of any time they spend working for other employers if they are engaged in road transport activities. Driving and other activities must be declared when working for employers involved in road transport.

Record Keeping

Irrespective of which of the three Directives (the WTD, HAD or RTD) applies in any particular work situation, employers must keep detailed records of employee working time and provide copies of such records to their employees when asked for them. There is no officially prescribed system for record keeping or special format for individual records, but whatever system is used the records must be kept for two years and be made available to DVSA enforcement officers on request. This means that if tachograph records are used to record working time details they must be retained for two years and not just 12 months.

Health Assessments

Employers will be required to provide free health assessments for night workers. Employers have a duty to determine exactly who is a night worker for this purpose and provide the health assessment accordingly. The assessment should include a questionnaire devised and monitored by a qualified health professional and, where necessary, be backed up by a medical examination.

Enforcement

The RTD regulations will be enforced mainly by the DVSA, most likely when they are checking compliance with the EU drivers' hours and tachograph rules, or as a result of complaints made to them.

Self-Employed Workers

The original intention of the Directive was that it should apply to self-employed drivers from 23 March 2009. This was fiercely opposed by many EU member states but, after much debate and a vote in the European Parliament, the European Commission removed a proposal to exempt the self-employed and they have been included as a group of drivers who, since 11 May 2012, do now need to comply by observing the 48-hour average working week and 60-hour limit and the associated provisions listed below.

The Horizontal Amending Directive (HAD)

The WTD referred to above originally excluded the transport sector, but publication of an amending Directive, 2000/34/EC (the so-called Horizontal Amending Directive – HAD), which took effect from 1 August 2003, brought all employed road transport personnel, including office-based staff, referred to collectively as 'non-mobile workers', and other previously exempted employment categories, into line.

This Directive, which has applied to all employed road transport personnel (ie apart from those subject to the EU/AETR drivers' hours rules) since 1 August 2003 as mentioned above, requires all relevant transport employees to comply with the provisions set out below.

Four particular provisions of the HAD apply to drivers who fall outside the scope of the RTD – ie drivers of smaller vehicles and drivers of other vehicles that are exempt from the EU/AETR drivers' hours rules. These are:

- the 48-hour average working week;
- the requirement to have four weeks' paid annual leave;
- regular health checks for night workers;
- the need for 'adequate rest'.

Under these regulations, workers are allowed to opt out of the 48-hour average working week. However, mobile workers covered by the RTD are only entitled to the annual leave and health checks provisions (see above).

The Working Time Directive for Non-Mobile Workers

The Working Time Directive (Directive 93/104/EC) of November 1993 introduced a number of provisions to control working time for employees, including the concept of a maximum 48-hour working week and shift working restrictions under which night workers may not work more than a specified average number of working hours in any 24-hour period. This Directive specifically excluded the transport sector (eg road, rail, sea, air, inland waterway, etc), which is now covered by other, subsequently published Directives, namely the RTD and HAD described above.

Under the WTD provisions:

- Employers are required to limit average weekly working time to a maximum of 48 hours, including overtime, calculated over successive periods of 17 weeks (ie four months), or for the period of employment where this is less than 17 weeks.
- The opt-out clause which would have allowed non-mobile workers to exceed the average 48-hour working week has now been withdrawn by the European Parliament.
- Employers are required to limit night working to no more than eight hours in 24 hours taken as an average over a 17-week reference period (see sections above regarding the RTD and HAD on this topic). For night workers (ie those who work for at least three hours at night) whose work involves special hazards or heavy physical or mental strain, the limit is a straight eight hours in 24 hours with no averaging out.
- Employers are required to provide free health assessments for night workers, and the opportunity for employees to transfer to day work if their health is affected by night working.

- Employers are required to allow workers a daily rest period of at least 11 consecutive hours in each 24-hour period and an uninterrupted rest break of at least 20 minutes when their daily work exceeds six hours.
- Employers are required to allow workers a weekly rest period of not less than 24 hours in each seven days.
- Employers are required to allow workers who have been employed continuously for 13 weeks to have at least four weeks' paid annual leave, which may not be exchanged for payment in lieu except where it occurs on termination of the employment.
- Employers are required to keep records of workers' hours of work that are adequate to show that the legal requirements are complied with, and retain these records for at least two years from the date on which they were made.

The WTD regulations set more restrictive standards for young workers and exempt certain special classes of worker such as Crown servants, the police, trainees and agricultural workers.

Unfair Dismissal

The Employment Rights Act 1996 is amended by the addition of new provisions to make it unfair to dismiss an employee for refusing to comply with a requirement contrary to the working time regulations, or to forgo his rights.

The National Minimum Wage

The National Minimum Wage provisions introduced by the National Minimum Wage Regulations 1999 under the National Minimum Wage Act 1998, which came into force in the UK on 1 April 1999, have been further amended by the National Minimum Wage Regulations 1999 (Amendment) Regulations 2008. Since April 2018, these require that workers (other than self-employed persons) aged 25 years and over be paid a minimum 'Living Wage' rate of £8.21 per hour. Workers aged 21–24 years of age must be paid at least £7.70 per hour, and workers aged from 18 to 20 years at least £6.15 per hour. The development rate for 16–17-year-olds is £4.35 per hour and the apprentice rate is £3.90 per hour. The minimum wage applies to most workers in the UK, including agency workers (eg agency drivers), part-time and casual workers and those paid on a commission basis.

NB: The National Minimum Wage rates and the National Living Wage rates are now both changed in April each year.

Assessing Minimum Pay

For the purposes of assessing minimum pay, payments to employees comprising bonuses, incentives and performance-related awards count as part of the pay package, but other allowances not consolidated into an employee's pay are not counted. Similarly, overtime payments and shift payments do not count. Benefits in kind, such as the provision of overnight subsistence, meals, uniforms and workwear allowances, are also excluded. Gross pay, with all deductions and reductions subtracted, should be divided by the number of hours worked to determine whether the resulting hourly pay rate at least matches, if not exceeds, the national minima stated above.

Types of Work

The work hours for which an employer has to pay are calculated according to the type of work employees are engaged upon. Mainly this is as follows:

- time work, where an employee is paid for working a set number of hours or a set period of time;
- salaried work, where an employee has a contract to work a set number of basic hours annually in return for an annual salary paid in equal instalments;
- unmeasured work, where employees are paid to do specific tasks (eg driving), but are not set specific hours for the work.

NB: In this case the employer must agree with the employee (in writing) a daily average of hours to be spent carrying out the assigned tasks. The employer must be able to show that the number of hours agreed is realistic.

Exemptions from the rates above apply to the self-employed, company directors and volunteers, and where an employee receives housing as part of their employment package there is a daily off-set allowance.

Enforcement and Penalties

Enforcement of the minimum and living wage provisions is by HM Revenue & Customs and by the employees themselves, who have a right to complain if they are not being paid the National Minimum/Living Wage levels.

Employers obviously need to keep accurate records of the hours worked and hourly rates paid to employees in case such information is called into question later – for a minimum of three years. An employee (or any other qualifying worker) may make a written request for access to his own records, and this must be allowed within 14 days unless extended by agreement. Should a dispute arise, the burden of proof is on the employer to show that the National Minimum/Living Wage has been paid, not on the employee to prove that it has not.

Refusal to pay the National Minimum/Living Wage is a criminal offence carrying a maximum fine of up to £5,000 on conviction. Dismissal of an employee who becomes eligible for the National Minimum/Living Wage or for a higher rate of pay will constitute unfair dismissal, with no qualifying period to be served by workers to secure protection against this form of unfair dismissal.

Self-Employment

The road haulage industry is renowned for the number of self-employed workers, especially owner-driver lorry operators. However, not all such so-called self-employed persons are genuinely self-employed in terms that meet legal requirements of HMRC in regard to payment of tax and National Insurance contributions.

To satisfy HMRC a self-employed person needs to meet a series of so-called 'tests' under which the self-employed person:

- decides, broadly, how and when specified work is to be carried out, the actual hours he works and when breaks and holidays are taken, and is not subject to the disciplinary provisions of an employer;
- provides his own tools and equipment and is free to send another person (or sub-contractor) in his place to carry out work where necessary;
- has no entitlement to payment for public or annual holidays or sickness, is not included in an employer's pension scheme, and has no rights to claim redundancy payments, unfair dismissal or any entitlement to unemployment benefit if his services are no longer required;
- takes financial risk with the aim of making a profit, is responsible for paying his own income tax and National Insurance contributions, and charges for the services provided by submitting an invoice;
- is free to work for other employers as required if he so wishes (a self-employed person who works for only one employer is likely to be considered to be an employee of that employer).

A number of instances have arisen in transport where the self-employed status of owner-drivers has been questioned by HMRC (mainly because they work for only one firm). In such cases, where HMRC has ruled that owner-driver agreements are merely employment contracts, the employer becomes liable for back tax and National Insurance contributions for its sub-contractors. This is especially so where the owner-driver works under the 'O' licence of the employing company – and if he is genuinely self-employed, then, in any event, this practice is illegal under 'O' licensing legislation. This specific issue is currently being investigated in depth by HMRC.

NB: This issue is currently being investigated in depth by HMRC.

Tax Relief on Driver Allowances

Sleeper Cab Allowances

The amount paid to drivers for overnight subsistence varies considerably from area to area but HM Revenue & Customs has agreed that (November 2017 and still in force) LGV drivers can be paid night-out allowances on a tax-free basis amounting to £34.90 per night where the vehicle does not have a sleeper cab, reducing to £26.20

(approx 75 per cent of the figure) per night where a sleeper cab is available. These levels of payments are considered by HMRC to reimburse a driver and do not prevent an employer from paying an additional allowance although any additional allowance will normally be subject to tax. Payment of such amounts is subject to the employer being satisfied that:

- the individual did necessarily spend the night away from his home and normal place of work and that he used a sleeper cab;
- the employee necessarily incurred extra expense in doing so; and
- the amounts paid are no more than reasonable reimbursement of the average allowable expenses of the driver (ie for payment of an evening meal, breakfast, washing facilities and the upkeep of bedding).

Owner-drivers are dealt with differently for tax purposes and may *not* claim such night-out allowances against their tax liability.

These payments should only be made where the employee does actually spend the night away and incurs extra expense. If he uses the bunk in a sleeper cab the allowable amount is only that required to meet the expenses he incurs, not the full night-out allowance.

HM Revenue & Customs may refuse claims for tax-free payments of night-out allowances above the general limit. Employers who have paid in excess of this amount (or a locally agreed rate) without deduction of tax may find themselves liable to meet the tax due on the additional amounts paid, except where it can be proved that the expense was genuinely incurred (by production of a valid receipt); alternatively, they should include it as part of the wages within PAYE.

Records Retained for Tax Purposes

Where tachograph records are used to justify payment of night-out and other subsistence expenses to drivers these become part of the tax record and as such must be retained for six years instead of the normal one year.

Personal Incidental Expenses

Employee drivers may be paid additional amounts by way of 'personal incidental expenses' in relation to genuine expenditure (eg newspapers, laundry and calls home) during a qualifying absence (ie when working away from home) up to a tax-free limit, without any tax or National Insurance consequences for the employer up to the value of £5 per day if in the UK, or £10 per day outside the UK (source: GOV.UK website).

Benchmark Scale Rate Payments

Where an employee has to spend money as a result of a business journey in the UK, and incurs an allowable expense while on that journey, employers are allowed to make the following subsistence payments, in relation to travel time:

Minimum journey time	Maximum amount of meal allowance
5 hours	£5
10 hours	£10
15 hours (and ongoing at 8pm)	£25

Tax Relief for International Drivers

International LGV drivers who spend fewer than 91 days in the UK during a tax year (ie from 6 April to 5 April annually) can claim 'non-resident' status and qualify for their wages to be paid tax-free.

Goods Vehicle Drivers' Records

04

Drivers of goods vehicles and other vehicles used for the carriage of goods (eg off-road vehicles and so-called 4 × 4s) over 3.5 tonnes gross weight must keep records of the time they spend driving such vehicles and their working times. Most drivers are also required to record breaks taken during driving periods, over the working day and their daily and weekly rest periods. Where vehicles fall within the scope of the EU drivers' hours rules or the AETR rules as described in Chapter 3 (ie unless they are specifically exempt as shown in the relevant exemptions list) the record-keeping requirement is based on the mandatory use of tachographs as described in Chapter 5.

Where a vehicle is outside the scope of the EU or AETR rules then the British domestic (ie 1968 Transport Act – as amended) driving hours rules normally apply (see Chapter 3) and the driver of such a vehicle is required to keep written records by means of a 'log-book' system. The requirement is that the record must be a written record (in order to meet the requirements of the operator's licence) but it must be a record that is capable of accurately capturing a driver's activities. Suppliers of these log books can be found on the internet but the trade associations (FTA/RHA) do also supply them.

It should be noted that some operators operating under British domestic driving hours rules do choose to use tachographs instead of 'log books' as they feel that the information available through the use of a tachograph enables them to better control and monitor fleet and driver activity and Working Time compliance. Where this is done the rules on tachograph operation and inspection/calibration apply.

To summarize the main record-keeping alternatives, these are as follows:

- Goods vehicles not exceeding 3.5 tonnes permissible maximum weight – NO RECORDS.*
- Goods vehicles over 3.5 tonnes permissible maximum weight (including the weight of any trailer drawn) operating within EU rules – TACHOGRAPH RECORDS (ie either analogue or digital).
- Goods vehicles over 3.5 tonnes permissible maximum weight exempt from EU rules – WRITTEN 'LOG-BOOK' RECORDS (but subject to further exemption in certain cases). (See note above in relation to tachographs.)

- Goods vehicles over 3.5 tonnes permissible maximum weight exempt from both EU and British domestic rules (eg military vehicles, etc) – NO RECORDS.

**Currently records are required when driving in Germany, and if the proposed lower weight of 2,400 kg is adopted by the EU then vehicles exceeding this lower weight will also be required to keep records when on international hire and reward operations from the UK to the EU. Note also that alternatively fuelled vans are currently able to operate up to 4,250 kg in the UK without the need for a tachograph.*

This chapter describes the record-keeping requirements applying to drivers falling within the third item above, namely those operating under the British domestic rules, who must keep written 'log-book' records.

Exemptions from Written Record Keeping

Written records do not have to be kept in the following cases:

- by drivers of vehicles being operated by, or under the control of, the armed forces, the police or the fire brigade;
- by drivers of goods vehicles that do not drive on public roads;
- by drivers who do not drive in connection with a business or commercial activity;
- by drivers voluntarily using an EU/AETR tachograph for record-keeping purposes which has been calibrated and sealed at a DVSA-approved tachograph centre.

Record Books

Ready-printed record books can be purchased 'off the shelf' or firms can have their own version pre-printed with their own name and logo if desired. In the latter case it is important that the specific requirements of the regulations are observed in both the format and the printing of the book.

The book must be a standard A6 format (105 mm × 148 mm) or it may be larger if preferred. It must comprise a front sheet on which is entered relevant information, a set of instructions for the use of the book, and a number of individual weekly record sheets with facilities for completing these in duplicate (ie with carbon paper or carbonless copy paper) and for the duplicate sheet to be detached for return to the employer when completed.

There is no legal requirement for the numbering of record books or for their issue against an entry in a register of record book issues as previously required.

Weekly record sheets in the book must follow the format set out in the regulations with appropriate spaces for entries to be made under the following headings:

- driver's name;
- period covered by sheet week commencing… week ending… ;
- registration number of vehicle(s);
- place where vehicle(s) based;
- time of going on duty;
- time of going off duty;
- time spent driving;
- time spent on duty;
- signature of driver;
- certification by employer (ie signature and position held).

Issue and Return of Record Books

Employers must issue their employee drivers with record books when they are required to drive vehicles to which the British domestic driving hours regulations apply and where records must be kept. Before issuing the book, the employer must complete the front cover to show the firm's name, address and telephone number, preferably with a rubber stamp if he has one.

When a record book is issued to the driver he should complete the front cover with his surname, first name(s), date of birth and home address, and the date he first used the book. When the book is completed he should also enter the date of the last entry (ie date of last use). There is space to record the name and address of a second employer.

Books issued by an employer to an employee-driver must be returned to that employer when complete (subject to the requirement for the driver to retain it for two weeks after use) or when the employee leaves that employment. He must not take it with him to his new employer. Any unused weekly sheets and all duplicates must be included when the book is returned.

Two Employers

Where a driver has two employers who employ him to drive goods vehicles to which the British domestic hours rules apply, the first employer must issue the record book as described (completed weekly record sheets and completed record books must be returned to this employer), and the second employer must write or stamp his firm's name and address on the front cover of the record book with a statement that the holder is also a driver in his employment. When the driver does part-time driving work for another employer he must disclose to each employer, if requested, details of his working and driving times with the other employer. Similarly, when a driver changes to a new employer the former employer must give the new employer details of the driver's previous driving and working times if requested.

Record Book Entries

The driver must make entries on the weekly sheet for each day on which a record is required (instructions on the correct use of the book are printed inside the cover). Care must be taken to ensure that an exact duplicate of the entry is made simultaneously (ie two separately written repeat entries are *not* acceptable even if no carbon paper is available). When completing a daily sheet he must enter all the required details under each of the headings. If he changes vehicles during the day he must write in the registration number for each vehicle. He must then sign the sheet before returning it to his employer.

Completion of the record is straightforward, the driver having to enter the vehicle registration number, the time of coming on duty, and at the end of the day the time at which he went off-duty, and he must sign the sheet. He may enter any remarks concerning his entries, or point out corrections which should be made, in the appropriate box at the foot of the record. The employer may also use this space if required for making comments regarding the record. This space may also be used for recording the name of a second driver.

Corrections

Entries in the record book must be in ink or made by a ballpoint pen and there must be no erasures, corrections or additions. Mistakes may only be corrected by writing an explanation or showing the correct information in the remarks space. Sheets must not be mutilated or destroyed.

Return and Signing of Record Sheets

On completion of the weekly sheet, and after it has been signed by the driver, the duplicate copy must be detached from the book and handed to the employer within seven days of the date of the last entry on the sheet, and then within a further seven days the employer must have examined and signed the duplicate sheet. However, if in either case it is not reasonably practicable to do so within this time, these actions must be carried out as soon as it is possible to do so.

Retention and Production of Record Books

The driver should carry his record book with him at all times when working and must produce it for inspection at the request of an authorized examiner. The book should be shown to the employer at the end of every week or as soon as possible after the week so he can examine and countersign the entries. Following completion of the book the driver must continue to keep it with him for a further 14 days (available for inspection by the enforcement authorities) before returning it to his employer.

Completed record books must be retained by the employer, also available for inspection by the enforcement authorities, for not less than 12 months. As stated earlier, if the books are to be used to record compliance with a Working Time Directive then they need to be retained for 24 months not just 12.

FIGURE 4.1 Simplified record sheet for British domestic transport operations

WEEKLY RECORD SHEETS

WEEKLY SHEETS								
1. DRIVER'S NAME			2. PERIOD COVERED BY SHEET WEEK COMMENCING (DATE) .... TO WEEK ENDING (DATE)					
DAY ON WHICH DUTY COMMENCED	REGISTRATION NO OF VEHICLE(S) 3.	PLACE WHERE VEHICLE(S) BASED 4.	TIME OF GOING ON DUTY 5.	TIME OF GOING OFF DUTY 6.	TIME SPENT DRIVING 7.	TIME SPENT ON DUTY 8.	SIGNATURE OF DRIVER 9.
MONDAY							
TUESDAY							
WEDNESDAY							
THURSDAY							
FRIDAY							
SATURDAY							
SUNDAY							
10. CERTIFICATION BY EMPLOYER				I HAVE EXAMINED THE ENTRIES IN THIS SHEET SIGNATURE .... POSITION HELD			

Records for Germany

Currently, the German authorities require, under their own domestic legislation, foreign drivers of goods vehicles of between 2.8 tonnes and 3.5 tonnes gross weight to either use a tachograph to produce a record of their activities or to carry and complete AETR-type log books. AETR-type log books are available from the Road Haulage Association (RHA) Tel: 01733 261131 or email rhashop@rha.co.net. In addition, drivers of these vehicles are required to comply with the EU/AETR rules relating to driving and rest times. Failure to produce a record, carry a log book or comply with the required driving and rest rules could result in delays and penalties.

Following Brexit, and planned changes to the 'Germany only' requirement for log books, tachograph records may be required in UK based vehicles to replace log books for vehicles exceeding 2,400 kg engaged in international hire and reward operations.

Tachographs – Fitment and Use Requirements

05

Tachograph instruments installed in goods and passenger vehicles must be capable of at least producing a record that enables drivers' working activities, breaks, rests and driving practices to be monitored to ensure that legal requirements – especially observance of the drivers' hours rules – have been met.

There are now two very distinctly different and separate tachograph recording systems legislated for use both in the UK and across the EU. First is the analogue system which has been in existence for many years (originating as the so-called hated 'spy in the cab'), and a digital system which came into force from May 2006. These two systems run in parallel; drivers of older vehicles having to use the former system and those driving post-May 2006 registered over 3.5 tonne gross weight vehicles using the latter system. Some drivers, however, encounter both older and newer vehicles in their work and thus have to contend with both systems – changing as often as daily when swapping from one vehicle to another, and producing, as a consequence, both round, flat wax-coated charts which must be kept flat to avoid damage, and till-roll printouts which instantly roll up and are very difficult to keep flat.

The original EEC Regulation 3821/85 covering tachographs was repealed in March 2015. It was replaced by EU Regulation 165/2014 which brought many changes aimed at reducing fraud and allowing new specification, new generation, 'smarter' tachographs to be introduced. EU Regulation 165/2014 still contains much of the content from the old EEC Regulation 3821/85 but it was also the driver of changes, noted earlier, particularly in relation to derogations from Regulation EC 561/2006. In practice the details, requirements and rules within these EEC and EU Regulations are now accepted by the UK authorities in spite of Brexit.

The main changes for operators and drivers were that there is now no longer a need for drivers to carry a statutory Letter of Attestation relating to drivers' records (note the word 'statutory' as Letters of Attestation are still required but it is the nature and format of these letters which have been relaxed) and, by an amendment affecting Regulation EC 561/2006, that many restrictions relating to operations 'within 50 km of base' have been extended to 100 km from base. Full details are included below in the appropriate sections. We will begin by looking at the older analogue tachographs

Legal Requirements for Analogue Tachographs

The fitment of tachographs and their use, particularly insofar that a chart of the correct type must be used, in relevant vehicles (ie those operating within the scope of the EU driving hours rules – see Chapter 3) for record-keeping purposes originally became a legal requirement in the United Kingdom on 31 December 1981.

The legislation requires the fitment and use of tachographs in most goods vehicles and other vehicles used for the carriage of goods over 3.5 tonnes permissible maximum weight with certain EU-approved exemptions as listed in the following section of this chapter. Since the list of exemptions is limited, many categories of goods vehicle which may be thought to be exempt are not so.

It should be stressed that unless a vehicle is used for private purposes only or is specifically exempted as shown by the exemption list, the law applies to:

- any goods vehicle over 3.5 tonnes gvw,* or a combination of a goods vehicle and goods-carrying trailer which together exceed 3.5 tonnes permissible maximum weight; and
- any other vehicle (such as off-road vehicles and so-called 4 × 4s) used for the carriage of goods which when towing a trailer has a combined permissible maximum weight exceeding 3.5 tonnes.

* Note: The 4,250 kg weight limit for alternatively powered vehicles means that these vehicles are currently also exempt from the need for a tachograph.

In particular, it should be noted that:

- vehicles carrying postal articles exceeding 3.5 tonnes permitted maximum weight, whilst exempt from EU drivers' hours rules, must be fitted with tachographs;
- there is no exemption for short-distance operations, infrequent-use vehicles or occasional driving under the EU rules. Once a relevant vehicle is on the highway the law applies in full.

This means that a tachograph instrument must normally be installed in the vehicle and that whosoever drives it must keep a tachograph record and observe the EU/AETR drivers' hours rules in full both for the day on which the driving takes place and for the week in which that day falls. It should also be noted that vehicles which are exempt from the tachograph rules are not necessarily exempt from record-keeping requirements (for example, those operating under the British domestic hours rules). See Chapter 4 for details of activities where written records must be kept.

Under the EU regulations a number of specific basic requirements relating to tachograph use must be met as follows:

- The tachograph instrument must conform to the technical specification laid down in the EU regulation 165/2014.

- The instrument must be calibrated and officially sealed at an approved calibration centre to ensure that accurate (ie legally acceptable) records are made.
- The instrument must be used in accordance with the regulations, with individual responsibilities being observed by both employer and driver.
- Electronic tachographs must be capable of detecting interruptions in the power supply.
- Driving time must be recorded automatically.
- Facilities must be provided for the removal and subsequent refitting, by an approved centre, of recording equipment seals to enable speed limiters to be fitted.
- Cables connecting electronic tachographs to the transmitter (ie sender unit) must be protected by a continuous steel sheath (ie a tamper-proof armoured cable).

Exemptions

There is no requirement for the fitment and use of tachographs in vehicles in the following list or in vehicles used in connection with the particular transport operations specified in the exemption list.

Changes in regulations (ie the Community Drivers' Hours and Recording Equipment (Amendment) Regulations 1998 – effective from 24 August 1998) brought within the scope of the tachograph rules vehicles which are not in themselves considered to be goods vehicles (eg four-wheel-drive off-road vehicles) and therefore were previously exempt from the rules. However, when such vehicles are drawing a trailer for the carriage of goods for commercial purposes, and the combined weight of the towing vehicle and trailer exceeds 3.5 tonnes, the fitment and use of tachographs as described in this chapter is necessary and the driver must observe the EU drivers' hours rules as set out in Chapter 3.

National and International Exemptions

1. Vehicles not exceeding 3.5 tonnes gross weight including the weight of any trailer drawn.
2. Passenger vehicles constructed to carry not more than nine persons including driver.
3. Vehicles on regular passenger services on routes not exceeding 50 km.
4. Vehicles with legal maximum speed not exceeding 40 kph (approx 25 mph).
5. Vehicles used by the armed services, civil defence, fire services, forces responsible for maintaining public order (ie police).

NB: Item 4 above includes certain works trucks and industrial tractors which have a statutory 30 kph speed limit imposed upon them but this does not include forklift trucks, which may come within the scope of the rules.

Under a European Court ruling, British Gas had to fit tachographs to vehicles it uses for the delivery of gas appliances, gas cylinders and meters to ensure fair competition with private transport operators. The point at issue, and contended by British Gas, was that its vehicles engaged on such deliveries were being used in connection with gas services. This was not accepted by the European Court.

Also: Vehicles used for private waste collection (ie not on behalf of local authorities) on journeys exceeding a 100 km radius from the place where they are normally based must be fitted with a fully calibrated tachograph, following a European Court of Justice ruling.

6 Vehicles used in emergencies or rescue operations, including humanitarian aid.

7 Specialized vehicles used for medical purposes.

8 Vehicles transporting circus and funfair equipment.

9 Specialized breakdown vehicles operating within 100 km of their base.

10 Vehicles undergoing road tests for technical development, repair or maintenance purposes, and new or rebuilt vehicles which have not yet been put into service.

11 Vehicles used for non-commercial carriage of goods for personal use (ie private use).

12 Vehicles used for milk containers or milk products intended for animal feed.

Further Derogations in National Operations Only

13 Vehicles with between 10 and 17 seats used exclusively for the non-commercial carriage of passengers.

14 Vehicles used by public authorities to provide public services which are not in competition with professional road hauliers.

15 Vehicles used by agricultural, horticultural, forestry or fishery* undertakings, for carrying goods within a 100 km radius of the place where the vehicle is normally based, including local administrative areas the centres of which are situated within that radius.

** To gain this exemption the vehicle must be used to carry live fish or to carry a catch of fish which has not been subjected to any process or treatment (other than freezing) from the place of landing to a place where it is to be processed or treated.*

16 Vehicles used for carrying animal waste or carcasses not intended for human consumption.

17 Vehicles used for carrying live animals from farms to local markets and vice versa, or from markets to local slaughterhouses within a radius of 100 km.

18 Vehicles used in connection with sewerage; flood protection; water, gas and electricity services; highway maintenance and control; refuse collection and disposal; telephone and telegraph services; carriage of postal articles*; radio and television broadcasting; detection of radio or television transmitters or receivers.

** This does not apply to vehicles operated by universal service providers (only Royal Mail at the present time within the UK) who must have a tachograph fitted in spite of operating under British driving rules.*

19 Vehicles specially fitted for and used:

- as shops at local markets and for door-to-door selling;
- for mobile banking, exchange or savings transactions;
- for worship;
- for the lending of books, records or CDs;
- for cultural events or exhibitions.

20 Vehicles (not exceeding 7.5 tonnes gvw) carrying materials or equipment for the driver's use in the course of his work within a 100 km radius of base provided the driving does not constitute the driver's main activity and does not prejudice the objectives of the regulations.

21 Vehicles operating exclusively on islands not exceeding 2,300 sq km not linked to the mainland by bridge, ford or tunnel for use by motor vehicles (this includes the Isle of Wight, Arran and Bute).

22 Vehicles used to collect sea coal due to the effect of salt water on the equipment.

23 Vehicles (not exceeding 7.5 tonnes gvw) used for the carriage of goods propelled by natural or liquefied gas or by electricity.

24 Vehicles used for driving instruction (but not if carrying goods for hire or reward).

25 Tractors used after 1 January 1990 exclusively for agricultural and forestry work.

26 Vehicles used by the RNLI for hauling lifeboats.

27 Vehicles manufactured before 1 January 1947.

28 Steam-propelled vehicles.

29 Vintage vehicles (ie over 25 years old) not carrying more than nine persons including the driver, not being used for profit, and being driven to or from a vintage rally, museum, public display or a place where it has been or is to be repaired, maintained or tested.

NB: In the exemption above relating to vehicles used by public authorities, the exemption applies only if the vehicle is being used by:

a *a health authority in England and Wales, a health board in Scotland or a National Health Service (NHS) Trust:*

- *to provide ambulance services in pursuance of its duty under the NHS Act 1977 or NHS (Scotland) Act 1978; or*
- *to carry staff, patients, medical supplies or equipment in pursuance of its general duties under the Act;*

b *a local authority to fulfil social services functions, such as services for old persons or for physically and mentally handicapped persons;*

- **c** *HM Coastguard or lighthouse authorities;*
- **d** *harbour authorities within harbour limits;*
- **e** *airports authority within airport perimeters;*
- **f** *any holder of a rail network licence, Transport for London, holders of network licences wholly owned by the HM Government, a Passenger Transport Executive or local authority for maintaining railways;*
- **g** *Canal and River Trust for maintaining navigable waterways.*

It can clearly be seen that the exemptions outlined above generally mirror the exemptions contained within the earlier content relating to Goods Vehicle Drivers' Hours and Working Time. This is mainly because the original EEC Regulations 3820/85 and 3821/85 were meant to complement each other.

Declaration of Exemption

When presenting a vehicle for the goods vehicle annual test which the operator believes is exempt from the tachograph regulations in accordance with the list above, a 'Declaration of Exemption' form has to be completed. Forms can be downloaded from the GOV.UK website.

Employers' Responsibilities

The employer needs to determine whether his transport operation and his vehicles fall within scope of the EU tachograph requirements – by reference to the exemption list above – and take appropriate steps regarding the fitment and calibration of instruments as described in this chapter. He must also instruct his drivers accordingly. Additionally, the regulations place specific responsibilities on the employer of a driver who drives within the EU rules as follows:

- The employer must ensure that the tachograph is sealed and calibrated in accordance with the rules (see below).
- The employer must organize the driver's work in such a way that he is able to comply with both the drivers' hours and tachograph rules.
- The employer must ensure that the driver understands the tachograph requirements and uses the equipment properly to provide accurate records.
- The employer must supply drivers with sufficient numbers of the correct type of tachograph charts (ie one chart for the day, one spare in case the first is impounded by an enforcement officer, plus any further spares which are necessary to account for any charts which become too dirty or damaged to use), and he must ensure that completed charts are collected from drivers no later than 42 days after use.
- The employer must periodically check completed charts to ensure that the law has been complied with (ie that the driver has made a chart for the day, that he has completed it fully and properly, and that he has observed the

driving hours rules). If breaches of the law are found, the employer must take appropriate steps to prevent their repetition.

- The employer must retain completed charts for 12 months for inspection by DVSA examiners, if required.
- The employer must give copies of the record to drivers concerned who request them.

A number of court cases have highlighted the extent of employer responsibilities for tachograph operation as follows:

- It has been made clear that employers who do not check tachograph records are permitting drivers' hours offences and can be prosecuted and convicted accordingly.
- Employers can be charged with failing to use the tachograph in accordance with the regulations in cases where a driver is unable to produce charts to show his driving and other work activities (eg when requested to do so in a roadside check).
- Where employers allow drivers to take their tractive units home after their day's work they must ensure that such driving is recorded on a tachograph chart and is counted as part of the driver's legally permitted driving and working time for that day – it is not part of his rest period.
- Employers who do not take action against drivers found to have repeated infringements when their tachograph records are analysed can be held to account by the Traffic Commissioners for having a system of analysis that in itself does nothing to reduce infringements or improve compliance.

Drivers' Responsibilities

Drivers of vehicles operating within the EU rules must observe the tachograph requirements. In particular this means understanding what the law requires and how to comply with it. The specific responsibilities of the driver in regard to the law are as follows:

- Drivers using tachograph charts must ensure that a proper record is made by the instrument:
  - that they enter the correct personal details, places of start and finish of duty, the vehicle registration number, date and time and odometer readings of any change of vehicle;
  - that it is a continuous record;
  - that it is a 'time right' record (ie recordings are in the correct 12-hour section of the chart – daytime or night-time hours – and that the time recorded is that of the country of origin, if on an international journey).
- In the event of instrument failure or in circumstances where no vehicle is available when the driver is working he must make manual recordings of his activities on the chart 'legibly and without dirtying' it.

- Drivers must produce for inspection on request by an authorized inspecting officer a current chart/record for that day plus the charts relating to the previous 28 days (see section below on Production of Charts/Records).
- Drivers must return completed charts and/or records to their employer no later than 42 days after use.
- Drivers must allow any authorized inspecting officer to inspect the charts and tachograph calibration plaque, which is usually fixed inside the body of the instrument.

In cases where drivers take their tractive units home at the end of their working shift, this time must be recorded on the tachograph chart and counted as part of the daily maximum driving time and the driver's day's work – it is not part of his rest period.

Production of Charts/Records

When driving vehicles with analogue tachographs the driver must be able to produce:

- The record sheet (ie chart/s) for the current day and those used in the previous 28 calendar days.

NB: The 28-day timescale referred to above means the records made during the previous 28 days of working/driving. It does not mean the previous 28 sets of records. Thus, for example, if the driver has not worked at all during those previous 28 days he will have no records to produce or, if he has worked on only some of the days, he will need to produce records for those days but not the other days.

Previously drivers driving abroad have been required to produce a model Letter of Attestation to the enforcement authorities if they could not produce a full set of records for the 28-day period due to holiday or sickness, etc in order to explain why there are 'gaps' in their records. The actual format that these letters should take is not actually specified under EU Regulation 165/2014 but many EU member states and AETR countries do still require an agreed layout and format. In this case operators are advised to use model Letters of Attestation which can be freely downloaded from many websites or from bodies such as the RHA and FTA. (See later also for digital tachographs.)

Two-Crew Operation

Reference above to a driver also includes any other driver who is carried on the vehicle to assist with the driving. In this case a two-man tachograph must be fitted and both drivers must use it to produce records as follows:

- The person who is driving must have his chart located in the uppermost (ie number 1) position in the instrument and use the number 1 activity mode switch to enable his activities and vehicle speed and distance recordings to be made on the chart as appropriate.

- The person who is riding passenger must have his chart in the rearmost (ie number 2) position and must use the number 2 activity mode switch to record his other work activities, or break or rest periods. Only time-group recordings are made on this chart; driving, speed and distance traces are *not* produced on the second-man chart.

NB: Following a High Court ruling it has become clear that the second man on a double-manned vehicle operation must insert his chart in the second-man position of the instrument from the commencement of the journey, or at the time he boards the vehicle, not from the later time when he commences his period of driving. The time of boarding is relevant because under the regulations the physical presence of the second driver is not required for the first hour of the journey.

Tachograph Calibration, Sealing and Inspection

To make legally acceptable records, tachograph installations in vehicles must be calibrated initially at an approved tachograph centre (a list of D*f*T-approved tachograph fitting and calibration centres can be found on the GOV.UK website at: www.gov.uk/find-approved-tachograph-centre-atc (archived at https://perma.cc/NWH5-36V7)). Subsequently, analogue tachographs must be inspected every two years and fully re-calibrated every six years or after repair at an approved centre whilst digital tachographs must be re-calibrated after two years, following any repair, if the UTC time is incorrect by more than 20 minutes, if the vehicle registration number is changed or if the circumference of the tyres is changed.

The DVSA specifies and approves the premises (and the display of approved signs), equipment, staff (including their training) and procedures for the installation, repair, inspection, calibration and sealing of tachographs. Such centres must be approved to the BS 5750 Part 2 quality assurance standard before they can gain DVSA approval. No other workshops or individuals are permitted to carry out such work and any work carried out by unauthorized agents would render the installation incapable of producing legally acceptable records.

Tachograph Installation Offences

It is an offence for any unauthorized person to carry out work on tachograph installations. It is also an offence for a vehicle operator (maximum fine £5,000) to obtain and use a tachograph instrument repaired by a firm which is not BS 5750 approved.

Calibration

The calibration process requires the vehicle to be presented to an approved tachograph centre in normal road-going trim, complete with body and all fixtures, unladen, and with tyres complying with legal limits as to tread wear and inflated to manufacturer's recommended pressures. At the centre, the necessary work on the analogue installation is carried out to within specified tolerances.

The regulations specify tolerances within which the tachograph installation must operate and are valid for temperatures between 0 °C and 40 °C as follows:

TABLE 5.1 Calibration process

	On bench test	On installation	In use
Speed	3 kph	4 kph	6 kph
Distance	1%	2%	4%
Time	in all cases, ± 2 minutes per day with a maximum of 10 minutes per seven days		

NB: In the case of both speed and distance figures shown above, the tolerance is measured relative to the real speed and to the real distance of at least 1 km.

Calibration and Periodic Inspection Fees

As of 1 January 2012 tachograph fees have been deregulated.

Sealing of Analogue Tachographs

Approved centres seal analogue tachograph installations after calibration or two-yearly inspections with their own official seals (each of which is coded differently) and details of all seals are maintained on a register by the DVSA. The seals are of the Customs type whereby a piece of wire is passed through each of the connecting points between the vehicle and the tachograph itself and then a lead seal is squeezed tight on to the wire with special pliers which imprint the centre code number in the metal. Attempts to remove any of the seals or their actual removal will show and need to be accounted for.

The purpose of sealing is to ensure that there is no tampering with the equipment or any of its drive mechanism or cables which could either vary the recordings of time, speed or distance or inhibit the recording in any way. Such tampering is illegal and once seals are broken the installation no longer complies with the law and legally acceptable records cannot be made.

Besides the seals inside the body of the instrument head, the following points are sealed:

- the installation plaque;
- the two ends of the link between the recording equipment and the vehicle;
- the adaptor itself and the point of its insertion into the circuit;
- the switch mechanism for vehicles with two or more axle ratios;
- the links joining the adaptor and the switch mechanism to the rest of the equipment;
- the casings of the instrument;
- any cover giving access to the means of adapting the constant of the recording equipment to the characteristic coefficient of the vehicle.

Seal Breakage

Obviously, there are occasions when certain of the seals have to be broken of necessity to carry out repairs to the vehicle and replacement of defective parts (eg the vehicle clutch or gearbox). The only seals which may be broken in these circumstances are as follows:

- those at the two ends of the link between the tachograph equipment and the vehicle;
- those between the adaptor (ie the tachograph drive gearbox) and the point of its insertion into the circuit;
- those at the links joining the adaptor and the switch mechanism (ie where the vehicle has a two-speed rear axle) to the rest of the equipment.

With the introduction of statutory speed-limiters operators are permitted to break tachograph seals for the purpose of fitting such devices, but the seals must be replaced at an approved tachograph centre within seven days.

While it is permitted to break the particular seals listed above for other authorized purposes (eg in connection with vehicle maintenance), a written record must be kept of the seal breakage and the reason for it. The installation must be inspected or re-calibrated and fully sealed following repair or seal breakage as soon as 'circumstances permit' and before the vehicle is used again. It is illegal to remove any of the other seals and tampering with seals by drivers is tantamount to committing fraud (ie for the purposes of making fraudulent records, which is an offence liable to lead to a prison sentence).

DVSA vehicle examiners check that all tachograph head seals are intact when vehicles are submitted for their annual goods vehicle test. This tough regime is intended to crack down on rogue operators who are fiddling their tachographs to avoid compliance with statutory speed limits and the drivers' hours and working time rules.

Analogue Tachograph Calibration Plaques

When an analogue tachograph has been inspected or re-calibrated, the approved centre must fix, either inside the tachograph head or near to it on the vehicle dashboard in a visible position, a plaque giving details of the centre, the 'turns count' and the calibration date. The plaque is sealed and must not be tampered with or the sealing tape removed. When an instrument is subjected to a two-year inspection or re-calibration a new plaque must be fitted. If a vehicle is found on the road with an 'out-of-date' plaque an offence will have been committed and prosecution may follow.

The normal sequence for plaques is that one will show the initial calibration date, the next (two years later), which is fitted alongside the first plaque, will show the date of the two-year inspection and a third plaque will show the second two-year inspection. After a further two years a six-year re-calibration of the installation will be due and at this time all the previous plaques will be removed, the new calibration plaque will be fitted and the procedure described above starts again. In between times, following certain repairs, a 'minor work' plaque may be fitted but this does not alter the sequence of dates for the two-year inspection and the six-year re-calibration plaques.

The two-year and six-year periods referred to above for inspections and calibrations are counted to the actual day/date, not to the end of the month in which that day/date falls.

Tachograph Breakdown

If analogue tachograph equipment becomes defective the driver must continue to record manually on the chart all necessary information regarding his working, driving, breaks and rest times which are no longer being recorded by the instrument. There is no requirement to attempt to record speed or distance.

Once a vehicle has returned to base with a defective tachograph, it should not leave again until the instrument is in working order and has been re-calibrated (if necessary) and the seals replaced. If it cannot be repaired immediately, the vehicle can be used so long as the operator has taken positive steps (which he can satisfactorily prove later if challenged by the enforcement authorities – see paragraph below) to have the installation repaired as soon as reasonably practicable.

If a vehicle is unable to return to base within *one week* (ie seven days) counting from the day of the breakdown, arrangements must be made to have the defective instrument repaired and re-calibrated as necessary at an approved centre en route within that time.

Defence

There is a defence in the regulations against conviction (ie not against prosecution) for an offence of using a vehicle with a defective tachograph. This has the effect of allowing subsequent use of a vehicle with a defective tachograph provided steps have been taken to have the installation restored to a legal condition as soon as circumstances permit and provided the driver continues to record his driving, working and break period times manually on a tachograph chart. In such circumstances it will be necessary to satisfactorily prove to the enforcement authorities – and to the court if they proceed with prosecution – that a definite booking for the repair had already been made at the time the vehicle was apprehended and that this appointment was for the repair to be carried out at the earliest possible opportunity.

It is also a defence to show that at the time it was examined by an enforcement officer the vehicle was on its way to an approved tachograph centre to have necessary repairs carried out. However, this defence will fail if the driver did not keep written records of his activities in the meantime.

Use of Analogue Tachographs

Drivers are responsible for ensuring that the tachograph instrument in their vehicle functions correctly throughout the whole of their working shift in order that a full and proper recording for a full 24 hours can be produced. They must also ensure that they have sufficient quantities of the right type of charts (see below) on which to make recordings.

NB: Some prolonged activities away from the vehicle may need to be recorded manually.

Time Changes

Drivers must ensure that the time at which the instrument clock is set and consequently recordings are made on the chart agree with the official time in the country of registration of the vehicle. This is a significant point for British drivers travelling in Europe, who may be tempted to change the clock in the instrument to the correct local European time rather than, for example, having it indicate and record the time in Britain. To re-emphasize the point, this means that for British drivers in British-registered vehicles the tachograph chart recording must accord with the official time in Britain regardless of the country in which that recording was made – the tachograph clock must *not* be reset to show local time when travelling abroad.

Dirty or Damaged Charts

If a chart becomes dirty or damaged in use, it must be replaced and the old chart should be securely attached to the new chart which is used to replace it. When doing this, care must be taken not to mark either chart so that any recordings are further damaged or obscured, etc.

Completion of Centre Field

Before starting work with a vehicle in which tachograph charts are to be used, the driver must enter on the centre field of his chart for that day the following details:

- his surname and first name (not initials);
- the date and place where use of the chart begins;
- vehicle registration number;
- the distance recorder (odometer) reading at the start of the day.

At the end of a working day, the driver should then record the following information on the chart:

- the place and date where the chart is completed;
- the closing odometer reading;
- by subtraction, the total distance driven – in kilometres (it is not a legal requirement for the driver to carry out this calculation).

Making Recordings

When the centre field has been completed the chart should be inserted in the tachograph instrument, ensuring that it is the right way up (it should be impossible to fit it wrongly) and that the recording will commence on the correct part of the 24-hour chart (day or night). The instrument face should be securely closed. The activity mode switch (number 1) should be turned as necessary throughout the work period to indicate the driver's relevant activities, namely driving, other work, break or rest periods. While some drivers find difficulty in getting into the habit of turning the switch to coincide with each change of activity, nevertheless this is what the law requires and it is an offence to fail to do so (ie not keeping proper records).

Recording Rules

Regulation 561/2006/EC specifies in Article 26 that the use to which the tachograph crossed hammers and rectangle symbols are put must, from 1 May 2006, be as follows:

use to record 'other work' (ie any activity other than driving) done for both the driving employer and any other employer outside of transport;

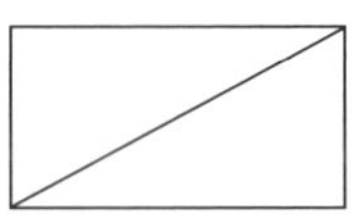

use to record 'periods of availability' as defined in EU Directive 2002/15/EC – The Road Transport Directive – and as described on p 115.

Other Work and Overtime Recordings

The High Court has ruled that drivers must record *all* periods of work on their tachograph charts. This makes it clear that work undertaken for the employer after the daily driving shift has been completed (eg in a yard, warehouse, workshop or office), and whether deemed part of the normal day or overtime working, must be recorded on the chart for that day – ie either by the instrument if this is convenient or otherwise manually. A contention that since tachographs were intended primarily to record driving time in the interests of road safety they should be used for that purpose only and not for recording other working activities was ruled to be contrary to the provisions of both the EU legislation and section 97 of the Transport Act 1968.

Where manual recordings are entered onto the tachograph to record other work, etc they are permitted to be either on the front or rear of the chart providing that they do not deface or obscure any details made by the recording equipment.

Overnight Recordings

At the end of his shift the driver can leave the chart in the instrument overnight to record the daily rest period or alternatively it can be removed and the rest period recorded manually on the chart. Generally, enforcement officers prefer an automatic recording of daily rest made by the instrument but this is not always practicable where the vehicle may be used on night-shift work, may be driven for road testing or other purposes by workshop staff, or moved around the premises by others when the driver is at home having the rest period. Also, if the driver is scheduled to start work later on the following day, there will be an overlap recording on the chart which is illegal. It is also recommended that the driver manually enters the start and finish times of every daily duty on the chart as this will effectively provide an accurate 24-hour record. Again, in so doing the driver must not make an entry that could obscure a part of the chart where the machine trace will be made.

Vehicle Changes

If the driver changes to another vehicle during the working day he must take the existing chart with him and record details of the time of change, the registration number of the further vehicle(s) and distance recordings in the appropriate spaces on the chart. He then uses that chart in the next vehicle to record his continuing driving, working activities and break periods. This procedure is repeated no matter how many different vehicles (except those not driven on the public highway) are driven during the day so the one chart shows all of the driver's daily activity. This assumes that the tachograph chart is compatible with the tachograph instrument. If the chart and the instrument are not compatible, a new chart must be used by the driver. The charts used by the driver must be kept together to show a complete day's work.

Mixed Tachographs

It is important to note that, although now few in number, there are still various makes and models of analogue tachograph currently available in the UK that need different charts and they cannot all be interchanged. So, the driver who switches from a vehicle with one make of instrument to a vehicle with a different make during the working day will have to make fresh entries on a second or even third chart. At the end of the day all the charts used should be put together to present a comprehensive (and legal) record for the whole day. However, there are some charts now available on the market suitable for dual use in different makes of tachograph. It is the employer's duty to issue drivers with the correct charts (ie with matching type approval numbers to those on the tachograph instrument in use) in sufficient numbers for the schedule which the driver has to operate.

There are also different tachographs for use in vehicles with different speed limits. This means that, whilst most tachographs are designed to be fitted with charts capable of recording up to 125 kph, there are charts capable of recording up to 140 kph and even 180 kph. It is the operator's responsibility to issue the correct type of chart to the driver but it is also the driver's responsibility to ensure that a proper record is made, and using a differently calibrated chart in a differently calibrated tachograph head would certainly not produce a proper record.

NB: Where instruments are standardized in a fleet, one chart will suffice for the whole day and the driver must take this with him from one vehicle to the next, recording changes as previously described.

Manual Records

Drivers are responsible for ensuring that the instrument is kept running while they are in charge of the vehicle and should it fail or otherwise cease making proper records they should remove the chart and continue to record their activities manually on it as previously described. They must also make manual recordings on the chart of work done or time spent away from the vehicle (for example, periods during the day spent working in the yard, warehouse or workshop). Manual recordings must be made legibly and in making them the chart must not be 'dirtied'.

Records for Part-time Drivers

The rules on the use of tachographs described in the foregoing text apply equally to part-time or occasional drivers such as yard and warehouse staff, office people and even the transport manager. The rules also apply fully even if the driving on the road is for a very short distance or period of time; a five-minute drive without a tachograph chart in use would be sufficient to break the law and risk prosecution. Vehicle fitters and other workshop staff who drive vehicles on the road for testing in connection with repair or maintenance are specifically exempt from the need to keep tachograph records when undertaking such activities but this exemption *does not* apply to them when using vehicles for other purposes (eg collecting spare parts, ferrying vehicles back and forth, taking replacement vehicles out to on-road breakdowns, taking and collecting vehicles to and from goods vehicle test stations, etc).

Retention, Return and Checking of Tachograph Charts

Drivers must retain and be able to produce, on request by authorized examiners (including the police), completed tachograph charts for the current day and for the previous 28 days.

Charts must be returned by drivers to their employer no later than 42 days after use and on receiving the charts the employer must periodically check them to ensure that the drivers' hours and record-keeping regulations have been complied with. Failure by an operator to check charts for possible offences by drivers can lead to charges of 'permitting' the commission of certain tachograph and drivers' hours offences (should such offences be proven) – in one case a transport manager was held to be 'reckless' because his chart-checking system was not sufficiently thorough. Charts must then be retained, available for inspection if required, for a period of one year (see below).

Where a driver has more than one employer in a week (eg as with agency drivers), he must return the tachograph charts to the employer who first employed him in that week. This provision clearly presents a problem for those firms which regularly employ agency drivers and which may find difficulty in securing the return of charts for driving work done with their vehicles and operators should try to include this requirement when considering using a driver agency.

Retention of Charts for Tax Records

Where tachograph charts are used by employers to justify payment of driver night-out and other subsistence expenses for tax purposes, then the charts constitute part of the legal recording system for tax purposes and as such must be retained for six years instead of the normal one-year period as described above.

Retention of Charts for Working Time Records

Where tachograph charts are used by employers to record compliance with either the Road Transport Directive (RTD) or the Horizontal Amending Directive (HAD) they must be retained for two years.

Non-Driving Days (all Tachographs)

Drivers must make records for work completed on any non-driving days, within a working week, when they have undertaken some driving that comes within the scope of the EU drivers' hours rules, since their last weekly rest.

For example, a driver who drives a vehicle within the scope of the EU rules on a Monday, and then works in a warehouse from Tuesday to Friday, of the same week, must complete non-driving records for the work completed from Tuesday to Friday.

The driver can make the record in a number of ways by:

- making manual records on a tachograph chart;
- making manual records on a printout from a digital tachograph;
- using the manual input facility on a digital tachograph;
- making manual records in a domestic log book for days when they are working under the domestic drivers' hours rules and a record is legally required.

Records for non-driving days do not need to be complex. They may merely show the name of the driver, the date, and the start and finish of the shift. The driver should always carry these records on the vehicle (for the previous 28 days) to be able to produce them to enforcement officers for the relevant period.

Official Inspection of Charts

An authorized inspecting officer (which means a DVSA traffic examiner or a person authorized by a TC, in either case on production of their authority if requested, or a police officer) may require any person to produce for inspection any tachograph chart or record on which recordings have been made. This includes:

- any charts for the current day and for the previous 28 *calendar* days;
- any legally required manual records made in the previous 28 days.

Further, he may enter a vehicle to inspect a chart or a tachograph instrument (he should be able to read the recordings relating to the nine hours prior to the time of his inspection) and the calibration plaques and detain a vehicle for this purpose. At any reasonable time he may enter premises on which he believes vehicles or tachograph charts are kept and inspect the instruments in such vehicles and the completed charts. He can require (by serving a notice in writing) charts to be produced at a Traffic Area Office at any time on giving at least 10 days' notice in which to do so. Where a chart is suspected of showing a false entry he may 'seize' the chart (but not for reasons other than evidence of a false entry, or an entry intended to deceive or an entry altered for such purposes) and retain it for a maximum period of six months, after which time, if no charges for offences have been made, the chart should have been returned. If not, the person from whom it was taken can apply to a magistrate's court to seek an order for its return.

In practice, TCs regularly ask operators to provide batches of tachograph charts covering one or more of their vehicles for a short period or possibly some months either on a routine basis or following investigations into, or leads about, hours law or tachograph infringements – and where it is suspected that drivers are regularly exceeding speed limits. These charts are then analysed for contraventions of the law. The courts have ruled that examiners do have powers to remove tachograph charts from operators' premises when acting on the instructions of a TC – this follows the successful prosecution of a haulage firm that refused to allow charts to be removed from its premises.

Cases have been reported where the police have demanded that operators should send in to them, by post, tachograph charts required for inspection. This has been shown to be an illegal practice: there is no provision in the law which allows random collection of charts by the police or demands for charts to be submitted by post. Only in cases where an on-the-spot examination reveals possible offences can the police then request copies of the relevant chart for that day, other charts for that week and for the last day of the previous week. DVSA enforcement officers, on the other hand, may take random selections of charts away for examination.

It is an offence to fail to produce records for inspection as required or to obstruct an enforcement officer in his request to inspect records or tachograph installations in vehicles.

The Analogue Tachograph Instrument

A tachograph is a cable or electronically driven speedometer incorporating an integral electric clock and a chart recording mechanism. It is fitted into the vehicle dashboard or in some other convenient visible position in the driving cab. The instrument indicates time, speed and distance, and permanently records this information on the chart as well as the driver's working activities. Thus, the following factors can be determined from a chart:

- varying speeds (and the highest speed) at which the vehicle was driven;
- total distance travelled and distances between individual stops;
- times when the vehicle was being driven and the total amount of driving time;
- times when the vehicle was standing and whether the driver was indicating other work, break or rest period during this time.

Recordings

Recordings are made on special circular charts, each of which covers a period of 24 hours (Figure 5.1), by three styli. One stylus records distance, another records speed and the third records time-group activities as determined by the driver turning the activity mode switch on the head of the instrument (ie driving, other work, breaks and rest periods). The styli press through a wax recording layer on the chart, revealing the carbonated layer (usually black) between the top surface and the backing paper. The charts are accurately pre-marked with time, distance and speed reference radials and when the styli have marked the chart with the appropriate recordings these can be easily identified and interpreted against the printed reference marks.

Movement of the vehicle creates a broad running line on the time radial, indicating when the vehicle started running and when it stopped. After the vehicle has stopped, the time-group stylus continues to mark the chart but with an easily distinguishable thin line. The speed trace gives an accurate recording of the speeds attained at all times throughout the journey, continuing to record on the speed base line when

FIGURE 5.1 A typical tachograph chart showing recordings of times, distance and speed

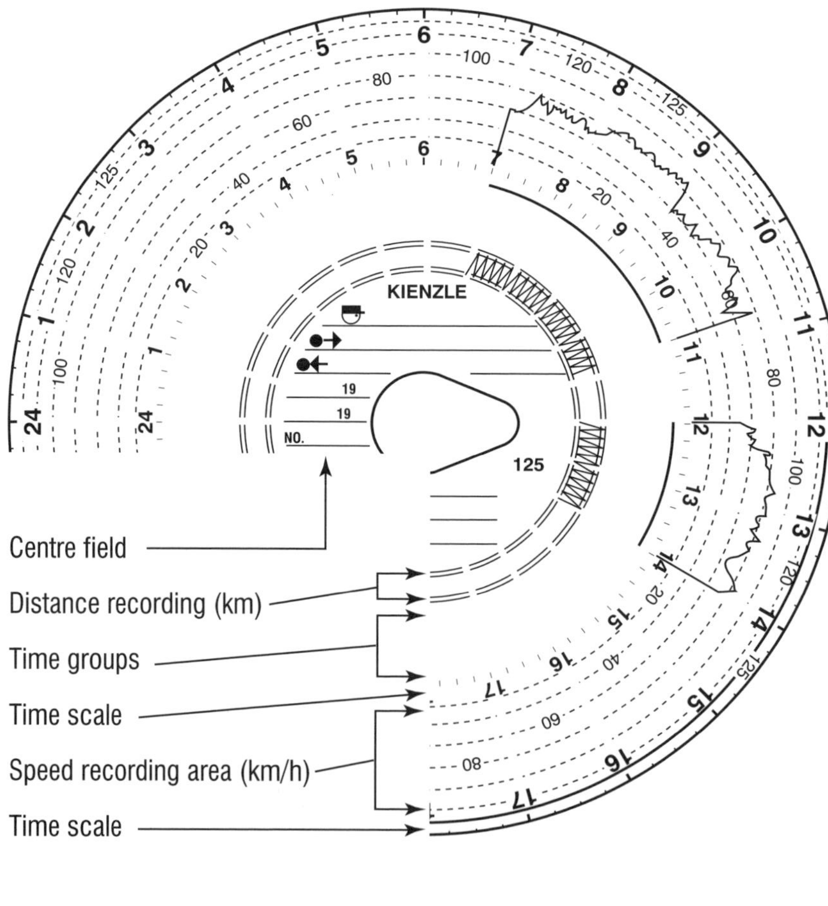

the vehicle is stationary to provide an unbroken trace except when the instrument is opened. The distance recording is made by the stylus moving up and down over a short stroke, each movement representing 5 kilometres travelled; thus, every 5 kilometres the stylus reverses direction, forming a 'V' for every 10 kilometres of distance travelled. To calculate the total distance covered the 'V's are counted and multiplied by 10 and any 'tail ends' are added in, the total being expressed in kilometres.

When a second chart is located in the rear position of a two-man tachograph, only a time recording of the second man's activities (ie other work, break or rest) is shown. Traces showing driving, vehicle speed or distance cannot be recorded on this chart.

Precautions against interference with the readings are incorporated in the instrument. It is opened with a key and a security mark is made on the chart every time the instrument is opened and/or when the power supply is interrupted. When checking the chart it can be easily established at what time the instrument was opened or the power interrupted and thus whether this was for an authorized reason or not. Interference with the recording mechanism to give false readings, particularly of speed, can be determined quite simply by an experienced chart analyst.

Faults

Tachographs are generally robust instruments, but listed below are some of the faults which may occur:

- failure of the cable drive at the vehicle gearbox;
- failure of the cable drive at the tachograph head;
- failure of the adaptor/corrector/triplex gearbox;
- cable breaking or seizure;
- electrical faults affecting lights in the instrument or the clock;
- incorrect time showing on the 24-hour clock (eg day-shift work becomes shown against night hours on the charts);
- failure of the tachograph head;
- damage to the recording styli;
- failure of the distance recorder;
- damage to charts because of incorrect insertion.

Fiddles

A key feature of tachograph recordings is that careful observation will show results of the majority of faults in recordings as well as fiddles and attempts at falsification of recordings by drivers. The main faults likely to be encountered will show as follows:

- Clock stops – recordings continue in a single vertical line until the styli penetrate the chart.
- Styli jam/seize up – recordings continue around the chart with no vertical movement.

- Cable or electronic drive failure – chart continues to rotate and speed and distance styli continue to record on base line and where last positioned respectively. Time-group recordings can still be made but no driving trace will appear.

Attempts at falsification of charts will appear as follows:

- Opening the instrument face will result in a gap in recordings.
- Interrupting the power supply will lead to incomplete records being produced.
- Winding the clock backwards or forwards will leave either a gap in the recording or an overlap. In either case the distance recording will not match up if the vehicle is moved.
- Stopping the clock will stop the rotation of the chart so all speed and distance recordings will be on one vertical line (see the first item in the previous list about how faults in instruments show on charts).
- Restricting the speed stylus to give indications of lower than actual speed will result in flat-topped speed recordings while bending the stylus down to achieve the same effect will result in recordings below the speed base line when the vehicle is stationary.
- Written or marked-in recordings with pens or sharp pointed objects are readily identifiable by even a relatively unskilled chart analyst.

NB: This is only an outline list of a large number of possible faults and attempts at falsification likely to be encountered. Some driver fiddles are one-off attempts, crudely and clumsily executed and naively obvious; others are much more sophisticated in their execution, often as part of an ongoing violation of legal requirements. These are more difficult, but not impossible, for the transport manager or fleet operator to detect and would certainly be picked up quickly by an experienced chart analyst.

EU Instruments and Charts

Tachographs may only be used for legal record-keeping purposes if they are type-approved and comply with the detailed EU specification. This specification has been adopted by the UK authorities. Such instruments have provision for indicating to the driver, without the instrument being opened, that a chart has been inserted and that a continuous recording is being made. They also provide for the driver to select, by an activity mode switch on the instrument, the type of recording which is being made. In the UK this must be one of the following:

- driving time;
- other work time;
- break and rest periods.

Two-man instruments are also provided with a means of simultaneously recording the activities of a second crew member on a separate chart located in the rear position in the instrument.

The charts used for legal purposes must also be type-approved as indicated by the appropriate 'e' markings printed on them. It is illegal to use non-approved charts or charts which are not approved for the specific type of instrument being used. Care should be taken that charts used have accurate time registration – cheap and non-type-approved versions, which are illegal anyway, have been found in the past to be significantly inaccurate in the way they are printed, thus producing inaccurate and worthless records. It was noted earlier that one of the most common problems is drivers using charts that are not calibrated for the tachograph (for example, using a 140 kph or 180 kph chart in a 125 kph tachograph).

Chart Analysis

Analysis of the information recorded on tachograph charts can provide valuable data for determining whether drivers have complied with the law on driving, working, break and rest period times, and have conformed to statutory speed limits. The data can also be extremely useful as a basis for finding means of increasing the efficiency of vehicle operation and for establishing productivity monitoring and payment schemes for drivers.

Many fleet operators use and rely upon the services of tachograph analysis agencies for checking their charts for conformity with the law. However, it should be noted that should such firms fail to recognize and notify the operator of deficiencies in their records, it is the operator who is at risk and his licence, not the analysis bureau. The TCs repeatedly remind operators that responsibility for driver compliance with the hours law rests entirely with them, not outside agencies. Generally, also, the checking carried out by such firms is for standard hours law infringements only, which are mainly picked up by computerized analysis and may not include identification of other irregularities or cleverly executed false entries or fraudulent recordings. Similarly, such analysis may not identify driver abuse of vehicles or frequent and excessive speeding.

Tachograph manufacturers supply accessories to enable detailed chart analysis to be carried out. A chart analyser magnifies the used chart to the extent that detailed analysis beyond the scope of a normal visual examination can be made of the vehicle's minute-by-minute and kilometre-by-kilometre progress. Journey times, average running times and speeds, delivery times, route miles, traffic delays and many other relevant factors can be readily established. With the aid of a fixed hairline cursor on the magnifier to allow precise definition of the time and speed scales and recordings on the chart, even vehicles' rates of acceleration and deceleration can be determined.

The German company Siemens VDO (formerly Kienzle), which is the leading tachograph manufacturer, has undertaken considerable research into chart analysis and is able to offer users the service of its analysis experts both in Germany and the UK as well as in other countries to determine the activities of vehicles and particularly the progress of a vehicle immediately prior to an accident and at the point of impact. In some instances such analysis has shown that witnesses' accounts of the speed of the vehicle and its braking force just before the accident have been far from correct. Whilst Siemens VDO offer this service, it must also be noted that similar services are offered by the FTA and RHA and by several independent tachograph analysis service providers.

It is also claimed that by detailed analysis of the charts and by keeping drivers aware of the information obtained, driving methods can be improved, thus saving fuel and cutting down on the wear and tear on vehicle brakes, tyres, transmission and other components.

It should be noted that for operators an important point relating to chart analysis is that where infringements are detected and the driver informed it is not sufficient to simply file the record away, as remedial actions are expected where infringements exist. In short, operators need to ensure that drivers improve their compliance and that the numbers and types of infringements reduce over time. Having a system of detection but failing to act on what is detected is simply not good enough for operator licensing purposes.

Offences (all Tachographs)

Some tachograph-related offences have already been mentioned in connection with specific requirements of the law but there are other overriding, and very serious, offences to be considered. In particular, it is an offence to use or cause or permit the use of a vehicle which does not have a fully calibrated tachograph installed; for the driver to fail to keep records by means of a tachograph (or manually if the instrument is defective) and to make false recordings. Further, it is an offence for the driver to fail to return used charts to his employer within 42 days after use of an analogue tachograph or 28 days for a digital tachograph, or to fail to notify his first employer of any other employer for whom he drives vehicles to which the regulations apply.

In many cases offences committed by the driver result in charges against the employer for 'causing' or 'permitting' offences. For example, where tachograph records go missing and cannot be produced for examination by the enforcement authorities, the employer may be charged with any one of three (or even all three) relevant offences: namely, failing to cause the driver to keep a record, failing to preserve the record or failing to produce the record. It is in such cases that sound legal representation should be sought and a good defence put forward where possible.

Two other types of offence that have come to the forefront in recent times and have featured in extensively reported prosecutions concern:

- missing mileages when charts are compared;
- use of illegal/cloned digi-cards by drivers;
- interference of tachograph systems by various means of wires and so-called 'magic buttons' and magnets.*

Penalties on summary conviction for offences under these regulations can be a fine of up to level 4 on the standard scale (currently £2,500) and conviction for such offences can jeopardize both the employer's 'O' licence (by seriously impacting on the OCRS) and the driver's LGV driving entitlement. Conviction for the more serious offences of making false entries on a tachograph chart and forgery can result in level 5 fines of up to £5,000 (per offence) or imprisonment for up to two years. Since

April 1998 tachograph falsification has been a 'recordable' offence, meaning that a person convicted of such an offence carries a criminal record.

** TCs have made it clear that LGV drivers convicted for using equipment to interfere with their tachograph will be disqualified from holding an LGV driving licence for a period of one year. These types of offences where it is clear that the recording instrument has been 'compromised' are included in the DVSA list of 'most serious infringements' and will also normally result in prosecution of the driver and the operator.*

Heavy penalties are also likely for those transport operators and LGV drivers found guilty in UK courts of forging tachograph entries relating to international journeys. These penalties are contained in the provisions of the Forgery and Counterfeiting Act 1981, which the Court of Appeal now allows the police to use for bringing prosecutions for tachograph offences committed outside the UK. Fines may be in excess of the current level 5 standard scale maximum of £5,000, and custodial sentences longer than those available to the courts under other legislation.

The courts have ruled that in cases where a driver or transport operator claims not to have known that the tachograph instrument in a vehicle had been fitted with a device intended to interfere with its operation (ie a trip device to aid the production of false records) this was no excuse and an offence of 'strict liability' was committed, to which there is no defence.

Tachograph Records as Evidence

In the past it has been made clear that tachograph records, while providing evidence of 'the facts shown' for drivers' hours purposes, would not be used by the police and enforcement authorities as evidence to bring prosecutions against drivers. However, since October 2015, it is worthy of note that tachograph records going back up to 28 days may now also be used as evidence of further infringements or offences by drivers facing prosecution for drivers' hours-related offences identified at roadside checks. This 'historic offence' provision means that fixed penalty notices may now not only be issued for previous offences committed by UK drivers but also that fixed penalty notices can be issued to foreign drivers who have committed earlier offences whilst in the UK. This was not possible before this change. In addition, the TCs may also impose short-term LGV driving bans on drivers found from their records to have regularly exceeded maximum speed limits.

Note: Clearly, analogue tachographs are being replaced by both digital and fourth generation tachographs but there is no set date, as yet, for them to be statutorily replaced by the newer technology.

Production of Records (all Tachographs)

Under digital tachograph legislation (ie Regulation 561/2006/EC – Article 26) drivers must be able to produce records (ie charts or digital printouts) to the enforcement authorities (eg the DVSA and the police) as follows:

When driving vehicles with digital tachographs or a combination of both digital and analogue types

- Record sheets (ie charts) for the day of driving with the analogue instrument and for the previous 28 days.
- Any manual record and printout made by a digital instrument during the current week and for the previous 28 days.

Drivers who drive vehicles fitted with digital tachographs must also be able to produce on request their driver smart card.

Digital Tachographs

Regulation 561/2006/EC was published on 15 March 2006, with its various provisions relating to the introduction of digital tachographs and the drivers' hours law effective from 1 May 2006 and 11 April 2007 respectively. The drivers' hours law issues contained in this regulation (which replaces the repealed Regulation 3820/85/EEC) are dealt with in Chapter 3.

It is important to note that despite the introduction of the digital tachograph from May 2006 in all new goods vehicles over 3.5 tonnes gross weight (apart from those specifically exempt under the legislation), existing analogue tachographs fitted to goods vehicles will remain valid and effective until such time as the vehicle reaches the end of its useful life or the analogue tachograph instrument itself ceases to function. In the latter case, where the vehicle exceeds 12 tonnes maximum weight, the replacement tachograph fitted must be of the digital type. On this basis, it is clear that analogue (or chart-type) tachographs will continue in use for at least a few years, giving both fleet operators and their drivers the headache of dealing with a dual system, both of which will have to be operated correctly within the law and adequately integrated to provide a full statutory record of driver activities as required by the European legislation. This is compounded by the recent introduction of fourth generation tachographs (see below) where the operator requires a different Company Card in order to download all the information from the unit in the vehicle.

A driver who has failed to obtain a digital 'smart card' cannot legally drive a vehicle fitted with a digital tachograph unless the driver in question is specifically exempted, as in the case of a driver operating under British domestic driving rules and using a 'log book'.

Further changes to the tachograph rules were introduced by EU Regulation 1266/2009/EC with effect from 1 October 2011. These were technical changes revising the existing tachograph specification contained in Annex 1B, including the so-called 'one minute rule' which is described on p 158 of this *Handbook*. Also, this regulation introduced a requirement for information from the motion sensor to be capable of being checked against vehicle data, thus showing any discrepancies and attempts at tampering.

The Regulations

Regulation (561/2006/EC) which is outlined here was introduced for a number of reasons including:

- to prevent infringement and fraud in application of the driving hours rules;
- to monitor automatically driver performance and behaviour;
- to overcome problems of monitoring compliance due to the numbers of individual record sheets (charts) that have to be held in the vehicle cab;
- the need to introduce advance recording equipment with electronic storage devices and personal driver cards to provide an indisputable record of work done by the driver over the last few days and the vehicle over a period of several months; and
- to devise a system which ensures total security of the recorded data.

Definitions for Digital Tachographs and Ancillaries

The digital equipment features a number of key components defined in the technical Annex of the Regulation as follows:

- *Recording equipment* means the total equipment intended for installation in road vehicles to show, record and store automatically or semi-automatically details of the movement of such vehicles and of certain work periods of their drivers. This equipment includes cables, sensors, an electronic driver information device, one (two) card reader(s) for the insertion of one or two driver memory card(s), an integrated or separate printer, display instruments, facilities for downloading the data memory, facilities to display or print information on demand, and facilities for the input of the places where the daily work period begins and ends.
- *Data memory* means an electronic storage system built into the recording equipment, capable of storing at least 365 calendar days from the recording equipment. The memory should be protected in such a way as to prevent unauthorized access to and manipulation of the data and detect any such attempt.
- A *'driver card with memory'* means a removable information transfer and storage device allocated by the authorities of the member states to each individual driver for the purposes of identification of the driver and storage of essential data. The format and technical specifications of the driver card must meet the requirements laid down in the technical annex to the regulations.
- A *'control card'* means a removable data transfer and storage device for use in the card reader of the recording equipment, issued by the authorities of the member states to competent authorities to get access to the data stored in the data memory or in the driver cards for reading, printing and/or downloading.
- A *'company data card'* means a removable data transfer device issued by the member state's authorities to the owner of vehicles fitted with recording

equipment. The company data card allows for displaying, downloading and printing of the data.

- *A 'workshop data card'* means a removable data transfer device for use by vehicle and equipment manufacturers and authorized personnel operating in a DVSA approved workshop. It is valid for one year and allows the equipment to be tested, calibrated and the downloading of data. With the introduction of the fourth generation of tachographs it is most likely where a fleet of vehicles is operated with a mixture of digital and fourth generation tachographs that the workshop will require two cards. This 'non-compatibility' issue is planned to be resolved some time in 2020.
- *Downloading* means the copying of a part of or a complete set of data stored in the data memory of the vehicle or in the memory of the driver card, but which does not alter or delete any stored data, allows for the origin of downloaded data to be authenticable and to be kept in a format that can be used by any authorized person, and ensures that any attempts to manipulate data are detectable.

Function and Use of Digital Instruments

The regulations require digital instruments to be able to record, store, display and print out specified statutory information as follows.

Recording and Storing in the Data Memory

The instrument is required to record and store:

- Distance travelled by the vehicle with an accuracy of 1 km.
- Speed of the vehicle:
  - momentary speed of the vehicle at a frequency of 1 second for the last 24 hours of use of the vehicle;
  - exceeding the authorized speed of the vehicle, defined as any period of more than 1 minute during which the vehicle speed exceeds 90 kph for N3 vehicles or 105 kph for M3 vehicles (with time, date, maximum speed of the over-speeding, average speed during the period concerned).
- Periods of driving time (times and dates), with an accuracy of one minute.
- Other periods of work or of availability (times and dates) with an accuracy of one minute.
- Breaks from work and daily rest periods (times and dates) with an accuracy of one minute.
- For electronic recording equipment which is equipment operated by signals transmitted electrically from the distance and speed sensor, any interruption exceeding 100 milliseconds in the power supply of the recording equipment (except lighting), in the power supply of the distance and speed sensor, and any interruption in the signal lead to the distance and speed sensor, with date, time, duration and driver card issue number.

- The driver card issue number with times and dates of insertion and removal.
- For each driver card that is inserted for the first time after it was used in another item of recording equipment:
  - current driving time since the last break or rest period;
  - driving time for the day after the last rest period of at least eight hours;
  - driving times for the day between two rest periods of at least eight hours for the preceding 27 calendar days with date, time and duration;
  - total of the driving times for the current week and the preceding week and the total of the driving times of the two completed preceding weeks;
  - rest periods of at least eight hours' duration for the day and the preceding 27 calendar days in each case with date, time and duration;
  - the VRN (vehicle registration number) of the vehicles driven.
- Date, time and duration of driving without an inserted or a functioning driver card.
- Data recorded on the places at which the daily work period began and ended.
- Automatically identifiable system faults of the recording equipment with date, time and driver card issue number.
- Faults in the driver card with date, time and driver card issue number.
- Workshop card number of the authorized fitter or workshop with date of at least the last installation inspection and/or periodic inspection of the recording equipment.
- Control card number with date of control card insertion and type of control (display, printing, downloading). In the case of downloading, the period downloaded should be recorded.
- Time adjustment with date, time and card issue number.
- Driving status (single/crew driving – driver/co-driver).

Storage on the Driver Card

The driver card must be capable of storing:

- the essential data for a period of at least the last 28 days combined with the VRN identification of the vehicle driven and the data as required above;
- the events and faults mentioned above with the VRN identification of the vehicle driven;
- the date and time of insertion and removal of the driver card and distance travelled during the corresponding period;
- the date and time of insertion and removal of the co-driver card with issue number.

Data must be recorded and stored on the driver card in such a way as to rule out any possibility of falsification.

Recording and Storing for Two Drivers

Where vehicles are used by two drivers the driving time must be recorded and stored on the driver card of the driver who is driving the vehicle. This means that the cards need to be changed over from their slats on the vehicle unit (VU) when the drivers change over. The equipment must record and store in the data memory and on the two driver cards simultaneously, but distinctly, details of the information listed above.

Recording Driver Walkaround

Increasingly, DVSA examining officers are checking on recordings of the time that drivers spend doing their daily walkaround checks of the vehicle before starting out on their journey. Where no such recording is shown, their assumption is that no such check was carried out, which could lead to further enquiries by the DVSA. Conversely, if the driver insists he did check his vehicle this may lead the examiner to allege that the driver has failed to keep a proper record or has falsified his record, both of which are offences for which prosecution may follow.

Recording Multi-Drop Deliveries

The accuracy of digital tachograph recording within an accuracy of 'one minute' has caused problems and concerns in the past over what was termed 'the one-minute rule'. However, since 2012, for tachograph recording purposes, a 'minute' has been defined as 'the same type of activity as the longest activity within the minute'. This means that if a driver records driving for 25 seconds within a minute and 'other work' for 35 seconds within that same minute, the whole minute will be recorded as 'other work'. This is accepted by the authorities as being acceptable for recording the activities of drivers who need to stop and start the vehicle repeatedly during their periods of duty.

Displaying or Printing for an Authorized Examiner

The equipment must be capable of displaying or printing, on request, the following information:

- Driver card issue number, expiry date of the card.
- The surname and first name of the driver who is the cardholder.
- Current driving time since the last break or rest period.
- Driving time for the day after the last rest period of at least eight hours.
- Driving times for the day between two rest periods of at least eight hours for the preceding 27 calendar days on which the driver has driven, with date, time and duration.
- Total of the driving times for the current week and the preceding week and the total times for the two completed preceding weeks.
- The other periods of work and availability.
- Rest periods of at least eight hours' duration for the day and the preceding 27 days in each case with date, time and duration.

- VRN identification of vehicles driven for at least the last 28 calendar days with the distance travelled per vehicle and day, time of first insertion and last removal of the driver card and the time of change of vehicle.
- Time adjustment with date, time and card issue number.
- Interruption of power supply to the recording equipment with date, time, duration and driver card issue number.
- Sensor interruption with date, time, duration and driver card issue number.
- The VIN and/or VRN identification of the vehicle driven.
- Driving without driver card as defined above for the last 28 calendar days.
- Details of the information stored concerning the driver.
- Recorded data on the places where the daily work period began and ended.
- The automatically identifiable system faults of the recording equipment with date, time and driver card issue number.
- The faults in the driver card with date and time and driver card issue number.
- Control card number with date of control card insertion and type of control (display, printing, downloading). In the case of downloading, the period downloaded should be recorded.
- Exceeding the authorized speed as defined above, with date, time and driver card issue number for the current week and in any case including the last day of the previous week.
- Summary reports to permit compliance with the relevant regulations to be checked.

Figure 5.2 shows a list of the pictograms used in digital tachographs, both on-screen and on the printouts while Figure 5.3 is a sample printout with the explanation of the coding (both courtesy of Siemens VDO).

Smart Cards

Crucial to the whole system is the driver ('smart') card, often referred to as a 'digi-card', which is personal to the individual and carries identification information and other essential data about him. It has a capacity to store relevant data on driving and working times, breaks and rest periods covering at least 28 days, and comprises the legal record in place of the current tachograph chart. The card itself is tamper-proof, and strict regulatory systems are established by national governments to prevent fraudulent issue, use and transfer of cards within their territories. Cards are valid for five years, after which time they should be renewed by application to the DVLA no later than 15 days before the expiry of the card.

Once issued, a digi-card must be able to be produced by the driver even when driving a vehicle with an analogue tachograph in order to allow the enforcement authorities to make a full check on the driver's activities. Failure to produce upon request could lead to the driver being prosecuted.

A tachograph 'digi-card' (officially called a 'tachograph card') is a plastic card similar in size to a photocard driving licence or credit card, with a microchip embedded

FIGURE 5.2 Pictograms used in digital tachographs

Basic pictograms		Pictograms list
	People	**Actions**
	Company	
	Controller	Control
	Driver	Driving
	Workshop/ test station	Inspection/ calibration
	Manufacturer	
	Activities	**Duration**
	Available	Current availability period
	Drive	Continuous driving time
	Rest	Current rest period
	Work	Current work period
II	Break	Cumulative break time
?	Unknown	
	Equipment	**Functions**
1	Driver slot	
2	Co-driver slot	
	Card	
	Clock	
	Display	
	External storage	Downloading
	Power supply	
▼	Printer/ Print-out	Printing
	Sensor	
	Vehicle/ vehicle unit	
	Miscellaneous	
!	Event	
×	Fault	
●	Location	
	Security	
>	Speed	
	Time	
Σ	Total/summary	
	Qualifiers	
24h	Daily	
I	Weekly	
II	Two weeks	
→	From or to	

Pictogram combinations

	Control pace
● →	Location begin
→ ●	Location end
	From time
	To time
>>	Overspeed
	Cards
	Driver card
	Company card
	Control card
	Workshop card
	Driving
	Crew driving
	Driving time for one week
	Driving time for two weeks
	Print-outs
24h ▼	Daily driver activities from driver card print-out
24h ▼	Daily driver activities from VU print-out
! × ▼	Events and faults from driver card print-out
! × ▼	Events and faults from VU print-out
▼	Technical data print-out
>> ▼	Overspeed print-out
	Faults
× 1	Card fault (driver slot)
× 2	Card fault (co-driver slot)
×	Display fault

FIGURE 5.3 Example of a typical printout from a digital tachograph

Driver Activities Card Daily Print-Out

Print-out	Explanation
▼ 15/10/1997 15:15 (UTC)	1 Printing - Date & Time (UTC)
-----------▼-----------	Delimiter Print-out general information
# DavidFish	2 Controller - Name
#▮B/4803992633	Controller - Card Number
#→	3 Control Place (Hand written)
▯ WALSTER	5 Driver - Last Name
Nick D.	Driver - First Name
▯▮GB/135798642	6 Driver Card - Number
14/05/2004	Driver Card - Expiry Date
⛟ XAD1117483A	7 Vehicle - VIN
B/PV1772	Vehicle - Nation + VRN
Tacho-Manufacturer	8 Tachograph - Manufacturer Name
Tacho-Part-Number	Tachograph - Part Number
T Workshop-Name	Last Inspection/Calibration - Workshop Name
T▮GB/159482637	Workshop Card Number
T 05/03/1997	Date
-----------▯-----------	Delimiter driver information
▮▼14/10/1997	4 ***Type of Print-Out (Card) & Enquiry date***
? 00:00 06:17 06h18	9 Card not inserted. Activity unknown
-------------------	10 Card insertion
⛟ B/PV1772	Insertion in VRN No
42000 km	Odometer at card insertion
⊚ 14:12 16:03 01h52	11 Detailed activities
⚒ 16:04 18:00 01h57	
⊢ 18:01 18:01 00h01	
81111 km; 111 km	12 Odometer, Distance travelled at Card withdrawal
? 18:02 23:59 05h58	9 Card not inserted. Activity unknown
-----------Σ-----------	Summary information
→⚒06:19 F	13 Start daily work time Country/Region Odometer
⚒→18:00 E CAT	End daily work time Country/Region Odometer
⊚ 04h59 374 km	14 Activity totals
⚒ 03h42 ⊠ 00h11	
⊢ 01h14 ? 13h54	
▯2 05h25	15 Duration of crew status
-----------!▮×-----------	16 Delimiter Cards Events and Faults
!S12/09/1997 18:24	Event Security breach attempt **and VRN number**
B/PV1772	**of the vehicle in which this event/fault occurred**
!⏚12/09/1997 18:23	Event Power supply interruption **and VRN**
B/PV1772	**number of the vehicle in which this event/fault occurred**
-----------!⛟×-----------	17 Delimiter Vehicle Unit Events and Faults
!⎍05/09/1997 06:35	Event Sensor interruption
▯▮IT/836254363	Driver Card Number
×⛟21/08/1997 12:45	Fault VU
▯▮---	No card inserted
×▼21/08/1997 12:46	Fault Printer
▯▮---	No card inserted

▯	18 Driver's signature ***if applicable***
#	19 Controller's signature ***if applicable***

into it. There are four such differently coloured cards for use with digital tachographs as follows:

- driver cards – which the driver inserts at the commencement of his journey to record driving and working activities (see Figures 5.4 and 5.5);
- company cards – for use by vehicle operators to protect and download the data;
- workshop cards – available only to approved tachograph calibration centres;
- control cards – for use only by DVSA examiners and the police for carrying out enforcement activities.

Before commencing a journey the driver is required to insert his driver card into the 1st (driver) or 2nd (co-driver) slot on the front of the vehicle unit (VU). Where the vehicle has two drivers (ie multi-crewing) the D*f*T has advised that both drivers must insert their respective driver cards into the vehicle unit when they start using the vehicle. While the vehicle is moving, time spent as the second driver will be recorded as a period of availability and the mode cannot be changed to other work or to a break until the vehicle comes to rest. The time setting (and all manual entries) must be in UTC (Universal Time Coordinated), which replaced Greenwich Mean Time (GMT), and must remain so both in the UK and throughout Europe. The 'centre field' details, with digital instruments, will be recorded automatically by the tachograph – ie driver name, vehicle registration number, start and finish odometer readings and name of place code.

In the same way that drivers and co-drivers currently record their different activities – driving, other work, breaks and rest – by changing the mode switch and by swapping the position of charts in the tachograph head, with digital tachographs the mode switch will have to be turned and digital smart cards will need to be swapped between driver and co-driver slots in the instrument when double-manning a vehicle.

Details of time spent working away from the vehicle that are currently written on the rear of the tachograph chart (ie record sheet) will have to be input manually into the digital tachograph. However, time spent embarking and disembarking ferries where this interrupts a driver's daily rest can be entered using the 'ferry flag' facility. The system will also record details of any faults, interference, errors and overspeeding that occur.

NB: To select the 'Ferry Flag' the driver needs to select the ferry/train mode on the digital tachograph. Actions then depend upon the particular journey. For example, if the ferry crossing is going to be part of the driver's daily rest, the driver needs to select daily rest whilst in the ferry queue and then select the ferry mode for actual embarkation. Embarkation will automatically be shown as driving. Once on the ferry the driver needs to select rest mode again and the record will have been made.

If the driver has finished their daily rest whilst on the ferry, the tachograph should be used as if the driver was starting the working day as usual. However, if the driver needs to finish their daily rest immediately following disembarkation they need to select ferry mode immediately prior to disembarkation, disembark, park up and re-select rest mode.

Note also that ferry mode is to be used when these circumstances apply to train journeys.

All this information will be stored for at least 28 days on the driver's personal smart card and for at least a year in the VU. It is also worthy of note that the driver's digi-card is planned to be merged with the driver's driving licence to form a single card to be used in future 'smart' tachographs.

Recording Rules

Regulation 561/2006/EC specifies in Article 26 that the use to which the tachograph crossed hammers and rectangle symbols are put must, from 1 May 2006, be as follows:

The crossed hammers, used to record 'other work' (ie any activity other than driving) done for both the driving employer and any other employer outside of transport.

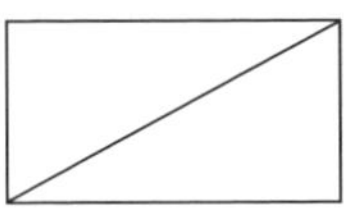

The rectangle, used to record 'periods of availability' as defined in EU Directive 2002/15/EC – The Road Transport Directive – and as described on p 115.

Fees for Digital Tachograph Cards (ie Digi-Cards)

Applications for new or replacement driver digi-cards are made using form D777B, whilst applications for new or replacement company cards are made using form D779B.

The following table of fees has been set by the DVLA for digital tachograph 'smart' cards.

NB: Further information on digital tachographs can be found on the official Government website: www.gov.uk/tachographs (archived at https://perma.cc/X2LP-8CKQ).

TABLE 5.2 Table of fees

Transaction	Driver card	Company card	Workshop card	Control card
Card application	£32	£32	£0	£0
Renewal after 5 years	£19	£19	£0	£0
Replacement – lost/stolen	£19	£19	£0	£0
Exchange	£0	£32	£0	£0
Malfunction	£0	£0	£0	£0

The fees above were correct in 2018 but are under review by the DVLA as part of a major review of fees and may be reduced or abolished as the review progresses.

FIGURE 5.4 Front view of driver 'smart' card

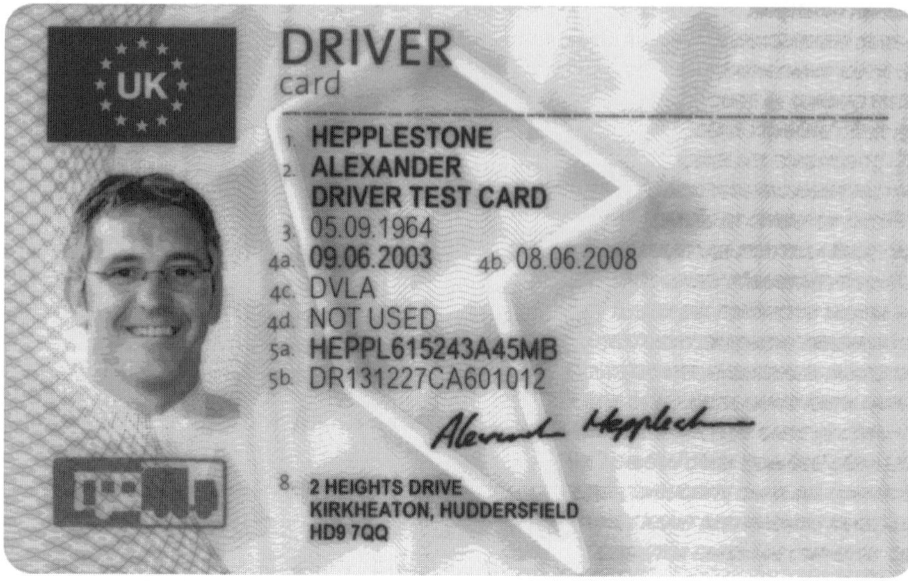

FIGURE 5.5 Rear view of driver 'smart' card

Typical Digital Equipment

Typical equipment comprises a recording unit (ie the VU) incorporating a mass memory fitted into the vehicle instrument panel. This is connected to an intelligent sensor to enable transmission of 'driving' pulses to the recording unit and to the instrument cluster for displaying road speed, time and distance travelled. Connections are provided (ie data interfaces) to allow readout of the stored data via an office PC or a laptop computer, and for it to be printed out to hard copy via a suitable printer where required. Various warning functions are incorporated and a keypad connection can be made to input additional commands and relevant data.

Production of Digital Records

Operator Responsibility for Digital Records

For road safety reasons, and to ensure compliance with legal requirements regarding the monitoring and preservation of digital tachograph records, operators should ensure that they follow the guidance given by the DVSA in its Safe Operator's Guide, which is summarized below. In particular, it is important that the operator can show that his drivers are keeping to the hours and record-keeping regulations by having a good monitoring and control system in place. Digital tachographs require the electronic downloading of data from driver digi-cards and from tachograph instruments; this will support improved methods of analysis but requires different administrative processes to those used for analogue tachograph records. The downloading and monitoring system should cover the following requirements, which are the responsibility of the transport manager or a delegated person.

Inspection and Calibration

Digital tachographs need to be inspected every two years. At the time of inspection they must also be calibrated, unlike analogue tachographs which are normally only calibrated every six years.

Issue of Tachograph Record Print Rolls

- Record the quantity and type of print rolls* (see below) issued (ie make and type approval number).
- Record the driver's name and date of issue.

** Drivers must have a spare print roll available to use should the roll in the printer be removed and retained by the enforcement authorities or if the roll in the printer is completely used up, in the same way as drivers using analogue tachographs need to have at least one spare chart. Should the print roll be removed by the enforcement authorities and the driver does not have a replacement, they will be unable to continue to drive until a replacement roll has been fitted*

Return of Record Sheets and Printouts

- Record the date and time of chart returns and/or printouts.
- Record other relevant details (eg damaged or defaced charts and missing records).

Checking and Downloading of Driver Digi-Cards

- Download data from driver digi-cards at regular intervals – ie at a maximum of 28-day intervals and sufficiently often that no data are lost (NB: digi-cards generally hold up to 28 days' data, overwriting the oldest records when the card is full).
- Routinely check and download digi-cards, particularly for agency and part-time drivers, to ensure that the cards are valid and that drivers have adequate time to complete their duties.

NB: Most digital tachograph manufacturers and suppliers also supply equipment to download digi-cards, as do many of the industry trade associations.

Locking-in and -out of Digital Tachographs with a Company Card

Company cards allow operators to download data from the digital tachograph (ie the VU), which should be done routinely within the legal maximum time, ie at a maximum of 90-day intervals, to ensure that data is complete and accurate and to enable operators to take timely action to remedy any problems. However, DVSA do recommend that data should be downloaded before the maximum 90-day limit to ensure no data is lost. This download will identify all driving activities, driver cards used and driving where no card has been used, and any 'events' or 'faults' recorded by the instrument. Company cards can also be used to 'lock out' third parties who may want unauthorized access to the records produced.

Analysing Digital Data

Digital data downloading from the instrument itself or from driver smart cards requires IT equipment and software to analyse the data. Alternatively, analysis can be carried out remotely by a third party. Such data must be available from the operator to anybody authorized to inspect the data.

Records of Analysis of Driver Record

Records should be kept of the analysis and the results from both analogue and digital tachographs, particularly why journeys were not completed as scheduled, breakdown, traffic delays, etc, and whether the driver has endorsed the back of the chart or the printout as appropriate.

Lists of Faults and Offences

Lists should be kept of all drivers' hours and records of offences, occurrences of tachograph faults and instances of speeding found during analysis. A procedure should be in place to bring these promptly to the attention of the person running the operation (ie the CPC holder) and the drivers. The monitoring and control system should also include informing the drivers of any issues and the drivers in question acknowledging that they have been so informed.

Monitoring and Training of Drivers

A system should be in place to interview drivers when offences are discovered with a view to arranging suitable training programmes and, where necessary, imposing sanctions.

Repairing Tachographs

Adequate procedures should be in place for ensuring that tachograph malfunctions are dealt with, bearing in mind that it is an offence to use a vehicle with a defective tachograph. Any breakdown of the equipment must be dealt with as soon as possible but, in any case, the repairs must be carried out en route within seven days if the vehicle is not to return to base within that time.

Storing Record Sheets and Printouts

It is a legal requirement that tachograph records (ie both charts and printouts) are kept for at least one year* from the date they were made – filed in date order under either the driver's name or the vehicle registration numbers.

**As noted above, this may be extended to two, or even six, years depending upon the purpose for which the records are kept.*

Storing Digital Data

This data must be stored in its downloaded format (in accordance with the technical data in Regulation 1360/2002/EC) and operators are legally required to ensure that the downloading equipment used (by themselves or by contracted outside agencies) can fulfil this requirement. The data may be stored remotely from the operating centre (eg at the premises of an analysis bureau), provided it can be made readily available on request (eg by email transfer if necessary).

Working Time Records

Where records of work by employees working under the provisions of the Working Time Directives are maintained by employers and stored for at least two years following the period to which they relate, they may be stored as part of the payroll system. Under Working Time regulations, workers must, on request, be given copies of the records of hours worked.

Production of Digital Records

Drivers working with digital tachographs must be able to produce for inspection on request by an inspecting officer:

- their digital tachograph card;

- any printouts and manual records for the current day and for the previous 28 calendar days;
- any analogue tachograph charts relating to the use of such instruments during this period.

See also p 155.

Drivers who fail to produce such records on request may find themselves prohibited from driving for a period of time and fined. Such actions will also be recorded against the Operator Compliance Risk Score (OCRS) and may result in vehicles being pinpointed more frequently during roadside enforcement checks.

Signing of Digital Records

In instances where their smart card malfunctions, drivers are required by law to produce two copies of the digital printout from the tachograph each day, one at the beginning of the journey and the other at the end. These copies must be annotated to show the date and driver's name or driver's licence number, and he must sign each copy. If the printer is also malfunctioning then a written record needs to be kept but this too must be signed at commencement and at the finish of duty.

Return of Records

Digital records (ie printouts and downloads) must be returned by the driver to his employer or the vehicle operator, normally within 28 days, but this may vary according to circumstances. Where this is not possible, the enforcement authorities will require evidence that the employer/operator has adequate alternative systems in place for controlling drivers' compliance with the driving hours and working time regulations.

Fourth Generation Smart Tachographs

These long-planned 'smart' tachographs are the first 'smart' tachographs to enter service and were introduced into the UK as a fitment to new vehicles from 15 June 2019. At introduction the old argument about 'spy in the cab' was raised but not with anything like the degree it was when tachographs in general were initially introduced. These new generation machines are designed to reduce the levels of record falsification and to improve the overall administration of drivers' hours and driver activity. Their 'smart' functions are that they:

- have a Global Positioning System (GPS) function which allows the location of the vehicle to be determined when away from base and also allows tracking throughout a journey;
- have the capability to be able to be linked to the telematics systems fitted to the vehicle. This enables the operator to determine exactly what activities the driver is performing at any given time.

In relation to the GPS function the fourth generation machine automatically records the vehicle's position at various times of the day. These include:

- At the starting location of the daily work period.
- Every time three hours of accumulated driving has been amassed.
- At the location where the daily work period finishes.

The machine also automatically records the country in which the vehicle is located and operating. This can help in cases where the true location of a vehicle may need to be proven.

In relation to the capture of data, the new machines allow the enforcement authorities to scan data held by the tachograph without stopping the vehicle in question. This in turn allows them to concentrate on vehicles where the data may show some sort of irregularity or infringement of the regulations.

This data capture facility is not being taken up by all European enforcement agencies and the DVSA has stated that it does not intend to use this 'remote detection' facility for several years as there are too few vehicles fitted with the new fourth generation machines. Other European agencies may do otherwise but the decision of when to begin remote detection is a matter for individual countries.

Data able to be scanned includes:

- the latest attempted security breach;
- the longest interruption of the power supply;
- sensor faults;
- motion data errors;
- vehicle motion recording conflicts;
- driving without a valid card;
- crew member card insertion whilst driving;
- time adjustment data;
- calibration data including the dates of the two most recent calibrations;
- vehicle registration data;
- speed recorded by the tachograph.

In order to comply with data protection legislation and in order to protect drivers the data captured does not include details about typical driver's hours offences, such as failing to take a break or exceeding the daily driving limit. In addition, the data can only be retained for a total of three hours unless some sort of offence or irregularity is detected. Even where this is detected the data cannot, by itself, lead to automatic penalties but it can be used towards further action being taken. The whole issue of data protection is deemed to be the main area where future challenges will arise relating to the capture of personal data by various bodies without verifiable consent being given by the driver. There are other concerns relating to telematics capturing personal data and proof of authenticity of the data captured, but it is expected that these types of 'teething problems' will be solved over time.

Overall, the new tachographs will enable improved journey planning, routeing and scheduling and should also assist in locating stolen or broken down vehicles, protecting drivers whilst away from base and improving the standards of record keeping.

As a final point it must be noted that there is, to date, no requirement to retro-fit the new generation machines into vehicles currently fitted with older type machines and that the UK authorities have declared that retro-fitting will not be compulsory until 2034, by which time fifth generation machines will have been introduced and so this too may be a date which means very little.

Anti-Fraud Measures

The EU has adopted a two-part package of measures aimed at:

- detecting and preventing abuses of the tachograph system; and
- providing the use of dedicated, type-approved adaptors for light vehicles that are required to comply with the drivers' hours and tachograph rules.

First, member states are required to develop dedicated equipment and software that can be used to analyse the data from the digital tachograph. Additionally, best practice guidance is given for national control authorities when carrying out checks of vehicles and the recording equipment, whether at the roadside, at company premises or at workshops.

Second, in the case of certain light vehicles (ie vehicles in classes M1 and N1) in which it was technically not possible to install tachograph equipment so that it could meet the necessary requirements, the use of dedicated, type-approved adaptors for these vehicles is allowed. It is these adapters that may be used if, or when, drivers' hours regulations are amended to include lighter vehicles.

Driver Licensing and Licence Penalties

06

Driver Licensing

Any person wishing to drive a motor (ie mechanically propelled) vehicle on a public road in the UK or within Europe must hold a licence showing a driving entitlement (either full or provisional) for the relevant category of vehicle. Specifically in the case of medium and large goods vehicle driving, drivers must hold a current licence showing a relevant vocational driving entitlement (either full or provisional). This is the legal responsibility of the individual concerned and heavy penalties are imposed on any person found to be driving either without a licence, whilst suspended from driving, without a licence covering the correct category of vehicle or while disqualified from driving by a court.

Furthermore, it is the responsibility of the employer of any person required to drive for business purposes to ensure that such employee-drivers, irrespective of their function, status or seniority, are correctly licensed to drive company vehicles. The fact that a driver may be disqualified or has allowed his licence to lapse without the employer knowing is no defence for the employer against prosecution on a charge of allowing an unlicensed person to drive a vehicle.

Offences

The law states that it is an offence to drive, or to cause or permit another person to drive, a vehicle on the road without a current and valid driving licence. In the case of LGVs it is an offence to drive, or to cause another person to drive, without a valid licence (ie full or provisional) giving entitlement to drive vehicles in categories C or C+E.

Checking Licences

Haulage employers are advised by the police and the Traffic Commissioners to check their drivers' licences on a regular basis – always initially when giving a driver a job and then at least once every three to six months – otherwise they leave themselves wide open to prosecution for a range of licensing offences and for the vehicle insurance to be invalidated. When checking licences only an original licence should be accepted, never a photocopy. Check that all of a driver's given names shown on the licence match those in the company record, and that the date of birth shown also coincides with that recorded at the time of employment.

Employers can check the validity of a driving licence and verify the holder's driving entitlements by contacting the DVLA in several different ways.

First, online by using the 'View Driving Licence' system (www.viewdrivingrecord.service.gov.uk (archived at https://perma.cc/W9FC-HQCC)). This allows drivers to gain access to their driving licence details which they can share with an employer.

Second, by using another online service which allows 3rd parties (usually employers) to gain access to the 'Check Driving Licence' option (www.gov.uk/check-driving-information (archived at https://perma.cc/L86R-HQA9)). For this method the driver provides some details and a code number which the employer/3rd party can use to access the details themselves directly from the 'View Driving Licence' system.

Third, there is the 'Share Driving Licence Service' which allows UK licence holders to share their information (including DCPC and tacho card information) online using a code number from the DVLA which is valid for 21 days.

Fourth, there is a telephone service where the employee needs to call 0300 790 6801 to give permission for the check and where the employer then calls 0906 139 3837 to get the information.

Fifth is to use the postal service using form D888/1, completed by the driver, to request the information.

Finally, there is the DVLA Access to Driver Data service (ADD) which is a business-to-business facility allowing employers to access live licence data relating to their employees with permission by the employees.

Operators wishing to check licences of non-UK nationals can get the driver to contact the DVLA on 0300 790 6801 to give permission for the check by allowing the employer to call the same number within seven days of permission being granted or the operator can call the same number with the driver involved in the conversation.

With the 'View Driving Licence' system it works in the following way. A driver can view their driving licence including the vehicle categories they are entitled to drive and any endorsement or penalty points that they may have by using the free View Driving Licence service. This can be found at www.gov.uk/view-driving-licence (archived at https://perma.cc/72VQ-7BCS). Once the site is accessed the driver needs to enter:

- their driving licence number;
- their National Insurance number; and
- their home address postcode.

They then tick a box to confirm that they have read the privacy notice and click 'View Now' and the licence details are displayed and can be printed off.

Should the driver then wish to share the details they select the 'Share your information' tab and click on the 'Get a code' box. A case-sensitive code will be displayed that will enable the person the driver wishes to share the details with to access the information on a single occasion any time up to 21 days after the code has been issued.

Note: In May 2015 the Senior Traffic Commissioner made it clear that whilst employers should check driving licences at least every six months, three-monthly intervals would be preferred. However, if three-monthly checks were introduced it was also stated that whilst the six-monthly check should be made on all licences, the three-monthly check should also be made on all licences but 'could' be a check on a random sample of licences. The main point being that the six-monthly check would remain and would be supported by the three-monthly random sampling where an organization deemed it to be more appropriate, or practical, than carrying out a full check every three months.

Invalidation of Insurance

Driving without a current and valid driving licence covering the category of vehicle being driven can invalidate insurance cover (which is itself an offence and is usually included among the charges for an unlicensed person driving) and could result in any accident or damage claim being refused by the insurance company under the terms of its policy contract – which is invariably conditional upon the law being complied with in full.

Licensing Provisions

The licensing provisions described in this chapter are principally contained in:

- the Road Traffic Act 1988;
- the Road Traffic (Driver Licensing and Information Systems) Act 1989;
- the Road Traffic (New Drivers) Act 1995;
- the Third European Directive on Driving Licences (3EUD) (2006/126/EC);

and the following regulations:

- the Motor Vehicles (Driving Licences) (Large Goods and Passenger Carrying Vehicles) Regulations 1990 (which deal with entitlements to drive LGVs over 7.5 tonnes gross weight and passenger-carrying vehicles which are used for hire and reward operations), plus a number of subsequent amendments;
- the Motor Vehicles (Driving Licences) Regulations 1999;
- the Motor Vehicles (Driving Licences) Amendment Regulations (updating fees);
- the Motor Vehicles (Driving Licences) (Amendment) Regulations 2018.

The licence-scheme changes brought about by this legislation involved significant change in the old vocational (ie HGV/PSV) licensing. In particular, the terminology changed so that heavy goods vehicles (HGVs*) and public service vehicles (PSVs) as they were previously known are now called large goods vehicles (LGVs) and passenger-carrying vehicles (PCVs), respectively, and goods vehicles are no longer classified by the number of axles. In addition, licences to drive medium-sized goods vehicles and minibuses (Category C1 and Category D1 respectively) and all categories for larger vehicles such as C, CE, D and DE are now most commonly referred to as 'vocational' driving licences.

* *Unfortunately, when the UK road user levy was introduced in 2014, for some reason it was actually termed the HGV Road User Levy.*

For driver licensing purposes:

- a large goods vehicle is a motor vehicle (not being a medium-sized goods vehicle) which is constructed or adapted to carry or haul goods and the permissible maximum weight of which exceeds 7.5 tonnes;
- a medium-sized goods vehicle is defined as one having a permissible maximum weight exceeding 3.5 tonnes but not exceeding 7.5 tonnes;
- a large passenger-carrying vehicle is a vehicle constructed or adapted to carry more than 16 passengers;
- a small passenger-carrying vehicle is a vehicle which carries passengers for hire or reward and which is constructed or adapted to carry more than eight but not more than 16 passengers.

Driving Licences

Major changes to Britain's ordinary and vocational driving licence schemes were introduced in 1990–91 as the UK harmonized with EU requirements. Since 1 April 1991 the pink and green European model, 'unified' driving licence (Euro-licence), which showed all of an individual's entitlements to drive (ie for motorcycle, car, light and large goods vehicles, and passenger carrying vehicles as appropriate), was replaced by the introduction of the Third European Directive on Driving Licences which sought to standardize driving licences across the EU and improve security in relation to fraudulent use of driving licences. This 'pink' card was replaced early in 2014 by a pastel-coloured card with even greater security features.

The new vocational Euro-licences also show, where appropriate, provisional driving entitlements and now include a clearer list of entitlements. They operate using universal medical requirements for drivers and universal periods of validity for licences of five years with universal validity for photographs of 10 years. These 'Euro-licences' will remain valid for the UK but may not be valid in all European countries post-Brexit (see later).

Green and Pink Licences Still Valid

National driving licences issued in EU member states are still recognized throughout the EU and existing British 'green' or 'pink' ordinary driving licences continue to be valid both in Britain and in other countries which recognize British licences. However, vocational drivers requiring a DQC card will not be able to use the old 'green' licence as it will need to be surrendered before a DQC card, which requires a photograph of the driver, can be issued.

Existing UK Licence Holders

For a large proportion of British ordinary driving licence holders (ie those who have no vocational entitlements) who currently hold 'licences-for-life', the changes mentioned above will not be noticed unless or until they apply to change the details on their licence (eg to record a new address), when they will be issued with the Euro-licence.

The DVLA no longer issues paper driving licences. An EU directive required all member states to issue driving licences in a card format containing the licence holder's photograph and signature. Because of this the paper 'counterpart' licence was no longer relevant, because any endorsements on the licence could not be viewed. This means that drivers hoping to hire vehicles need to get proof of their entitlement to do so by contacting the DVLA to download a copy of their licence details which shows endorsements, or not. This is done by accessing the 'view-driving-licence' system mentioned above.

The photocard Category B (car) driving licence, which is made entirely from polycarbonate (and is valid for 10 years, after which it has to be surrendered for renewal or when the holder reaches the age of 70, when it also requires renewal), has a number of enhanced security features that were not available on the older licences. One of the main differences between the two is that the current photocard has a black and white photo while the older version had a coloured one.

The photocard driving licence is said to offer numerous benefits as follows:

- A secure format reduces the chance for misrepresentation.
- It makes certain that the person getting a provisional licence, taking the test and getting a full driving licence is one and the same.
- It makes certain that the person obtaining the licence is the right age to do so.
- It cuts the chances of a person holding more than one licence, either by accident or design.
- It increases the accuracy of the DVLA database, which will in turn provide better information to the police and courts.

The exact form that UK driving licences will take following Brexit is unclear, although UK drivers driving within the EU will require International Driving Permits (IDPs) in addition to their UK licence (see later in this section).

Organ Donor Option

Euro driving licences originally incorporated an organ donor consent section (in the green counterpart of the licence document). Previously, only provisional driving licences had this facility and separate donor cards were enclosed by the DVLA when sending out full driving licences. As the paper counterpart is now phased out it is the responsibility of the potential donor to ensure that their wishes to donate are recorded using an alternative method. It should be noted that in Scotland and Wales, organ donor consent is assumed unless the person actually physically opts out of the scheme. At the time of writing England is also considering an'opt out' scheme, which is expected to be in place some time during 2020.

The Issuing Authority

Responsibility for the issue of vocational driving entitlements rests with the DVLA, Swansea. However, the TCs still retain a disciplinary role in regard to vocational entitlements as described on p 187.

All applications in connection with driver licensing (ie for both ordinary and vocational driving entitlements) should be addressed to the DVLA, Swansea followed by the appropriate postcode, ie:

- SA99 1BN for replacement licences and
- SA99 1DH for licence renewal.

A full list of DVLA postcodes (including vehicle related issues) is available on the DVLA website, but also see below.

Online licence applications are encouraged by the DVLA and are quick and relatively simple. They can be made using the website at www.gov.uk/contact-the-dvla (archived at https://perma.cc/JW6W-UVM9).

Further information on driver licensing can be obtained from the Customer Services Unit, DVLA, Swansea SA6 7JL (tel: 0300 790 6801 for general enquiries about driver licensing).

Over the past few years the DVLA has been re-structuring and, as a part of that re-structuring, in addition to making most licence procedures accessible through the internet, it has closed all its local offices and centralized its activities in Swansea. This has meant that the many sections of the DVLA in Swansea now have different identification postcodes for correspondence and enquiries. These are below:

- Changes to a V5C = DVLA SA99 1BA
- First Registration = DVLA SA99 1BE
- Enforcement Enquiries = DVLA SA99 1AH
- Medical Enquiries = DVLA SA99 1TU
- Applications using V11 or V890 = DVLA SA99 1AR
- Vehicle and Driver Record Enquiries = DVLA SA99 1BP
- Replacement Driving Licences = DVLA SA99 1BN
- Renewal of Driving Licences (10 years) = DVLA SA99 1DH
- Trade Licensing = DVLA SA99 1DZ
- Trade Disposals = DVLA SA99 1BD
- Trade Personalized Number Plates = DVLA SA99 1DP
- Private Personalized Number Plates = DVLA SA99 1DS

NB: DVLA is now actually requesting that most enquiries be done using its website as part of the modernization of its services. The website can be accessed through the GOV.UK website or the DVLA's own website.

Minimum Age for Drivers of Small, Medium and Large Vehicles

Certain minimum ages are specified by law for drivers of small, medium and large motor vehicles as follows:

Small Goods Vehicle

- Small goods vehicle not exceeding 3.5 tonnes maximum authorized mass and alternatively fuelled small goods vehicles up to 4.25 tonnes maximum authorized mass (including the weight of a trailer not exceeding 750 kg maximum authorized mass (MAM))

  Category B *17 years**

  **16 if receiving a Disability Living Allowance (ie mobility allowance)*

- Small goods vehicle not exceeding 3.5 tonnes MAM (including the weight of a trailer exceeding 750 kg MAM)

  Category B + E *17 years*

NB: To take advantage of the increased weight allowance to 4.25 tonnes drivers need to have undertaken at least five hours of training in an alternatively fuelled vehicle of that size. The training must be delivered by either an instructor on the National Register of LGV Instructors or an instructor on the National Vocational Driving Instructors Register.

Medium Goods Vehicles

- Medium-sized goods vehicle constructed or adapted to transport goods which exceeds 3.5 tonnes MAM but not 7.5 tonnes MAM (including the weight of a trailer not exceeding 750 kg MAM)

  Category C1 *18 years**

  **17 if member of the armed services*

- Combinations of vehicles where the towing vehicle is in subcategory C1 and its trailer has a MAM of more than 750 kg MAM, provided that the MAM of the combination thus formed does not exceed 12,000 kg and the MAM of the trailer does not exceed the unladen mass of the towing vehicle. (If driver passed category B test prior to 1 January 1997 he will be restricted to a total weight not more than 8,250 kg)

  Category C1 + E *21 years** **

  **17 if member of the armed services*

  *** 18 if:*

  – *after passing a driving test for this category and Driver CPC initial qualification;*

- *learning to drive or taking a driving test for this category or Driver CPC initial qualification;*
- *while undergoing a national vocational training course to obtain a Driver CPC initial qualification.*

Large Goods Vehicles

- Vehicles over 3,500 kg MAM with a trailer up to 750 kg MAM

  Category C *21 years** **

  **17 if member of the armed services*

  *** 18 if:*

  - *after passing a driving test for this category and Driver CPC initial qualification;*
  - *learning to drive or taking a driving test for this category or Driver CPC initial qualification;*
  - *while undergoing a national vocational training course to obtain a Driver CPC initial qualification.*

- Vehicles over 3,500 kg MAM with a trailer over 750 kg MAM

  Category C + E *21 years** **

  **17 if member of the armed services*

  *** 18 if:*

  - *after passing a driving test for this category and Driver CPC initial qualification;*
  - *learning to drive or taking a driving test for this category or Driver CPC initial qualification;*
  - *while undergoing a national vocational training course to obtain a Driver CPC initial qualification.*

NB: Drivers with vocational entitlement to drive medium and large goods vehicles who have passed their vocational tests since 19 January 2013 need to renew their vocational entitlements every five years irrespective of their age at the time of passing the test. The medical requirements for these renewals entail 'self-certification' declarations by drivers up until the age of 45, after which time full medicals will be required.

Road Rollers

A person under 21 but not less than 17 years old may drive a road roller if it:

- is propelled by means other than steam;
- has an unladen weight of not more than 11,690 kg;*
- is fitted with metal or hard rollers;

- is not constructed or adapted to carry a load other than water, fuel, accumulators and other equipment used for the purpose of propulsion, loose tools, loose equipment and any object which is specially constructed for attachment to the vehicle so as to increase, temporarily, its unladen weight.

* *If this weight is exceeded, the minimum age for driving a roller is 21 years.*

Agricultural Tractors

A person under 17 but over 16 may drive an agricultural tractor only if it is:

- of the wheeled type;
- not more than 2.45 metres wide including the width of any fitted implement;
- specially licensed for excise duty purposes as an agricultural machine;
- not drawing a trailer other than one of the two-wheeled or close-coupled four-wheeled type which is not more than 2.45 metres wide.

A 16-year-old must not drive an agricultural tractor on a road unless he has passed the appropriate test.

Tracked Vehicles

A person under 21, but over 17, may drive a tracked machine providing that the MAM of the machine does not exceed 3,500 kg.

Vehicle Categories/Groups for Driver Licensing

Under the Euro-licensing system where vehicle groups are categorized we, and all EU member states, no longer refer to the 'traditional' groups of vehicles but use categories to denote the sizes and types of vehicles that may be driven. Euro-licences also show moped and motorcycle categories but these are not included in detail as they do not relate to vehicles. A list of the categories is below:

Category	Vehicle type
Cars and light vans	
B	Motor vehicles not exceeding 3.5 tonnes mass and with not more than eight seats (excluding the driver's seat) including drawing a trailer not exceeding 750 kg mass. Including combinations of category B vehicles and a trailer where the combined weight does not exceed 3.5 tonnes and the weight of the trailer does not exceed the unladen weight of the towing vehicle.* Note also the concession to 4.25 tonnes, above. *Additional categories covered: F, K, P*
B + E	Motor vehicles in category B drawing a trailer over 750 kg where the combination does not come within category B.

Category	Vehicle type
Medium goods vehicles	
C1	Medium goods vehicles between 3.5 tonnes and 7.5 tonnes (including drawing trailer not exceeding 750 kg) – maximum weight of the combination must not exceed 8.25 tonnes.
C1 + E	Medium goods vehicles between 3.5 tonnes and 7.5 tonnes and drawing a trailer over 750 kg but does not exceed the unladen weight of the towing vehicle – maximum weight of the combination must not exceed 12 tonnes. *Additional category covered: B+E*
Large goods vehicles	
C	Large goods vehicles over 3.5 tonnes (but excluding vehicles in categories D, F, G and H) including those drawing a trailer not exceeding 750 kg.
C + E	Large goods vehicles in category C drawing a trailer exceeding 750 kg. *Some C+E licences, where the holder was previously qualified to drive vehicles in old HGV class 2 or 3, show a restriction limiting driving to drawbar combinations only. This is coded as a Restriction 102* *Additional category covered: B+E*
Minibuses	
D1	Passenger vehicles with between 9 and 16 seats including drawing trailer not exceeding 750 kg.
D1 + E	Motor vehicles in category D1 drawing a trailer over 750 kg – the weight of the trailer must not exceed the unladen weight of the towing vehicle and the maximum weight of the combination must not exceed 12 tonnes. *Additional category covered: B+E*
Passenger vehicles	
D	Passenger vehicles with more than eight seats including drawing a trailer not exceeding 750 kg.
D + E	Passenger vehicles in category D drawing a trailer over 750 kg. *Additional category covered: B+E*
Other vehicles	
A	Mopeds, motorcycles and tricycles.
F	Agricultural or forestry tractors but excluding any vehicle in category H.
G	Road rollers.
H	Track-laying vehicles steered by their tracks.
K	Mowing machine or pedestrian-controlled vehicle with up to three wheels and not over 410 kg.
L	Electrically propelled vehicles.

*The concession relating to trailers in Category B (above) came as part of the 2013 EU Directive which now allows post 1997 Category B drivers to pull trailers, exceeding 750 kg, under some circumstances, providing the drawing vehicle has a Maximum Authorized Mass (MAM) of less than 3,500 kg. For example, if a Category B driver, who passed their driving test after 1 January 1997, drives a van with a MAM of 2,300 kg they can now tow a trailer up to a combination weight of 3,500 kg. This means that the driver could tow a 1,200 kg MAM trailer. This provision is not available for drivers driving vehicles with a MAM of 3,500 kg, who are still restricted to drawing trailers not exceeding 750 kg MAM.

In any case it is worthy of note that if the trailer MAM cannot be accurately determined, the DVSA recommend that the trailer weight should not exceed more than 70 per cent of the weight of the drawing vehicle.

NB: In the above table, vehicle/trailer weights, unless otherwise specified, are to be taken as the MAM, which is the same as the permissible maximum weight (pmw) for the vehicle/trailer – commonly referred to as the 'gross weight'.

Restricted Category for Pre-1997 Drivers

Drivers of goods vehicles with trailers in category C1+E who passed their category B test prior to 1 January 1997 are restricted to a total combination weight of 8,250 kg. The restriction is marked on the driver's licence with the code 107. Driving a combination up to the 12-tonne limit requires an additional test.

NB: A full list of licence restrictions and information codes can be found on the GOV.UK website at: https://www.gov.uk/driving-licence-codes (archived at https://perma.cc/L9GN-9KS9).

Restricted Categories for Post-1997 Drivers

Since 1 January 1997, new drivers passing the car and light vehicle test (ie with vehicles not exceeding 3.5 tonnes permissible maximum weight) for the first time are not permitted to drive vehicles above this weight without securing additional driving categories on their licence. It is stressed that this restriction to 3.5 tonne driving applies *only* to those who first pass their test since this date; it will not be applied retrospectively to existing licence holders – their existing entitlements are preserved.

Drivers who pass their car test (ie category B) are not permitted to:

- drive minibuses (in category D1);
- drive medium-sized goods vehicles (in category C1); or
- tow large (ie over 750 kg) trailers (in categories B+E, C1+E and D1+E).

They must take a further test if they wish to drive such vehicles or vehicle combinations.

Any driver wishing to drive a vehicle towing a heavy trailer (ie one with a gross weight over 750 kg) must not drive a combination exceeding 3,500 kg MAM without first having passed a test in the associated rigid vehicle towing an appropriate trailer. Learner drivers in categories B, C1, C, D1 and D cannot drive a vehicle towing a trailer of any size.

Towed and Pushed Vehicles

It has been ruled that a person who steers a vehicle being towed (whether it has broken down or even has vital parts missing, such as the engine) is 'driving' the vehicle for licensing purposes and therefore needs to hold current and valid driving entitlement covering that category of vehicle. Conversely, it has been held that a person pushing a vehicle from the outside (ie with both feet on the ground) is not 'driving' a vehicle, nor are they 'using' the vehicle.

Incomplete Vehicles

Drivers of incomplete goods vehicles comprising a chassis and cab only (ie before bodywork is fitted) and of articulated tractive units not yet fitted with a fifth-wheel coupling must (from 1 January 1998) hold either a category C1 driving entitlement for such vehicles weighing between 3.5 and 7.5 tonnes, or a category C entitlement for such vehicles weighing over 7.5 tonnes. Prior to this date incomplete vehicles could be driven on a category B licence covering motor cars and light vans.

Tractive Units

Drivers of heavy (ie over 3.5 tonne) articulated tractive units with no semi-trailer attached need hold only a category C driving entitlement – contrary to popular misconception, a category C+E driving entitlement is not required.

Fitters

In the past, fitters who had held their category C vocational licence for at least two years were also entitled to drive category D vehicles (buses and coaches) on road tests, for repair or for annual tests, etc providing no passengers are carried.

However, in December 2014, there was an amendment published as the Motor Vehicle (Driving Licences) Amendment Regulations 2014, which deleted this relaxation. In effect this means that since 29 December 2014 a category D vehicle cannot now be driven by a category C licence holder, whether or not the person in question is a fitter/mechanic.

Learner Drivers

Learner drivers must hold a provisional driving entitlement to cover them while driving under tuition.

Full category C (rigid LGV) entitlement holders can use this entitlement in place of a provisional entitlement for learning to drive vehicles in category C+E (ie drawbar combinations and articulated vehicles). But it should be noted that full entitlements in categories B and C1 *cannot* be used as a provisional entitlement for learning to drive vehicles in categories C or C+E respectively. A proper provisional entitlement for these classes is required.

Learner drivers must be accompanied, when driving on public roads, by the holder of a full entitlement covering the category of vehicle being driven (see also below) and must not drive a vehicle drawing a trailer, except in the case of articulated vehicles or agricultural trailers. (*NB: Full licence holders must have held the licence for three years.*)

An 'L' plate of the approved dimensions must be displayed on the front and rear of a vehicle being driven by a learner driver (see Chapter 7). Learners driving in Wales may alternatively display a 'D' plate.

Since June 2018 learner drivers of category B vehicles are now allowed to drive on motorways in order to gain 'high speed' driving skills. However, there are some rules which must be obeyed. Firstly, the car must be fitted with dual controls and the driver must be having a lesson with an official, approved driving instructor. It is the instructor who must assess whether or not the learner driver in question is safe to drive if motorway instruction is planned. However, learner drivers seeking a licence for category C1, C and C+E vehicles and who hold full entitlements in licence categories B, C1 or C, as appropriate, may drive such vehicles on motorways while under tuition as a normal part of their training.

Compulsory Re-tests for Offending New Drivers

From 2 June 1997, newly qualified drivers who tot up six or more penalty points on their licence within two years of passing the test revert to learner status (ie with the display of 'L' plates and the need to be accompanied by a qualified driver) and have to repass both the theory test and the practical driving test before regaining a full licence.

Supervision of 'L' Drivers

Qualified drivers who supervise learner drivers in cars and in light, medium and large goods vehicles must:

- Be at least 21 years old.
- Have held a full driving entitlement for a continuous period of at least three years (excluding any periods of disqualification).
- For accompanying learner vocational drivers, have held a relevant entitlement (ie for the type of vehicle on which they are supervising) for at least three years.
- Have passed a test for the category of licence being taught. Drivers acquiring an entitlement by 'grandfather rights' cannot supervise learner drivers.

Contravention of these requirements could lead to prosecution of the supervising driver and, on conviction, a fine, penalty points and possibly licence disqualification.

Insurance Schemes for New Drivers

A Government scheme of insurance incentives was launched in 1995 to encourage newly qualified drivers to take additional lessons after passing their driving test. The 'Pass Plus' scheme is aimed particularly at young drivers who have not previously taken out motor insurance. It comprises six hours of training, under the supervision of an ADI, normally taken within 12 months of passing the test, and includes driving in all weather conditions, at night, on motorways and dual carriageways and in town. Many insurance companies offer preferential insurance premiums to 'Pass Plus' certificate holders and some local authorities offer discount schemes for drivers wishing to take the training. A list of these local authorities can be found on the GOV.UK website by typing in 'Pass Plus'.

Many insurance companies also offer discounts to young drivers who agree to have their driving monitored using a 'black box' fitted to the vehicle which effectively records their driving and their mileage. Compliance with speed limits, driving smoothly, driving within set time parameters and low mileage can all contribute towards possible discounts.

Full details can be found by contacting the DVSA Pass Plus Team on 0115 936 6504.

Exemptions from Vocational Licensing

Exemptions from the need to hold a vocational driving entitlement (ie in categories C1, C or C+E) apply when driving certain vehicles as follows (in most cases such vehicles may be driven by the holder of a category B licence):

1. Steam-propelled vehicles.
2. Road construction vehicles used or kept on the road solely for the conveyance of built-in construction machinery.
3. Engineering plant, but not mobile cranes.*
4. Works trucks.
5. Industrial tractors.
6. Agricultural motor vehicles which are not agricultural or forestry tractors.
7. Digging machines.
8. Vehicles used on public roads only when passing between land occupied by the vehicle's registered keeper and which does not exceed an aggregate of 9.7 km in a calendar week.
9. Vehicles, other than agricultural vehicles, used only for the purposes of agriculture, horticulture or forestry, between areas of land occupied by the same person and which do not travel more than 1.5 km on public roads.
10. Vehicles used for no purpose other than the haulage of lifeboats and the conveyance of the necessary gear of the lifeboats which are being hauled.
11. Vehicles manufactured before 1 January 1960 used unladen and not drawing a laden trailer.
12. Articulated goods vehicles with an unladen weight not exceeding 3.05 tonnes.
13. Vehicles in the service of a visiting military force or headquarters as defined in the Visiting Forces and International Headquarters (Application of Law) Order 1965.

14 Any vehicle being driven by a police constable for the purpose of removing it to avoid obstruction to other road users or danger to other road users or members of the public, for the purpose of safeguarding life or property, including the vehicle and its load, or for other similar purposes.

15 Breakdown vehicles which weigh less than 3.05 tonnes unladen, provided they are fitted with apparatus for raising a disabled vehicle partly from the ground and for drawing a vehicle when so raised, are used solely for the purpose of dealing with disabled vehicles, and carry no load other than a disabled vehicle and articles used in connection with dealing with disabled vehicles.

16 A passenger-carrying vehicle recovery vehicle other than an articulated vehicle with an unladen weight of not more than 10.2 tonnes which belongs to the holder of a PSV 'O' licence, when such a vehicle is going to or returning from a place where it is to give assistance to a damaged or disabled passenger-carrying vehicle or giving assistance to or moving a disabled passenger-carrying vehicle or moving a damaged vehicle.

17 A mobile project vehicle, which is defined as a vehicle exceeding 3.5 tonnes pmw constructed or adapted to carry not more than eight persons in addition to the driver and which carries mainly goods or burden comprising play or educational equipment for children or articles used for display or exhibition purposes.

** Drivers of mobile cranes must hold a full vocational entitlement covering vehicles in category C1 for driving cranes between 3.5 and 7.5 tonnes and category C for driving cranes over 7.5 tonnes mpw (applicable since 1 January 1999).*

Application for Licences and Vocational Entitlements

Applications for driving licences have to be made to Swansea on form D1 for ordinary licences and forms D2 and D4 for vocational licences. Forms are obtainable from main post offices or direct from Swansea via the internet (at www.gov.uk/contact-the-dvla (archived at https://perma.cc/JW6W-UVM9)).

Questions on the form are concerned with personal details of the applicant, the type of licence required, any previous licence held and whether the applicant is currently disqualified. Vocational entitlement applicants are asked about any convictions they may have recorded against them.

Health Declaration

Applicants for ordinary licences (Group One) are asked to declare information about their health, particularly as to whether they have:

- had an epileptic event (ie seizure or fit);
- sudden attacks of disabling giddiness, fainting or blackouts;

- severe mental handicap;
- had a pacemaker, defibrillator or anti-ventricular tachycardia device fitted;
- diabetes controlled by insulin;
- angina (heart pain) while driving;
- had a major or minor stroke;
- Parkinson's disease;
- any other chronic neurological condition;
- a serious problem with memory;
- serious episodes of confusion;
- had any type of brain surgery, brain tumour or severe head injury involving hospital in-patient treatment;
- any severe psychiatric illness or mental disorder;
- continuing or permanent difficulty in the use of arms or legs which affects the ability to control a vehicle safely;
- been dependent on or misused alcohol, illicit drugs or chemical substances in the previous three years (excluding drink-driving offences);
- any visual disability which affects both eyes (short/long sight and colour blindness do not have to be declared);
- Obstructive Sleep Apnoea Syndrome (OSAS) (this does not have to be reported unless the driver shows symptoms such as daytime sleepiness).

In addition, Group Two applicants for vocational entitlements (unless submitting a medical report – form D4 – see below) are required to state whether they have:

- sight in only one eye;
- any visual problems affecting either eye;
- angina;
- any heart condition or had a heart operation;
- OSAS.

Applicants for vocational licences must be able to demonstrate visual acuity of at least Snellen 6/7.5 in at least one eye and Snellen 6/6.0 in the other eye.

Where licence applicants have previously declared a medical condition, they are required to state what the condition is, whether it has worsened since it was previously declared and whether any special controls have been fitted to their vehicle since the last licence was issued.

The DVLA's Considerations for Vocational Entitlements

Applicants for vocational driving entitlements must meet specified conditions as follows:

- They must be fit and proper persons.
- They must meet laid-down eyesight requirements.

- They must satisfy a medical examination and specifically must not
  - have had an epileptic attack in the previous 10 years (see below), or
  - suffer from insulin-dependent diabetes.*

** There is some slight relaxation, in certain cases, for some drivers who require insulin treatment, but the DVLA require notification in all cases and will then consider each case on merit (see below).*

The decision as to whether or not an applicant will be granted a vocational driving entitlement rests entirely with the DVLA and in making this decision it will take into account any driving convictions for motoring offences, drivers' hours and record offences, and offences relating to the roadworthiness or loading of vehicles against the applicant in the four years prior to the application, and any offence connected with driving under the influence of drink or drugs during the 11 years prior to the application. The applicant has to declare such convictions on the licence application form (D2) but the DVLA has means of checking to ensure that applicants have declared any such convictions against them.

TCs' Powers in Respect of Vocational Entitlements

Although the issue of vocational (ie C1, C, C1E, CE, D1, D1E, D and DE) entitlements is the prerogative of the DVLA, TCs still have powers to consider the fitness of persons applying for or holding such entitlements. This disciplinary role allows a TC to call upon applicants or entitlement holders to provide information as to their conduct (and if necessary to appear before him to answer in person at a Driver Conduct Hearing), to refuse the grant of an entitlement, and to suspend or disqualify a person from holding such an entitlement. The TC's decision must be communicated to the person concerned, upon whom it is binding, and to the Secretary of State for Transport (effectively the DVLA).

Date for Vocational Applications

Application for a vocational driving entitlement should be made not more than three months before the date from which the entitlement is required to run. Reminders will be sent out by the DVLA to existing licence/entitlement holders two months prior to the expiry date of their existing licence/entitlement.

Medical Requirements for Vocational Entitlements

Strict medical standards for vocational entitlement holders are legally established to ensure that those wishing to drive large goods or passenger-carrying vehicles are safe to do so and are not suffering from any disease or disability (especially cardiovascular disease, diabetes mellitus, epilepsy, neurosurgical disorders, excessive sleepiness, nervous or mental disorders, vision problems, or the excessive use of prescribed medicines or illicit drugs, for example) which would prevent them from driving safely.

Even tougher medical standards for vocational entitlement holders were brought in from 1 January 1997 when the EU's 'second' driver licensing Directive came into force. In particular these concerned eyesight (see p 195) and a number of other serious problems which are added to the list of medical disabilities that may result in failure of the medical examination and refusal of a driving licence (see below).

UK applicants for vocational driving entitlements must satisfy such medical standards on first application and subsequently. To do so, they must undergo a medical examination and have their doctor complete the medical certificate portion of the application form D4 not more than four months before the date when the entitlement is needed to commence.

For drivers who passed their vocational before 19 January 2013, a further examination and completed medical certificate is required for each five-yearly renewal of the entitlement after reaching age 45 years. After reaching the age of 65 years a medical examination is required for each annual renewal of the entitlement. Further medical examinations may be called for at any time if there is any doubt as to a driver's fitness to drive.

The form D4 requests applicants' consent to allow the DVLA's medical adviser to obtain reports from their own doctor and any specialist consulted if this helps to establish their medical condition.

Drivers passing their test after 19 January 2013 will still need an initial medical examination using form D4 but will then 'self-certificate' their medical condition every five years until attaining the age of 45 when full medicals will be required in the same way as drivers passing pre-January 2013.

Driving Following Medical Disqualification

Where an application for a full driving licence is made following the revocation of a licence or the refusal of its renewal on medical grounds, the applicant may be required to take a driving test (or an 'on-road assessment') to determine whether he is fit to regain his licence. A provisional licence may be granted for this purpose (ie to authorize driving on the road), but its use is restricted to driving only during the period preceding and while taking the test, and its authority ceases immediately upon conclusion of the test or assessment.

Medicals for Category C1 Drivers

Since 1 January 1997 new drivers of vehicles over 3.5 tonnes gross weight (ie covered by driving licence category C1) require the same medical examination that previously applied only to over 7.5 tonnes vocational licence holders and must follow the same regime as described above for subsequent medical examinations.

Medical Examination Fees

Doctors charge a fee for conducting such medical examinations, which the candidate must pay himself. These examinations are not available on the National Health Service in the UK – current fees are around £120 to £200. The medical fee for licence/entitlement renewal can be claimed as an allowable expense for income tax purposes.

Diabetes

Insulin-dependent diabetes sufferers were usually barred from holding vocational entitlements. However, this 'blanket ban' has now been lifted and some drivers with insulin-dependent diabetes may now be allowed to drive medium and large goods vehicles, although there is often a requirement that the driver needs to renew the licence more frequently than would otherwise be the case. Diabetes sufferers where the diabetes is controlled by diet and who are 'stable' are not normally affected by driver licensing restrictions, but see below.

Rules for Diabetics

Note: In June 2016, the DVLA announced a new regime for LGV and coach/bus drivers with diabetes. The advice given is as follows.

If you are NOT insulin treated but there is a change in your condition you need to inform the DVLA if:

- you have suffered two episodes of severe hypoglycaemia within the last 12 months (the term 'severe' is normally interpreted as suffering hypoglycaemia where assistance was needed from a second person);
- you have developed impaired awareness of hypoglycaemia;
- you are experiencing visual problems.

In cases where the driver is reliant on insulin, they:

- need to have three months of continuous blood glucose readings available on a memory meter every time they apply for a licence;
- must test their blood glucose no more than two hours before the start of the first journey and every two hours through the day (they will also need to test their blood glucose and record the readings at least twice a day even when not driving).

Finally, because most insulin treated Group 2 licence holders need to renew their vocational entitlements every 12 months there is now a set three-year routine to be followed. This is outlined below:

- First application or Year One – Self-declaration, GP examination and independent diabetologist examination.
- Year Two – Self-declaration and independent diabetologist examination.
- Year Three – Self-declaration, GP examination and independent diabetologist examination.

Following the cycle above, it simply repeats itself. For full information visit the diabetes and driving pages on GOV.UK.

Epilepsy

A person will now be prevented from holding a vocational entitlement *only* if he has a 'liability to epileptic seizures'. An applicant must satisfy the DVLA that:

- he has not suffered an epileptic seizure during the 10 years prior to the date when the entitlement is to take effect;
- no epilepsy treatment has been administered during the 10 years prior to the starting date for the entitlement; and
- a consultant nominated by the DVLA has examined the medical history and is satisfied that there is no continuing liability to seizures.

Car, light vehicle and certain other drivers (ie in licence categories A, B, B+E, F, G, H, K, L and P), but not vocational drivers, who suffer from epilepsy can obtain a licence to drive such vehicles provided:

- they have been free from an epileptic attack during the period of one year from the date the licence is granted; or,
- if not free from such an attack, they have had an asleep-attack more than three years before the date on which the licence is granted and have had attacks only while asleep between the date of that attack and the date when the licence is granted; and
- the DVLA is satisfied that driving by them will not cause danger.

Coronary Health Problems

Drivers who have suspected coronary health problems are permitted (since April 1992) to retain their vocational driving entitlements while medical enquiries are made. (Previously the rule was to revoke the licence pending enquiries into the holder's health.) Such drivers no longer have to submit to coronary angiography (ie angiogram testing). The DVLA says that ECG exercise tests will be undertaken no earlier than three months after a coronary event and providing the driver displays no signs of angina or other significant symptoms, he is allowed to keep his driving entitlement while investigations are made, but subject to the approval of his own doctor.

Drivers who have suffered, or are suffering from, the following heart-related conditions must notify the DVLA:

- heart attack (myocardial infarction, coronary thrombosis);
- coronary angioplasty;
- heart valve disease/surgery;
- coronary artery bypass surgery;
- angina (heart pain);
- heart operation (other than a heart transplant).

The DVLA's Drivers Medical Branch has the following advice for heart sufferers:

- Following a heart attack or heart operation, driving should not be recommenced for at least one month following the attack or operation. Driving may be resumed after this time if recovery has been uncomplicated and the patient's own doctor has given his approval.
- A driver suffering from angina may continue to drive (whether or not he is receiving treatment) unless attacks occur while driving, in which case he must notify the DVLA immediately (see below) and *stop driving*.

- A driver who suffers sudden attacks of disabling giddiness, fainting, falling, loss of awareness or confusion must notify the DVLA immediately (see below) and *stop driving*.

Any driver who has doubts about his ability to continue to drive safely is advised to discuss the matter with his own doctor, who has access to medical advice from the DVLA.

Alcohol and Drug-Related Problems

Persons with repeated convictions for drink-driving or drug-driving offences may be required to satisfy the DVLA (with certification from their own doctor) that they do not have an 'alcohol/drug problem' before their licence is restored to them.

Note: Operators checking licences held by some non-UK, EU drivers may see a Restriction 69. This restriction means that the driver has been convicted of drinking and driving in an EU member state and needs to have a breathalyser fitted into the vehicle which must be used before they are allowed to take the vehicle on the public road.

Other Medical Conditions

Other disabilities which may cause failure of the driver's medical examination include:

- sudden attacks of vertigo ('dizziness');
- OSAS;
- heart disease which causes disabling weakness or pain;
- a history of coronary thrombosis;
- the use of hypertensive drugs for blood pressure treatment;
- serious arrhythmia;
- severe mental disorder;
- severe behavioural problems;
- alcohol dependency;
- inability to refrain from drinking and driving;
- drug abuse and dependency;
- psychotrophic medicines taken in quantities likely to impair fitness to drive safely.

A licence will be refused to a driver who is liable to sudden attacks of disabling giddiness or fainting unless these can be controlled.

Those who have had a cardiac pacemaker fitted are advised to discontinue vocational driving, although driving may be permitted if a person who has disabling attacks which are controlled by a pacemaker has made arrangements for regular review from a cardiologist and will not be likely to endanger the public.

Notification of New or Worsening Medical Conditions

Once a licence has been granted (ie whether ordinary or covering vocational entitlements), the holder is required to notify the Drivers Medical Group, DVLA at Swansea

SA99 1TU (Tel: 0300 790 6806) of the onset, or *worsening*, of any medical condition likely to cause him to be a danger when driving – *failure to do so is an offence*. (The Medical Group is also the contact point for any enquiries relating to medical issues.)

Examples of what must be reported are:

- giddiness;
- fainting;
- blackouts;
- epilepsy;
- diabetes;
- strokes;
- multiple sclerosis;
- Parkinson's disease;
- OSAS (where symptoms are present);
- heart disease;
- angina;
- 'coronaries';
- high blood pressure;
- arthritis;
- disorders of vision;
- mental illness;
- alcoholism;
- drug-taking;
- loss, or loss of use, of any limb.

In many cases the person's own doctor will either advise reporting the condition to the DVLA himself, or the doctor (or hospital) may advise the DVLA direct. In either case the driving licence will have to be surrendered until the condition clears.

There is no requirement to notify the DVLA of temporary illnesses or disabilities such as sprained or broken limbs where a full recovery is expected within three months.

Most notifiable conditions are now able to be sent to DVLA after downloading the notification form from the DVLA website. For example, OSAS is notified by completing form SL1 for car drivers and SL1V for vocational drivers.

EU Health Standards for Drivers from 2013

The UK aligned the current driver health standards in 2013 with those contained in EU Directive 2006/126/EC. Principally, the changes concern eyesight, diabetes and epilepsy as follows:

- The eyesight requirements were reduced – licence applicants now only have to read a number plate from 17.5 m instead of a distance of 20 m. Bus and lorry drivers are now able to take vision tests wearing glasses or contact lenses, and the rules for drivers who have reduced sight in one eye were relaxed.
- LGV drivers who are being treated with insulin are now able to apply to drive provided strict medical monitoring is carried out (as noted above). Previously they could only drive vehicles up to 7.5 tonnes gross weight.
- The 2013 rules set out a definition of epilepsy under which drivers will have to surrender their licence if they have two or more epileptic seizures in five years and that they will not be able to reapply for their licence for a further five years. The UK proposed that two attacks in 10 years means the loss of a licence and a driver not being able to reapply for 10 years.
- Drivers are still required to notify the DVLA of any health issues, including heart problems, that their doctor has warned could affect their ability to drive.

The general understanding is that the currently agreed medical requirements will remain in force after Brexit and 'may' lead to some EU member states accepting UK driving licences as valid for their country.

Medical Appeals and Information

The final decision on any medical matter concerning driving licences rests with the Drivers Medical Group of the DVLA. However, there is the opportunity of appeal, within six months, in England and Wales to a magistrate's court, and within 21 days in Scotland to a sheriff's court. In other cases the refused driver may be given the opportunity to present further medical evidence which the medical adviser will consider.

Further information on medical conditions relating to driving are to be found in a Government booklet, *Guide to the current medical standards of fitness to drive*. This can be found on www.gov.uk/government/publications/at-a-glance (archived at https://perma.cc/359F-MG7Z). Useful information for diabetic drivers may also be obtained from Diabetes UK Central Office, Macleod House, 10 Parkway, London, NW1 7AA. Tel: 0345 123 2399; info@diabetes.org.uk.

Drugs and Driving

Drug-driving offences are on the increase with many claims being made by the press and media stating that the increase in prosecutions for drug-driving rises year on year at an alarming rate. In order to try to counter this, the UK authorities advise that it is illegal to drive if either:

- you are unfit to do so because you are on legal or illegal drugs;
- you have certain levels of illegal drugs in your blood (even if they haven't actually affected your driving).

For these purposes, legal drugs are classed as prescription or what are known as over-the-counter medicines.

Should a driver be stopped by the police and it is suspected that drugs may be an issue, the police can make the driver perform a 'field impairment assessment'. This assessment is a series of physical tests to assess a driver's capability to perform certain tasks. Alternatively, the police may also use a roadside drug kit to screen for cannabis and cocaine.

Drivers who are suspected of drug-driving and being unfit to drive will be arrested and will have to take a blood or urine test at a police station.

Prescription medicines

In England and Wales it is currently illegal to drive with legal drugs in your body if they act to impair your driving. It is also an offence to drive in some European countries without carrying a current medical prescription or if you have over the specified limits of certain drugs in your blood and you haven't been prescribed them.

Drivers need to consult their GP if they have been prescribed any of the following:

- amphetamine, eg dexamphetamine or selegiline;
- clonazepam;

- diazepam;
- flunitrazepam;
- lorazepam;
- methadone;
- morphine or opiate and opioid-based drugs, eg codeine, tramadol or fentanyl;
- oxazepam;
- temazepam.

However, you can drive after taking these drugs providing that you've been prescribed them, and followed advice on how to take them, by a healthcare professional or if they are not causing you to be unfit to drive even if you may be above the specified limits. Where a driver may have taken drugs which were not personally prescribed to them, and the levels are above certain limits for the drugs in question, prosecution is generally the resulting action.

At the roadside the police are now able to test for cannabis, cocaine, ecstacy, ketamine, benzodiazepines, methadone, morphine and opiates. If suspected of taking drugs, a 'field impairment test' is carried out and if the police are not satisfied with the results the driver is taken to a police station for tests of blood and urine.

Where prosecutions for drug-driving are made, drivers may suffer a minimum driving ban of 12 months, an unlimited fine or up to six months in prison. In addition, the offence and conviction will be recorded on the driver's licence for a period of 11 years. However, where death is caused by dangerous driving whilst the driver is under the influence of drugs a custodial sentence of up to 14 years can be given.

Note: The law does not apply to Scotland or Northern Ireland although drivers in these countries who are deemed 'unfit' to drive may still be arrested.

Drug testing of vocational drivers by their employers is also becoming an increasing practice in the UK, following the pattern in the United States which has had mandatory testing since 1992. In fact, Unilabs UK, one of the leading drug-testing laboratories, has reported a substantial increase in requests for testing by haulage companies in recent times. While there is no suggestion at this stage that the practice should become mandatory in this country, most of Britain's major oil companies now carry out random testing for both alcohol and drug problems – Shell has produced a staff booklet identifying 11 banned substances (including amphetamines) and warning of the consequences of drink or drug abuse.

Join the Fight against Drugs

If you have any information about drugs or drug smugglers, HM Revenue & Customs request that you ring the 24-hour hotline 'Customs Confidential' on 0800 788 887. You don't have to tell them who you are, but for important information you may be eligible for a cash reward.

Eyesight Requirement

The statutory eyesight requirement mentioned above for ordinary (ie car and light goods vehicle) licence holders is for the driver to be able to read, in good daylight (with glasses or contact lenses if worn), a standard motor vehicle number plate from 20.0 metres (ie 65.6 feet). A 120°-wide field of view is also required. It is an offence to drive with impaired eyesight and the police can require a driver to take an eyesight test on the roadside. If glasses or contact lenses are needed to reach these vision standards they must be worn at all times while driving. It is an offence to drive with impaired eyesight. There are proposals for drivers to undergo regular eye tests.

Eyesight Standards for Vocational Licence Holders

Tougher eyesight standards for vocational drivers were introduced from 1 January 1997. Specifically, drivers of vehicles in categories C, C1, C+E, C1+E, D, D1, D+E and D1+E (effectively trucks over 3.5 tonnes and passenger vehicles with more than nine seats) must have eyesight which is at least:

1. 6/7.5 on the Snellen scale in the better eye* and
2. 6/6.0 on the Snellen scale in the other eye* and
3. 3/60 in each eye without glasses or contact lenses.

* *These standards may be met with glasses or contact lenses if worn but the glasses must not have a corrective power greater than (+8) dioptres.*

To achieve these standards means being able to read the top line of an optician's chart (ie Snellen chart) with each eye from a distance of *at least* 3 metres without the aid of glasses or contact lenses – if it can only be read from, say, 2.5 metres or less, the test is failed. Wearers of spectacles or contact lenses must have vision of at least 6/7.5 in the better eye and at least 6/6.0 in the weaker eye, which means being able to read the sixth line of an optician's chart at 6 metres. Besides these requirements, all drivers must meet existing eyesight standards, which include having a field of vision of at least 120° (horizontal) and 20° (vertical) in each eye with no double vision.

Drivers who held a licence before 1 January 1997 and who do not meet these higher standards are advised to check their licensing position with the Drivers Medical Group at the DVLA (see above for address and telephone number).

NB: Different EU/EFTA and EEA member states have different requirements relating to the need for a driver to carry a spare pair of spectacles in case the usual pair becomes lost or damaged. Drivers are advised to carry a spare pair for all EU member states, but this is compulsory in France, Spain and Switzerland.

Licence Fees and Validity

Current fees for driving licences are as follows:

Licence type	Online	Post
First provisional		
Car	£34.00	£43.00
Bus or lorry (costs are taken in initial theory test, etc)	FREE	FREE
First full		
Car	FREE	FREE (£17.00 to use a different photo from the provisional)
Bus or lorry	FREE	FREE
Renewal		
After expiry	£14.00	£17.00
From age 70	FREE	FREE
For medical reasons	N/A	FREE
Bus or lorry	N/A	FREE
After disqualification	N/A	£65.00
HRO* disqualification	N/A	£90.00
After revocation	N/A	£50.00
Duplicate		
Replace lost or stolen licence	N/A	£20.00
Paper licence for photocard licence no change of details	N/A	£20.00
Paper licence for photocard licence with change of name	N/A	FREE
Paper licence for photocard licence with change of address	FREE	FREE
Exchange		
Add or remove entitlement	N/A	FREE
Remove expired endorsements	N/A	£20.00
Change photo on licence	£14.00	£17.00
Northern Ireland Licence for a full GB licence	N/A	FREE
Other Fees		
Car theory test	£23.00	£23.00
Motorcycle theory test	£23.00	£23.00

* High-risk offender disqualified for drink-driving convictions.

Licence Validity

As discussed earlier, vocational driving entitlements are normally valid for five years or until the holder reaches the age of 45 years under the self-certification scheme. After the age of 45 years, five-year entitlements are granted subject to medical fitness declared by a doctor, but may be for lesser periods where the holder suffers from a relevant or prospective relevant disability. From the age of 65 years, vocational entitlements are granted on an annual basis only.

Ordinary driving licences are valid until age 70 years after which they may be reviewed at three-yearly intervals subject to meeting the health requirements. Photocard driving licences need to be renewed at 10-yearly intervals and this can now be done online.

To renew online, you need:

- a valid UK passport;
- to be a resident of Great Britain (there's a different service in Northern Ireland);
- to pay £14 by MasterCard, Visa, Electron, Maestro or Delta debit or credit card (there's no fee if you're over 70);
- addresses of where you've lived over the last 3 years;
- your current driving licence;
- your National Insurance number (if you know it);
- to not be disqualified from driving.

Tax Deductions

The cost of renewing vocational driving entitlements and of undergoing medical examinations in connection with licence renewals is income tax deductible against earnings – but not the cost of first obtaining such an entitlement.

Lost or Mislaid Licences

Drivers who lose or mislay their driving licences should apply for a duplicate licence in the normal way using the standard application form, form D2, at a cost of £20.00.

UK drivers moving to live abroad who have mislaid their driving licence may obtain a temporary 'Certificate of Entitlement' (commonly referred to as a cover note), valid for one month from the DVLA at Swansea (free of charge), subject to proof of their identity. This document is valid for proving entitlement to drive to enable such persons to apply for and obtain an equivalent driving entitlement in their new country of residence. Applicants for these certificates will need to apply to the DVLA, or download an application from their website and then return it to the DVLA in Swansea for processing.

Production of Driving Licences

Both the police and enforcement officers of the DVSA can request a driver – and a person accompanying a provisional entitlement holder – to produce his licence showing ordinary and vocational entitlements to drive. If he is unable to do so at the time, it may be produced without penalty if the request was by a police officer, at a police station of his choice within seven days.

If the licence cannot be produced within the seven days it can be produced as soon as reasonably practicable thereafter. A TC can also require the holder of any vocational driving entitlement to produce his licence at a Traffic Area Office for examination. Failure to produce a licence on request is an offence.

A police officer can ask a driver to state his date of birth – British ordinary driving licences carry a coded number which indicates the holder's surname and date of birth. The name and address of the vehicle owner can also be requested.

When required by a DVSA examiner to produce his licence, a vocational entitlement holder may be required to give his date of birth and to sign the examiner's record sheet to verify the fact of the licence examination. This should not be refused.

Licence holders apprehended for endorsable fixed penalty (ie yellow ticket) offences are required to produce their driving licence to the police officer at that time or later (ie within seven days) to a police station and surrender the licence, for which they will be given a receipt. Failure to produce a licence in these circumstances means that the fixed penalty procedure will not be followed and a summons for the offence will be issued requiring a court appearance. Drivers summoned to appear in court for driving and road traffic offences must produce their driving licence to the court on, at least, the day before the hearing.

International Driving Permits

Certain European countries do not accept British ordinary driving licences (see the AA website for a list of such countries: www.theaa.com/getaway/idp (archived at https://perma.cc/DT5H-6RJP)). This may include any of the EU member states depending upon Brexit, in which case an International Driving Permit (IDP) will be required by British licence holders wishing to drive in those countries. The DVLA do actually advise all UK drivers to carry an IDP if going abroad as the picture is somewhat unclear and if an IDP is carried it could prevent problems at some borders and with some enforcement authorities.

There are two types of ID which need to be discussed.

First, there are IDPs which are issued under the 1949 Geneva Convention on Road Traffic. There are the original IDPs which remained valid after 29 March 2019 as they are valid for 12 months. These are recognized in Ireland, Spain, Cyprus and Malta.

Second, there will be new IDPs issued under the 1968 Vienna Convention on Road Traffic. These are valid for three years and are recognized in all EU countries plus Norway and Switzerland. These IDPs have been valid from 29 March 2019 and were originally made be available from 1 February 2019. (IDPs applied for in February had a start date of 29 March.)

These are now only obtainable from around 2,500 post offices for a statutory fee of £5.50. A passport-type photograph is required for attachment to the permit.

Applicants must be UK residents, over 18 years of age and hold full driving entitlements for the category of vehicle which the IDP is required to cover.

NB: Drivers needing to drive to, say, France, Germany and Spain will need both types of IDP as they will be driving in two different IDP areas.

Exchange of Driving Licences

British driving licence holders can exchange their licence if necessary in order to:

- record changes of personal details;
- add new categories to a full licence;
- remove out-of-date endorsements or suspension details;
- add or take off provisional motorcycle entitlement;
- exchange an old-style pink or green licence for a new-style one.

Exchanging a Foreign Licence for a GB Licence

Northern Ireland Licences

Full NI driving licences or a test pass can be exchanged for a GB licence. Alternatively, a driver can continue to use an NI licence in Britain until it expires.

EU/EEA Licences

A valid full licence issued in any EU or EEA country (ie all EC countries plus Liechtenstein, Iceland and Norway) need not be changed immediately for a GB licence. So long as such a licence remains valid, the holder can drive in Great Britain until he reaches 70 years of age or for three years after becoming resident in Great Britain, whichever is the longer period. This concession may or may not continue after we leave the EU as it will depend upon reciprocal concessions being agreed and granted for UK licence holders driving abroad.

Currently, foreign drivers of large goods vehicles can drive in Great Britain until aged 45 or for five years after becoming resident, whichever is the longer period. Drivers aged over 45 years but under 65 can drive until their 66th birthday or for five years after becoming a GB resident, whichever is the shorter. Drivers aged 65 years or older may drive for 12 months after becoming a resident in Great Britain.

In order to continue driving after this time, a British driving licence must be obtained by making application on form D2. Application can be made for a British licence at any time, even after expiry of the foreign national licence. (The procedures for foreign vocational licence holders may also change following our EU departure.) Again these rules and parameters may also change as Brexit becomes more deeply ingrained into UK law and operations.

Non-EC (Designated) Countries and Gibraltar

A full valid car (Category B) licence issued in any of the following countries can be exchanged for a British licence: Australia, Barbados, British Virgin Islands, Gibraltar, Hong Kong, Japan, Kenya, New Zealand, Singapore and Zimbabwe.

Holders of any vocational licences from any of the above countries should contact DVLA Driver Licensing Enquiries 0300 790 6801 for further information.

Full Jersey or Isle of Man car, lorry or bus licences, or a full Guernsey car licence, can be exchanged for a British licence if they were valid within the past 10 years.

Certain driving licences for vehicles up to 3.5 tonnes issued in South Africa and Canada may now be exchanged for an equivalent GB licence.

A foreign car (category B) driving licence can be used in Great Britain for one year only provided it remains valid, but exchange of a driving licence issued in any of the above-listed countries can be made up to five years after taking up residence in Great Britain.

Visitors from other countries not mentioned above cannot exchange their national licence for a British equivalent but they can drive Category B vehicles in Great Britain on such licences (or on an International Driving Permit) for up to one year.

All foreign licence holders who for various reasons cannot obtain an exchange licence or who wish to drive vehicles which their national licence does not cover must apply for provisional entitlement in the normal way using form D1.

Full GB driving licences can only be issued to foreign nationals who become normally resident in Great Britain.

Visitors Driving in the UK

Visitors to the UK may drive vehicles in the UK provided they hold a domestic driving licence issued in their own country (ie outside the UK and the EU) or a Convention Driving Permit (issued under the 1949 Geneva Convention on Road Traffic by a country outside the UK). Holders of such permits are entitled to drive vehicles of a class which their own national or international licence covers for a period of 12 months from the date of their entry into the UK.

Driving While Tired

Drivers must be encouraged to *stop* when they feel tired, whether during the night-time hours or during daytime, and rest for a short while, no matter what the pressures of the job or the particular journey in which they are engaged. Employers have responsibilities under health and safety legislation to assess such potential risks and take proper action to eliminate them. (The *Highway Code* recommends that car drivers stop for a short break after every two hours of driving.)

Think! – Driving Tiredness Campaign

Since tiredness has been established as the principal factor in around 10 per cent of all accidents the D*f*T made obstructive sleep apnea syndrome (OSAS) a notifiable condition and launched a Think! campaign to combat tiredness among both car and vocational drivers. The main points for drivers to observe are that they should:

- Make sure they are fit to drive, particularly before undertaking any long journeys (over an hour) – avoid such journeys in the morning without a good night's sleep or in the evening after a full day's work.
- Avoid undertaking long journeys between midnight and 6 am, when natural alertness is at a minimum.
- Plan their journey to take sufficient breaks. A minimum break of at least 15 minutes after every two hours' driving is advised.

- If they feel at all sleepy, stop in a safe place and either take a nap for not more than 15 minutes, or drink two cups of strong coffee.

Advice on taking regular breaks and not driving whilst tired is also regularly featured on information boards alongside motorways.

NB: Think! was expanded in 2016 and is now responsible for many of the drink-drive and general road safety campaigns, advertisements and posters seen in and around the UK.

Driving Licence Penalty Points and Disqualification

In some circumstances, driving licence penalty points can be completely avoided if a driver agrees to attend a corrective 'workshop' where re-training and training is given in an attempt to prevent any re-occurrence of a similar contravention of the rules. Currently, 'speed awareness workshops' and 'seat belt awareness workshops' are offered to some drivers. This offer is dependent upon the nature of the offence and serious contraventions will not normally be eligible for this concession. The price for these workshops varies but is approximately £100 for speed awareness and £40 for seat belt awareness. The speed awareness workshop requires the driver to attend a formal group workshop whilst the seat belt awareness workshop can be undertaken online. The seat belt awareness workshop is an internet-based workshop which requires delegates to take, and pass, an assessment on completion.

In other cases, driving licence holders may be penalized following conviction by a court for offences committed on the road with a motor vehicle. These penalties range from the issue of fixed penalty notices for non-endorsable offences, which do not require a court appearance unless the charge is to be contested, and incur no driving licence penalty points, although the relevant fixed penalty has to be paid; to those for endorsable offences when penalty points are added on the licence and the fixed penalty is incurred or a heavy fine imposed on conviction if a court appearance is made.

Licence disqualification for a period (extending to a number of years in serious cases) may also be an option – especially for drink-driving-related offences, and in very serious instances imprisonment of the offender may follow conviction in a magistrate's court or indictment for the offence in a higher court. Holders of vocational driving entitlements may be separately penalized for relevant offences which could result in such entitlements being suspended or revoked and in serious circumstances the holder being disqualified from holding a vocational entitlement – see below.

The Graduated Fixed Penalty Scheme

The Graduated Fixed Penalty Scheme relates to a 'sliding scale' of penalties for breaches of regulations by commercial vehicles. It especially focuses on areas such as drivers' hours and tachograph infringements, loading and overloading, and road-worthiness. It allows DVSA officials and police officers to vary the fixed penalty levied in relation to the seriousness of the incident. It also allows the enforcement authorities to secure a financial guarantee of payment from foreign drivers who cannot supply a reliable address within the UK.

Fixed penalties can range from £50 to £300 and be non-endorsable or endorsable with £100 and £200 fines also carrying three penalty points. This 'flexibility' allows the enforcement authorities to make allowances for minor infringements without having to treat each case using 'the full weight of the law'. Further information can be found by downloading the DVSA Guide to Graduated Fixed Penalties and Financial Deposits from the DVSA website.

The Penalty Points System on Conviction and Disqualification

Driving licence endorsement of penalty points following conviction for motoring offences is prescribed by the Road Traffic Offenders Act 1988 with further provisions relating to driving offences being contained in the Road Traffic Act 1991 – see list below.

The penalty points system grades road traffic offences according to their seriousness by a number or range of penalty points, between 2 and 11, imposed on the driving licence of the convicted offender. Once a maximum of 12 penalty points has been accumulated within a three-year period counting from the date of the first offence to the current offence (not from the date of conviction), disqualification of the licence for at least six months will normally follow automatically (see below).

Most offences rate a fixed number of penalty points to ensure consistency and to simplify the administration; but a discretionary range applies to a few offences where the gravity may vary considerably from one case to another. For example, failing to stop after an accident which only involved minor vehicle damage is obviously less serious than a case where an accident results in injury.

Unless the court decides otherwise, when a driver is convicted of more than one offence at the same hearing, only the points relative to the most serious of the offences will normally be endorsed on the licence. Once sufficient points (ie 12) have been endorsed on the driving licence and a period of disqualification has been imposed (six months for the first totting-up of points), the driver will have his 'slate' wiped clean and those points will not be counted again. Twelve more points would have to be accumulated before a further disqualification would follow, but to discourage repeated offences the courts will impose progressively longer disqualification periods in further instances (minimum 12 months for subsequent disqualifications within three years and 24 months for a third disqualification within three years).

Legislation (October 2015) allows DVSA enforcement officers to issue fixed penalty notices for 'historic' offences. This means that offences and infringements detected within the last 28 days can now be used to form a prosecution if a prosecution is to be brought for an offence being committed at the time the vehicle was stopped. The main reason for this change was to enable the DVSA to prosecute non-UK drivers at the roadside for offences committed whilst in the UK, a power which it previously did not have.

It is also important to note that following some tragic road accidents and a general lack of regard for other road users, drivers caught using a mobile phone whilst driving now receive a fine of £200 (maximum £1,000) and get six penalty points on their licence. LGV drivers also receive six penalty points and a £200 fine but the maximum fine for them is £2,500. In addition the Senior TC has issued guidance that LGV drivers should have their vocational entitlement suspended, with immediate effect, for 21 days for a first offence, 2 × 21 days for a second offence and 3 × 21 days for a third offence.

Licence Endorsement Codes and Penalty Points

Following conviction for an offence, the driver's licence record will be endorsed by the convicting court with both a code (to which employers and prospective employers should refer, with the driver's permission, so they can assess the offences which drivers have committed) and the number of penalty points imposed as follows:

Code		Penalty points
	Accident offences	
AC 10	Failing to stop after an accident	5–10
AC 20	Failing to report an accident within 24 hours	5–10
AC 30	Undefined accident offence	4–9
	Disqualified driver	
BA 10	Driving while disqualified	6
BA 30	Attempting to drive while disqualified	6
BA 40	Causing death by driving whilst disqualified	3–11
BA 60	Causing serious injury by driving whilst disqualified	3–11
	Careless driving	
CD 10	Driving without due care and attention	3–9
CD 20	Driving without reasonable consideration for other road users	3–9
CD 30	Driving without due care and attention or without reasonable consideration for other road users	3–9
CD 40	Causing death through careless driving when unfit through drink	3–11
CD 50	Causing death by careless driving when unfit through drugs	3–11
CD 60	Causing death by careless driving with alcohol level above the limit	3–11
CD 70	Causing death by careless driving then failing to supply a specimen	3–11
CD 80	Causing death by careless, or inconsiderate, driving	3–11
CD 90	Causing death by driving: unlicensed, disqualified or uninsured drivers	3–11

Code		Penalty points
	Construction and use offences	
CU 10	Using a vehicle with defective brakes	3
CU 20	Causing or likely to cause danger by reason of unsuitable vehicle or using a vehicle with parts or accessories (excluding brakes, steering or tyres) in a dangerous condition	3
CU 30	Using a vehicle with defective tyre(s)	3
CU 40	Using a vehicle with defective steering	3
CU 50	Causing or likely to cause danger by reason of load or passengers	3
CU 80	Breach of the requirements as to control of the vehicle, mobile phone etc	3
	Reckless/dangerous driving	
DD 10	Causing serious injury by dangerous driving	3–11
DD 40	Dangerous driving	3–11
DD 60	Manslaughter or culpable homicide while driving a vehicle	3–11
DD 80	Causing death by dangerous driving	3–11
DD 90	Furious driving	3–9
	Drink or drugs	
DG 40	In charge of a vehicle while drug level above specified limits	10
DG 60	Causing death by careless driving with drug level above the limit	3–11
DR 10	Driving or attempting to drive with alcohol level above limit	3–11
DR 20	Driving or attempting to drive while unfit through drink	3–11
DR 30	Driving or attempting to drive then failing to supply a specimen for analysis	3–11
DR 40	In charge of a vehicle while alcohol level above limit	10
DR 50	In charge of a vehicle while unfit through drink	10
DR 60	Failure to provide a specimen for analysis in circumstances other than driving or attempting to drive	10
DR 70	Failing to provide a specimen for breath test	4
DR 80	Driving or attempting to drive when unfit through drugs	3–11
DR 90	In charge of a vehicle when unfit through drugs	10
	Insurance offences	
IN 10	Using a vehicle uninsured against third-party risks	6–8

Code		Penalty points
	Licence offences	
LC 20	Driving otherwise than in accordance with a licence	3–6
LC 30	Driving after making a false declaration about fitness when applying for a licence	3–6
LC 40	Driving a vehicle having failed to notify a disability	3–6
LC 50	Driving after a licence has been revoked or refused on medical grounds	3–6
	Miscellaneous offences	
MS 10	Leaving a vehicle in a dangerous position	3
MS 20	Unlawful pillion riding	3
MS 30	Contravention of the Road Traffic Regulations provisions on street playgrounds	2
MS 50	Motor racing on the highway	3–11
MS 60	Offences not covered by other codes as appropriate	–
MS 70	Driving with uncorrected defective eyesight	3
MS 80	Refusing to submit to an eyesight test	3
MS 90	Failure to give information as to identity of driver, etc	3
	Motorway offences	
MW 10	Contravention of Special Roads Regulations (excl speed limits)	3
	Pedestrian crossings	
PC 10	Undefined contravention of Pedestrian Crossing Regulations	3
PC 20	Contravention of Pedestrian Crossing Regulations with moving vehicle	3
PC 30	Contravention of Pedestrian Crossing Regulations with stationary vehicle	3
	Provisional licence offences	
PL 10	Driving without 'L' plates	3–6
PL 20	Not accompanied by a qualified person	3–6
PL 30	Carrying a person not qualified	3–6
PL 40	Drawing an unauthorized trailer	3–6
PL 50	Undefined failure to comply with conditions of a provisional licence	3–6
	Speed limits	
SP 10	Exceeding goods vehicle speed limits	3–6
SP 20	Exceeding speed limit for type of vehicle (excluding goods or passenger vehicles)	3–6

Code		Penalty points
SP 30	Exceeding statutory speed limit on a public road	3–6
SP 40	Exceeding passenger vehicle speed limit	3–6
SP 50	Exceeding speed limit on a motorway	3–6
SP 60	Undefined speed limit offence *NB: Disqualification is obligatory where the relevant speed is in excess of 30 mph over the statutory limit.*	3–6
	Traffic directions and signs	
TS 10	Failing to comply with traffic light signals	3
TS 20	Failing to comply with double white lines	3
TS 30	Failing to comply with a 'Stop' sign	3
TS 40	Failing to comply with direction of a constable or traffic warden	3
TS 50	Failing to comply with a traffic sign (excluding 'Stop' signs, traffic lights or double white lines)	3
TS 60	Failing to comply with a school crossing patrol sign	3
TS 70	Undefined failure to comply with a traffic direction or sign	3
	Special code	
TT 99	To signify a disqualification under 'totting up' procedure. If the total of penalty points reaches 12 or more within three years, the driver is liable to be disqualified	
	Theft or unauthorized taking	
UT 50	Aggravated taking of a vehicle	3–11

NB: These codes relate to the driver only and do not take account of any subsequent effect the offence may have on the Operator Compliance Risk Score (OCRS) in cases such as vehicles with defective brakes, steering or tyres.

Where the offence is one of aiding or abetting, causing or permitting or inciting, the codes are modified as follows:

Aiding, Abetting, Counselling or Procuring

Offences as coded, but with zero changed to 2, eg UT 50 becomes UT 52.

Causing or Permitting

Offences as coded, but with zero changed to 4, eg LC 20 becomes LC 24.

Inciting

Offences as coded, but with zero changed to 6, eg DD 40 becomes DD 46. The length of time for periods of disqualification is shown by use of the letters D = days, M = months and Y = years. Consecutive periods of disqualification are signified by an asterisk (*) against the time period. The symbol + means that 3 to 11 points are added to a licence if for exceptional reasons disqualification is not imposed.

Disqualification

The endorsing of penalty points will also arise on conviction for offences where disqualification is discretionary and where the court has decided that immediate disqualification is not appropriate (for example if acceptable 'exceptional' reasons are put forward – see also below). In this case the offender's driving licence will be endorsed with four points. The courts are still free to disqualify immediately if the circumstances justify this.

Offences carrying obligatory disqualification are shown in the following list:

- causing death by dangerous driving and manslaughter;
- dangerous driving within three years of a similar conviction;
- driving or attempting to drive while unfit through drink or drugs;
- driving or attempting to drive with more than the permitted breath-alcohol level;
- failure to provide a breath, blood or urine specimen;
- racing on the highway.

Driving while disqualified is a serious offence which can result in a fine at level 5 on the standard scale (see below), currently £5,000 maximum, or six months' imprisonment, or both.

Special Reasons for Non-Disqualification

The courts have discretion in exceptional mitigating circumstances (ie when there are 'special reasons') not to impose a disqualification. The mitigating circumstance must not be one which attempts to make the offence appear less serious and no account will be taken of hardship other than exceptional hardship. Pleading that you have a wife and children to support or that you will lose your job is not generally considered to be exceptional hardship for the purposes of determining whether or not disqualification should be imposed.

If account has previously been taken of circumstances in mitigation of a disqualification, the same circumstances cannot be considered again within three years.

Where a court decides, in exceptional circumstances as described above, not to disqualify a convicted driver, 3 to 11 penalty points will be added to the driver's licence in lieu of the disqualification.

Driving Offences

Dangerous Driving

A person is to be regarded as driving dangerously if the way he drives 'falls far short of what would be expected of a competent and careful driver, and it would be obvious to a competent and careful driver that driving in that way would be dangerous'. Driving would be regarded as dangerous 'if it was obvious to a competent and careful driver that driving the vehicle in its current state would be dangerous' – this obviously applies to the vehicle's mechanical condition or the way it is loaded. Also, 'dangerous' refers to danger either of injury to any person or of serious damage to property. The principal offences to which this relates are dangerous driving and causing death by dangerous driving. The offence of causing serious injury by dangerous driving was introduced in 2012.

Interfering with Vehicles, etc

It is an offence for any person to cause danger to road users by way of intentionally and without lawful authority placing objects on a road, interfering with motor vehicles, or directly or indirectly interfering with traffic equipment (eg road signs, etc).

Penalties

Penalties for these offences are heavy. For example, causing death by careless driving while under the influence of drink or drugs carries a maximum penalty of up to five years in prison and/or a fine. For causing a danger to road users the maximum penalty is up to seven years' imprisonment and/or a fine.

In addition to disqualification and the endorsement of penalty points on driving licences, courts may impose fines and, for certain offences, imprisonment. The maximum fine for most offences is determined by reference to a scale set out in the Criminal Justice Act 1991 as follows:

Level 1	£200
Level 2	£500
Level 3	£1,000
Level 4	£2,500
Level 5	Unlimited

Serious offences such as dangerous driving, failing to stop after an accident or failure to report an accident, and drink-driving offences, carry the current maximum fine which used to be £5,000 but is now unlimited, as do certain vehicle construction and use offences (eg overloading, insecure loads, using a vehicle in a dangerous condition, etc) and using a vehicle without insurance.

Under provisions included in the Criminal Justice Act 2003, the maximum penalty for the offence of causing death by dangerous driving was increased from a 10-year prison sentence to 14 years. This measure was taken, according to the then Home Secretary, to ensure that drivers who kill can be 'properly punished'.

Driver Penalties for New Drivers

The Road Traffic (New Drivers) Act 1995 concerns new drivers who first passed their driving test on or after 1 June 1997. Where such drivers acquire six or more penalty points on their licence within two years of passing that test (the so-called 'probationary period') the DVLA will automatically revoke the licence on notification by a court or fixed penalty offence. Such drivers have to surrender their full licence and obtain a provisional licence to start driving again as a learner. They will have to pass both the theory and practical tests again in order to regain their full driving licence.

Penalty points counting towards the total of six include any incurred before passing the test, if this was not more than three years before the latest penalty point offence. Points imposed after the probationary period will also count if the offence was committed during that period.

Passing the re-test will not remove the penalty points from the licence; these will remain and if the total reaches 12, the driver will be liable to disqualification by a court.

Removal of Penalty Points and Disqualifications

Since the abolition of the paper counterpart driving licence, penalty points endorsed on driving licences are removed automatically when they expire, free of charge. However, it may be that drivers should check with the DVLA on the 'view-driving-licence' system, mentioned earlier, in order to confirm the removal.

The waiting period for removal is four years from the date of the offence, except in the case of reckless/dangerous driving convictions when the four years is taken from the date of conviction. Endorsements for alcohol-related and drug-related offences must remain on a licence for 11 years.

Application may be made by disqualified drivers for reinstatement of their licence after varying periods of time depending on the duration of the disqualifying period as follows:

- less than two years – no prior application time;
- less than four years – after two years have elapsed;
- between four years and 10 years – after half the time has elapsed;
- in other cases – after five years have elapsed.

The courts are empowered to require a disqualified driver to retake the driving test before restoring a driving licence, and following the introduction of provisions contained in the Road Traffic Act 1991 it is now mandatory for them to impose 'extended' re-tests following disqualification for the most serious of driving offences, namely, dangerous driving, causing death by dangerous driving and manslaughter by the driver of a motor vehicle (in Scotland, the charge is culpable homicide).

The fee charged for replacement licences following disqualification under the New Drivers Act is £50.00. For other disqualifications the cost is £65.00, but where the disqualification was for drink-driving-type offences the fee for a replacement is £90.00.

NB: These fees have been held for some years but they are expected to change as part of the phased review being undertaken by the DVLA.

Re-tests for Offending Drivers

Where drivers are convicted of the offences of manslaughter, causing death by dangerous driving, or dangerous driving, and mandatory disqualification is imposed, an 'extended' re-test (involving at least one hour's driving) must be taken before the driving licence is restored. This also applies to drivers disqualified under the penalty points totting-up procedure. Courts may also order drivers disqualified for lesser offences to take an appropriate (ie ordinary) driving test.

Drink-Driving and Breath Tests

It is an offence to drive or attempt to drive a motor vehicle when the level of alcohol in the breath is more than 35 micrograms per 100 millilitres of breath. This is determined by means of an initial breath test, conducted on the spot when the driver is stopped, and later substantiated by a test on a breath-testing machine (eg Lion Intoximeter) at a police station. The breath/alcohol limit mentioned above equates to the blood/alcohol limit of 80 milligrams of alcohol in 100 millilitres of blood or the urine/alcohol limit of 107 milligrams of alcohol in 100 millilitres of urine.

NB: Under legislation approved in 2014, a reduced drink-drive limit has been in force in Scotland from 5 December 2014. This means that the blood alcohol limit in Scotland has been reduced from 80 mg in every 100 ml of blood, to 50 mg in every 100 ml of blood, bringing Scotland into line with most other European countries.

Failure to Produce a Breath Sample and Low Breath-Test Readings

If those suspected of an alcohol-related offence cannot, due to health reasons, produce a breath sample, or if a breath test shows a reading of not more than 50 micrograms of alcohol per 100 millilitres of breath, they are given the opportunity of an alternative test, either blood or urine, for laboratory analysis. This test can only be carried out at a police station or a hospital and the decision as to which alternative is chosen rests with the police (unless a doctor present determines that for medical reasons a blood test cannot or should not be taken). Similarly, if a breath test of a driver shows the proportion of alcohol to be no more than 50 micrograms in 100 millilitres of breath, the driver can request an alternative test (ie blood or urine) as described above for those who cannot provide a breath sample for analysis.

A House of Lords ruling says that a driver recording a breath sample that does not exceed 50 micrograms in 100 millilitres of breath must be given a police statement to this effect.

Prosecution for Drink-Driving Offences

Prosecution will follow a failure to pass the test, which will result in a fine or imprisonment and automatic disqualification from driving. Failure to submit to a breath test and to a blood or urine test are serious offences, and drivers will find themselves liable to heavy penalties on conviction and potentially long-term disqualification or driving licence endorsement (endorsements for such offences remain on a driving licence for 11 years).

The police *do not have* powers to carry out breath tests at random but they *do have* powers to enter premises to require a breath test from a person suspected of driving while impaired through drink or drugs, or who has been driving, or been in charge of a vehicle which has been involved in an accident in which another person has been injured.

In a highly publicized case in 1991, charges against an LGV driver breathalysed by police having been woken from sleep on the sleeper berth of his vehicle cab (and with his tachograph set to record rest) were dismissed by the court. Although presumably over the statutory limit (otherwise no charge would have been brought), the driver was clearly making no attempt to drive his vehicle and the vehicle was parked in a proper (ie non-public) place. Since the court dismissed the case there was no opportunity to obtain a ruling from a higher court as to the precise legal position of drivers in such circumstances. It is considered that drinking and then sleeping in a vehicle cab does not present risk of prosecution for drivers providing the vehicle is properly parked.

Note: Whilst 'drink-driving' must never be condoned, as 'being at the controls of the vehicle with the ignition keys in' has been interpreted as 'driving' (as in cases of mobile phone use) then it follows that a driver who may be drinking alcohol and/or exceed the drink-drive limits should never sit in the driving seat of a vehicle cab without properly securing the vehicle and removing the keys from the ignition.

This scenario does seem at some odds with other circumstances. For instance, if 'sitting in the driver's seat with the keys in' is termed driving then surely if a driver is in a vehicle with the keys in and parked in a restricted area they cannot be prosecuted for illegal parking as they must be driving! (This may be logical but not practicable.)

Drink-Driving Disqualification

Conviction for a first drink-driving offence will result in a minimum one-year period of disqualification and for a second or subsequent offence of driving or attempting to drive under the influence of drink or drugs longer periods of disqualification will be imposed by the court. If the previous such conviction took place within 10 years of the current offence the disqualification must be for at least three years.

Drivers convicted twice for drink-driving offences may have their driving licence revoked altogether. Offenders who are disqualified twice within a 10-year period for any drink-driving offences and those found to have an exceptionally high level of alcohol in the body (ie more than 2½ times over the limit) or those who twice refuse to provide a specimen will be classified as high-risk offenders (HROs) by the DVLA. They will be required to show that they no longer have an 'alcohol problem' by means of a medical examination (including blood analysis of liver enzymes) by a DVLA-approved doctor before their licence will be restored to them. A higher than normal fee (ie £90) will be charged for the renewal of such licences.

Drink-Driving Courses

The Road Traffic Act 1991 contained provisions whereby certain (but not all) drink-driving offenders may have the period of their disqualification reduced if they agree to undertake an approved rehabilitation course and satisfactorily complete it. The provision applies only where the court orders the individual (who must be over 17 years of age) to be disqualified for at least 12 months following conviction under the Road Traffic Act 1988 for:

- causing death by careless driving when under the influence of drink or drugs;
- driving or being in charge of a motor vehicle when under the influence of drink or drugs;
- driving or being in charge of a motor vehicle with excess alcohol in the body; or
- failing to provide a specimen (of breath, blood or urine) as required.

The court has a duty to ensure that a place on an approved course is available for the offender. It must explain to the offender 'in ordinary language' the effect of the order (to reduce the disqualification period), the amount of the fees and that these must be paid in advance and it must seek the offender's agreement that the order should be made – in other words, it is a completely voluntary scheme and there is no question of force.

Given these provisos, the court can order the period of disqualification to be reduced by not less than three months and not more than one-quarter of the unreduced period (for example, with a 12-month disqualification, the reduction will be three months, leaving a nine-month disqualification period to be served).

The latest date for completion of one of these rehabilitation courses is two months prior to the last day of the reduced disqualification period (so, in the nine-month example given above, the course would have to be completed by the last day of the seventh month). On completion of the course the offender is given a certificate which must be returned to the clerk of the supervising court (named in the order) in order to secure the reduction. Failure to complete the course or to produce the certificate on time will result in the loss of this facility.

A number of approved courses have been established around the country (with fees of between £150 and £200 with a legally set limit of £250 being in force). These require attendance for at least 16 hours, which is normally spread over three days, over three weeks. There are additional fees if the candidate arrives late, misses a session, changes dates, etc. The course is made up of a number of separate sessions, during which the offender will learn about the effects of alcohol on the body and on driving performance and behaviour, about drink-driving offences, and about the alternatives to drinking and driving. A range of relevant advice will also be given. (Courses in Wales and Northern Ireland vary slightly but details are available on the GOV.UK website.)

Drug-Driving Code of Practice

A Code of Practice has been established to tackle the dangers caused by drivers under the influence of drugs. This includes prescription drugs and medicines as well as illegal drugs. The Code requires suspected drivers to submit to a roadside impairment test by the police. This test will be carried out in accordance with the Code and will include the 'field impairment assessment'. Refusal to participate in the test will render a driver liable to the same penalty as refusal to undertake a breath test. This testing is in addition to the new drug testing equipment used by police traffic patrols at roadside checks and now carried in some police vehicles.

It should be noted that drug tests that indicate excessive use of prescription drugs are included in the overall drug testing scheme and the driver may be required to produce the prescription in order to prove that he has not exceeded a prescribed limit.

Penalties against Vocational Entitlements

Where a licence holder is disqualified from driving following conviction for offences committed with cars or other light vehicles, or as a result of penalty point totting-up, any vocational entitlement which that person holds is automatically lost until the licence is reinstated. Additionally, the holder of any vocational entitlement may have this revoked or suspended by the DVLA without reference to the TC – see below – and be disqualified from holding such entitlement, for a fixed or an indefinite period, at any time on the grounds of misconduct or physical disability. Furthermore, a person can be refused a new vocational driving entitlement following licence revocation, again either indefinitely or for some other period of time which the Secretary of State (ie via the DVLA) specifies. A new vocational test may be ordered before the entitlement is restored – see further below.

Disqualification from holding a vocational entitlement as described above does not prevent a licence holder from continuing to drive vehicles within the category B entitlement that he holds.

The TCs continue to play a disciplinary role under the new licensing scheme in regard to driver conduct, but only at the request of the DVLA. They have powers under the new provisions to call drivers to public inquiry (PI) to give information and answer questions as to their conduct. Their duty is to report back to the DVLA if they consider that a vocational entitlement should be revoked or the holder disqualified from holding an entitlement. The DVLA must follow the TCs' recommendation in these matters.

Failure to attend a PI when requested to do so (unless a reasonable excuse is given) means that the DVLA will automatically refuse a new vocational entitlement or suspend or revoke an existing entitlement.

Rules on disciplining vocational entitlement holders require TCs to follow a set of recommended guidelines in imposing penalties against such entitlements. Under these rules, and where there are no aggravating circumstances, a driver being disqualified for 12 months or less should be sent a warning letter, with no further disqualification of the vocational entitlement. Where a driving disqualification is for more than one year, offenders should be called to appear before the TC and should incur an additional suspension of their vocational entitlement, amounting to between one month and three months. The intention here is to allow them to regain their driving skills and road sense in a car before driving a heavy vehicle again. Where two or more driving disqualifications of more than eight weeks have been incurred within the past five years, and the combined total of disqualification exceeds 12 months, the driver should be called to PI and a further period of vocational driving disqualification imposed amounting to between three and six months.

In the case of new vocational entitlements, for applicants who already have nine or more penalty points on their ordinary licence, the guidelines recommend that the TC should issue a warning as to future conduct or suggest that the applicant tries again when the penalty points total on his licence has been reduced.

Removal of Vocational Driving Licence Disqualification

Drivers disqualified from holding a vocational entitlement, as described above, may apply to have the disqualification removed after two years if it was for less than four years, or after half the period if the disqualification was for more than four years but less than 10 years. In any other case including disqualification for an indefinite period an application for its removal cannot be made until five years have elapsed. If an application for the removal of a disqualification fails another application cannot be made for three months.

The DVLA will not necessarily readily restore vocational driving entitlements on application following disqualification of a driving licence. An applicant may be called to PI by a TC, who will inquire into the events which led to the disqualification and at which he may also decide that the applicant must wait a further period before applying again, must spend a period driving small (ie up to 3.5 or 7.5 tonnes) vehicles or must take a new vocational driving test in order to regain the vocational entitlement.

Appeals

If the DVLA refuses to grant an application for a vocational driving entitlement or revokes, suspends or limits an existing entitlement, the applicant or entitlement holder may appeal against the decision under the Road Traffic Act 1988. The first step is for them to notify the DVLA, and any TC involved in consideration of the applicant's conduct, of their intention to appeal. The appeal can then be made to a magistrate's court in England or Wales within six months of the DVLA decision, or in Scotland to the local sheriff's court, within 21 days of the DVLA decision. However, the revocation will remain in force pending the outcome of the appeal.

Driver Testing and Training

07

This chapter deals with the legal requirements for driving tests, including the IAM 'RoadSmart', RTITB training for the use of lorry loaders, LGV Apprenticeships and training for the carriage of dangerous goods.

Driving Tests

The main purpose of driver testing is to ensure that all drivers taking a vehicle on the road:

- are safe and competent to do so;
- know the rules of the road and the significance of traffic signs and signals; and
- appreciate the dangers arising from moving vehicles.

NB: During 2016, the DVSA carried out trials of a revised driving test for car drivers at 32 different centres across the UK. These trials, which involved over 4,300 learner drivers and over 860 driving instructors, are now complete and changes were intro duced on 4 December 2017. It is expected that further changes to the driving test will be made when the effects of Brexit highlight a need for new, or different, skills.

The four major 2017 changes are outlined below:

1. The independent driving part of the test that lasted around 10 minutes was increased to 20 minutes and the driver on test has to drive without turn-by-turn directions from the driving examiner.
2. During the independent driving part of the test, most candidates are asked to follow directions using a sat nav. The sat nav is set up by the examiner. The driver on test must use the sat nav supplied by the examiner and cannot use their own. However, approximately one in five examinations will not use a sat nav. In these cases, the driver on test needs to follow given traffic signs instead.
3. The 'reverse around a corner' and 'turn-in-the-road' (three point turn') manoeuvres were no longer included in the test although learner drivers

should still be taught them. In the 2017 test, drivers on test are asked to do one of three possible reversing manoeuvres. These are:

- parallel parking at the side of the road;
- parking in a bay – either driving in and reversing out, or reversing in and driving out;
- pulling up on the right-hand side of the road, reversing for two car lengths and rejoining the traffic.

4 The examiner now asks two vehicle safety questions during the test – (these are known as the 'show me, tell me' questions).

Typically the driver on test is asked:

- a 'tell me' question (where the driver needs to explain how they would carry out a safety task) at the start of their test;
- a 'show me' question (where the driver needs to carry out a safety task) whilst driving such as washing the windscreen or demisting the rear screen, etc using the controls on the vehicle.

The DVSA have made these changes in response to the fact that over a quarter of deaths from road collisions involve young people aged 15–19 and because over 50 per cent of car drivers now have a sat nav. In spite of the changes the new test still takes around 40 minutes.

Note: The changes above apply to tests in England, Scotland and Wales only. In Northern Ireland the system is different and details can be found by visiting the GOV.UK website and typing in 'Driving Test Changes: 4 December 2017' and following the link.

Driver testing procedures following the requirements of the EU's 'second driver' licensing Directive were originally introduced into the UK for car and light vehicle drivers from 1 July 1996 and from 1 January 1997 for large goods and passenger vehicle drivers – including car and LGV theory tests. These were followed by the 'third' Directive which came into force on 19 January 2013 which standardized driving licence formats across the EU and made the category expiry dates more clearly defined. It also brought in changes to medical procedures for drivers gaining vocational entitlements since that date.

The main objective of the vocational test remains, which is to ensure that goods and passenger vehicle drivers are competent to drive large vehicles on the roads in safety. It also provides a measure of professionalism among commercial vehicle drivers. The test is more comprehensive and more complex than the ordinary (ie car and light goods) driving test and, consequently, demands greater skill and knowledge from the driver who wishes to pass.

Proof of Identity

Candidates for both ordinary and vocational (ie C1, D1, C1E, D1E, LGV and PCV) driving tests must produce satisfactory photographic evidence of identity when arriving for a test. Acceptable identity documents for this purpose include existing driving licences (ordinary, vocational or an overseas driving licence), a passport or an employer-issued identity card bearing the holder's name, signature and photograph. If a test candidate cannot produce satisfactory means of identification the test will not be conducted and the fee forfeited.

This measure is necessary to combat a rising incidence of persons with false identities taking multiple driving tests on behalf of others who cannot themselves pass the test, but are prepared to pay large sums to acquire a test pass certificate.

Ordinary Driving Test

Before persons can be granted a licence to drive a motor vehicle on the road they must pass both a written theory test, which includes a hazard perception test, and a practical driving test on the class of vehicle for which they require the licence. For a car licence (Category B) a provisional licence needs to be applied for using Form D1 available from post offices or online at www.gov.uk/apply-first-provisional-driving-licence (archived at https://perma.cc/6BL5-CA49). For a provisional vocational licence a vocational licence form D2 is used and the hazard perception element of theory testing can be taken at a different time from the pure theory element of the test. An entitlement to drive will not be gained until both parts of the test are passed – the theory test having to be passed before the practical driving test can be taken.

NB: Theory and practical driving tests must now be taken in English and not by using the services of a translator. This change was felt necessary following several incidents and prosecutions relating to fraudulent practices by some translators.

The Theory and Hazard Perception Tests

Driving test candidates must take and pass a 'touch screen' theory test and a hazard perception test – which replaces the old, verbal, questioning to test the candidate's knowledge of the *Highway Code* – carried out on behalf of the Driving and Vehicle Services Agency (DVSA – an Executive Agency of the D*f*T) at a network of practical test centres across Britain.

The test, which was revised in 2018 in order to use plain English and to make the options and answer clearer, comprises 50 multiple-choice questions of which the candidate must get at least 43 correct to achieve a pass certificate. The questions concern such matters as driver attitude, traffic signs and regulations, the effects of alcohol and drugs, driver fatigue and safety, and environmental aspects of vehicles. All these topics are covered in the *Highway Code* and the DVSA's *Driving Goods Vehicles: The Official DVSA Syllabus*. The DVSA has also published *The Official Theory Test for Drivers of Large Vehicles*, which explains the test and lists the 900-odd bank of questions from which test papers are set, together with the correct answers. All these publications are available from The Stationery Office or main booksellers. It should be noted that there are constant updates to the Highway Code, with, for instance, information on 'hard shoulder' driving on motorways being added in 2019.

The theory test is an online test offered by many companies and organizations, with the questions appearing on screen, which the candidate has only to touch to indicate the correct answer. This system makes the test more accessible to the general public, and is particularly helpful for people with special needs. Candidates are advised of the result of their theory test immediately.

Online versions of sample theory test questions can be found at: www.gov.uk/practise-your-driving-theory-test (archived at https://perma.cc/YA59-B6LD).

The hazard perception part is also computerized, and the candidate responds by clicking a button on the mouse. There are 14 separate video clips featuring everyday road scenes and in each one there will be at least one developing hazard – one of the clips features two such hazards. To achieve a high score the candidate must respond to the hazards quickly; the maximum score on each is five. The pass mark for the car hazard perception test is 44 out of 75.

Practical Driving Tests

The practical driving test (lasting approximately 38–40 minutes) is carried out by examiners from the DVSA. Candidates must present a theory test pass certificate – practical driving tests will not be carried out without the candidate having first passed the theory test.

Test candidates have to meet the following requirements:

- They must show that they are fully conversant with the contents of the *Highway Code*.
- They must prove that they are able to read in good daylight (with the aid of spectacles, if worn) a motor vehicle's registration number in accordance with the vision requirements (see p 195).
- They must show that they are competent to drive without danger to and with due consideration of other users of the road, including being able to:
  - start the engine of the vehicle;
  - move away straight ahead or at an angle;
  - overtake, meet or cross the path of other vehicles and take an appropriate course;
  - turn right-hand and left-hand corners correctly;
  - stop the vehicle in an emergency and in a normal situation, and in the latter case bring it to rest at an appropriate part of the road;
  - answer two safety questions;
  - drive independently for about 20 minutes;
  - follow directions using a sat nav (4 out of 5 drivers only);
  - carry out a reverse parking manoeuvre which involves stopping the vehicle next to and parallel with a parked vehicle, then reversing to position and park the vehicle in front of or behind the other vehicle, level with and reasonably close to the kerb, and/or parking in a bay and/or parking on the left and the right side of the road*;
  - indicate their intended actions at appropriate times by giving appropriate signals in a clear and unmistakable manner (in the case of a left-hand-drive vehicle or a disabled driver for whom it is impracticable or undesirable to give hand signals there is no requirement to provide any signals other than mechanical ones);

- act correctly and promptly on all signals given by traffic signs and traffic controllers and take appropriate action on signs given by other road users.

** In December 2017, the 'three point turn' and 'reversing round a corner' were taken out of the test (see earlier).*

The driving test may be terminated in the event of a serious driving error which jeopardizes public safety.

Cars used for the ordinary (ie category B) driving test must be fitted with a seat belt and a head restraint for the front seat passenger and an additional rear view mirror for use by the examiner.

Candidates who fail the driving test are given an oral explanation of the reasons for their failure.

Extended Driving Tests

Since 6 January 1992 the courts have been vested with powers to impose an extended driving test on any person who has been convicted of dangerous driving offences, or convicted of other offences involving obligatory disqualification.

Loss of a driving licence for dangerous driving or related offences involving obligatory disqualification means that the licence holder returns to 'learner' status and has to conform to the normal rules applicable to provisional licence holders. This also applies to new drivers who incur six penalty points within two years of passing the driving test.

In these cases, a theory test must be taken and passed for the category of vehicle on which the extended practical driving test is to be taken. There are currently two schemes of re-testing: an ordinary re-test, and an extended re-test. This extended driving test is longer and therefore more demanding than the normal, lasting for about 70 minutes and covering a wide variety of roads, usually including dual carriageways. Candidates for the extended re-test are advised to prepare by taking suitable instruction from an Approved Driving Instructor (ADI). The higher fee (as indicated below) reflects the length of the test.

Drivers, especially new drivers, incurring penalty points can also take re-training under the 2Pass scheme to reinforce the required standards to help prevent further penalty points being amassed.

The purpose of re-testing is not intended to be punitive; rather it is a road safety measure, designed to recheck the driver's competence.

Driving Test Fees

The fee for an ordinary driving test (conducted on weekdays up to 4.30 pm) is £62.00, or £75.00 if conducted on a weekday evening or on a Saturday. The extended test for a disqualified driver (as above) costs £124.00 on weekdays and £150.00 at weekends. Car theory tests are currently £23.00.

The fee for lorry and bus multiple choice theory tests is £26.00 and the hazard perception test is £11.00.

Physical driving tests for cars and trailers, lorries and buses cost £115.00 on weekdays (up to 4.30 pm) and £141.00 if conducted in the evening or on a Saturday.

Higher test fees of £124.00 on weekdays (up to 4.30 pm) and £150.00 on Saturdays are payable where an extended re-test is ordered following obligatory disqualification of a driving licence (see above).

Driver CPC tests cost £26.00 for the multiple choice theory test, £23.00 for the theory case studies, £11.00 for the hazard test and £55.00 (or £63.00 for evening and weekend testing) for the practical test – this includes the issue of a Driver Qualification Card (DQC).

Test fees are forfeited unless at least 10 clear days' notice of cancellation is given.

NB: These fees, and others, were reduced to the current levels in 2016 in order for the UK to align its charges with the charges levied for similar testing undertaken by EU member states. At the time of writing there has been no announcement of any planned increase following Brexit.

Driving Instruction

Only ADIs approved by the DVSA are permitted to give driving instruction for payment on vehicles legally defined as 'motor cars', which basically means the following classes of vehicle:

- private cars;
- goods vehicles not exceeding 3,050 kg unladen weight.

In August 2017, following consultation, the DVSA announced that at 'some time' in 2018 learner drivers would be allowed to take instruction on motorways for the first time. This is now a reality and learners are now allowed to drive on motorways providing they are under the instruction of an approved instructor and the car is fitted with dual controls. The training is still voluntary and it is the instructor who decides whether or not the learner driver is able to cope with motorway conditions. Trainee driving instructors are not allowed to offer this training and it only applies to cars and not motorcycles. The DVSA do not give additional training to approved driving instructors, but offer learning materials and have updated the learner driving syllabus.

Tuition given for payment on heavy goods vehicles does not come within the scope of this legislation despite a certain amount of transport industry opinion that it should do so. However, to ensure that the level of driving instruction available to learner LGV drivers is of a consistently high standard a new scheme for the voluntary registration of LGV driving instructors has been established. Entry to the register is currently via a three-part examination of both driving and instructional abilities.

LGV Driver Testing

In order to drive a large vehicle (ie goods or passenger) it is usually necessary to pass the large vehicle theory test, a hazard perception test, a case study test, a practical demonstration and a practical driving test on either a large goods or passenger vehicle of the appropriate category for which a licence is required. These four elements of the driving test combine to meet the requirements of the Driver Certificate of Professional Competence (DCPC) initial qualification.

Some vocational drivers may not need a DCPC in order to drive a 'vocational' vehicle. Exemptions include the following activities:

- non-commercial carriage of passengers or goods for personal use;
- carrying material or equipment for the driver's use (but driving the vehicle can't be the main part of the driver's job);
- driving lessons for anyone who wants to get a driving licence or a Driver CPC;
- driving to or from pre-booked appointments at official vehicle testing centres;
- driving within 100 kilometres of base – but the vehicle can't be carrying passengers or goods, and driving a lorry, bus or coach can't be the driver's main job;
- maintaining public order – and the vehicle is being used or controlled by a local authority;
- rescue missions or in states of emergency.

In addition, the driver does not need the full Driver CPC if the vehicle is:

- limited to a top speed of 28 mph;
- being used or controlled by the armed forces, police, fire and rescue service, prison service or people running a prison or young offender institution.

Some existing vocational drivers who have yet to require a DCPC because they didn't need one, but now find that they would like to acquire their first DCPC, have an option of either completing 35 hours of Periodic DCPC training or completing Element Two (Case Studies) and Element Four (Practical Demonstration) (see below) of the vocational driving test. This concession is only offered to existing vocational drivers who wish to apply for an initial DCPC.

Theory and Hazard Perception Testing (Element One)

Since 1 January 1997 large vehicle (ie LGV/PCV) driving test candidates must take and pass a 'touch screen' theory test – which has replaced the old, verbal, questioning to test the candidate's knowledge of technical and safety matters and the *Highway Code*. This test is in two parts – Module 1a and Module 1b – and has been expanded with the inclusion of a wider range of topics such as fuel economy, environmentally sensitive driving and safety issues, and is available online.

Theory tests (Module 1a) are carried out on behalf of the DVSA at their dedicated test centres nationwide. The test takes 1 hour and 55 minutes and comprises 100 multiple-choice questions; a pass is achieved with 85 correct answers. It is worthy of note that, due to allegations and actual proof of fraud, theory tests are now only permitted to be taken in English or Welsh and not in one of 19 foreign languages as was previously the case.

The hazard perception test (Module 1b) is as previously described on pp 217–18, with the exception that for bus and lorry drivers there will be 19 video clips, with a pass mark of 67 out of 100.

The pass certificate issued for these tests is valid for two years. In turn, it also means that the hazard perception element must be taken within a period of two years of passing the theory element.

The Case Studies (Element Two)

The case study test lasts for 1 hour and 15 minutes and is comprised of seven case studies that the candidate works through on a computer. The case studies are scenarios which have been developed to relate to real life vocational driving and work situations. The candidate is asked six to eight multiple-choice questions on each case study and needs to score 40 marks from a total of 50 in order to pass.

The successful candidate will need the pass reference number in order to book Element Four of the overall test (Practical Demonstration). The pass reference number is valid for two years.

The Physical Test (Element Three)

See below for detailed information.

The Practical Demonstration (Element Four)

As mentioned earlier, the practical demonstration is only required by vocational drivers requiring a DCPC initial qualification; it is not required to be taken as a part of a Category B (car) driving test.

The practical demonstration cannot be taken until the driver in question has completed Part 2 of the driving test (Case Studies). The test is aimed at demonstrating that the driver is able to:

- load the vehicle following safety rules and keep it secure;
- stop trafficking in illegal immigrants;
- assess emergency situations;
- do a walkaround vehicle safety check.

The test, which takes approximately 30 minutes, is made up of five topics from the Driver CPC syllabus, and the driver is able to score up to 20 points for each topic. In order to pass, the driver must score at least 15 out of 20 in each topic area and have an overall score of at least 80 out of 100.

The Vocational Driving Test (Element Three)

In order to undertake a large goods or passenger vehicle (vocational/LGV/PCV) driving test, candidates will need their large vehicle theory test pass certificate when booking. Without this the examiner will not conduct the practical driving test. This requirement applies to drivers who are applying for a C1 or D1 category licence and only hold category B licences.

The 90-minute large goods vehicle practical driving test is conducted by DVSA examiners and booking has to be made directly through the DVSA. Certain test centres offer Saturday morning vocational driver testing. This test has to be taken within two years of the candidate passing the theory tests

The staged system of testing means that:

- Applicants for vocational tests must already hold a full category B (car and light vehicle) driving entitlement before taking a test to obtain a category C entitlement.

- Category B entitlement holders have to pass a test on a rigid goods vehicle in category C before being able to take a test to qualify for driving articulated vehicles and drawbar combinations in category C+E.
- Category C1 entitlement holders wishing to drive vehicles in category C1+E must take a further test for this type of vehicle combination.

In each case the driver must hold a provisional entitlement for the category of vehicle on which he wants to be tested.

Application

Applications for the large vehicle practical driving test can be made online through the GOV.UK website or by contacting the DVSA on 0300 200 1122.

Applicants are warned to apply for a test in good time. This is important if a vocational driving entitlement is required – subject to passing the test – from a particular date; and applicants must also ensure that their driving is of a sufficiently high standard to be able to pass the test.

Test Cancellation

Should a candidate need to cancel a test appointment this should be done at least 10 clear working days in advance, otherwise the fee will be forfeited.

Identification

Test candidates must be able to produce satisfactory photographic identification on arrival at the test centre, otherwise the examiner may refuse to conduct the test and the fee will be forfeited (see p 216).

Vehicles for the Vocational Driving Test

The candidate has to provide the vehicle (or arrange for the loan of a suitable vehicle) on which he wishes to be tested and it must comply with the following requirements:

- it must be laden (see below) and of the category (ie a 'minimum test vehicle') for which an LGV driving entitlement is required – see below;
- it must display 'L' plates front and rear;
- it must be in a thoroughly roadworthy condition;
- seating accommodation with a seat belt in a cab must be provided for the examiner;
- it must have sufficient fuel for a test lasting up to two hours.

Minimum Test Vehicles

All vehicles used for Categories C1, C1+E, C and C+E tests must:

- have externally mounted nearside and offside mirrors;
- have seat belts fitted to seats used by the examiner or any person supervising the test;

- be fitted with a tachograph;
- have an anti-lock braking system (ABS).

NB: Trailers don't need ABS.

All vehicle combinations must operate the appropriate service brakes and utilize a heavy duty coupling arrangement suitable for the weight.

NB: An articulated tractor unit is not considered to be a suitable vehicle for category C or C1 test.

Category C1

- A medium-sized lorry with a MAM of at least 4 tonnes;
  - at least 5 metres in length;
  - capable of 80 kph (50 mph); and
  - with a closed box cargo compartment at least as wide and as high as the cab.

Category C1+E

- A drawbar combination comprising a Category C1 vehicle;
  - towing a trailer of at least 2 tonnes MAM;
  - with a combined length of at least 8 metres;
  - capable of 80 kph (50 mph);
  - with a closed box trailer slightly less wide than the towing vehicle, but rearview must be by external mirrors only; or
- A medium-sized articulated lorry with a MAM of at least 6 tonnes;
  - with a combined length of at least 8 metres;
  - capable of 80 kph (50 mph);
  - with a closed box trailer slightly less wide than the towing vehicle, but rear view must be by external mirrors only.

Category C

- A rigid goods vehicle with a MAM of at least 12 tonnes;
  - at least 8 metres in length;
  - at least 2.4 metres in width;
  - capable of 80 kph (50 mph);
  - with at least eight forward gears*;
  - a closed box cargo compartment at least as wide and as high as the cab; and
  - a maximum length of 12 metres (39 ft 4 in).

Category C+E

- A drawbar outfit comprising a combination of a Category C vehicle and trailer with a MAM of 20 tonnes;
  - with a combined length of at least 14 metres;
  - with a trailer at least 7.5 metres in length from coupling eye to extreme rear;
  - at least 2.4 metres in width;
  - capable of 80 kph (50 mph);
  - with at least eight forward gears*;
  - with a closed box cargo compartment at least as wide and as high as the cab; and
  - a maximum length of 18.75 metres (61 ft 5 in); or
- An articulated lorry with a MAM of at least 20 tonnes;
  - with a minimum length of 14 metres;
  - a maximum length of 16.5 metres (54 ft);
  - at least 2.4 metres in width;
  - capable of 80 kph (50 mph);
  - with at least eight forward gears*;
  - with a closed box cargo compartment at least as wide and as high as the cab.

** Since 10 April 2014, the vehicle can now either have eight forward gears or an automatic gearbox. If an automatic gearbox is used the driver, should they pass the practical test, will gain a C or D category entitling them to drive manual gearboxes in that category providing that they initially passed either a category B, B+E, C1, C1+E, C, or C+E, D, D1+E or D+E test in a vehicle with a manual gearbox. Existing drivers holding a manual entitlement in any of these categories may also upgrade to a full manual entitlement either by paying a fee or waiting until the next five-yearly renewal.*

Real Total Mass

Since November 2013, some goods vehicles and/or trailers and some passenger carrying vehicles used for practical driving tests need to be loaded to set minimum levels in order to achieve Real Total Mass requirements.

These loading levels are as follows:

- Category B+E – The trailer must be loaded with at least 600 kg in the form of sealed bags of sand or one Intermediate Bulk Container (IBC) filled with water.
- Category C1 – No load requirement.
- Category C1+E – The trailer must be loaded with at least 600 kg in the form of sealed bags of sand or one IBC filled with water.

- Category C – The vehicle must be loaded with at least 5,000 kg in the form of five IBCs filled with water.
- Category C+E (artic.) – The trailer must be loaded with at least 8,000 kg in the form of eight IBCs filled with water.
- Category C+E (drawbar) – The vehicle must be loaded with at least 5,000 kg in the form of five IBCs filled with water and the trailer must be loaded with at least 3,000 kg in the form of three IBCs filled with water.
- Category D1 – No load requirement.
- Category D – No load requirement.
- Category D1+E – The trailer must be loaded with at least 600 kg in the form of sealed bags of sand or one IBC filled with water.
- Category D+E – The trailer must be loaded with at least 600 kg in the form of sealed bags of sand or one IBC filled with water.

The Vocational Driving Test Syllabus

The recommended syllabus should be studied by candidates preparing for the C1, C1E or LGV driving test. It is available in the DVSA publication *The Official Guide to Driving Goods Vehicles* (available from The Stationery Office and most good bookshops) and *The Professional LGV Drivers' Handbook* (by David Lowe, available from Kogan Page).

Vocational Tests – Current Situation

Drivers seeking vocational licence entitlement are expected to be experienced and technically expert. Test candidates are asked at least one 'show me' and one 'tell me' type question when taking the physical driving test, with a driving fault being recorded for each incorrect answer up to a maximum of four driving faults. If all five answers are given incorrectly, a serious fault will be recorded. These 'show me' and 'tell me' questions are necessary where a driver does not intend to drive professionally, or is exempted from Driver CPC, and does not require to pass Module 4 of the Initial Driver CPC which includes the same types of questions.

Examples of safety check questions are as follows.

Identify where:

- you would check the engine oil level and tell me how you would check that the engine has sufficient oil;
- you would check the engine coolant level and tell me how you would check that the engine has the correct level;
- the windscreen washer reservoir is and tell me how you would check the windscreen washer level.

Tell me how you would check:

- your tyres to ensure that they are correctly inflated, have sufficient tread depth and that their general condition is safe to use on the road;

- that the brake lights are working;
- the condition of the reflectors on this vehicle;
- the condition of the windscreen and windows on this vehicle;
- the condition of the windscreen wipers on this vehicle;
- the condition of the suspension on this vehicle;
- that the condition of the body is safe on this vehicle;
- that the power-assisted steering is working.

Tell me:

- how you would operate the loading mechanism on this vehicle (vehicle-specific, ie tail lift);
- the main safety factors involved in loading this vehicle.

Show me how you would check:

- that the headlamps, sidelights and tail lights are working;
- that the direction indicators are working;
- the operation (specify) of the audible warning devices on this vehicle;
- the wheel nuts are secure on this vehicle;
- the condition of the mudguards on this vehicle;
- for the correct air pressure on this vehicle;
- for air leaks on this vehicle;
- that your cargo doors are secure;
- that your cab locking mechanism is secure.

Show me how you would:

- replace the tachometer disc on this vehicle;
- insert your driver digital tachograph card.

Show me:

- what instrument checks you would make before and after starting the engine on this vehicle;
- where the emergency exits are and how you would check that they are operating correctly;
- where the first-aid equipment is on this vehicle;
- where the fire extinguishers are on this vehicle.

The Braking Exercise

From 2011, drivers undertaking the vocational driving test are no longer required to carry out off-road braking tests. These tests will be carried out on the road in normal traffic conditions. This is thought to be a more realistic test of a driver's ability to bring his vehicle to rest in a safe and timely manner taking account of prevailing road and traffic conditions.

The Safe Parking Test

Candidates will be asked to carry out the current reversing exercise, but at the end of the reversing bay there will be a simulated loading platform up to which the candidate will be required to reverse (stopping with the extreme rear of the vehicle within a stopping area marked by black and yellow hatched lines) and park safely for loading and unloading.

Stopping short of the marked stopping area will be assessed as a serious fault. Reversing through the marked stopping area and dislodging the simulated loading/unloading platform will be assessed as a serious fault. Stopping within the marked stopping area but unacceptably short of the platform will be assessed as a driving fault. A total loss of vehicle control, which causes actual danger to the driver, examiner or another road user, will be assessed as a dangerous fault.

It is recognized that some professional drivers reverse, under control, up to a loading/unloading platform until they gently touch the platform. This will be acceptable on test as long as the platform is not dislodged.

The Uncoupling and Recoupling Exercise

After uncoupling the candidate will be required to park the towing vehicle alongside the trailer and then realign the towing vehicle with the trailer before recoupling. The competencies of control, accuracy and effective observation will be assessed during the exercise. A fault involving actual danger to the driver or another road user will be assessed as a dangerous fault. A fault that would be potentially dangerous to the driver or another road user will be assessed as a serious fault. Faults that reflect that the driver does not have the required competencies to carry out the exercise following industry best practice and recognized procedures will be assessed as driving or serious faults, depending upon the severity of the fault.

EU Vocational Driving Test Standards

Under European Commission Directive 2000/56/EC, which amended an earlier Directive on driving licences (91/439/EEC), the conduct of the practical driving test itself was revised and applied to tests conducted from September 2003. As current licence holders in the UK have clearly passed using an EU syllabus and standards it would seem that these UK licences will be recognized throughout the EU and, providing the UK continues to use the EU based testing system, this should remain the position. However, as noted in the previous chapter, in the case of a no-deal Brexit IDPs will need to be carried by UK drivers where some EU member states decide to introduce it as a requirement to enter their country.

The following text summarizes Annex II to the Directive in so far as it applies to vocational driving tests only.

Driving Skills and Behaviour for Vocational Drivers

Driving test candidates must demonstrate the following key skills:

- Preparation and technical check of the vehicle for the purposes of ensuring road safety. Applicants must demonstrate that they are capable of preparing to drive safely by satisfying the following requirements:
  - adjusting the seat as necessary to obtain a correct seated position;
  - adjusting rear-view mirrors, seat belts and head restraints if available;
  - random checks on the condition of the tyres, steering, brakes, lights, reflectors, direction indicators and audible warning device;
  - checking the power-assisted braking and steering systems;
  - checking the condition of the wheels, wheel nuts, mudguards, windscreen, windows and wipers, fluids (eg engine oil, coolant, washer fluid);
  - checking and using the instrument panel including the recording equipment (ie the tachograph);
  - checking the air pressure, air tanks and the suspension;
  - checking the safety factors relating to vehicle loading: body, sheets, cargo doors, loading mechanism (if available), cabin locking (if available), way of loading, securing load;
  - checking the coupling mechanism and the brake and electrical connections (categories C+E, C1+E only);
  - reading a road map, route planning, including the use of electronic navigation systems (optional).
- Special manoeuvres to be tested with a bearing on road safety:
  - coupling and uncoupling, or uncoupling and recoupling a trailer from its motor vehicle;
  - the manoeuvre must involve the towing vehicle being parked alongside the trailer (ie not in one line) (categories C+E, C1+E only);
  - reversing along a curve;
  - parking safely for loading/unloading at a loading ramp/platform or similar installation.
- Behaviour in traffic. Applicants must perform all the following actions in normal traffic situations, in complete safety and taking all necessary precautions:
  - driving away: ie after parking, after a stop in traffic, when exiting a driveway;
  - driving on straight roads;
  - passing oncoming vehicles, including in confined spaces;
  - driving round bends;
  - crossroads: approaching and crossing of intersections and junctions;
  - changing direction: left and right turns; changing lanes;

- approach/exit of motorways or similar (if available): joining from the acceleration lane;
- leaving on the deceleration lane;
- overtaking/passing: overtaking other traffic (if possible);
- driving alongside obstacles, eg parked cars;
- being overtaken by other traffic (if appropriate);
- special road features (if available): roundabouts;
- railway level crossings;
- tram/bus stops;
- pedestrian crossings;
- driving up/downhill on long slopes;
- taking the necessary precautions when alighting from the vehicle.

NB: As mentioned, the on-road braking exercise will be carried out away from the test centre but the examiner will determine at what stage of the test this exercise happens, bearing in mind traffic conditions and the safety of all road users and pedestrians.

Marking of the Skills and Behaviour Tests

In assessing driver competence, the examiner will be looking for the ease with which the applicant handles the vehicle controls and his capacity to drive in complete safety in traffic. Importantly, the examiner must be made to feel safe throughout the test. The examiner will also pay special attention as to whether the applicant shows defensive and social driving behaviour, in particular ensuring the safety of all road users, especially those who are the weakest and most exposed, by showing due respect for others. Overall, drivers are expected to make progress in an economically and environmentally friendly manner.

During the test, the examiner will be checking to ensure that the test candidate makes proper use of safety belts, rear-view mirrors, head restraints; driving seat; lights and other equipment; clutch, gearbox (if applicable), accelerator, braking systems (including third braking systems, if available); and the steering. He will also be checking the driver's control of the vehicle under different circumstances and at different speeds; his steadiness on the road (this means no fast acceleration, smooth driving and no hard braking); the weight and dimensions and characteristics of the vehicle; the weight and type of load.

Additionally, drivers must show that they are capable of detecting any major technical faults in their vehicles, especially those posing a safety hazard, and know how to have them remedied in an appropriate fashion.

Vocational Test Passes and Failures

A driver who passes the vocational driving test is issued with a certificate to that effect, valid for a period of two years, and the holder can apply for a vocational driving entitlement of the appropriate category to be added to his unified driving licence.

A driver who fails the vocational driving test is given a written statement of failure and an oral explanation of the reasons for his failure. He may apply for an immediate re-test to be taken after an interval of at least three days.

Advanced Commercial Vehicle Driving

For many years the advanced driving courses and tests organized by the Institute of Advanced Motorists (IAM) (now IAM RoadSmart) have been looked upon as a severe test of driving skills requiring a high degree of knowledge of the 'rules of the road' for private car drivers. Commercial vehicle drivers who wish to show that they too have attained an exceptional level of proficiency can also take the advanced driving courses and tests designed specially for commercial vehicles.

The advanced commercial vehicle driving test is organized by the Institute of Advanced Motorists at IAM RoadSmart, 1 Albany Place, Hyde Way, Welwyn Garden City, AL7 3BT (tel: 0300 303 1134; website: www.iam.org.uk (archived at https://perma.cc/4SUM-9GPN)) and is open to any heavy goods vehicle driver, subject to certain conditions as follows:

- Loads, if carried on test vehicles, must be properly secured.
- A safe seat at the front of the vehicle, including seatbelt, must be available for the examiner.
- The driver must not, by taking the test, contravene the drivers' hours and record-keeping rules.

On passing the test, the applicant becomes eligible for admission to membership of the IAM.

Fees

The IAM has introduced a combined fee of £149 under its *Skills for Life* programme, which includes the following:

- a copy of the IAM's *Advanced Driving/Motorcycling Manual*;
- associate membership of one of the many local IAM Groups;
- a place on an IAM course to prepare for the Advanced Driving Test;
- the fee for the IAM Advanced Test;
- a first-year membership of the IAM after passing the Advanced Test.

They also offer a number of courses and tests as packages all at different prices. Details on IAM RoadSmart tests and courses can be found on the IAM website.

Exemption from the Test

Certain specially qualified drivers may apply to become members of the Institute without taking the advanced driving test:

- Royal Navy, Army and Royal Air Force LGV instructors and qualified testing officers who have passed an LGV instructor's course and whose application is supported by the recommendation of the applicant's commanding officer.

- Holders of the Road Transport Industry Training Board Instructor's Certificate.
- Fire Service LGV instructors who have completed an LGV instructor's course, and whose application is supported by the senior instructor.
- LGV driving examiners.

The Advanced Test

To pass the test the driver should show 'skill with responsibility', and any driver of reasonable experience and skill should be able to pass without difficulty. The Institute's RoadSmart examiners test candidates on routes located all over Britain.

The test lasts about two hours, during which the test route of some 35–40 miles is covered. The route incorporates road conditions of all kinds including congested urban areas, main roads, narrow country lanes and residential streets. Candidates are not expected to display elaborate driving techniques. Examiners prefer to see the vehicle handled in a steady, workmanlike manner without exaggeratedly slow speeds or excessive signalling. Speed limits must be observed (driving in excess of any limit results in test failure) and the driving manner must take into consideration road, traffic and weather conditions. However, the examiners expect candidates to drive briskly within the limits and to cruise at the legal limit (ie either on the road or the vehicle, whichever is lower) whenever circumstances permit.

Drivers will be asked to reverse around a corner and to make a hill start. There will be spot checks on the driver's power of observation (ie the examiner will ask questions about road signs or markings recently passed or about other significant landmarks).

Examiners ask a number of questions of candidates but these are not trick questions. The previous requirement for the driver to give a running commentary during a portion of the route no longer exists – although the test regulations do state that candidates are free to give a commentary if they wish to make extra clear their ability to 'read the road'.

Test Requirements

The examiner will consider the following aspects of driving:

- *Acceleration*: must be smooth and progressive, not excessive or insufficient, and must be used at the right time and place.
- *Braking*: must be smooth and progressive, not fierce. Brakes should be used in conjunction with the driving mirror and signals. Road, traffic and weather conditions must be taken into account.
- *Clutch control*: engine and road speeds should be properly coordinated when changing gear. The clutch should not be 'ridden' or slipped and the vehicle should not be coasted with the clutch disengaged.
- *Gear changing*: should be smooth and carried out without jerking.
- *Use of gears*: the gears should be correctly selected and used and the right gear engaged before reaching a hazard (obviously, where a vehicle with an automatic gearbox is used some of these requirements are not applicable).

- *Steering*: the wheel should be correctly held with the hands and the 'crossed-arm' technique should not be used except when manoeuvring in confined spaces.
- *Driving position*: the driver should be alert and should not slump at the wheel. Resting an arm on the door while driving should be avoided.
- *Observation*: the driver should 'read' the road ahead and show a good sense of anticipation and the ability to judge speed and distance.
- *Concentration*: the driver should keep his attention on the road and should not be easily distracted.
- *Maintaining progress*: taking account of the road, traffic and weather conditions, the driver must keep up a reasonable pace and maintain good progress.
- *Obstruction*: the candidate must be careful not to obstruct other vehicles by driving too slowly, taking up the wrong position on the road or failing to anticipate and react correctly to the traffic situation ahead.
- *Positioning*: the driver must keep to the correct part of the road, especially when approaching and negotiating hazards.
- *Lane discipline*: the driver must keep to the appropriate lane and be careful not to straddle white lines.
- *Observations of road surfaces*: the driver must keep an eye on the road surface, especially in bad weather, and should watch out for slippery conditions.
- *Traffic signals*: signals, signs and road markings must be observed, obeyed and approached correctly and the driver should show courtesy at pedestrian crossings.
- *Speed limits and other legal requirements*: these should be observed. The examiner cannot condone breaches of the law.
- *Overtaking*: must be carried out safely and decisively, maintaining the right distance from other vehicles and using the mirror, signals and gears correctly.
- *Hazard procedure and cornering*: road and traffic hazards must be coped with properly, and bends and corners taken in the right manner.
- *Mirror*: the mirror must be used frequently, especially in conjunction with signals and before changing speed or course.
- *Signals*: direction indicator, and hand signals when needed, must be given at the right place and in good time. The horn and headlamp flasher should be used as per the *Highway Code*.
- *Restraint*: the driver should show reasonable restraint, but not indecision, at the wheel.
- *Consideration*: sufficient consideration and courtesy should be shown to other road users.
- *Vehicle sympathy*: the driver should treat the vehicle with care, without overstressing it by needless revving of the engine and by fierce braking.

- *Manoeuvring*: manoeuvres (reversing) should be performed smoothly and competently.

'Trailblazer' LGV Driver Apprenticeships

This apprenticeship was designed by employers within the supply chain and logistics industry, and is suitable for apprentices employed in a wide variety of organizations. It provides the foundation knowledge, skills and experience for the role of LGV driver within occupational areas in the supply chain and logistics industry.

This is seen as vital because LGV drivers are responsible for ensuring that the right products are delivered at the right time. They need to be skilled and careful drivers and maintain the integrity of their load and vehicle at all times. LGV drivers also need to be able to drive in many different conditions, circumstances and locations both home and abroad.

The apprenticeship is phased and logical to ensure that it adds value to both the apprentice and the employer, to ensure that it is relevant and to ensure the apprentice is sufficiently developed to begin a career as an LGV driver. It is based on learning relevant core competencies and assessment of these using a properly developed training plan where the apprentice needs to demonstrate continual development towards a final end point assessment.

The apprenticeship takes 12 months in total with quarterly progress assessments recommended. Apprentices will need to have passed either Category C or C+E tests before final assessment and will also need to have passed relevant English and maths qualifications before final assessment. The final assessment covers both a knowledge test and a behaviours test which covers possible actions in different scenarios.

'Some firms have said the new Trailblazer apprenticeship is not for them – until they find out that it can take new recruits through to driving 44 tonnes vehicles,' said Colin Snape, the RHA's Deputy Director of Policy at the time. 'That totally changes their level of interest. Firms should realize that the funding of £4,500 (up to £5,000 for firms with fewer than 50 employees or Levy Payers) is suitable for their businesses. A higher level of funding is available for firms taking on young drivers.'

Given the critical shortage of LGV drivers at the current time, it appears that there has never been a better time to become a trainee LGV driver in the UK. Full details can be found on the internet by typing in 'Trailblazer LGV driver apprenticeship'.

Driver Training

Driver Training for Lorry Loaders

No mandatory requirements exist at the present time for goods vehicle drivers to hold certificates of competence to operate lorry-mounted cranes. However, they do need to be 'competent' and under the Health and Safety at Work Act 1974 employers have a statutory duty to provide adequate instruction and safety training for all employees. Details of training providers can be obtained from the Association of Lorry Loader Manufacturers and Importers (ALLMI) – see below.

There is also a voluntary certification scheme run by the Construction Industry Training Board (CITB) to improve safety on construction sites. This scheme is strongly supported by the construction industry, which may refuse entry to its own sites to non-certified lorry drivers. Mainly, the Board's scheme is concerned with ensuring a sound understanding of safety procedures for the use of a wide range of equipment, including lorry-mounted cranes and skip loaders. Under the scheme, the Board provided certification of existing lorry-loader and skip-loader operators who could show by means of employer confirmation that they were experienced in the use of such equipment.

Newcomers seeking first-time certification and drivers renewing grandfather rights certificates have to undergo (re-) training and site-based assessment to show that they can operate such equipment with complete safety. CITB safety certificates are renewable at five-yearly intervals.

Another scheme is run by the Contractors' Mechanical Plant Engineers (CMPE), although this requires no specific training, certification being based solely on employers' references. Training is also provided by most member firms of ALLMI. Additionally, the Association itself publishes a Code of Practice for safe application and use of loaders. ALLMI has also been issued with the Health and Safety Executive's logo of recognition to reflect the standards of the training courses offered by its members. ALLMI offers a 15-module suite of operator training courses as well as slinger and crane supervisor training, appointed person, load test course and courses aimed at instructor accreditation and managers. Details of ALLMI training courses are available from the Association at Unit 7b, Cavalier Court, Bumpers Farm, Chippenham, Wiltshire SN14 6LH (0844 858 4334) www.allmi.com (archived at https://perma.cc/U48W-PJPC). Other organizations providing suitable lorry-loader training include the Freight Transport Association, the RTITB and a number of commercial training firms.

Driver Training for ADR

The Carriage of Dangerous Goods and Use of Transportable Pressure Equipment Regulations 2009 (regulation 5) replace previous regulations of this title. These regulations require that dangerous goods drivers are trained in accordance with section 8.2.1 of the European Agreement Concerning the International Carriage of Dangerous Goods by Road (commonly referred to as the ADR 2017) and that they hold Vocational Training Certificates issued by the DVLA, Swansea, and gained by attending an approved course and passing a written examination. Courses are offered by most transport training providers and the trade associations.

Relevant Vehicles

The regulations apply broadly to the carriage of specified dangerous goods in:

- road tankers with a capacity exceeding 1,000 litres; or
- tank containers with a capacity greater than 3,000 litres (with certain exceptions); or
- vehicles carrying radioactive materials or explosives; or
- vehicles carrying packed dangerous goods the amount of which exceeds certain thresholds, as set down by the ADR regulations.

Driver Responsibilities

Vocational training certificates are valid for a period of five years and are renewable, subject to the holder attending an approved refresher course and taking a further examination within the 12 months prior to the expiry date of an existing certificate. The driver must hold a valid certificate for the actual class and group of dangerous goods being carried at the time. Drivers must carry the certificate with them when driving relevant vehicles and must produce it on request by police or a goods vehicle examiner. It is an offence to drive a dangerous goods vehicle without being the holder of a certificate, or to fail to produce such a certificate on request.

Employer Responsibilities

It is the responsibility of the employer to ensure that dangerous goods drivers receive training so they understand the dangers arising from the products they are carrying and what to do in an emergency situation, and that they hold relevant certificates covering the vehicle being driven and the products carried. The employer has a duty to provide necessary training leading to the certificate. The employer must retain records of all instruction and training given to drivers.

Approved Training and Examination

The Department for Transport has approved suitable establishments where dangerous goods driver training and DGSA training can be obtained. These include the CILT, FTA, RHA and many private training organizations. ADR training is also now able to be delivered as DCPC training offered by some JAUPT approved training centres.

The syllabus for the examination involves both theoretical sessions and practical exercises. The examination itself comprises a core element designed to assess candidates' practical and legal knowledge plus a specialist element for either road tanker and tank container drivers or packaged goods drivers (or both if required). Additionally, candidates have to pass individual 'dangerous substance' examination papers, which cover each of nine classes of dangerous goods, to test their specialist knowledge of the products they carry in their work.

Candidates who pass the examination (by achieving a pass mark of at least 75 per cent in each element – ie core, tanker/package and substance) will receive their certificate (similar to a photo card-style driving licence) direct from the DVLA, Swansea. Those who fail can apply to resit the examination without further training within a period of 16 weeks from receipt of the notification of failure.

Transport Training

NVQs in Transport

NVQ training standards for the road haulage industry are overseen and largely controlled by Skills for Logistics, a not-for profit assessment, consultancy and research organization which does not offer training but which is able to advise and assist in developing training.

Actual NVQ training courses are now widely available through the trade associations (FTA and RHA), the CILT and many private transport training organizations throughout the UK. The standards underpin a number of National Vocational Qualifications (NVQs) which have been developed for use within the industry as follows:

- NVQ level 1

  Assisting in road haulage and distribution operations

  – covers basic operational skills which may involve helping other more skilled staff.
- NVQ level 2

  Transporting goods by road (inc Driver CPC)

  – aimed at the driver of a small or large goods vehicle.

  Distribution and warehousing

  – aimed at someone engaged in the storage and despatch of goods.

  Organizing road transport operations

  – aimed at the traffic planner or clerk who is concerned with traffic operations.
- NVQ level 3

  Supervisory management (inc Operator CPC)

  – aimed at supervisors within the road haulage and distribution industry performing road haulage and distribution operations.
- NVQ level 4

  Management

  – aimed at managers in the road haulage and distribution industry.

There are also levels 5 and 6 which are for senior managers, where level 5 is equivalent to a first degree.

Continuing Professional Development

Constant changes in business, industry and technology mean that executives need to keep their skills and knowledge up to date in order to maximize professional opportunities and their market value. Continuing professional development (CPD) schemes, such as those operated by the CILT in the UK for its members, enables individuals to improve their knowledge and competence systematically throughout their working life – a concept supported by the Government.

Professional development is the key to career enhancement. Although it is possible to train as and when suitable courses become available, this approach can leave the individual with key needs unfulfilled. A CPD scheme offers personal development solutions structured to fit around a certain career and lifestyle. Planning career development in this systematic way brings the following developments:

- It makes the best use of training and learning opportunities.
- It encourages the individual to look for alternative ways of meeting training/learning needs.
- It enables the individual to become aware of less obvious knowledge or skills gaps.
- By periodic evaluation of development individuals can judge whether they are meeting their personal objectives.
- Records are kept to track progress.

Learning Activities

Formal learning usually comprises:

- company training;
- study courses including open learning;
- teaching and making presentations;
- attendance at conferences, seminars and meetings related to the individual's work or professional interests.

Informal learning includes:

- reading;
- networking;
- mentoring and coaching;
- project work.

CPD places emphasis on helping individuals to plan and progress their professional future. Normally, schemes focus on outputs without prescribing a minimum number of hours or particular courses to attend; professional persons are expected to take responsibility for their own learning. The CILT, for example, helps members to identify opportunities and provides accreditation of their learning log.

Further details of the CILT and its CPD scheme can be obtained from:

Personal Development Dept
The Chartered Institute of Logistics and Transport in the UK
Earlstrees Court
Earlstrees Road
Corby
Northants NN17 4AX
Tel: 01536 740100
www.ciltuk.org.uk (archived at https://perma.cc/4UWQ-TSNH)

08

Vehicle Registration, HGV Road User Levy, Excise Duty and Trade Licences

Vehicle Registration

New vehicles must be registered with the DVLA at Swansea and a registration number obtained for each. A one-off first registration charge of £55 is made to cover the DVLA's administrative costs. A list of new vehicle registration marks is also described on pp 417–19.

The registration number must be displayed on plates mounted on the front and rear of the vehicle. These must conform to legal requirements as specified in the Road Vehicles (Display of Registration Marks) Regulations 2001 as amended (see p 418 for full details).

Annual registration prefix changes were replaced by six-monthly changes from 1 March 1999 (prefix 'T') until 1 September 2001, when an entirely new format for registration plates was introduced. This comprises two letters representing the place of registration (ie one of 19 areas followed by a letter for the office of registration). Two numbers denote the year of registration. The last three letters are randomly selected.

Form V55/4, which is used for motor vehicle registrations, consists of a single sheet used for first-licensing and registration purposes. This is sent to the DVLA and will form a part of the national vehicle statistics.

The form includes questions about the purchaser's occupation and previous vehicle and about the main use to which he intends to put the new vehicle, and detailed information on the vehicle design and construction.

Whilst most of the main vehicle manufacturers and importers will have entered the details of each vehicle on the form before it reaches the dealer, the purchaser will also need to complete details. If the manufacturer or importer has not completed the form in advance, copies are available on demand at licensing offices.

Documents

A completed form V55/4, a copy of the supplier's invoice and an appropriate Type Approval Certificate for goods vehicles subject to the type approval regulations are required when first registering a new goods vehicle (a certificate of insurance is only required if registering a new vehicle in Northern Ireland). When an excise licence is required for vehicles exempt from annual testing a completed form V112G (Declaration of Exemption) must also be produced.

Since the phasing out of the UK's existing Goods Vehicle National Type Approval (GVNTA) scheme in 2012, EU Directives relating to EU-wide type approval are now in place. These changes to the vehicle type approval scheme in the UK mean that a new vehicle may be certificated under either the EC Whole Vehicle Type Approval system (ECWVTA), for vehicles which are produced in large numbers, the UK National Small Series Type Approval (NSSTA) for vehicles produced in small batches or the Individual Vehicle Approval (IVA) scheme for special 'one-off' vehicles.

At the time of writing, the EU is working on a planned regulation that would mean, following Brexit, UK vehicle manufacturers will need to use a new type approval system. The outline of the Regulation is below:

> Manufacturers of UK type approved products will need to apply for a new type of EU type approval. These manufacturers will be able to use reports used for UK type approval by the Vehicle Certification Agency (VCA) in the UK, but they will have to apply again to the EU. This makes it somewhat unfair in relation to trade with the EU and it is hoped that a compromise may be found.

In addition, some 'specialized vehicles' which were exempt from type approval under the GVNTA do, from October 2014, need to be approved under the ECWVTA scheme and operators using 'specialized vehicles' need to check this requirement with the DVLA as these requirements are subject to change. Typically these include vehicles such as:

- recovery vehicles exceeding 12,000 kg MAM;
- engineering plant vehicles using truck chassis;
- crash cushion vehicles used by highway maintenance;
- vehicles used for AIL work;
- vehicles with moving mounted platforms on booms;
- highway testing vehicles based on truck chassis.

The issue of type approval post-Brexit is likely to see the UK adopting the EU's standards of type approval in order to ensure that UK vehicles are able to meet EU type approval standards.

Vehicle Registration Documents

A Registration Document/Certificate shows the registered keeper of a vehicle. The registered keeper is the person who keeps the vehicle on a public road, but is not necessarily the legal owner. The Certificate gives the keeper's name and address, the registration mark and other details of the vehicle, including engine, VIN and type approval numbers, the category into which it falls, its body type, maximum mass (ie weight) etc. A new Registration Certificate is issued each time the DVLA updates the record with any change to the existing details. The vehicle keeper should make sure that the details on this certificate are accurate and must tell the DVLA immediately if any changes are necessary. It may be difficult to sell the vehicle if any of the information is inaccurate. However, it is important to note that the Registration Document/ Certificate is *not* a document of title (ownership).

Since January 2004 anyone applying for a V5 Registration Document will have been issued with the new-style Vehicle Registration Certificate (V5C). This new Registration Certificate has been developed to comply with European Directive 1999/37/EC, which required member states to introduce a common format for Registration Certificates no later than June 2004, with the aim of helping to identify vehicles in international traffic and to allow for the re-registration of vehicles throughout the EU, including the UK. This is not likely to change.

Issues of the V5C document also show (where applicable) the vehicle engine's Euro status (eg currently Euro VI for new vehicles). This enables operators to show the vehicle's compliance with emission standards for road tax and toll-charging purposes.

NB: Whilst the statutory charge of £55.00 is made by the DVLA for first registration of a new vehicle, the DVLA also charges £25.00 for replacing a lost, stolen, destroyed or damaged vehicle registration document.

Police officers and enforcement officers of the DVSA may request production of the registration document for inspection at any reasonable time.

Issue of the Licence

Paper discs are no longer issued and proof of licensing is now carried out electronically by the DVLA. On payment of the relevant amount of Vehicle Excise Duty (VED) for a vehicle, the DVLA will register on a central database that the vehicle is properly licensed. This 'no disc' scenario also means that when a vehicle is sold the existing licence cannot be transferred. The old owner automatically receives a refund of any unused months and the new owner needs to make a new application to the DVLA. Other changes which accompanied the 'no disc' scenario included the facility to pay for VED monthly, bi-annually or annually by direct debit, but there is a 5 per cent surcharge for using this facility if the monthly or bi-annual options are used.

Number Plates

As part of the DVLA's measures to combat vehicle crime, it has been a requirement since the beginning of 2003 that vehicle number (registration) plates may be produced only by registered manufacturers, who must keep records of the plates they sell, to whom they are sold and whether that person is authorized to require the plates. Purchasers of plates need to produce evidence as to who they are (a passport or photocard driving licence) and that they have a right to the plates for the vehicle in question (generally by producing the vehicle registration document (form V5C) or a letter of authorization from the vehicle owner). Drivers of vehicles with dirty or fancy number plates caught on ANPR (Automatic Number Plate Recognition) systems may be prosecuted under rules introduced in 2006.

An issue yet to be resolved relates to number plates with the letters GB inside the EU circle of stars as this will be incorrect when the UK becomes a non-EU country. Whether or not these plates will need to be changed or allowed to continue appears to be an issue for individual EU member states. Currently, it appears that if you have a Euro number plate with a GB symbol you will be OK to travel through the EU but if you have a number plate without the Euro symbol you will need a GB sticker in addition to your number plate. This information came from the GOV.UK website and only applies to EU travel.

Trailer Registration

As a result of Brexit, and in order to comply with the Vienna Convention, all UK based trailers used on commercial international operations to the EU now need to have proof of their identity and be registered. This was required to be completed by December 2018 for implementation in March 2019.

Registration applies to all trailers used commercially over 750 kg and is optional for non-commercial trailers 750 kg to 3,500 kg. Registration can be done online using the GOV.UK website and submitting the application to the Technical Application System (TAS) at the DVSA via www.dvsa.gov.uk (archived at https://perma.cc/RZU8-4MWM), although the actual registration document will be issued and sent via the post.

Details required to register a trailer include the keeper's details, trailer manufacturer, trailer VIN/chassis number, trailer gross vehicle weight (GVW) and trailer unladen weight (ULW), number of axles, etc. Details of any change of ownership are also to be recorded. Costs are £26.00 for first registration, £21.00 for following registrations and £10.00 for a replacement certificate.

When the Trailer Registration Certificate is issued it is to travel with the trailer and a trailer identity registration plate with one alpha and seven numeric figures on it is to be displayed at the rear of the trailer in addition to the number plate of the drawing vehicle. Forms to be used to apply for a new trailer ID number for a new build trailer and for a 'Ministry Number' for a new trailer to be used on the road are Forms TES1 and TES2 respectively.

Advice and further details are available through the DVSA at enquiries@dvsa.gov.uk or on 0300 123 9000.

Registration of 'O' Licence Vehicles

The TCs have ruled that vehicles specified on British 'O' licences must be registered in the UK.

The DVLA has also warned that British VED must be paid on vehicles unless the operator has a genuine business abroad.

HGV Road User Levy

Following the Heavy Goods Vehicle Road User Act 2013, mainland UK introduced the Heavy Goods Vehicle Road User Levy in April 2014. The DVA in Northern

Ireland extended the levy to cover Northern Ireland from 17 November 2014. The introduction of the levy also brought about major changes to VED, the abolition of some reduced pollution certificates, leading to their final abolition in 2017, and new vehicle banding for taxation purposes. For UK operators, the levy, which only applies to goods vehicles with a revenue weight of 12,000 kg MAM, or above, is based upon time (six months or 12 months in line with VED), the weight of the vehicle and the number of axles. It is paid as an integral component of the overall VED charge for applicable vehicles.

The British Government estimated that the levy would collect over £27 million per year and that around £21 million would be net revenue to be deposited into the Consolidated Fund. These figures were based on their forecasting that there were approximately 260,000 UK registered vehicles that are covered by the levy at the time it was introduced and approximately 130,000 foreign vehicles would enter the country every year and account for approximately 1.5 million trips. In general terms, whilst the number of UK registered LGVs fell slightly in 2017–18, there is also a slight fall in the numbers of foreign registered vehicles entering the country. (Source: D*f*T UK road traffic statistics 2017–18).

The levy has to be applied to both foreign vehicles and UK registered goods vehicles 12,000 kg MAM and above in order to comply with the EU's Eurovignette Directive (Directive 1999/62/EC) which forbids unfair treatment where domestic transport operators are able to receive additional benefits and gain unfair advantage over and above any benefits or advantages enjoyed by international operators from other EU member states. It also states that member states intending to introduce road levies such as this can only set the threshold weights at either 3,500 kg or 12,000 kg and, given the nature of international trade in the UK, the British Government felt that 12,000 kg would be more appropriate as most movements are undertaken by larger vehicles.

The main aim of the levy is to ensure that visiting vehicles operating in the UK pay a proportion towards the infrastructure costs and pollution they cause, in a similar fashion to levies charged to UK operators by many governments, whilst working in EU member states and foreign countries.

In reality, in order to satisfy the EU Eurovignette Directive, the UK (and the EU member states who operate vignette systems of road charging) reduce the amount of VED paid by domestic operators in order to offset the cost of the levy to their own operators.

For UK-based operators, the levy is paid at the same time as the first VED renewal after 1 April 2014, or application for initial VED authorization. It is considered that, whilst many operators benefit from reductions in the new VED/levy rates, some do see increases and, where this does happen, operators are advised to consider voluntary down-plating to reduce the combined cost. The actual levy charge varies for UK operators from around £85 per year, up to around £1,000 for the largest vehicles. For operators applying to renew the VED, the rate also includes a reduced pollution grant or discount for vehicles with Euro IV–VI engines. The grant or discount replaces the reduced pollution certificates for vehicles exceeding 12,000 kg MAM, which were previously required in order to pay a reduced VED fee.

In relation to reduced pollution certificates, no more reduced pollution certificates for Euro II and Euro III engine vehicles have been issued since 31 March 2016. This means that the latest possible expiry date for these certificates was the end of

February 2017. Euro IV, V and VI engine vehicles were given their last reduced pollution certificates at the end of December 2016, meaning that the complete 'certificate' scheme came to a close at the end of December 2017. Further details can be found on the GOV.UK website. To balance this in an environmentally focused manner, the UK now gives a 10 per cent discount on the LGV Road User Levy to UK operators operating Euro VI vehicles but charges an additional 20 per cent on UK registered vehicles with Euro V or less emission standards.

Foreign operators need to pay before they enter the UK. Their charges also vary from around £10 per day, up to around £1,000 per year. They are able to purchase short-term vignettes (daily, weekly, monthly, etc) but there are surcharges for the shorter terms. Payment can be made online but there are also payment facilities at truck-stops close to the channel ports, at the ports and actually on the ferries and Channel Tunnel link.

The DVSA are the enforcement arm in mainland UK, with the DVA undertaking enforcement in Northern Ireland. Enforcement is largely in relation to non-payment, or under-payment of the levy. As there are no discs or other physical proof of payment, enforcement is largely carried out through the use of ANPR cameras to identify vehicles that either have not paid or have underpaid. In these cases a fixed penalty of £300 is charged and the vehicle can be immobilized if the driver cannot pay at the roadside, cannot pay a Fixed Penalty Deposit (FPD) or cannot provide details of a suitable UK address. There are additional costs to operators to have vehicles immobilized, to have the immobilization lifted, for vehicles requiring to be stored and for vehicles that are ultimately disposed of. These costs are in line with the charges levied by the London Congestion Charging Scheme. Ultimately, a fine of up to £5,000 can be imposed if the issue is sufficiently serious as to warrant court action.

Rebates are available in the same way as rebates for VED and vehicles which are exempt from VED (military vehicles, vehicles operating under trade licences, etc) are also exempt from the levy. Further information can be found in the HGV Road User Levy Bill explanatory notes (www.publications.parliament.uk/pa/bills/lbill/2012-2013/0082/en/2013082en.htm (archived at https://perma.cc/T7VU-EBZY)). Full details are available in the HGV Road User Levy Act 2013.

The HGV Road User Levy is now an integral element of the UK's VED system for vehicles of 12,000 kg MAM and above, and needs to be considered by relevant operators when replacing or renewing vehicles and trailers. Tables showing the actual costs of the levy to foreign operators (daily, monthly, etc), and the six monthly and annual costs for UK operators, are contained in the tables below, which were taken from Schedule 1 of the Act and include notes for clarification of certain pertinent points in relation to the levy.

Schedule 1 – Rates of HGV Road User Levy

Table 8.1 sets out the rates of levy for each of the bands given by Tables 8.2 to 8.5.

TABLE 8.1 Rates for each band

Band	Daily rate	Weekly rate	Monthly rate	Yearly rate
A	£1.70	£4.25	£8.50	£85.00
B	£2.10	£5.25	£10.50	£105.00
C	£4.80	£12.00	£24.00	£240.00
D	£7.00	£17.50	£35.00	£350.00
E	£10.00	£32.00	£64.00	£640.00
F	£10.00	£40.50	£81.00	£810.00
G	£10.00	£50.00	£100.00	£1,000.00
B(T)	£2.70	£6.75	£13.50	£135.00
C(T)	£6.20	£15.50	£31.00	£310.00
D(T)	£9.00	£22.50	£45.00	£450.00
E(T)	£10.00	£41.50	£83.00	£830.00

Table 8.2 applies to a rigid goods vehicle (whether or not used for drawing a trailer) other than one to which Table 8.3 applies.

TABLE 8.2 Rigid goods vehicle

Revenue weight of vehicle		2 axle vehicle Band	3 axle vehicle Band	4 or more axle vehicle Band
More than (kg)	Not more than (kg)			
11,999	15,000	B	B	B
15,000	21,000	D	B	B
21,000	23,000	–	C	B
23,000	25,000	–	D	C
25,000	27,000	–	D	D
27,000	44,000	–	–	E

TABLE 8.3 Rigid goods vehicle with trailer over 4,000 kg

Revenue weight of vehicle		2 axle vehicle	3 axle vehicle	4 or more axle vehicle
More than (kg)	Not more than (kg)	Band	Band	Band
11,999	15,000	B(T)	B(T)	B(T)
15,000	21,000	D(T)	B(T)	B(T)
21,000	23,000	–	C(T)	B(T)
23,000	25,000	–	D(T)	C(T)
25,000	27,000	–	D(T)	D(T)
27,000	44,000	–	–	E(T)

Table 8.3 applies to a rigid goods vehicle within paragraph 10 of Schedule 1 to the 1994 Act (rigid goods vehicles used for drawing trailers of more than 4,000 kilograms).

The appropriate band for a vehicle to which Table 8.2 or 8.3 applies depends on:

(a) the revenue weight of the vehicle; and

(b) the number of axles on the vehicle, ignoring any trailer.

Table 8.4 applies to a tractive unit on which there are two axles.

TABLE 8.4 Tractive unit with two axles

Revenue weight of tractive unit		Any no of semi-trailer axles	2 or more semi-trailer axles	3 or more semi-trailer axles
More than (kg)	Not more than (kg)	Band	Band	Band
11,999	25,000	A	A	A
25,000	28,000	C	A	A
28,000	31,000	D	D	A
31,000	34,000	E	E	C
34,000	38,000	F	F	E
38,000	44,000	G	G	G

Table 8.5 applies to a tractive unit on which there are three or more axles.

TABLE 8.5 Tractive unit with three or more axles

Revenue weight of tractive unit		Any no of semi-trailer axles	2 or more semi-trailer axles	3 or more semi-trailer axles
More than (kg)	Not more than (kg)	Band	Band	Band
11,999	28,000	A	A	A
28,000	31,000	C	A	A
31,000	33,000	E	C	A
33,000	34,000	E	D	A
34,000	36,000	E	D	C
36,000	38,000	F	E	D
38,000	44,000	G	G	E

The appropriate band for a vehicle to which Table 8.4 or 8.5 applies depends on:

(a) the revenue weight of the tractive unit; and

(b) the number of axles on the semi-trailers that are to be drawn by the tractive unit.

The appropriate band for any heavy goods vehicle with a revenue weight of more than 44,000 kilograms is Band G.

In this Schedule:

(a) 'axle', 'rigid goods vehicle' and 'tractive unit' each has the same meaning as in the 1994 Act (see section 62(1) of that Act);

(b) a reference to a revenue weight of more than 11,999 kilograms is to be read as a reference to a revenue weight of 12,000 kilograms or more.

More comprehensive combined tables, taken from the Government website, which incorporate both the VED and levy costs are to be found below.

Vehicle Excise Licences

This section relates to the vehicle excise of all road vehicles and will, where appropriate, include reference to the HGV Road User Levy (above).

All mechanically propelled vehicles, whether used for private or business purposes, which are used or parked on public roads in Great Britain, must be covered by a vehicle excise licence indicating that the appropriate amount of VED has been paid – except when being driven, by previous appointment, to a place to have their annual test.

It is an offence to use or keep an unlicensed vehicle on the road for any period, however short. Conviction for such an offence will result in heavy fines, and back duty may be claimed (see also p 270). Furthermore, vehicle licensing rules mean that the registered keeper of a vehicle (the person named on DVLA's record) remains responsible for taxing a vehicle (or making a SORN declaration) until that liability is formally transferred to a new keeper. To avoid liability for taxing it, the keeper needs to inform DVLA when the vehicle is off the road, or has been sold, transferred, scrapped or exported. Once DVLA has been notified about a sale/transfer or that the vehicle is off-road they will issue an acknowledgement letter, which should be kept as proof that the vehicle record has been changed. Failure to re-license a vehicle or make a SORN declaration will incur an automatic penalty of £80 (there are also fines for having an uninsured vehicle). Determined offenders will be faced with prosecution and could be fined a minimum of £1,000. Operators' licence holders also jeopardize their 'O' licences when committing excise duty offences.

Vehicles registered after April 2017 are taxed differently. They now need to pay their first year of VED based on their emissions standards. In addition, new vehicles costing more than £40,000 need to pay an additional rate of £310.00 per year for the first five years, after which they pay the normal rate for their emissions standards.

The present system of excise licences for most goods vehicles is based on gross weights (ie the 'revenue weight') and axle configurations, while goods vehicles not exceeding 3,500 kg gross weight are in the same class as private vehicles, which is called private/light goods (PLG) (see p 593 for full details).

Exemptions

Exemption from VED (as specified in the Vehicle Excise and Registration Act 1994) applies to the following:

1. Vehicles used for police, fire brigade, ambulance or health services (including veterinary ambulances).
2. Mines rescue vehicles.
3. Vehicles used for the haulage of lifeboats and lifeboat gear.
4. Vehicles for disabled people, including mobility scooters and powered wheelchairs with a maximum speed of 8 mph for road use.
5. Vehicles used solely for forestry, agriculture or horticultural purposes travelling on public roads to pass between land occupied by the same person and the distance travelled on public roads is not more than 1.5 km per journey.
6. Vehicles travelling to or from a place where they are to have an annual roadworthiness test by prior appointment.

7 Vehicles for export.
8 Vehicles in the service of a visiting force or headquarters.
9 Historic vehicles manufactured before 1 January 1976.

The special concessionary rate which formerly applied has been abolished and the following vehicles that were included in this class are now free of VED and are thus added to the exempt class along with the above-listed vehicles:

- An agricultural or off-road tractor which is a tractor used on public roads only for purposes relating to agriculture, horticulture, forestry or cutting verges, hedges or trees bordering public roads. An off-road tractor is one which is not an agricultural tractor but which is designed and constructed primarily for use otherwise than on roads and is incapable of exceeding 25 mph on the level.
- A light agricultural vehicle which is a vehicle with a revenue weight not exceeding 1,000 kg which is designed and constructed to seat only the driver and primarily for use otherwise than on roads; and is used only for agriculture, horticulture or forestry.
- An agricultural engine.
- Mowing machines.
- Steam-powered vehicles.
- Electrically propelled vehicles where the source of power is not connected to any other source of power when the vehicle is moving.
- Vehicles when used, or going to or from a place for use, or kept for use, for clearing snow on public roads by means of a snow plough or similar device.
- Vehicles constructed or adapted and used only for the conveyance of machinery for spreading material on roads to deal with frost, ice or snow.

Special Vehicles

Special vehicles over 3.5 tonnes – current and annual rate of duty £165. This class includes mobile cranes, digging machines, works trucks, road rollers and showmen's goods and haulage vehicles. Vehicles classed as 'mobile pumping vehicles' have been added to this category. However, some 'special vehicles' are currently being reviewed and the list of vehicles above may change.

Rates of Duty

The rate of duty payable varies depending on the way in which the vehicle is constructed, the way that it is used and, in the case of light vehicles, their unladen weight, and for heavy goods vehicles, their 'revenue' weight and the number of axles. The current rates of duty shown below in the tables are the new rates following the introduction of the HGV Road User Levy in 2014. Because this levy only applies to vehicles 12,000 kg MAM and above, the rates for lighter vehicles are shown on separate tables.

Revenue Weight

Revenue weight means either the 'confirmed maximum weight' as determined under the plating and testing regulations (ie by the issue of a plate and plating certificate), or the 'design weight' for vehicles not subject to plating and testing and currently known as restricted LGVs (this is the maximum laden weight at which non-plated vehicles can legally operate on roads in the UK).

Down-Plating

For various operational reasons heavy goods vehicles are specified to a higher standard and gross weight than payload weights demand. However, to avoid the higher rates of VED (and reduce HGV Road User Levy costs) that would normally be payable, such vehicles may be down-plated without making any technical change to the specification – see pp 443–44 for details of how this can be done.

Reduced Pollution Vehicles

Reduced rates of VED applied to certain buses, haulage vehicles and heavy goods vehicles which were built or adapted to ensure reduced pollution exhaust emissions under the provisions of the Vehicle Excise Duty (Reduced Pollution) Regulations 1998 (as amended). These regulations:

- set out the reduced pollution requirements to be satisfied in order for a vehicle to qualify for reduced rates of excise duty;
- provided for the issue of reduced pollution certificates (but see earlier) for vehicles not exceeding 12,000 kg MAM, or grants/discounts for vehicles which do exceed 12,000 kg MAM, where the specified requirements have been met;
- set out the procedure for applying for a vehicle examination in order to obtain a reduced pollution grant.

Note: As discussed earlier, reduced pollution certificates and grants were phased out completely at the end of 2017.

Articulated Combinations

In the case of articulated tractive units which are used with a variety of trailers, the determining factor for taxation purposes is the number of axles on the trailer likely to be used with it. This is so that the maximum amount of duty is paid to prevent a vehicle operating on the road at a rate less than that which is applicable. In general terms, the system operates so that the fewer the axles the greater the duty payable and vice versa. This is because the duty relates to the road damage caused and greater damage arises with fewer axles. In consequence of this it is illegal to operate a vehicle on a road for which the incorrect (ie insufficient) excise duty has been paid.

Trailers

Where drawbar trailers are drawn, if the gross weight of the trailer exceeds 4 tonnes and the gross weight of the towing vehicle exceeds 12 tonnes, additional duty is payable in accordance with published duty tables but not otherwise. So, if the towing vehicle or the trailer falls below these weights, no trailer duty is payable. This difference is reflected in the tables below.

Goods-Carrying Vehicles

The goods vehicle rate of duty is payable if the vehicle is built or has been converted to carry goods, and is actually used to carry goods in connection with a trade or business. In general this rate of duty applies to all types of lorries, vans, trucks, estate cars, dual-purpose vehicles and also passenger vehicles if they are converted for carrying goods. If, however, dual-purpose vehicles (see below) and goods vehicles (over 3.5 tonnes) are never used for carrying goods in connection with a trade or business they may be licensed at the private heavy goods rate of duty, which is currently £165 per year if paid as a single payment. Payments by monthly/half-yearly direct debit attract a surcharge.

Following a High Court ruling in March 1999, heavy vehicles carrying wide loads in excess of 4.3 metres must be taxed at the 'Special Types' rate of duty, irrespective of their gross weight. This duty is based on the use of a vehicle rather than its construction, and when carrying a wide load under the Motor Vehicles (Authorisation of Special Types) General Order 2003, the relevant Special Types duty rate must be applied.

In yet another interpretation case, the Crown Court has ruled that concrete-pumping vehicles must be taxed at the goods vehicle rate of duty, and not at the reduced rate applicable to mobile cranes.

Driver Training and Non-Goods-Carrying Vehicles

Heavy goods vehicles which are used exclusively for driver training purposes may be licensed at the private heavy goods rate of duty even if they carry ballast (eg IBCs filled with water, or other loads such as bags of sand) to simulate driving under loaded conditions – *but not other 'commercial' loads*. Similarly, other goods vehicles used for private purposes (ie carriage of goods but not in connection with a trade or business – for example, privately used horseboxes) may be licensed at the private heavy goods vehicle rate of duty – currently £165 for vehicles over 3.5 tonnes (note the point about single payment above).

Private-Rate Taxation of Heavy Vehicles on International Work

The use of heavy vehicles for goods carrying in the UK or within EU member states while taxed only at the private heavy goods rate of duty is illegal both in the UK and in Europe (see also section on penalties, p 270). Furthermore, running a vehicle on the Continent with VED that has expired, on the assumption that the tax can be renewed on the vehicle's return to the UK, is also illegal. Under the provisions of bilateral agreements and under International Conventions on the Taxation of Road Vehicles, vehicles on which the correct rate of Vehicle Excise Duty has been paid in their country of registration are exempt from payment of further duty (but not tolls or other road charges) on being temporarily imported into the territories of other parties to the agreements. Where the correct duty is not paid in the 'home' country, there is a liability for payment of additional duty in each other country through which the vehicle travels.

Dual-Purpose Vehicles

For the purposes of the regulations a dual-purpose vehicle (as referred to above) is defined as a vehicle, built or converted to carry both passengers and goods of any description, which has an unladen weight of not more than 2,040 kg and has either four-wheel drive or:

- has a permanently fitted roof;
- is permanently fitted with one row of transverse seats (fitted across the vehicle) behind the driver's seat (the seats must be cushioned or sprung and have upholstered back-rests);
- has a window on either side to the rear of the driver's seat and one at the rear.

The majority of so-called estate cars, SUVs, station wagons, hatchbacks, certain Land Rovers and Range Rovers are dual-purpose vehicles under this definition. It should be noted, however, that vehicles used for *dual operations* are not dual-purpose vehicles in terms of the legal requirements.

The rates below show the cost of road tax for cars, vans and light goods vehicles starting from 1 April 2014. Medium sized goods vehicles and large goods vehicles not exceeding 12,000 kg MAM are shown on later tables.

NB: If you already know the vehicle details, you can find out its vehicle tax rate online at the DVLA website. Otherwise, you can check the vehicle tax rates in the tables below. They also show the tax class (TC) of the vehicle type they are for. The information in these tables is taken directly from the GOV.UK website, to whom thanks are due.

Vehicles registered after 1 April 2017

TABLE 8.6 First tax payment when you register the vehicle

CO_2 emission (g/km)	Petrol cars (TC48)	Diesel cars (TC49)	Alternative fuel cars (TC59)
0	£0	£0	£0
1–50	£10	£25	£0
51–75	£25	£110	£15
76–90	£110	£130	£100
91–100	£130	£150	£120
101–110	£150	£170	£140
111–130	£170	£210	£160
131–150	£210	£530	£200
151–170	£530	£855	£520
171–190	£855	£1,280	£845
191–225	£1,280	£1,815	£1,270
226–255	£1,815	£2,135	£1,805
Over 255	£2,135	£2,135	£2,125

NB: This payment covers your vehicle for 12 months.

TABLE 8.7 Rates for second tax payment onwards

Fuel type	Single 12-month payment	Single 12-month payment by direct debit	Total of 12 monthly payments by direct debit	Single 6-month payment	Single 6-month payment by direct debit
Petrol or diesel	£145	£145	£152.25	£79.75	£76.13
Electric	£0	N/A	N/A	£0	N/A
Alternative	£135	£135	£141.75	£74.25	£70.88

NB: Alternative fuel vehicles include hybrids, bioethanol and liquid petroleum gas.

Cars Registered on or between 1 March 2001 to 31 March 2017

The rate of vehicle tax is based on fuel type and CO_2 emissions for cars registered on or after 1 March 2001 to 31 March 2017.

The rates are split into bands depending on CO_2 emissions – the lower the emissions, the lower the vehicle tax.

CO_2 emission details are shown on the car's V5C Registration Certificate, or you can find emission details online.

The following two tables contain the 'standard' rates of vehicle tax for cars that are already registered.

TABLE 8.8 Petrol car (TC48) and diesel car (TC49)

Band	CO_2 emission (g/km)	Single 12-month payment	Single 12-month payment by direct debit	Total of 12 monthly instalments by direct debit	Single 6-month payment	Single 6-month payment by direct debit
A	Up to 100	£0	N/A	N/A	N/A	N/A
B	101–110	£20	£20	£21	N/A	N/A
C	111–120	£30	£30	£31.50	N/A	N/A
D	121–130	£125	£125	£131.25	£68.75	£65.63
E	131–140	£145	£145	£152.25	£79.75	£76.13
F	141–150	£160	£160	£168	£88	£84
G	151–165	£200	£200	£210	£110	£105
H	166–175	£235	£235	£246.75	£129.25	£123.38
I	176–185	£260	£260	£273	£143	£136.50
J	186–200	£300	£300	£315	£165	£157.50
K*	201–225	£325	£325	£341.25	£178.75	£170.63
L	226–255	£555	£555	£582.75	£305.25	£291.38
M	Over 255	£570	£570	£598.50	£313.50	£299.25

* Includes cars with a CO_2 figure over 225g/km registered before 23 March 2006.

TABLE 8.9 Alternative fuel car (TC59)

Band	CO_2 emission (g/km)	Single 12-month payment	Single 12-month payment by direct debit	Total of 12 monthly instalments by direct debit	Single 6-month payment	Single 6-month payment by direct debit
A	Up to 100	£0	N/A	N/A	N/A	N/A
B	101–110	£10	£10	£10.50	N/A	N/A
C	111–120	£20	£20	£21	N/A	N/A
D	121–130	£115	£115	£120.75	£63.25	£60.38
E	131–140	£135	£135	£141.75	£74.25	£70.88
F	141–150	£150	£150	£157.50	£82.50	£78.75
G	151–165	£190	£190	£199.50	£104.50	£99.75
H	166–175	£225	£225	£236.25	£123.75	£118.13
I	176–185	£250	£250	£262.50	£137.50	£131.25
J	186–200	£290	£290	£304.50	£159.50	£152.25
K*	201–225	£315	£315	£330.75	£173.25	£165.38
L	226–255	£545	£545	£572.25	£299.75	£286.13
M	Over 255	£560	£560	£588	£308	£294

* Includes cars with a CO_2 figure over 225 g/km registerec before 23 March 2006.

TABLE 8.10 Private or light goods (TC11)

Engine size (cc)	Single 12-month payment	Single 12-month payment by direct debit	Total of 12 monthly payments by direct debit	Single 6-month payment	Single 6-month payment by direct debit
Not over 1549	£160	£160	£168	£88	£84
Over 1549	£265	£265	£278.25	£145.75	£139.13

TABLE 8.11 Light goods vehicles (TC39)

Registered on or after 1 March 2001 and not over 3,500 kg revenue weight (also known as maximum or gross vehicle weight).

Vehicle	Single 12-month payment	Single 12-month payment by direct debit	Total of 12 monthly payments by direct debit	Single 6-month payment	Single 6-month payment by direct debit
Light goods vehicle	£260	£260	£273	£143	£136.50

TABLE 8.12 Euro IV light goods vehicles (TC36)

Registered between 1 March 2003 and 31 December 2006, Euro IV compliant and not over 3,500 kg revenue weight.

Vehicle	Single 12-month payment	Single 12-month payment by direct debit	Total of 12 monthly payments by direct debit	Single 6-month payment	Single 6-month payment by direct debit
Euro IV light goods vehicles	£140	£140	£147	£77	£73.50

TABLE 8.13 Euro V light goods vehicles (TC36)

Registered between 1 January 2009 and 31 December 2010, Euro V compliant and not over 3,500 kg revenue weight.

Vehicle	Single 12-month payment	Single 12-month payment by direct debit	Total of 12 monthly payments by direct debit	Single 6-month payment	Single 6-month payment by direct debit
Euro V light goods vehicles	£140	£140	£147	£77	£73.50

Where the vehicle weight exceeds 44,000 kg the 'special types vehicles' rate is charged. This is currently £2,485 VED for 12 months or £1,332.50 for 6 months plus Levy rates of £900 for 12 months and £540 for 6 months for Euro VI vehicles. Euro 0-V vehicles pay £2,785 VED for 12 months and £1,512.50 for 6 months plus Levy rates of £1,200 for 12 months or £720 for 6 months.

In respect of recovery vehicles, they have their own tax class under this new regime and need to pay £165 per year or £90.75 for six months if their revenue weight is over 3,500 kg but no more than 25,000 kg and £410 per year or £225.50 for six months if their revenue weight exceeds 25,000 kg. Should the payments be made by direct debit then the annual costs for a total of 12 monthly payments, or for a single six-month payment, will be £173.25 and £86.63 respectively for recovery vehicles no more than 25,000 kg and £430.50 and £215.25 respectively for recovery vehicles exceeding 25,000 kg.

Combined transport is also treated separately so that a Euro VI tractive unit with a trailer with three or more axles operating at over 41,000 kg but not over 44,000 kg will need to pay a combined VED and Levy rate of £586 per year or £350.60 for six months, whilst a Euro 0-V vehicle will pay £778 and £465.80.

VED Tables for Goods Vehicles Exceeding 3,500 kg MAM, Including Details of VED and Levy Bands

TABLE 8.14 VED and Levy rates Euro VI

VED band and rate	Total 12 months VED and Levy	Total 6 months VED and Levy	12 month VED rate	6 month VED rate	Levy bands	12 month Levy rate (Euro VI)	6 month Levy rate (Euro VI)	12 and 6 months Euro 0-V	6 month RPC discount or grant
AO	N/A	N/A	£165	£90.75	N/A	N/A	N/A	N/A	£2.75
BO	N/A	N/A	£200	£110	N/A	N/A	N/A	N/A	£22
A1	£156.50	£87.90	£80	£40	A	£76.50	£45.90	£102 and £61.20	£2.50
A2	£160.50	£87.90	£84	£42	A	"	"	"	"
A3	£176.50	£95.90	£100	£50	A	"	"	"	"
A4	£222.50	£118.90	£146	£73	A	"	"	"	"
A5	£227.50	£121.40	£151	£75.50	A	"	"	"	"
B1	£189.50	£104.20	£95	£47.50	B	£94.50	£56.70	£126 and £75.60	£20
B2	£199.50	£109.20	£105	£52.50	B	"	"	"	"
B3	£219.50	£119.20	£125	£62.50	B	"	"	"	"

C1	£426	£234.60	£210	£105	C	£216	£129.60	£288 and £172.80	£120
C2	£481	£262.10	£265	£132.50	C	"	"	"	"
C3	£505	£274.10	£289	£144.50	C	"	"	"	"
D1	£615	£339	£300	£150	D	£315	£189	£420 and £252	£185
E1	£1,136	£625.60	£560	£280	E	£576	£345.60	£768 and £460.80	£250
E2	£1,185	£650.10	£609	£305.50	E	"	"	"	"
F	£1,419	£782.40	£690	£345	F	£729	£437.40	£972 and £583.20	£250
G	£1,750	£965	£850	£425	G	£900	£540	£1,200 and £720	£250

* Inverted commas (") indicate the same cost as in the last figure above. For example, all Levy Band A vehicles pay the same levy rates irrespective of whether or not they are banded as A1 or A5. This follows for the other bancs where the band is sub-divided.

In order to calculate the VED/Levy cost operators will need to know the band(s) relevant to their vehicle(s). Tables 8.15 to 8.21 give that information.

TABLE 8.15 Rigid goods vehicles

Weight over (kg)	Weight not over (kg)	Two axles	Three axles	Four, or more, axles
3,500	7,500	AO	AO	AO
7,500	11,999	BO	BO	BO
11,999	14,000	B1	B1	B1
14,000	15,000	B2	B1	B1
15,000	19,000	D1	B1	B1
19,000	21,000	D1	B3	B1
21,000	23,000	D1	C1	B1
23,000	25,000	D1	D1	C1
25,000	27,000	D1	D1	D1
27,000	44,000	D1	D1	E1

NB: The bands above also apply to rigid goods vehicles that are used to pull trailers that do not exceed 4,000 kg. Where rigid vehicles do tow trailers exceeding a weight of 4,000 kg a different banding system is used and a higher rate of duty is applied. These bands and rates are below.

TABLE 8.16 Levy bands for rigid vehicles towing trailers exceeding 4,000 kg

Weight of vehicle (not trailer) over (kg)	Weight of vehicle (not trailer) not over (kg)	Two axles	Three axles	Four axles
11,999	15,000	B(T)	B(T)	B(T)
15,000	21,000	D(T)	B(T)	B(T)
21,000	23,000	E(T)	C(T)	B(T)
23,000	25,000	E(T)	D(T)	C(T)
25,000	27,000	E(T)	D(T)	D(T)
27,000	44,000	E(T)	E(T)	E(T)

TABLE 8.17 Rigid vehicles towing trailers exceeding 4,000 kg Levy rate and RPC grant

Levy band	Euro VI levy rate for 12 months	Levy rate 6 months	Euro 0-V levy rate for 12 months	Levy rate 6 months
B(T)	£121.50	£72.90	£162	£97.20
C(T)	£279	£167.40	£372	£223.20
D(T)	£405	£243	£540	£324
E(T)	£747	£448.20	£996	£597.60

TABLE 8.18 Tractive unit with two axles

Weight over (kg)	Weight not over (kg)	Two axles	Three axles	Four, or more, axles
3,500	11,999	AO	AO	AO
11,999	22,000	A1	A1	A1
22,000	23,000	A2	A1	A1
23,000	25,000	A5	A1	A1
25,000	26,000	C2	A3	A1
26,000	28,000	D1	B3	B1
28,000	31,000	D1	C1	B1
31,000	33,000	E1	E1	C1
33,000	34,000	E1	E2	C1
34,000	38,000	F	F	E1
38,000	44,000	G	G	G

TABLE 8.19 Tractive unit with three or more axles

Weight over (kg)	Weight not over (kg)	Two axles	Three axles	Four, or more, axles
3,500	11,999	AO	AO	AO
11,999	25,000	A1	A1	A1
25,000	26,000	A3	A1	A1
26,000	28,000	A4	A1	A1
28,000	29,000	C1	A1	A1
29,000	31,000	C3	A1	A1
31,000	33,000	E1	C1	A1
33,000	34,000	E2	D1	A1
34,000	36,000	E2	D1	C1
36,000	38,000	F	E1	D1
38,000	44,000	G	G	E1

TABLE 8.20 VED and Levy costs for rigid vehicles pulling trailers exceeding 4,000 kg with road friendly suspension

HGV axles	Levy band	Trailer weight (kg)	Gross train weight not over (kg)	VED band and rate number	VED and Levy 12 months (Euro VI)	VED and Levy 6 months (Euro VI)	VED and Levy 12 months (Euro 0-V)	VED and Levy 6 months (Euro 0-V)
2	B(T)	4,001–12,000	27,000	B(T)1	£351.50	£187.90	£392	£212.20
2	B(T)	12,000+	33,000	B(T)3	£416.50	£220.40	£457	£244.70
2	B(T)	12,000+	36,000	B(T)6	£522.50	£273.40	£563	£297.70
2	B(T)	12,000+	38,000	B(T)4	£440.50	£232.40	£481	£256.70
2	B(T)	12,000+	40,000	B(T)7	£565.50	£294.90	£606	£319.20
2	D(T)	4,001–12,000	30,000	D(T)1	£770	£425.50	£905	£506.50
2	D(T)	12,000+	38,000	D(T)4	£835	£458	£970	£539
2	D(T)	12,000+	40,000	D(T)5	£849	£465	£984	£546

TABLE 8.20 *continued*

HGV axles	Levy band	Trailer weight (kg)	Gross train weight not over (kg)	VED band and rate number	VED and Levy 12 months (Euro VI)	VED and Levy 6 months (Euro VI)	VED and Levy 12 months (Euro 0-V)	VED and Levy 6 months (Euro 0-V)
3	B(T)	4,001–12,000	33,000	B(T)1	£351.50	£187.90	£392	£212.20
3	B(T)	12,000+	38,000	B(T)3	£416.50	£220.40	£457	£244.70
3	B(T)	12,000+	40,000	B(T)5	£513.50	£268.90	£554	£293.20
3	B(T)	12,000+	44,000	B(T)3	£416.50	£220.40	£457	£244.70
3	C(T)	4,001–12,000	35,000	C(T)1	£584	£319.90	£677	£375.70
3	C(T)	12,000+	38,000	C(T)2	£649	£352.40	£742	£408.20
3	C(T)	12,000+	40,000	C(T)3	£671	£363.40	£764	£419.20
3	C(T)	12,000+	44,000	C(T)2	£649	£352.40	£742	£408.20
3	D(T)	4,001–12,000	33,000	D(T)1	£770	£425.50	£905	£506.50
3	D(T)	4,001–12,000	36,000	D(T)3	£806	£443.50	£941	£534.50
3	D(T)	10,001–12,000	38,000	D(T)1	£770	£425.50	£905	£506.50
3	D(T)	12,000+	44,000	D(T)4	£835	£458	£970	£539
4	B(T)	4,001–12,000	35,000	B(T)1	£351.50	£187.90	£392	£212.20
4	B(T)	12,000+	44,000	B(T)3	£416.50	£220.40	£457	£244.70
4	C(T)	4,001–12,000	37,000	C(T)1	£584	£319.90	£677	£375.70
4	C(T)	12,000+	44,000	C(T)2	£649	£352.40	£742	£408.20
4	D(T)	4,001–12,000	39,000	D(T)1	£770	£425.50	£905	£506.50
4	D(T)	12,000+	44,000	D(T)4	£835	£458	£970	£539
4	E(T)	4,001–12,000	44,000	E(T)1	£1,282	£715.70	£1,531	£865.10
4	E(T)	12,000+	44,000	E(T)2	£1,347	£748.20	£1,596	£897.60

TABLE 8.21 VED and Levy costs for rigid vehicles pulling trailers exceeding 4,000 kg without road friendly suspension

HGV axles	Levy band	Trailer weight (kg)	Gross train weight not over (kg)	VED band and rate number	VED and Levy 12 months (Euro VI)	VED and Levy 6 months (Euro VI)	VED and Levy 12 months (Euro 0-V)	VED and Levy 6 months (Euro 0-V)
2	B(T)	4,001–12,000	27,000	B(T)1	£351.50	£187.90	£392	£212.20
2	B(T)	12,000+	31,000	B(T)3	£416.50	£220.40	£457	£244.70
2	B(T)	12,000+	33,000	B(T)6	£522.50	£273.40	£563	£297.70
2	B(T)	12,000+	36,000	B(T)10	£730.50	£377.40	£771	£401.70
2	B(T)	12,000+	38,000	B(T)7	£565.50	£294.90	£606	£319.20
2	B(T)	12,000+	40,000	B(T)9	£725.50	£374.90	£766	£399.20
2	D(T)	4,001–12,000	30,000	D(T)1	£770	£425.50	£905	£506.50
2	D(T)	12,000+	33,000	D(T)4	£835	£458	£970	£539
2	D(T)	12,000+	36,000	D(T)8	£1,014	£547.50	£1,149	£628.50
2	D(T)	12,000+	38,000	D(T)5	£849	£465	£984	£546
2	D(T)	12,000+	40,000	D(T)7	£1,009	£545	£1,144	£626
3	B(T)	4,001–12,000	29,000	B(T)1	£351.50	£187.90	£392	£212.20
3	B(T)	4,001–12,000	31,000	B(T)2	£410.50	£217.40	£451	£241.70
3	B(T)	10,001–12,000	33,000	B(T)1	£351.50	£187.90	£392	£212.20
3	B(T)	12,000+	36,000	B(T)3	£416.50	£220.40	£457	£244.70
3	B(T)	12,000+	38,000	B(T)5	£513.50	£268.90	£554	£293.20
3	B(T)	12,000+	40,000	B(T)8	£663.50	£343.90	£704	£368.20
3	C(T)	4,001–12,000	31,000	C(T)1	£584	£319.90	£677	£375.70
3	C(T)	10,001–12,000	33,000	C(T)4	£680	£367.90	£773	£423.70
3	C(T)	4,001–12,000	35,000	C(T)1	£584	£319.90	£677	£375.70
3	C(T)	12,000+	36,000	C(T)2	£649	£352.40	£742	£408.20
3	C(T)	12,000+	38,000	C(T)3	£671	£363.40	£764	£419.20
3	C(T)	12,000+	40,000	C(T)5	£821	£438.40	£914	£494.20

TABLE 8.21 *continued*

HGV axles	Levy band	Trailer weight (kg)	Gross train weight not over (kg)	VED band and rate number	VED and Levy 12 months (Euro VI)	VED and Levy 6 months (Euro VI)	VED and Levy 12 months (Euro 0-V)	VED and Levy 6 months (Euro 0-V)
3	D(T)	4,001–12,000	31,000	D(T)1	£770	£425.50	£905	£506.50
3	D(T)	4,001–12,000	33,000	D(T)3	£806	£443.50	£941	£524.50
3	D(T)	4,001–12,000	35,000	D(T)8	£1,014	£547.50	£1,149	£628.50
3	D(T)	12,000+	36,000	D(T)1	£770	£425.50	£905	£506.50
3	D(T)	12,000+	37,000	D(T)2	£797	£439	£932	£520
3	D(T)	12,000+	39,000	D(T)1	£770	£425.50	£905	£506.50
3	D(T)	12,000+	40,000	D(T)4	£835	£458	£970	£539
4	B(T)	4,001–12,000	35,000	B(T)1	£230	£115	£135	£81
4	B(T)	12,000+	40,000	B(T)3	£295	£147.50	£135	£81
4	C(T)	4,001–12,000	37,000	C(T)1	£444	£222	£135	£81
4	C(T)	12,000+	40,000	C(T)2	£649	£352.40	£742	£408.20
4	D(T)	4,001–12,000	36,000	D(T)1	£770	£425.50	£905	£506.50
4	D(T)	4,001–12,000	37,000	D(T)5	£849	£465	£984	£546
4	C(T)	10,001–12,000+	39,000	D(T)1	£770	£425.50	£905	£506.50
4	D(T)	12,000+	40,000	D(T)4	£835	£458	£970	£539
4	E(T)	4,001–10,000	38,000	E(T)1	£1,282	£715.70	£1,531	£865.10
4	E(T)	4,001–10,000	40,000	E(T)3	£1,351	£750.20	£1,600	£899.60
4	E(T)	10,001–12,000	40,000	E(T)1	£1,282	£715.70	£1,531	£865.10

It is noticeable that these tables are quite complex and it is possible for operators to make mistakes and to risk underpaying the correct VED/Levy fee. Operators who may be uncertain are advised to contact the DVLA (DVA in Northern Ireland) to seek clarification. There is also help on the Government website to help operators calculate the correct tax: www.gov.uk/calculate-vehicle-tax-rates (archived at https://perma.cc/4PHD-JGQU). Operators can also download form V149 which gives expanded views of all the VED tables.

Payment of Duty

Excise duty is payable once annually, every six months or monthly. Application for initial registration or renewal of duty is made either online, or on the appropriate form as follows:

TABLE 8.22 Payment of duty

• First registration	- form VE 55/4 for new vehicles - form VE 55/5 for reimported and rebuilt vehicles
• Renewal of duty	- form V10 for all vehicles up to 3,500 kg - form V11 renewal reminder, which enables vehicles to be re-licensed at a post office - form V85 for heavy goods vehicles, which may be re-licensed at the DVLA in Swansea or at some post offices

The DVLA is also promoting its 'Fleet Scheme' introduced in 2015 as it does take a lot of the administrative burden away from operators of large fleets. The scheme means that the form V5 is not automatically issued to fleet operators. The DVLA retains the V5 unless it is requested. DVLA states that the scheme has the following advantages for fleet operators:

- Operators receive documentation (V11, V85 and V5C) in bulk and not 'piecemeal'.
- Operators are able to tax vehicles in bulk at post offices.
- There is access to a dedicated helpdesk within the DVLA.
- Issues are more easily and speedily resolved.
- Operators have access to the DVLA 'View Vehicle Record' (VVR) service on the GOV.UK website, enabling them to see, at a glance, what information is held on each vehicle.

Further information can be obtained from the DVLA website or by emailing the DVLA directly.

Reduced, Extended Periods and Refunds

A vehicle may be licensed for only six months at a time if this is preferred but this method of licensing, as the tables above show, means that a higher amount of duty is paid annually. All licences are valid only from the first day of the month in which they come into force. Alternatively, new vehicles may be licensed part-way through a month (but only at the DVLA) with the duty period commencing on the 10th, 17th or 24th day of the month and continuing through to the end of the 12-month period from the first day of the following month.

In cases where a vehicle is to be used for a shorter period than either six or 12 months or is taken out of service during the currency of the licence, a licence has to be taken out for one or other of these periods and then the DVLA informed in order for the owner or operator to receive their refund.

Statutory Off-Road Notification Scheme (SORN)

This scheme requires registered vehicle keepers to notify the DVLA whenever a vehicle is off the road untaxed. By law, vehicle keepers must provide a Statutory Off-Road Notice (SORN) declaring to the DVLA that the vehicle is not being used and is not being kept on a public road and is therefore not liable to VED.

The Government introduced new vehicle tax rules from 1 January 2004 under which keepers of vehicles who have not paid their tax (VED) within the month would be identified from the DVLA computer database and receive an *automatic* £80 fixed penalty. But persistent offenders could face prosecution and a minimum fine of £1,000. The changes meant that for the first time registered keepers of vehicles were now legally responsible for taxing them. If they did not tax their vehicle, or failed to inform the DVLA that the vehicle was off-road or had had a change of keeper, then they were liable for the fixed penalty – even if the vehicle belonged to someone else.

This scheme enabled the Government to crack down further on 'vehicle cheats' who did not tax their vehicles, many of whom also drove without insurance or a valid test certificate. At the time of these tax rules, there were estimated to be some 1.75 million untaxed vehicles on UK roads. As a test certificate (for light vehicles over three years old and LGVs over one year old) and insurance certificate are needed to purchase vehicle road tax, this measure, according to the Government, not only cut the number of untaxed vehicles, but also cut the number of unsafe and illegal vehicles on our roads.

Making a false 'off-road' declaration can result in prosecution and a maximum fine of £5,000 or two years' imprisonment on conviction.

Renewal of Vehicle Licences

When the licence expires after six months or 12 months it has to be renewed by completing renewal form V10 (cars and light goods vehicles) or form V85 (vehicles exceeding 3,500 kg). Renewal reminders are sent out from the DVLA on form V11 and this may be used as an alternative to form V10 to renew the licence at certain post offices (provided the vehicle is not over 3,500 kg gross weight where form V10 is used, there is no change in ownership or address which has not been recorded and no change to the vehicle or its use), or by telephone or online direct to the DVLA. The vehicle registration document and the appropriate fee are all that is normally required at post offices as they can check insurance details and annual test validity through their link at the DVLA. However, at some smaller post offices, a valid certificate of insurance and, if the vehicle is subject to annual testing, a current test certificate, may need to be shown. The necessary insurance and annual test details are held electronically by the DVLA for online renewals.

Form V85 is used for goods vehicles over 3,500 kg gross weight. Using this form, in addition to the registration document and fee, a valid certificate of insurance and a current test certificate need to be produced at the post office. Renewing tax can also be done online at the DVLA in the same way as for smaller vehicles, although you may need the insurance policy holder's permission to allow the DVLA to conduct the electronic check.

Where to Apply

Applications for renewal of duty may be made as follows:

TABLE 8.23 Applications for renewal of duty

• If you have the official licence renewal reminder, form V11 (provided there is no change in the details on the form)	In person to main post offices or online.
• If you have form V11 but there are changes in the details	In person or online.
• If the vehicle is a heavy goods vehicle for which no form V11 has been received	In person or online.

Payment of Vehicle Excise Duty, either online or at a post office, can now be made by credit card, for which a statutory extra charge of £2.50 is made. Re-licensing of vehicles online can be completed via the Government website at: www.gov.uk/renew-driving-licence (archived at https://perma.cc/WGM4-MD5E).

Replacement Licences

Replacements for lost, stolen or destroyed vehicle registration documents/certificates (or the new keeper supplement) can be obtained by applying to the DVLA using form V62 (Vehicle Registration Certificate V5C Application Form), which is available from certain post office branches, or can be downloaded from the Government website at: www.gov.uk/government/publications/application-for-a-vehicle-registration-certificate (archived at https://perma.cc/4BPF-XYXZ). An existing registered vehicle keeper on the DVLA computer may apply by telephoning 0300 123 4321 at any time 24 hours a day using a debit/credit card for payment, provided there are no changes in the registration details. A statutory administration fee is also charged.

Alteration of Vehicles

If a vehicle is altered during its life by adding or removing equipment, by changing the type of body or even the colour of the vehicle, by changing the plated weight or increasing the unladen weight by fitting a heavier body or heavier components, the DVLA must be advised of the changes at once. If the changes mean that the vehicle goes into a higher weight range, then the additional licence duty becomes payable from the date of the changes.

If a van is converted to carry passengers or has side windows fitted to the body behind the driver's seat the owner becomes liable to pay car tax to HM Revenue & Customs. The amount of tax payable is based on the current wholesale value of the vehicle. Any person making such a conversion must report the fact to the HM Revenue & Customs authorities immediately.

Sale of Vehicles

When a vehicle is sold, the seller must notify the DVLA by completing the bottom tear-off portion of the registration document (form V5), which is perforated for this purpose, with the name and address of the new owner of the vehicle. It is an offence to fail to notify a change of vehicle ownership (maximum fine £1,000) and it can lead to the original owner being prosecuted for offences committed with the vehicle by the new owner and leaving the previous owner to pay any fixed penalty fines incurred. The new owner has to fill in his name and address in the changes section of the registration document and send the document to the DVLA for registration in his name. If a vehicle is sold for scrap or is broken up, the registration document has to be sent to the DVLA with a note advising them of this.

Under a new vehicle keepership scheme, the police and the DVLA will combine reporting of the offences of failing to register a vehicle (ie by the new owner) and VED evasion. This scheme is intended to clamp down on those who fail to notify disposal or acquisition of a vehicle.

Where a vehicle is sold the DVLA will refund any full months VED remaining to the seller and the new owner must re-tax the vehicle before using it.

Production of Test Certificates

A valid goods vehicle test certificate has to be produced at the time of re-licensing any goods vehicle over one year old (ie vehicles over 3,500 kg gross weight and articulated vehicles which are subject to the goods vehicle annual test) at a post office, and a light vehicle or private car type (ie MoT) test certificate when re-licensing any vehicle not over 3,500 kg gross weight which is over three years old and is subject to the light vehicle annual test scheme at a post office. At the time of writing it is unclear which test certificate will apply to alternatively powered vans operating up to 4,250 kg as they may not be able to be MOT'd as they exceed the 3,500 kg weight limit for this test. Clarification is awaited from the D*f*T.

Vehicles Exempt from Plating and Testing

When applying to licence or re-licence medium and large goods vehicles which are exempt from plating and testing, a declaration has to be made on form V112G to cover the non-production of a valid test certificate. Light goods vehicles use form V112.

Where a person does not intend to use a vehicle during the period of an excise licence except for a purpose which is specifically exempt from testing requirements (see list on pp 446–48), a 'Form of Declaration' must be made as specified in the Goods Vehicles (Evidence of Test Certificates) Regulations 2004 (SI 2004 No 2577).

Penalties and Payment of Back Duty

Offenders prosecuted for evasion of VED face fines of up to £1,000 for cars and £25,000 for heavy goods vehicles. This also applies to payment at an incorrect (ie too low) rate of duty or payment by means of a cheque which defaults, while making a false 'off-road' declaration will lead to a fine of up to £5,000 or two years' imprisonment on conviction, as previously mentioned. Additionally, an offender may be ordered to pay any amount of back duty. Previously the amount of back duty payable could be reduced if the offender could prove non-use of the vehicle during any particular month, but this provision was rescinded. Failure by a vehicle keeper to notify the DVLA of a change of name or address could result in a £1,000 fine on conviction.

Foreign-Registered Vehicles in Great Britain

Foreign-registered cars and light vehicles brought into Great Britain temporarily by overseas residents are exempt from UK registration and licensing. See p 593 for further details.

Data Protection

In accordance with the provisions of the General Data Protection Regulation (GDPR) and the Data Protection Act the DVLA at Swansea is registered as a Data User and as such must make available, on request, details held on file concerning individual persons. Such information is normally shown on driving licences and vehicle registration documents but an enquiry to establish details held on file can be made through the Driver Licensing Share Scheme (covered earlier) in relation to driver licensing and by using the DVLA's online service that can provide details on vehicles including when the VED expires, the VED rate payable, when the annual test expires, the vehicle colour, SORN status, engine size, year of manufacture, year of first registration, etc. To access this service go to the GOV.UK website and type 'Get vehicle information from DVLA'.

Trade Licences

Trade licences (trade plates) are available for use by motor traders and vehicle testers to save them the inconvenience of having to license individually every vehicle which passes through their hands.

Different forms are required for new and existing trade licence applications and changes. For example:

- Form VTL301 to apply for a first trade licence.
- Form VTL305 to renew an existing trade licence.
- Form VTL308 to surrender a trade licence (refund of duty).
- Form VTL310 to apply for a duplicate or replacement trade licence or trade plates.

A trade licence can be obtained from the DVLA. Replacements for lost or defaced trade plates (which remain the property of the DVLA) cost £13.50. Besides the 12-month and six-month licences, it is now possible to obtain such a licence for periods between seven months and 11 months at pro-rata rates to the six-monthly rate (ie 55 per cent of the annual rate for six months, plus one-sixth of this amount for every month in excess of six months). See below:

TABLE 8.24 Trade licences

Month you apply	When the licence expires	How long it's valid for	Rate of duty for all vehicles
January	June	6 months	£90.75
January	December	12 months	£165
February	December	11 months	£165
March	December	10 months	£151.25
April	December	9 months	£136.10
May	December	8 months	£121
June	December	7 months	£105.85
July	December	6 months	£90.75
August	June	11 months	£165
September	June	10 months	£151.25
October	June	9 months	£136.10
November	June	8 months	£121.00
December	June	7 months	£105.85

Display of Trade Licences

The DVLA will, when they have approved the application, issue a pair of special number plates with the registration number in red letters on a white background – an additional plate is available in certain circumstances. Since the paper VED discs were discontinued, paper trade licence discs are also no longer issued.

Issue of Licences

There are considerable restrictions on the issue and use of trade licences; as already mentioned they are issued only to:

- motor traders, defined as 'manufacturers or repairers of, or dealers in mechanically propelled vehicles' (this also includes dealers who are in business consisting mainly of collecting and delivering mechanically propelled vehicles), plus those who modify vehicles (eg by fitting accessories) and those who provide valet services for vehicles, who may use the licence for all vehicles which are from time to time temporarily in their possession in the course of their business as motor traders;
- vehicle testers for all vehicles which are from time to time submitted to them for testing in the course of their business as vehicle testers.

Vehicles such as service vans or general runabout vehicles owned by motor traders cannot be used under trade licences; the full rate of duty has to be paid for such vehicles.

Use of Trade Licences

The following are the purposes for which vehicles operated under a trade licence may be used by a motor trader or vehicle tester:

- for test or trial in the course of construction or repair of the vehicle or its accessories or equipment and after completing construction or repair;
- travelling to or from a weighbridge to check the unladen weight or travelling to a place for registration or inspection by the council;
- for demonstration to a prospective customer and for travelling to or from a place of demonstration;
- for test or trial of the vehicle for the benefit of a person interested in promoting publicity for the vehicle;
- for delivering the vehicle to a purchaser;
- for demonstrating the accessories or equipment to a prospective purchaser;
- for delivering a vehicle to, or collecting it from, other premises belonging to the trade licence holder or another trader's premises;
- for going to or coming from a workshop in which a body or equipment or accessories are to be or have been fitted, or where the vehicle is to be or has been valeted, painted or repaired;
- for delivering the vehicle from the premises of a manufacturer or repairer to a place where it is to be transported by train, ship or aircraft or for returning it from a place to which it has been transported by these means;
- travelling to or returning from any garage, auction room or other place where vehicles are stored or offered for sale and where the vehicle has been stored or offered for sale;
- travelling to a place to be tested (and returned), dismantled or broken up.

It should be noted that the use of a vehicle on trade plates does not exempt the driver or operator from the need to ensure that it is in sound mechanical condition when on the road, even if being driven for the purposes of road testing or fault-finding prior to repair or after repair. The police can prosecute if they find trade-licensed vehicles on the road in an unsafe or otherwise illegal condition.

Carriage of Goods on a Trade Licence

Goods may only be carried on a vehicle operating under a trade licence:

- when a load is necessary to demonstrate or test the vehicle, its accessories or its equipment – the load must be returned to the place of loading after the demonstration or test unless it comprised water, fertilizer or refuse;
- when a load consists of parts or equipment designed to be fitted to the vehicle being taken to the place where they are to be fitted;
- when a load is built in or permanently attached to the vehicle;
- when a trailer is being carried for delivery or being taken to a place for work to be done on it;
- if the goods are another fully licensed vehicle being carried for the purpose of travel from or to the place of collection or delivery (ie the driver's own transport to get him out or back home).

Carriage of Passengers on a Trade Licence

The only passengers who are permitted to travel on a trade-licensed vehicle are:

- the driver of the vehicle, who must be the licence holder or his employee – other persons may drive the vehicle with the permission of the licence holder but they must be accompanied by the licence holder or his employee (this latter proviso does not apply if the vehicle is only constructed to carry one person);
- persons required to be on the vehicle by law; a statutory attendant, for example;
- any person carried for the purpose of carrying out his statutory duties of inspecting the vehicle or trailer;
- any person in a disabled vehicle being towed including persons from the disabled vehicle being carried provided this is not for hire or reward;
- a prospective purchaser or his servant or agent;
- a person interested in promoting publicity for the vehicle.

NB: It is illegal for transport fleet operators to road-test their own vehicles on trade plates. This has been established on the grounds that the vehicles are not 'temporarily' in their possession and are therefore outside the permitted terms of trade licence use.

Recovery Vehicles

A separate class of VED at an annual rate of duty of £165 or £410* currently applies to these vehicles. Any vehicle used for recovery work which does not conform to the definition given below must be licensed at the normal goods vehicle rate according to its class and gross weight.

**The total annual rates of duty for recovery vehicles based on design weights are as follows although these fees can be paid in monthly instalments in the same way as VED:*

- *3.5 to 25 tonnes* *£165.00 (£90.75 for six months)*
- *over 25 tonnes* *£410.00 (£225.50 for six months)*

Definition of Recovery Vehicle

For the purpose of this taxation class, a recovery vehicle is one which is 'either constructed or permanently adapted primarily for the purpose of lifting, towing and transporting a disabled vehicle, or for any one or more of those purposes'. A vehicle will no longer be a recovery vehicle under the regulations (ie the Vehicle Excise and Registration Act 1994, Schedule 1 part V) if at any time it is used for a purpose other than:

- the recovery of a disabled vehicle (a maximum of two disabled vehicles may be recovered at any one time);
- the removal of a disabled vehicle from the place where it became disabled to premises at which it is to be repaired or scrapped;
- the removal of a disabled vehicle from premises to which it was taken for repair to other premises at which it is to be repaired or scrapped;
- carrying fuel and other liquids required for its propulsion and tools and other articles required for the operation of, or in connection with, apparatus designed to lift, tow or transport a disabled vehicle;
- travelling to a place where it will be available to recover or remove a disabled vehicle and to go from a place where it has recovered a disabled vehicle or to any place to which it has removed a disabled vehicle;
- repairing a vehicle at the place at which it became disabled or to which it had been taken for safety;
- towing or carrying one trailer which had previously been towed or carried by the vehicle immediately prior to it becoming disabled;
- removing a vehicle from the road to a nominated place on the instruction of a police constable or a local authority under their statutory powers.

The Act allows the carriage of people and/or goods on a recovery vehicle under the first two items listed above, provided they were either a driver or passenger in the vehicle immediately prior to it becoming disabled, or goods being carried on the vehicle immediately prior to it becoming disabled. The driver and/or passenger of a disabled vehicle (and his personal effects) may also be carried from the place where the disabled vehicle is to be repaired or scrapped to his original destination.

The use of a recovery vehicle, subject to VED at the recovery vehicle rate, for purposes other than those described above is illegal and may lead to prosecution and demands for payment of duty (and back duty) at the full goods vehicle rate.

Operation of Recovery Vehicles

Recovery vehicles licensed under the recovery vehicle taxation class are not exempt from goods vehicle plating and testing unless they satisfy the definition of a 'recovery vehicle' (see above). In addition, recovery vehicles exceeding 12,000 kg MAM are now subject to type approval at first registration. Such vehicles, however, are currently exempt from 'O' licensing. However, recovery vehicles exceeding 7,500 kg are subject to speed restrictions. These are:

- Recovery vehicles exceeding 7,500 kg but not exceeding 44,000 kg: 60 mph on motorways, 50 mph on dual carriageways and 40 mph on any other roads.
- Recovery vehicles exceeding 44,000 kg: 40 mph on motorways, 30 mph on dual carriageways and 30 mph on any other roads.

Recovery vehicles operating within 100 km of their base are also exempted from the EU drivers' hours rules and the tachograph requirements but those persons who drive them must comply with the British domestic driving hours' rules (see pp 110–13 for details). The driver of such vehicles must also be in possession of a driving licence that enables them to drive a vehicle at a weight that equals the combined weight of the recovery vehicle and any vehicle being towed. For example the driver of a rigid (Category C) 12,000 kg gvw recovery vehicle performing a suspended tow of a vehicle exceeding 750 kg must be in possession of a Category C+E licence.

Rebated Heavy Oil (Red Diesel)

Commercial vehicles powered by diesel (heavy oil) engines must use diesel fuel on which the full rate of duty has been paid. A lower rate of duty is payable on fuel used for purposes other than driving road vehicles, such as driving auxiliary equipment, for contractors' plant which does not use public roads, bench-testing of engines and space heating. Fuel on which the lower rate of duty has been paid is known as rebated heavy oil but is more commonly called gas oil or red diesel (known as Solvent Red). It is illegal to use this type of fuel, or kerosene, in road vehicles, as is the use of other marked diesel such as that with the Solvent Yellow 124 marker (known as Solvent Yellow) used in most EU member states.

Rebated heavy oil must be marked, when delivered from bonded oil warehouses, with a red dye so that its use can easily be detected, and the supplier must deliver to the recipient a delivery note bearing a statement that the oil is 'not to be used as road fuel'. If both rebated and unrebated oils are stored in the same place a notice bearing the same wording must be placed at the outlet of the rebated oil supply.

Supplies of so-called 'green' diesel have become available from the Irish Republic. This fuel is to be regarded in the same way as 'red' diesel. In other words, it is illegal for normal goods vehicle use on UK roads and in Europe.

Road fuel testing units staffed by officers of HM Revenue & Customs (HMRC) operate throughout the UK to test fuel in vehicles and in storage tanks. Under the Hydrocarbon Oil Regulations 1973 and the Hydrocarbon Oil (Marking) Regulations 2002, HMRC officers are empowered to examine any vehicle and any oil carried in it or on it and may also enter and inspect any premises and inspect, test or sample any oil on the premises whether the oil is in a vehicle or not. Vehicle owners and drivers must give the officers facilities for inspecting oils in vehicles or on premises.

The following vehicles may use rebated heavy oil as fuel:

- vehicles not used on public roads and not licensed for road use;
- road rollers;
- road construction machinery (vehicles used or kept on a road solely for carrying built-in road construction machinery);
- vehicles licensed as 'limited use vehicles' and used for agriculture, horticulture or forestry which pass only between areas of land occupied by the same person and which travel on public roads between such places for no more than 1.5 km;
- agricultural machines (ie tractors);
- trench digging and excavating machines;
- mobile cranes;
- mowing machines;
- works trucks.

All other vehicles must use unrebated (full-duty paid) oil at all times. Heavy penalties, including fines of up to £5000, repayment of duty and even arrest and impounding of vehicles, are imposed on offenders convicted of using illegal diesel fuel. Clearly there will also be a major impact on the operator licence and OCRS.

It should be noted particularly by international hauliers that use of 'red diesel' (ie untaxed diesel fuel) carried in reserve or 'belly' tanks or fed from diesel tanks on refrigerated semi-trailers and used once outside the UK is an illegal practice (NB: red diesel can legally be used for powering refrigeration units on vehicles). It is also illegal to carry red diesel in unconnected or disconnected additional vehicle tanks. Although Customs checks abroad on vehicle fuel tanks are limited, any operator found running on or illegally carrying such fuel within the EU is likely to face heavy penalties.

Customs may question operators with unusually large diesel tanks mounted on reefer semi-trailers to determine whether such fuel is being illegally used to power the vehicle as well as the fridge unit.

The maximum legal capacity for an engine-connected diesel tank on a vehicle is 1,500 litres. HMRC policy is that vehicle manufacturer-fitted fuel tanks are acceptable, but any additional tank fitted to the vehicle, or the exchange of a standard manufacturer tank for a large-capacity tank, infringes the rules and will incur a penalty. Above 1,500 litres it is considered that the vehicle would have to operate under ADR regulations (see Chapter 20). It should also be noted that transferring fuel purchased abroad for use in another vehicle is illegal and may result in charges for evasion of duty.

With estimated losses of some £600 million annually through illegal use of duty-free red diesel, and to eliminate unfair commercial advantage gained through its use, HMRC is anxious to implement further controls over its permitted use. It has already deliberated on:

- banning road construction vehicles from using red diesel unless they can be classed as 'works vehicles' operating within 1 km of a site;
- banning lorry or van-mounted elevated working platforms from using red diesel but allowing mobile cranes to continue the use of this fuel;
- banning the use of red diesel in unlicensed vehicles that are not used on public roads unless a SORN has been made;
- continuing to allow agricultural tractors and agricultural engines to use this fuel, but subject to a definition for their legitimate use in agriculture; and
- deciding what legislative changes (if any) are needed in relation to the defined use of farm vehicles, subject to discussions with interested parties.

Operators in doubt about the use of rebated fuel or wishing to report illegal use of rebated fuel should contact HMRC Tax Evasion Hotline on 0800 788 887 or visit the HMRC website.

Oil Storage

Many haulage firms need to store oil in large quantities and will therefore need to be aware of the Control of Pollution (Oil Storage) (England) Regulations 2010, which came into effect in 2011. These regulations apply to all types of oil (with the exception of waste mineral oil) stored above ground in containers of more than 200 litres at industrial or commercial premises. The regulations set minimum standards for oil storage (ie tanks to have a 110 per cent bund capacity) with the objective of preventing pollution and protecting the environment, oil being a major pollutant of watercourses and toxic to plants and animals. Fines for non-compliance are up to £5,000 but if pollution is caused they could be up to £20,000 or three months' imprisonment. In addition, if the pollution causes damage to the environment, the costs of remedial actions, such as soil sterilization or the re-planting of poisoned plant life can also be levelled at the 'polluter'. Further information can be obtained from the GOV.UK website or the DEFRA website.

Insurance (Vehicles and Goods in Transit) and Conditions of Carriage

09

Owners and operators of motor vehicles using the public highway must insure against third-party* injury and passenger claims. Further, an essential part of any investment in property (buildings, vehicles, plant, etc) is to obtain protection by insurance against loss or damage by theft, fire or other eventuality. Today it is also wise to be protected against claims (often spurious claims) made by third parties for compensation following injury to themselves or damage to their property as a result of some occurrence involving you, your employees, your property or taking place on your premises.

**The insurance company is the first party, the insured person(s) is the second party and anybody else involved (particularly if they make a claim for compensation) is termed the third party.*

Motor Vehicle Insurance

Third-Party Cover

The Road Traffic Act 1988 (as amended) (s143) requires that all motor vehicles, except invalid carriages and vehicles owned by local authorities or the police, used on a road must be covered against third-party risks. (Exact details of bodies exempted under these broad categories can be found in the Act itself.) This can be achieved by means of a conventional insurance policy or, alternatively, by a deposit of £500,000 in cash or securities to the Accountant-General of the Supreme Court but this is only applicable if authorization is granted by the Secretary of State for Transport. Normally, such authorization is only granted to public bodies and authorities and to major organizations with access to the substantial funds which may be needed to meet major accident claims.

Where the cover is obtained by conventional insurance means the Road Traffic Act 1988 stipulates that such cover is valid only if taken out with insurers who are members of the Motor Insurers' Bureau (MIB), which is a body established to meet claims for compensation (in respect of death or personal injuries only) by third parties involved in accidents with motor vehicles which subsequently prove to be uninsured against third-party risks.

Sections 145 (3a) and (3c) of the 1988 Act state that the insurance policy:

> must insure such person, persons or classes of persons as may be specified in the policy in respect of any liability which may be incurred by him or them, in respect of the death or bodily injury to any person or damage to property caused by, or arising out of, the use of the vehicle on a road in Great Britain... [and] must also insure him or them in respect of any liability which may be incurred by him or them... relating to payment for emergency treatment.

NB: In April 2000, the term 'on a road' (used above) was extended to include 'or other public place'.

Passenger Liability

Passenger liability insurance cover for motor vehicles is compulsory. This requirement applies to all vehicles which are required by the Road Traffic Act to have third-party insurance and the cover must extend to authorized passengers (other than employees of the insured, who are covered separately by the compulsory employers' liability insurance), other non-fare-paying passengers and also to what may be termed 'unauthorized passengers' such as hitchhikers and other people who are given lifts.

Unauthorized Passengers

The display in a vehicle of a sign which says 'No passengers' or 'No liability' does not indemnify a vehicle operator or driver from claims by so-called 'unauthorized' passengers who may claim for injury or damage received when travelling in or other wise in connection with the vehicle resulting from the driver's or vehicle operator's negligence. The law ensures that such liabilities are covered within the vehicle policy of insurance.

Property Cover

In accordance with an EU Directive (EC 5/84), from 1 January 1989 all UK motor insurance policies were required to cover liability for damage to property (up to a maximum liability of £250,000 arising from one accident or a series of accidents from one cause. This requirement was later raised to a maximum liability of £1,000,000). Damage to property in this context includes that caused by the weight of vehicle (eg to road surfaces, paving slabs, etc) and by vibration which may damage services (eg gas and water mains, gullies and sewers, telephone cables, etc) below the road surface, and third parties whose property is damaged in a vehicle accident have the right to request details of the vehicle insurance. Additional insurance cover would be necessary should these types of damage be caused by vehicles operating under Special Types General Orders (STGOs).

Certificate of Insurance

A policy of insurance does not provide the cover required by the Act until the insured person or organization has in their possession a Certificate of Insurance. Possession means, in this context, exactly what it says: 'promised' or 'in the post' is not sufficient to satisfy the law. The policy itself is not *proof* of insurance cover; it only sets out the terms and conditions for the cover and the exclusion and invalidation clauses.

The Certificate (or a temporary cover note proving cover until the Certificate is issued), which is *proof* (or at least evidence) of cover, must show the dates between which the cover is valid, give particulars of any conditions subject to which the policy is issued (eg the permitted purposes for which the vehicle may be used and those which are not permitted) and must relate to the vehicles covered, either individually by registration number or by specification, and to the persons who are authorized to drive them.

Note: Where the vehicles are covered by the operator depositing £500,000 with the Supreme Court the certificate issued is not a Certificate of Insurance; it is known as a Certificate of Deposit, although the rules relating to production, etc, are the same.

Production of Insurance Certificate

Unless applying online to the DVLA or at a main post office, it is necessary to produce a current Certificate of Insurance when making an application for an excise licence (road tax) for a vehicle. Alternatively, a temporary cover note may be produced and this will be accepted, but the insurance policy document itself is not acceptable.

Note: Under the Vehicle Excise and Registration Act 1994, where a fleet comprises 250 vehicles or more, the normal requirement for the production of individual Certificates of Insurance for fleet vehicles when applying for vehicle excise licences does not apply.

The owner (ie registered keeper) of a motor vehicle must produce a Certificate of Insurance relating to the vehicle if required to do so by a police officer. If he is not able to produce the Certificate on the spot, or if an employed driver is required to produce a Certificate of Insurance for the vehicle he is driving, it may be produced for inspection, no later than seven days from the date of the request by the police officer, at any police station which the owner or driver chooses. These same time limits apply to the production of Certificates of Deposit. The person to whom the request is made does not have to produce the Certificate personally, but may have somebody else take it to the nominated police station for him. A valid temporary cover note would suffice instead of the Certificate if this has not yet been issued.

Duty to Give Information

If requested to do so, the owner of a vehicle must give the police any information they request to help determine whether on any particular occasion a vehicle was driven without third-party insurance cover in force. The owner must also give information about the identity and address of a driver who may at any time have been driving a vehicle which is registered in his name, or information which may lead to identification of a driver if he is asked to do so by the police.

When the vehicle or vehicles concerned in such a request are the subject of a hiring agreement, the term 'owner' for the purposes of these insurance provisions includes each and every party to the hiring agreement.

The Motor Insurance Database

Under European law (the Fourth Motor Insurance Directive), vehicle fleet operators are required to register with the Motor Insurance Database (MID), which will hold details of the insurance arrangements for every vehicle on our roads. Failure to register will result in prosecution for the fleet operator, whose duty it is to provide details of the current fleet and any subsequent changes including the use of any temporary vehicles. Information about privately owned vehicles is provided to the MID directly by the insurer and vehicle owners can access the MID by using the Motor Insurers' Bureau (MIB) although there are charges for some enquiries.

Registration of details may be made via the internet to, and further details obtained from, the Motor Insurers' Bureau at: www.mib.org.uk (archived at https://perma.cc/2LLL-5MV6).

NB: Failure to notify the MID can lead to a fine of up to £5,000, and whilst it is the motor insurer who will normally notify the MID, individual operators should check that this is the case.

Continuous Insurance Enforcement

With over an estimated 1 million uninsured people reportedly driving on UK roads, the police are anxious to identify and seize uninsured vehicles, for which they have been given powers and for which they have been supplied with the technology to establish the insurance status of vehicles without the need to actually stop them. With the introduction of legislation in February 2011 (The Motor Vehicles (Insurance Requirements) Regulations 2011 – SI 2011 No 20) establishing a system of Continuous Insurance Enforcement (CIE), it is now a legal requirement for registered vehicle keepers to insure their vehicle(s) at *all* times (see above). The registered keeper does not have to be driving the vehicle to be caught. It is an offence to *keep* a vehicle without insurance unless the DVLA has been notified that the vehicle is being kept off the road and a valid Statutory Off Road Notification (SORN) has been obtained.

Since 2012, a SORN is now valid until the vehicle is next taxed, scrapped or permanently exported. SORNs can now be made online by going to www.dvla.gov.uk (archived at https://perma.cc/BW2S-5RYT). They can also be made by using a form

V11 reminder at a post office or by completing form V890 and posting it to the DVLA.

Under the 2011 system, the Motor Insurers' Bureau (MIB) and the DVLA work in partnership to identify uninsured vehicles by comparing DVLA vehicle records against those held on the MID. The registered keeper will be sent an Insurance Advisory Letter (IAL) telling them that their vehicle appears to be uninsured and warning them that they will be fined unless they take action. If the keeper fails to comply with the advice set out in the letter they will face the prospect of:

- the vehicle being clamped, seized and disposed of;
- prosecution with an unlimited maximum fine.

The driver will face:

- a fixed penalty notice of £300 and six penalty points;
- possible disqualification from driving.

Vehicle owners and keepers wishing to check that their vehicles are recorded as insured may do so by accessing the MID via its website at: www.askMID.com (archived at https://perma.cc/2NEU-ZRP2).

Invalidation of Cover

Insurance cover may be invalidated and claims for compensation refused if policy conditions are not strictly adhered to. In particular, these circumstances may arise if the vehicle is operated illegally (for example, in excess of its permissible weight, without a valid test certificate, in an unsound mechanical condition, outside the terms of an 'O' licence, if the driver is deemed incapable through drink or drugs or is incorrectly licensed or unlicensed, or one who is disqualified or if replacement components fitted to the vehicle are not to manufacturer's specification).

In some cases, where authorized drivers are actually listed and named on a policy, an un-named driver would also invalidate cover. These examples are not meant to be comprehensive, merely to give typical examples. A full list can be found within the RTA 1988 (as referenced above).

It is important to stress the need to examine carefully all the clauses contained in a motor insurance policy and to take steps to avoid any action which may invalidate the policy. This can include ascertaining whether or not a spouse or partner, who is a named driver but not an actual policy holder, is covered to drive other vehicles with the owners' consent when not holding an actual policy in their own name.

The employment of unlicensed or incorrectly licensed drivers or the use of unroadworthy vehicles (ie vehicles which do not comply with legal requirements or are found to be on the road in a dangerous condition) are two examples of the most likely ways of invalidating a motor insurance policy. Similarly, the policy should cover *all persons* who may be required (or may need in an emergency) to drive vehicles, not just employees.

Use of Unfit Drivers

It is important not to use drivers who are, or who are believed to be, medically unfit to drive. Insurance companies have a duty to notify the Secretary of State for Transport of the names and addresses of people refused insurance cover on medical grounds so their driving licences can be withdrawn. The standards of fitness are constantly changing and operators need to check that their understanding of what constitutes a 'notifiable' condition is up to date. Details can be found on the DVLA website.

Payment to Travel

Previously, motor insurance cover could be invalidated if passengers paid towards the cost of car-running expenses. As a result of provisions in the Transport Act 1980, the receipt of travel expenses contributions from passengers in private cars does not invalidate insurance policies provided no profit is made and that the payment is only deemed to be an 'appropriate contribution to the running costs of the vehicle'.

Cancellation of Insurance

When an insurance policy is cancelled, the Certificate of Insurance – there may be one or more depending on the number of vehicles covered by the policy – relating to that policy must be surrendered to the insurer within seven days of the cancellation date.

Cover in EU Countries

It is a requirement under the EU's Directive 2009.103 on Motor Insurance that every motor insurance policy issued in an EU country and the European Economic Area (EEA) countries of Iceland, Liechtenstein, Norway and Switzerland, must include cover against those liabilities which are compulsorily insurable under the laws of every other EU member state (*Article 7 (2) of the EEC Directive on Insurance of Civil Liabilities arising from the use of Motor Vehicles (No 72/166/EEC)*).

Motor policies issued in the UK contain provisions for such cover but this only provides very limited legal (usually third party only) minimum cover and, while an international motor insurance Green Card is no longer essential for some European countries, it is strongly recommended that one is obtained by all UK based drivers intending to drive on mainland Europe as Brexit will mean that all EU individual member states will be free to decide whether or not UK insurance meets their requirements. Although the EU has indicated that it will not require Green Cards to be held by UK drivers abroad, individual member states may act independently, and so the future remains uncertain.

Possession of a Green Card provides adequate evidence of a minimum of third-party insurance when abroad and it also eliminates problems of language and different procedures in foreign countries. However, drivers and/or operators may wish to check the level of cover they will be provided with by their insurers when planning to go abroad as it may not reflect the level of cover they enjoy within the UK as many 'comprehensive' UK policies only offer third-party cover when the vehicle is used abroad.

International Accident Report Form

A special accident report form has been devised by the European Insurance and Pensions Authority (EIOPA) for use as an agreed statement and accident report to be completed by drivers at the time of an accident when travelling in a foreign country (ie country other than that in which the vehicle is insured). The form is generally known as the European Accident Statement (EAS) and is a two-part form allowing each driver to complete the required sections on the form and exchange them with the other party. In this way the insurance companies get the information they require and the whole process is speeded up and simplified. The use of such a form (available from insurers), particularly when dealing with persons from other countries who cannot speak your language, is strongly recommended.

Fleet Insurance

Most large fleet operators obtain insurance cover on a 'blanket' basis. Under this arrangement vehicles are not specified on the Certificate of Insurance by registration number but there is a statement on the Certificate to the effect that cover is provided for any vehicle owned, hired or temporarily in the possession of the insured person or company. With blanket insurance it is normal to advise the insurance company by means of a quarterly return of the registration numbers of all vehicles added to or deleted from the fleet strength during that period.

The basic insurance premium is calculated on the total fleet at the beginning of the policy year and adjustments are made by the insurance company issuing debit or credit notes as necessary following receipt of the quarterly returns. This system saves the insurance companies having continually to issue and cancel cover notes and Certificates for vehicles in fleets where there may be many changes during a year because of staggered replacement programmes. The insured company also benefits by not having to get in touch with its insurers every time a vehicle is obtained or disposed of and, further, by being able to obtain an excise licence for a new vehicle without having to wait to receive a cover note from the insurance company.

Additional Insurance Cover

Extended Cover

The minimum cover against third-party risks mentioned above is not sufficient protection for the owner of a vehicle in the event of it being involved in an accident. To obtain extra protection against such contingencies it is necessary to extend the insurance cover beyond the third-party legal minimum. This can be done in varying stages depending on what the vehicle owner considers necessary for his purpose.

The basic policy can be extended to cover loss of any no-claims bonus and can be further extended to give additional limited cover (fire and theft) or comprehensive cover which provides protection against third-party claims, fire and theft risks, and accidental damage to the vehicle itself.

Guaranteed Auto Protection (GAP) Cover

This is an extra insurance policy, usually taken out when buying a vehicle by means of hire purchase. In the event of a total loss claim, it is intended to cover the difference between the current market value of the vehicle (ie the amount the insurance company pays out) and the amount still owing under the finance agreement.

Loading and Unloading Risks

Goods vehicle insurance policies should include clauses which give protection against claims arising from the loading or unloading of vehicles or the activities of employees engaged on such work.

Loss of Use

Most motor vehicle policies do not include cover for the loss of use of a vehicle or for the hire of a replacement vehicle following an accident. If the accident proves to be the fault of the third party, a claim has to be made against the third party for the loss of use or the hiring charges incurred but such claims are often difficult to substantiate (particularly the value of loss of use of the vehicle) and may result in only meagre awards. An extension to the policy covering such eventualities is the most satisfactory means of protection against this type of loss. This 'loss of use' is similar to the loss of use charges made by hire companies whilst repairs are made to their vehicles following damage caused by the hirer. In recent years this 'loss of use' has been extended to cover the loss of use of a hire car by the hire company because the car required valeting following the hire period. Typically, this is because the driver had been smoking in the vehicle.

Mechanical Failure

Mechanical failure is another item which is not normally included in motor insurance policies and generally it is not possible to obtain this type of cover for motor vehicles (although it is for some items of heavy engineering plant). Damage to engines caused by frost is covered in the majority of commercial vehicle insurance policies although there are certain qualifications. It is necessary, for example, if a claim is to be met, for the vehicle to have been sheltered in a properly constructed garage between specified hours of the night and for the anti-freeze solution to be of a set level of concentration. It is a condition of all policies that all reasonable steps should be taken to safeguard the vehicle from such loss or damage, and this clause particularly is one which the insurance company can use to escape a claim if it feels the policy conditions were not complied with. Most of these policy extensions will specify the exact types of oils, fuel, spare parts, etc that need to be used in order for the extension to be valid.

Windscreen Breakage

Insurance companies normally provide cover for windscreen breakage within the standard motor insurance policy. Claims made for broken windscreens are generally limited to a fixed amount (often set at a level where the vehicle owner will be expected to pay a proportion of the cost), but are paid to the policy holder without detriment to any existing no-claims bonus and irrespective of whether or not an 'excess' clause is in force on the policy. Similar cover applies on most goods vehicle policies providing for the cost of replacement of the broken windscreen and for repairs to paintwork damaged by the broken glass.

Medical Expenses

When professional drivers are required to travel abroad they should be covered for medical expenses incurred in foreign countries, for compensation for taking relatives out to visit them if they are detained in hospital and for bringing the patient back to the UK for further treatment if necessary. Compensation for the loss of drivers' personal effects and baggage can usually be included in this type of policy.

For more than 45 years, the Transmed scheme, purpose-designed for the international road transport industry, has been rescuing drivers from abroad. Transmed is based in Surbiton, Surrey and can be contacted on 0845 612 1003. The scheme is now also available through insurance brokers where individual packages need to be discussed.

This extended cover is over and above the level of cover provided by the European Health Insurance Card (EHIC), which is issued by the NHS and covers the driver for the cost of 'emergency' treatment in EU member states. In relation to 'emergency' this means that things like mountain rescue costs, repatriation flight costs and costs of any lost or stolen property are not covered.

It should be noted that the cost of treating existing conditions is not covered by the EHIC and that the EHIC will need to be renewed at five-yearly intervals. It should also be noted that EHIC only covers the costs to state provided healthcare on a 'national basis' and so if nationals have to pay for emergency treatment then the EHIC holder will also have to pay at the same rate.

Towing

Insurance cover for towing a vehicle which has broken down is normally provided under a goods vehicle policy, but the cover does not extend to damage caused to the vehicle while it is being towed, or to loss or damage of any goods being carried by the broken-down vehicle.

Damage by Weight

A goods vehicle insurance policy should provide cover against claims for damage caused to roads, bridges, manhole covers and suchlike by the weight of the vehicle passing over them. Some policies have a limit on the maximum liability acceptable for damage to property and this amount should be checked to ensure that it is adequate to meet likely claims in this respect.

Defence Costs

A motor insurance policy can be extended to cover legal costs incurred in defending a driver faced with manslaughter or causing death by reckless driving charges.

Goods in Transit Insurance

Motor vehicle insurance does not provide cover for claims made for damage or loss to goods carried on or in the vehicle. Goods in transit (GIT) insurance cover is needed to provide protection for this eventuality, in spite of not actually being required under UK law. In fact many own-account operators, carrying their own goods, include GIT insurance within their general business insurance.

Most GIT insurance policies provide cover in accordance with the limits included in the Road Haulage Association, or Freight Transport Association/Chartered Institute of Purchasing and Supply, Conditions of Carriage, which is normally a maximum liability of £1,300 per tonne for goods carried within the UK. If goods are of relatively low value (bulk traffics, such as coal, gravel and other excavated materials, for example) a lower limit of liability and consequently a lower premium can be considered. However, in many cases the £1,300 per tonne limit can be totally in adequate. Many loads these days are valued at tens of thousands of pounds with an equivalent value per tonne way in excess of the RHA, or FTA/CIPS, level and it is necessary to ensure that the insurance is adequate to cover the value of such loads. Owner-drivers, in particular, are advised to examine their GIT policies with great care; many such policies become automatically invalidated if high-value loads are left unattended (some loads must be accompanied *at all times*), approved routes are not taken or approved stopping points are not used, etc.

When goods of this level of value are carried regularly the insurance company will provide suitable annual cover but in some instances goods vehicle operators may find that a lower level of cover is suitable for most of their activities since they only occasionally carry high-value loads. It is important when this happens that the haulier makes himself aware of the load value and that the insurance company is advised of such loads and the appropriate cover obtained. Failure to do so could leave a haulier facing expensive loss or damage claims from his own pocket.

Some GIT policies specifically exclude certain high-risk loads such as cigarettes, tobacco, spirits, livestock, computers, etc, so the operator faced with a request to carry such a load should check that his policy covers the value and consult his insurers before accepting an order to move the goods.

The GIT policy can be on an 'All-Risks' basis but it is usual for the policy to meet the particular requirements of the operator to give him protection against the liabilities he assumes when he accepts goods for carriage. Such liabilities may be accepted under conditions of carriage (see later in this chapter) or under a contract or agreement or, in the absence of any specific contract or conditions, at common law. If the operator is carrying his own goods in addition to other people's he should make sure that these are also covered under the policy.

Carrier Liability for Goods

Most transport managers are aware that it is essential that they should effect a GIT insurance policy in respect of the goods carried, but it is most important to consider very carefully the liabilities which are assumed for the goods handled on behalf of customers and that there is full understanding of the GIT insurance contract which has been arranged.

If transport contractors for commercial reasons assume total responsibility for very high-value loads and do not in any way limit their liability by contract or by the application of conditions of carriage (see below), they will soon realize that the claims which are being handled by their GIT insurers become so expensive that the premium subsequently demanded will be far too high to bear.

Some third-party logistics providers (3PLs), under contract to distribute goods for a specific client, may well be able to negotiate that the client remains responsible for their own goods whilst in transit although this fact must be ascertained and not assumed.

High-Value Loads

There may be a temptation for haulage contractors to accept high-value loads because the freight rate being offered by the consignor is generous in comparison to normal haulage rates. Such loads, however, are notoriously attractive to thieves so it is important before accepting them to examine the GIT insurance policy to make sure that such high-value goods are not specifically excluded and that any special requirements which the insurance company may have imposed regarding routes, schedules, overnight parking and general vehicle specification, security and protection are complied with.

Night Risk and Immobilizer Clauses

Insurance policies frequently contain clauses requiring vehicles carrying high-value goods to be securely parked in locked or guarded premises overnight (known as the 'Night Risk' clause) or to be of a secure nature (box body), fitted with approved vehicle protection devices such as steering column and fifth wheel locks, engine immobilizers and alarm systems (known as the 'Immobilizer' clause). It is a condition of the insurance that such devices must be maintained in good working order and must be put into effect when the vehicle is left unattended. Failure to comply with such conditions can render the cover invalid.

Note: Other policies may insist that tracker devices and electronic seals are used.

Sub-Contracting

Care must also be taken when an operator uses a sub-contractor to move, or carry, goods on their behalf, as the sub-contractor must have adequate insurance to meet the terms of any contract formed between the principal carrier and the owner of the goods. This is particularly important as in the UK it is the principal carrier who will be liable to the customer and, in the case of any problems, will then need to pursue the sub-contractor in order to try to recover any financial losses incurred through a claim made by the customer.

Before valuable loads are sub-contracted to other hauliers, operators should take considerable pains to satisfy themselves as to the genuineness of any driver calling at their premises for a load (telephoning the driver's employer is one suggested method of checking). Experience shows that drivers with criminal intent will state that they are employed by a certain firm and that they require a return load; documents are frequently handed to the driver in such cases; he picks up the load and disappears. A few days later, when investigations are made, it is only then discovered that the driver obtained the load by false pretences. GIT insurers may not accept responsibility for such losses, or indeed any losses involving sub-contracted loads unless they have had prior notification of the loads and the circumstances.

GIT on Hired Vehicles

The increasing use of vehicles on contract hire raises an important issue regarding liabilities for goods carried. Normally under the terms of the hire contract it is made quite clear by the hire company supplying the vehicle that it assumes no responsibility for loss or damage to the goods which are carried on the vehicle.

Vehicles Hired with Drivers

If, however, under the terms of the contract the hire company offers to provide a driver, the driver acts under its instructions. Should he act in a way which would be considered contrary to normal reasonable action (for example, leaving a fully laden vehicle overnight in the open when he had been specifically instructed to empty the vehicle or to place it in a locked garage), the hire company may find itself held liable at law for a 'fundamental breach of contract' and be faced with having to pay the full amount of any loss incurred. A method of overcoming this difficulty is for the hire company to arrange with the owner of the goods for a GIT insurance policy to be effected in their joint names and for the owners of the goods to pay the premium in the contract hire agreement.

Conditions of Carriage

An operator carrying goods for hire or reward is advised to set out conditions of carriage under which he contracts to carry goods. In these conditions the carrier can define his liabilities by stipulating limits on the value of goods for which he will normally accept responsibility, with goods of higher value being carried only on special terms, and stating circumstances and provisions under which no compensation is payable. For example, an operator could make it a condition that he accepts no liability under the following circumstances:

- force majeur;
- act of war or civil war;
- seizure under legal process;
- act or omission of the trader, his employees or agents;
- inherent liability to wastage in bulk, or weight; latent defect, inherent defect, vice or natural deterioration of the merchandise;
- insufficient or improper packing;
- insufficient labelling or addressing;
- riots, civil commotions, strikes, lock-outs, stoppage or restraint of labour from whatever cause;
- consignee not taking or accepting delivery within a reasonable time;
- loss of a particular market whether held daily or at intervals;
- indirect or consequential damages;
- fraud on the part of the trader (in this context trader means either consignor or consignee);
- if non-delivery of a consignment, whether in part or whole, is not notified in writing within a specified number of days of despatch and a claim made in writing within a further specified number of days of despatch;
- if pilferage or damage is not notified in writing within a specified number of days of delivery, and a claim made in writing within a further specified number of days of delivery.

A note to the effect that goods are carried only under the Conditions of Carriage should be made on all relevant business documents, particularly consignment and delivery notes, invoices and quotations. Conditions of Carriage should always be drawn to the customer's attention and copies made available for customers to examine before they give orders for movements to commence. Conditions of carriage are 'usually' found on the reverse side of quotations or other paperwork used by hauliers and/or on their websites.

RHA/FTA Conditions of Carriage

The majority of transport contractors find it sensible to limit their liability in accordance with Conditions of Carriage such as those published by the RHA (these are the copyright of the RHA and may not be used by non-members) where the liability is based on a value of £1,300 per tonne on the actual weight of the goods carried or on the computed weight if the volume of the goods exceeds 80 cubic feet per tonne. This limit can be varied on the insurance policy to suit individual demands but otherwise retaining for the operator the legal liability limitations. Further sets of conditions for livestock carrying and sub-contracting are also prepared for members.

Conditions have also been drawn up by the Freight Transport Association (FTA) in conjunction with the Chartered Institute of Purchasing and Supply (CIPS), and these also specify a liability limit of £1,300 per tonne. These are not copyright and may be used by hauliers although legal difficulties may arise where RHA conditions and the new FTA/CIPS conditions are applied to the same movement contract (ie one set by the customer and one by the haulier).

Unfair Contract Terms

The long-standing Unfair Contract Terms Act 1977, and subsequent Acts of 2014 and 2015, are aimed at consumer rights when contracts may be drawn up and affect such contracts as conditions of carriage. The effect of this legislation is to increase the liability of transport operators, particularly in respect of instances where liability for negligence is disclaimed by contract or by notice. Further, it prevents a business from excluding its liabilities for breach of contract when dealing with the general public. Consequently, any term in a contract purporting to exclude liability for personal injury by negligence is void. Any term excluding liability for damage to property by negligence is also void unless the term used is reasonable as between the parties to the contract.

Cover for International Haulage Journeys (not Own-Account)

The GIT cover described above is not sufficient or even legally acceptable where vehicles are engaged on international haulage work. In most cases, such operations are governed by the provisions of the Convention on the Contract for the International Carriage of Goods by Road, commonly known and referred to as the CMR Convention. This Convention automatically applies where an international haulage journey takes place between different countries at least one of which is party to the Convention (with the exception of UK–Eire and UK mainland–Channel Islands journeys, which are ruled not to be international journeys for this purpose).

Road hauliers who carry goods on any part of an international journey, whether they choose to know it or not, fall within the legal confines of the CMR Convention under which compensation levels for loss of or damage to goods are much higher than the standard Conditions of Carriage GIT cover applicable in national transport operations. CMR levels of cover vary according to a set standard which is published daily in the financial press. For this reason it is important to obtain adequate cover when involved in international transport.

Additionally, where hauliers undertake cabotage* operations they should discuss the levels of cover required with their insurers – indeed, they should see if extended cover is available to cover certain liabilities such as losses from unattended vehicles. Difficulties may arise where local conditions of carriage are imposed, and claims and legal wrangling arise under law other than English law. For example, under French law, minimum liability is set at such a high value that it may well exceed the amount per tonne covered by a UK haulier's CMR policy (see pp 671–74).

* The EU has indicated that cabotage will become illegal for UK operators operating within the EU as we will no longer be an EU member state and it is only

permitted as an 'EU activity'. That said, there 'should' be a transition period to allow any formed contracts, etc, to be changed and, of course, it also means that foreign operators will not be allowed to undertake cabotage operations in the UK. Once again the 'deal/no-deal' scenario means that this could all change.

Own-Account

The GIT cover described above for hauliers is not necessarily required by own-account operators, although it could be used if the operator felt it appropriate. However, most own-account operators limit the value of the load to the actual value of their goods being carried, or to another set limit below that of the requirements under CMR. Some actually set the limit extremely low as many own-account loads of items such as component parts or raw materials have little monetary value until later in the production cycle.

Security

Insurance claims relating to vehicle thefts are a serious problem and are of concern to insurance companies as well as to vehicle operators and the police. It is important that when away from base drivers should be encouraged to park their vehicles, especially if they are loaded with valuable goods, in guarded security parks. While the number of suitable security parks is limited and they are not always conveniently located, it is nevertheless in everybody's interest that vehicles should not be left parked overnight on the roadside or on pieces of wasteland. Some insurers are now refusing to pay out on loss or theft claims if keys are left in or on a vehicle, if a fitted immobilizer or tracker is not used or if the driver fails to undertake a check or security procedure that they were supposed to.

Additional security measures need to be taken to prevent illegal immigrants from entering vehicles returning to the UK from Europe and operators and drivers are required to have suitable laid-down security procedures, including regular and ongoing vehicle checks both on a daily basis and en route, and to maintain records of checks, if they are to be seen to be acting properly in relation to this problem. Guides on these procedures and checks are available from HMRC, the UK Border Force, the RHA and the FTA. It is proof that approved guides were being used and checks carried out accordingly that is often the main factor taken into account by HMRC when considering prosecution for illegal immigrants entering the UK in goods vehicles.

Security Warning

The RHA issues 'best practice' advice on vehicle security as follows:

- Make every effort to ensure you are employing honest staff. Take up references over at least the previous five years and be suspicious of unexplained gaps. When checking references by telephone be sure to look in the telephone directory yourself for the number. A number supplied by a dishonest applicant could connect you to his accomplices. A staff enrolment form is available on application to RHA Area Offices and this form or a similar one should be completed.

- Until you have seen his driving licence and have in your possession his P45 tax form and photograph, do not allow a newly engaged driver to take out a vehicle.
- Fit a vehicle immobilizer and/or alarm in as inaccessible a position as possible. Choose one which provides protection without the driver having to perform any operation which he normally would not have to do to stop his vehicle. Inspect the device frequently.
- Drivers of vehicles carrying valuable loads should not get out of their cab if stopped. Even if a police officer requests them to do so, they should offer to go to the nearest police station. Electronic locking or even bolts on the inside of the cab doors give added protection against hijackers.
- A trouble-free cash bonus, from which a driver can be fined if he does not observe your security drill, is helpful.
- Vehicles should not be left unattended for long periods, especially at night. At no time should keys be left in an unattended vehicle. Remember, a stationary vehicle with its windscreen wipers or indicators operating gives a clear signal to any watching criminal that it is his for the taking.
- Discourage drivers from using the same cafés at the same time each day, particularly where their vehicles are not parked within sight.
- Starter or ignition switches, security lock keys: remove numbers and keep the keys for each vehicle on a ring which is welded so that they cannot be separated.
- If a vehicle's keys are lost, change switches and locks. It is much cheaper than losing a load.
- Invite drivers to report to the police any suspicious circumstances, such as transfer of goods from one vehicle to another without apparent reason, which they might see on their travels, or the registration number of any vehicle which is persistently following them.
- When disposing of a vehicle, remove the name of your firm so that a thief cannot use it to secure a load by false pretences.

TruckPol

With the closure of the National Stolen Lorry Load Desk in 2003, the Metropolitan Police in partnership with the RHA established TruckPol, an intelligence unit dedicated to cutting road freight crime across the United Kingdom. TruckPol acts as a single point of contact, collating crime reports and intelligence from a variety of sources.

TruckPol actually closed down in 2012 but it was announced in March 2014 that it was to be re-opened after funding was secured. TruckPol is now available through its own website: www.truckpol.org.uk (archived at https://perma.cc/26RN-NQ4Y). Details on TruckPol can also be accessed through www.nationalbusinesscrimesolution.com/truckpol (archived at https://perma.cc/26RN-NQ4Y) or by calling 0333 136 3191.

Both the RHA and FTA support TruckPol and frequently update on security problem areas and locations, and provide advice for their members, in their newsletters and member briefings.

NB: Incidents of truck crime or suspicious behaviour, etc should first be reported to the police locally or to Crimestoppers (0800 555 111).

Road Traffic Law

10

Road traffic regulations are very complex and are to be found in a number of Acts and statutory instruments relating to all aspects of road use by pedestrians, cyclists and motorcyclists, motorists and, of course, small, medium and large goods vehicles and passenger vehicle drivers and operators. In recent years new traffic offences have been introduced along with tougher measures to deal with drink-drivers (with up to 10 years' imprisonment for drink-drivers who cause a death), drivers driving under the influence of drugs, 'historic offences' and with vandals who place road users' lives at risk by placing dangerous objects on a road or interference with traffic signs or signals (with up to seven years' imprisonment for convicted offenders).

One of the most important pieces of legislation concerning traffic law is the Traffic Management Act 2004 (as updated). Guidance notes on this large act can be found on the GOV.UK website. While the Act is predominantly concerned with traffic management matters, reducing congestion and roads issues, one of the key provisions that relates more specifically to transport operators is the establishment of a uniformed on-road traffic officer service to manage the traffic consequences of such incidents as accidents, vehicle breakdowns, obstructions and debris on the carriageway, etc. These traffic officers operate under the auspices of the Highways Agency and have the power to stop and direct traffic in the interests of keeping traffic flowing.

Definition of Roads

For the purposes of most aspects of road traffic law a 'road' is defined in the Road Traffic Act 1988 (section 192) for England and Wales as 'any highway and any other road to which the public has access, and includes bridges over which a road passes'. In Scotland, the Roads (Scotland) Act 1984 applies and defines a public road as 'any road and any other way to which the public has access, and includes bridges over which a road passes'.

NB: It has been held that so-called 'private' dock roads at ports from which ferry services operate are in fact 'open to the public' and therefore public roads on which drivers are subject to the normal road traffic rules applicable to all other public roads. This includes driving under Regulation EC 561/2006 and AETR rules. However, breaking daily rests for ferry embarkation and disembarkation can be recorded on the digital tachograph and is permitted (as detailed in Chapter 4).

The term 'highway' has its meaning in common law as a way over which all members of the public have the right to pass and repass. This might be on foot, on horseback, accompanied by a beast of burden or with cattle, or with a vehicle. For the purposes of the Highways Act 1980 a 'highway' includes the whole or part of the highway other than a ferry or waterway, and where it passes over a bridge or through a tunnel, the bridge or tunnel is part of the highway. This Act makes it an offence for a person, without lawful authority or excuse, in any way wilfully to obstruct free passage along the highway of whatever type.

The Highway Code

Many of the particular legal requirements relating to the use of vehicles on the road are identified in the *Highway Code*, along with much useful advice on driving and road usage, although it should be remembered that the *Code* is intended for guidance and is not, in itself, a book of definitive traffic law. However, many of the rules in the *Code* are legal requirements and failure to comply with these will render a driver liable for prosecution, and if convicted he may face a fine, penalty points being imposed on his driving licence and even disqualification from driving. In any case, even where a specific offence has not been committed, such as in the event of an accident, failure to follow advice given in the *Code* on safe driving may still result in attachment of blame.

A revised edition of the *Code** (latest edition updated on 20 August 2019) is currently published by the DVSA and is available online. Among recent changes were the legal requirements for drivers to comply with the flashing red X lane closure lights found on motorways (Rule 258) and advice in relation to the treatment of burns (Annex 7). Drivers are also advised to always carry high-visibility jackets in the vehicle for use during breakdowns, and there is also information on what to do when becoming tired while driving. Also included is a kilometres-to-miles conversion table. Both imperial and metric measures are stated throughout the text.

It is intended that future editions of the *Code* will include a section/sections on LGVs. A book covering the LGV sector that supports the main *Highway Code* is a DVSA publication entitled *Your Lorry on the Road – Safe Driving for Life*.

The main *Code* is broken down into subject areas and annexes as follows:

- Introduction.
- Rules for pedestrians (1 to 35).
- Rules for users of powered wheelchairs and mobility scooters (36 to 46).
- Rules about animals (47 to 58).
- Rules for cyclists (59 to 82).
- Rules for motorcyclists (83 to 88).
- Rules for drivers and motorcyclists (89 to 102).
- General rules, techniques and advice for all drivers and riders (103 to 158).
- Using the road (159 to 203).
- Road users requiring extra care (204 to 225).
- Driving in adverse weather conditions (226 to 237).

- Waiting and parking (238 to 252).
- Motorways (253 to 273).
- Breakdowns and incidents (274 to 287).
- Road works, level crossings and tramways (288 to 307).

In addition it covers:

- Light signals controlling traffic, light signals used to control traffic, including traffic light signals, flashing red lights, motorway signals and lane control signals.
- Signals used to alert other road users, including direction indicator signals, brake light signals, reversing light signals and arm signals.
- Signals used by authorized persons, including police officers, arm signals by persons controlling traffic, Driver and Vehicle Standards Agency officers and traffic officers and school crossing patrols.
- Traffic signs used, including signs giving orders, warning signs, direction signs, information signs and road works signs.
- Road markings used, including those across the carriageway, along the carriageway, along the edge of the carriageway, on the kerb or at the edge of the carriageway and other road markings.
- Vehicle markings used, including large goods vehicle rear markings, hazard warning plates, projection markers and other markings.
- Annex 1: You and your bicycle. An annex of the *Code* with information and rules about you and your bicycle.
- Annex 2: Motorcycle licence requirements. An annex of the *Code* with information and rules about motorcycle licence requirements.
- Annex 3: Motor vehicle documentation and learner driver requirements. An annex of the *Code* with information and rules about motor vehicle documentation and learner driver requirements.
- Annex 4: The road user and the law. An annex of the *Code* with information about the road user and the law.
- Annex 5: Penalties. An annex of the *Code* with information and rules about penalties, including penalty points and disqualification, a penalty table, new drivers and other consequences of offending.
- Annex 6: Vehicle maintenance, safety and security. An annex of the *Code* with information and rules about vehicle maintenance, safety and security.
- Annex 7: First aid on the road. An annex of the *Code* with information about first aid on the road, including dealing with danger, getting help, helping those involved, and providing emergency care.
- Annex 8: Safety code for new drivers. An annex of the *Code* with information about the safety code for new drivers, including the New Drivers Act and further training.
- Other information provided by the *Code*, including metric conversions, useful websites, further reading, the blue badge scheme and code of practice for horse-drawn vehicles.

* *Available from The Stationery Office and via its website* www.tsoshop.co.uk (archived at https://perma.cc/H94Q-6F23), *the Safe Driving for Life website, most booksellers and many newsagents, price around £2.50. It can also be downloaded free of charge as a PDF file.*

There is a separate Highway Code for Northern Ireland available through www.nidirect.gov.uk (archived at https://perma.cc/48MF-USE4).

Speed Limits

Excessive speed is said to be a contributory factor in one in three road casualties. How fast we drive is crucially important to how safe our roads are, and the Government's message for many years has been to 'Kill your Speed'. A new system of speed enforcement has been introduced – see below.

Five levels of speed limit for vehicles are imposed on road users:

- limits applying to vehicles using particular roads;
- limits applying to particular classes of vehicle (including limits imposed by the mandatory fitment of speed limiter devices);
- temporary speed limits on vehicles introduced for special reasons such as in potentially hazardous situations;
- average speed limits for vehicles transiting hazards and sites such as roadworks;
- variable speed limits which are set on major routes and determined by the volume of traffic and/or a temporary hazard at a given location.

Speed Limits on Roads

On roads where street lights are positioned at intervals of not more than 200 yards (defined as a 'restricted' road), an overall speed limit of 30 mph applies to all classes of vehicle unless alternatively lower speeds are indicated by signs or unless the vehicle itself is subject to a lower limit by reason of its construction or its use. In some instances, speeds in excess of 30 mph are permitted on such roads and this is indicated by appropriate signs showing the higher maximum limits.

The present maximum speed limits on roads outside built-up areas for cars and car-derived vans are 60 mph on single-carriageway roads and 70 mph on dual-carriageway roads and motorways, except where specified temporary or permanent lower limits are in force. In certain high-accident risk areas (eg housing estates and roads near schools) 20 mph speed-limit zones have been introduced in conjunction with road humps. Local authorities can introduce 20 mph zones, and their introduction is becoming ever more popular with many new ones being introduced right across the country and being applied to an ever wider range of types of roads.

Other so-called 'traffic calming' measures being increasingly used to improve road safety include road-narrowing chicanes, enforcement cameras and reductions from 60 mph to 50 mph on sections of roads with sharp bends. A 50 mph limit is also used, especially in Wales, as a measure to improve air quality.

Advisory speed limits on motorways should be observed. These are shown by illuminated signs which indicate hazardous situations and roadworks ahead and by temporary speed limit signs at roadworks. The amber flashing warning lights positioned on the nearside of motorways (two lights, one above the other) indicate an advisory slowing down until the danger, and the next non-flashing light, is passed. Mandatory speed limits may also be seen where 'variable' speed limits are enforced, especially on motorways at peak travel times or at roadworks sites on motorways (indicated by white signs with black letters and a red border). There are also an increasing number of roadworks where average speed limits apply. These speed limits calculate the time it takes for a vehicle to travel between two, or more, set points thereby enabling the average speed to be calculated for the distance travelled. Failure to comply with these mandatory motorway speed warning signs and limits can result in prosecution. Average speed limits are also used extensively in Europe for measuring average speeds between toll booths.

Speed Limits on Vehicles

Vehicles are restricted to certain maximum speeds according to their construction, weight or use but when travelling on roads which themselves are subject to speed restrictions it is the lowest permitted speed (ie of the vehicle or of the section of road) which must be observed.

Special Types Vehicles

Vehicles operating outside the Road Vehicles (Construction and Use) Regulations 1986 (C&U) for the purposes of carrying abnormal indivisible loads come within scope of the Special Types General Order (STGO) as described in Chapter 19 and must conform to specified speed limits depending on their category. These speed limits were stated earlier but are repeated here with other speed limits for ease of reference:

Works Trucks and Industrial Tractors

The maximum speed limit for works trucks and industrial tractors is 18 mph but the latter are not permitted on motorways.

Wheeled Vehicles not Fitted with Pneumatic Tyres on All Wheels and Track Laying Vehicles

Where such vehicles are used there is a 20 mph speed limit on all types of roads, although permission is normally required for these vehicles to use motorways. Advice on this is available from the RHA or FTA.

TABLE 10.1 Table of vehicle speed limits

	Motorway (mph)	Dual carriageway (mph)	Other roads (mph)
Private cars			
– solo	70	70	60
– towing caravan or trailer	60	60	50
Buses and coaches			
– not over 12 metres length	70 (65)*	60	50
– over 12 metres length	60	60	50
** Coaches over 7.5 tonnes subject to speed limiter legislation are restricted to 65 mph.*			
Goods vehicles			
Car-derived vans			
– solo	70	70	60
– towing caravan/trailer	60	60	50
Not exceeding 7.5 tonnes mlw			
– solo	70	60	50
– articulated	60	60**	50
– drawbar	60	60**	50
*** In Northern Ireland the speed limit for vehicles in these two categories is 50 mph only.*			
Over 7.5 tonnes mlw			
– solo	60	60#	50#
– articulated	60	60#	50#
– drawbar	60	60#	50#

NB: m/w means maximum laden weight (ie maximum gross weight for a vehicle as specified in Construction and Use Regulations).
See text below for speed limits for Special Types and other vehicles.
Transport Scotland announced that there is no plan to follow England and Wales by implementing the increased limits in Scotland at the present time in spite of a pilot scheme on the A9 using average speed enforcement and analysis of the effects of the rises in England and Wales. This means that the speed limit on a single carriageway for an LGV in Scotland remains at 40 mph, as of late 2019.
Operators and drivers are advised to inform their drivers who drive in both England and Scotland to reinforce the difference and prevent unnecessary speeding fines when vehicles are operated in Scotland.

Emergency Vehicles

Fire, police and ambulance service vehicles are exempt from all speed limits if, by observing the speed limit, they would be hampered in carrying out their duties. However, drivers of such vehicles have a duty to take particular care when exceeding statutory limits and could face proceedings if an accident results while exceeding the limits.

TABLE 10.2 Special Types vehicles

Vehicle category	Motorways	Dual carriageways	Single carriageways
Category 1	60 mph	50 mph	40 mph
Category 2 and 3	40 mph	35 mph	30 mph

Speed-Enforcement Cameras

The Road Traffic Act 1991 legally authorized the use of photographs as evidence by courts in cases of alleged speeding ('Yellow Box' offences, illegal bus lane use and traffic-light jumping, etc). Cameras have been installed at key sites since 1 July 1992 to catch speeding drivers and other offenders. The so-called Gatso cameras (named after their inventor, Dutch ex-racing driver Maurice Gatsonides) produce film showing the vehicle and its number plate (which can be enhanced by scientific means for purposes of clarity – and can even decipher the registration number of vehicles fitted with plates which have been photo-reflective sprayed), date, time and the vehicle speed.

However, digital speed-enforcement cameras have been progressively introduced to overcome the physical constraints of the old system, which requires the manual loading, unloading, removal and storage of film from the roadside units – a costly and time-consuming operation for already hard-pressed police forces.

More recently, because legislation allows for a prescribed device which 'captures and records images of motor vehicles at two positions on the road and calculates the average speed of the vehicle between those positions' we see average speed cameras. Where the statutory speed limit has been exceeded the vehicle and registered keeper are identified from DVLA records and a relevant penalty is imposed. In the case of hire vehicles, the hire company, as the registered owner, is informed and the driver contacted. There is usually an administration fee levelled by the hire company in these cases.

Average speed limit cameras are known as SPECS (speed-enforcement cameras) and were launched in Nottingham on 28 July 2000. The system measures average speeds between pairs of cameras mounted on distinctive columns a distance apart which create Speed Controlled Zones. Clearly since 2000 there has been extensive expansion of this type of enforcement and it will continue to increase as the UK Government strives to reduce annual road casualty and injury rates.

It is also worth noting that the enforcement authorities have recently been supported in the move against speeding drivers and the fixed penalty for speeding offences is now £100 and three penalty points.

Lighting-Up Time

All mechanically propelled vehicles must display front and rear position lights and headlamps (where required by regulations) between sunset and sunrise and during daytime hours when visibility is seriously reduced (see Chapter 13 for lighting details).

Night Parking

Goods vehicles not exceeding 2,500 kg gross vehicle weight do not require lights at night when standing on restricted roads (ie on which a 30 mph speed limit – or lower limit – is in force) if they are parked either in a recognized parking place (ie outlined by lamps or traffic signs) or on the nearside, close to and parallel to the kerb, facing the direction of travel and with no part of the vehicle within 10 metres of a junction (ie on the same side as the vehicle or on the other side of the road). On any road where these conditions are not met lights must be shown (ie front and rear position lights).

All goods vehicles exceeding 1,525 kg unladen weight must display lights at all times when parked on roads between sunset and sunrise. Trailers and vehicles with projecting loads must not be left standing on roads at night without lights.

Vehicles should be parked on the nearside of the road when left standing overnight except when parked in a one-way street or in a recognized parking place and they must not cause obstruction.

Increasing attention is being given by the police and local authorities to drivers sleeping overnight in heavy vehicles with sleeper cabs while parked in lay-bys. Drivers should be warned against this practice, which is usually considered illegal on the grounds that the vehicle is causing an obstruction. A similar situation applies when drawbar trailers and semi-trailers are left in lay-bys.

Parking in lay-bys, separated from the main carriageway only by a broken white line, without sidelights and other obligatory lights as appropriate being lit after lighting-up time, is an offence and the driver will be prosecuted if caught. This does not apply where the lay-by is segregated from the highway.

Stopping, Loading and Unloading

Leaving Engine Running

Whenever a driver leaves his vehicle on a road, the engine must be stopped (except in the case of fire, police or ambulance service vehicles or when the engine is used to drive auxiliary equipment or to power batteries to drive such equipment). Hitherto, the requirement for stopping a vehicle engine when stationary was to prevent noise, but an amendment to the C&U Regulations, effective from 2 February 1998, made preventing exhaust emissions an additional reason for the requirement.

Increasing numbers of vehicles fitted with stop–start technology and locally introduced stop–start areas are to be found in many UK cities and London boroughs, where failure to comply by switching the engine off if the vehicle is to be stationary for more than one or two minutes, can mean a fine.

A word of caution could be noted here as some people who have stopped a vehicle and left the engine running while they either made or received a mobile phone call whilst in the driving seat have been deemed to have been driving as they were deemed to have been 'at the controls of the vehicle for the purpose of controlling the motion.'

Obstruction

A vehicle must not be left in a position where it is likely to cause obstruction or danger to other road users, eg near an entrance to premises, near a school, a zebra crossing or a road junction.

Trailers (including articulated semi-trailers) must not be left on a road when detached from the towing vehicle.

Where a vehicle left in a dangerous position is found to have been the cause of an accident, the driver can be prosecuted irrespective of whether or not he was actually in the vehicle at the time of the accident.

Loading and Unloading Restrictions

Vehicles must not stop or park on clearways to load or unload unless specifically authorized to do so. In some areas loading and unloading restrictions are indicated by yellow lines painted on the kerb at right angles to it as follows:

- A single yellow line at intervals indicates a ban on loading and unloading between the times shown on a nearby plate (eg Mon–Sat 0830–1830).
- Double yellow lines at intervals indicate a complete ban on loading and unloading at any time.

The precise terms of the restriction are indicated on signs mounted on nearby lamp posts, walls, etc. Delivery drivers should check these carefully to avoid any infringement of the law. Delivery drivers may also need to contact the local police or traffic warden in order to get permission to load or unload if there is no alternative location to undertake these tasks. Operators also need to note the move towards low emission vehicles being required in order to load or in some areas where Ultra-Low Emission Zones (ULEZs) have been created.

Waiting and Parking Restrictions

Single, double or broken yellow lines painted on the road parallel to the kerb apply to waiting and parking at various times, but they do not indicate a ban on loading or unloading and the same applies to 'no waiting' prohibitions indicated by 'no waiting' signs (see the *Highway Code* for full details of waiting and parking restrictions).

Drivers should also be aware that loading and unloading and waiting and parking restrictions also apply to Red Routes where red lines are painted on the road at the kerbside, especially in cities such as London, areas such as the West Midlands, and to the Greenways of Edinburgh to allow traffic to flow more freely on major routes in to, and out of, the cities and area. There are also similar restrictions applying to bus lanes and multi-occupancy vehicle (MOV) lanes.

Parking Meter Zones

Loading and unloading in parking meter zones during the working day (the times are indicated on signs) is not allowed unless a gap between meter areas or a vacant meter space can be found. A vehicle using a meter space for loading or unloading can stop for up to 20 minutes without having to pay the meter fee (this does not apply when parking for any purpose other than loading or unloading the vehicle).

Tramways

With the increased use of trams in many of our towns and cities the Government issued guidance for all drivers in relation to what actions to take, and not to take, when driving on roads that are also tramways. Whilst this may appear straightforward to those of us who regularly encounter trams on a daily basis, for many drivers not used to operating around tramways, this guidance may be valuable. There is also guidance to be found in the *Highway Code*.

In summary the guidance states that:

You **MUST NOT** enter a road, lane or other route reserved for trams. Take extra care where trams run along the road. You should avoid driving directly on top of the rails and should take care where trams leave the main carriageway to enter the reserved route, to ensure you do not follow them. The width taken up by trams is often shown by tram lanes marked by white lines, yellow dots or by a different type of road surface. Diamond-shaped signs and white-light signals give instructions to tram drivers only.

Take extra care where the track crosses from one side of the road to the other and where the road narrows and the tracks come close to the kerb. Tram drivers usually have their own traffic signals and may be permitted to move when you are not. Always give way to trams. Do not try to race or overtake them or pass them on the inside, unless they are at tram stops or stopped by tram signals and there is a designated tram lane for you to pass.

You **MUST NOT** park your vehicle where it would get in the way of trams or where it would force other drivers to do so. Do not stop on any part of a tram track, except in a designated bay where this has been provided alongside and clear of the track. When doing so, ensure that all parts of your vehicle are outside the delineated tram path. Remember that a tram cannot steer round an obstruction.

Tram stops. Where the tram stops at a platform, either in the middle or at the side of the road, you **MUST** follow the route shown by the road signs and markings. At stops without platforms you **MUST NOT** drive between a tram and the left-hand kerb when a tram has stopped to pick up passengers. If there is no alternative route signed, do not overtake the tram – wait until it moves off.

Look out for pedestrians, especially children, running to catch a tram approaching a stop.

Always give priority to trams, especially when they signal to pull away from stops, unless it would be unsafe to do so. Remember that they may be carrying large numbers of standing passengers who could be injured if the tram had to make an emergency stop. Look out for people getting off a bus or tram and crossing the road.

All road users, but particularly cyclists and motorcyclists, should take extra care when driving or riding close to or crossing the tracks, especially if the rails are wet. You should take particular care when crossing the rails at shallow angles, on bends and at junctions. It is safest to cross the tracks directly at right angles. Other road users should be aware that cyclists and motorcyclists may need more space to cross the tracks safely.

Tramway overhead wires are normally 5.8 metres above any carriageway, but can be lower. You should ensure that you have sufficient clearance between the wire and your vehicle (including any load you are carrying, or fixed equipment) before driving under an overhead wire. Drivers of vehicles with extending cranes, booms, tipping apparatus or other types of equipment should ensure that the equipment is fully lowered. Where overhead wires are set lower than 5.8 metres, these will be indicated by height clearance markings – similar to 'low bridge' signs. The height clearances on these plates should be carefully noted and observed. If you are in any doubt as to whether your vehicle will pass safely under the wires, you should always contact the local police or the tramway operator. Never take a chance as this can be extremely hazardous.

Motorway Driving

Motorway driving requires special care and observance of the motorway regulations. In particular, vehicles not capable of exceeding 25 mph on the level are generally prohibited from using motorways, including vehicles operating under the Special Types General Order (see also Chapter 19) if they cannot exceed this speed.

Vehicles must not stop on motorways except when instructed to stop by a police or traffic officer, through mechanical defect or lack of fuel, water or oil, due to an accident, the illness of a person in the vehicle or for other emergency situations (including giving assistance to other persons in an emergency), or to permit a person from the vehicle to recover or remove objects from the carriageway. It is illegal to drive on the hard shoulder (unless the hard shoulder is being used as an additional traffic lane during peak periods) or the central reservation, to reverse or to make a 'U-turn' on a motorway. Vehicles which must use the hard shoulder for emergency reasons as described above must remain there only for so long as is necessary to deal with the situation and the driver and any passengers should move away from the vehicle and stay behind the protective barrier of the hard shoulder.

Use of Lanes

Goods vehicles with maximum laden weights in excess of 7.5 tonnes and vehicles drawing trailers (and certain other heavy motor cars not included in the categories mentioned) must not use the outer or offside lane of three- and four-lane motorways.

On some steep slopes of two-lane motorway sections large goods vehicles (ie over 7.5 tonnes) are banned from using the outside lane; these bans are clearly signposted on the approaches to the appropriate section indicating the extent of the banned section and the vehicles prohibited from using the outer lane.

From 1 January 2005 the range of vehicles prohibited from using the outer (offside) lane of three-lane motorways was extended to include goods vehicles with a maximum laden weight exceeding 3.5 tonnes which are fitted with speed limiters as required by the Road Vehicles (Construction and Use) Regulations 1986 (C&U) (see also p 383).

Note: Lane departure warning systems (LDWS) need to be fitted to all new goods vehicles over 3,500 kg MAM since 1 November 2015. These systems warn the driver that they have strayed out of the limits of the lane they are travelling in. This is a requirement under EC Regulation 661/2009 which also brought advanced emergency braking systems (AEBS) to the UK.

Temporary Speed Limits

Where carriageway repairs take place on motorways or where contraflow traffic systems are used an *advisory* 50 mph speed limit is usually imposed. The 50 mph limit can be lowered if the workforce needs to work in close proximity to the passing traffic. These limits are considered by the police to be a maximum speed, and they may prosecute drivers found speeding in these sections for a 'driving without due consideration' type of offence. However, it is becoming more common for a *mandatory* temporary speed limit to be imposed in such cases and where drivers are detected speeding in these sections they will be prosecuted for this offence.

Other Vehicles on Motorways

Light and heavy locomotives which do not comply with C&U Regulations, dump trucks, engineering plant and vehicles for export which do not comply with the C&U Regulations may be driven on motorways provided they are capable of attaining a speed of 25 mph on the flat when unladen and not drawing a trailer.

Learner Drivers on Motorways

Category B learner drivers are now allowed to drive on motorways, providing that they are accompanied by a driving instructor approved to accompany them and the car has dual controls. Holders of provisional LGV and PCV driving entitlements may drive heavy goods vehicles or large passenger carrying vehicles on motorways provided they hold a full ordinary driving entitlement (ie category B, if you passed your test before 1 January 1997 or B and C1 if passed later) and are accompanied by a suitably qualified driver.

Lights, Markings and Signs on Motorways

Hazard Warning

Motorways are equipped with amber hazard warning lights located on the nearside verge and placed at 1-mile intervals. When these lights flash, vehicles must slow down until the danger which the lights are indicating, and a non-flashing light, has been passed.

Rural Motorways

Rural motorways have amber lights, placed at not more than 2-mile intervals and usually located in the central reservation, which flash and indicate either a maximum speed limit or, by means of red flashing lights, that one or more lanes ahead are closed. The speed limit indicated applies to *all* lanes of the motorway and should not be exceeded.

Urban Motorways

Urban motorways have overhead warning lights placed at 1,000-yard intervals. Amber lights flash in the event of danger ahead and indicate a maximum speed limit or an arrow indicating that drivers should change to another lane. If red lights flash above any or all of the lanes, vehicles in those lanes must stop at the signal. It is as much of an offence to fail to stop at these red lights as it is to ignore automatic traffic signals.

Information Signs

New systems using overhead information signs have been installed on many of the UK's motorways. These are generally controlled from control centres operated by Highways England or Transport Scotland and the police to notify drivers of incidents and conditions on the road ahead and warn of delays, closures and diversions. They are also used to inform drivers of times and distances to major junctions.

Motorway Road Markings

Road markings designed to reduce the risk of nose-to-tail collisions are being increasingly used on some sections of the motorway network. The chevron-shaped markings are painted on the road surface at 10-metre intervals for 5 kilometres (ie 3 miles). Drivers are advised to keep at least two chevrons (ie two seconds) between themselves and the vehicle in front.

Local Radio Station Frequency Signs

Under arrangements with the D*f*T, local radio stations can have their broadcasting frequencies indicated on motorway signs. It is a condition of such signposting that the station in question provides traffic news relevant to the location of the signs and of benefit to long-distance travellers 24 hours a day, seven days a week with at least four broadcasts per hour at peak times and two per hour during off-peak times, with programme interruptions for important announcements. The signs do not carry the station name or logo, only the broadcasting frequency, enabling drivers quickly to tune into the appropriate wavelength.

Emergency Telephones on Motorways

Emergency telephones are located at 1-mile intervals on the hard shoulders of each side of motorways – there is no need (and it is both dangerous and illegal) to cross the carriageways to reach an emergency telephone. Arrows on the back of posts on the hard shoulder indicate the direction to the nearest telephone. The telephone box itself also has a code number written on it and the caller will be asked for this code number when making the call. The code number tells the operator the exact location of the telephone and on which carriageway it is sited. This enables the emergency services to attend with minimal delay. The use of the telephone is free, and it connects directly to the police, who should be given full details of the emergency, who is calling and the vehicle involved. A person travelling alone or drivers with a young child or children are advised to tell the police of this fact. After making the call you should return immediately to the location of your vehicle to await help but stand outside of the crash barrier, where one is fitted.

Driving in Fog

To help drivers avoid the grave hazards of driving in fog, the *Highway Code* clearly advises, in Rule 235, that drivers should:

- use headlights as required by the *Code* (ie switch them on when visibility is reduced to 100 m – 328 ft);
- keep a safe distance behind the vehicle in front, remembering that the other vehicle's rear lights can give a false sense of security;
- be able to pull up within the distance they can see clearly, especially on motorways and dual carriageways, where vehicles are travelling much faster;
- use the windscreen wipers and demisters;
- beware of other drivers not using headlights;
- not accelerate to get away from a vehicle which is being driven too close behind;
- check mirrors before slowing down and use the brakes so the brake lights warn drivers behind that their vehicle is slowing down;
- stop in the correct position at a road junction with limited visibility and listen for traffic until it is safe to cross, then do so positively without hesitating in a position directly in the path of approaching vehicles.

The *Code* also states that drivers MUST NOT use front or rear fog lights unless visibility is seriously reduced as they dazzle other road users and can obscure the brake lights. These lights must be switched off when visibility improves.

Automatic Fog-Warning System

Automatic fog-warning systems operate on several motorways. Detectors installed alongside the motorway identify when visibility falls below 300 metres and automatically switch on the existing matrix signals to display the message 'FOG'. These systems are now largely incorporated into the 'Variable Message' systems used on many motorways and major trunk roads. The signals are located at strategic points where unexpected pockets of fog may occur as identified by the Meteorological Office. When the fog signs are on, drivers should slow down and proceed at a speed where they can safely stop within their range of vision.

Hazard Warning Flashers

Four-way direction-indicator flasher systems fitted to vehicles may be legally used to indicate that a vehicle is approaching slowed or stationary traffic, when a vehicle is temporarily obstructing the road or any part of the carriageway either while loading or unloading, when a vehicle is broken down or for any other emergency reasons (previously their use was only permitted in emergencies). Further details of vehicle lighting requirements are to be found in Chapter 13.

Temporary Obstruction Actions

The Highway Code gives the following advice for when a vehicle breaks down:

- get your vehicle off the road if possible;
- warn other traffic by using your hazard warning lights if your vehicle is causing an obstruction;
- help other road users see you by wearing light-coloured or fluorescent clothing in daylight and reflective clothing at night or in poor visibility;
- put a warning triangle on the road at least 45 metres (147 feet) behind your broken-down vehicle on the same side of the road, or use other permitted warning devices if you have them. Always take great care when placing or retrieving them, but never use them on motorways;
- if possible, keep your sidelights on if it is dark or visibility is poor;
- do not stand (or let anybody else stand) between your vehicle and oncoming traffic;
- at night or in poor visibility do not stand where you will prevent other road users seeing your lights.

Drivers can also place, on the vehicle itself, a 'Road Vehicle Sign', described as a highly visible flexible yellow sheet depicting a red warning triangle.

The person in charge of, or accompanying, an emergency or breakdown vehicle that is causing an obstruction is authorized to place a 'keep right' sign to indicate a route past the vehicle.

In the case of an LGV breaking down, the following is recommended:

- If the ground is sufficiently firm, get the vehicle off the road if possible, preferably at least 3 metres from any passing traffic.
- Put the hazard warning lights on.
- Exit the vehicle on the side away from passing traffic, wearing a hi-visibility vest or tabbard.
- Don't stand in front of your lights and obscure them from other road users.
- Place hazard warning triangles at 100–200 metres behind the vehicle and one at the rear of the vehicle but don't use hazard warning triangles on a motorway if they are likely to impede any recovery vehicles.

NB: Goods vehicles operating under ADR carrying dangerous goods must also carry warning triangles or amber flashing lights in order to conform with these regulations.

Lights During Daytime

If visibility during the daytime is poor, because of adverse weather conditions, drivers of all moving vehicles must switch on both front position lights and headlamps or front position lights and matched fog and spotlights. This applies in the case of heavy rain, mist, spray, fog or snow or similar conditions. When vehicles are equipped with rear fog lights (see pp 411–12) these should be used when the other vehicle lights are switched on in poor daytime visibility conditions. Further details of vehicle lighting requirements are to be found in Chapter 13.

Parking

Drivers who park their vehicles in a position which causes danger or obstruction to other road users can be prosecuted and their driving licence endorsed with penalty points on conviction (usually three) or they can be disqualified from driving. This rule applies even if the driver is not in the vehicle at the time of any accident that may be caused.

The *Highway Code* lists the many places where drivers should not or must not park. Drivers should study these lists to avoid causing danger or committing an offence.

There are not many parking places for the goods vehicle driver who has collections or deliveries to make, particularly in town, and for this reason drivers should be instructed to take reasonable care when parking in congested areas to avoid causing obvious obstruction or danger. Drivers needing to park to unload heavy items or high-value items should enlist the help of the police, traffic wardens or a local authority parking enforcement officer in order to make a space available. In any case, drivers should not double-park, block entrances and exits of business or private premises, or park near dangerous junctions or near pedestrian crossings, as well as avoiding the areas mentioned in the *Highway Code*.

Parking on Verges

The Road Traffic Act 1988 (sections 19 and 20) makes it an offence to park a heavy commercial vehicle (ie a vehicle over 7.5 tonnes maximum laden weight including the weight of any trailer) on the verge of a road, on any land between two carriageways or on a footway whether the vehicle is totally parked on those areas or only partially so.

There are exemptions to this: when a vehicle is parked on such areas with the permission of a police officer in uniform, or in the event of an emergency, such as for the purposes of saving life or extinguishing fire, or for loading and unloading, provided that the loading or unloading could not have been properly performed if the vehicle had not been so parked and that the vehicle was not left unattended while it was parked.

It is an offence (under the Road Traffic Act 1988 section 34) for any person to drive a motor vehicle onto common land, moorland or other land which does not form part of a road, or on any footpath or bridleway beyond a distance of 15 yards, except where legal permission exists to do so, but then only for the purposes of parking or to meet an emergency such as saving life or extinguishing fire.

Lorry Road User Charging

LKW-Maut and GO-Box Systems

Germany, Austria, Switzerland and now Norway have their own lorry road toll (Maut) systems. Germany's LKW-Maut scheme, which applies solely to heavy trucks over 12 tonnes gross weight using the country's motorways, was finally inaugurated on 1 January 2005 after two previous false starts due to technological hiccups. Austria's Maut system, colloquially known as the GO-Box system, was introduced in 2004 to replace both that country's former Eco-points and 'vignette' systems. Switzerland's system is a mileage-based truck tax. This tax goes by the acronym LSVA. The Norwegian system, which was introduced in 2015, is aimed at reducing the numbers of goods vehicles avoiding the tolls on the major routes within the country using Autopass on-board units. It applies to goods vehicles exceeding 3.5 tonnes gvw and is known as a 'bar-tag'. There are similar systems operated in many EU member states, including the Eurovignette system which is applied in Luxembourg, the Netherlands, Denmark and Sweden, and the UK's HGV Road User Levy which uses a very similar system to the Swiss LSVA, although electronic enforcement is more widespread in the UK. Further details of these systems and others can be found in Chapter 26.

NB: Belgium changed the system of tolling on 1 April 2016 to include all goods vehicles over 3.5 tonnes gvw and the requirement that all vehicles subject to the new tolling must be fitted with an on board unit (OBU). This also meant that Belgium left the Eurovignette scheme. This change is also detailed in Chapter 26.

In addition to the road charges above, there are road tolls throughout Europe with additional charges made for many major tunnels and estuarial crossings.

Lorry Routes and Controls

Whilst there are many major route markers with the green capital 'R', many local authorities identify preferred routes for heavy vehicles passing through their areas and display on them appropriate signs that:

- mark the most suitable route between dock areas and the nearest convenient connection with the primary route/motorway network;
- mark a suitable alternative route at any place on the primary route network where drivers of goods vehicles might be advised to avoid a particular part of that route, but where it is not appropriate to direct all traffic onto the alternative route, or to the primary route itself;
- mark routes from the primary/motorway route system to local inland centres which generate a high level of goods vehicle traffic (industrial estates, for example).

Certain areas, especially London and an increasing number of towns and cities, impose controls on the movement of goods vehicles and the parking of goods vehicles. These controls and restrictions are always marked with appropriate signs and operators are advised to ensure that their drivers observe them.

London Controls

Vehicles over 18 tonnes pmw are prohibited from travelling along many routes through Greater London at certain times unless the operator holds an exemption permit (issued under the London Lorry Control Scheme), which must be carried on the vehicle in a conspicuous position. Vehicles are also required to be fitted with air-brake silencers (hush kits).

The routes on which the controls apply are well signposted and the times at which it applies are also given on the signs. It is an offence for a driver of a goods vehicle over 18 tonnes pmw to travel on the controlled routes at the relevant times unless a valid exemption permit has been issued and is carried on the vehicle. Application for exemption permits and vehicle plates should be made to the London Lorry Control Team; email: lorry.control@londoncouncils.gov.uk.

The London scheme applies (to vehicles without permits) at the following times:

TABLE 10.3 London scheme times

• Sunday	at all times
• Monday to Friday	midnight to 7 am and 9 pm to midnight
• Saturday	midnight to 7 am and 1 pm to midnight

Red Route Schemes

The Red Route scheme to prevent traffic congestion on certain primary routes in London has been extended. Originally about 6.5 miles of roadway between Archway Road and the Angel, Islington, was designated as a Red Route but other sections have been, and are being, progressively introduced until the full 315-mile Red Route network is complete. Each section is identified by single or dual red road markings and accompanying Red Route signs. Vehicles may only stop to collect or deliver at specified times (or not at all), only for limited periods (ie 20 minutes only between the hours of 10.00 am and 4.00 pm) and only in marked (ie white-painted) loading bays. Generally the Red Route bans will apply between 7.00 am and 7.00 pm.

Failure to comply with the restrictions can lead to severe penalties. A red Penalty Charge Notice (PCN) (penalty currently £130) will be issued by police or traffic wardens. If this is paid within 14 or 21 days, depending upon the terms of the Penalty Charge Notice, it is reduced to £65.

Similar schemes operate in other cities where the penalty is usually £70.00 or £50.00, which is reduced to £35.00, or £25.00 if paid within a set number of days (14, 21 or 28). Operators visiting UK towns and cities should check whether or not the city/town in question does operate such a scheme.

London Congestion Charging

Congestion charges of £11.50 on the day (but only £10.50 for fleet vehicles using auto-pay), and £14.00 per day, if made on the day following entering the Congestion Zone area, apply in a central area of London on weekdays only (Monday to Friday) between the hours of 7.00 am and 6.00 pm excluding public holidays.

The charging zone covers any route that crosses the River Thames by Lambeth, Westminster, Waterloo, Blackfriars, Southwark or London Bridges. Not included in the charging area are Euston Road, Tower Bridge, Elephant and Castle, and Vauxhall Bridge. The operating hours of the Congestion Charging Scheme are 7.00 am to 6.00 pm. Cameras are located at 85 per cent of the boundary intersections and at random points within the zone. These cameras record vehicle registration numbers and cross-check via computer with records of charges paid.

Vehicles running on gas or electricity are exempt after paying a £10 registration fee. All other commercial vehicles are included, unless they are emergency service vehicles or are vehicles on municipal duty, not competing with private firms.

Drivers who regularly enter the charging zone may pre-register and autopay, otherwise payment of the daily fee may be made by credit card – a call centre processes credit-card numbers. Since May 2011 the charge cannot be paid at places such as newsagents and convenience stores, etc. Any driver who has not paid prior to entry into the charging zone may pay later that day – up to midnight – or pay £14 until midnight on the following charging day. Payment can be made by calling 0343 222 2222 or through the Transport for London (T*f*L) website at: www.tfl.gov.uk/modes/driving/congestion-charge (archived at https://perma.cc/93F6-6UZS).

Failure to pay the daily charge will result in evaders incurring a £130 penalty, issued to the vehicle owner (not necessarily the driver). This is halved to £65 if paid within two weeks, but will rise to £195 if it is not paid within 28 days. There is an appeals procedure.

Low and Ultra-Low Emission and Clean Air Zones (LEZs, ULEZs and CAZs)

The Low Emission Zone (LEZ), now termed the Clean Air Zone (CAZ), across London commenced on 4 February 2008 although the current zone is larger than the original as it now covers an area stretching from Enfield to Dartford, Croydon and Hayes. According to T*f*L, the aim of the LEZ/CAZ is to improve air quality in London by deterring users of the most polluting vehicles from driving them in the area. The vehicles affected are older diesel-engined lorries, buses, coaches, large vans, minibuses and other heavy vehicles that are derived from lorries and vans such as motor caravans and motorized horseboxes not able to meet Euro IV emission standards. There was a phased introduction of the scheme from 4 February 2008 which continued through to January 2012.

Compliance with the emission zone requirement is by reference to particulate emissions from vehicle exhausts.

Following a lead by London which has operated a ULEZ for the central zone since April 2019, cities such as Birmingham, Brisol, Cardiff, Leeds, Manchester Sheffield, many Scottish cities, and others, are all currently evaluating and planning introducing emissions controls within their areas. The main impact for haulage and distribution operators who operate vehicles which cannot meet EuroVI emission standards will be the need to either pay to enter the areas concerned, retro-fit or purchase new vehicles.

In London generally, it is Transport for London (TfL) who operate and control the main emissions standards and are the lead body in these initiatives and the body that controls the main ULEZ and the planned LEZ covering an area bounded by the North and South Circular roads. Operators planning to serve London or go to London should contact TfL for clarification on standards and charges in the areas they intend to visit or traverse.

Whilst TfL leads the controls, the London boroughs have some degree of independence in their decision making. This allows different boroughs to plan and introduce different emissions controls regimes. For example, the latest ULEZs are those covering Hackney and Islington in London which have been in force since September 2018 and effectively mean that only ultra-low emissions vehicles are allowed in certain streets and roads at some peak travel times in these boroughs.

Contact before visiting is recommended because, if non-compliance is detected, the operator only gets a warning letter, but if further detection is recorded there is a daily charge of £200. This charge can be paid in advance, if required, although non-payment of the initial £200 leads to the 'fine' of £1,000 a day for an LGV. This is reduced by 50 per cent if paid within 14 calendar days, but increased by 50 per cent if not paid within 28 calendar days. The zone operates 24 hours a day, 7 days a week (including bank holidays).

It is also important that operators realize that there are actually two zones planned with the second zone planned to be in general operation right across the capital.

The standards for the second ULEZ are:

- Euro 4 for petrol cars, vans, minibuses and other specialist vehicles;
- Euro 6 for diesel cars, vans and minibuses and other specialist vehicles;
- Euro VI for lorries, buses and coaches and other specialist heavy vehicles.

Expansion of the ULEZ from Central London up to, but not including, the North and South Circulars originally planned for 2021 is now planned for 2020 and being trialled. It is intended that it will operate on a seven-day, 24-hour basis and will apply to LGVs and 'large vans'. Vehicles wishing to enter the zone will require Euro VI engines or pay a daily charge of between £12.50 and £100.

Currently, once the operator has paid for a day the vehicle can be driven within the Zone as many times as the operator wishes on that day. Payment will need to be made for every day that the vehicle is used in the Zone. For example, a vehicle being driven within the Zone at 10 pm on one day but leaving at 2 am the next day would need to pay for two days. Payment can be made by cheque or using a debit or credit card, or online.

LEZ/CAZ Compliance Test

Hauliers can book low-emission certificate (LEC) tests to prove their older vehicles comply with the requirements of London's LEZ/CAZ, which began in February 2008. These LEC tests are available at DVSA goods vehicle testing stations and ATFs and discounts are offered where the test is taken at the same time as the annual test.

Exemptions

Certain vehicles are exempt from the zones as follows:

- Specialist non-road going vehicles designed and built for mainly off-road use, but which may use the road for limited purposes (including agricultural and forestry tractors, mowing machines, agricultural and farm machinery and equipment, mobile cranes, and road and building construction machinery).
- Historic vehicles built before 1 January 1973.
- Vehicles operated by the Ministry of Defence.

If such vehicles meet any of the above criteria and are registered in Great Britain, they are automatically exempt and need not be registered with T*f*L. Such vehicles meeting any of the above criteria which are registered *outside* Great Britain (including Northern Ireland) are also exempt, but need to be registered with T*f*L. However, operators need to ensure that local London boroughs do not introduce their own exemptions.

Discounts

Some showman's vehicles are eligible for a 100 per cent discount from the daily charges they are registered to a person following the business of a travelling showman and have been modified or specially constructed.

Contact Website for Further Information

The T*f*L website at: www.tfl.gov.uk (archived at https://perma.cc/4CJS-DTMM) provides details of emissions requirements for most vehicle types, how to register, how to make payments and the penalty charges payable in a case of failure to comply.

LoCity

Although the original implementation date for the ULEZ/CAZ of 2020 was brought forward, the five-year scheme called 'LoCITY' is still in place. This scheme, operated by T*f*L, is a five-year programme in London aimed at reducing air pollutants and improving carbon efficiency. LoCITY is in place to help operators understand alternative low carbon and fuel technologies prior to the ULEZ/UCAZ requirement for Euro VI vehicles for operation within the ULEZ/UCAZ. It also enables London boroughs to upgrade to cleaner vehicles and provides information and training in modern technologies and infrastructure, all as preparatory actions prior to the ULEZ/UCAZ going live and is linked to the Fleet Operator Recognition Scheme (FORS).

Further information can be obtained from the T*f*L website: www.tfl.gov.uk/modes/driving/low-emission-zone (archived at https://perma.cc/9Z53-N6H6).

London Safer Lorry Scheme

Most operators using vehicles in Greater London now have to comply with the 'London Safer Lorry Scheme' which is overseen by T*f*L. The scheme operates 24 hours a day, seven days a week and applies to all goods vehicles exceeding 3.5 tonnes gvw. The scheme requires goods vehicles to be fitted with sideguards (unless specifically exempted) and Class V and Class VI mirrors to give a better view of pedestrians and cyclists in the proximity of the vehicle.

NB: In the case of fitting sideguards, it has been agreed that extendible trailers (trombones) will only need to 'fully comply' when the trailer is in the closed (unextended) position and that only the actual extended section will be subject to the exemption. This exemption is also subject to review and technological advances which may enable extended trailers to be fully fitted with sideguards in the future.

The scheme is being enforced by the police, the DVSA and the TfL-funded industrial HGV Taskforce (IHGV Taskforce). The maximum fine for contravention is £1,000 and the operator concerned will be referred to the Traffic Commissioner. Vehicles that do contravene will be banned from the Greater London area. Further information on the controls and exemptions can be found on the TfL website.

Note: It should also be noted that the T*f*L London 'Direct Vision Standards' for Euro VI LGVs exceeding 12,000 kg are progressing and that permits are available through T*f*L for vehicles meeting a 'one star' rating. Ratings of 0 to 5 have now been agreed, with the implementation date for the issue of permits last year being 26 October 2019. Operators of vehicles rated with 'zero stars' need to apply to T*f*L for a Safe System in order to obtain a permit. Vehicle 'star ratings' are available from the vehicle manufacturers (see below).

Zero-rated vehicles without a Safe System will then be banned from 26 October 2020, and 0 star and 1 star rated vehicles will be banned from 2024 unless they can prove a Progressive Safe System. The standards use 'star' ratings of 0–5 which are dependent upon the extent of 'direct' vision the driver has from the cab, mirrors and the fitting of certain equipment.

In relation to the equipment, the standards do require a camera monitor fitted to the nearside, a proximity sensor that gives an audible warning to the driver of a 'vulnerable' road user on their nearside and another audible warning which is able to be heard outside of the vehicle stating 'Warning this vehicle is turning left'.

Permits for 'Safe Systems' cover issues such as blind spot elimination and minimization, warning devices for intended manoeuvres and minimization of the physical impact of dangers presented by the vehicle itself. In addition, it will be recommended that the drivers of these 'Safe System' vehicles undergo specific training in the safety of 'vulnerable' road users and the use of safety equipment. Progressive Safe Systems will be introduced following a major review of the scheme planned for 2024, when the proposal is to increase the minimum star rating from 1 stars to 2 stars.

As mentioned above, DVS star ratings for vehicles are available from the vehicle manufacturers, but operators will need to supply the manufacturer with the age of the vehicle and the chassis number in order for the DVS rating to be confirmed.

NB: Whilst the majority of the content above relates to London other cities are monitoring the performance of these initiatives and the successes, or not, of similar schemes.

Bus Lanes

Traffic lanes on urban roads reserved solely for use by buses are a common feature in many towns and cities. Uniform traffic signs and road markings indicate bus lanes. A single wide solid white line is used to mark the edge of the reserved lanes. Upright signs incorporating international symbols combined with arrows show to other traffic the number of lanes available for their use. When the signs and restrictions are in operation on a road, all other vehicles, except for pedal cycles (and taxis if signed to this effect), are prohibited from using the bus lane. Although contra-flow bus lanes are still used, increasingly many towns and cities have ceased to use them on road safety grounds.

High-Occupancy Vehicle (HOV) Lanes

HOV lanes are a method of utilizing spare capacity in existing bus lanes used by some UK towns and cities. They are also used where the introduction of new bus-only lanes cannot be justified on bus frequency grounds, or as part of a policy to encourage car sharing. The basic principle is that only vehicles carrying two or more people, buses and two-wheeled vehicles are permitted to use the lanes during the hours of operation. Large goods vehicles may or may not be allowed access. Currently, some pilot schemes allowing goods vehicles access to these lanes are in operation.

Level Crossings

Most railway level crossings are now fitted with automatic half-barrier crossing gates and appropriate warning signs are given in advance. When a train is approaching such crossings, red lights flash and a bell rings to warn drivers and pedestrians. Once these warnings start the barrier comes down immediately, and drivers should not zig-zag around the barriers. When the train has passed, the barriers will rise unless another train is following, in which case the warnings will continue.

Drivers of vehicles which are large or slow (ie that with their loads are more than 2.9 metres (9 ft 6 in) wide or more than 16.8 metres (55 ft) long or weighing more than 38 tonnes gross or incapable of a speed of more than 5 mph) wishing to cross one of these crossings must, before attempting to cross, obtain permission to do so from the signalman by using the special telephone which is provided at the crossing. Failure to do this is an offence. In the event of a vehicle becoming stuck on the crossing the driver should advise the signalman immediately by using the telephone.

Level and Tram Crossings

Many cities now use trams and there are also rules in the *Highway Code* relating to encountering and crossing tramways. The *Highway Code* treats level crossings and tram crossings in similar ways. In short, the rules state that a driver crossing a level crossing or tramway must take care when approaching a crossing point, never enter a crossing unless the exit is clear, never get too close to the vehicle in front and never park or stop on a crossing.

In addition, in relation to trams, where they share the road with other vehicles, the rules state that care must be taken not to enter a road reserved for trams, not to park where it could obstruct a tram, to take care where tramways cross from one side of the road to another, to be aware of overhead clearance of any electrical wires and to look out for pedestrians who may be running to catch a tram.

Weight-Restricted Roads and Bridges

Where signs indicate that a particular section of road or a bridge is restricted to vehicles not exceeding a specified weight limit or axle weight limit, unless otherwise expressly stated, the weight limit shown relates to the actual weight of the vehicle or to an individual axle of the vehicle, not the relevant plated weights.

Signs protect weak bridges by restricting vehicles according to their maximum authorized gross weight (ie their plated weight) – indicated as 'mgw'. These have replaced existing signs as described above where the weight shown relates only to the actual weight of the vehicle and load at the time. The new signs apply even if the vehicle, with a plated weight greater than the limit shown, is unladen at the time and therefore well below the maximum weight limit for the bridge (unless the sign permits 'empty vehicles'). Where doubt exists about any particular sign it is advisable to consult the local authority responsible for its erection and to determine the precise wording of the Traffic Management Order under which authority the sign would have been erected.

Note: The Forth Road Bridge authority in Scotland currently enforces a maximum weight limit of 196 tonnes on the bridges for a single movement. In addition, vehicles exceeding 80 tonnes are subject to a speed limit and need to be escorted whilst vehicles exceeding 44 tonnes or more than 27.4 metres in length need to notify and have indemnity in advance of crossing, and vehicles over 2.9 m wide or over 18.65 m in length just need to give notification. Further information is available on the Transport Scotland website, www.theforthbridges.org (archived at https://perma.cc/P2WA-34W2) or by calling 0131 319 3083.

Owner Liability

Under the Road Traffic Offenders Act 1988 responsibility for payment of fixed penalty fines or excess parking charges, etc rests with the registered vehicle owner (ie the keeper of the vehicle, not necessarily the legal owner), if the driver who committed the offence cannot be identified or found. The registered owner of the vehicle is sent details of the alleged offence and is obliged to pay the fine or submit a 'Statutory Statement' of ownership in which he states whether he was the vehicle owner at the time of the alleged offence (in which case he should name the driver), had ceased to be the owner at that time or had not yet become the owner at that time. Where the person was not the owner he must give the name of the previous owner or the new owner to whom he transferred the vehicle, if he knows it.

When a vehicle is hired out for less than six months, and such an incident arises, the hiring company can declare that the vehicle was on hire and send a copy of the hiring agreement together with a signed statement of liability from the hirer accepting responsibility for the fine or excess parking charge. Such a clause is normally included in the hiring agreements which the hirer signs. Failure to pay a fixed penalty or excess charge, or to give information as required by the police in such matters, can result in a fine of up to £1,000 on conviction (or even £5,000 in certain circumstances).

Fixed Penalties

In order to reduce the pressure on the courts, a system of fixed penalties exists by which both civil enforcement officers (CEOs) (see below) and, in a limited way, police community support officers (PCSOs) as well as the police can issue fixed penalty notices requiring the vehicle driver or owner to pay the fixed penalty or to elect to have the case dealt with in court in the normal way. The fixed penalty system operates on two levels: non-endorsable offences (mainly dealt with by CEOs), and driving licence endorsable offences which only the police can deal with since CEOs have no general authority to request the production of driving licences.

Non-Endorsable Offences

For non-endorsable offences a white ticket/notice (penalty £50) is issued either to the driver if present or is fixed to the vehicle windscreen. Since no driving licence penalty points are involved for such offences there is no requirement to examine the licence. CEOs have authority to issue fixed penalty tickets for the following non-endorsable offences:

- leaving a vehicle parked at night without lights or reflectors;
- waiting, loading, unloading or parking in prohibited areas;
- unauthorized parking in controlled parking zone areas;
- contravention of the Vehicle Excise and Registration Act 1994 by not displaying a current licence disc;

- making 'U' turns in unauthorized places;
- lighting offences with moving vehicles;
- driving the wrong way in a one-way street;
- overstaying on parking meters, returning to parking places before the expiry of the statutory period or feeding meters to obtain longer parking facilities than those permitted in a meter zone;
- parking on pavements or verges by commercial vehicles exceeding 3,050 kg unladen weight (see pp 310–11).

Endorsable Offences

The extended fixed penalty system covers driving licence endorsable offences, which can be dealt with only by the police (ie not PCSOs) – this includes some driving and vehicle use offences. For endorsable offences a yellow ticket/notice with a different level of penalty applies as described below.

For driving licence endorsable offences the police issue a yellow ticket/notice for which a penalty of £100 is payable and three penalty points are issued. These tickets are only issued after the police officer has seen the offender's driving licence and has established that the addition of penalty points appropriate to the current offence, when added to any points already on the licence, will not result in automatic disqualification under the 12-point totting-up procedure. If this is the case, the ticket will be issued and the driving licence will be confiscated (an official receipt, covering the holder for non-possession or production of his licence, will be given – valid for two months), being returned to the holder with the appropriate penalty points added when the penalty has been paid.

If the offender does not have his driving licence with him at the time the penalty notice will not be issued on the spot but will be issued at the police station if the driving licence is produced there within seven days – subject again to the number of penalty points already on the licence.

Where the addition of further points in respect of the current offence would take the total of penalty points on the licence to 12 or more, thus leading to automatic disqualification, the ticket will not be issued and the offence will be dealt with by the offender being summoned to appear in court in the normal manner.

Note: There are a limited number of non-endorsable and endorsable offences that carry a £100, £200, or even a £300 fine.

London Area Parking Offences

The fixed penalty system includes specific London area parking offences, namely parking on a Red Route (see pp 312–13), for which the penalty is currently up to £130. This is reduced to £65 if the fine is paid within 14 or 21 days (this time limit will be entered into the Parking Charge Notice), and parking in other prohibited places, for which the penalty is levelled by the borough concerned. Currently these offences attract a fine of between £80 and £130.

Payment or Election to Court

Fixed penalty notices, often referred to as Parking Charge Notices (PCNs), must be paid in accordance with the instructions on the notice and, in any case, within the specified time limit of 28 days. Alternatively, the offender can elect to have the charge dealt with by a court so he has the opportunity of defending himself against the charge or, even if he accepts that he is guilty of the offence, of putting forward mitigating circumstances which he feels may lessen any penalty which may be imposed.

The address of the fixed penalty office to which the penalty payment should be sent is given in the notice together with instructions for making application for a court hearing if this course of action is chosen.

Failure to Pay

With both the white and yellow ticket systems, failure to pay the statutory penalty within the requisite period of 28 days will result in the offender being automatically considered guilty and the penalties being increased by 50 per cent (ie to £75 and £150 respectively). These increased amounts become fines and continued non-payment will lead to the arrest of the offender and appearance before a court in the district where the offence was committed. This could be many miles from where the offender lives and may necessitate him being transported there under arrest and possibly held overnight.

Summary of Offences

Among the many offences covered by the fixed penalty scheme are the following:

- parking at night without lights or reflectors;
- waiting, parking, loading or unloading;
- breach of controlled parking zone regulations;
- failing to display a current excise licence disc;
- making 'U' turns in unauthorized places;
- lighting offences with a moving vehicle;
- driving the wrong way in a one-way street and making banned right turns;
- contravening traffic regulation orders;
- breach of experimental traffic orders;
- breach of experimental traffic schemes in Greater London;
- contravening motorway traffic regulations;
- using a vehicle in contravention of a temporary prohibition or restriction of traffic on a road;
- driving in contravention of an order prohibiting or restricting driving on certain classes of road;
- breach of pedestrian crossing regulations;
- contravention of a street playground order;

- breach of parking orders on roads, and of parking place designation orders and other offences committed in relation to them, except failing to pay an excess charge;
- contravening minimum speed limits;
- speeding;
- driving or keeping a vehicle not showing a registration mark;
- driving or keeping a vehicle with a registration mark or hackney carriage sign obscured;
- failing to comply with traffic directions or signs;
- leaving a vehicle in a dangerous position;
- failing to wear a seat belt;
- breach of a restriction on carrying children in the front or rear of vehicles;
- driving a vehicle elsewhere than on the road;
- parking a vehicle on a footpath or verge;
- breach of Construction and Use Regulations;
- contravening lighting restrictions on vehicles;
- driving without a licence;
- driving whist using a mobile phone;
- breach of provisional driving licence conditions;
- failing to stop when required to do so by a uniformed police officer;
- obstructing the highway with a vehicle;
- overtaking on a pedestrian crossing;
- failing to display a registration mark (ie number plate) on a vehicle;
- driving on a footpath.

NB: In October 2015, the UK introduced a system allowing the issue of fixed penalty notices for offences detected on a driver's tachograph records at any time over the previous 28 days. However, this can only be done in cases where the DVSA are conducting a roadside check and find, at the time, that there is a current offence being committed and that that offence is prosecutable. This 'historic offence' provision was introduced, in the main, in order to allow the DVSA to issue fixed penalties against foreign drivers who had previously been unable to be charged for previous offences committed whilst the vehicle was in the UK.

The Graduated Fixed Penalty and Deposit Scheme

A scheme of graduated fixed penalties (GFP) and deposits for both UK and foreign truck drivers who break the law was introduced from 1 April 2009 in an amendment to the Fixed Penalty Order 2000. The scheme is operated by the police and by DVSA examiners who have the power to issue such notices.

Fixed penalties, issuable by police, already exist for a range of traffic and roadworthiness offences for all categories of vehicle. Their use provides a quick and effective method of dealing with minor offending which reduces the burden on the courts and saves police time. Acceptance of a fixed penalty provides the offender with the opportunity of discharging all liability for that offence, requires no admission of guilt, results in no criminal record and saves him the need to attend court.

The fixed penalty provisions created powers to introduce fixed penalties for commercial vehicles as a means of dealing effectively with cases such as multiple offences arising from the commercial operation of vehicles which proved cumbersome and time-consuming to process. Certain penalties are now graduated to reflect the number and severity of the offences.

The scheme covers offences, mainly relating to commercial vehicles, as follows:

- drivers' hours and tachograph record offences;
- overloading;
- roadworthiness;
- construction and use of vehicles;
- driver licensing;
- community authorizations;
- goods vehicle plating and testing;
- Vehicle Excise Duty;
- vehicle exhaust emissions.

The amounts of the graduated fixed penalty payable vary according to the type and degree of the alleged offence at three main levels, namely, £100, £200 and £300.

Additionally, powers are included in the legislation to:

- enable the number of penalty points endorsed on driving licences to be varied according to type, location and severity of offence;
- require operators to notify the TC of fixed penalty notices issued against them under the new GFP scheme;
- allow enforcement officers to issue endorseable fixed penalties to non-GB driving licence holders through checks of their 'driving record';
- require financial deposit payment (£300 up to £900) by drivers who do not have a satisfactory UK address (intended to enforce against foreign drivers who otherwise have been able to avoid a fixed penalty or prosecution in the UK);
- immobilize vehicles subject to a prohibition (again, primarily directed at foreign drivers).

NB: Where these requirements cannot be met the police and DVSA officials have the right to impound the vehicle concerned.

Civil Enforcement Officers

In addition to the powers of CEOs (traffic wardens) (from 31 March 2008) to issue fixed penalty tickets as described in the previous section, they also have powers to act as parking attendants at street parking places, to carry out special traffic control duties, to inquire into the identity of drivers of vehicles, to act in connection with the custody of vehicles at car pounds and to act as school crossing patrols.

They may demand to know the names and addresses of those believed to have committed parking, obstruction, traffic sign and excise licence offences and to see the driving licence of any person who is reasonably suspected of such offences. If the licence cannot be produced at that time the CEO may issue a form HO/RT 1 requiring its production at a police station within seven days. CEOs have no powers to request the production of insurance certificates or vehicle test certificates.

CEOs' powers were extended to include stopping vehicles for testing and other purposes and escorting abnormal loads – duties previously the prerogative of the police only (and where they are often referred to as PCSOs).

Pedestrian Crossings

There are several types of pedestrian crossing. Zebra crossings are bounded on either side by areas indicated by zig-zag road markings in which overtaking, parking and waiting are prohibited. The marked areas extend to about 60 ft on either side of the crossing. A 'give way' line 3 ft from the crossing is the point at which vehicles must stop to allow pedestrians to cross. Pelican crossings are controlled by traffic lights which vehicle drivers must observe and pedestrians should cross only when the green light signal indicates that they should do so (at many pelican crossings an audible bleeper is provided to assist blind people to cross with safety). With this type of crossing, if there is a central refuge for pedestrians, each side of the refuge is still considered to be part of a single crossing. Only if the two parts of the crossing are offset does it become two separate crossings. There are other types of pedestrian crossings in the UK including 'Puffin' crossings with red and green figures above the control box and 'Toucan' crossings (where both pedestrians and cyclists may cross). Further information is available in the *Highway Code*.

Builders' Skips

Provisions are contained in the Highways Act 1980 to control the placing of builders' skips on the road. Before such a skip is placed on the road, permission must be obtained from the local authority. This will be given subject to conditions relating to the size of the skip, its siting, the manner in which it is made visible to oncoming traffic, the care and disposal of its contents, the manner in which it is lit or guarded and its removal when the period of permission ends.

Owners must ensure that skips carry proper reflective markers (see p 427), are properly lit at night, are clearly marked with their name and telephone number or address, and that they are moved as soon as is practical after they have been filled.

The police and highway authorities have powers to reposition or remove a skip from the road and recover the cost of doing so from the owner, and a penalty may be imposed.

For the purposes of the Act the definition of a builder's skip is 'a container designed to be carried on a road vehicle and to be placed on a highway or other land for the storage of builders' materials, or for the removal and disposal of builders' rubble, waste, household and other rubbish or earth'.

Abandoned Motor Vehicles

It is an offence under the Road Traffic Regulation Act 1984 to abandon a motor vehicle or any part of, or part removed from, a motor vehicle in the open air or on any other open land forming part of a highway. Such offences, on conviction, can lead to fines for a first offence and fines and a term of up to three months' imprisonment or both for a subsequent offence.

Vehicles which are illegally or obstructively parked can be removed and a statutory charge imposed. An additional charge for storage of a removed vehicle can be made and, since the de-criminalization of many parking offences, many local authorities have their own levels of charges. Removed and impounded vehicles are not released until all relevant charges have been paid.

Retention and Disposal of Seized Vehicles

Where a police officer has seized and removed a vehicle as authorized under section 165A of the Road Traffic Act 1988, certain legal procedures must be followed; namely, the constable must give a seizure notice to the driver (unless it is impracticable to do so) and must also give a seizure notice to the registered keeper and the owner (where that appears to be someone different) requiring him to claim the vehicle within a specified period (but not less than seven working days). The notice must indicate the charges payable to reclaim the vehicle. These now vary depending on the police authority concerned but are comprised of a seizure fee and a charge for each 24 hours or part thereof that the vehicle is in custody when the vehicle is claimed back after 24 hours of seizure, counting from noon on the first day after the seizure – and the person claiming the vehicle must produce a valid driving licence and certificate of insurance at a specified police station, the vehicle being retained until these conditions are met. Where the police cannot issue a seizure notice or the conditions of the notice are not met, the vehicle may be disposed of after 14 days. If disposal is by means of a sale, the net proceeds must be paid to the owner if he makes a claim within one year of the sale.

Wheel Clamps

Vehicles which are illegally parked or which cause obstruction in a wide area of Central London and in some other towns and cities, will be immobilized by the Police or by contractors on their behalf. A wheel clamp, originally known as the 'Denver Boot', will be fixed to one wheel of the vehicle, thereby preventing it being driven away. A notice will be stuck to the vehicle giving the driver notice of the offence committed and instructions for securing release from the clamp.

It is an offence to try to remove a wheel clamp or to attempt to drive off with one fitted. In London, vehicle drivers finding a clamp fixed to their vehicle must go to the Metropolitan Police pound in Hyde Park underground car park and request removal of the clamp. Both a removal charge and a fixed penalty have to be paid before the clamp is removed. If the vehicle has been removed by the police a removal charge is payable, in addition to any fixed penalty, to secure its release.

The actual rates for the removal of wheel clamps fitted by the police vary across the country but information on where to contact to have the clamp removed, the fees and any fixed penalty will be available on the INF32 leaflet which is left on the vehicle by the wheel clamping team.

It is worthy of note that many local authorities now prefer to remove illegally parked vehicles and impound them as opposed to fitting wheel clamps to vehicles which may be causing an obstruction.

Overloaded Vehicles

It is an offence to drive an overloaded vehicle on a road. Under the Road Traffic Act 1988 (sections 70 and 71) an authorized examiner or police officer may prohibit the use of an overloaded vehicle on the road until the weight is reduced to within legal limits and may direct, in writing, the person in charge of an overloaded vehicle to remove the vehicle to a specified place. See also p 355.

A driver may be instructed (normally by the issue of a form GV3) to drive for a distance of up to 5 miles to a weighbridge for the weight of his vehicle and load to be checked. If he is directed to drive more than 5 miles to the weighbridge and his vehicle is found to be within the maximum permitted weights then a claim may be made against the appropriate highway authority for the costs incurred.

The DVSA and police also use mobile vehicle weighing equipment for roadside checks and a 'weighing in motion' system which operates by having 'weigh strips' in the surface of the road and number plate recognition cameras. In practice, the axle weights are recorded as the vehicle passes over the weigh strip (an electronic strain gauge) in the road and the registration number is recorded at the same time. This enables enforcement officers to identify overloaded vehicles and to later pull them over at a suitable stopping place in order to carry out a full weight check.

The maximum fine for an overloading offence is £5,000 but any one instance of an overloaded vehicle could result in conviction for more than one offence, each of which carries this maximum penalty. Subsequent convictions for such offences could lead to higher fines. Convictions for overloading offences also jeopardize the operator's licence (see also Chapter 11 on vehicle weights and overloading and the potential impact on the Operator Compliance Risk Score (OCRS)).

Road Traffic Accident Procedure

Road accidents are said to cause many thousands of fatalities across the EU at a cost of hundreds of billions of euros. The relevant figures for the UK alone for 2018, released in 2019, were 165,100 injuries with 1,770 people being killed and 26,610 people seriously injured.

Any driver involved in a road accident in which personal injury is caused to any person other than himself, or damage is caused to any vehicle other than his own vehicle, or damage is caused to any animal* other than animals carried on his own vehicle, or to any roadside property (see below for definition) MUST STOP. Failure to stop after an accident is an offence and fines of up to £5,000 can be imposed on conviction.

The driver of a vehicle involved in an accident must give to anybody having reasonable grounds for requiring them his own name and address, the name and address of the vehicle owner and the registration number of the vehicle.

If the accident results in injury or damage to any person other than the driver himself or to any other vehicle or to any reportable animal,* or to roadside property, then the details of the accident must be reported to the police *as soon as reasonably practicable afterwards, but in any case no later than 24 hours after the event.* This obviously does not apply if police at the scene of the accident take all the necessary details. Failure to report an accident is an offence which also carries a maximum fine of £5,000.

* *For these purposes an animal means any horse, ass, mule, cattle, sheep, pig, goat, dog (in Northern Ireland only, a 'hinnie' is added to this list).*

Reportable incidents include those that occur 'in any public place' as well as on the road. Any public place would include, for example, supermarkets, railway stations and multi-storey car parks.

Under the Road Traffic Act 1988 the need to stop following accidents extends to cover any damage caused to any property 'constructed on, fixed to, growing on, or otherwise forming part of the land in which the road is situated or land adjacent thereto'. This means that if a vehicle runs off the road and no other vehicles or persons are involved the driver still has to report damage to fences, hedges, gateposts, street bollards, lamp posts, and so on.

Third parties injured in accidents who find when making claims for damages that the vehicle was uninsured at the time can make a claim for their personal injuries to the MIB (see also Chapter 9). More recently the MIB compensation scheme has been extended to cover claims for damage to property by uninsured vehicles. Such claims for property damage will only be accepted if the vehicle driver is traced – not otherwise – and provided no claim for the damage can be made elsewhere. There is a limit of £250,000 on claims and they are subject to a £300 excess clause.

Road Humps – Traffic Calming

Regulations permit the construction of road humps on sections of the highway where a 30 mph speed limit or less is in force. The road hump will be treated as part of the highway provided it complies with the regulations. Regulations were introduced as far back as 1989 to enable local authorities to reduce pedestrian casualties by the introduction of more road humps (see also p 298 regarding 20 mph speed limit zones). It is to be noted that some roads at the entrance to villages on 'A' class roads now also have raised areas to act to slow traffic down as it enters the built up area.

Increasing use is being made of a variety of so-called 'traffic-calming' measures to reduce vehicle speeds and cut accident risks. Besides road humps other measures include rumble strips which draw the driver's attention by extra road noise and vibration, mini-roundabouts and 'pinch points' using steel poles to produce a narrow access point. However, these steps are seen in some quarters as being a counter-measure, driving fast traffic on to other vulnerable routes and impeding emergency vehicles.

Sale of Unroadworthy Vehicles

It is an offence to sell, supply, offer to sell or expose for sale a vehicle in such a condition that it does not comply with the Construction and Use Regulations, and is therefore legally unroadworthy. Under the Road Traffic Act 1988 offenders are liable to a fine of up to £5,000.

This means that to display a vehicle for sale which needs attention to bring it up to the required standard is an offence, even though the intention would have been to remedy any defects before a purchaser paid for or took the vehicle away. However, it would not be an offence if the buyer was made aware of the defects and he intended to remedy them or have them remedied before using the vehicle on the road.

It is also an offence to fit any part to a vehicle which, by its fitting, makes the vehicle unsafe and causes it to contravene the regulations. For example, fitting a tyre which is below the limits regulating tread depth would be to commit such an offence.

Under the Road Traffic Act 1991 the law relating to the sale of unroadworthy vehicles has been tightened: in particular, the seller of such a vehicle now has a statutory duty to take steps to ensure that the buyer is aware that the vehicle is in an unroadworthy condition. Previously the seller could rely on the defence that he believed that the vehicle was not to be used on the road until made roadworthy.

Seat Belts

Legislation specifying the compulsory wearing of seat belts in motor vehicles came into force on:

- *31 January 1983*
  for drivers and front-seat passengers of motor cars, light vehicles not exceeding 1,525 kg unladen weight registered on or after 1 April 1967 and vehicles not exceeding 3,500 kg gross weight registered since 1 April 1980.
- *1 July 1991*
  for adults (ie persons aged 14 years or over) travelling in the rear of motor cars to wear seat belts where they are fitted – irrespective of the age of the car.

- *2 February 1993*
  for the driver and any person sitting in a seat which is equipped with a seat belt (even on a voluntary basis) to wear the belt provided – this includes drivers of goods vehicles over 3.5 tonnes gross weight which are fitted with seat belts on a voluntary basis since there is no legal requirement for such vehicles to be so fitted. Also, from this date:
  - It is illegal to carry any unrestrained child in the front seat of a motor vehicle.
  - Children under three years of age travelling in the front seat of a vehicle must be restrained by a suitable child restraint.
  - Children under 12 years of age and under 1.35 metres (approx 4 ft 5 in) tall travelling in vehicles must be restrained by an approved device adapted to their weight.
  - Children over 1.35 metres tall may use an adult seat belt.

NB: Seat belts have been fitted to all new cars and taxis since 1987.

Legislation requiring compulsory fitment of seat belts in new goods vehicles over 3.5 tonnes gross weight came into effect from 1 October 2001. Belts must be fitted to all forward-facing front seats and exposed rear seats.

Responsibility for Seat Belt Wearing

It is the individual responsibility of the vehicle driver and any adult passengers (ie persons 14 years of age and over) to wear the seat belt provided for the seat in which they are sitting (ie front or rear). The driver is *not* liable where adult passengers fail or refuse to comply with the law in this regard. However, in the case of children under 14 years of age it is the driver's responsibility to ensure that the law is complied with, irrespective of whether the child's parents, guardians or other responsible person in whose charge they are, are in the vehicle.

Bench-Type Seats

Where a light goods vehicle is fitted with a bench-type or double front passenger seat, it is illegal to occupy the centre part of the seat (ie next to the driver), where a lap belt, or no belt may be provided, if the outer part of the seat with the full belt provided is unoccupied.

Failure to Wear Seat Belts

Failure by a person to wear a seat belt as required by law could result in a fixed penalty (currently £100) or a fine of up to £500 if convicted by a court. In a case relating to illegally carrying an unrestrained child a fine of up to £200 could be imposed.

A court has ruled that if, as a result of an accident, injuries were sustained which might have been prevented or lessened had the injured person been wearing a seat belt, then the damages awarded to that person in any claim should be reduced by an appropriate amount. Subsequently, other cases involving motor accident claims have followed the same lines.

Drivers caught not wearing a seatbelt can, in some circumstances, elect to complete a seatbelt awareness course of corrective training instead of paying the fine and having penalty points added to their driving licence. The internet-based 'Your Belt – Your Life' programme is offered by the police and the driver in question needs to score a minimum of 7/10 on an assessment at the end of the course. The fee is currently £36.00. It has been held down for some time.

Exemptions

Exemption from seat belt wearing applies:

- When holding a valid medical certificate giving exemption (see further details below).
- When driving a vehicle constructed or adapted for the delivery or collection of goods or mail to consumers or addresses, while engaged in making local rounds of deliveries or collections, but only where such journeys do not exceed 50 metres in length.
- When driving a vehicle at the time of carrying out a manoeuvre which includes reversing.
- When accompanying a learner driver as a qualified driver and supervising the provisional entitlement holder while that person is performing a manoeuvre which includes reversing.
- In the case of a driving test examiner (but *not* an instructor) who is conducting a test of competence to drive and who finds that wearing a seat belt would endanger himself or any other person.
- In the case of a person who is driving or riding in a vehicle being used for fire brigade or police purposes, or for carrying a person in lawful custody, including a person being so carried.
- In the case of a driver of a licensed taxi who is seeking hire, answering a call for hire, or carrying a passenger for hire; or of a driver of a private hire vehicle which is being used to carry a passenger for hire.
- When *riding** in a vehicle being used under a trade licence for the purposes of investigating or remedying a mechanical fault in the vehicle.

** This particular exemption refers specifically to 'riding' in a vehicle and does not include 'driving' a vehicle for the same or similar purposes – therefore, it must be concluded that the driver of a vehicle using it for the purpose described would not be exempt from wearing a seat belt whereas a passenger riding in the vehicle for the same purpose would be exempt.*

- In the case of a disabled person, wearing a disabled person's seat belt.
- In the case of a person *riding* (see note above) in a vehicle while it is taking part in a procession organized by or on behalf of the Crown. This exemption also applies to a person riding in a vehicle which is taking part in a procession held to mark or commemorate an event which is commonly or customarily held in the police area in which it is being held, or for which a notice has been given under the Public Order Act 1986.

The regulations also do not apply to a person who is:

- driving a vehicle if the driver's seat is not provided with an adult seat belt;
- riding in the front of a vehicle in which no adult belt is available to him;
- riding in the rear of a vehicle in which no adult belt is available to him.

It should be noted that these exemptions relate to the non-wearing of seat belts where they are not provided, but this circumstance may involve other infringements of the law relating to the non-fitment of seat belts.

Stowaways

The UK Border Force manages border control and enforces immigration and Customs regulations – including dealing with applications for permission to enter or stay in the UK, citizenship and asylum issues, smuggling and border tax fraud. The Force, previously know as the Border Agency, was split into two distinct units within the Home Office on 1 April 2013. One unit operates the visa and immigration service, and the other unit operates an immigration law enforcement division.

Concern about the number of illegal immigrants (legally termed 'clandestine entrants') entering this country stowed away in heavy goods vehicles has resulted in severe penalties being imposed on drivers and operators caught with such stowaways hidden in their vehicles. The Immigration and Asylum Act 1999 sets penalties of £2,000 for each immigrant found in a lorry trailer, with confiscation of the vehicle as the sanction should the fine not be paid. However, under existing legislation (ie the Immigration Act 1971, section 25) it is already an offence to aid illegal immigrants to enter Great Britain. On conviction, an offending driver could face a heavy fine or up to seven years' imprisonment.

Despite a Court of Appeal ruling in February 2002 that these illegal immigrant fines are contrary to human rights and therefore illegal, the Home Office has continued to impose them on drivers and operators caught with illegal stowaways in their vehicles.

Proof of 'due diligence' may be accepted in defence of any charges under the legislation, but it is important for an accused driver to clearly show that he followed one of the Codes of Practice produced by the Border Force, HMRC or the trade associations. In the meantime, the RHA provides the following advice to its members to pass on to their drivers:

- Never leave ignition keys in the vehicle. Lock cab doors and secure the vehicle's load space whenever the vehicle is unattended.
- Avoid routine stops for papers, cigarettes, etc, particularly within 100 km of Channel ports.
- Always ensure windows are closed when away from your vehicle.
- If sleeping in the vehicle, lock all doors and try to block access to the rear doors by parking up against a wall or other secure barrier.
- Be on the lookout for bogus officials or staff.

- Never leave keys hidden for a relief driver.
- On arrival at your destination, do not leave your vehicle in someone else's care.
- Look out for and report any security defects on your vehicle, such as faulty locks or straps.
- Use pre-planned secure overnight parking wherever possible.
- Try to keep your vehicle in sight if you leave it unattended.
- Make sure your vehicle is correctly loaded.
- If you make the same journey frequently, consider whether the route or schedule can be varied.
- Report any irregularity of loading, sealing or documentation.
- Never accept unsolicited offers of assistance.
- Avoid talking about your route over the radio.
- When returning to a vehicle, check for suspicious vehicles/people nearby and if concerned note descriptions, registration numbers, etc.
- After every stop, and throughout the journey, look for signs of tampering with doors, straps, curtains, etc.
- Ensure that you properly record all the checks you make in order to provide an audit trail.
- Managers should ensure that operational procedures are constantly reviewed.
- Report to base when you arrive at an unoccupied site, or when you see suspicious activity.
- If you are concerned that there may be illegal stowaways on the vehicle report to the nearest authorites and, at ports, make use of any detection facilities available.
- If you are uncomfortable opening your vehicle for potentially bogus authorities, ask for their details so you can check up on them and offer to open your vehicle at the nearest police station.

HMRC summarize these procedures with their own 'Secure – Check – Record' advice for drivers. In addition, in an attempt to reduce the problem the UK's Border Force have increased investment in enforcement and are now using drones to detect 'illegals' who would otherwise not be detected from the ground.

Hauliers are advised to turn in any stowaways found in their vehicles, despite the onerous civil penalties involved. Facilitating the entry of illegal immigrants is a serious criminal offence that carries a maximum prison sentence of 10 years.

Home Office Civil Penalty Code of Practice

This Code of Practice is issued in accordance with section 33 of the Immigration and Asylum Act 1999, now amended by the Immigration, Asylum and Nationality Act 2006. This sets out the measures to be taken and the procedures to be followed by persons operating a system for preventing the carriage of clandestine entrants to the United Kingdom in respect of road vehicles.

Under section 34(3) of the 1999 Act, where it is alleged a person is liable to a penalty under section 32 of that Act for bringing a clandestine entrant to the United Kingdom, it is a defence to show that:

- he did not know and had no reasonable grounds for suspecting that a clandestine entrant was, or might be, concealed in the transporter;
- there was an effective system in operation in relation to the transporter to prevent the carriage of clandestine entrants;
- on the occasion concerned, the person or persons responsible for operating that system did so properly.

Regard will be had to this Code of Practice in determining whether such a system is effective (section 34(4) of the 1999 Act) which bears out the need for effective driver checking and recording procedures.

Part 1: Road Haulage and Other Commercial Vehicles

'Commercial vehicle' means any vehicle excluding buses, coaches, cars, taxis, mobile homes and caravans.

'Vehicle' refers to the entire vehicle, including any attached trailer(s) and any container carried. It also refers to a detached trailer, in the case of which any reference to 'driver' is to be read as 'operator'.

1.1 *Measures to be taken to secure vehicles against unauthorized entry*

1.1.1 Before final loading takes place, all existing cuts or tears in the outer shell or fabric of the vehicle that exceed 25 centimetres in length must be repaired and sealed so as to prevent unauthorized entry. If present at the time of final loading, the owner, hirer or driver of the vehicle must check it to ensure that no persons have gained entry and are concealed within. It must then be locked, sealed or otherwise made secure to prevent unauthorized entry.

1.1.2 If not present at the time of final loading, the owner, hirer or driver must, where possible, ensure that such checks are conducted at that point by reputable persons. The owner, hirer or driver must then obtain written confirmation from those persons that these checks were properly conducted and that the vehicle did not contain concealed persons at the time of final loading and securing.

1.1.3 When the final loading has been completed, the load space must be secured immediately by lock, seal or other security device that will prevent unauthorized entry.

1.1.4 Tilt cords and straps, where used, must be undamaged, pass through all fastening points, made taut and be secured by lock, seal or other security device.

1.1.5 There must be no means of entry to the load space, other than via access points which have been secured by lock, tilt cord/strap and seal, or other security device.

1.1.6 Locks, tilt cords, straps and other devices used to secure the load space must be effective and of robust quality.

1.1.7 Seals, other than Customs seals, must be distinguished by a number from a series that is unique to the owner, hirer or driver. This must be recorded in the documentation accompanying the vehicle.

1.1.8 When a sealed container (except a container sealed by Customs) is loaded onto a vehicle, the owner, hirer or driver must, where possible, check to ensure that it does not contain unauthorized persons. It must then be resealed and made secure in accordance with the above requirements. These actions and the number of the new seal used must be recorded in documentation accompanying the vehicle.

1.1.9 The same checking, securing and recording procedure detailed in paragraph 1.1.8 above must be followed when the load space in the vehicle has been opened by the owner, hirer, driver or any other person before the final checks detailed in section 1.2 below are carried out.

1.1.10 Where a new driver becomes responsible for the vehicle en route to the United Kingdom, he should ensure that it does not contain unauthorized persons and that the requirements detailed above have all been met.

1.1.11 Paragraphs 1.1.1–1.1.10 above will not apply in relation to any vehicle that it is not possible to secure by means of lock, seal or other security device. However, in such circumstances, it will be for the owner, hirer or driver concerned to establish alternative arrangements to prevent unauthorized entry, and to be able to demonstrate that such arrangements have been made and complied with.

1.2 Measures to be taken immediately prior to the vehicle boarding the ship, aircraft or train to the United Kingdom, or before arrival at immigration departure/control location in mainland Europe.

1.2.1 Where used, check tilt cords and straps for evidence of tampering, damage or repair.

1.2.2 Where used, check that seals, locks or other security devices have not been removed, damaged or replaced. In order to ensure that there has been no substitution, numbers on seals must be checked to confirm that they correspond with those recorded on the documentation accompanying the vehicle.

1.2.3 Check the outer shell/fabric of the vehicle for signs of damage or unauthorized entry, paying particular attention to the roof, which may be checked from either inside or outside the vehicle.

1.2.4 Check any external storage compartments, toolboxes, wind deflectors and underneath the vehicle.

1.2.5 Check inside the vehicle. Effective detection devices may be used for this purpose at the discretion of the owner, hirer or driver, but this will not obviate the requirement that the other checks be carried out (detailed above). Where it is not possible to secure a vehicle lock, seal or other security device, a thorough manual check of the load and load space must be conducted.

1.2.6 Use any of the available facilities at the port that are in place to help detect clandestine entrants (X-ray, CO_2 detectors, etc).

1.3 *General principles*

1.3.1 Vehicles should be checked regularly en route to the United Kingdom to ensure that they have not been entered, particularly after stops when left unattended. These checks need to be effective and comprehensive.

1.3.2 A document detailing the system operated to prevent unauthorized entry must be carried with the vehicle, so that it may be produced immediately on demand to an immigration officer in the event of a possible liability to a penalty.

1.3.3 A report detailing the checks that were carried out must be carried with the vehicle. If it is possible to arrange it, the report should be endorsed by a third party, who has either witnessed or carried out the checks himself by arrangement with the owner, hirer or driver, as the report will then be of greater evidential value.

1.3.4 While owners, hirers or drivers may contract with other persons to carry out the required checks on their behalf, they will nevertheless remain liable to any penalty incurred in the event of failure to have an effective system in place or to operate it properly on the occasion in question.

1.3.5 Where the checks conducted suggest that the security of the vehicle may have been breached, or the owner, hirer or driver otherwise has grounds to suspect that unauthorized persons have gained entry to the vehicle, it must not be taken onto the ship, aircraft or train embarking area in Europe for the journey to the United Kingdom. Any such circumstances must be reported to the police in the country concerned at the earliest opportunity, or at the latest, to the passport control authorities at the port of embarkation. In the event of difficulties arising, owners, hirers or drivers should contact the UK Immigration Service at the proposed port of arrival for advice.

Use of Radios and Telephones in Vehicles

The *Highway Code* contains advice against using a hand-held microphone or telephone handset while the vehicle is moving except in an emergency because it is generally illegal to do so. Drivers should not stop on the hard shoulder of a motorway to answer or make a call, no matter how urgent. The *Code* recommends that a driver should only speak into a fixed, neck-slung or clipped-on microphone when it would not distract his attention from the road.

Penalties for Mobile Phone Use

Under provisions contained in the Road Safety Act 2006, penalties for the illegal use of mobile phones or other similar hand-held devices by vocational drivers were increased to a £100 fixed penalty notice and a three-point penalty added to the driver's licence. These limits were increased to a fine of £200 and six penalty points in 2017. Should offenders decide to take the case to court rather than accept the fixed penalty, on conviction they could face a maximum fine of £1,000 but, with penalty points, this could also mean disqualification.

Drivers who stop the vehicle, even in a safe place such as a lay-by, must apply the handbrake, switch off the engine and remove the ignition keys, if possible, in order to avoid any charge that they were 'driving' when using the telephone. Several drivers have stopped and failed to secure the vehicle and stop the engine and have been charged because they are at the controls of the vehicle with the engine running which 'can' be construed as 'driving'.

Traffic and Weather Reports

Drivers concerned about prevailing or likely weather conditions prior to making a journey, or even while en route, can check forecasts from local and national newspapers and get an update of the current situation by using a laptop, smartphone or listening to radio and television bulletins. In particular, the following are useful for traffic and weather forecasts.

Radio

BBC Radios 1, 2, 4 and 5 and local BBC and commercial radio stations broadcast regular weather and traffic bulletins.

The D*f*T signposts show tuning frequencies for local radio stations on some motorways. These wavelengths broadcast 24 hours a day, seven days a week, giving as many as four local traffic and weather reports an hour at peak times, and two during off-peak times, with programme interruptions for important traffic announcements.

National radio covers major traffic and weather problems, and the Radio Data System (RDS) originally developed by the BBC enables drivers listening to BBC radio to be interrupted with relevant travel news. Receivers using additional data, Enhanced Other Networks (EON), which is a component of the European Radio Data System (EDS) can switch drivers from a BBC national radio station, or CD, to a BBC local radio station for a travel bulletin.

Online

AA Roadwatch (www.theaa.com/traffic-news (archived at https://perma.cc/2W7X-VALA)) provides national motorway and A-road information, also call 84322 – 'the AA' on your mobile or 0906 88 84322 from a land line. The RAC Traffic News (http://www.rac.co.uk/route-planner/traffic-news (archived at https://perma.cc/582A-BBZK)) also provides information on route planning and traffic throughout the UK. In addition there are online information systems, available with a smartphone or laptop, operated by national broadcasters (BBC, etc), local and regional government, and others covering individual motorways. They are even available through commercial organizations such as Michelin.

On-Board Traffic Information

Sophisticated modern technology can now also provide drivers with on-board (ie in-vehicle) visual information on traffic routes and conditions. Typical systems currently available include the following.

AA Roadwatch Twitter

The AA Roadwatch Twitter page displays dynamic traffic news on the screen and provides live information and advice from fellow travellers.

Trafficmaster (part of the Teletrac Navman organization)

Despite what many road users think, the blue poles sprouting up on Britain's roadsides are not speed cameras. They are part of the Teletrac live traffic-monitoring network of infrared sensors and roadside beacons on over 8,000 miles of motorway and trunk roads. The system provides information on traffic flow and conditions and real-time information on journey times on over 95 per cent of the country's main roads and can predict when traffic is at its worst – and therefore enable drivers to determine when is the best time to travel. The Trafficmaster map is updated every 30 seconds.

The system works by using specially developed infrared sensors, installed approximately 4 miles apart, to measure the time taken for a vehicle to travel between each sensor site. Computers at each site continuously transmit this information back to Teletrac's National Control Centre in Milton Keynes, where it is processed and transmitted directly to vehicles fitted with Trafficmaster receivers.

Trafficmaster claims that its technology is playing a key role in helping to cut the cost and time wasted in congestion by providing accurate, high-quality, dynamic information directly to drivers, resulting in significant reductions in both journey times and stress levels.

Trafficmaster can be contacted through www.teletracnavman.co.uk (archived at https://perma.cc/CZ6E-MTQA) or call 0345 521 1144.

The two systems above are only examples and many drivers are able to receive tweets and text messages from fellow drivers and the trade associations during their driving duty time, allowing them live, up-to-date information and enabling them to take countermeasures to avoid delays and/or other problems. In addition, many fleets also operate communication systems which allow the traffic/transport office to contact drivers en route.

Smuggling

The Customs authorities are becoming increasingly concerned about the volumes of smuggled goods, particularly tobacco products, being brought into the UK. It is estimated that tobacco smuggling alone amounts to some £3.5 billion annually.

Besides new measures to detect smuggling such as the use of sophisticated X-ray equipment, tougher new penalties have been introduced which could result in convicted offenders losing their vehicles (all goods vehicles found to be carrying contraband goods are seized: 300 LGVs were impounded in the first year of operation) and their driving licences, and facing up to seven years in prison. Smuggling also applies to 'people trafficking', where custodial sentences are the usual penalty for any driver who knowingly attempts to traffic illegal immigrants into, or out of, the UK.

The limits* for personal importation of goods into the UK are as follows.

Currently from within the EU:

TABLE 10.4 Personal importation of goods

800 cigarettes	400 cigarillos
200 cigars	1 kg of smoking tobacco
110 litres of beer	10 litres of spirits
90 litres of wine	20 litres of fortified wine (eg port or sherry)

**Although there are no actual 'maximum' limits in place you are likely to be asked questions if you carry more than the figures above.*

Post-Brexit, the levels for bringing in duty-free items from Europe will be:

TABLE 10.5 Personal importation of goods Post-Brexit

200 cigarettes or 100 cigarillos	16 litres of beer
50 cigars or 250 grams of tobacco	4 litres of non-sparkling wine
2 litres of fortified wine	1 litre of spirits

These figures are those 'expected' to be used unless individual EU member states decide to set individual specific limits for the UK post-Brexit.

Any amounts of such goods brought in exceeding these limits may be confiscated and penalties imposed.

The High Court (in August 2002) ruled that UK Customs & Excise policing of cross-Channel shopping expeditions by means of random searches and routine confiscations caused 'injustice and hardship'. Instead of random checks, the court said that Customs officers should act only when there are reasonable grounds for suspicion that excise goods have been acquired for commercial purposes. It also held that travellers should no longer bear the burden of proving that their excise goods fall within acceptable limits 'and the mere fact that a traveller is transporting a significant cargo does not constitute a "persuasive presumption" that he has acquired them for commercial purposes'.

Transporting large quantities of excise goods into this country may suggest a possible commercial intent. But that should be for Customs to prove, beyond reasonable doubt, in court. Why should citizens be forced to justify their appetite for wine, consumption levels of beer or fondness for cigarettes to outside authority to prevent their purchases being impounded? Citizens have a right to be presumed dissolute before any court may find them guilty of criminality.

In a more recent ruling, the European Court of Justice has determined that truck drivers caught with smuggled goods on their vehicles are to be held responsible for the duty payable even if they are proven to be the innocent victims of deceit.

To report suspected smuggling call HMRC on 0800 788 887.

Goods Vehicle Dimensions and Weights

11

European and British law relating to the weights and dimensions of goods vehicles and trailers is extremely complex. Much of it is difficult for operators to comprehend and apply, and even worse for their drivers, who may, when loading, have to make on-the-spot decisions which could later prove to be wrong, thereby breaching the law and bringing possible prosecution for themselves and their employers. We have seen many weight and dimensional changes in recent years which have been documented in previous editions of this *Handbook*.

Interest is still being shown for increased overall lengths for vehicle and trailer combinations up to 25.25 metres. Currently vehicles at this length can operate legally in Sweden (where there are also trials using two 13.6 trailers, operating up to 32 metres) and Finland whilst Denmark allows road trains up to 20.75 metres and is trialling electrically powered LGVs powered by overhead cabling whilst Germany and the Netherlands also allow car transporters (including overhang) up to the Danish limit of 20.75 metres.

The UK 'long trailer' evaluation exercise has been extended (excuse the pun) to run until 2027 and is continuing with very positive results to date, with no increased safety risk issues reported and is expected to reduce CO_2 emissions by 3,000 tonnes with economic benefits expected to reach £33 million. As part of the extended evaluation trailers of 14.6 metres and 15.65 metres are being used with the original number of extended trailers on trial raised from 1,800 to 2,800 (see below).

The normal maximum permitted dimensions and maximum weight limits for goods vehicles and trailers in Great Britain are set out in the Road Vehicles (Construction and Use) Regulations 1986 (C&U Regulations), as amended, and the Road Vehicles (Authorised Weight) Regulations 1998, which introduced from 1 January 1999 the following specific weight limits:

- two-axle rigids (including buses) 18 tonnes;
- three-axle goods vehicles (without road-friendly suspension) 25 tonnes;
- three-axle goods vehicles (with road-friendly suspension) 26 tonnes;
- three-axle articulated buses 28 tonnes;

- four-axle goods vehicles (without road-friendly suspension) 30 tonnes;
- four-axle goods vehicles (without road-friendly suspension) 32 tonnes;
- four-axle combinations 36 tonnes;
- four-axle articulated vehicles fitted with road-friendly suspension on the drive axle, where the tractor unit does not exceed 18 tonnes and the trailer does not exceed 20 tonnes, 38 tonnes;
- four-axle articulated vehicles fitted with road-friendly suspension on the drive axle 38 tonnes;
- five-axle combinations 40 tonnes;
- five-axle (3+2) articulated vehicles at 44 tonnes permitted for the carriage or delivery of 'loading units' (a loading unit is normally an ISO container, swap body or semi-trailer) on international combined transport operations;
- drive axles at 11.5 tonnes for all the above except 41-tonne combinations (see next page).

These changes are detailed in this chapter, along with existing C&U regulation limitations on vehicle weights which remain in force. Information on weights and dimensions for vehicles carrying abnormal indivisible loads under other legislation is to be found in Chapter 19.

A 10.5-tonne maximum drive axle weight applies to vehicles grossing 40 tonnes or more; otherwise the limit is 11.5 tonnes. Tractive units of combinations operating at 44 tonnes gross weight must have engines that are regarded as meeting low pollution emission standards – ie either a gas-fuelled or dual fuelled engine or a diesel engine that complies with at least the Euro-II emission standard.

European limits on vehicle weights and dimensions are to be found in EC Directive 96/53/EC of 25 July 1996, which repeals previous Directive 85/3/EEC on this subject and its various amendments. They are also free to download from the International Transport Forum (ITF) website.

NB: In late September 2016, the Department for Transport announced that EU Directive 2015/719 would be introduced into the UK (following consultation) in relation to the maximum weights and dimensions of some goods vehicles. This has now been done and means that the maximum authorized weight is increased by up to one tonne for vehicles powered by compressed natural gas (CNG), liquefied natural gas (LNG), biomethane liquefied petroleum gas (LPG), electricity, hydrogen, and natural gas plus mechanical energy from on-board storage or on-board sources, including waste heat.

In turn, this means that 'relevant' vehicles with a maximum weight of 18 tonnes are increased to 19 tonnes and vehicles with a maximum weight of 26 tonnes are increased to 27 tonnes.

The idea behind this directive was to ensure that operators running 'greener'/cleaner vehicles are not disadvantaged because their vehicles have a smaller payload than conventional goods vehicles.

In addition, the plans allow articulated two-axle units with three-axle trailers on intermodal journeys to operate at a maximum weight of 42 tonnes although the 44 tonne maximum weight limit remains in place. This also allows articulated vehicles to carry two containers or swap bodies providing that the combined overall length does not exceed 45 feet. In relation to containers and swap bodies, the directive states that, in order to reduce cases of overloading, shippers should give a 'statement of weight' to the haulier used to transport them.

The directive also allows aerodynamic kits and equipment exceeding 500 mm in length and motor vehicles equipped with cabs that improve their aerodynamic performance to be able to be type approved before being placed on the market. There are also relaxations for rear folding aerodynamic devices which means that vehicles so fitted are permitted to operate at an increased length.

In addition to the details above, there is also the increase from 3,500 kg up to 4,250 kg for vans powered by electricity and other alternative fuels.

Definitions

The following definitions apply when considering the lengths, widths and weights of goods vehicles and trailers:

Overall length – the distance between the extreme forward and rearward projecting points of the vehicle/trailer inclusive of all parts, but excluding load-securing sheets and flexible coverings, receptacles for Customs seals and tailboards (provided they are not supporting the load in which case they are included in the overall length). In the case of drawbar trailers overall length *excludes* the length of the coupling.

Overall width – the distance between the extreme projecting points on each side of the vehicle/trailer inclusive of all parts but excluding driving mirrors, distortion of the tyres caused by weight, receptacles for Customs seals, load-securing sheets and flexible coverings.

Weight – the maximum gross (or design) weight (gvw) for a vehicle/trailer is that at which it has been designed to operate. The permissible maximum weight (pmw) for a vehicle/trailer is the limit set by law (and is shown on the 'Ministry' plate attached to the vehicle), which must not be exceeded on the road in Great Britain.

Length

Rigid Vehicles

The maximum overall length permitted for rigid vehicles, including draw bar trailers, is 12 metres.

Articulated Vehicles

For certain articulated vehicles the maximum permitted length is 16.5 metres (see also below), provided the combination can turn within minimum and maximum swept inner and outer concentric circles of 5.3 metres radius and 12.5 metres radius respectively (see Figure 11.1); otherwise the maximum permitted length is 15.5 metres. The swept circle requirements do not apply to:

- low loader or step-frame low-loader combinations;
- car transporters;
- articulated vehicles constructed to carry indivisible loads of exceptional length;
- articulated vehicles with semi-trailers built or converted to increase their length prior to 1 April 1990;
- articulated vehicles not exceeding 15.5 metres overall length.

Articulated vehicles first used since 1 June 1998 which are fitted with a lift axle must meet the turning circle requirement (described below) both with and without all the wheels in contact with the ground.

For the purposes of enforcement of the turning circle requirements, DVSA has notified vehicle manufacturers that it will take a notional measurement from the kingpin to the centre-line of the semi-trailer bogie. Where such a dimension does not exceed 8.155 metres the combination will be assumed to comply in the case of 2.5-metre wide semi-trailers; 8.135 metres if 2.55 metres wide and 8.115 metres if 2.6 metres wide. Where this dimension exceeds 7.8 metres DVSA reserves the right to demand a turning circle demonstration on a steering pad.

The maximum overall length for an articulated vehicle incorporating a low-loader semi-trailer, manufactured after April 1991 (but not a step-frame semi-trailer), is 18 metres. Such vehicles do not have to meet the turning circle requirements described above.

Where an articulated vehicle is designed to carry indivisible loads of exceptional length there is no length restriction (an indivisible load means 'a load which cannot without undue expense or risk of damage be divided into two or more loads for the purpose of conveyance on a road').

D*f*T Trial of Longer Semi-Trailers

An extended trial of longer semi-trailers mentioned above is being conducted by the Department for Transport (starting from January 2012). The trial involves semi-trailers of 14.6 metre length (ie 1 metre longer than the former maximum length) and semi-trailers of 15.65 metre length (ie 2.05 metres longer than the former standard). These increases take the maximum overall lengths of articulated vehicles in the United Kingdom to 17.5 metres and 18.55 metres respectively. The trial is aimed at evaluating their contribution to reducing vehicle movements and is expected to save 3,000 tonnes of CO_2. The voluntary trial has been planned over the extended 15 year period and the number of trailers increased by 1,000, in order to allow those operators wishing to take part to recover the cost of their investment in the longer trailers and for meaningful data to be collected from all sectors of the transport industry.

It is stressed that the increased lengths apply only to those vehicles approved by the D*f*T. Maximum weights for such vehicles remain within current UK limits (ie 44 tonnes on six axles). Operators taking part in the trial had to apply to the D*f*T for an allocation and, when granted, needed to also apply to the Vehicle Certification

FIGURE 11.1 The maximum and minimum outer and inner swept circles within which articulated vehicles over 15.5 metres long and certain other vehicles (see text for details and exceptions) must be able to turn

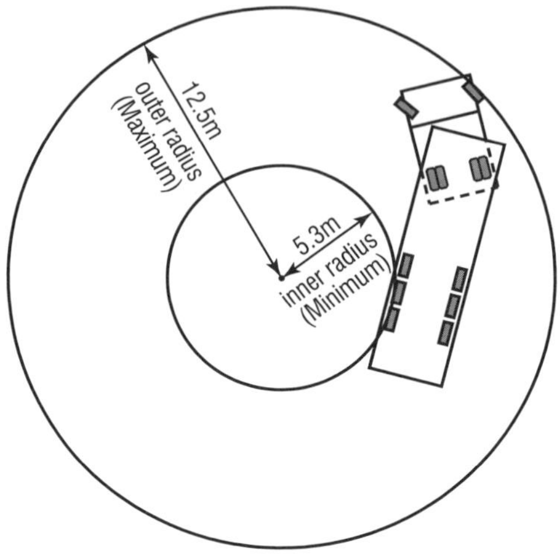

Agency (VCA) for Vehicle Special Orders (VSOs) permitting the operation of the longer vehicles in commercial service.

Vehicle and Trailer Drawbar Combinations (Road Trains)

When a rigid motor vehicle is drawing a trailer the maximum overall length for the combination is 18.75 metres, subject to certain other minimum dimensional requirements being met (see below).

The 18.75-metre maximum length for road train combinations incorporates:

- a maximum loadspace of 15.65 metres to be shared between the two bodies;
- a minimum gap of 0.75 metres (to provide a 16.4-metre 'envelope' of load and coupling space); and
- a minimum cab length of 2.35 metres (see Figure 11.2).

When a trailer is designed for carrying indivisible loads of exceptional length the length of the drawing vehicle must not exceed 9.2 metres and the whole combination must not exceed 25.9 metres.

When two or more trailers are drawn, the overall length of the combination must not exceed 25.9 metres unless an attendant is carried and two days' notice is given to the police. When two trailers are drawn within the 25.9 metre limit mentioned here (ie only legally permissible with a vehicle classed as a motor tractor or locomotive), only one of the trailers may exceed an overall length of 7 metres. When three trailers are drawn (ie only legally possible with a vehicle classed as a locomotive), none of the trailers may exceed a length of 7 metres.

FIGURE 11.2 The maximum dimensions for drawbar vehicle combinations

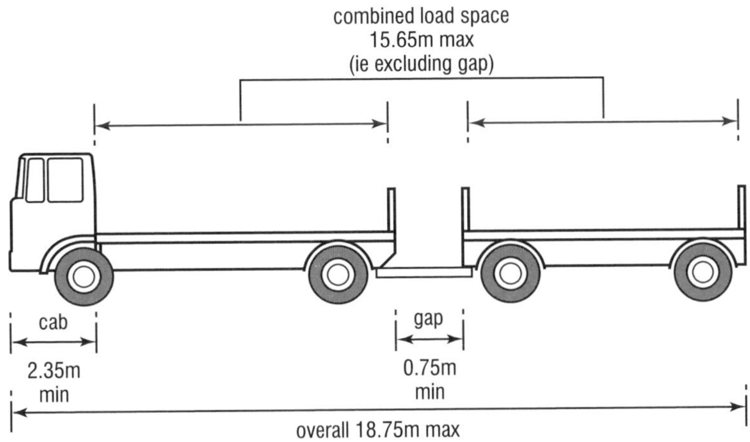

NB: The term 'loading area' includes the thickness of the bulkhead. Towing equipment is not counted in the measurement of the truck-trailer gap.

The limits do not apply when a broken-down vehicle (which is then legally classed as a trailer) is being towed.

Trailers

The maximum length for any drawbar trailer which has four or more wheels and is drawn by a vehicle which has a maximum gross weight exceeding 3,500 kg is 12 metres. The same 12-metre maximum length limit also applies to agricultural trailers.

NB: Although the maximum individual lengths for both rigid drawing vehicles and trailers are 12 metres as stated, two such maximum-length units obviously cannot be combined within the overall 18.75-metre limit for drawbar combination described above.

The maximum permitted length for all other drawbar trailers is 7 metres.

Composite trailers (see p 362) having at least four wheels and drawn by a goods vehicle over 3,500 kilograms permissible maximum weight or by an agricultural vehicle, may be up to 14.04 metres long.

Articulated Semi-Trailers

The maximum permitted length for certain articulated combinations is 16.5 metres. This applies where such vehicles include a semi-trailer with a distance from the centre-line of the kingpin to the rear of the trailer which does not exceed 12 metres and where the distance from the kingpin (or foremost kingpin if more than one) to *any point* on the front of the trailer does not exceed 2.04 metres. Car transporter

FIGURE 11.3 The maximum dimensions for articulated vehicles and semi-trailers (see above for details and exceptions)

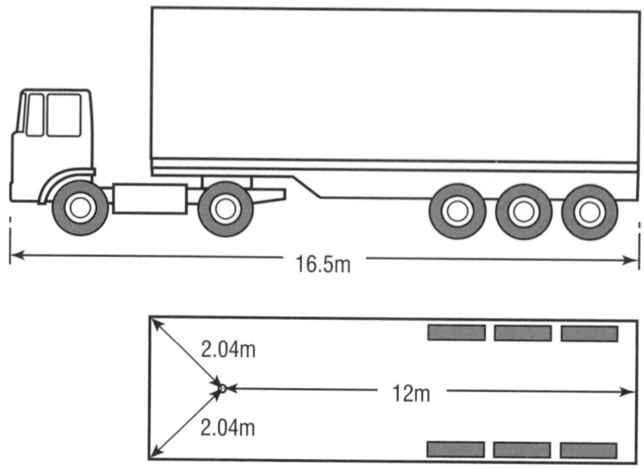

semi-trailers are slightly different insofar that the distance from the kingpin to the rear of the trailer can be up to 12.5 metres and the distance from the kingpin to any point on the front of the trailer can be up to 4.19 metres – see Figure 11.3.

Articulated semi-trailers built since 1 May 1983 are limited to a maximum length of 12.2 metres. There is no specified length limit for semi-trailers built prior to this date. In measuring the 12.2-metre dimension no account need be taken of the thickness of front or rear walls or any parts in front of the front wall or behind the rear wall or closing device (ie door, shutter, etc). The thickness of any internal partitions must be included in the length measurement. This means effectively that the dimension relates only to load space between the front and rear walls.

The 12.2-metre length limit for semi-trailers as described does not apply to a trailer which is normally used on international journeys, part of which is outside the UK. Similarly, articulated vehicles operating within the 15.5-metre limit on international journeys do not have to meet the turning circle requirements described on p 342 for 16.5-metre-long vehicles.

The 13.7 Metre Container Problem

The carriage of standard 13.7 metre pallet-wide ISO-type shipping containers cannot be carried out legally on maximum-length articulated vehicles on account of the limitation on swing radius as set out in Community Directive 96/53/EC. This was particularly worrying for European intermodal road hauliers who needed to use the 13.7 metre pallet-wide container, the only size longer than 12.1 metres that would enable them to compete effectively against the traditional road hauliers using 13.6-metre-long semi-trailers. However, this problem has been overcome by use of the Geest (ie Geest North Sea Line bv)-designed 'Euro-Casting' fitted to the front end of a 13.7 metre container, which successfully meets the crucial swing radius of 2.04 metres – measured from the centre of the kingpin to any point at the front end of the container or skeletal semi-trailer – as well as the 12.0-metre length requirement measured from the centre of the kingpin to the rearmost point of the semi-trailer (see Figure 11.3).

NB: Please see below (after Weight Limits) in respect of proposed increases to the lengths of some vehicles.

Measurement of Length

In measuring vehicle or trailer length account must be taken of any load-carrying receptacle (eg demountable body or container) used with the vehicle and any bridging plates used for loading and unloading, but not for carrying the load. Excluded from the overall length measurement are such things as rubber or resilient buffers and receptacles for Customs seals. Also excluded are forklifts that fit onto the rear of trailers for unloading and which are carried at the rear of the trailer when the vehicle is in motion; these are commonly used for unloading palletised loads. In the case of drawbar combinations the length of the drawbar is excluded from overall length calculations. With dropside-bodied vehicles the length of the tailboard in the lowered (ie horizontal) position is excluded unless it is supporting part of the load, in which case it must be included in the overall length measurement and for the purposes of establishing overhang limits (see below).

Overhang

Overhang is the distance by which the body and other parts of a vehicle extend beyond the rear axle. The maximum overhang permitted for rigid goods vehicles (ie motor cars and heavy motor cars) is 60 per cent of the distance between the centre of the front axle and the point from which the overhang is to be measured. The point from which the overhang is measured is, in the case of two-axled vehicles, the centre line through the rear axle, and in the case of vehicles with three or more axles two of which are non-steering rear axles, 110 millimetres to the rear of the centre line between the two rear axles (Figure 11.4).

This regulation does not apply to vehicles used solely in connection with street cleansing; the collection or disposal of refuse; the collection or disposal of the contents of gullies or cesspools; works trucks; or tipping vehicles, provided the total overhang does not exceed 1.15 metres (3 ft 9 in approx). There is no specified overhang limit on trailers.

NB: Overhang is not always measured from the rear axle but from the turning axis of the vehicle – as the caption to Figure 11.4 points out. In other words, this is not always the middle of the rear bogie of a six- or eight-wheeler: when one of the axles steers or is lifted, the turning centre becomes the driven axle. There is also an alternative to the 60 per cent of the distance from front axle to vehicle turning point. It can instead conform to European Directive 92/27/EEC, in accordance with which the swing-out of a rear corner is limited to 0.8 metres when the vehicle is following the 12.5-metre radius swept circle.

FIGURE 11.4 How to measure body overhang on vehicles with two axles, three axles and more (this measurement applies equally to two- and three-axle tractive units) (see details and exceptions in text above)

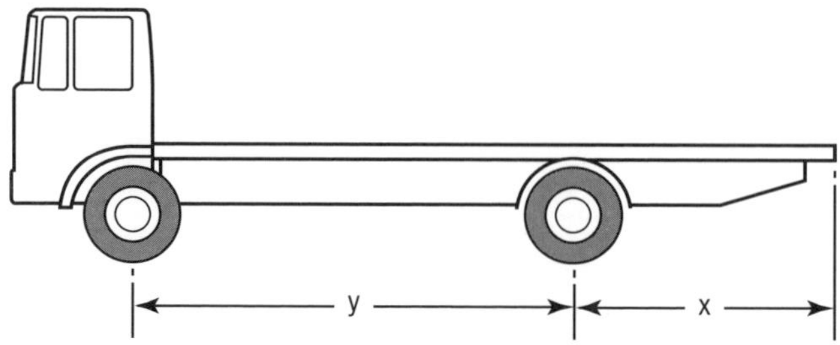

Two-axled vehicles: Overhang 'x' must not exceed 60 per cent of length 'y'

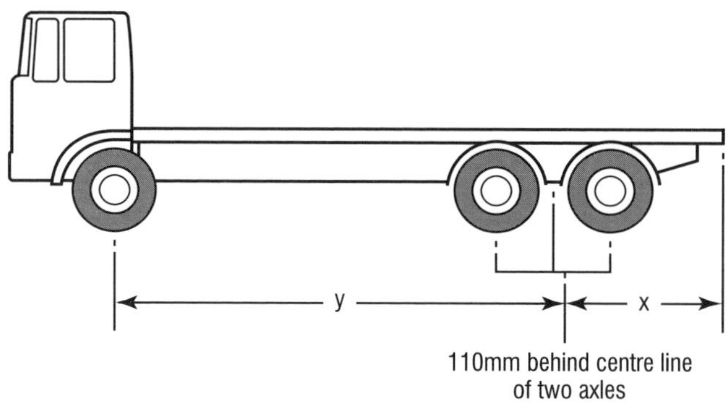

Vehicles with three axles or more: Overhang 'x' measured from 110mm behind the centre-line of the two rear axles must not exceed 60 per cent of the length of 'y', which is the distance between the centre-line of the front wheel to the centre-line of the two rear axles plus 110mm

Width

Motor Vehicles

The overall width of motor tractors, motor cars and heavy motor cars (most goods vehicles are included in these classifications) must not be more than 2.55 metres (see note below about refrigerated vehicles) and the maximum width of locomotives must not be more than 2.75 metres.

Trailers

The maximum permissible width for standard trailers is 2.55 metres (also note refrigerated vehicles below) provided the drawing vehicle has a maximum permissible weight exceeding 3,500 kilograms. If the towing vehicle is below this weight, the width of the trailer must not exceed 2.3 metres.

Refrigerated Vehicles

The maximum permitted width for refrigerated (ie reefer) vehicles, semi-trailers and drawbar trailers is 2.6 metres provided that the thickness of the side walls (inclusive of insulation) is at least 45 millimetres. For the purposes of this regulation 'refrigerated vehicle' means a vehicle (or trailer) specially designed to carry goods at low temperature.

Height

There are currently no legal maximum height limits for goods vehicles or for loads in Britain (see below) but these are, obviously, governed by the height of bridges on the routes on which the vehicles are operated. For general information, the minimum height of bridges on motorways is normally 4.8 metres to 5 metres and the maximum heights for buses is 4.57 metres (see also item regarding high loads on p 551).

NB: The Blackwall Tunnel (on the A102(M)), the River Thames crossing to the east of London, is limited to a maximum height of 4 metres northbound and 4.70 metres southbound. The Dartford Tunnels are also subject to a 4.8 metre height limit (west tunnel) and a 5.0 metre height limit (east tunnel).

The operator must bear in mind, however, that if he loads vehicles to a height which could cause danger he would be liable to prosecution under the Construction and Use Regulations. Also, if a vehicle were to be loaded to a height whereby the load hit a bridge on the route being used, the operator could be accused under these regulations of using a vehicle on a road for a purpose for which it was unsuitable so as to cause, or to be likely to cause, danger.

EU regulations specify a general height limit of 4 metres but this does not apply in the UK and some member states continue to have their own height limits, such as Sweden where although the height is unrestricted, most main routes have a practical height limit of 4.5 metres.

Height Marking and Route Descriptions

Since 1 October 1997 all vehicles with an overall travelling height of more than 3 metres must have a notice prominently displayed in the driver's cab indicating the actual travelling height of the vehicle, its load or equipment in feet and inches (or in both feet and inches and metres).

The height marking, where this is shown in feet and inches only, must be in letters and figures at least 40 mm tall. Where the height is shown in both imperial and metric measures the figures shown must not differ by more than 50 mm.

As an alternative to the height marking described above, in circumstances where the driver is operating on a particular journey during which he is unlikely to be confronted with any bridge or overhead structure which does not exceed the maximum travelling height by at least 1 metre, a document may be carried on the vehicle (within easy reach of the driver) which describes the route, or a choice of routes, which the driver must follow in order to avoid any risk of the vehicle, its load or equipment colliding with any bridge or overhead structure.

Where vehicles are fitted with 'high-level equipment' (defined as power-operated equipment) with a maximum height of more than 3 metres they must have a warning device which gives visible warning to the driver if the height of the vehicle exceeds a predetermined level. This applies to vehicles first used and trailers first made from 1 April 1998.

Bridge Bashing

Bridge bashing remains a major problem despite new legislation on height marking as described above. Network Rail reports an average of 1,800 strikes every year, with one bridge being struck 32 times in one year. Network Rail also states that there are an average of 5 strikes every day costing the taxpayer around £23 million a year. Some key railway bridges have been identified as providing risk of potential disaster, should they be struck by a large vehicle. Infrared warning systems have been installed at many of these key sites, which trigger alarms when over-height vehicles approach.

The *AA Trucker's Atlas of Britain* (scale 3 miles to 1 inch), recommended by both Network Rail and the RHA, shows 1,700 road and bridge and tunnel heights. It contains useful advice on how not to be a 'bridge basher' and suggests that by not knowing their vehicle height, drivers risk the consequences of bridge bashing from causing rush-hour chaos to losing their job, or even causing loss of life. It warns that drivers should not hit and run but should report incidents – failure to do so being an offence. Most rail bridges have a sign indicating the Network Rail Helpline contact number (03457 11 41 41) to be telephoned following contact with a bridge structure and advising that the police should also be notified immediately by dialling 999. The seriousness of bridge bashing in relation to costs to the economy and disruption to the networks cannot be over-stressed and operators are asked (particularly by Network Rail) to take appropriate actions in order to ensure that drivers are made aware of this.

Vehicles for Combined Transport

Swap-body and container-carrying goods vehicles running to and from rail terminals on intermodal operations may operate at up to 44 tonnes gross weight provided they are:

- articulated vehicles and drawbar combinations equipped with:
  - at least six axles; and
  - road-friendly suspensions (or having no axle exceeding 8.5 tonnes); and

- articulated vehicles comprising specially built bimodal semi-trailers (ie capable of running on road or rail).

For these purposes, containers and swap-bodies are defined as being receptacles at least 6.1 metres long designed for repeated carriage of goods and for transfer between road and rail vehicles.

To comply with the law, the driver must carry with him documentary evidence to show that the swap-body or container load is on its way to a rail terminal (the document must show the name of the rail terminal, the date of the contract and the parties to it), or is on its way back from a rail terminal (in which case the document must show the terminal and the date and time that the unit load was collected). There is no restriction on the distance that may be travelled to or from a rail terminal for the purposes of complying with this legislation.

Authorized Weight Regulations

UK lorry weights have been aligned with EC Directive 96/53/EC since 1 January 1999 under the Road Vehicles (Authorized Weight) Regulations 1998 (SI 1998 No 3111), which specify maximum authorized weights for vehicles (ie weights not to be exceeded in any circumstances). These regulations make new provision for the weights of vehicles and trailers of the types defined in EC Directive 70/156/EEC (see list on pp 352–53) but they do not apply to vehicle combinations that meet the requirements for combined transport in the C&U Regulations. Vehicles that comply with C&U are taken to comply with the Authorised Weight Regulations.

The pre-existing vehicle and axle weight limits set out in the C&U Regulations (as amended) remain in force largely unchanged, apart from three particular provisions listed below which were implemented when these regulations were amended in consequence of the making of the new authorized weight regulations:

- An increase in the maximum total weight of all trailers drawn at any one time by a locomotive.
- An increase in the maximum weight permitted for uncompensated steering axle from 7,120 kg to 8,500 kg.
- Amendments to the provisions relating to vehicles used in combined transport operations.

Maximum Weight Determined by Axle Spacing

The authorized weight (in kg) for the vehicles shown below must equal the product of the distance measured in metres between the foremost and rearmost axles of the vehicle multiplied by the factor specified in the third column and rounded up to the nearest 10 kg, if that number is less than the 'maximum authorized weight' (ie in accordance with Table 11.1).

TABLE 11.1 Maximum weight determined by axle spacing

Description of vehicle	Number of axles	Factor to determine maximum authorized weight
Rigid motor vehicle	2	6,000
Tractor unit	2	6,000
Trailer which is not a semi-trailer or centre-axle trailer	2	6,000
Rigid motor vehicle	3	5,500
Tractor unit	3 or more	6,000
Trailer which is not a semi-trailer or centre-axle trailer	3 or more	5,000
Rigid motor vehicle	4 or more	5,000
Articulated bus	any number	5,000

Maximum Authorized Weights for Vehicle Combinations

TABLE 11.2 Maximum authorized weights for vehicle combinations

Description of combination	Number of axles	Maximum authorized weight (kg)
Articulated vehicle	3	26,000
Rigid motor vehicle towing a trailer	3	22,000
Rigid motor vehicle towing a trailer (1)	3	26,000
Articulated vehicle	4	36,000
Articulated vehicle (2)	4	38,000
Rigid motor vehicle towing a trailer	4	30,000
Rigid motor vehicle towing a trailer (1)	4	36,000
Articulated vehicle	5 or more	40,000

TABLE 11.2 *continued*

Description of combination	Number of axles	Maximum authorized weight (kg)
Rigid motor vehicle towing a trailer	5 or more	34,000
Rigid motor vehicle towing a trailer (1)	5 or more	40,000
Articulated vehicle (3)	6 or more	41,000
Rigid motor vehicle towing a trailer (1 & 3)	6 or more	41,000
Rigid motor vehicle towing a trailer (1, 3 & 4)	6 or more	44,000

(1) Applies to vehicles that have a distance between the rear axle of the motor vehicle and the front axle of the trailer of not less than 3 m.

(2) Applies to combinations where:
- (a) the combination is a 2-axle tractor unit and 2-axle semi-trailer;
- (b) the weight of the tractor unit comprised in the combination does not exceed 18,000 kg;
- (c) the sum of the axle weights of the semi-trailer does not exceed 20,000 kg; and
- (d) the driving axle is fitted with twin tyres and road-friendly suspension.

(3) Applies to vehicles where:
- (a) the weight of each driving axle does not exceed 10,500 kg; and
- (b) either
  - (i) each driving axle is fitted with twin tyres and road-friendly suspension; or
  - (ii) each driving axle that is not a steering axle is fitted with twin tyres and does not exceed 8,500 kg;
- (c) each axle of the trailer is fitted with road-friendly suspension; and
- (d) each vehicle comprised in the combination has at least 3 axles.

(4) Applies to vehicles powered by low pollution engines (ie gas or diesel complying with emission requirements).

Weight by Reference to Axle Spacing

The maximum authorized weight in kg for an articulated vehicle 'shall be the product of the distance measured in metres between the kingpin and the centre of the rearmost axle of the semi-trailer multiplied by the factor specified and rounded up to the nearest 10 kg, if that number is less than the 'maximum authorized weight' (ie in accordance with Table 11.3).

TABLE 11.3 Weight by reference to axle spacing

Description of vehicle combination	Number of axles	Factor to determine maximum authorized weight
Articulated vehicle	3 or more	5,500

Maximum Authorized Axle Weights

TABLE 11.4 Maximum authorized axle weights

Description of axle	Maximum authorized weight (kg)
Single driving axle	11,500
Single non-driving axle	10,000
Driving tandem axle	18,000
Driving tandem axle (1)	19,000
Non-driving tandem axle	20,000
Tri-axle	24,000

(1) Applies to axles where:

(a) the driving axle is fitted with twin tyres and road-friendly suspension; or

(b) each driving axle is fitted with twin tyres and no axle has an axle weight exceeding 9,500 kg.

Where maximum weights are less than those in Table 11.4, see Table 11.5.

TABLE 11.5 Maximum authorized axle weights

Description of axle	Specified dimension	Length (metres)	Maximum authorized weight (kg)
Driving tandem axle	Distance between the 2 axles	Less than 1	11,500
Driving tandem axle	Distance between the 2 axles	Not less than 1 but less than 1.3	16,000
Non-driving tandem axle	Distance between the 2 axles	Less than 1	11,000
Non-driving tandem axle	Distance between the 2 axles	Not less than 1 but less than 1.3	16,000
Non-driving tandem axle	Distance between the 2 axles	Not less than 1.3 but less than 1.8	18,000
Tri-axle	Distance between any 1 axle and the nearer of the other 2 axles	1.3 or less	21,000

Overall Weight Limits

The total weight of the load on a vehicle, together with the weight of the vehicle itself, must not exceed the maximum permitted weight for each individual axle or for the vehicle.

NB: In relation to both length and weight limits, the European Council of Ministers approved a revised weights and dimensions limits directive. The directive allows lorry and bus manufacturers to exceed current length and weight limits in order to use designs that improve road safety and/or increase fuel efficiency. The Regulation from the initial Directive came into force in 2017 and allows things such as 'crumple zones' and rounded front cabs to be added to vehicles and weight increases permitted for vehicles using alternative fuels such as electricity or hydrogen, etc as mentioned earlier.

Load Movements – C&U Regulations versus Special Types Order

The majority of general haulage loads moved in this country fall within scope of the weights, lengths and width limitations set out in the Road Vehicles (Construction and Use) Regulations 1986 (C&U) as described in this chapter. However, an increasing number of long, heavy and/or wide loads are being transported which, due to C&U restrictions on load lengths, widths and weights, are required to be moved under the abnormal indivisible loads (AIL) provisions of the Road Traffic Act 1988 Section 44(1) detailed in the Motor Vehicle (Authorisation of Special Types) General Order 2003 (STGO) as described in Chapter 19 of this *Handbook*. In particular, it should be noted that maximum vehicle and load lengths permitted under Regulation 7 of C&U must not be confused with those authorized under the STGO.

ISO Container Dimensions and Weights

Shipping containers to ISO standards present a complexity of dimensions and weights, mainly identified by a 'Type Designation'. A table showing the relevant internal and external heights, widths and lengths plus maximum gross weights and cubic capacity in metric and imperial measures is to be found in Appendix IX. Since July 2016, it is also now a requirement that ISO containers that are to travel by sea (but not ro-ro or short sea ferry crossings) must have proof of a certified gross weight before they will be loaded onto the container ship.

Weight Offences

It is an offence on the part of both the driver and the vehicle operator (ie the driver's employer) to operate a goods vehicle on a road laden to a weight above that at which it has been plated by the DVSA (ie above the maximum permitted gross and individual axle weights) and both are liable to prosecution. Such offences are 'absolute' in that once the actual overweight has been established the fact that it was a deliberate action to gain extra revenue or purely accidental, unintentional, outside the driver's or vehicle operator's control or loading was in a place where no weighing facilities existed, is of no consequence in defending against the charge.

Currently, the policy adopted by the DVSA is that if a vehicle exceeds its weight limits by more than 5 per cent (up to a maximum of 1 tonne) it will be prohibited from proceeding on its journey until the weight is reduced to within legal limits – see below. Where an overload exceeds 10 per cent of the vehicle's legal limits or a maximum of 1 tonne, a prosecution will follow with heavier penalties being imposed on conviction. Trading Standards Officers may not take such a lenient view in their dealing with overloaded vehicles.

Vehicles can be diverted to a point of weighing by the enforcement authorities issuing a Form PG3. This form gives the issuing officer the right to divert the vehicle for up to a distance of 5 miles. Should that distance be exceeded and the vehicle is found not to be overloaded then the operator may claim for the disruption caused.

Defence

There is no defence of 'due diligence' against charges of overloading, something for which the RHA has been campaigning, but it is a defence under the Road Traffic Act 1988 (section 42) to prove that at the time the contravention was detected the vehicle was proceeding to the nearest available weighbridge or was returning from such a weighbridge to the nearest point at which it was reasonably practicable to remove the excess load. There have also been instances reported where successful defences have been made against conviction where the operator was able to show that he had no way of knowing or controlling the weight placed on a vehicle.

It is a further defence, where the weight exceeds maximum limits by not more than 5 per cent, to prove that the weight was within legal limits at the time of loading the vehicle and that no person had since added anything to the load. This defence is typically aimed at protecting loads such as hay, straw, aggregates and bricks, etc, which may have been subject to rain, hail, sleet or snow whilst in transit and absorbed the moisture.

Penalties

Overloading offences are looked upon very seriously by the enforcement authorities and by the courts and very heavy penalties are imposed on offenders. In addition to punitive fines (currently a maximum of £5,000 per offence – an overloaded vehicle could result in a number of individual offences related to gross and axle weights), the operator risks a reduced OCRS rating, losing his 'O' licence and/or the driver could put his LGV driving entitlement in jeopardy.

Prohibition of Overweight Vehicles

Any vehicle on a road found by a vehicle examiner to be overloaded to the extent that it could endanger public safety will be ordered off the road immediately. The necessary powers to enable this step to be taken are included in section 70 (2) and (3) of the Road Traffic Act 1988 and they empower an authorized officer to prohibit the driving of a goods vehicle on a road if after having it weighed it appears to him that the vehicle exceeds the relevant weight limits imposed by the Construction and Use Regulations 1986, and as a result would be an immediate risk to public safety if it were used on a road. The officer may be one of the DVSA's examiners or a specially authorized weights and measures inspector or a police constable.

A prohibition notice, form TE160P, will be issued to the driver of a vehicle found to be overweight and it is the driver's responsibility to remove the excess weight to his own satisfaction and clear the TE160 P before proceeding on his journey. The penalty for ignoring a prohibition notice is a fine of up to £5,000.

Under changes to the OCRS system, serious cases of overloading can now constitute a Most Serious Offence (MSO). These are classed as offences where:

- a vehicle with a gross weight not exceeding 12,000 kg is overloaded by a factor of 25 per cent or more; or where
- a vehicle with a gross weight exceeding 12,000 kg is overloaded by a factor of 20 per cent or more.

In these cases the operator's OCRS will be seriously affected and the operator and driver will usually face prosecution.

Official Weighing of Vehicles

Under the Road Traffic Act 1988 an authorized officer can request the person in charge of a vehicle to drive it to a weighbridge to be weighed. It is an offence to refuse to go to a weighbridge if requested (maximum fine currently £5,000). Once a vehicle has been weighed the official in charge should give the driver a 'certificate of weight' (whether it is overloaded or not) and the vehicle will be exempt from further requests for weighing while carrying the same load on that journey.

The following Codes of Practice are currently in use by the DVSA for vehicle weighing.

Code of Practice for Conventional Weighing

The procedure will be as follows:

- Normally only one authorized officer will check-weigh a vehicle.
- The driver and any passengers should remain in the vehicle during weighing as they are part of the weight transmitted to the road.
- When requested, the driver should move the vehicle smoothly onto the weighbridge plate or pads.
- The engine should be switched off but left in gear during weighing. When a vehicle's individual axles are being check-weighed both the hand and foot brakes should be released.
- If the vehicle is too long to go on the weighing plate or is over the weight capacity of the machine it may require two or more weighings to get a total weight for the vehicle (see note below).
- The driver may be required to have the axle weights checked, and in positioning the vehicle he should carefully follow instructions given by the authorized officer.

- A certificate of weight will be issued for each vehicle weighed and will be handed to the driver. In some cases, where circumstances permit, he may be invited to see the weight recorded on the indicator. The certificate of weight exempts a vehicle from being weighed again on the same journey *with the same load* if stopped at another weight check. The driver should give the certificate of weight to his employer as soon as he reaches his base (see below).
- The driver should also note that previous overloading offences may be detected by checks on weighbridge records.

NB: Operation of Vehicle Weighing Equipment

Weighbridges will be operated only by or under the supervision of a duly authorized officer fully conversant with the operation of the weighing equipment and with approved methods of weighing. Weighing by the method known as 'double-weighing' will only be carried out by a Trading Standards Officer whose professional qualifications and experience will enable him to give expert evidence as to the accuracy of this weighing procedure; or by a duly authorized officer at sites which have been examined and approved as suitable for double-weighing by the local Trading Standards Officer, and who will if necessary be available to give expert evidence in court. Double-weighing occurs when the results of two or more individual weighings of a vehicle's axles are summated to produce the total gross weight of the vehicle.

Dynamic Weighing

The use of dynamic axle weighing machines is permitted under regulations (the Weighing of Motor Vehicles (Use of Dynamic Axle Weighing Machines) Regulations 1978), which specify that an enforcement officer can require a vehicle to be driven across the weighing platform of a machine for this purpose. The permitted weights for the vehicle are measured to within plus or minus 150 kg for each axle and within plus or minus 150 kg multiplied by the total number of axles to determine the tolerance on the total vehicle weights.

The D*f*T has a 'Code of Practice for Weighing Goods Vehicles on Dynamic Axle Weighers' (see below), which must be followed by enforcement officers to secure a successful prosecution for vehicle overloading. This Code supplements the regulations and provides enforcement officers as well as vehicle operators and drivers with information on the correct setting up and operational use of weighing machines and on periodical (ie maximum six-monthly) accuracy tests which must be carried out. Among other things, the Code specifies standards for the approach and exit from the concrete apron of the equipment (ie plus or minus 3 mm for a distance of 8 metres on each side of the weigh beam, and the finished surface must not deviate from the level by more than 3 mm under a 3-metre-long straight edge).

Portable Weighers

Trading Standards Officers and DVSA inspectors in some areas use portable axle weigh-pads as a means of checking vehicle/axle weights and have brought overloading prosecutions against operators based on such weighings. In spite of their increased use, especially at temporary roadside vehicle check-points, there is some doubt about the accuracy of such machines although later equipment is more accurate than some earlier weigh-pads.

Code of Practice on Dynamic Weighing

The following procedure should be adopted for weighing vehicles:

- The vehicle to be weighed is to be stopped a minimum distance of 6 metres from the weigh beam on a level approach; avoid stopping on uneven ground, eg with one or more wheels on the kerb.
- Possible errors caused by surges in the liquid load of a single compartment unbaffled tanker should be taken into account.
- The enforcement officer operating the console is to recheck and reprint the Low and High indication, set the equipment in the dynamic mode and, where appropriate, set the direction selector switch to suit the vehicle approach. He must also press the totalizer button to ensure that any residual information in the totalizer has been cleared.
- Where vehicles under 3 tonnes unladen weight are to be checked, and the equipment has a 'low weight' mode, this button should be depressed before weighing commences.
- An enforcement officer should then instruct the driver of the vehicle to drive across the weigh beam at a steady speed not exceeding 2.5 miles per hour; during this run the driver must neither accelerate nor use his brake. This can normally be achieved by engaging the lowest forward gear and driving at tick-over speed across the weighbridge.
- The vehicle is to be observed at all times during the weighing procedure to ensure that a consistent speed is maintained. In the case of a foreign driver who cannot speak English it is desirable for him to be guided by an enforcement officer walking alongside the vehicle.
- If at any time during the weighing a driver accelerates above the permitted speed, thus causing a red printout, or no printout, to be registered, or if he uses his brakes to cause a sharp deceleration, the weighing should be disregarded and the vehicle weighed again until a satisfactory weighing and an all-black printout is achieved.
- At the conclusion of a satisfactory weighing, with an all-black printout showing axle weights, the operator should press the appropriate button to give a summation of the axle weights. The registration number of the vehicle should then be written on the printout adjacent to the readout.
- Each weighing is to be followed by a zero and high indication check which will be shown on the print-roll.
- Following weighing of the vehicle, normal Road Traffic Act procedures are to be followed in the light of the Weighing of Motor Vehicles (Use of Dynamic Axle Weighing Machines) Regulations 1978. The prescribed Certificate of Weight should be issued to the driver. The driver needs to retain this

certificate to prevent the need to be weighed again on the same journey and to hand it in to the transport operator on return to base in order for it to be stored in the vehicle history file. The recorded weights should be assessed in the light of the presumed accuracy limits, laid down in the regulations, of ±150 kg per axle, with a consequent accuracy limit on gross vehicle weight of ±150 kg, multiplied by the number of axles; compensating axles as usual should continue to be assessed as a combined weight against the combined plated weights.

- The print-roll should be left intact for the complete day's weighings, then removed, dated and retained by the enforcement staff.

On-Board Vehicle Weighing

Operators of tippers and other vehicles where it is often impossible to measure the weight of the load being loaded may wish to fit an on-board weighing system which is capable of measuring gross weight and/or individual axle weights. These systems are widely available and, over the life of the vehicle, could prove cost effective if they prevent even a single prosecution. They operate in different ways with some being operated by hydraulics and others by systems of sensors.

Construction and Use of Vehicles

12

In constructing goods vehicles and trailers, manufacturers and bodybuilders must observe requirements regarding the specification and standards of construction of components and the equipment used in the manufacture. While some of these items are covered by the type approval schemes (see pp 402–05), the majority are included in the Road Vehicles (Construction and Use) Regulations 1986, Statutory Instrument (SI) 1078/1986 (available from The Stationery Office or free to download from the GOV.UK website) and the many subsequent amendments to these regulations, which, collectively, are commonly referred to as the C&U Regulations. Certain EU legislation also applies, as indicated in the text. It should be noted that the rules have not had major change in recent years although this may alter when the UK finally leaves the EU and new trading patterns and requirements become clearer.

Once a goods vehicle or trailer has been built and put into service, it is the operator as the vehicle user (see p 17) who must then ensure that it complies fully with the law regarding its construction and use when on the road. It is worth pointing out that where a vehicle on the road is found to contravene the constructional aspects of the regulations, it is the operator who will be prosecuted and if convicted he will be liable to meet the penalty and may find that it jeopardizes his 'O' licence. It is no defence or excuse to say that the fault with the vehicle rests with the manufacturer, bodybuilder or even the supplying dealer.

Only the main items from the regulations and amendments which concern the goods vehicle operator and transport manager are included in this chapter. Those aspects of the regulations dealing with the limitations on vehicle weights and dimensions are covered in Chapter 11. The provisions of the C&U Regulations dealing with safe operation and safety of vehicles and loads are explained in Chapter 17. Many other points relating to a wide variety of other types of vehicle (motor bicycles and invalid carriages, for example) are not included because they are not generally thought to be relevant to the reader of this *Handbook*.

Definitions of Vehicles

For the purpose of these regulations the following definitions, as given in the Road Traffic Act 1988, apply:

- A **goods vehicle** is a vehicle or a trailer adapted or constructed to carry a load.
- A **motor car** is a vehicle which, if adapted for the carriage of goods, has an unladen weight not exceeding 3,050 kg but otherwise has an unladen weight not exceeding 2,540 kg.
- A **heavy motor car** is a vehicle constructed to carry goods or passengers with an unladen weight exceeding 2,540 kg. Note: This definition may change when alternatively fuelled vehicles are allowed to operate at 4,250 kg, up from 3,500 kg, and operators need to monitor this situation.
- A **motor tractor** is a vehicle which is not constructed to carry a load and has an unladen weight not exceeding 7,370 kg.
- A **light locomotive** is a vehicle which is not constructed to carry a load and which has an unladen weight of more than 7,370 kg but not exceeding 11,690 kg.
- A **heavy locomotive** is a vehicle which is not constructed to carry a load and which has an unladen weight exceeding 11,690 kg.
- An **articulated vehicle** as defined in the C&U Regulations is a motor car or heavy motor car with a trailer so attached that when the trailer is uniformly loaded at least 20 per cent of the weight of the load is imposed on the drawing vehicle.
- A **composite trailer** is a combination of a converter dolly and a semi-trailer, and is treated as one trailer only when considering the number of trailers which may be drawn.
- **Engineering plant** means movable plant or equipment in the form of a motor vehicle or trailer which is specially designed and constructed for the purposes of engineering operations and which cannot, for this reason, comply with the C&U Regulations. Also, it is constructed to carry only materials which it had excavated from the ground and which it is specially designed to treat while being carried. It also means mobile cranes which do not conform in all respects with the C&U Regulations but not mobile cranes based on a LGV chassis.
- An **agricultural motor vehicle** means a motor vehicle that is constructed or adapted for use off roads for the purposes of agriculture, horticulture or forestry and which is primarily used for one or more of those purposes.
- A **pedestrian-controlled vehicle** means a motor vehicle which is controlled by a pedestrian and which is not constructed or adapted to carry a driver or passenger.
- A **works truck** means a motor vehicle (other than a straddle carrier) designed for use in private premises and used on a road only in delivering goods from or to such premises, or from a vehicle on a road in the immediate neighbourhood, or in passing from one part of the premises to another or to other private premises in the immediate neighbourhood, or in connection with roadworks or in the immediate vicinity of the site of such works.
- A **works trailer** means a trailer used for the same purposes as a works truck.

International Vehicle Classifications

Goods vehicles are classified according to the following international categories:

- Category M: Motor vehicles having at least four wheels, or having three wheels when the maximum weight exceeds 1 metric ton, and used for the carriage of passengers:
  - *Category M1*: Vehicles used for the carriage of passengers and comprising no more than eight seats in addition to the driver's seat;
  - *Category M2*: Vehicles used for the carriage of passengers, comprising more than eight seats in addition to the driver's seat, and having a maximum weight not exceeding 5 metric tons;
  - *Category M3*: Vehicles used for the carriage of passengers, comprising more than eight seats in addition to the driver's seat, and having a maximum weight exceeding 5 metric tons.
- Category N: Motor vehicles having at least four wheels, or having three wheels when the maximum weight exceeds 1 metric ton, and used for the carriage of goods:
  - *Category N1*: Vehicles used for the carriage of goods and having a maximum weight not exceeding 3.75 metric tons;
  - *Category N2*: Vehicles used for the carriage of goods and having a maximum weight exceeding 3.75 but not exceeding 12 metric tons;
  - *Category N3*: Vehicles used for the carriage of goods and having a maximum weight exceeding 12 metric tons.
- Category O: Trailers (including semi-trailers):
  - *Category O1*: Trailers with a maximum weight not exceeding 0.775 metric tons;
  - *Category O2*: Trailers with a maximum weight exceeding 0.775 metric tons but not exceeding 3.75 metric tons;
  - *Category O3*: Trailers with a maximum weight exceeding 3.75 but not exceeding 10 metric tons;
  - *Category O4*: Trailers with a maximum weight exceeding 10 metric tons.

Constructional and Maintenance Requirements

Brakes

All goods vehicles must meet specified braking efficiencies. The regulations state minimum efficiencies for the service brake, for the secondary brake and for the parking brake or handbrake. On pre-1968 vehicles the secondary brake can be the handbrake and on post-1968 vehicles it can be a split or dual system operated by the footbrake. If it is the latter it must be capable of meeting the secondary requirement if part of the dual system fails. The parking brake must achieve the required efficiency by direct mechanical action or by the energy of a spring without the assistance of stored energy.

Every vehicle must have a parking brake system to prevent at least two wheels from turning when it is not being driven. All vehicles first used after 1 January 1968 must have an independent parking brake.

Anti-lock (ie anti-skid) braking systems are required on certain later articulated vehicles and drawbar trailer combinations under EU legislation (for which Category 1 – wheel-by-wheel systems are necessary) and under British C&U Regulations. The vehicles affected are articulated tractive units and rigid goods vehicles over 16 tonnes equipped to draw trailers and first used from 1 April 1992, and trailers over 10 tonnes built on or after 1 October 1991.

From 1 March 2002 anti-lock braking systems (ABS) were required to be fitted on all newly registered goods vehicles over 3.5 tonnes gross weight. Today these ABS systems have been superseded by electronic braking systems (EBS) which are found on many new large goods vehicles produced by the major manufacturers.

Advanced Emergency Braking Systems (AEBS)

Under EC Regulation 661/2009, there has been a phased-in introduction of AEBS systems on goods vehicles exceeding 3.5 tonnes, minibuses, buses and coaches. These systems of collision avoidance warn the driver of a possible collision and, if the driver fails to take action, apply the brakes automatically.

The phasing-in meant that Level 1 AEBS systems were required to be fitted to all new vehicles by 1 November 2015, where the vehicles were either a goods vehicle exceeding 8,000 kg gvw, fitted with a pneumatic/air or hydraulic braking system and pneumatic rear-axle suspension, or a passenger-carrying vehicle with more than eight seats and a maximum authorized mass of more than 5,000 kg. Since that date, mandatory fitment of Level 2 AEBS applies to all new types of vehicles (vehicles launched for the first time) from November 2016 and all new vehicles (vehicles registered for the first time) from November 2018. There are some exemptions for off-road vehicles and urban buses.

Note: Under EC Regulation 661/2009, lane departure warning systems (LDWS) also need to be fitted to all new goods vehicles over 3.5 tonnes gvw, minibuses, buses and coaches as a mandatory requirement since 1 November 2015. Although not a braking issue, this is also linked to collision avoidance.

Specified Braking Efficiencies

Goods vehicles used before 1 January 1968:

TABLE 12.1 Specified braking efficiencies

Two-axle rigid vehicles	Service brake	45 per cent
	Secondary brake	20 per cent
Multi-axled rigid vehicles, trailer combinations and articulated vehicles	Service brake	40 per cent
	Secondary brake	15 per cent

Goods vehicles first used on or after 1 January 1968:

TABLE 12.2 Specific braking efficiencies

All vehicles	Service brake	50 per cent
	Secondary brake	25 per cent
	Parking brake must be capable of holding the vehicle on a gradient of at least 1 in 6.25 without the assistance of stored energy (1 in 8.33 with a trailer attached)	16 per cent

Maintenance of Brakes

The braking system on a vehicle, including all of its components and means of operation, must be maintained in good and efficient working order and must be properly adjusted at all times.

Braking Standards

The regulations reflect the requirements for braking standards laid down in EC Directives 320/1973, 524/1975 and 489/1979 (as amended). These call for the fitment of load sensing valves or anti-lock braking on drive axles – most modern tractive units already comply with these requirements – and the overall emphasis is on stability, eliminating jack-knifing and trailer swing. EU rules permit the use of two-line air braking systems instead of the traditional British three-line systems. Most older tractive units in the UK have three-line braking systems fitted with yellow, blue and red couplings.

Vehicles built to the European standard have only two lines (red and yellow or two black). Coupling three-line tractive units to three-line trailers, two-line tractive units to two-line trailers and two-line tractive units to three-line trailers presents no difficulties. Problems arise when coupling three-line tractive units to two-line trailers. Such combinations must not be used unless they are specially designed or modified by fitting a fourth coupling or internal valves and connecting pipework.

Failsafe Handbrake Alarms

Whilst still not mandatory, these alarms are often fitted as standard by some manufacturers and are also available from several different suppliers. They are available as either electronic alarms or as real speech alarms.

Anti-Lock Brakes

The following goods vehicles must be fitted with anti-lock brakes:

- Motor vehicles first registered on or after 1 April 1992 with design gross vehicle weight greater than 16,000 kg and authorized to tow trailers with total design axle weight exceeding 10,000 kg.

- Trailers with total design axle weight exceeding 10,000 kg manufactured on or after 1 October 1991.
- New Category N vehicles from 1998 were required to have anti-lock braking fitted as part of their type approval.
- All Category N2 and N3 vehicles and Category O3 and O4 trailers registered from April 2002 were required to have anti-lock braking systems fitted.

Anti-lock systems must conform to Annex 10 of the EU braking directive (Council Directive 71/320/EEC).

A journey in a vehicle with a faulty anti-lock braking system may be completed if the fault arose en-route, or the vehicle may be driven to a place where the fault is to be repaired. However, this does not apply if the defective braking system does not meet specified braking efficiency requirements.

Endurance Braking Systems

From 1 January 1995 UK braking requirements were harmonized with those of the EU, thereby requiring new vehicles from this date carrying dangerous goods to be fitted with endurance braking systems. Whilst many of the early systems were less than effective, since the date of introduction, endurance braking technology has become a standard fitment to most new vehicles and has developed into sophisticated systems able to effectively retard the forward motion of a loaded vehicle, reduce fuel usage, reduce brake pad wear and reduce general wear and tear on braking system components. Many systems now automatically apply retardation whenever pressure is taken off the accelerator pedal.

Automatic Brake Adjusters

N1 vehicles (light goods vehicles) first used since 1 April 1995 must have automatic brake adjusters on the front axle. All goods vehicles and trailers exceeding 3,500 kg mpw first used since that date are required to be fitted with automatic brake adjusters on all brakes. There are a few limited exceptions for specialized vehicles and electrically powered vans operating at 4,250 kg.

Brakes and Couplings on Trailers

Trailers constructed before 1 January 1968 must have an efficient braking system on half the number of wheels. Trailers constructed after this date must be fitted with brakes operating on all wheels which are capable of being applied by the driver of the drawing vehicle and having maximum efficiencies matching the braking requirement for the drawing vehicle, emergency brakes operating on at least two wheels and a parking brake capable of holding the trailer on a gradient of at least 1 in 6.25.

New lightweight trailers (ie weighing not more than 750 kg) made after 1 January 1997 must be fitted with a secondary safety coupling. Such trailers must also be marked with their date of manufacture.

Overrun Brakes

Overrun brakes may be fitted to trailers not exceeding 3,500 kg gross weight (or 3,560 kg if made before 27 February 1977). Overrun brake couplings must be damped and matched with the brake linkage. Normally, to ensure that these standards are met, the coupling design needs to be type approved. Trailer braking efficiency must be at least 45 per cent and the parking brake must be capable of holding the laden trailer on a gradient of 1 in 6.25 (ie 16 per cent). Modern braked trailers must also be fitted with an emergency device (normally operated by a wire) which automatically applies the brakes if the trailer becomes uncoupled from the towing vehicle. This does not apply to single axle trailers up to 1,500 kg gross weight provided they are fitted with a safety chain or cable to stop the coupling head touching the road if the trailer becomes detached.

Light Trailer Brakes

Light trailers must be fitted with brakes if:

- their maximum gross weight exceeds 750 kg and their unladen weight exceeds 102 kg;
- their maximum gross weight exceeds 750 kg and they were built on or after 1 October 1982; or
- their laden weight on the road exceeds half the towing vehicle's kerbside weight (this does not apply to agricultural trailers or to trailers whose unladen weight does not exceed 102 kg and which were built before 1 October 1982).

Parked Trailers

When trailers are detached from the towing vehicle they must be prevented from rolling by means of a brake, chain or chock applied to at least one of their wheels.

Braking Coils

Braking coils to ISO 7638 standard (standards for trailer connectors) must be used when both drawing vehicle and trailer are fitted with suitable electrical connections. A prohibition notice will be issued where these coils are found unconnected in roadside checks.

Exhaust Emissions

Since 1 April 1991 newly registered diesel-engined goods vehicles exceeding 3.5 tonnes gross weight have been required to comply with EC Directive 88/77, which sets gaseous emission (ie exhaust emission) limits (see Chapter 21 for details of emission requirements for fleet cars and light vans). These limits have already been applied in type approval regulations to vehicles first used from 1 April 1991 (later for cars/vans with engines over 1,400 cc and those with diesel engines).

The purpose of the EU's legislative programme (under EC Directive 91/542) was to reduce the amount of nitrogen oxide (NO_x), carbon monoxide (CO) and unburned hydrocarbons (HC) blown into the atmosphere from vehicle exhausts. The first stage of this programme (ie the so-called Euro-I standard) applied to all new Type Approved goods vehicles from 1 July 1992 (and to earlier Type Approved vehicles from 1 October 1993). Tougher Euro-II standards applied to new vehicles over

3.5 tonnes pmw from 1 October 1996; and progressively more stringent emission controls have applied since 1 October 2000. Euro-IV limits have been in force since 1 October 2005. The Euro-V standard came into force from 1 October 2008. Euro-VI has applied since 1 January 2014.

The following table indicates the relevant emissions standards with the date of implementation and the emissions and smoke limits.

TABLE 12.3 Emissions standards

Tier	Date	CO	HC	NOx	PM	Smoke
Euro IV	10.2005	1.5	0.46	3.5	0.02	0.5
Euro V	10.2008	1.5	0.46	2.0	0.02	0.5
Euro VI	01.2014	1.5	0.13	0.4	0.01	–

The vehicle user is required by law to keep the engine of his vehicle and any emission control equipment (ie catalytic converter) in good working order and in tune.

Euro-VI Standard

Euro-VI emissions standards implemented from 1 January 2014 for new vehicle type approvals apply to all newly registered diesel-engined goods vehicles over 3.5 tonnes maximum laden (ie gross) weight.

Basically, the Euro-VI standard seeks to achieve a halving of particle emissions from the previous Euro-V standard of 0.02 g/kWh to a maximum of 0.01 g/kWh and a reduction in nitrogen oxide (NO_x) of some 77 per cent. These reductions are important because they are the component gases of the exhaust emission that do most harm both to people and to the atmosphere, plus of course, there are the emissions of unburnt hydrocarbons (reduced to 0.13 for Euro-VI from 0.46 for Euro-V) and carbon monoxide (one of the so-called greenhouse gases). As a notable point, they are also the gases that most town and city authorities target when considering low emission solutions and Euro-VI standard is normally a pre-requisite for vehicles hoping to enter such zones. In addition, some ECMT permits will be limited to vehicles able to meet Euro-VI emission standards (see Chapter 26).

To put these reductions into context, information disseminated by Volvo Trucks via the internet shows that, whereas the environmental footprint of exhaust emissions for a Euro-I diesel engine in 1993 equated roughly to the area of a tennis court, the exhaust emissions for a Euro-VI diesel engine will equate to the miniscule area of a postage stamp. The technology needed to achieve this reduction involves the use of existing exhaust gas recirculation (EGR) systems combined with selective catalyst reduction (SCR) technology together with variable geometry turbo-charging, a diesel particulate filter, and an ammonium slip catalyst to effect a further clean-up of NO_x emissions at the tailpipe.

Emissions Developments

The Euro-VI standards saw the legislation change from an EU Directive to an EU Regulation and it is expected that this will remain a regulatory standard for future UK domestic legislation, thereby aligning the UK standards with those of the EU in order to reduce possible 'incompatibility' problems when UK vehicles are operating in Europe. However, the EU Commission dropped the idea of proposing Euro VII at the same time as Euro VI but the drive towards reduced emissions will continue despite the fact that stricter limits are said to be likely to cause a mild rise in CO_2 from trucks and buses.

EGR v SCR

For vehicles to achieve the Euro-IV standard – from 1 October 2005 and Euro-V from 1 October 2008, necessary for all vehicles over 7.5 tonnes gross weight – operators have needed to choose between two technologies: EGR, which requires no additions to either engine or silencer box, or SCR, which achieves its effect through the addition of a chemical substance generally called 'AdBlue'. Current opinion suggests that EGR is preferable because it is cheaper, has no additional maintenance, has an absence of moving parts and is a proven technology. AdBlue is a synthetic urea solution which, when used with SCR engine technology, converts exhaust pollutants (mainly nitrogen oxides and particles) into water vapour and harmless nitrogen. It requires intervention from the driver, by way of regular topping up of the AdBlue tank, otherwise the engine will run at reduced power. It also relies on the driver being able to source AdBlue when away from base.

Euro-VI and EGR/SCR

By way of an example of manufacturers meeting the tough Euro-VI emission standard, in some of its most developed engines Swedish manufacturer Scania uses the vehicle's existing EGR system and is also using variable geometry turbo-charging, a diesel particulate filter, SCR and an ammonium slip catalyst to clean up exhaust emissions. The new engines are designed to give the same performance and fuel efficiency as their older Euro-V counterparts. These engines, Scania says, make it possible for operators to take the next step and invest in the greenest technology available. This enables them to benefit from lower motorway charges and other incentives that may be introduced by the authorities and also commands a higher second-hand value on resale.

On-Board Diagnostic Equipment

All heavy diesel-engine vehicles complying with Euro-IV, Euro-V and Euro-VI emissions standards must be fitted with onboard diagnostics (OBD) or onboard management (OBM) equipment to monitor their emissions performance. If this diagnostic equipment fails or it records a malfunction in the emissions system the vehicle can only be operated at very much reduced power levels… and the driver has a slow journey home in what is termed 'limp mode'!

Public Service Vehicle Emissions

Many vehicles operating within the public service sector need to comply with tougher emissions standards. Vehicles owned or used under contract by Government departments or local authorities are required to meet the European EEV (enhanced environmental vehicle) standard, which is tougher than Euro-V on particulates, smoke and, for gas engines, tailpipe methane. Many local authorities are also now insisting on vehicles with low emissions for use in city and town centre areas. In turn this has led to the introduction of the 'bio-bus' (powered by human waste) operating between Bristol and Bath and the many electric bus routes now open in London. Since the first introduction of electric buses into the capital, T*f*L now operates a combined fleet which includes electric buses, hybrid buses and hydrogen-powered buses. Clearly this trend will continue and spread to many more authorities and operators.

London 'T' Charge

The London 'T' Charge (a toxicity charge known as an emissions surcharge) was launched on 23 October 2017 and wound up when the ULEZ was introduced. It covered the entire London Congestion Charge area. The charge was mainly levied on the most pollutive diesel and petrol vehicles, registered before 2006, seeking to enter and operate within the Congestion Charge area and was a charge of £10.00 per day (Monday to Friday 0700–1800).

London Safer Trucks Programme

Transport for London announced that, following a report by the Transport Research Laboratory, London's Safer Trucks Programme is to bring forward requirements for safer heavy goods vehicles.* One of the main aims is to improve the safety performance of vehicles during low-speed manoeuvres, which involve, and lead to, the death and injury of vulnerable road users (VRUs), namely, pedestrians and cyclists. Research has found that blind spots on large vehicles are often the cause of these types of accidents and it is proposed to introduce a 'Direct Vision Standard' (DVS) for vehicles operating in London. (A Direct Vision Standard for heavy goods vehicles assesses and rates how much the driver can see directly from their cab in relation to other road users.)

**The report uses the term heavy goods vehicles and not large goods vehicles.*

Following this assessment, heavy goods vehicles will be rated, using stars; where zero stars = the lowest (poorest) standard of direct vision, three stars = good direct vision, and five stars = the highest (best) direct vision.

In addition, the Mayor of London has asked T*f*L to consult on how the Direct Vision Standard may be able to be used in order to remove the most unsafe HGVs from the capital by 2020 and to radically improve the safety standards of all other HGVs by 2024. Trials on trucks with extended windscreens and glass panel doors are already being undertaken and a 'star-rating' system will be used to grade LGVs when the system goes live. The outlined programme for introduction is below.

- 26 October 2019: permit issuing commences.
- Scheme 'go-live' 26 October 2020: all 0-star HGVs over 12 tonnes would be banned unless they prove a Safe System.

- 2024: all 0 to 2-star HGVs banned unless they prove a 'Progressive Safe System'.

More information is available on the T*f*L website and through the trade associations (FTA and RHA).

Local Authority Emissions Testing

Throughout the UK, local authorities are empowered, and currently operate, roadside emission testing schemes under section 83 of the Environment Act 1995. Drivers of vehicles that fail the test are issued with a prohibition notice giving them 10 days to fix the problem and (usually) a fixed penalty notice requiring payment of £60, rising to £90 if unpaid within 28 days. The test levels are the same as those that vehicles would be expected to meet at annual test. The scheme covers all types of vehicles, including commercial vehicles, but excludes hybrid engines, three-wheeled vehicles and two-stroke engines.

Smoke

Vehicles must not emit smoke, visible vapour, grit, sparks, ashes, cinders or oily substances that might cause damage to property or injury or danger to any person.

Excess Fuel Devices

Excess fuel devices must not be used on diesel vehicles while the vehicle is in motion. Such devices are incorporated in the vehicle fuel pump to enable extra fuel to be fed to the engine to aid cold-starting. Their use when the engine is warm slightly increases the power of the engine, but in doing so black smoke is emitted from the exhaust. For this reason their use is forbidden while the vehicle is in motion. These devices are not now commonly found on modern diesel engines with improved fuel management technology.

Smoke Opacity Limits

Diesel-engined vehicles first used after 1 April 1973 (but not manufactured before 1 October 1972) must comply with smoke opacity limits specified in BS AU 141a/1971. Engines fitted to such vehicles must be of a type for which a type test certificate in accordance with the British Standard Specification for *The Performance of Diesel Engines for Road Vehicles* has been issued by the Secretary of State. The certificate indicates that engines of that type do not exceed the emission of smoke limits set out in the BS Specification.

Offences

It is an offence to use a vehicle to which this type test applies if the fuel injection equipment, the engine speed governor or other parts of the engine have been altered or adjusted in such a way that the smoke emission of the vehicle is increased. An offence is committed if a vehicle emits black smoke or other substances even without alteration or adjustment of the parts (eg as a result of lack of maintenance). The DVSA has promised tougher enforcement of goods-vehicle smoke emissions, particularly at the time of submitting vehicles for annual test, and operators are encouraged to use Euro VI standard vehicles if at all possible.

Control of Fumes

Petrol-engined vehicles first used after 1 January 1972 must be fitted with a means of preventing crankcase gases escaping into the atmosphere except through the exhaust system.

Fuel Tanks

Vehicle fuel tanks must be constructed so as to prevent any leakage or spillage of fuel. In particular, there is concern about leakage from heavy vehicle fuel tanks onto the road, where it causes exceptional danger to cyclists, motorcyclists and other road users. Checking the fuel tank filler cap seal is now included as a part of many drivers' daily checks.

NB: Drivers operating internationally are also advised to check the tank by opening the filler cap in order to ensure that no drugs/packages have been lowered into the tank prior to border crossings.

Failure to maintain diesel fuel tanks in good condition (and especially filler caps) is now an offence in its own right and gives the police the opportunity to prosecute without having to actually observe spillage from the tank. Fines of up to £2,000 could be imposed on conviction for such offences.

Vehicles first used since 1 July 1973 and manufactured since 1 February 1973 that are propelled by petrol engines must have metal fuel tanks fitted in a position to avoid damage and prevent leakage. This provision does not apply where the vehicle complies with relevant EU regulations (EC 221/70) and is marked accordingly.

Ground Clearance for Trailers

Minimum ground clearances are specified for goods-carrying trailers manufactured since 1 April 1984. Such trailers must have a minimum ground clearance of 160 mm if they have an axle interspace of more than 6 metres and not more than 11.5 metres. If the interspace is more than 11.5 metres, the minimum clearance is 190 mm.

Measurement of the axle interspace is taken from the point of support on the tractive unit in the case of semi-trailers or the centre line of the front axle in other cases to the centre line of the rear axle or the centre point between rear axles if there is more than one.

In determining the minimum ground clearance no account should be taken of any part of the suspension, steering or braking system attached to any axle, any wheel and any air skirt. Measurement of the ground clearance is taken in the area formed by the width of the trailer and the middle 70 per cent of the axle interspace.

Horn

All vehicles with a maximum speed exceeding 20 mph, except works trucks and passenger-controlled vehicles, must be equipped with an audible warning instrument.

The sound emitted by a horn must be continuous and uniform and not strident. Gongs, bells, sirens and two-tone horns are only permitted on emergency vehicles, though a concession allows similar instruments, except two-tone horns, to be used on vehicles from which goods are sold to announce the presence of the vehicle to the public. Any vehicle first used since 1 August 1973 must not be fitted with multi-toned or musical horns.

Regulations effective from October 2005 permit the fitting of a bell, gong, siren or two-tone horn to vehicles used by HM Revenue & Customs when used for investigating serious crime, and defence vehicles used in case of a radiation accident or emergency.

Restriction on Sounding Horns

Audible warning instruments must not be sounded at any time while the vehicle is stationary or in a built-up area (ie where a 30 mph speed restriction is in force) between 11.30 pm and 7.00 am (see also item about reversing alarms on p 399). The use of the horn on a stationary vehicle in an emergency situation (ie 'at times of danger due to another, moving vehicle on or near the road') is allowed.

Horns Used as Anti-Theft Devices

Audible warning instruments that are gongs, bells or sirens may be used to prevent theft or attempted theft of a vehicle provided a device is fitted that will stop the warning sounding continuously for more than five minutes. Hazard lights and interior lights may be set to operate continuously for (a maximum of) five minutes if the vehicle is tampered with.

Mirrors

Goods vehicles and dual-purpose vehicles must be fitted with at least two mirrors. One of these must be fitted externally on the offside and the other must, in the case of vehicles first used since 1 June 1978, be fitted in the driver's cab or driving compartment. When an interior mirror does not provide an adequate view to the rear, a mirror must be fitted externally on the nearside. The mirrors must show traffic to the rear or on both sides rearwards. Mirrors fitted to vehicles over 3,500 kg must conform to at least Class II and those fitted to other vehicles to Class II or III as described in EC Directive 2003/97/EC. Since 2012 it has been compulsory for all LGVs to be fitted with 'Cyclops mirrors' which are front facing mirrors to eliminate the driver's blind spot directly in front of the vehicle. These are Class VI mirrors now fitted to all new LGVs over 7,500 kg.

Definitions for Classes of Mirrors

Classes of mirrors are defined in EC Directive 2003/97/EC as follows:

- Class I – being an interior rear-view mirror;
- Classes II and III – being main exterior rear-view mirrors;
- Class IV – being a wide-angle exterior mirror;
- Class V – being a close-proximity exterior mirror;

- Class VI – being a front mirror (ie one that gives a view across the front of the vehicle).

In all these cases very specific and detailed angles of vision are prescribed and illustrated in the Directive.

Fitment of Mirrors

Type approved, external mirrors with a bottom edge less than 2 metres from the ground (when the vehicle is loaded) must not project more than 20 cm beyond the overall width of the vehicle or vehicle and trailer. Mirrors fitted on the offside must be adjustable from the driving seat unless they are of the spring-back type. Type approved internal mirrors fitted to vehicles first registered on or after 1978 must be framed with material (usually plastic beading) which will reduce the risk of cuts to any passenger who may be thrown against the mirror.

Close-Proximity and Wide-Angle Mirrors

Goods vehicles over 12 tonnes maximum permissible weight first used since 1 October 1988 must be fitted with additional mirrors that provide close-proximity and wide-angle vision for the driver in accordance with EC Directives 205/85 and 562/86.

Since January 2007 all new trucks have required more mirrors as a result of two EU Directives (ie Directives 2003/97/EC as amended by 2005/27/EC). Besides the existing requirements described in this section:

- Vehicles between 3.5 tonnes and 7.5 tonnes gross weight need two Class IV (wide-angle) mirrors and a Class V (close-proximity) mirror.
- Vehicles between 7.5 tonnes and 12 tonnes gross weight need two Class IV (wide-angle) mirrors, a Class V (close-proximity) mirror and a Class VI (front) mirror.
- Heavy vehicles over 12 tonnes gross weight need additional Class IV (wide-angle) and Class V (close-proximity) mirrors plus a Class VI (front) mirror.

Fresnel Lenses

A great danger caused by left-hand drive (ie foreign) vehicles on British roads – and conversely by British vehicles driving on continental roads – is that of 'side-swiping' vehicles overtaking in the passenger-side blind spot.

Fresnel lenses placed on the passenger-side window are said to give the driver a wider view of overtaking vehicles that would otherwise be lost in the driver's blind spot. The DVSA investigated the use of these lenses, hoping to help reduce the 400-odd side-swipe incidents that occur annually on British roads as an increasing number of foreign vehicles enter the UK year on year and also to help UK drivers improve visibility when reversing. They are now widely available within the UK, often as small plastic 'stick on' patches which can be applied to external mirrors. It should also be noted that many vehicles now have reversing cameras and front-viewing or side viewing cameras which, in addition to preventing accidents, also increase the all-round vision for the driver.

Safety Glass

Goods vehicles must be fitted with safety glass (ie toughened or laminated glass which, when fractured, does not fly into fragments likely to cause severe cuts) for windscreens and windows in front of and on either side of the driver's seat. The windscreen and all windows of dual-purpose vehicles must be fitted with safety glass. Glass bearing an approval mark under EC Directive 92/22 is regarded as meeting the requirement stated above for safety glass.

The glass must be maintained so as not to obscure the vision of the driver while the vehicle is being driven on the road. This means that a driver could be prosecuted for having a severely misted up, iced up or otherwise dirty windscreen.

Seat Belts

Seat belts for the driver and one front-seat passenger must be fitted to goods vehicles not exceeding 1,525 kg unladen registered since 1 April 1967 and goods vehicles not exceeding 3,500 kg gross weight first used since 1 April 1980. From 1 October 1988 goods vehicles over 3,500 kg must be fitted with seat belt anchorage points for each forward-facing seat to which lap-strap type seat belts can be fixed (see Chapter 10 for details of seat-belt fitment requirements in fleet cars).

Since 1 March 2001 seat belts have been required by law to be fitted in new goods vehicles over 3.5 tonnes gross weight (although many new vehicles were fitted with seat belts by manufacturers on a voluntary basis long before this date).

Vehicles to which this regulation applies, first used since 1 April 1973, must be fitted with belts that can be secured and released with one hand only and also with a device to enable the belts to be stowed in a position where they do not touch the floor. Vehicles to which this requirement applies will fail the annual test if seat belts are not fitted, are permanently obstructed or are not in good condition.

The legal requirement for drivers and passengers to wear seat belts came into effect in January 1983 with certain exemptions (see p 330).

Since 1 February 1997 it has been illegal to use a minibus or coach for carrying a group of three or more children (aged between three and 16 years) on an organized trip unless as many forward-facing passenger seats as there are children are fitted with seat belts.

Seat belt use is now often mandatory for construction workers driving mechanical plant equipment and the flashing green lights seen on some of these vehicles are used to indicate that the seat belt is actually in use. Whilst they should only be used on-site, they are seen on the road and it is likely that they contravene the Lighting Regulations insofar that a vehicle with a flashing green light indicates a doctor on call.

Sideguards

Most heavy vehicles and trailers must be fitted with sideguards to comply with legal requirements except certain vehicles and trailers that are exempt from the fitting requirement as listed at the end of this section.

Sideguards must be fitted to the following vehicles and trailers:

- goods vehicles exceeding 3.5 tonnes maximum gross weight manufactured since 1 October 1983 and first used since 1 April 1984;
- trailers exceeding 1,020 kg unladen weight manufactured since 1 May 1983 and which, in the case of semi-trailers, have a distance between the foremost axle and the centre line of the kingpin (or rearmost kingpin if there is more than one) exceeding 4.5 metres (Figure 12.1);
- semi-trailers made before 1 May 1983 with a gross weight exceeding 26,000 kg and used in an articulated combination with a gross train weight exceeding 32,520 kg.

FIGURE 12.1 Measurements of relevant distance between foremost axle and centre of kingpin for semi-trailers to determine if sideguards must be fitted

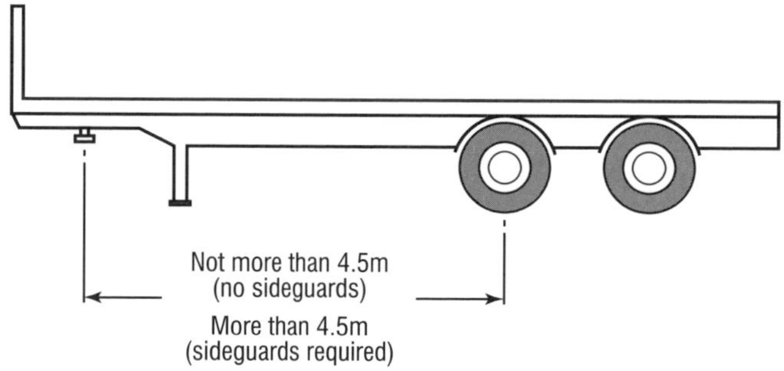

NB: The IVA type approval scheme takes the definition of 'unprotected road users' from Directive 89/297/EEC and enforces the need for sideguards that protect these users (cyclists, pedestrians, motorcyclists) from falling under the sides of the vehicle to be caught in the wheels of the vehicle.

The London Safer Lorry Scheme requires sideguards to be fitted to some goods vehicles that would otherwise be exempt and operators of goods vehicles and combinations exceeding 3.5 tonnes gvw should check on the Transport for London (T*f*L) website for clarification if they operate, or intend to operate, in the Greater London area. Currently the full sideguard requirement only applies to sliding bogie/extendible trailers (trombones) when they are in the non-extended (closed) position, although this is being monitored to see whether or not it is acceptable on safety grounds. Sideguards are not required on vehicles and trailers, other than semi-trailers, where the distance between any two consecutive (ie front and rear) axles is less than 3 metres (Figure 12.2).

FIGURE 12.2 Measurements of two consecutive axles on drawbar trailers – the same dimension applies to rigid vehicles – to determine if sideguards must be fitted

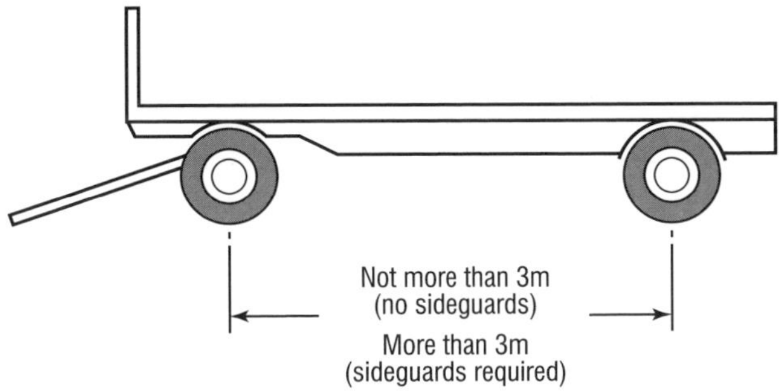

Strength of Sideguards

Sideguards must be constructed so they are capable of withstanding a force of 200 kg (2 kilonewtons) over their length, apart from the rear 250 mm, without deflecting more than 150 mm. Over the last 250 mm the deflection must not be more than 30 mm under such force (Figure 12.3). These force resistance requirements *do not* apply where sideguards were fitted to existing semi-trailers (ie those built before 1 May 1985, and which were used at weights above 32,520 kg).

FIGURE 12.3 How force resistance applies to sideguard on new vehicles and trailers (it does not apply to sideguard fitted to existing semi-trailers)

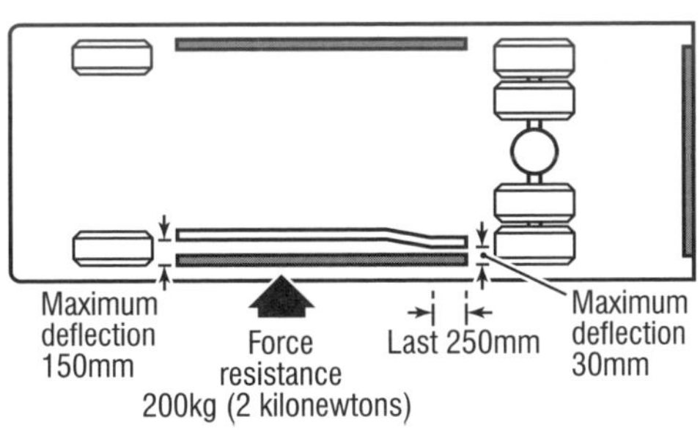

Fitment of Sideguards

The fitting position for sideguards depends on the type of vehicle or trailer as follows:

- Rigid vehicles: at front – not more than 300 mm behind the edge of the nearest tyre and the foremost edge of the sideguard; at rear – not more than 300 mm behind the rearmost edge of the sideguard and the edge of the nearest tyre (Figure 12.4).

FIGURE 12.4 Fitting position for sideguard on rigid vehicles

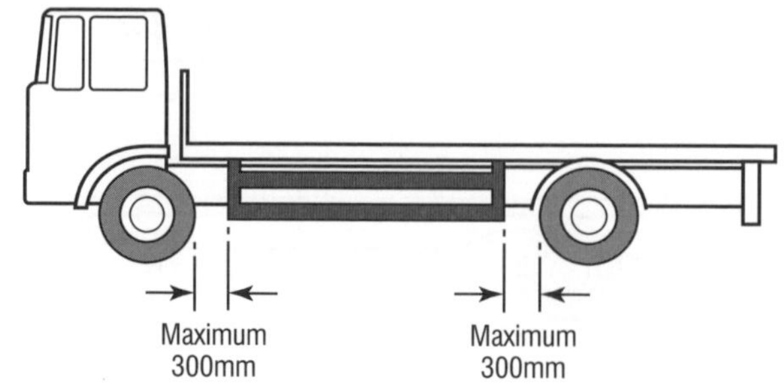

- Trailers: at front – not more than 500 mm behind the edge of the nearest tyre and the foremost edge of the sideguard; at rear – not more than 300 mm behind the rearmost edge of the sideguard and the edge of the nearest tyre (Figure 12.5).

FIGURE 12.5 Fitting position for sideguard on trailers

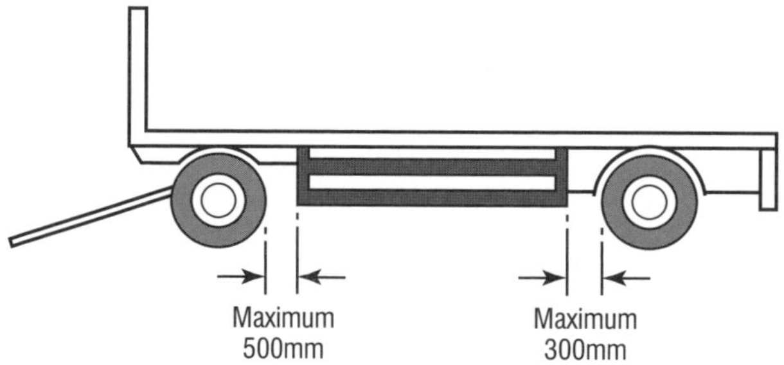

- Semi-trailers with landing legs: at front – not more than 250 mm behind the centre line of the landing legs and the foremost edge of the sideguard; at rear – not more than 300 mm behind the rearmost edge of the sideguard and the edge of the nearest tyre (Figure 12.6).

FIGURE 12.6 Fitting position for sideguard on semi-trailers with landing legs

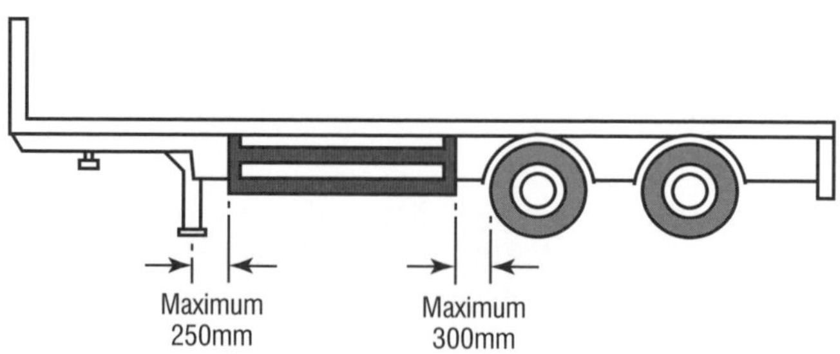

- Semi-trailer without landing legs: at front – not more than 3 metres behind the centre line of the rearmost kingpin and the foremost edge of the sideguard; at rear – not more than 300 mm behind the rearmost edge of the sideguard and the edge of the nearest tyre (Figure 12.7).

FIGURE 12.7 Fitting position for sideguard on semi-trailers without landing legs

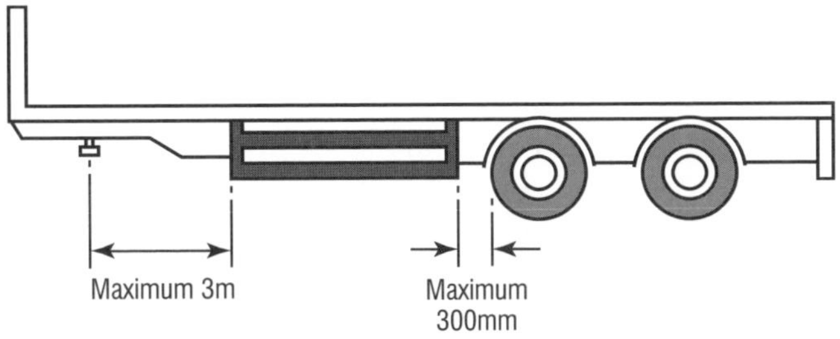

In all cases sideguards must be fitted so they are not inset more than 30 mm from the external face of the tyre, excluding any distortion due to the weight of the vehicle (Figure 12.8).

FIGURE 12.8 Inboard mounting position for sideguards – all vehicles and trailers

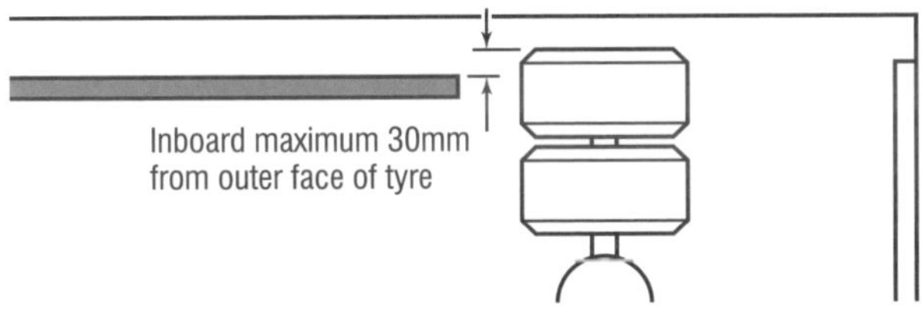

The upper edge of sideguards must be positioned as follows:

- In the case of vehicles or trailers with a body or structure that is wider than the tyres, no more than 350 mm from the lower edge of the body or structure (Figure 12.9).

FIGURE 12.9 Fitting position for sideguards where body or structure is wider than the tyres

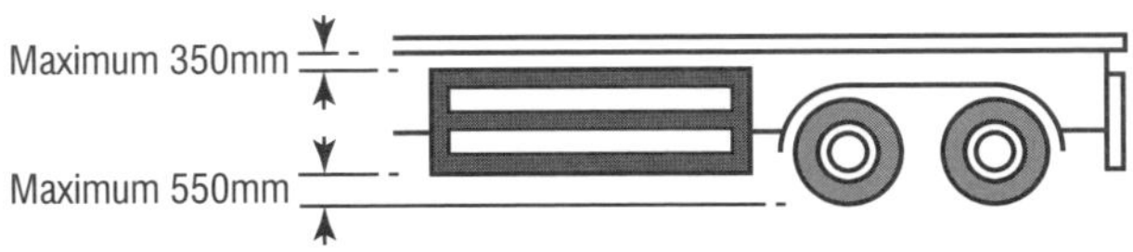

- In the case of vehicles or trailers with a body or structure that is narrower than the tyres or that does not extend outwards immediately above the wheels, a vertical plane taken from the outer face of the tyre must be measured upwards for 1.85 metres above the ground. If this plane is dissected by the vehicle structure within 1.85 metres from the ground, the sideguard must extend up to within 350 mm of the structure where it is cut by the vertical plane (Figure 12.11); if the vertical plane is not dissected by the vehicle structure, the upper edge of the sideguard must extend to be level with the top of the vehicle structure to a minimum height of 1.5 metres from the ground (Figure 12.10).

FIGURE 12.10 Fitting position for sideguards where body or structure is narrower than the tyres up to a height of 1.85 metres

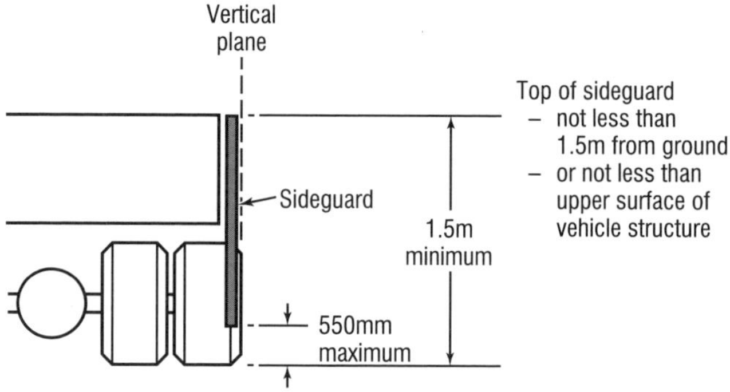

The lower edge of sideguards must not be more than 550 mm from the ground. This dimension is to be measured on level ground and, in the case of a semi-trailer, when its load platform is horizontal.

FIGURE 12.11 Fitting position for sideguards where body or structure is narrower than the tyres

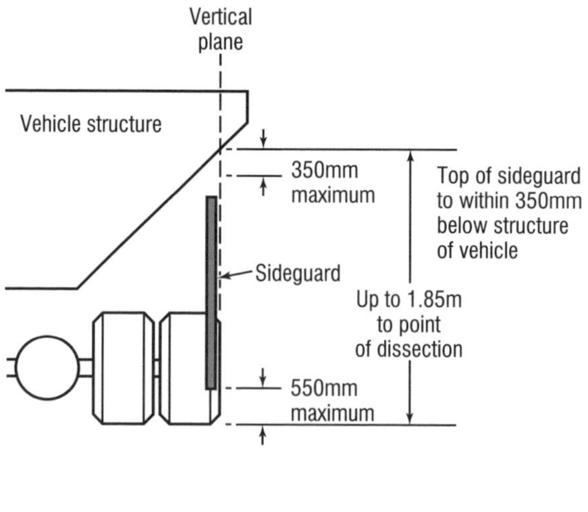

When sideguards are to be fitted to extendible trailers and to vehicles and trailers designed to carry demountable bodies or containers, the following fitting provisions apply:

- Sideguards must be fitted to extendible trailers in compliance with the original fitting specifications in regard to spacings from the nearest wheel, kingpin or landing leg when the trailer is at its shortest length. When the trailer is extended beyond its minimum length the spacings between the front edge of the sideguard and the semi-trailer landing legs or kingpin (if it has no landing legs) and the rear edge of the sideguard and the foremost edge of the tyre nearest to it are no longer applicable. (These circumstances are the ones being monitored/evaluated by Transport for London.)
- Sideguards must be fitted to vehicles and trailers that are designed and constructed (not merely adapted) to carry demountable bodies or containers so that when the body or container is removed the sideguards remain in place.

This means that if the vehicle runs without a body or container it must still comply with the sideguard requirements.

Vehicles that are fitted with sideguards complying with EC Directive 89/279 do not have to comply with the fitting requirements specified in the UK regulations as detailed above.

Construction of Sideguards

All parts of the sideguard that face outwards must be 'smooth, essentially rigid and either flat or horizontally corrugated'. Each face of the guard must be a minimum of 100 mm wide (including the inward face at the forward edge) and the vertical gaps between the bars must not be more than 300 mm wide.

Maintenance of Sideguards

Sideguards must be maintained free of any obvious defect that would impair their effectiveness. It is important to ensure that the fitting dimensions are observed, particularly when the sideguards are damaged (eg by forklift truck impact).

Exemption to Fitting Dimensions

The specific requirements relating to the fitting positions for sideguards as previously described only apply so far as is practicable in the case of the following vehicles and trailers:

- Those designed solely for the carriage of a fluid substance in closed tanks permanently fitted to the vehicle and provided with valves and hose or pipe connections for loading and unloading.
- Those vehicles that require additional stability during loading and unloading or while working and which are fitted with extendible stabilizers on either side (eg lorry-mounted cranes, tower wagons, inspection platforms).

Exemptions

Sideguards do not have to be fitted to vehicles and trailers in the following list:

- vehicles incapable of a speed of more than 15 mph on the level under their own power;
- agricultural trailers;
- engineering plant;
- fire engines;
- land tractors;
- side and end tipping vehicles and trailers;
- vehicles with no bodywork fitted and being driven or towed for the purposes of a quality or safety check by the manufacturer, distributor or dealer in such vehicles, or being driven by prior arrangement to have bodywork fitted;
- vehicles being driven or towed to a place by prior arrangement to have sideguards fitted;
- vehicles designed solely for use in connection with street cleansing, the collection or disposal of refuse or the collection or disposal of the contents of gullies or cesspools;
- trailers specially designed and constructed to carry round timber, beams or girders of exceptional length;
- articulated tractive units;
- naval, military or air-force vehicles;
- trailers specially designed and constructed (not merely adapted) to carry other vehicles loaded from the front or rear (eg car transporters);
- temporarily imported foreign semi-trailers;
- low-loader trailers where:
  - the upper surface of the load platform is not more than 750 mm from the ground; and
  - no part of the edge of the load platform is more than 60 mm inboard from the external face of the tyre (discounting the distortion caused by the weight of the vehicle).

Note the possible requirement in order to comply with the London Safer Lorry Scheme (as mentioned earlier).

Silencer

An adequate means of silencing exhaust noise and of preventing exhaust gases escaping into the atmosphere without first passing through a silencer must be fitted to all vehicles. Silencers must be maintained in good and efficient working order and must not be altered so as to increase the noise made by the escape of exhaust gases.

Speedometer

Speedometers (and/or tachographs, as appropriate – see Chapter 5) must be fitted to all vehicles registered since 1 October 1937 except those that cannot or are not permitted to travel at more than 25 mph, agricultural vehicles that are not driven at more than 20 mph and works trucks first used before 1 April 1984. In the case of vehicles first used since 1 April 1984 the speedometer must indicate speed in both miles per hour and kilometres per hour. The instrument, either mechanical or electronic, must be maintained in good working order at all material times and kept free from any obstruction that might prevent it being easily read.

Defence

It is a defence to be able to show that a defect to a speedometer or a tachograph occurred during the journey when the offence was detected or that at that time steps had been taken to get the defect repaired with all reasonable expedition (ie as soon as reasonably practicable). In relation to tachographs, the defect must be rectified within seven days and if the vehicle is not expected to return to base within that time, the repair must be undertaken en route.

Speed Limiters

In a move to reduce the number and severity of road accidents, legislation requires certain heavy vehicles to be fitted with speed limiters. The Government also believes that speed limiters have beneficial effects for operators in terms of fuel economy – possibly saving as much as 150 million litres annually when all relevant vehicles are fitted – and benefit the environment by an annual reduction of an estimated 0.5 million tonnes of carbon monoxide (CO) pumped, by way of exhaust emission, into the atmosphere. At the same time, the EU requires certain vehicles also to be fitted with speed limiters set to a maximum of 90 kph (approx 56 mph), and this has led to no end of confusion since the two sets of requirements do not align.

The UK regulations, which came into effect on 1 August 1992, limited relevant vehicles to a maximum speed of 60 mph (ie 96.5 kph). They applied to all new goods vehicles exceeding 7.5 tonnes permissible maximum weight that were capable of a speed in excess of 60 mph on the flat and which were first registered on or after 1 August 1992.

In recent years some operators have reduced the set maximum speed to 50 mph for vehicles operating in the urban cycle or on relatively local work. In a similar way, some van operators have also voluntarily fitted speed limiters to delivery vans.

Vehicles not capable of travelling at or above 60 mph (eg some highway maintenance vehicles) are exempt from the regulations, as are the following vehicles:

- those being taken to a place to have a speed-limiter device fitted or calibrated;
- those owned and being used by the army, navy or air force;
- those being used for military purposes while driven by a person under military orders;
- those being used for fire brigade, ambulance or police purposes;

- those exempt from excise duty because they do not travel more than 6 miles per week on public roads.

Speed limiter equipment must comply with BS AU 217 (or some acceptable equivalent), be calibrated to a set speed not exceeding 60 mph and be sealed by an 'authorized sealer'. Existing speed limiters, fitted on a voluntary basis prior to 1 August 1992, were permitted and did not have to be sealed by an 'authorized sealer' as stated above.

Speed limiters must be maintained in good working order, though it is a defence to show that where a vehicle is driven with a defective limiter, the defect occurred during that journey or that at the time it is being driven to a place for the limiter to be repaired.

EU Requirements

The speed limiter requirements of EC Directive 92/6/EEC apply from 1 January 1994 and require new goods vehicles first registered from this date and which exceed 12 tonnes gross weight to be fitted with speed limiters. Speed limiters should be set at a speed of not more than 85 kph (52.8 mph), allowing a stabilized speed of not more than 90 kph (56.0 mph). An extension to the regulations in 2007 saw goods vehicles first used on or after 1 October 2001 up to and including 31 December 2004, exceeding 3.5 tonnes also brought into scope. Speed limiters for these vehicles needed to be set at 90 kph (56 mph) and goods vehicles exceeding 7.5 tonnes gvw up to 12 tonnes gvw were required to have their speed limiters re-set at 90 kph from 100 kph. It is unlikely that the UK will change these current requirements.

Speed Limiter Plates

Vehicles that are required to be fitted with speed limiter equipment must carry a plate (fitted in a conspicuous and readily accessible position in the vehicle cab) on which are shown the words:

- 'SPEED LIMITER FITTED' (in large letters at the top);
- the Standard with which the installation complies (eg BS AU 217 Part 1A 1987);
- the speed setting in mph/kph;
- the vehicle registration number;
- the name/trademark of the firm which carried out the calibration; and
- the place where the speed limiter was fitted and the date of fitment.

Plates that referred to a maximum speed of 56 mph had to be changed (as of 1 September 1997) to show 85 kph. Replacement plates were normally supplied (free of charge) by the then VOSA when relevant vehicles were presented for their annual test after this date.

Speed Limiters for Larger Vans and Light Trucks

Since 1 January 2007 all goods vehicles over 3,500 kg gvw fitted with Euro-III engines and first registered from 1 October 2001 to 31 December 2004 should have been fitted with a speed limiter calibrated to a maximum speed not exceeding

56 mph (90 kph). Euro-III vehicles already have the facility to have a top speed limiter built into the engine electronic control unit, thus ensuring that the calibration procedure does not involve the fitment of brackets, air cylinders or piping.

The same date, 1 January 2007, was also the date from which over 3.5 tonne gross weight vans have been prohibited from using the outside lane of a three- or more lane motorway. Many operators of goods vehicles not exceeding 3.5 tonnes are now also fitting speed limiters in order to save fuel and to increase the life of the vehicle. Where this is done and the vehicle becomes unable to travel at 70 mph on a motorway, the vehicle is also prohibited from using the outside lane of a motorway with three or more lanes, in the same way as any vehicle towing a trailer is, due to it not being able to achieve the maximum speed limit for that class of road.

Spray Suppression

Regulations require certain vehicles and trailers to be equipped with anti-spray devices. The following vehicles and trailers must be fitted with approved equipment from the dates shown:

- N2: Motor vehicles for transporting goods with a maximum mass exceeding 7.5 tonnes.
- N3: Motor vehicles for transporting goods with a maximum mass exceeding 12 tonnes.
- O3: Trailers and semi-trailers with a maximum mass between 3.5 and 10 tonnes.
- O4: Trailers and semi-trailers with a maximum mass exceeding 10 tonnes.

These requirements came into force with effect from 9 April 2011.

Exemptions

Anti-spray requirements do not apply to those vehicles and trailers that are fitted with such devices in accordance with EC Directive 91/226 (and marked accordingly) and to those that are exempt under the C&U Regulations from the need for wings. Further exemptions are as follows:

- four-wheel and multi-wheel drive vehicles;
- vehicles with a minimum of 400 mm (approximately 16 in) ground clearance in the middle 80 per cent of the width and the overall length of the vehicle;
- works trucks;
- works trailers;
- broken-down vehicles;
- vehicles that cannot exceed 30 mph on the level under their own power owing to their construction;
- vehicles specified in regulations as exempt from sideguards:
  - agricultural trailers and implements;
  - engineering plant;
  - fire engines;

  - side and end tippers;
  - military vehicles used for military, naval or air-force purposes;
  - vehicles with no bodywork fitted being driven on road test or being driven by prior appointment to a place where bodywork is to be fitted or for delivery;
  - vehicles used for street cleansing, or the collection or disposal of the contents of gullies or cesspools;
  - trailers designed and constructed to carry round timber, beams or girders of exceptional length;
  - temporarily imported foreign semi-trailers.
- concrete mixers;
- vehicles being driven to a place by prior arrangement to have anti-spray equipment fitted;
- land locomotives, land tractors and land implement conveyors;
- trailers forming part of an articulated vehicle or part of a combination of vehicles having, in either case, a total laden weight exceeding 46,000 kg.

British Standard

The British Standard on spray suppression was originally contained in two documents, BS AU 200 (parts 1 and 2) 1984, which applied to vehicles fitted before 1 May 1987. This was replaced by BS AU 200 (parts 1a and 2a) 1986, which apply to fitment since this date. The regulations require anti-spray devices to conform to the Standard set out in these documents.

In order to comply with the law, relevant vehicles and trailers must be fitted with anti-spray systems that fall into one of two main categories:

- a straight valance across the top of the wheel and a flap hanging vertically behind the wheel, all made from approved spray-suppressant material; or
- a semi-circular valance following the curvature of the wheel with either:
  - air/water separator material round the edge; or
  - a flap of spray suppressant material hanging from the rear edge.

Spray-Suppressant Material

Two types of material are referred to in the Standard. These are generally identifiable as follows:

- spray-suppressant material – designed to absorb or dissipate the energy of water thrown up from the tyre in order to reduce the degree to which water shatters into fine droplets on hitting a surface;
- air/water separator – 'a device forming part of the valance and/or wheel flap which permits air to flow through while reducing the emission of spray'.

Maintenance of Anti-spray Equipment and Devices

The regulations stipulate that all devices fitted to comply with the legal requirement (and every part of such a device) must be maintained, when the vehicle is on the road, so that they are free from 'any obvious defect which would be likely to affect adversely the effectiveness of the device'. It is also important that fitting dimensions are maintained, especially if the flaps are damaged.

Fitment – Valances and Flaps

Where the choice is for spray suppression to be achieved by the use of valances and flaps (particularly on rear vehicle wheels and trailer wheels) the specific requirements for fitment are as follows:

NB: Capital letters in brackets in the following text refer to items on the adjacent diagrams illustrating fitment details.

- Valances of spray-suppressant material must extend across the top of the tyre from a line vertical with the front edge of the tyre (A) to a line beyond the rear wheel which will allow the rear flap to be suspended no more than 300 mm from the rear edge of the tyre (B). The valance must be at least 100 mm deep (C).

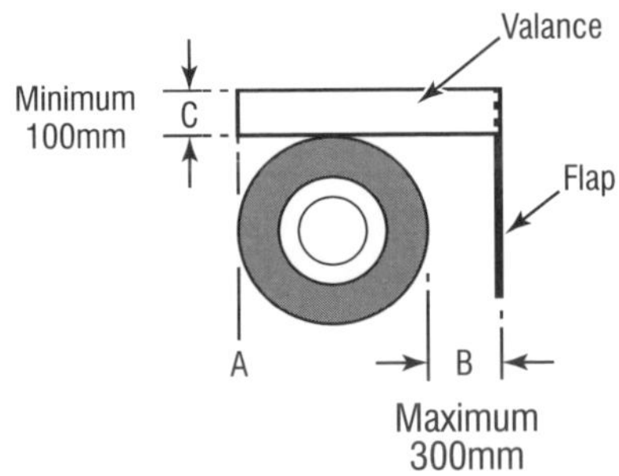

- The valance must extend downwards to be level with the top of the tyre (D) or it may overlap the top of the tyre (E).

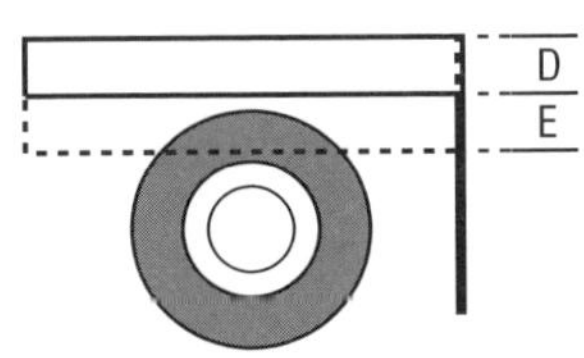

- In the case of multiple-axle bogies the relevant dimensions are shown below with the additional requirement that where the gap between the rear edge of the front tyre and the front edge of the rear tyre is greater than 250 mm (F) a flap must be fitted between the two. Note: No middle flap is required if the distance does not exceed 250 mm.

NB: The top of the valance may be in two separate sections (see shaded part) so long as it otherwise conforms to the dimensions.

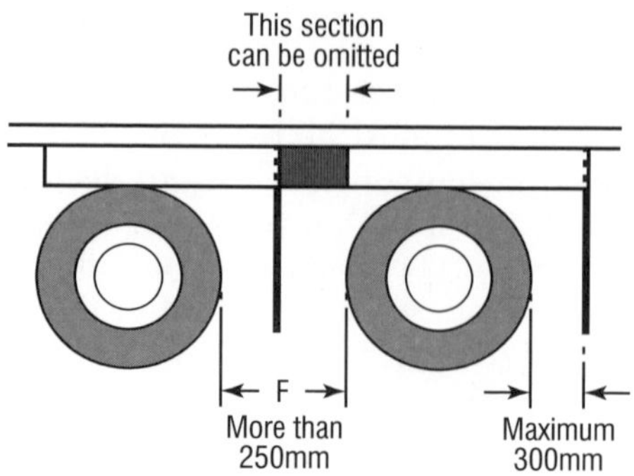

- Valances must extend the full width of the tyre and beyond to a maximum of 75 mm (G) in the case of the rear wheels (non-steerable) and 100 mm (H) in the case of steered wheels.

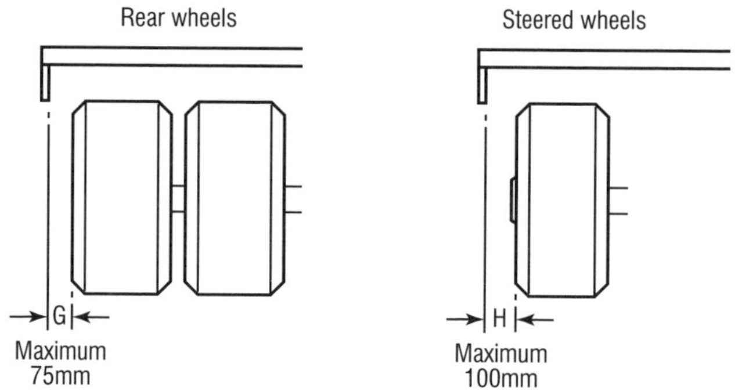

- If the valance extends below the level of the tyre on fixed wheels, the gap between the tyre face and the valance can be extended to 100 mm (J). There must be no gaps between the valance and the vehicle body.

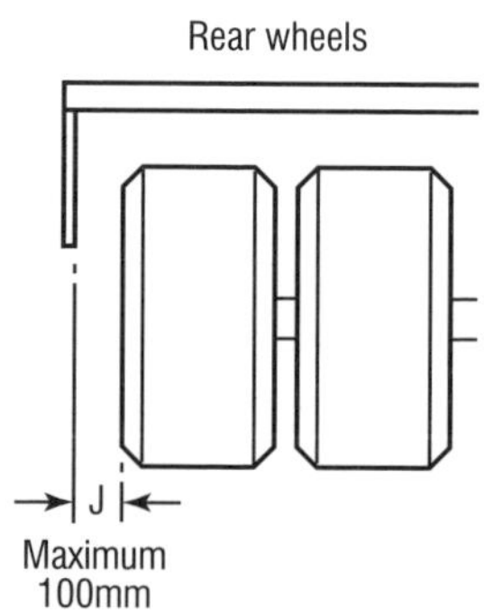

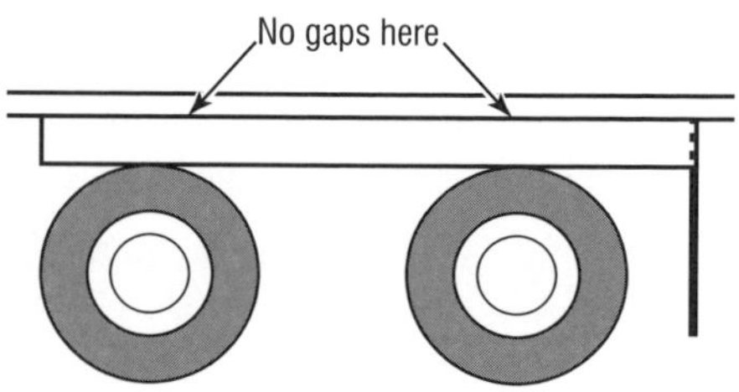

- Flaps used in conjunction with valances as described above must conform to the following dimensions:
  - They must extend to the full width of the tyre/tyres (K).
  - They must reach down to within 200 mm of the ground (L) when the vehicle is unladen (300 mm on rearmost axles of trailers used on roll-on/roll-off ferries or on any axle where the radial distance of the lower edge of the valancing does not exceed the radius of the tyres fitted).

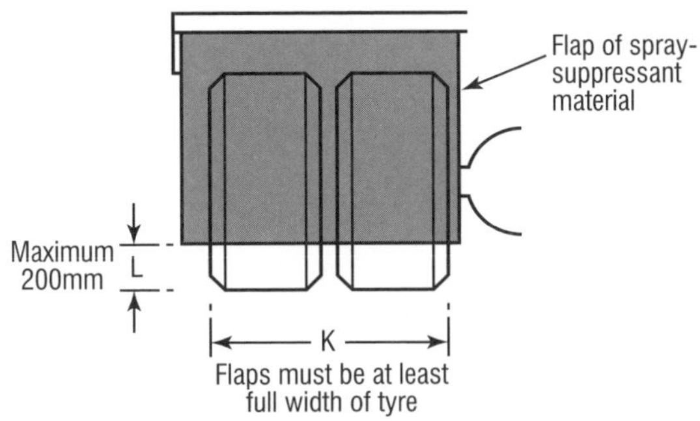

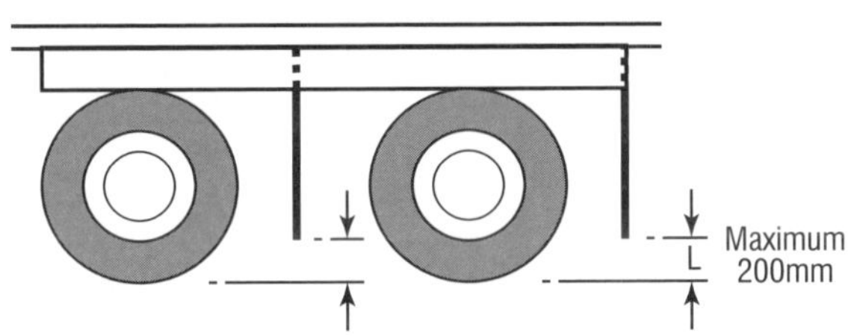

  - When flaps are used in conjunction with mudguard valances the top of the flap must extend upwards at least to a point 100 mm above the centre line of the wheel irrespective of the position of the lower edge of the mudguard.
  - Where the flap extends inside the guard it must be at least the width of the tyre tread pattern.

Flap used in conjunction with mudguard valance

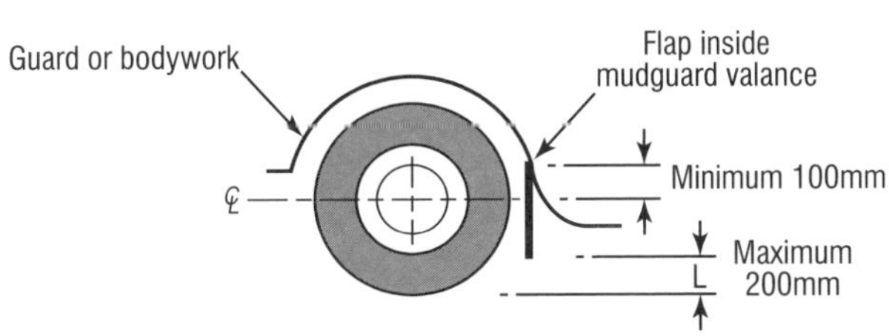

- If the flap used is of a type with an air/water separator device (ie bristles) fitted to the bottom edge, the following dimensions apply:
  - Rear edge of tyre to flap – maximum distance 200 mm (M).
  - The edge of the device must come to within 200 mm of the ground (N).

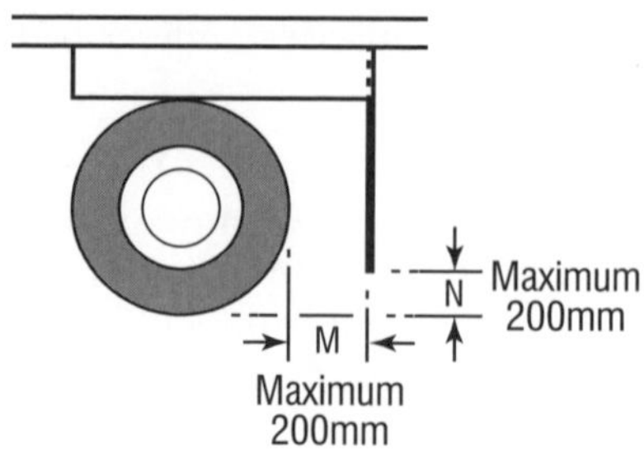

Deflection of Flaps

Wheel flaps must not be capable of being deflected rearwards more than 100 mm when subjected to a force of 3N (ie 4 lb) applied near the bottom of the flap.

Fitment – Mudguards and Air/Water Separator Devices

Where the choice for compliance with the regulations is by means of conventional mudguarding there are specific dimensions to be observed:

- If the mudguard is covering a steerable wheel (see later note about steerable axles on drawbar trailers), the radius of the edge of the valance must be not more than 1.5 times the radius of the tyre measured at three points (P) and in the case of non-steerable wheels, 1.25 times the same radius.
  - Vertically above the centre of the tyre.
  - A point at the front of the tyre 20 degrees above the horizontal centre line of the tyre (non-steerable wheels) or a point 30 degrees above the horizontal centre line of the tyre (steerable wheels).
  - A point at the rear of the tyre 100 mm above the horizontal centre line of the tyre.

Three points of measurement of radial for mudguards (P)

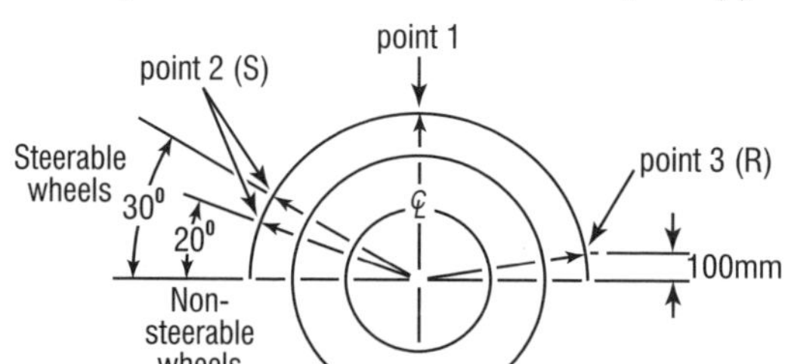

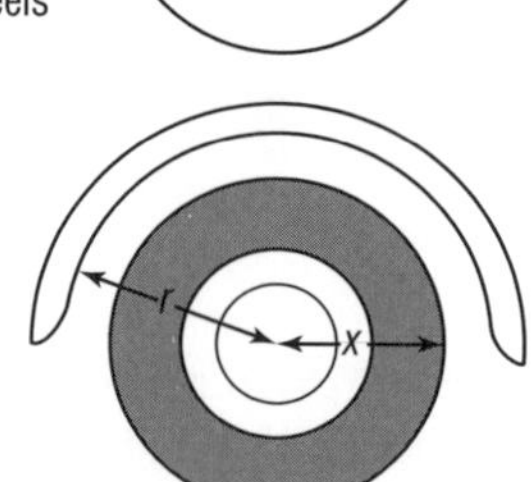

Steerable wheels
r = maximum 1.5 x x

Non-steerable wheels
r = maximum 1.5 x x

- Mudguard valances must be at least 45 mm deep behind a point vertically above the wheel centre. They may reduce in depth forward of this point (Q).

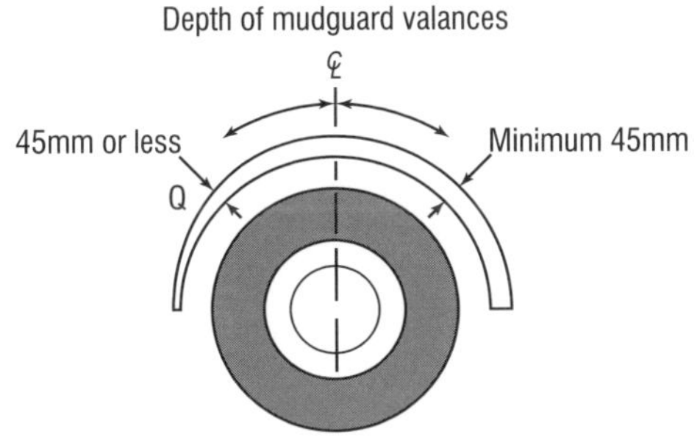

- In the case of drawbar trailers and rear-steer trailers, the 1.5 times radius dimension applies as above for the front steerable axle or rear steering axle unless the mudguards are fitted to the turntable and/or can turn with the wheels, in which case the maximum radius for the valance is 1.25 times the tyre radius.
- If the valancing on fixed-wheel mudguards is provided by means of air/water separator material (ie bristles), the edge must follow the periphery of the tyre. On steerable wheels the edge must be not more than 1.05 times the tyre radius.

  The valances on mudguards must extend downwards at the front and rear to at least the following dimensions:
  - at rear – to within 100 mm above the centre line of the axle (point 3) (R);
  - at front – to within a line 20 degrees above the centre line of the axle. In the case of steerable wheels this dimension is raised to 30 degrees (point 2) (S).

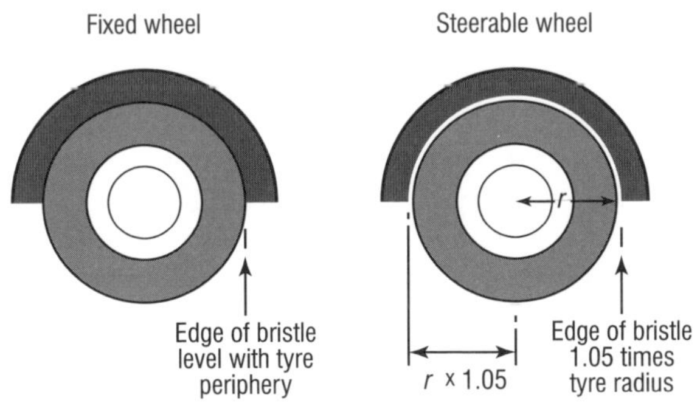

- In the case of multi-mudguarding over tandem axles or bogies, the intersection of the guards between the wheels must conform to one of the two dimensions:
  - the gap between the guards at the valance edges must not exceed 60 mm (T); or
  - the edges must come down to within 150 mm of the horizontal centre line across the wheels (V).

- If the gap between the tyre edges is greater than 250 mm, a flap must be provided between the wheels. If the gap is more than 300 mm, the wheels should be treated as though separate for mudguarding purposes (W).

Notes

- All dimensions in the regulations are to be taken when the vehicle is unladen, when steerable wheels are straight ahead and when the load platforms of articulated semi-trailers are level.
- All suppression material or devices and air/water separator material or devices must be permanently and legibly marked with the following mark: BS AU 200/2, plus 'the name, trademark or other means of identification of the responsible manufacturer'.

Tyres

It is an offence to use, or cause or permit to be used on a road, a vehicle or a trailer with a pneumatic tyre which is unsuitable for the use to which the vehicle is being put. It is also an offence to have different types of tyres fitted to opposite wheels of the vehicle or trailer; for example, radial-ply tyres must not be fitted to a wheel on the same axle as wheels already fitted with cross-ply tyres and vice versa. Tyres must be inflated to the vehicle or tyre manufacturers' recommended pressures so as to be fit for the use to which the vehicle is being put (for example, motorway work or cross-country work). No tyre must have a break in its fabric or a cut deep enough to reach the body cords, more than 25 mm or 10 per cent of its section width in length, whichever is the greater; also there must be no lump, bulge or tear caused by separation or partial fracture of its structure; neither must there be any portion of the ply or cord structure exposed.

In 2019 the DVSA announced that where they find an operator is fitting tyres that are more than 10 years old to their vehicles or trailers they will be subject to an investigation which could lead to the operator concerned being referred to the Traffic Commissioner. Whilst this is serious it should be noted that there is an exception for tyres fitted to inner rear wheels but the operator concerned must be able to demonstrate that they operate a tyre management risk assessment regime which is aimed at assessing the condition of the tyres used or stocked.

Shortly after the announcement in 2019 the DfT announced that recent research had actually shown that there was some degree of corrosion to tyre cords in tyres that were only eight years old and so it is expected that the 10-year benchmark may be reduced in the near future.

Approval Marks on Tyres

It is an offence to sell motor car tyres unless they carry an 'E' mark to show compliance with EU load and speed requirements. It is also an offence to sell re-tread car or lorry tyres unless they are manufactured and marked in accordance with British Standard BS AU 144b 1977.

Since 1 October 1990 it has been a requirement for tyres on heavy goods vehicles to show load and speed markings in accordance with UN ECE Regulation 30 or 54.

It is a legal requirement that these limits of both loading and speed performance are strictly observed. Failure to do so can result in prosecution and could invalidate insurance claims in the event of an accident to a vehicle loaded above the weight limit of the tyres or travelling at a speed in excess of the tyre limit.

Tread Depth

All tyres on goods vehicles of over 3,500 kg gross weight must have a tread depth of at least 1 mm across three-quarters of the breadth of the tread and around the entire circumference of the tyre. This 1 mm tread depth must be in a continuous band around the entire circumference of the tyre. Further, on the remaining one-quarter of the width of the tyre where there is no requirement for the tread to be 1 mm deep, the base of the original grooves must be clearly visible.

Most tyres for heavier vehicles have a depth/wear indicator bar in the bottom of the tread. This gives a quick check on tyre wear but it must be remembered that on tyres which have been re-cut the wear bars will not be present.

The minimum tread depth for cars, light vans (not exceeding 3,500 kg gross weight) and light trailers was increased to 1.6 mm from 1 January 1992, and this applies across the central three-quarters of the width of the tyre and in a continuous band around the entire circumference. The 1 mm limit stated above remains in force for heavy goods vehicles.

Re-Cut Tyres

Re-cut tyres may be fitted to goods vehicles of over 2,540 kg unladen weight which have wheels of at least 405 mm rim diameter and to trailers weighing more than 1,020 kg unladen weight and electric vehicles. They must not be used on private cars, dual-purpose vehicles, goods vehicles or trailers of less than the weight or wheel size specified.

Run-Flat and Temporary-Use Spare Tyres

The regulations permit the legal use of 'run-flat' tyres in a partially inflated or flat condition and what are described as temporary-use spare tyres. Where a temporary-use spare tyre is being used the vehicle speed must not exceed 50 mph otherwise the legal provision which permits their use ceases to apply. The temporary-use spare tyre or the wheel to which it is fitted must be of a different colour to the other wheels on the vehicle and a label must be attached to the wheel giving clear information about the precautions to be observed when using the wheel. There are also compounds available (for smaller vehicle tyres) that can be used to fill the tyre to enable it to be used following a puncture although many of these compounds cannot be removed from the tyre and, once the vehicle gets to a suitable tyre replacement facility the tyre with the compound must be replaced.

Lightweight Trailer Tyres

Tyres fitted to lightweight trailers since 1 April 1987 must be designed and maintained to support the maximum axle weight at its maximum permitted speed (ie 60 mph).

Front Under-Run Protection

Since August 2003 it is a requirement under EC Directive 2000/40/EC that all goods vehicles exceeding 3.5 tonnes gross weight should be fitted with an approved form of front under-run protection (ie bumper) system (FUPS). This bumper must extend to the full width of the vehicle, must be fitted no higher than 400 mm from the ground when the vehicle is unladen and must meet the same strength requirements specified for rear under-run bumpers (see below). Vehicles over 16 tonnes gross weight used for off-road purposes (ie principally tippers – in European category N2G and N3G) and vehicles whose 'use is incompatible with the provisions of front under-run protection' are exempt from the legal requirements.

Rear Under-Run Bumpers

Rear under-run bumpers (referred to in legislation as rear under-run protection (RUPS)) must be fitted to most rigid goods vehicles over 3.5 tonnes gross weight manufactured since 1 October 1983 and first used since 1 April 1984. Trailers, including semi-trailers, over 1,020 kg unladen weight manufactured since 1 May 1983 must also be fitted with bumpers. Certain vehicles and trailers are exempt (see below) from the fitting requirements and there were no retrospective fitting requirements for existing vehicles.

Strength of Bumpers

Rear under-run bumpers must be constructed so they are capable of withstanding a force equivalent to half the gross weight of the vehicle or trailer or a maximum of 10 tonnes, whichever is the *lesser*, without deflecting more than 400 mm measured from the rearmost point of the vehicle or trailer – not from the original vertical position of the bumper.

Fitment of Bumpers

Bumpers must be fitted as near as possible to the rear of the vehicle and the lower edge must be not more than 550 mm from the ground (see Figure 12.12). Normally, only one bumper would be fitted, but where a tail-lift is fitted or the bodywork or other parts of the vehicle make this impracticable, two or more bumpers may be fitted. When a single full-width bumper is fitted it must extend on each side of the centre to within at least 100 mm from the outermost width of the rear axle, but must not in any case extend beyond the width of the rear axle measured across the outermost face of the tyres. When two or more bumpers are fitted, for the reasons mentioned above, the space between each part of the bumper must not exceed 500 mm and the outermost edge of the bumpers must extend to within at least 300 mm from the outermost width of the rear axle (see Figure 12.13). Bumpers must not protrude beyond the width of the vehicle or trailer and the outside ends of the bumper must not be bent backwards.

FIGURE 12.12 Illustration of the rear under-run bumper force resistance requirements and ground clearance dimension

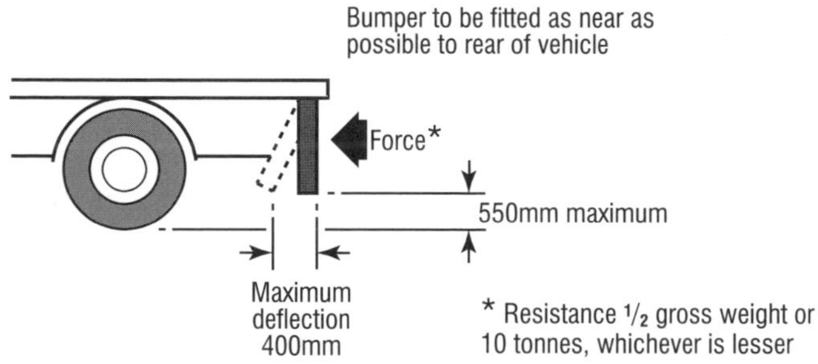

FIGURE 12.13 Illustrations of the fitting dimensions for single and multiple rear under-run bumpers

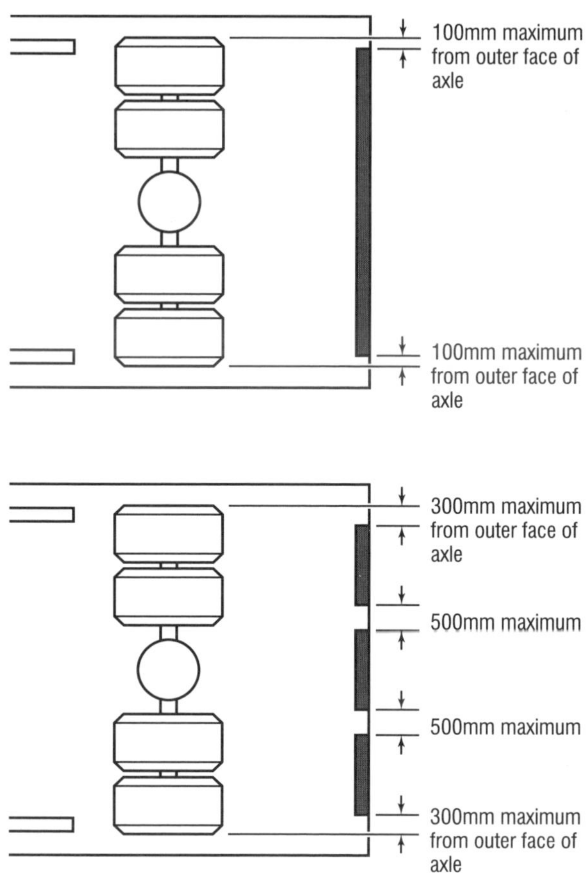

Maintenance of Bumpers

Rear bumpers must be maintained free from any obvious defect that would adversely affect their performance in giving resistance to impact from the rear. It is also important to ensure that the dimensional requirements are met, particularly if the bumper is damaged (for example by forklift truck impact or reversing onto loading bays).

Exemptions

Rear under-run bumpers do not have to be fitted to vehicles and trailers in the following list:

- vehicles incapable of a speed exceeding 15 mph on the level under their own power;
- tractive units of articulated vehicles;
- agricultural trailers, trailed appliances and agricultural motor vehicles;
- engineering plant;
- fire engines;
- road spreading vehicles (ie for salt and grit);
- rear tipping vehicles;
- military, naval or air-force vehicles;
- vehicles being taken to have bodywork fitted, or being taken for quality or safety checks by the manufacturer, distributor or dealer in such vehicles;
- vehicles being driven or towed to a place to have a rear under-run bumper fitted by prior arrangement;
- vehicles designed to carry other vehicles which are loaded from the rear (eg car transporters);
- trailers designed and constructed (not just adapted) to carry round timber, beams or girders of exceptional length;
- vehicles fitted with tail-lifts where the tail-lift forms part of the floor of the vehicle and extends to a length of at least 1 metre;
- temporarily imported foreign vehicles and semi-trailers;
- vehicles specially designed (not just adapted) for carrying and mixing liquid concrete;
- vehicles designed and used solely for the delivery of coal by means of a conveyor fixed to the vehicle so as to make the fitment of a rear under-run bumper impracticable.

View to the Front

Drivers must have a full view of the road and traffic ahead at all times when driving. Obstructing the windscreen with mascots, stickers, stone guards and other such things could result in prosecution and/or failure of the vehicle when it is presented for annual test.

Vehicles with closed-circuit television (CCTV) rear-view monitors mounted in the cab in such a position that the driver's view to the front is obscured, or partly obscured, will normally be failed in their annual test by the DVSA. This particularly applies to refuse collectors and ambulances, which traditionally use such equipment (see also p 400).

This provision may seem at odds with the use of TomTom-type devices in cars and portable front facing cameras where the equipment screen is often fixed to the front windscreen of the vehicle concerned, but this does seem to be acceptable to the enforcement authorities although some concerns have been raised.

NB: Note the 'deeper' windscreen requirements for access to the London Direct Vision Standard area.

Windscreen Wipers and Washers

Windscreen Wipers

All vehicles must be fitted with one or more efficient automatic windscreen wipers capable of clearing the windscreen to provide the driver with an adequate view to the front and sides of the vehicle. They must be maintained in good and efficient working order and must be adjusted properly. This provision does not apply if the driver has an adequate view of the road without looking through the windscreen.

Windscreen Washers

Vehicles required to be fitted with windscreen wipers must be fitted with a windscreen washer that is capable, in conjunction with the wipers, of clearing the area of the windscreen swept by the wipers of mud or dirt. Washers are not required on land tractors, track-laying vehicles and vehicles that cannot travel at more than 20 mph.

A vehicle should not be driven on the road with defective windscreen wipers or washers. This is an offence which could result in a fine of up to £1,000 (as with many other C&U regulation offences). Washers and wipers which may be frozen and unable to operate can be deemed to be defective and also be subject to enforcement.

Note: Many operators now insist that drivers only use a proper screen wash solution, and not tap water, following concerns about the possibility of contracting Legionnaire's Disease from coming into contact with water which may have been in the washer system for some time whilst also having been warmed by the heat of the engine.

Wings

Goods vehicles and trailers must be fitted with wings to catch, as far as practicable, mud and water thrown up by the wheels unless adequate protection is provided by the bodywork.

Articulated vehicles and trailers used for carrying round timber are exempt from these requirements in respect of all except the front wheels of the tractive unit.

Vehicles and trailers in an unfinished condition that are proceeding to a bodybuilder for work to be completed and works trucks are also exempt from the need to have wings.

Use of Vehicles

In addition to the foregoing constructional requirements, which are mainly the responsibility of the vehicle manufacturer or the person building the bodywork, there are requirements regarding the use of vehicles which are the responsibility of the operator. However, as mentioned earlier, the vehicle user carries full legal responsibility for the mechanical condition of a vehicle on the road and its compliance with the constructional requirements even if the fault which led to an offence could be laid at the door of the chassis manufacturer, the bodybuilder, an ancillary equipment supplier or the dealer.

These requirements cover such items as vehicle weights (which were dealt with earlier), towing, fumes, the condition and maintenance of vehicles and their components, noise, smoke and general safety in the use of vehicles. They also include the regulations regarding the number of trailers which a vehicle may draw. The regulations also clearly state that any vehicle used must be 'fit for purpose' and not present any hazard to any other road users.

Gas and Electric Powered Vehicles

Regulations specify technical standards for fuel tanks or containers, the filling system and valves and general requirements for gas propulsion systems in motor vehicles. The regulations permit the use of LPG only in gas-propelled vehicles, though this may be combined with petrol fuel systems, and the sole use of methane or hydrogen is prohibited. The D*f*T publishes free guides on fitting and operating both LPG and CNG (see below) and information is available through the GOV.UK website.

Article (17A) and schedules (5A and 5B) to the Motor Vehicles (Authorisation of Special Types) General Order 1979 – inserted by virtue of Amendment No 2 of 1 December 1998 to the Order – authorize the use on roads of vehicles propelled by compressed natural gas (CNG), notwithstanding that they do not comply with the requirements of the C&U Regulations. They must, however, comply with the provisions of the new schedules as to constructional requirements and the requirements for testing gas containers used in these systems.

Since that date CNG engines and multi-fuel vehicles have been introduced as research and development continues in an attempt to reduce the use of carbon based liquid fuels. However, whilst the C&U Regulations will apply to these alternative fuel engines, Commission Regulation (EU) No 630/2012 also covers the specification of vehicles powered by all types of gas and mixtures of hydrogen with natural gas.

More and more electric goods vehicles are entering service and, whilst originally exempted from many regulations, they are now increasingly included in C&U standards and operators need to be aware of changing standards for these vehicles. That said, it is to be noted that electrically powered vans are now permitted to operate at weights up to 4,250 kg and not 3,500 kg in order to take account of the additional weight of the batteries without reducing payload.

Noise

It is an offence to use, or cause or permit to be used, on a road a motor vehicle or trailer which causes an excessive noise because of a defect, lack of repair or faulty adjustment of components or load. Also, no motor vehicle must be used on a road in such a manner as to cause any excessive noise which could have been reasonably avoided by the driver. Noise for these purposes is the combined noise emitted by the exhaust plus that from the tyres, engine, bodywork and equipment, and the load. Noise levels for goods vehicles are measured by special meters either by the police or by DVSA examiners at goods vehicle testing stations and occasionally on roadside tests. The noise measured is that of the 'whole' vehicle, not just the exhaust and engine. Refrigerator compressors, reversing bleepers (see below) and warning devices also constitute noise emitted from a vehicle and care needs to be taken if these are used during the silent hours and/or in residential areas.

Noise Limits

It is no longer a legal requirement for goods vehicles to maintain the noise standards set when the vehicle was manufactured. The regulations covering noise emissions are adequately covered under other provisions (see above).

The European Commission was proposing to reduce the maximum noise limits for heavy lorries from the current level of 79 decibels (dBa) to 77 dBa over a three-year period stretching from 2015 to 2017. However, to date nothing has been decided although this initiative includes a further reduction from 77 dBa to 75 dBa by 2020–22.

Reversing Alarms

It is legally permissible to fit reversing alarms to certain goods and passenger vehicles if desired – *the regulations do not make it mandatory to do so*. Such alarms may be voluntarily fitted and may be either a warning buzzer or horn, etc, or a verbal recording. They may be used on the following vehicles:

- commercial vehicles over 2 tonnes gross weight;
- passenger vehicles with nine or more seats;
- engineering plant;
- works trucks.

Time Restriction on Use of Reversing Alarms

The alarms are subject to the same night-time restrictions that apply to the sounding of horns in built-up areas (ie not after 11.30 pm and before 7.00 am) and the sound emitted must not be capable of being confused with the pelican crossing 'safe to cross' signal. If a vehicle fitted with a reversing alarm is to be used during these 'silent hours' the alarm must be capable of being switched off.

Restriction on Fitment of Reversing Alarms

Such alarms *must not* be fitted to light goods vehicles below 2 tonnes gross weight or to motor cars.

Advice on Use of Alarms

A number of cases have arisen following reversing accidents resulting in death or injury where the Health and Safety Executive (HSE) has prosecuted the vehicle operators concerned for not voluntarily fitting reversing alarms. In other words, the HSE line is that the offenders had not taken sufficient steps to ensure safety when their vehicles were reversing by fitting equipment which the law permits, but does not mandatorily require them to do.

Televisions in Vehicles

It is illegal for a vehicle to be fitted with television receiving apparatus where the driver can see the screen either directly or by reflection, except where such equipment displays nothing other than information:

- about the state of the vehicle or its equipment;
- about the location of the vehicle and the road on which it is located;
- to assist the driver to see the road adjacent to the vehicle (eg to the rear when reversing); or
- to assist the driver to reach his destination.

NB: See also p 397.

Towing

Goods vehicles (not showmen's vehicles) may draw (ie tow) only one trailer. An exception to this is when a rigid goods vehicle tows a broken-down vehicle on a towing ambulance or dolly, in which case although this is counted as towing two trailers it is allowed. In a case where an articulated vehicle has broken down, this may be towed by a rigid goods vehicle so long as the articulated vehicle is not loaded. In these circumstances the outfit is treated as one trailer only, but if it is loaded, an articulated outfit being towed is considered to be two trailers and it would be illegal for a normal goods vehicle (ie a heavy motor car) to tow it. Only a locomotive (this definition normally applies to recovery vehicles which can only tow and that are unable to carry goods; further information can be found in the VOSA publication *Guide for Recovery Operations* or in the *Association of Vehicle Recovery Operators (AVRO) guide*) can tow a broken-down articulated vehicle which is laden (see below).

Motor tractors may draw one laden or two unladen trailers, and locomotives may draw three trailers (see p 361 for definitions).

Composite Trailers

The C&U Regulations make it permissible for rigid goods vehicles (apart from locomotives and motor tractors) to draw two trailers instead of only one, when one of

FIGURE 12.14 A conventional six-wheeled rigid vehicle drawing a dolly mounted semi-trailer for which the maximum overall length is 18.35 metres

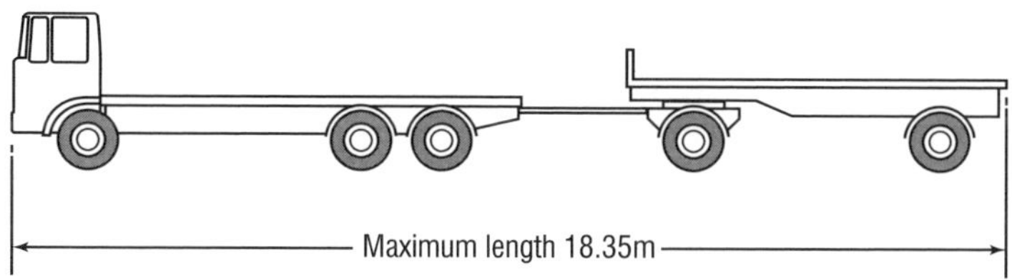

the trailers is a towing implement (ie a dolly) and the other is an articulated-type semi-trailer secured to and resting on, or suspended from, the dolly. This combination of dolly and semi-trailer is known as a composite trailer (Figure 12.14).

To comply with the regulations, the dolly needs to have two or more wheels and be specifically designed to support a superimposed semi-trailer. Dollies must display a manufacturer's plate and they are subject to the annual heavy goods vehicle test.

Towing Distance

The distance between the nearest points of two vehicles joined by a tow rope or chain must not exceed 4.5 metres. When the distance between the two vehicles exceeds 1.5 metres the rope, chain or bar must be made clearly visible from both sides of the vehicles. There is no specified maximum distance limit if a solid tow bar is used for towing.

Trailer and Semi-Trailer Coupling and Uncoupling

Over time, the procedure of coupling and uncoupling trailers and semi-trailers has proved to be a high-risk activity, prone to accident and dangerous incident, unfortunately costing far too many lives. Because of this it is now an integral part of the Category C+E driving test. In 2006 a new Code of Practice was launched by the Society of Operations Engineers (SOE) in conjunction with the Institute of Road Transport Engineers (IRTE) and the Health and Safety Executive (HSE) in an effort to ensure that safe practices are adopted and followed by drivers and others when carrying out this high-risk procedure. The Code is divided into five sections dealing with safe procedures for standard and close-coupled semi-trailers and both centre-axle and turntable drawbar trailers.

Copies of the Code are available from the SOE and online at: www.soe.org.uk (archived at https://perma.cc/5DZU-EY95). Copies of an HSE guide and the HSE 2016 guide *Safe Coupling and Uncoupling Guide* are available on the HSE website: hse.gov.uk (archived at https://perma.cc/6XUW-QZCQ).

Type Approval

Type approval is a scheme which requires vehicle manufacturers to submit new vehicles (ie new designs, new models and changes of specifications for existing approved models) for approval before they are put on the market. The Department for Transport examines the vehicle submitted to ensure that it meets all legal requirements and also meets minimum standards of construction and performance. When a vehicle has been approved the manufacturer is then required by law to build all vehicles of a similar type to exactly those standards and certify this fact to the customer by the issue of a Certificate of Conformity.

An EU directive lays down the basic procedures for the type approval schemes for vehicles and components. Subsidiary directives have also been issued setting out agreed standards on some aspects of vehicle safety or pollution. They cover the same ground as existing national regulations. The directives do not yet cover all vehicle features which need to be regulated so until the programme is complete both EU directives and national regulations apply to relevant items. The UK established a non-compulsory scheme to enable exporting vehicle manufacturers to gain the necessary type approval in order to sell their products in EU countries.

Vehicles Covered

EC approval of most road vehicles is based around a 'Whole Vehicle' framework directive, Directive 70/156/EEC as most recently amended by Directive 2007/46/EC – implemented in all EU member states from 29 April 2009 – which specifies the range of aspects of the vehicle that must be approved under separate technical directives.

This Directive is known as ECWVTA (EC Whole Vehicle Type Approval) and applies to manufacturers of large numbers of vehicles. Where a manufacturer may only produce a few vehicles the type approval procedure is known as National Small Series Type Approval (NSSTA). Both these schemes are overseen in the UK by the Vehicle Certification Agency (VCA), which is an executive agency of the D*f*T.

In order to gain EC Whole Vehicle Type Approval, a vehicle must first be approved in regard to its brakes, emissions, noise, etc – in fact, up to 48 different standards for a typical vehicle. The issuing of the whole vehicle approval does not in itself involve testing, but *a production* sample of the complete vehicle is inspected to check that its specification matches the specifications contained in all the separate directive approvals.

Broadly, the whole vehicle framework document covers any vehicle with four or more wheels intended for use on roads, except agricultural or forestry tractors, mobile machinery and vehicles with a design maximum speed of less than 25 kph. Separate technical directives and regulations allow (or require) the approval of individual vehicles and systems as part of a type of vehicle, and some allow for the approval of separate devices. Where this is used for 'one-off' vehicles it is known as Individual Vehicle Approval (IVA). System and component approval requires that a sample of the type to be approved is tested by the Technical Service to the requirements of the relevant Directive. Its technical specification is documented and that specification forms part of the approval.

From 29 October 2014, before a vehicle can be registered at the DVLA it will have to be able to prove that it complies with ECWVTA in at least one of the following ways:

- It complies with full EU type approval through the Vehicle Certification Agency (VCA).
- It complies with NSSTA through the VCA.
- It complies with the rules of the IVA scheme through the DVLA.

Exemptions from Type Approval

Type approval does not apply to the following vehicles:

- vehicles manufactured before 1 October 1982, whenever they are first registered;
- vehicles manufactured on or after 1 October 1982, providing they were first licensed before 1 April 1983;
- temporarily imported vehicles;
- vehicles proceeding for export from the UK;
- vehicles in the service of visiting forces or headquarters;
- certain vehicles which are, or were formerly, in use in the public service or the Crown;
- prototypes which are not intended for general use on the roads;
- motor tractors, light locomotives and heavy locomotives;
- engineering plant (provided it does NOT have a truck chassis), pedestrian-controlled vehicles, straddle carriers, works trucks and track-laying vehicles;
- vehicles specially designed and constructed for use in private premises for moving excavated materials, vehicles fitted with movable platforms and vehicles designed and constructed for the carriage of abnormal indivisible loads;
- tower wagons;
- fire engines;
- road rollers;
- steam-propelled vehicles;
- vehicles constructed for the purpose of preventing or reducing the effect of snow or ice on roads;
- two-wheeled motorcycles with or without sidecars;
- electrically propelled vehicles;
- breakdown vehicles (providing they are NOT recovery vehicles exceeding 12,000 kg MAM);

- any vehicle not exceeding 3,500 kg maximum gross weight which is constructed or assembled by a person not ordinarily engaged in the manufacture of goods vehicles of that description;
- vehicles not exceeding 3,500 kg maximum gross weight provided that:
  - the vehicle has been purchased outside the UK for the personal use of the individual importing it or his dependants;
  - the vehicle has been so used by that individual or his dependants on roads outside the UK before it is imported;
  - the vehicle is intended solely for such personal use in the UK; and
  - the individual importing the vehicle intends, at the time when the vehicle is imported, to remain in the UK for not less than 12 months from that date.

For clarification purposes, the following vehicles which were exempted from type approval before October 2014 are now no longer excluded:

- crash cushion vehicles;
- vehicles used for AIL work;
- vehicles with moving mounted platforms on booms;
- highway testing vehicles based on a truck chassis.

Responsibility for Compliance

Responsibility for complying with the complex construction standards rests with the manufacturer although users are still responsible for maintaining vehicles in roadworthy condition. The construction standards applied by the scheme are limited to those which can be approved during the primary stage of manufacture. The standards are identical to those already required under the Construction and Use Regulations but under this scheme vehicles have to be approved before they can be used on the road.

Effects on Plating and Testing

The scheme requires plated weights for heavy goods vehicles to be set during the type approval process instead of waiting until the first annual plating and testing examination. This means that heavy vehicle operators need a Type Approval Certificate in order to get a Ministry plate for display in the vehicle cab (see Chapter 14). However, annual testing is retained so as to check the condition of vehicles and to ensure that plated weights are accurate.

Responsibility for Type Approval

All aspects of type approval are the responsibility of the DVSA, who remind operators that in order to obtain an annual test or a plating certificate for a type approved vehicle they need to use form VTG788 for ECWVTA and NSSTA vehicles and form VTG789 for IVA vehicles.

The Standards Checked

To obtain goods vehicle national type approval it is first necessary to obtain individual systems approvals for the following items:

- power-to-weight ratio (not applicable to petrol-engined vehicles or dual-purpose vehicles);
- gaseous exhaust emissions (petrol-engined vehicles only);
- particle emission (ie exhaust smoke) (diesel-engined vehicles only);
- external noise level;
- radio-interference suppression (petrol-engined vehicles only);
- brakes.

NB: As the whole Type Approval scheme currently applying to UK vehicles and vehicle components is based on EU standards and requirements it is likely (depending upon a deal or no-deal Brexit) that the UK will have to develop its own new Type Approval standards and regime although it could simply adopt what we have. In any case interested parties need to monitor this requirement closely either by contacting the trade associations or by following developments on the DVSA website www.gov.uk/government/organisations/driver-and-vehicle-standards-agency (archived at https://perma.cc/PG6H-U4KG).

Arrangements for First Licensing of Vehicles

For vehicles over 1,525 kg unladen weight or which form part of an articulated vehicle, application for first licensing on form V55 must be accompanied by two copies of the Type Approval Certificate, which should have been supplied with the vehicle. On one of these the applicant must complete a declaration saying whether or not the vehicle is exempt from the plating and testing regulations (see Chapter 14 for full details) and whether it has been altered in any way that has to be notified to the DVSA under the type approval regulations and, if so, whether any action arising from the notification has been satisfactorily completed.

Issue of Plates

When application is made for first licensing a vehicle which is subject to plating and testing, the DVLA will send a copy of the Type Approval Certificate and the Certificate of Conformity (CoC) with the applicant's declaration to the Goods Vehicle Centre (GVC) at Swansea. The second copy will be stamped and returned to the applicant to serve as a temporary Ministry plate. When the GVC receives the copy of the certificate, and if the details compare satisfactorily with those on the copy sent direct by the vehicle manufacturers, it will issue a Ministry plate and laminated plating certificate. These will be sent direct to the person or company in whose name the vehicle is registered. Thus, operators buying new vehicles receive their first plate and plating certificate for the vehicle from the GVC at the time of licensing rather than from the goods vehicle testing station when the vehicle is presented for its first annual test as under previous arrangements. This also means that trailers will be issued with paper plates and not paper discs and that the plates will need to travel with the trailers and that the trailers will also require their own registration plates. For further information go to the internet and type in 'Haulage Permits and Trailer Registration Act 2018'. When an application is made for licensing a vehicle which is exempt from plating and testing, a copy of the certificate and the declaration will be sent to the GVC so that it is aware that it is exempt.

Refusal to Licence

No vehicle subject to the type approval regulations will be first licensed unless the DVLA registration form V55 has a valid type approval number on it or it is an exempt vehicle.

Alteration to Vehicles

If a vehicle which has been issued with an Approval Certificate and supplied to a dealer or direct to an operator is modified by them, prior to first licensing, they must notify the VCA at Bristol (Vehicle Certification Agency, 1, The Eastgate Office Centre, Eastgate Road, Bristol, BS5 6XX (0300 330 5797) (www.dft.gov.uk/vca (archived at https://perma.cc/JUA4-R8L4))) and send the certificate for the vehicle together with a completed VTG10 form, full technical details, drawings of the alterations and details of the weights on the certificate which need, or may need, changing.

The VCA will judge whether the alterations affect the vehicle's compliance with the regulations; if they do not affect compliance the certificate will be returned so the vehicle can be licensed. If they do contravene compliance, the certificate will be cancelled and fresh approval will need to be obtained before the vehicle can be licensed. This is a complex and costly procedure that most operators will want to avoid; they can do so by registering and licensing the vehicle before any alterations are carried out.

Vehicle Lighting and Marking

13

The legal requirements for vehicles to be fitted with and to display lights at night and other times, and for the fitment of reflectors and other markings on vehicles, are contained in the Road Vehicles Lighting Regulations 1989 (as amended). These are now also complemented by conspicuity marking regulations introduced for new vehicles and trailers on 10 July 2011 under UNECE Regulation 48 (see below). These regulations specify in considerable detail all the requirements for the position of lamps and reflectors and the angles from which they must be visible. This chapter can only include a summary of the relevant requirements and dimensions as they apply to goods vehicles, which, for most normal purposes, is satisfactory because vehicles and trailers are generally ready-fitted with lamps and reflectors conforming to legal requirements when supplied from new. However, for a variety of reasons, operators may find it necessary to replace and relocate lamps from time to time when carrying out repairs and conversions, and at this time they are advised to check the regulations carefully to ensure strict compliance with the law. Advice can also be found in the revised *Heavy Goods Vehicle (HGV) Inspection Manual* which is free to download from the GOV.UK website. Not only can prosecution follow for incorrectly positioned or non-functioning lights and reflectors, but vehicles could fail their annual test on this account, which adds to operating costs and wastes time. There are also the safety considerations with the lives of both vehicle drivers and other road users at risk if vehicles are not showing correct or adequate lights.

The lighting regulations require that lights and reflectors which are fitted to vehicles must be maintained so as to enable them to be driven on a road between sunset and sunrise (times are published in most daily and local newspapers), or in seriously reduced visibility between sunrise and sunset, or to be parked on a road between sunset and sunrise without contravening the regulations. All lights must be kept clean and in good working order. It is an offence to cause undue dazzle or discomfort to other road users by the use of lights or through their faulty adjustment, or to have defective or obscured lighting on a vehicle at any time. There is no longer a defence to a charge of having defective lights on a vehicle (see below).

Obligatory Lights

Between sunset and sunrise vehicles used on a public road must display the following obligatory lights, other lights and reflectors:

- two front position lamps (ie sidelamps) showing white lights to the front;
- two rear position lamps (ie rear lamps) showing red lights to the rear;
- two headlamps showing white lights to the front (alternatively, the light may be yellow);
- illumination for the rear number (ie registration) plate when the other vehicle lights are on;
- certain goods vehicles and trailers additionally require side marker lamps plus side-facing reflectors and rear reflective markings – see below;
- one or two red rear fog lamps on post-1 April 1980 vehicles;
- two red reflex retro-reflectors at the rear;
- end-outline marker lamps;
- any other lights or lighting devices with which the vehicle is fitted (eg stop lamps, hazard warning signals, running lamps, dim-dip devices and headlamp levelling devices).

It is illegal except in certain specified cases for a goods vehicle to show a white light to the rear (showing such a light when reversing and indirect illumination of the rear registration plate are permitted, for example) or a red light to the front.

Daytime running lamps (DRLs), which switch on automatically when the vehicle ignition is switched on, have been required on new heavy vehicles since 7 August 2012.

NB: There was no requirement for such lamps to be fitted to existing vehicles at that time.

Headlamps

Motor vehicles must be fitted with two headlamps capable of showing a white or yellow light to the front – both lamps must emit the same colour light. Headlamps must be either permanently dipped or fitted with dipping equipment. Vehicles first used since 1 April 1987 must have dim-dip lighting devices unless their lighting equipment complies with EU requirements (see below). Vehicles must also have a warning device for the driver that indicates when full beam, and not dipped beam, is selected.

Headlamps must be mounted so that they are not lower than 500 mm from the ground and not higher than 1,200 mm. They must be placed on either side of the vehicle with their illuminated areas not more than 400 mm from the side of the vehicle. They must be equipped with bulbs or sealed-beam units of not less than 30 watts in the case of vehicles first used before 1 April 1986. For vehicles used since this date no minimum wattage requirement is specified.

Vehicles that are used on international operations are often fitted with headlamps that can be set by operating a switch in the cab for either right hand side or left hand side driving.

Headlamp Exemptions

Certain vehicles are exempt from the headlamp requirements. These include vehicles with fewer than four wheels, pedestrian-controlled vehicles, agricultural implements, land tractors, works trucks, vehicles not capable of travelling at a speed of more than 6 mph and some military vehicles.

Headlamps on Electric Vehicles

Electrically propelled goods vehicles with four or more wheels registered before October 1969 and electric vehicles with two or three wheels first used before 1 January 1972 and capable of a speed of more than 15 mph are required to comply with the headlamp requirements. Those electrically propelled vehicles which are incapable of speeds of more than 15 mph are exempt from the headlamp requirements.

Use of Headlamps

Headlamps must be adjusted so that they do not cause undue dazzle or discomfort to other road users. When vehicles which require headlamps are being driven on unlit roads between sunset and sunrise and in seriously reduced daytime visibility the headlamps must be illuminated. They must be switched off when the vehicle is stationary except at traffic stops.

Incorrect aim of vehicle headlights is reported to be one of the most common reasons for annual goods vehicle test failure. Correction can be effected by simple adjustment, or by changing bulbs – inconsistent filament positioning on some low-quality bulbs being a possible cause of incorrect headlight aim.

It is to be noted that goods vehicles presented for annual test that require the headlights adjusting at the time of the test will be recorded as a PRS (pass after rectification at the station). In effect, this notes that the vehicle arrived at the test station in a 'fail' state and this is recorded and counts towards an operator's OCRS even if the vehicle is prepared and presented by a maintenance contractor.

NB: Unlit roads are roads on which there are no street lamps or on which the street lamps are more than 200 yards apart.

Headlamps in Daylight

It is a legal requirement for vehicles to use side-position lights (ie sidelights) and dipped headlights when travelling in seriously reduced daytime visibility conditions such as in fog, smoke, heavy rain, spray or snow. If matching fog or fog and spotlights are fitted in pairs these may be used instead of headlights, but sidelights must still be used and the other vehicle lights must be on (eg side marker lights).

There is no specific definition of 'seriously reduced visibility' in the regulations, although the *Highway Code* does state that: 'You **must** use headlights when visibility is seriously reduced, generally when you cannot see for more than 100 metres (328 feet)'.

Dim-Dip Lighting

Since 1 April 1987 newly registered vehicles must be fitted with dim-dip lighting devices which operate automatically when the obligatory lights of the vehicle are switched on and ensure that either 10 per cent (with halogen) or 15 per cent (with grading filament lamps) of the normal dipped beam intensity shows when the vehicle ignition key is switched on or the engine is running. The European Court of Justice has ruled that it is unfair for the British Government to legislate for the fitment of dim-dip lighting devices for vehicles which already comply with the EU Lighting Directive (EC 756/1976 as amended by EC 663/1991), which has no dim-dip requirement.

Front Position Lamps (sidelamps)

Two front position lamps (ie sidelamps) emitting a white light through a diffused lens must be fitted to all motor vehicles with three or more wheels and trailers (except those not more than 1,600 mm wide), those no longer than 2,300 mm (excluding the drawbar) built before 1 October 1985 and those used for carrying and launching boats. These are now usually incorporated into the headlight assembly. If such lamps are incorporated within a headlamp showing a yellow light then the side position lamps may be yellow. No minimum wattage is specified for these lights. The lights must be equal in height from the ground and mounted not more than 1,500 mm from the ground (in exceptional circumstances this height can be increased to 2,100 mm) in the case of vehicles first used on or after 1 April 1986 and 2,300 mm in other cases, and not more than 400 mm from the outer edge of the vehicle for vehicles first used since 1 April 1986 and 510 mm in other cases. No minimum height above the ground is specified.

Rear Position Lamps (rear lamps)

Two red rear position lamps (ie rear lamps) must be fitted to all motor vehicles and trailers. There is no specified wattage for these lights. They must be mounted not less than 350 mm and not more than 1,500 mm (2,100 mm in exceptional circumstances) from the ground. They must be at least 500 mm apart (no specified distance on pre-1 April 1986 registered vehicles) and not more than 400 mm (800 mm on pre-1 April 1986 registered vehicles) from the outside edge of the vehicle.

Stop Lamps

All goods vehicles (except those not capable of more than 25 mph) must be fitted with red stop lamps which are maintained in a clean condition and in good and efficient working order. Vehicles registered before 1 January 1971 need only one such lamp, which must be fitted at the centre or to the offside of the vehicle, although a second matching lamp may be fitted on the nearside. Vehicles registered since that date need two such lamps (specified wattage 15 to 36 watts except with pre-1 January 1971 registered vehicles) mounted not less than 350 mm from the ground and not more than 1,500 mm (in exceptional circumstances this may be increased to 2,100 mm) and they must be at least 400 mm apart. Such lamps must be visible horizontally from 45 degrees on either side and normally from 15 degrees above and below vertically (from only 5 degrees below where fitted less than 750 mm from the ground and only 10 degrees below when fitted not more than 1,500 mm from the ground).

Reversing Lamps

White reversing lamps (not more than two) may be fitted to vehicles provided they are only used while the vehicle is reversing and operate automatically only when reverse gear is selected. Alternatively, they may be operated manually by a switch (which serves no other purpose) in the driver's cab provided that a warning device indicates to the driver that the lights are illuminated. The lights must be adjusted so as not to cause dazzle to other road users. Such lamps when bearing an 'e' approval mark do not have to meet minimum wattage requirements but those without approval marks must not exceed 24 watts.

Number Plate Lamp

Rear number plates (ie registration plates) on vehicles must be indirectly illuminated when the other obligatory lamps on the vehicles are lit. The light must be white and must be shielded so that it only illuminates the number plate and does not show to the rear. At the time of writing it is unclear whether or not the new requirement for trailers to have their own number plate but also show the number plate of the drawing vehicle will require the fitting of two illuminated registration plate brackets.

Rear Fog Lamps

Rear fog lamps (at least one, but two may be fitted) must be fitted to new vehicles and trailers manufactured on or after 1 October 1979 and first used since 1 April 1980. There is no legal requirement to fit such lamps on pre-1 October 1979 registered vehicles but if they are fitted voluntarily they must comply with the regulations in regard to mounting position, method of wiring and use.

Rear Fog Lamps on Articulated and Towing Vehicles

In the case of articulated combinations, the relevant date in this connection is the date of the older of the tractive unit or semi-trailer. Thus, if a post-April 1980 registered tractive unit is coupled to a pre-October 1979-built trailer there appears to be no legal requirement for the vehicle to carry rear fog lamps. This means there is no retrospective fitting requirement for such lamps on older trailers. A broken-down vehicle being towed does not need rear fog lamps. However, it is important to remember the dangers which arise if such a combination is used when the tractive unit or towing vehicle itself has rear fog lamps which would, in some instances, be visible to following motorists who, in bad visibility, might not be aware of some 12 metres of trailer or another vehicle on tow behind the lights.

Mounting of Rear Fog Lamps

Rear fog lamps must be mounted either singly in the centre or on the offside of the vehicle or in a matched pair not less than 250 mm and not more than 1,000 mm from the ground (in the case of agricultural vehicles this height limit is increased to 1,900 mm or in cases where, because of the shape of the vehicle, 1,000 mm is not practical it may be increased to 2,100 mm). The lamps must be at least 100 mm from existing stop lamps.

Restriction on Wiring of Rear Fog Lamps

The lights must be wired so that they only operate when the other statutory lights on the vehicle are switched on; they must not be wired into the brake/stop light circuit and the driver must be provided with an indicator to show him when the lights are in use.

Use of Rear Fog Lamps

The lights should only be used in conditions affecting the visibility of the driver (ie in fog, smoke, heavy rain or spray, snow, dense cloud, etc), when the vehicle is in motion or during an enforced stoppage (a motorway hold-up, for example). They must not cause dazzle. The *Highway Code* recommends these lights should not be used unless visibility is below 100 metres (328 feet).

Side Marker Lamps

Side marker lamps must be fitted on vehicles and trailers as follows:

- Vehicles first used on or after 1 April 1991 and trailers made from 1 October 1990 and being over 6 metres long:
  - one lamp on each side within 4 metres of the front of the vehicle;
  - one lamp on each side within 1 metre of the rear of the vehicle;
  - additional lamps on each side at 3 metre intervals (or if impracticable 4 metres) between front and rear side marker lamps.
- Vehicles (including a combination of vehicles) over 18.3 metres long (including the length of the load):
  - one lamp on each side within 9.15 metres of the front of the vehicle;
  - one lamp on each side within 3.05 metres of the rear of the vehicle;
  - additional lamps on each side at 3.05-metre intervals between front and rear side marker lamps.
- Vehicles in combination between 12.2 metres and 18.3 metres long (but not articulated vehicles) carrying a supported load:
  - one lamp on each side within 1,530 mm of the rear of the rearmost vehicle in the combination;
  - one lamp on each side within 1,530 mm of the centre of the load, if the load extends further than 9.15 metres to the rear of the drawing vehicle.
- Trailers more than 9.15 metres long (6 metres for post-1 October 1990 trailers):
  - one lamp on each side within 1,530 mm of the centre of the trailer length.

Side marker lamps fitted to trailers built before 1 October 1990 may show white side marker lights to the front and red lights to the rear; in all other cases such lights must be amber. They must be positioned not more than 2,300 mm from the ground.

End-Outline Marker Lamps

Vehicles (except those less than 2,100 mm wide and those first used before 1 April 1991) and trailers (except those less than 2,100 mm wide and those built before 1 October 1990) must be fitted with two end-outline marker lamps visible from the front and two visible from the rear. They must be positioned no more than 400 mm in from the outer edges of the vehicle/trailer and mounted at the front at least level with the top of the windscreen. They must show white lights to the front and red lights to the rear.

Lighting Switches

On vehicles first used since 1 April 1991 a single lighting switch only must be used to illuminate all front and rear position lamps, side and end-outline marker lamps and rear number plate lamp although one or more front or rear position lamps may be capable of being switched on independently.

Visibility of Lights and Reflectors

A part, at least, of each front and rear position light, front and rear-mounted direction indicator lamp and rear retro-reflector required to be fitted to a vehicle/trailer must be capable of being seen from directly in front or behind the lamp or reflector when the vehicle doors, tailgate, boot lid, engine cover or other movable part of the vehicle is in a fixed open position.

Lights on Projecting Loads

Details of the requirements for the display of lights on projecting loads are given fully in Chapter 19, which covers this subject.

Direction Indicators

All goods vehicles must be fitted with amber-coloured direction indicators (on pre-September 1965 registered vehicles indicators can be white facing to the front and red facing to the rear) at the front and rear which must be fixed to the vehicle not more than 1,500 mm (2,300 mm in exceptional cases) and not less than 350 mm above the ground, at least 500 mm apart and not more than 400 mm from the outer edges of the vehicle. Side repeater indicators are required on vehicles first used since 1 April 1986 and these must be fitted within 2,600 mm of the front of the vehicle. Normally vehicles should have one indicator on each side at the front and rear but may have two on each side at the rear. They must not have more than one on each side at the front.

Indicators bearing approval marks do not have to meet minimum wattage requirements but those without such marks must be between 15 and 36 watts. They must flash at a rate of between 60 and 120 times a minute and a visible or audible warning must indicate to the driver when they are operating. The flash may be a single flash or a staggered sequence. The indicators must be maintained in a clean condition and in good and efficient working order.

Semaphore Arm Indicators

Vehicles first registered before 1 September 1965 are allowed to have either semaphore arm or flashing indicators. The semaphore arm type must be amber in colour but the flashing indicators may show a white light to the front and a red light to the rear.

Hazard Warning

Direction indicators operating on both sides of the vehicle simultaneously as a hazard warning to other road users are required by law on all vehicles first used since 1 April 1986. They must be actuated by a switch solely controlling that device and a warning light must indicate to the driver that the device is being operated. The hazard indicators may be used when the vehicle is stationary on a road, or any part of the road (ie not just the carriageway), because of a breakdown of it or another vehicle, an accident or other emergency situation, when encountering and slowing down for a barrier or slow or stationary traffic or when the vehicle is causing a temporary obstruction on a road when loading or unloading.

Emergency Warning Triangles

As an additional warning of a hazard drivers *may* (ie it is not compulsory to do so in the UK) place a red warning triangle on the road to the rear of a vehicle causing a temporary obstruction (eg through breakdown). The triangle must be made and marked to British Standard Specification BS AU 47: 1965. It must be placed upright on the road, 45 metres to the rear of the obstruction and on the same side. This requirement is compulsory in many EU member states and the requirements do vary in relation to both the distance the triangle(s) must be placed from the vehicle and the number of triangles to be used. Many EU countries also require the driver to wear a hi-visibility vest if they leave the cab in order to set out any triangle(s). Further advice can be obtained from the RHA or FTA.

Other safety devices may be used to warn of vehicles broken down on the roadside. These include traffic cones, warning lamps and traffic pyramids.

Optional Lamps

Optional main-beam headlamps (which includes spot lamps) may be fitted to a vehicle but they must be capable of being dipped, and if fitted as a matched pair they must also be capable of being switched off together – not individually. They must emit either a white or yellow light, must be adjusted so that they do not cause dazzle to other road users and must not be lit when the vehicle is parked. If optional front fog lamps are fitted and used singly, the headlamps must also be illuminated.

These optional lamps should be positioned not more than 1,200 mm from the ground and not more than 400 mm from the sides of the vehicle. They should be aligned so that the upper edge of the beam is, as near as practicable, 3 per cent below the horizontal when the vehicle is at its kerbside weight and has a weight of 75 kg on the driver's seat.

Vehicles first registered since 1 April 1991 may be fitted with only one pair of extra dipped-beam headlamps and then only on vehicles intended to be driven on the right-hand side of the road. They must be wired so that only one pair of dipped-beam headlamps can be used at any one time. Pre-April 1991 registered vehicles may have any number of additional dipped-beam headlamps.

Any number of extra main-beam headlamps (including spot/driving lamps) may be fitted and there is no restriction on their fitment or use except that they must not cause dazzle to other road users.

Blue Lights

There is an increasing trend towards the use of blue lights on the front of, or in the windscreens of, both cars and commercial vehicles, giving rise to questions about their legality. As the law stands at present it appears that it is not illegal to fit or use such lights as long as they do not flash in the same manner as those on emergency service vehicles. The police, however, are opposed to their use and are anxious to see them prohibited by law, because of the risk of confusion with emergency service vehicles and because of their potential use by criminals purporting to be police.

In defence of their use, many drivers believe that the ultraviolet light emitted by such lamps reduces in-cab white-light glare from oncoming vehicle headlights. Unfortunately, it is also thought that they help to 'confuse' roadside enforcement cameras.

Warning Beacons

Amber warning beacons must be fitted to vehicles with four or more wheels and having a maximum speed no greater than 25 mph when using unrestricted dual-carriageway roads except where such use is merely 'for crossing the carriageway in the quickest manner practicable in the circumstances'.

Amber warning beacons may also be fitted to vehicles used at the scene of an emergency, when it is necessary or desirable to warn of the presence of a vehicle on the road (eg Special Types vehicles carrying abnormal loads) and to breakdown vehicles used at the scene of accidents and breakdowns and when towing broken-down vehicles.

Green warning beacons may be used on vehicles by medical practitioners registered with the General Medical Council when travelling to or dealing with an emergency.

NB: Green beacons are now being used by some plant operators. They are supposed to indicate that the driver is wearing their seatbelt and should only be used on-site and not on the public highway as this may contravene the Lighting Regulations but the enforcement authorities appear to be unconcerned by this. It has also been reported that many operators of this plant merely fasten the seat belt to activate the beacon and then sit on the belt instead of wearing it. This sort of abuse does actually constitute an offence under HSE legislation.

Blue warning beacons and other special warning lamps may only be used on emergency vehicles (ie ambulance, fire brigade or police service vehicles; Forestry Commission fire-fighting vehicles; military bomb disposal vehicles; RAF Mountain Rescue vehicles; Blood Transfusion Service vehicles; Mines Rescue Service vehicles; HM Coastguard vehicles; RNLI vehicles; and those used primarily for transporting human tissue for transplanting).

In all cases such beacons should be fitted with their centres no less than 1,200 mm from the ground and visible from any point at a reasonable distance from the vehicle. The light itself must show not less than 60 and not more than 240 times per minute.

Swivelling Spotlights (Work Lamps)

White swivelling spotlights may be used only at the scene of an accident, breakdown or roadworks to illuminate the working area or work in the vicinity of the vehicle provided they do not cause undue dazzle or discomfort to the driver of any vehicle.

Working lights may also be fitted to articulated units in order to help the driver connect the air and electrical connections. These must also be actuated by a switch solely controlling them and a warning light must indicate to the driver that the device is being operated in order to prevent it being left on when the vehicle is in motion.

Rear Retro-Reflectors

Motor vehicles must be fitted with two red reflex retro-reflectors facing squarely to the rear. Reflectors must be fitted not more than 900 mm and not less than 350 mm from the ground. For normal goods vehicles and trailers they must be within 400 mm of the outer edge of the vehicle or trailer and not less than 600 mm apart. Reflectors must be capable of being seen from an angle of 30 degrees on either side.

Triangular Rear Reflectors

Triangular rear reflectors must not be used other than on trailers or broken-down vehicles being towed.

Side Retro-Reflectors

Vehicles more than 6 metres long first used since 1 April 1986 (more than 8 metres long if first used before 1 April 1986) and trailers more than 5 metres long must be fitted with two (or more as necessary) amber side retro-reflectors on each side. One reflector on each side must be fitted not more than 1 metre from the extreme rear end of the vehicle and another no more than 4 metres from the front of the vehicle with further reflectors at minimum 3-metre intervals (or can be 4-metre intervals) along its length. They must be mounted not more than 1,500 mm and not less than 350 mm from the ground. On pre-April 1986 vehicles one reflector must be positioned in the middle third of the vehicle length and the other within 1 metre of the rear. Where such reflectors are mounted within 1 metre of the rear of the vehicle/trailer they may be coloured red instead of amber.

Front Retro-Reflectors

Trailers built since 1 October 1990 must be fitted with two obligatory front retro-reflectors, white in colour and mounted facing forwards, at least 350 mm but not more than 900 mm from the ground and no more than 150 mm in from the outer edges of the trailer and at least 600 mm apart.

Vehicle Markings

Number (Registration) Plates

All vehicles first registered since 1 January 1973 and all registered semi-trailers and trailers must be fitted with number plates made of reflecting material complying with BS AU 145a. This requirement does not apply to goods vehicles over 7.5 tonnes gross weight which are required to display rear reflective markers (see p 421) or works trucks, agricultural machines and trailers or pedestrian-controlled vehicles. If a vehicle over 3,050 kg unladen is exempt from the requirement to fit rear reflective markers then it must be fitted with reflective number plates. Regulations specify the precise style of letters and numerals to be used on vehicle registration plates, in particular the spacing between each individual character. It is an offence to alter, rearrange or misrepresent the characters or to alter the spacings to form words or names. It is also an offence to use a number plate with a patterned or textured background. Three possible repercussions may result from the illegal presentation of vehicle registration numbers:

- a fine of up to £1,000 may be imposed on conviction;
- the registration number (mark) may be withdrawn;
- the vehicle may fail its MoT test.

From this it will be seen that the use of so-called ‘fun’ number plates in which spacings between letters and numbers are rearranged to produce key words is prohibited and will result in police action (usually an order to get the plates changed within five days, but possibly more serious consequences as listed above). Italicized, computer-type and shadow lettering on vehicle number plates will also invite police action. It is useful to note that the firms making and selling these plates commit no offence – only the person who uses them on the road.

The DVLA requires number plate manufacturers to be registered as part of the campaign to curb vehicle crime. Lists of your local authorized number plate manufacturers can be found on the DVLA website or by using a search engine, although any local garage would supply the information should you require it.

Vehicle Registration Numbers

From 1 September 2001 a new system of vehicle registration numbers was introduced in the UK requiring that number plates conform to a new British Standard (BS AU 145d) which replaces the previous standard referred to above. Since that date all new number (ie registration) plates must comply with the following format:

AB69 DVL

The letters 'AB' identify the local area in which the vehicle is registered. The number '69' identifies the date of first registration (ie 69 representing vehicles first registered on, or after, 1 September 2019) and will change every six months in September and March each year (eg 19 being March 2019 and 69 being September 2019, etc). The last three letters (in the above example DVL) are chosen at random.

Also from 1 September 2001, all new number plates must display the mandatory fonts (in both style and size – see below) specified in the Road Vehicles (Display of Registration Marks) Regulations 2001. No lettering other than in the specified standard font may be used (ie computer, script-type and other 'fun' lettering are banned). The name and trademark of the maker and the postcode of the supplying outlet may be used.

Mandatory Character Font

From 1 September 2001 all new number plates must display the new mandatory font as shown here and characters must be of the regulation size:

TABLE 13.1 Mandatory character font

123456789
ABCDEFGH
JKLMNOPQ
RSTUVWXYZ

TABLE 13.1 *continued*

Height	79mm
Width	50mm
Stroke	14mm
Side margin	11mm
Top and bottom margin	11mm
Space between characters	11mm
Space between groups	33mm
Vertical space between age and random numbers	19mm

(Applicable to all vehicles except motorcycles and vehicles manufactured before 1973.)

Existing number plates will not have to be changed to conform to the new style provided the font used is 'substantially the same' as the new style. However, number plates must be replaced if they have been customized with either:

- stylized letters and figures such as italics; or
- number plate fixing bolts that alter the appearance of the letters or numbers.

Failure to replace such number plates may result in the vehicle keeper risking prosecution.

Nationality Symbols

It is a legal requirement (under the Vienna Convention on Road Traffic) for vehicles travelling in a country other than that in which they are registered to display at the rear a nationality plate showing the official symbol for the country of registration (eg GB for Great Britain, F for France and D for Germany). These plates, usually in the form of a self-adhesive or magnetic sticker, should be of an approved pattern, oval in shape (at least 17.5 cm by 11.4 cm) and contain the relevant national symbol in black letters on a white background. A GB plate will need to be fitted to the vehicle if it is to travel abroad if the number plate does not include the EU symbol. Where the EU symbol is included in the number plate and contains a GB symbol these will be accepted by EU authorities but an additional GB plate will still be required for travel beyond or outside of the EU.

Vehicle owners/operators who wish to do so may now legally display their national flag on number plates (ie the union flag with 'GB' for Great Britain; the cross of St George with 'ENG' for England; the Saltire – the cross of St Andrew – with 'SCO' for Scotland; or the Red Dragon for Wales or Cymru) but these will not suffice if travelling to Europe.

Weight Markings

Goods vehicles must not display any weight markings other than their plated weights, any weights required to be displayed under the C&U Regulations, or weights required under other regulations (eg the Motor Vehicles (Authorisation of Special Types) General Order). This means that maximum weights shown on 'Ministry' plates and maximum laden weights (so long as these do not exceed 'Ministry' plated weights) may be shown on either one or both sides of a vehicle.

Motor tractors and locomotives must have their unladen weight shown in a conspicuous place on the outside of the vehicle where it can easily be seen.

Dimensions Marking

Goods vehicles over 3.5 tonnes and trailers made since 31 May 1998 must be fitted with a plate showing their length and width, unless this information is already shown on either the manufacturer's plate or a 'Ministry' plate.

'Ministry' Plates

Goods vehicles over 3,500 kg maximum gross weight and goods carrying trailers over 1,020 kg unladen weight must display a 'Ministry' plate and/or a manufacturer's plate showing the maximum permissible gross vehicle weight and individual axle weights (see Chapter 14). Trailer plates have been replaced, as noted earlier, and the current new 'MoT style' plate will now need to travel with the trailer when any existing trailer plate expires.

Special Types Plates

Vehicles carrying abnormal loads must display a manufacturer's plate showing the maximum weights at which the vehicle can operate and the relevant speeds for travel at those weights. The weights shown must be those approved by the vehicle or trailer manufacturer and the vehicle must not exceed specified Special Types speed limits when travelling loaded to the weight shown on the plate (see details of speeds for different classes of Special Types vehicles, p 300).

Food Vehicles

Vehicles which are used in connection with a food business or from which food is sold must display in a clearly visible place the name and address of the person carrying on the business and the address at which the vehicle is kept or garaged. If the vehicle bears a fleet number and is kept or garaged on that person's premises the garage address is not required but the local authority must be notified. Most vehicles operating under ATP regulations covering the international movements of perishable foodstuffs also show ATP approval marks of blue letters on a white background, although they may carry a certificate within the vehicle as an alternative.

Height Marking

The travelling height of vehicles and trailers carrying engineering equipment, containers and skips, where the height of the vehicle and load exceeds 3 metres, must be marked in the cab where the driver can see it. Further provisions extend this by requiring the fitment of warning devices where vehicles carry 'high-level equipment' (see p 350 for further details).

Hazard Marking

Vehicles which carry hazardous, radioactive or explosive loads must display appropriate hazard warning symbols on the vehicle, whether a bulk tanker, a tank container or a normal delivery vehicle used for carrying hazardous consignments, and on the individual packages too in the latter case. Further details are given in Chapter 20.

Rear Reflective Markings

All vehicles with a maximum permissible weight exceeding 7,500 kg and trailers with a maximum permissible weight exceeding 3,500 kg must be fitted with rear reflective markers which make them more conspicuous at night and in poor visibility (Figures 13.1 and 13.2). The markers may also be displayed on loads such as builders' skips (see below).

For new vehicles first used from 1 April 1996 and trailers manufactured on or after 1 October 1995, which under the regulations require the fitment of rear reflective markings as described below, fitment of a new type of rear marking (in accordance with ECE Regulation 70) is necessary.

Types of Markers

For pre-1 April 1996-used vehicles and pre-1 October 1995-built trailers, there are two types of markings, each in two sizes:

- alternating red fluorescent and yellow reflective diagonal strips – diagrams 1, 2, and 3 in Figure 13.1a;
- a central yellow reflective panel overprinted with the words LONG VEHICLE and having a red fluorescent surround – diagrams 4 and 5 in Figure 13.1a.

For post-1 April 1996-used vehicles and post-1 October 1995-built trailers, the markings comprise two types:

FIGURE 13.1a Rear reflective markers required on certain goods vehicles. The plates comprise red fluorescent material background. The lettering is in black on yellow reflex reflecting material

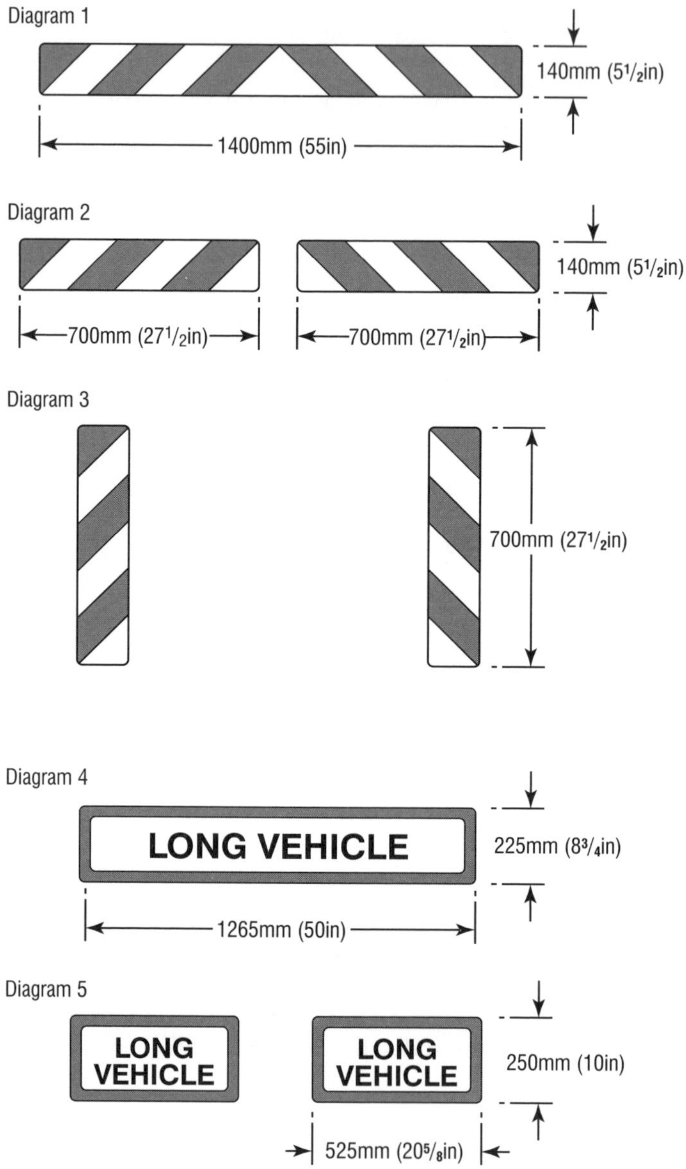

FIGURE 13.1b Rear markings for post-1 April 1996-used vehicles and post-1 October 1995-built trailers

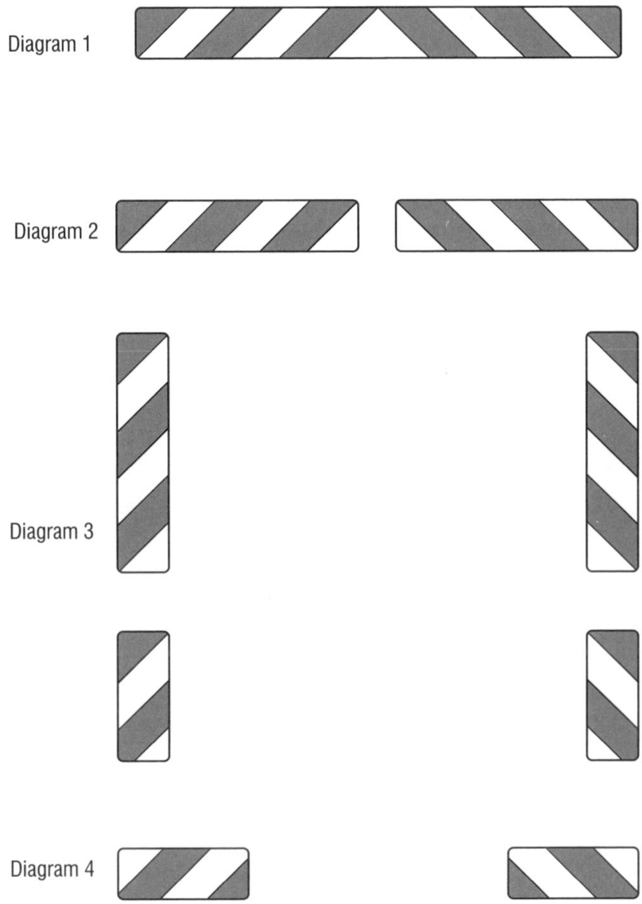

- alternating red fluorescent and yellow retro-reflective diagonal strips – diagrams 1, 2, 3 and 4 in Figure 13.1b;
- a central yellow retro-reflective panel surrounded by a red fluorescent border – diagrams 5, 6, 7 and 8 in Figure 13.1c.

Specification for Markers

Markers of the type illustrated in Figure 13.1a must comply with the regulations regarding size and colour and they must be in the form of durable plates stamped with the mark BS AU 152/1970. Those of the type illustrated in Figures 13.1b and 13.1c must also comply with the regulations as above and be stamped with a designated approval mark. They must not be simulated by being painted on the vehicle and the plates must not be defaced, cut or modified to aid fitting to the vehicle.

FIGURE 13.1c New-type rear markers for use on long vehicles first used from 1 April 1996 and trailers built since 1 October 1995

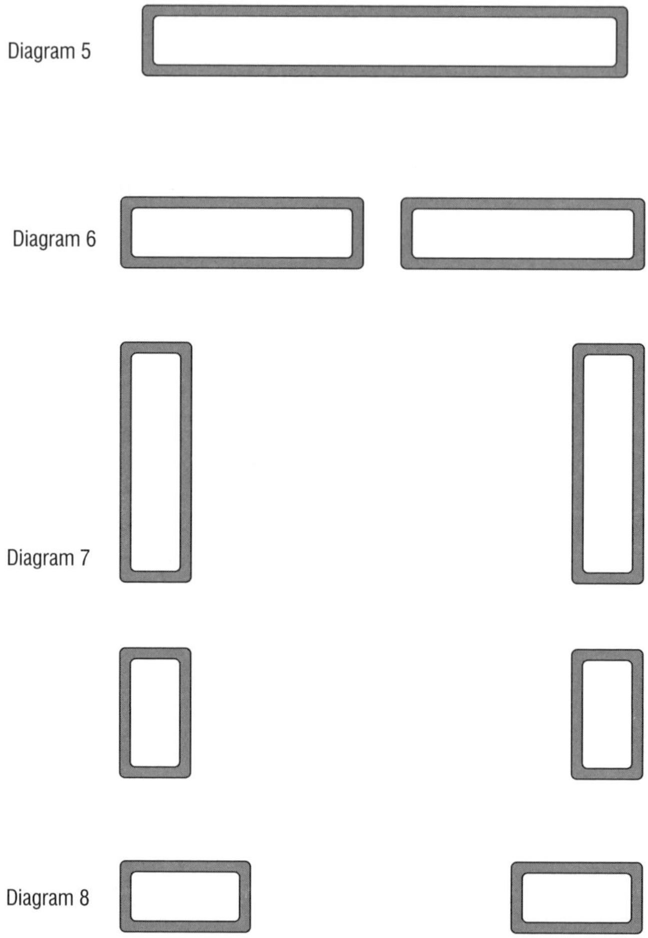

Which Markers to Be Fitted

Pre-1 April 1996-used Vehicles and Pre-1 October 1995-built Trailers

Vehicles not exceeding 13 metres in length and trailers in combinations not exceeding 11 metres must be fitted with the markers shown in diagrams 1, 2 or 3 in Figure 13.1a. Alternatively, they may be fitted with the markers shown in diagrams 1, 2, 3 or 4 in Figure 13.1b.

Vehicles more than 13 metres long and trailers in combinations more than 13 metres long must be fitted with the markers shown in diagrams 4 or 5 in Figure 13.1a (or alternatively those shown in diagrams 5, 6, 7 or 8 in Figure 13.1c).

Trailers in combinations of more than 11 metres but not more than 13 metres may be fitted with the markers shown in diagrams 1, 2, 3, 4 or 5 in Figure 13.1a or those in diagrams 1 to 8 in Figures 13.1b and 13.1c.

FIGURE 13.2 Vehicles which must carry reflective rear markers and the alternative fitting arrangements

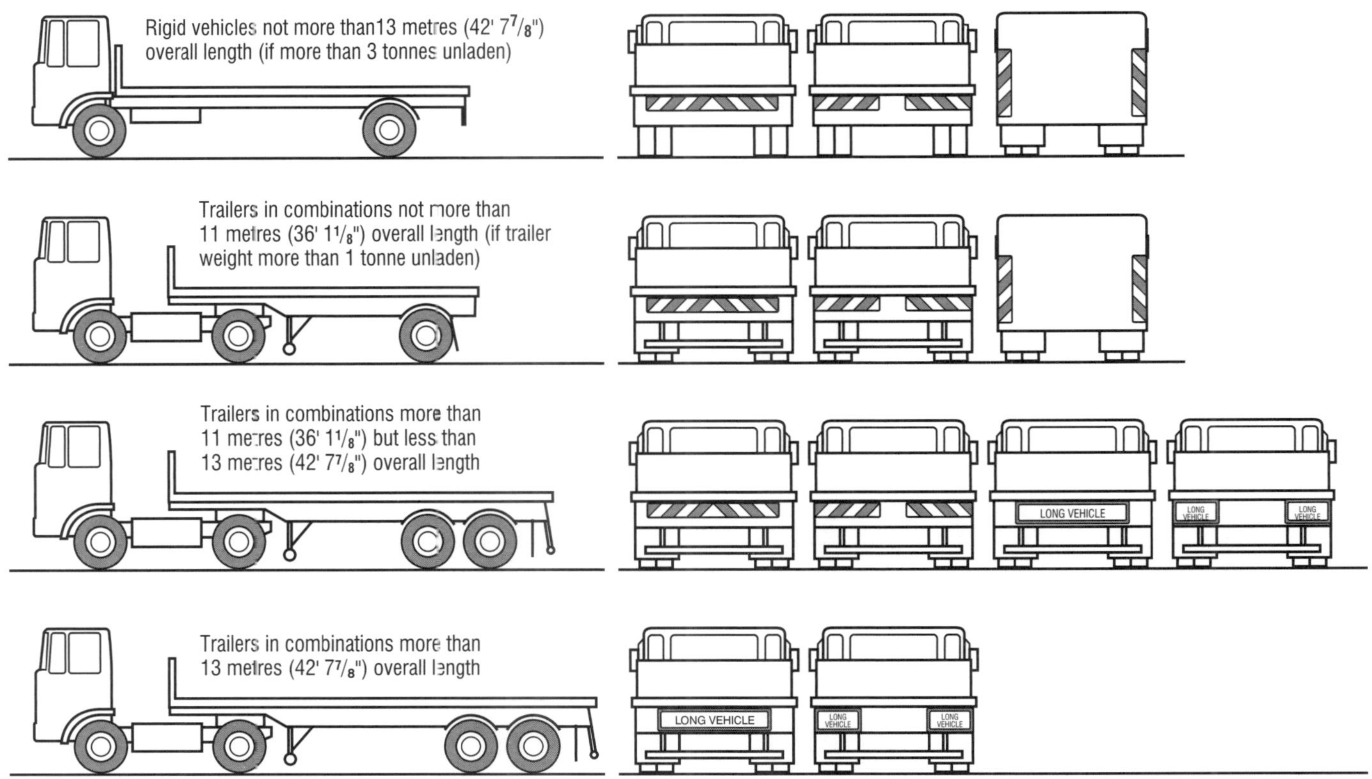

Post-1 April 1996-used Vehicles and Post-1 October 1995-built Trailers

Vehicles not exceeding 13 metres in length and trailers in combinations not exceeding 11 metres must be fitted with a marker or set of markers of the types shown in diagrams 1, 2, 3 or 4 in Figure 13.1b.

Vehicles more than 13 metres long and trailers in combinations more than 13 metres long must be fitted with the markers shown in diagrams 5, 6, 7 or 8 in Figure 13.1c. Trailers in combinations of more than 11 metres but not more than 13 metres must be fitted with a marker or set of markers of the types shown in diagrams 1 to 8 in Figures 13.1b and 13.1c.

Fitting Position

The height from the ground to the lower edge of the marker when fitted must not exceed 1,700 mm but must be at least 400 mm. It must be fitted parallel to the ground and be facing square to the rear.

Alternative Fitting Position

When a vehicle which by law requires rear reflective markers to be displayed is carrying a load which obscures partly or wholly the markers so that they are not clearly visible from the rear, the reflective markers may be fitted to the rear of the load.

Exemptions

Certain vehicles as indicated in the following list are exempt from the requirement to fit these markers:

- vehicles having a maximum speed not exceeding 25 mph;
- vehicles with a maximum gross weight not exceeding 7,500 kg;
- passenger vehicles other than articulated buses;
- land tractors, land locomotives, land implements, land implement conveyors, agricultural tractors or industrial tractors;
- works trucks or works trailers;
- vehicles in an unfinished condition proceeding to a works for completion or to a place where they are to be stored or displayed for sale;
- motor vehicles constructed or adapted for the purpose of forming part of articulated vehicles;
- broken-down vehicles while being drawn in consequence of the breakdown;
- engineering plant;
- trailers, not being part of an articulated bus, drawn by public service vehicles;
- vehicles designed for fire-fighting or fire salvage purposes;
- vehicles designed and used for the purpose of servicing or controlling aircraft;
- vehicles designed and used for the transportation of two or more motor vehicles carried thereon, or of vehicle bodies or two or more boats;
- vehicles proceeding to a place for export;
- vehicles brought temporarily into Great Britain by persons residing abroad;

- vehicles in the service of a visiting force or of a headquarters;
- motor vehicles first used before 1 January 1940;
- vehicles owned or in the service of the army, navy or air force;
- vehicles designed for heating or dispensing tar or similar material for road construction or maintenance;
- trailers being drying or mixing plant designed for the production of asphalt, bitumen or tarmacadam;
- trailers made before 1 August 1982 with an unladen weight not exceeding 1,020 kg;
- trailers with a gross weight not exceeding 3,500 kg.

Previously it was illegal to fit the markers to these vehicles, but a change in the regulations permits the fitting of such markers to exempt vehicles on a voluntary basis, provided the vehicles exceed the specified weight limit. It is illegal to display these markers on vehicles which do not require them by law except as mentioned above.

Builders' Skips

Rear reflective markings of the type described above (as shown in diagram 3, Figure 13.1a) must be fitted to the ends of builders' skips which are placed on the highway. They must be fitted as a matched pair as near to the outer edge as possible, mounted vertically and no more than 1.5 metres from the ground to the top edge. They must be kept clean, in good order and be visible from a reasonable distance. Such skips are required to be illuminated when standing on roads at night.

Conspicuity Markings

Conspicuity marking material is required to be fitted to new heavy goods vehicles and trailers from 10 July 2011. This requirement aligns the UK Road Vehicles Lighting Regulations (RVLR) with UNECE Regulation 48.

The legislation covers the following vehicles:

- goods vehicles with a gross vehicle weight exceeding 7,500 kg first used on or after 10 July 2011;
- trailers with a gross vehicle weight exceeding 3,500 kg manufactured on or after 10 July 2011.

Certain vehicles as follows are exempt from the requirements:

- a vehicle which is not a goods vehicle;
- goods vehicles not exceeding 7,500 kg gvw;
- trailers not exceeding 3,500 kg gvw;
- chassis cabs;
- incomplete vehicles proceeding to a works for completion or to a place where they are to be stored or displayed for sale;
- articulated tractive units;

- vehicles/trailers with an overall width not exceeding 2.1 metres do not require rear markings;
- vehicles/trailers with overall length not exceeding 6 metres do not require side markings.

In addition to covering the specification of lights and light components for new vehicles exceeding 7,700 kg MAM and trailers exceeding 3,500 kg MAM, the regulations state that, where applicable, vehicles and trailers must be fitted with horizontal and vertical reflective markings to the rear outline of the vehicle or trailer, as close to the edge of the vehicle or trailer as possible. Where the actual shape is impossible to define, lines produced by reflective tape are acceptable. Reflective tape needs to be red or yellow for rear markings and yellow or white for side markings and the tape must be at least 60 mm in width.

Goods Vehicle Plating, Annual Testing and Vehicle Inspections

14

Most goods vehicles are required to be tested annually to ensure they are safe to operate on the road and meet the legal requirements relating to mechanical condition. In particular, this annual inspection is intended to determine whether vehicles and trailers meet the standards specified in the Road Vehicles (Construction and Use) Regulations 1986 (as amended). Additionally, it is necessary for certain goods vehicles and trailers to be 'Ministry plated' to show the maximum permissible gross weight and maximum axle weights at which they may be operated on roads in Great Britain. The requirement for annual plating and testing of goods vehicles is contained in the Road Traffic Act 1988 and is detailed in the Goods Vehicles (Plating and Testing) Regulations 1988 as amended.

The Driver and Vehicle Standards Agency (DVSA) is responsible for the operation of goods vehicle testing stations – of which there are currently DVSA goods vehicle testing stations (GVTS) and privately operated, but DVSA controlled, 'designated premises' known as Authorized Testing Facilities (ATFs) in the UK. The DVSA is also the main enforcement authority involved in roadside checks on goods vehicles.

Since May 2009 the DVSA has been undertaking a programme of GVTS test centre closures. The stations concerned have largely been replaced by the privately run but DVSA-manned ATFs.

NB: Details of your local DVSA Goods Vehicle Testing Station (GVTS) or Authorized Testing Facility (ATF) can be found on the GOV.UK website.

Annual Testing

All articulated tractive units, rigid goods vehicles over 3,500 kg gross weight, goods carrying semi-trailers and drawbar trailers over 1,020 kg unladen weight and converter dollies must be tested annually at either a goods vehicle testing station or ATF. This annual test requirement from the date of first registration 'could' apply to the new electrically powered vans which are now permitted to operate at 4,250 kg instead of 3,500 kg but this issue is still being resolved at the time of writing.

Certain specialized vehicles are exempt from the test, as shown on pp 446–48, and the regulations do not apply to vehicles used under a trade licence. Goods vehicle test stations also carry out the Class V test, which is the MoT-type test, on large passenger vehicles which cannot get into normal MoT test garages (see also Chapter 15).

The Class VII test provides for MoT testing of goods vehicles of more than 3,000 kg but not more than 3,500 kg design gross weight which were formerly subject to goods vehicle plating and testing when they had an unladen weight exceeding 1,525 kg.

New requirements on annual roadworthiness testing were introduced from 1 January 2012 when revised European legislation (Directive 2010/48/EU) came into effect to reflect advances in technology. The changes included additional checks for some of the vehicle systems such as brakes, steering, suspensions and lighting. There were also new safety checks introduced on the increasing number of on-board electrical safety systems, including electronic stability control. Tests carried out on cars, vans, heavy goods vehicles, buses and coaches were all affected.

The new/additional checks included the following items:

- anti-lock braking systems;
- electronic stability control systems;
- tyre pressure monitoring systems;
- supplementary restraint systems including airbags and seat belt pre-tensioners;
- electronic power steering systems;
- electronic parking brakes.

These items are being added to all the time as new electronic packages such as AEBS and LDWS become standard fitment. The annual test (MOT) history of an LGV can now be checked online through the GOV.UK website.

Types of Test

There are various types of goods vehicle test as follows:

- *First test*: the first annual test of the vehicle or trailer (carried out no later than the end of the anniversary month in which it was first registered) at which the information shown on the vehicle's official (ie 'Ministry') plate (issued from Swansea) is verified.
- *Parts 2 and 3 re-tests*: re-examination of vehicles which have failed their first test or a re-test.
- *Periodical test*: the annual test which applies to all relevant vehicles after the first test.
- *Part 4 test*: a test provided for in the regulations which may be required if a notifiable alteration has been made to the vehicle, or if the operator wants the plating certificate amended to show different weights as a result of changes to the vehicle or, for example, if different tyre equipment has been fitted.

- *Re-test following appeal*: re-tests carried out following an appeal to the test station manager or subsequently the DVSA regional manager.

Test fees

The appropriate test fee(s) should be sent to the Goods Vehicle Centre with the first test application form (VTG1 or VTG2), while fees for subsequent tests should be sent direct to the test station. (Operators can open a direct debit account with the DVSA to enable any fee to be collected for any test station.)

Since October 2014 the fees charged for the various tests for vehicles exceeding 3,500 kg MAM, trailers exceeding 1,020 kg unladen weight and converter dollies were reduced as the DVSA sought to pass on some of the savings made by the introduction of ATFs and the re-allocation of some of the cost elements relating to operator licensing.

The fees for various HGV and trailer tests, re-tests and other services are tabled below.

TABLE 14.1 Test fees

NB: Previous charges relating to the cost of enforcement and compliance functions in relation to motor vehicles and trailers have been abolished.

Test Type	Vehicle Type	DVSA – normal hours	DVSA – out of hours	ATF – normal hours	ATF – out of hours
Motor Vehicles					
1st test, annual tests, prohibition clearances (full inspections), re-tests after 14 days	2 axles	£112.00	£150.00	£91.00	£129.00
1st test, annual tests, prohibition clearances (full inspections), re-tests after 14 days	3 axles	£144.00	£182.00	£113.00	£151.00
1st test, annual tests, prohibition clearances (full inspections), re-tests after 14 days	4+ axles	£177.00	£215.00	£137.00	£175.00
Re-tests within 14 days, prohibition clearances (partial inspections)	2 axles	£49.00	£69.00	£35.00	£55.00
Re-tests within 14 days, prohibition clearances (partial inspections)	3 axles	£69.00	£89.00	£49.00	£69.00

TABLE 14.1 *continued*

Test Type	Vehicle Type	DVSA – normal hours	DVSA – out of hours	ATF – normal hours	ATF – out of hours
Re-tests within 14 days, prohibition clearances (partial inspections)	4+ axles	£91.00	£111.00	£65.00	£85.00
Part-paid re-tests*	Any number of axles	£13.00	£13.00	£13.00	£13.00
Notifiable alterations		£27.00	£40.00	£27.00	£40.00
Replacement documents	£13.00				
Trailers					
1st test, annual tests, prohibition clearances (full inspections), re-tests after 14 days	1 axle	£51.00	£75.00	£41.00	£65.00
1st test, annual tests, prohibition clearances (full inspections), re-tests after 14 days	2 axles	£70.00	£94.00	£54.00	£78.00
1st test, annual tests, prohibition clearances (full inspections), re-tests after 14 days	3+ axles	£84.00	£108.00	£64.00	£88.00
Re-tests within 14 days, prohibition clearances (partial inspections)	1 axle	£25.00	£38.00	£18.00	£31.00
Re-tests within 14 days, prohibition clearances (partial inspections)	2 axles	£35.00	£48.00	£25.00	£38.00
Re-tests within 14 days, prohibition clearances (partial inspections)	3+ axles	£46.00	£59.00	£33.00	£46.00
Part-paid re-tests*	Any number of axles	£7.00	£7.00	£7.00	£7.00
Notifiable alterations		£27.00	£40.00	£27.00	£40.00
Replacement documents	£13.00				

* Part-paid re-tests are for failure items marked on the inspection document (PG14) which are re-tested on the same day as the test, or the next working day.

TABLE 14.2 Appeals

Fee Type	Fee
Appeal fee	£39.00

TABLE 14.3 TIR and ADR

TIR Fee Type	Fee
Initial application	£106.00
Re-inspection	£70.00
Type approval	£644.00
Type variation	£106.00
Certificate of conformity	£14
Duplicate certificate	£14

ADR Fee Type	Fee at DVSA Site	Fee at ATF Site
Initial application and full re-test	£116.00	£83.00
Re-test within 14 days	£63.00	£39.00
New type approved artic tractor certificate	£28.00	
Duplicate certificate	£14.00	

Hire of loaded trailers for solo tractor unit tests – all types of test £29.50 plus VAT.

TABLE 14.4 Pit fees which may be charged by some ATFs

Fee Type	Fee
Where a test is being carried out on an HGV	£55.00 + VAT*
Where a test is being carried out on a trailer	£40.00 + VAT*

* This fee, which is not always charged, is capped at these rates.

Test Dates

Vehicles may be submitted for test at any one of the full-time or part-time goods vehicle test stations selected by the vehicle operator. Vehicles are due for test each year no later than the end of the anniversary month in which they were first registered (eg a vehicle registered on 1 January 2019 would be due for its first test no later than 31 January 2020 and for subsequent tests by 31 January in each following year).

Trailer Test Dates

Since the introduction of ECWVTA (mentioned earlier) the DVSA now issue form VTG5B to the supplier of a new trailer prior to the trailer going to the customer. This form has a unique ID number, which must be prominently displayed on the trailer. The first annual test then becomes due before the end of the month of the anniversary of the issue of the form to the customer when the trailer is actually supplied.

Year of Manufacture/Registration

There is an anomaly with due test dates when a vehicle or trailer is manufactured in one year and is not registered before 1 July of the following year. In this case it must be tested by the end of December in the year in which it was first registered or sold.

Phased Programmes and Missed Test Dates

The DVSA allows vehicle operators the facility of having vehicles tested before their due date to accommodate phased programmes of test preparation, rather than having a large number of vehicles due for preparation and test in any particular month of the year.

Test Applications

Initial application for a first test of vehicles and trailers, and subsequent applications, can be made at any GVTS or ATF, or online at the GOV.UK website (the website also provides details of your nearest testing station or facility).

There are two schemes that can be used to book tests online. The first scheme is for booking single vehicles, for which the operator does not need to register with the DVSA. These single tests can be booked up to 93 days before the expiry date but apply only to DVSA test stations; ATF bookings need to be made with the ATF concerned. The second scheme allows the operator to book multiple vehicles at a DVSA test station and this scheme does require the operator to register with the DVSA. In order to use the single vehicle scheme or register on the multiple vehicle scheme, operators need to contact the DVSA and enquire about the 'electronic Test Booking Service (eTB)'. However, the eTB service cannot accommodate testing for ADR, undertaking voluntary test, or IVA tests.

NB: The DVSA have issued detailed guidance for operators seeking IVA for trailers due to the numbers of failures when the trailers are presented. Guidance is available on the GOV.UK website.

Tests can also be booked through the DVSA Contact Centre by calling 0300 123 9000. If this option is your preferred choice you will need to provide details of the vehicle concerned (registration number, number of axles, vehicle type, etc).

Application for subsequent tests can be made either to the Goods Vehicle Centre at Swansea or direct to any test station/facility. The following forms, which may be obtained from goods vehicle test stations, are used for making the application:

VTG1	First test of a vehicle
VTG2	First test of a trailer
VTG10	To inform of notifiable alterations to a vehicle
VTG40	For subsequent tests of both vehicles and trailers
VTG15	To be completed and submitted every time a dangerous goods vehicle is presented for test.

Time for Application

Applications can be made up to 93 days in advance of the due date. The DVSA recommends that applications for tests should be made as early as possible. They also state that, if this is the case, the testing station will try to arrange for a test within one month of receipt of the application.

Saturday and Out-of-Hours Testing

Saturday and out-of-hours testing is available at most test stations and facilities at an additional fee. Operators wishing to take advantage of this facility must mark their applications very clearly 'SATURDAY TEST' and show the appropriate date.

Testing for LEZ/CAZ Compliance

Hauliers can book low-emission certificate (LEC) tests at a GVTS or ATF to confirm whether their older vehicles comply with the London LEZ/CAZ requirement that began in February 2008. The cost for a test during normal working hours is £30 at an ATF or £42 at a GVTS.

Trailer Testing

Many operators have more semi-trailers and trailers than tractive units or drawing vehicles and in order to have these additional trailers tested it may be necessary for them to be submitted for test with a vehicle which has already been tested and has a current valid test certificate. In these cases only the trailer will be examined and the fee payable will be the trailer fee only.

Test Appointments

Following application for a first or subsequent test (see note above about Saturday testing facility), the test station selected by the operator will confirm the test booking in due course with an appointment letter, and all further communications regarding the test must be made with the test station, not with the Goods Vehicle Centre at Swansea. If, owing to excessive workload or staff shortage, the chosen test station cannot accommodate the test an appointment will be made at the nearest alternative test station and a letter will be sent from that station. The appointment letter and the vehicle registration document must be produced on arrival at the test station.

It is essential that vehicles arrive at the test station at the appointed time and in the condition required to enable the test to undertaken. Late or non-arrival of a vehicle can mean cancellation of the test and the fee will be forfeited unless an acceptable reason citing 'exceptional circumstances' is put forward. Exceptional circumstances include accident, fire, epidemic, severe weather, failure in the supply of essential services or other unexpected happenings. Breakdown, mechanical defect or non-availability of the vehicle because of shortages in spare parts supply or for operational reasons for example, are not looked upon as exceptional circumstances.

Cancellations

If it is necessary to cancel a test booking after making an application, provided seven days' notice is given to the test station, either a new test date will be arranged or the fee will be refunded after a small deduction for administration has been made. In exceptional circumstances, such as an accident to the vehicle on the way to the test station, if notification is given to the station within three days of the accident the fee will be carried forward or refunded less the small administration deduction. If other exceptional circumstances arise within seven days of the due date for the test, provided satisfactory evidence is given to the test station, the fee will be similarly carried forward or refunded less another small deduction.

Temporary Exemption

Should it ever be necessary for a test station or facility to cancel a test through exceptional circumstances such as a fire, severe weather conditions, flood, or staff sickness, etc, if an alternative station or facility cannot be found in time before the test is due, the station or facility concerned can issue a certificate of temporary exemption (form VTG33), which allows the vehicle to be used until a test can be arranged. This form can be produced either to the police or examiners of the DVSA if they ask for the test certificate, or when applying for an excise licence for the vehicle.

Refusal to Test

Test station officials have the right to refuse to test a vehicle or trailer for the following reasons, in which circumstances form VTG12 will be issued:

- Arrival after the appointed time.
- Appointment card or vehicle registration document not produced.
- If it is found that the vehicle brought to the test station does not conform to the details given on the application form.
- If the vehicle was booked for the test with a trailer but the trailer is not taken to the test station.
- If the chassis number cannot be found by the examiner or if the serial number given for the trailer by the DVSA is not stamped on it.
- If the vehicle is in a dirty or dangerous condition.
- If the vehicle does not have sufficient fuel or oil to enable the test to be carried out.

- If the test appointment card specified that the vehicle should be loaded for the test and it is taken to the test station without a load. Under normal circumstances the decision whether the vehicle is to be tested in a laden or unladen condition is left to the owner to suit his convenience but in some circumstances the test station may request that the vehicle is fully or partially loaded to enable the brakes to be accurately tested on the roller brake tester.
- In the case of a trailer, if the vehicle submitted with it is not suitable to draw it.
- If the vehicle breaks down during the test.
- If the vehicle is submitted for its annual test (ie not for the first test) or a re-test and the previous test and plating certificates are not produced.
- If the vehicle arrives and is loaded with some dangerous or toxic goods or goods that are comprised of human or animal waste, etc.

Test Procedure

Goods vehicle test stations and ATFs vary in size and in the number of examination staff. Testing normally takes approximately 45 minutes during which the driver must be available to assist and move the vehicle as required. Examination of vehicles is carried out by DVSA examiners based at the station, or ATF, in accordance with the *Heavy Goods Vehicle Inspection Manual* published by the DVSA and available free online at the GOV.UK website. All items which have to be inspected are listed in the *Manual* together with, where necessary, details of how the inspection of each item should be carried out and the reasons for failing the item. Under the 'reasons for rejection' column in the *Manual*, where the item inspected is one that is subject to wear, the maximum tolerance will be indicated. Also shown are the standards at which a prohibition notice may be issued during the Annual Test.

The Smoke Test

Free acceleration smoke emission testing of diesel engines by means of a calibrated smoke meter (to measure the density of smoke in a vehicle exhaust) was introduced as part of the goods vehicle annual test from 1 September 1992. Where it is necessary to carry out a purely visual test, the driver is asked to depress the accelerator pedal firmly from the engine idle position (preferably with the engine already warm) to the maximum fuel delivery position and, immediately the governor operates, release the pedal until the engine slows to a steady idling speed. Smoke emission from the first attempt at this procedure is ignored but the procedure has to be repeated for a maximum of 10 times until the smoke emission is considered to be of equal density for two successive accelerations.

Inspection Card

During the test the examiner has an inspection card on which all items in the *Inspection Manual* are listed and in the case of failure of any item the card is marked accordingly.

A computerized test card is used which allows the examiner to produce:

- a test 'pass' certificate;
- an advice note (for action required);
- a failure notice;
- a PG9 prohibition notice; or
- a PG14 refusal of test certificate.

Analogue Tachograph Testing

Tachograph testing is part of the annual test and comprises an inspection of the:

- tachograph scale marking in kph (additional mph marking is allowed);
- presence of the tachograph serial number and appropriate 'e' marking;
- tachograph installation/calibration plaque (its presence, condition and calibration date);
- 'K factor' plaque to ensure its presence, condition and that the 'K factor' is clearly visible;
- condition and presence of seals (checking particularly for evidence of interference).

Digital Tachograph Testing

Digital tachograph testing is also a part of the annual test. A digital tachograph is required to have a periodic inspection at least every 24 months. As part of this inspection, a full calibration of the system must be performed. As a part of the annual test, the nominated technician must check the integrity of the installation, and that it has not been the subject of tampering or manipulation. In particular he/she must ensure that:

- seals on the recording equipment/installation are not missing/improperly fitted or ineffective;
- the 'k' factor setting has not been altered, and that it corresponds to the vehicle parameters;
- there are no manipulation devices connected between the sender/motion sensor and the tachograph head/vehicle unit.

Note: It is expected that the new fourth generation tachographs will be tested in a similar manner to the older digital machines but as they have only recently entered service exact details are unknown.

Note Regarding Tachograph-Exempt Vehicles Using a Tachograph as a Speedometer

A vehicle must have a tachograph fitted unless the person presenting the vehicle for test claims that it is exempt from the tachograph regulations. If a tachograph is fitted on an exempt vehicle and used in place of a speedometer, the tachograph must be calibrated and sealed in accordance with the Community Recording Equipment

Regulations. However, provided the seals remain intact there will be no requirement for two-yearly inspections or further calibration. If the above vehicle legally requires a speed limiter and has the speed signal operating the limiter transmitted from the tachograph head, then all the seals including the gearbox sender unit must remain intact to avoid the requirement for re-calibration. If the vehicle does not legally require a speed limiter (or the speed limiter does not receive the speed signal from the tachograph head) then the tachograph head seals (excluding the gearbox sender unit seal) must remain intact to avoid the requirement for re-calibration.

Speed Limiter Checks

An electronic device is used during testing to check the function and setting of the speed limiter under test item 33 and failure of the item will jeopardize the whole vehicle test.

Dedicated ABS/EBS Cables

Where tractive units and trailers are fitted with ISO 7638 sockets to power ABS and/or EBS braking systems, these sockets must be connected by a dedicated ABS cable (where one or the other does not have an ISO 7638 socket, the ABS is powered through the stop light circuit). Vehicles presented for test after 1 April 2002 without such a cable receive notice VTG 14, 'refusal to test a vehicle'. Also from 1 April 2002, vehicles stopped at roadside checks that are found to have an ISO 7638 socket on both tractive unit and trailer, but do not have an ABS cable connecting them, receive a prohibition notice (PG9 – see p 455).

Where a vehicle and trailer are fitted with an EBS as well as ABS, a seven-core cable connection must be used instead of the normal ABS five-core cable. Vehicles found during roadside checks to have only a five-core instead of the requisite seven-core cable will receive a Defect Note (PGDN 35). On presentation at the test station or ATF such vehicles will receive an advisory notice to replace the cable.

Test Pass

When a goods vehicle is found to be in satisfactory order a test certificate is issued by the test station or ATF. For goods vehicles the certificate is form VTG5 and for goods-carrying trailers it is VTG5A. The trailer test disc is included with the certificate and this must be removed and fixed onto the trailer in a protective holder in a position where it is conspicuous, readily accessible and clearly visible from the nearside.

The heavy goods vehicle test certificate must be produced when applying for an excise licence for a vehicle which comes within the scope of these regulations and otherwise at the request of a competent authority.

Replacement Documents

Replacement test certificates, replacement plates and plating certificates (see later in chapter) may be obtained from local test stations or the Goods Vehicle Centre (GVC) at Swansea at a cost of £14.00 each. Application in both cases should be made on form VTG59, obtainable from goods vehicle test stations or the GVC. Automatic replacement of lost or defaced documents is not guaranteed. The Secretary of State has powers to order a re-test before issuing such replacements, in which case full test fees become payable.

Test Failure and Re-tests

When the vehicle is sent for test, it is recommended that a mechanic with a toolkit and minor spares items (light bulbs, for example) accompanies it so that any minor defects can be rectified on the premises and the test can be completed. The examiner may allow certain minor defects to be repaired during the test if they do not take up too much time (usually no more than 20 minutes) and delay the test schedule. In some instances the vehicle may be allowed to be taken out of the test line for minor repairs to be carried out but this again is at the discretion of the examiner.

As mentioned earlier, it should be remembered that, if minor repairs are allowed to be made at the time of the test, the fact that the vehicle arrived for test in a 'fail state' will be recorded and applied to the Operator Compliance Risk Score (OCRS).

If it is necessary to take the vehicle away to get the defects rectified and it is submitted again later that day or during the next working day, no additional charge is made. These free re-tests are restricted to those cases where the vehicle failed because of certain prescribed defects in items as follows:

- legal plate position;
- legal plate details;
- bumper bars;
- spare wheel carrier;
- cab doors;
- mirrors;
- view to front;
- speedometer;
- audible warning;
- oil leaks;
- fuel tanks, pipes and system;
- obligatory sidelamps;
- obligatory rear lamps;
- reflectors;
- direction indicators;
- headlamps – vertical aim;
- obligatory headlamps;
- obligatory stop lamps.

If the vehicle which fails the test is submitted to the same test station again within 14 days, a reduced re-test fee is charged and only the items on which the test was failed are re-examined. Arrangements for re-tests have to be made with the manager of the test station or ATF concerned. As with minor defects repaired at the time of the test, any test failure will also be recorded and applied to the operator's OCRS.

Appeals against Test Failure

If a vehicle or trailer undergoing test or re-test failed for a reason which the operator believes is not justified, he has a right of appeal to the test station or ATF manager or DVSA regional manager, by completing form VT17 within 14 days of the test. The form can be found on the GOV.UK website and can be emailed to csccomplaints@dvsa.gov.uk or posted to the DVSA in Swansea. The fee is usually the same as the cost of a test or re-test. The person who submitted the appeal will receive notification as to where and when he must submit the vehicle for re-examination.

Reduced Pollution Examination of Vehicles

Although reduced pollution certificates and grants are no longer generally used, they may be required for vehicles operating in LEZs and CAZs and operators may still submit their vehicles to a goods vehicle testing station for examination by the DVSA.

The reduced pollution requirement may be satisfied by:

- a new vehicle meeting the required standard;
- the fitting of a new engine to a vehicle; or
- the fitting of a type-approved device for which there is a Certificate of Conformity issued by the vehicle manufacturer.

The reduced pollution requirements are satisfied if the rate and content of a vehicle's particulate emissions do not exceed the number of grams per kilowatt-hour specified in the tables below.

TABLE 14.5 EU emission standards for HD diesel engines, g/kWh (smoke in m^{-1})

Tier	Date	CO	HC	NOx	PM	Smoke
Euro IV	October 2005	1.5	0.46	3.5	0.02	0.5
Euro V	October 2008	1.5	0.46	2.0	0.02	0.5
Euro VI	January 2014	1.5	0.13	0.4	0.01	

TABLE 14.6 Emission standards for diesel and gas engines, transient test, g/kWh

Tier	Date	CO	NMHC	CH_4a	NOx	PMb
Euro IV	October 2005	4.0	0.55	1.1	3.5	0.03
Euro V	October 2008	4.0	0.55	1.1	2.0	0.03
Euro VI	January 2014	4.0	0.16	0.5	0.46	0.01

Reduced Pollution Schemes for Lighter Vehicles

The introduction of the Euro VI standards and the continuing move towards reducing emissions is being extended to include lighter vehicles. The EU intends to introduce stricter limits on emissions from light road vehicles by making manufacturers change existing engine specifications and maintenance regimes for specifications and maintenance regimes that will make the vehicles more fuel efficient. Most manufacturers have already confirmed that they will be introducing or have introduced AdBlue and/or selective catalytic reduction (SCR) systems for light vehicles. Other considerations include fitting lighter vehicles with exhaust gas recirculation (EGR) systems in order to help meet the proposed new standards.

Plating of Goods Vehicles and Trailers

Manufacturer's Plating

All new goods vehicles and new trailers over 1,020 kg unladen weight must be fitted with a plate by the manufacturer which shows specified information as follows:

- the manufacturer's name;
- the date of manufacture;
- vehicle type;
- engine type and power rating;
- chassis or serial number;
- number of axles;
- maximum weight allowed on each axle;
- maximum gross weight for the vehicle (including the weight imposed on the tractive unit by a semi-trailer in the case of articulated vehicles);
- maximum train weight.

The plate containing this information is normally fitted inside the driver's cab on the nearside.

For trailers, the information shown on the plate is:

- the manufacturer's name;
- date of manufacture;
- chassis or serial number;
- number of axles;
- maximum weight allowed on each axle;
- maximum weight imposed on the drawing vehicle in the case of semi-trailers;
- maximum gross weight for the trailer.

The plate for trailers is usually riveted to the chassis frame on the nearside.

Design Weights

The weights stated are those at which the manufacturer has designed the vehicle to operate. Where these weights exceed those permitted by law (ie in the C&U Regulations) for the type of vehicle in question then, until such time as the vehicle is plated by the DVSA, the lower statutory weight limits apply. Conversely, if the manufacturer's design weight is lower than that permitted by law for the type of vehicle then it is the lower limit which applies.

Vehicle Dimensions

Goods vehicles over 3.5 tonnes gross weight and trailers manufactured since 31 May 1998 must be fitted with a plate showing their length and width, unless this information is already shown on either the manufacturer's plate or a 'Ministry' plate.

'Ministry' Plating

When Type Approved goods vehicles over 3,500 kg gross weight are first registered, an official plate (ie commonly referred to as a 'Ministry' plate) is issued showing the maximum permissible gross vehicle weight and individual axle weights at which the vehicle or trailer is allowed to operate within Great Britain.

A plating certificate (form VTG7 – for all vehicles and trailers) and a plate (form VTG6 – for pre-1 April 1983 vehicles; VTG6T – for post-1 April 1983 vehicles; VTG6A – for all trailers) and, on special request (apply on form VTG101), for older goods vehicles used in international operations, giving similar details to those on the manufacturer's plate, are issued by the Goods Vehicle Centre at Swansea after receipt of the necessary documents (including the Type Approval Certificate) when a new vehicle is first registered. The plating certificate must be retained by the vehicle operator but the plate (made of paper and protected in a laminated casing, not metal as is the manufacturer's plate) which is also issued must be fixed to the vehicle in an easily accessible position. Generally, it should be fitted inside the cab of vehicles on the nearside (but not affixed to the door) and in a suitable position on the nearside of trailers (it is usually fitted to the chassis frame). In all cases the plates should be protected against the weather, kept clean and legible, and secure against accidental loss.

Tractive units and semi-trailers in articulated outfit combinations are plated separately and the individual plates must be fixed separately to the tractive unit and the trailer.

NB: The new 'MoT style' printed plating forms for trailers have replaced the old 'plates' mentioned above for trailers being used on international operations and it may not be appropriate for the certificate to be left on a trailer, in which case the driver needs to carry it and it may need to be passed between different hauliers pulling the trailer in question.

Down-Plating of Vehicles

Down-plating to obtain the benefit of lower rates of Vehicle Excise Duty (VED) and to reduce the cost of the HGV Road User Levy will be carried out on request using form VTG10.

Where no alteration has been made to the vehicle, inspection by the DVSA will not normally be necessary. For example, in cases where:

- an articulated vehicle is down-plated to 23 tonnes gvw;
- a four-axle rigid vehicle is down-plated to 27 tonnes gvw;
- a three-axle rigid vehicle is down-plated to 19 tonnes; and
- a two-axle rigid vehicle is down-plated to 12 tonnes gvw,

the DVSA will not require any further information or action to be taken. Where these limits are exceeded the DVSA is expected to request the reason for operating at such low weights.

However, it should be noted that in no circumstances will a vehicle that has an inefficient braking performance, is not maintained to required safety standards or which otherwise does not comply with legal requirements be plated at lower weights to compensate for these defects. In such cases examiners at the Goods Vehicle Testing Station/ATF will refuse to issue the vehicle with a test (pass) certificate.

The procedure for down-plating is to complete the form for notifiable alterations (VTG10), obtainable from goods vehicle test stations and the Goods Vehicle Centre at Swansea, and then:

- hand it in at the time of presenting the vehicle for its annual goods vehicle test;
- contact the local goods vehicle test station at any time for an appointment to submit the vehicle for down-plating; or
- send the form and the fee (see below) to the Goods Vehicle Centre at Swansea.

The statutory fee is £27 if the down-plating is done at the time of the annual test. If not, then the fee is £40. The old vehicle plate will need to be returned and a new vehicle plate (to be fitted in the vehicle cab) and plating certificate will be issued.

International Plates

International Proof of Compliance plates are available and may be voluntarily fitted to vehicles by international hauliers. These plates show compliance with the weights and dimension requirements of EC Directive 96/53/EC. They have been introduced to speed up clearance times through Customs for vehicles on international journeys, showing that the vehicles to which they are fitted do meet the regulations on weights, widths and lengths. Operators wishing to fit these plates should apply to the Goods Vehicle Centre at Swansea using application forms (VTG101 for vehicles and VTG102 for trailers) obtainable from Swansea direct or from heavy goods vehicle testing stations.

Vehicles and trailers manufactured since 31 May 1998 should be fitted with these 'dimensions' plates, unless the information is already shown on the manufacturer's plate or on a 'Ministry' plate issued for the vehicle or trailer. Also note that since the introduction of the European Community Whole Vehicle Type Approval scheme (ECWVTA), and similar schemes, since 29 October 2012 international plates are automatically produced for all new trailers and since 24 October 2014 international plates are automatically produced for all new motor vehicles.

As mentioned earlier the position in relation to type approval will need to change due to Brexit and the position in relation to proof of compliance may also change following the new style MoT test certificates being issued to vehicles and trailers.

Notifiable Alterations

In addition to down-plating, operators who make any alteration to the structure of their vehicles must notify the DVSA before the vehicle is used on the road. Details of the alterations which require notification on form VTG10 are as follows:

a *Alterations to the structure or fixed equipment of a vehicle which vary its carrying capacity*
These include alterations to any of the following items:

(i) *Chassis frame or structure*
Any alteration which increases or decreases the front or rear overhang by more than 1 foot. Any structural alteration (other than normal adjustment of an extensible structure) which reduces or extends the wheelbase (or in the case of a semi-trailer the equivalent distance). Any other extension, deletion or alteration including cutting, welding, riveting, etc, which materially weakens the chassis frame or structure or changes its torsional stiffness.

(ii) *Steering suspension, wheels and axles (including stub axles and wheel hubs)*
The fitting of steering gear, axles, hubs or road springs of a different design or load-bearing capacity. The fitting of additional wheels and axles, or the removal of such items. Any addition, deletion or alteration which reduces the inherent strength of the above components.

(iii) *The fitting of an alternative body of different design, construction or type*
Any alteration which reduces materially the strength of the body structure or the means by which it is attached to the chassis. Any alteration which causes the body to extend beyond the rear of the chassis frame.

b *Alterations to braking system*
These comprise alterations which adversely affect either the braking system or the braking performance of the vehicle. They include the addition or deletion of components such as reservoirs, servomotors, brake actuators, exhausters and compressors. They would also include the addition of any equipment which it is necessary to connect to any part of the braking system, and the fitting of different brake drums or shoes or liners of a smaller contact area.

c *Other alterations to the structure or fixed equipment*
Any other alteration made in the load-bearing structure or fixed equipment of the vehicle, eg the coupling gear, which could make the vehicle unsafe to travel on roads at any weight shown on the plate and plating certificate. In the case of a motor vehicle this could include such alterations as changing the type of engine or repositioning the engine or its mountings (eg petrol to diesel, normal control to forward control, etc).

Notifiable alteration inspections and certification also attract a fee of £27.00 during normal working hours or £40.00 if conducted out of hours at DVSA test stations or ATFs.

NB: Any trailer that is over eight years old submitted for examination under the notifiable alterations procedure must have its braking system brought up to the latest standard applicable at the time of its rebuilding.

Exemptions from Plating and Testing

Vehicles which are subject to the Goods Vehicle (Plating and Testing) Regulations 1988 (as amended) are exempt from the need to hold current plating and testing certificates while being taken to a test station, when used on a road during the test, returning to base from the test station after a test and being taken (unladen) to a working or repair centre for work to be carried out on them in connection with the test.

Exempt Vehicles

Vehicles to which the regulations do not apply are as follows:

- dual-purpose vehicles not constructed or adapted to form part of an articulated vehicle;
- road rollers;
- vehicles designed for fire-fighting or fire salvage purposes;
- works trucks, straddle carriers used solely as works trucks and works trailers;
- motor vehicles used solely for clearing frost, ice or snow from roads by means of a snow plough or similar contrivance, whether forming part of the vehicle or not;
- vehicles constructed or adapted for, and used solely for, spreading material on roads to deal with frost, ice or snow;
- motor vehicles used for no other purpose than the haulage of lifeboats and the conveyance of the necessary gear of the lifeboats which are being hauled;
- living vans not exceeding 3,500 kg design weight;
- vehicles constructed or adapted for, and used primarily for the purpose of, carrying equipment permanently fixed to the vehicle which equipment is used for medical, dental, veterinary, health, educational, display or clerical purposes, such use not directly involving the sale, hire or loading of goods from the vehicle;
- trailers which have no other brakes than a parking brake and brakes which automatically come into operation on the overrun of the trailer;
- vehicles exempted from duty because they do not travel on public roads for more than 6 miles in any week and trailers drawn by such vehicles (Vehicle Excise and Registration Act 1994, Schedule 3);
- agricultural motor vehicles;

- agricultural trailers and trailed appliances drawn on roads only by a land tractor;
- passenger-carrying vehicles and hackney carriages;
- vehicles used solely for the purpose of funerals;
- goods vehicles proceeding to a port for export and vehicles in the service of a visiting force;
- unladen vehicles operating under a trade licence;
- vehicles equipped with new or improved equipment or types of equipment and used solely by a manufacturer of vehicles or their equipment or by an importer of vehicles, for or in connection with the test or trial of any such equipment;
- motor vehicles temporarily in Great Britain;
- motor vehicles for the time being licensed in Northern Ireland;
- trailers temporarily in Great Britain, a period of 12 months not having elapsed since the vehicle in question was last brought into Great Britain;
- track-laying vehicles;
- steam-propelled vehicles;
- motor vehicles manufactured before 1 January 1960 used unladen and not drawing a laden trailer, and trailers manufactured before 1 January 1960 and used unladen;
- three-wheeled vehicles used for street cleansing, the collection or disposal of refuse, and the collection or disposal of the contents of gullies;
- vehicles designed and used for the purpose of servicing or controlling aircraft, while so used on an aerodrome within the meaning of the Civil Aviation Act 1982 or on roads to such extent as is essential for the purpose of proceeding directly from one part of such an aerodrome to another part thereof or, subject as aforesaid, outside such an aerodrome unladen and not drawing a laden trailer;
- vehicles designed for use, and used on, an aerodrome mentioned in the preceding paragraph, solely for the purpose of road cleansing, the collection or disposal of refuse or the collection or disposal of the contents of gullies or cesspools;
- vehicles provided for police purposes and maintained in workshops approved by the Minister as suitable for such maintenance, being vehicles provided in England and Wales by a police authority or the receiver for the Metropolitan Police or, in Scotland, by a police authority or a joint police committee;
- heavy motor cars or motor cars constructed or adapted for the purpose of forming part of an articulated vehicle which are used for drawing only a trailer of a type described above or a trailer being used for, or in connection with, any purpose for which it is authorized to be used on roads under the Special Types General Order;
- play buses.

NB: The following definitions apply in the above exemptions:

- *'Works truck' means a motor vehicle designed for use in private premises and used on a road only in delivering goods from or to such premises, to or from a vehicle on a road in the immediate neighbourhood, or in passing from one part of any such premises to another or to other private premises in the immediate neighbourhood, or in connection with roadworks while at or in the immediate neighbourhood of the site of such works.*

Taxing Exempt Vehicles

When applying for a vehicle excise licence for a vehicle exempt from plating and testing, it is necessary to complete declaration form V112G (available from the GOV.UK website, the DVLA and main post offices) in order to obtain the licence without a valid test certificate.

Tachograph Testing

Operators submitting vehicles for test, which are exempt from the requirement for tachograph fitment, must declare the exemption on the appropriate form, which is form DVSA 75. The form is available on the GOV.UK website, which lists the exempt categories (see pp 132–35 for list of tachograph exemptions).

Production of Documents

The police and DVSA examiners can request production of both test and plating certificates for goods vehicles when such vehicles have been involved in an accident or if they believe an offence has been committed. If these documents cannot be produced at the time, they may be produced within seven days at a police station convenient to the person to whom the request was made, or as soon as reasonably practicable thereafter.

Enforcement Checks on Vehicles

The DVSA's Operator Compliance Risk Score Scheme

Using its Operator Compliance Risk Score (OCRS) system, a key element of its 'targeted enforcement' policy, the DVSA scores each 'O' licence holder from 0 to 10 to indicate how many times the holder has been caught breaking the rules. Operators are also graded red, amber and green – those with a higher score and a red coding are warned that they can expect much closer attention from the DVSA until they mend their ways. The scores are based on results from annual tests, vehicle inspections and prosecution records.

DVSA examiners have a small mobile compliance device (MCD) which they use when carrying out roadside checks on goods vehicles to identify those vehicles which should be checked. They key in vehicle registration numbers or operator licence information and the device displays information about the operator, including his

OCRS scores. This data also enables the DVSA to prioritize investigations of those operators most likely to be operating outside the law.

The DVSA changed the OCRS banding system on 30 April 2012. This change included the abolition of predictive scoring and the introduction of a new 'grey' band, and the practice of putting operators straight to red if they are prosecuted for an offence or are found to have committed serious infringements. This latter change was subsequently reversed in 2016.

More recently there is now also a 'blue' band (see below).

Currently, the historic score for an operator is calculated on data gathered over a three-year rolling period. There are actually two scores used to arrive at a historic score. There is a 'roadworthiness' score where points are issued for test failures, PG9s, etc and there is an 'enforcement' score for issues such as drivers' hours and tachograph offences.

Points for offences vary according to their severity and are banded. For example:

TABLE 14.7 Points for offences

Points	Offence	Band
300	Prosecution	5
200	£300 fixed penalty	4
100	£200 fixed penalty	3
50	£100 fixed penalty	2
25	£50 fixed penalty	1
0	Verbal warning	0

The actual historic score is arrived at by dividing the number of points accrued by the number of events over a three-year rolling reference period. Once this is done, each operator is allocated a 'risk band'. There are separate risk bands for roadworthiness and traffic enforcement scores as detailed in Table 14.8.

The DVSA also use a 'weighting factor' in relation to the length of time since an offence was recorded. By doing this, older offences accrue fewer points. Currently offences are weighted as follows:

- up to 12 months – multiplied by 1;
- over 12 months and up to two years – multiplied by 0.75;
- over two years – multiplied by 0.5.

Any operator prosecuted for an offence, or who commits what the DVSA regards as a most serious infringement (MSI), who is not prosecuted will be monitored closely. The infringements identified as MSIs by the DVSA have become known as the 'Seven Deadly Sins'.

TABLE 14.8 Risk band

Risk Band	Roadworthiness	Enforcement
Grey	no score	no score
Green	<10	<5
Amber	10–25	5–30
Red	>25	>30

These are set out in Annex 4 of Regulation 1071/2009 and are listed as:

- exceeding the six-day or fortnightly driving limits by more than 25 per cent;
- exceeding, during a daily working period, the maximum daily driving limit by a margin of more than 50 per cent or more without taking a break or without an uninterrupted rest period of at least 4.5 hours;
- using a fraudulent device able to modify the records of the recording equipment;
- not having a speed limiter as required by Community law;
- using a fraudulent device able to modify the speed limiter;
- falsifying the record sheets of the tachograph;
- falsifying data downloaded from the tachograph and/or the driver card;
- driving with a driver card that has been falsified;
- driving with a driver card belonging to another driver;
- transporting regulated dangerous goods, without identifying them on the vehicle as dangerous goods, thus endangering lives or the environment to such an extent that it leads to a decision to immobilize the vehicle;
- serious overloading of a vehicle with a gross weight not exceeding 12 tonnes by a factor of 25 per cent or more; and
- serious overloading of a vehicle with the gross weight exceeding 12 tonnes by a factor of 20 per cent or more.

(Clearly there are more than seven 'sins' listed but the term is still used!)

Operators can find out their current OCRS for the three-year period up to the end of the previous calendar month by emailing top.registrations@vosa.gov.uk (this email address is still valid (as of 10/18) in spite of it referring to VOSA and not the DVSA). As OCRS figures are updated weekly it is not possible to obtain backdated reports, and operators wishing to keep track of their performance should obtain their OCRS reports regularly. Information relating to OCRS is also available from the DVSA on 0300 123 9000.

Earned Recognition Scheme

The Earned Recognition Scheme (ERS) is operated by the DVSA and is a voluntary scheme designed to allow operators to verify that their operations comply with the required driver and vehicle standards. The scheme works by operators agreeing to use a DVSA IT system to continuously monitor their operations and share performance information with the DVSA.

Every four weeks the DVSA provide feedback on how well the operator has complied with the regulations and met key performance targets within the scheme. Where this information sharing shows problems the DVSA work with the operator to bring standards back to required levels. In volunteering to join the scheme the operators are graded into a 'blue' band of OCRS which means that they are less likely to be subject to roadside enforcement activity.

Further information is available on the GOV.UK website or through the trade associations.

Roadside Checks

In addition to carrying out annual vehicle tests at the goods vehicle testing stations, examiners of the DVSA operate roadside checks on commercial vehicles. These roadside checks are carried out at intervals on main roads by examiners who usually take over a lay-by which will accommodate several large vehicles. The DVSA has stepped up its normal system of roadside checks in recent times and occasionally carries out checks during the night and during weekends. Typically, vehicles which are required for examination are directed into a lay-by, where they are inspected mainly for visible wear and defects of the brakes, steering gear, silencers, tyres, lights and reflectors, and for the emission of black smoke when the engine is revved up. The examiners only have a limited amount of equipment on these checks so the extent of their examination is likewise limited but nevertheless the inspection is undertaken by skilled and observant people and very little escapes their attention.

NB: DVSA examiners use a guide called Categorisation of Defects *when considering the prohibition of vehicles found to be defective during roadside checks or while undergoing their annual test. Copies of this 198-page guide, which operators may find useful, can be downloaded from the GOV.UK website.*

Vehicle Inspections on Premises

Besides roadside checks, DVSA examiners and police officers in uniform are, at any reasonable time, free to enter any premises on which goods vehicles are kept and examine the vehicles. The owner's consent is not needed in this case but to examine any vehicle (ie other than goods vehicles) the owner's consent has to be obtained to carry out the examination or he must be given at least 48 hours' notice of such a proposal to carry out an examination; *if the notice is sent by recorded delivery post the period is increased to 72 hours*. In the latter case the consent of the owner of the premises, if different from the vehicle owner, must also be obtained. If on these inspections defects are found on the vehicles examined, the same procedure applies regarding the prohibition of their use as explained for roadside checks.

A police officer in uniform or a DVSA examiner, on production of suitable identification, can instruct a driver in charge of a stationary goods vehicle on a road (by the issue of form GV3) to take the vehicle to a suitable place to be examined but this must not be for a distance of more than five miles.

Prohibition notices can be issued by examiners at a goods vehicle test station if defects of a serious enough nature are found. Also, the police may be notified if prosecution is warranted, although it is not usual for vehicles in such a precarious state to be submitted for test.

NB: Three new EU Directives came into force in May 2014 relating to 'roadworthiness'. This EU package relates to periodic roadworthiness testing (Directive 2014/45/EU), registration documentation for vehicles and trailers (Directive 2014/46/EU) and roadside inspections (Directive 2014/47/EU). These harmonizing Directives were adopted by member states in 2018.

Powers of Police, DVSA Examiners and Certifying Officers

The Road Traffic Act 1988 gives authorized examiners (specifically, examiners of DVSA, London taxi examiners, authorized police officers and persons appointed for the purpose by a chief officer of police and certifying officers appointed under the Road Traffic Act 1991) powers to test and inspect vehicles (and examine vehicle records), on production of their authority, as follows:

- They can test any motor vehicle or trailer on a road to check that legal requirements regarding brakes, silencer, steering, tyres, lights and reflectors, smoke and fumes are complied with, and may drive the vehicle for this purpose.
- They can test a vehicle for the same purposes on premises if the owner of the premises consents or has been given at least 48 hours' notice, except where the vehicle has been involved in a notifiable accident, when there is no requirement to give notice. If the notice given is in writing it must be sent by recorded post and the time limit is extended to 72 hours.
- They may at any time enter and inspect any goods vehicle and goods vehicle records, and may at a reasonable time enter premises on which they believe a goods vehicle or goods vehicle records are kept.
- They can request a driver of a stationary goods vehicle to take the vehicle to a place for inspection up to five miles away.
- They can at any reasonable time enter premises where used vehicles are sold, supplied or offered for sale or supply or exposed or kept for sale or supply, to ensure that such vehicles can be used on a road without contravening the appropriate regulations. They may drive a vehicle on the road for this purpose.
- They may enter at any reasonable time premises where vehicles or vehicle parts are sold, supplied, offered for sale or supply, exposed or kept for sale or supply.
- They may require the person in charge of any vehicle to take it to a weighbridge to be weighed. If the vehicle is more than five miles from the place where the request is made and the vehicle is found not to be overloaded, the operator can claim against the highway authority for any loss sustained.

- When a goods vehicle has been weighed and found to exceed its weight limit and its use on a road would be a risk to public safety, they can prohibit its road use by the issue of form TE160P until the weight is reduced to within the legal limit.
- If they find that a goods vehicle is unfit or likely to become unfit for service they can prohibit the driving of the vehicle on the road either immediately or from a later date and time by the issue of a prohibition notice (form PG9 – see below).
- *NB: Police powers in this respect are restricted under the provisions of the Road Traffic Act 1991 (effective from 1 July 1992) to the issue only of immediate prohibitions in circumstances where they consider that the driving of a defective vehicle would involve a 'danger of injury to any person' as opposed to the DVSA examiner's right to prohibit a vehicle which is 'unfit for service'.*
- Where a prohibition order has been placed on a vehicle for various reasons, they are empowered to remove the prohibition (by the issue of form PG10) when they consider the vehicle is fit for use. *Where evidence of the vehicle's test certificate is required to be produced the vehicle will normally be subjected to a full roadworthiness test by the DVSA at a goods vehicle testing station or ATF – and payment of the current full test fee will be required.*
- They can ask the driver of a goods vehicle registered in an EU member state, fitted with a tachograph, to produce the tachograph record of the vehicle when it is used in this country and ask to examine the official calibration plaque in the instrument. They can at any reasonable time enter premises where they believe such a vehicle is to be found or that tachograph records are kept, and may inspect the vehicle and records (ie tachograph charts).

Powers of Police Constables

- A police constable or Highways England traffic officer *in uniform* can stop a moving vehicle on a road ('constable' includes any rank of uniformed police officer). They can direct the vehicle to a place of testing or test any motor vehicle or trailer on a road to check that legal requirements regarding brakes, silencer, steering, tyres, lights and reflectors, smoke and fumes are complied with. They may drive the vehicle for this purpose.
- They can test a vehicle for the same purposes on premises if the owner of the premises consents or has been given at least 48 hours' notice (or 72 hours if given by recorded post), except that consent is not necessary where the vehicle has been involved in a notifiable accident.

NB: This authority applies to all constables even if not specially authorized under the Road Traffic Act 1988 as mentioned above.

Enforcement Powers for DVSA Examiners

Specially selected and trained enforcement officers of the DVSA also have powers to stop moving vehicles. These officers, known as enforcement support officers (colloquially referred to as 'stopping officers') and accredited by chief constables under provisions contained in the Police Reform Act 2002, are uniformed and operate with liveried and fully marked vehicles (normally cars or 4 × 4s with amber beacons and 'follow me' lighting).

Further powers under The Road Vehicles (Powers to Stop) Regulations 2011 (SI 2011 No 996), which amended the Road Traffic Act 1988, came into effect from 30 March 2011. This allowed the Secretary of State for Transport to appoint DVSA 'stopping officers' throughout Great Britain (and in Northern Ireland) who may *stop* and inspect commercial vehicles for specified purposes as listed below. Under the previous legislation such officers in England and Wales had to be individually accredited by chief officers of police in the constabulary in which they operated once they had completed the necessary training.

These changes were designed to speed up the enforcement process and free up police involvement in the administration of the road stopping scheme. DVSA stopping officers have the powers to:

- stop commercial vehicles;
- carry out vehicle roadworthiness inspections;
- carry out vehicle weight checks;
- inspect documents, records and tachograph equipment;
- ensure that 'O' licence discs are correctly exhibited;
- ensure that a valid 'O' licence is held;
- ensure that drivers carry evidence of their Driver CPC training, or exemptions from such.

Resisting or obstructing a DVSA stopping officer is a criminal offence and can carry a fine of up to £5,000. The DVSA has published a guide on the policies and sanctions that may be applied when vehicles are stopped and problems, which may lead to action being taken against the driver and/or the operator, are encountered. This guide is available on the GOV.UK website and is entitled *DVSA Enforcement Sanctions Policy*.

NB: The 'power to stop' may be extended to some PCSO and CEOs in the future in order to free up police time.

Powers of Trading Standards Officers

Trading standards officers (ie employed by local authorities) can request the driver of a vehicle which is carrying goods that need an official conveyance note (ie ballast which includes sand, gravel, shingle, ashes, clinker, chippings, including coated material, hardcore and aggregates) to take that vehicle to a weighbridge to be weighed. Goods may have to be unloaded if necessary.

Inspection Notices and Prohibitions

Vehicle Inspection Notice – Form PGDN35

Following an inspection of a vehicle which is found to have no serious road safety defects, form PGDN35 (commonly known as an inspection notice) is issued to indicate to the user either that one or more minor defects were found which it is in his interest, and the interests of other road users, to have rectified at an early date – it is not actually a prohibition – or that the vehicle has no apparent defects – subject to a disclaimer – to save further inspection later on that journey or that day. This form is also issued when a vehicle is stopped but found to be defect-free to enable the driver to prove that this is the case should they be stopped again on the same journey.

NB: If this form is produced by a computer it is known as a Form PG35ECDN.

Direction Notice

As already mentioned, form GV3 is authorization for DVSA examiners to direct a vehicle to proceed to a specified place to be inspected (normally not more than five miles away).

Prohibition Notices

The driver of any vehicle found by DVSA examiners to have serious defects is given form PG9 on which these are listed. Form PG9 is the examiner's authority to stop the use of the vehicle on the road for carrying goods. Depending on how serious the defects are, the prohibition will either take effect immediately, in which case the vehicle, if loaded, has to remain where it is until either it is repaired or has been unloaded and then taken away for repair, for which the examiner will give authority by issuing form PG9B, or it may be delayed for 12 to 24 hours or more depending on the seriousness of the fault. In this case the vehicle may continue to operate until the limit of the period of exemption of the prohibition by which time, if it is not repaired and cleared, it must be taken off the road. If defects recorded as requiring immediate attention are repaired quickly on the roadside (either by the driver or by a mechanic or repair garage staff who come out to the vehicle) the examiner may issue a variation to the PG9 notice with form PG9A, which then allows the vehicle to be removed and used until the new time specified on the variation notice (the forms are described further individually below). In all cases where a PG9 is issued, details will be recorded on the operator's OCRS.

C&U Offences

If defects are found at a roadside check which make the vehicle unsafe to be on the road (usually tyres, brakes, steering or suspension defects) or if the defects are such that an offence under the Construction and Use regulations is committed (particularly in respect of lights, reflectors, smoke emission or the horn), DVSA examiners will report these items to the police in attendance for consideration for prosecution and the matter will be recorded on the operator's OCRS.

Prohibition Forms

A number of official forms as described below are used by DVSA examiners in the process of inspecting vehicles, recording defects and prohibiting the use of those which are defective. Any PG forms, or TE forms (see below) retained by the operator should be filed in the vehicle history file in the same way as periodic vehicle inspection sheets and retained for 15 months.

Form PG9

When an inspection by a DVSA examiner reveals defects of a serious nature form PG9 will be issued, specifying the defects and stating the precise time at which the prohibition preventing further use of the vehicle comes into force (which could be the time when the notice is written out – ie with immediate effect – or later). A copy of the PG9 is given to the driver and this must be carried on the vehicle until the prohibition is removed. Further copies of the notice are sent to the vehicle operator and, if the vehicle is specified on an 'O' licence, to the relevant TC.

If the PG9 has immediate effect, this means that the vehicle cannot be driven or towed away (see below).

Form PG9A

This form (Variation in the Terms of a Prohibition…) is issued if the DVSA examiner wishes to vary the terms of a PG9 notice by either suspending the PG9 until a future time (eg midnight on the day of issue), altering the time (which is effectively the same thing as suspending the notice as mentioned above) or altering the list of defects shown on the PG9 notice.

Form PG9B

A DVSA examiner may, after issuing a PG9, exempt the vehicle (Exemption from a Prohibition…) from the terms of the prohibition and permit its movement provided that the vehicle:

- is unladen;
- proceeds at a speed not in excess of a specified figure;
- does not tow a trailer;
- is towed on a rigid tow bar;
- is towed on a suspended tow;
- is not used after lighting-up time (if it has lighting defects);
- proceeds only between two specified points.

Other conditions may be added as appropriate.

Form PG9C

When a vehicle which is subject to a PG9 notice is presented to a DVSA examiner for clearance of the defect and the examiner is not satisfied that it is fit for service, he may issue form PG9C (Refusal to Remove a Prohibition…), which means that the original PG9 notice remains in force until the defects are satisfactorily rectified.

(Forms PG9 A, B and C are all actually different parts of the same form although they carry individual identities.)

Form PG10

If the defects specified in a PG9 notice have been repaired to the satisfaction of the DVSA examiner to whom the vehicle is presented for clearance and the examiner is satisfied that the whole vehicle is in a satisfactory condition for use on the road, he will issue a PG10 notice (Removal of Prohibition…), which removes the prohibition. The TC must be notified of the clearance if the vehicle is specified on an 'O' licence.

Form TE160P

This notice (*which does not have a PG prefix*) relates to prohibition on the use of overweight vehicles. It effectively requires the driver of the vehicle to take the vehicle to a weighbridge and, if it is found to be overloaded, reduce the gross weight to legal limits before proceeding on his journey.

NB: It is a defence to a charge of overloading that the vehicle was on its way to the nearest practicable weighbridge or that at the time of loading the weight was within legal limits and was subsequently not more than 5 per cent heavier despite not having any additions to the load en route.

Form TE160DH

This notice (*which also does not have a PG prefix*) relates to prohibition on the use of a vehicle for drivers' hours contraventions. It effectively requires the driver of the vehicle to park the vehicle and to take any statutory breaks, or rests, that are required before being allowed to continue their journey.

Effects of Prohibition

A vehicle must not, under any circumstances, be used to carry goods while it is the subject of a PG9 prohibition notice, but despite the prohibition notice a vehicle may be driven unladen to a goods vehicle test station or to a place agreed with a goods vehicle examiner (both by previous appointment only) in order to have the vehicle inspected. The vehicle may also be driven on the road for test purposes, provided it is unladen, within 3 miles of where it has been repaired.

Forms PG9 and PG9A have a panel of boxes identified by letters of the alphabet from A to M. These boxes are used by enforcement staff to codify certain aspects of the vehicle check as follows:

A Whether the vehicle was laden or unladen.

B Whether examination took place on the roadside, at a test station, during the annual test, following an accident, during a fleet check or on any other occasion.

C If defects appeared to be from a significant failure in maintenance arrangements a letter 'S' is entered; 'X' is used if the examiner can attach no undue significance to the defect (ie it could have happened on the journey); and the box is left blank if the examiner is not able to form an opinion as to the cause of the defect.

D To indicate whether a prosecution will follow (the letter 'P' in this box indicates prosecution by the police and 'V' by the DVSA).

E If the vehicle is issuing smoke ('S' equals smoking in service; 'S/A' equals smoking under free acceleration when vehicle is stationary).

L Indicates number of pages of prohibition notice served at the time (ie page 1 of 1, page 1 of 2). This indicates to the examiner who is asked to clear the prohibition whether there was another sheet(s) to the prohibition notice when it was issued.

NB: The letters A, B, C, D, E and L are the only identifiers currently used.

Appeals against the Issue of Prohibition Notices

There is no appeal against the imposition of a PG9 prohibition notice, but there is a right of appeal against refusal to remove a prohibition after repair.

Clearance of Prohibition

An operator having a vehicle placed under an immediate or a delayed prohibition notice has to get the defects repaired immediately, in cases where this is possible, or submit the vehicle to his local goods vehicle testing station or ATF either for a full roadworthiness examination in the case of serious defects (with payment of the relevant fees as shown on p 431) or, in the case of minor defects, a 'partial clearance' or 'mini' test. A clearance certificate, PG10, is issued if the examiner is satisfied with the repair. If the examiner is not satisfied with the repair he will issue a form PG9C Refusal to Remove a Prohibition, or form PG9A if some of the defects are cleared and others are not. If because of the better inspection facilities at the test station or ATF he finds further defects another form PG9 may be issued.

Light Vehicles Testing

Light goods vehicles up to 3,500 kg gross weight and dual-purpose vehicles (see p 252 for definition) under 2,040 kg unladen weight are required to be tested on the third anniversary (see Chapter 15) of the date of their original registration and annually thereafter (commonly known and referred to as the MoT test). The tests are carried out at private garages approved by the DVSA and displaying the blue and white triple-triangle sign. For full details of the testing scheme for these vehicles, see Chapter 15, which deals with light vehicle testing.

NB: The 3,500 kg weight limit rose to 4,250 kg when it was brought into UK law in 2018. Consultation through 2017 led to the Government agreeing that this would be appropriate for alternatively fuelled and electrically powered light vehicles in order that they are able to maintain their payload capacities. There will be no requirement for either a Category C1 licence, or for these heavier vans to be tested at LGV test stations. Operators wishing to use these heavier vehicles will need to ensure that the drivers have undertaken at least five hours of approved training before they are allowed to drive them unaccompanied.

Northern Ireland Certification of Vehicles

At the time of writing (late 2019) many of the previously proposed changes to the registration and licensing of vehicles in Northern Ireland have been implemented. The main thrust of the changes was to align the services available to Northern Irish drivers and operators with those available for mainland UK drivers and to transfer the administration of the NI vehicle registration and licensing to the DVLA in Swansea. The changes included an increase in the number of services available for NI drivers including access to DVLA to tax vehicles (form V85 for goods vehicles or the internet), the DVLA's fleet scheme and simplification of the procedure for moving vehicles between mainland UK and NI. In addition, an increased range of licensing transactions are now permitted at over 170 post offices across NI.

As indicated above, the United Kingdom system of goods vehicle plating and annual testing does not fully apply in Northern Ireland. The Province has its own Goods Vehicle Certification scheme (commonly known and referred to in the Province as the PSV test) which requires heavy goods vehicles to be submitted to the Department for Infrastructure (NI) for an annual mechanical examination. Under the Goods Vehicles (Certification) Regulations (Northern Ireland) 1982, owners of goods vehicles (other than those specifically exempted) must obtain a test certificate for each vehicle no later than one year from the date of first registration and annually thereafter.

Applications for a certificate can be made online, by post or in person to any of the test stations, or by telephone (0845 247 2471). Once you have applied you will be sent a reference number and will need to contact your chosen test centre to find out the time and date of the test. Postal applications should be sent as soon as the reminder is received and at least 28 days before the test is required to the Driver Vehicle Testing Agency, 66 Balmoral Road, Belfast BT12 6QL Tel: 028 9054 1410 (www.nidirect.gov.uk (archived at https://perma.cc/48MF-USE4)).

Whilst the DVA does still control much of the enforcement and vehicle testing, etc the operator licensing role is run by the Department for Infrastructure, Transport Regulation Unit. Email: dcu@infrastructure-ni.gov.uk (Tel: 028 9054 0540).

Applications and Certification by Non-NI-Based Bodies

Where an application is made by a corporate body with its principal or registered office outside Northern Ireland or by a person residing outside Northern Ireland the following conditions must be observed:

- During the currency of the certificate a place of business must be retained in NI.
- They must be prepared to accept, at such a place of business, any summons or other document relating to any matter or offence arising in NI in connection with the vehicle the certificate is applied for.
- They must undertake to appear at any court as required by such a summons or by any other document.
- They must admit and submit to the jurisdiction of the court relative to the subject matter of such summons or other document.

Failure to comply with any of the above-mentioned requirements will involve immediate revocation of the certificate.

Examination of Vehicle

When notified by the DVA the applicant must present the vehicle for examination, in a reasonably clean condition, together with the registration document and previous certificate, if any, at the time and at the centre specified in the notice.

Issue of Certificate

If, after examining the vehicle, the DVA is satisfied that it complies in all respects with the regulations in respect of the construction, use, lighting and rear marking, etc of vehicles, a certificate will be issued.

Refusal of Certificate

If the vehicle does not meet the requirements of the regulations a certificate will be refused and the applicant will be notified of the reasons why.

Re-examination of Vehicles

When a certificate has been refused and the defects specified in the notice have been put right, an application may be made for a further examination of the vehicle. A reduced re-test fee will be payable if the re-test is conducted within 21 days of the original test.

Refund of Fees

Prepaid test fees may be refunded in the following circumstances:

- If an appointment for an examination of a vehicle is cancelled by the DVA.
- If the applicant cancels the appointment by giving the DVA (at the centre where the appointment is made) three clear working days' notice.
- If the vehicle is presented to meet the appointment but the examination does not take place for reasons not attributable to the applicant or the vehicle.
- If the applicant satisfies the DVA that the vehicle could not be presented for examination on the day of the appointment because of exceptional circumstances which occurred no more than seven days before the day of the appointment, and providing notice is given to the centre where the examination was to take place within three days of the occurrence.

Duplicate Certificates

Duplicate certificates may be issued in replacement of those which have been accidentally lost, defaced or destroyed. A fee is payable for replacement certificates. If subsequently the original certificate is found, it must be returned to the nearest DVA examining centre or to any police station. Duplicates can also be obtained by completing Section 5 of form VT3 (MoT) or by calling the DVA on 0300 200 7861.

Display of Certificates

Since April 2015, there is now no requirement to display the certificate in the windscreen of the vehicle.

Conditions of Certificate

It is a condition of the certificate that the vehicle owner:

- must not permit the vehicle to be used for any illegal purpose;
- must not deface or mutilate the certificate or permit anybody else to do so;
- must, at all reasonable times, for the purpose of inspection, examination or testing of the vehicle to which the certificate relates:
  - produce the vehicle at such a time and place as may be specified by any inspector of vehicles;
  - afford to any inspector of vehicles full facilities for such inspection, examination or testing including access to his premises for that purpose;
  - ensure that the vehicle and all its fittings are maintained and kept in good order and repair and must take all practical steps to ensure that all parts of the mechanism, including the brakes, are free from defects and are in efficient working order;
  - immediately notify the nearest examination centre of any alteration in design or construction of the vehicle since a certificate was issued.

Transfer of Certificates

If a vehicle owner sells or changes the ownership of a vehicle, he must pass on the certificate or the new owner will need to apply for a duplicate.

If a vehicle owner dies or becomes infirm of mind or body, on application of any person the DVA may transfer the certificate to such a person.

Change of Address

If a certificate holder changes his address during the currency of a certificate, he must notify details of such changes to the nearest examination centre.

Offences

It is an offence to operate when a certificate has expired, or to alter, deface, mutilate or fail to display a certificate. Failure to observe such rules will result in the certificate being declared invalid. It is also an offence to assign or to transfer a certificate to another person without notification to the DVA, with the same resultant penalty. Fines or six months' imprisonment may be imposed on summary conviction for such offences or up to two years' imprisonment upon any further conviction or indictment.

Renewal of Certificates

Reminders of a forthcoming test are usually sent out about seven weeks before the test is due. However, they must be submitted at least one month before the expiry date of a certificate. If no reminder is sent, or if the vehicle has not been certificated in Northern Ireland before, the holder should apply for a certificate using an application form obtainable from any examination centre or the DVA office in Belfast (details on p 460).

Exemptions from Certification

The following vehicles are exempt from the requirements of NI certification:

- vehicles constructed or adapted for the sole purpose of spreading material on roads or used to deal with frost, ice or snow;
- a land tractor, land locomotive or land implement;
- an agricultural trailer drawn on a road only by a land tractor;
- a vehicle exempted from duty under section 7(i) of the Vehicles (Excise) Act (Northern Ireland) 1972 and any trailer drawn by such a vehicle;
- a motor vehicle for the time being licensed under the Vehicles (Excise) Act 1971, paragraph (a);
- a trailer brought into NI from a base outside NI if a period of 12 months has elapsed since it was last brought into NI;
- a pedestrian-controlled vehicle;
- a track-laying vehicle;
- a steam-propelled vehicle;
- a vehicle used within a period of 12 months prior to the date of it being registered for the first time in NI or the UK; or, where a vehicle has been used on roads in NI or elsewhere before being registered, the exemption applies for the period of 12 months from the date of manufacture rather than from the date of registration (for this purpose any use before the vehicle is sold or supplied retail is disregarded).

Light Vehicle (MoT) Testing

15

Private cars, motor caravans (irrespective of weight), dual-purpose vehicles (see p 252 for definition) under 2,040 kg unladen weight and light goods vehicles not exceeding 3,500 kg* gross weight are subject to annual testing (commonly referred to as the MoT test) at D*f*T-approved commercial garages, starting on the third anniversary of the date of their first registration and each year thereafter. (This is the fourth anniversary after registration for cars in Northern Ireland, although light goods vehicles are tested on their third anniversary in the same way as in the rest of the UK.) The weight has risen to 4,250 kg for vehicles powered by alternative fuels and electrically powered vehicles.

*NB: The timescale for cars and motorcycles (not light vans) in the rest of the UK is currently being reviewed under a proposal to extend it to the fourth anniversary. This was announced as far back as the July 2015 Budget but, to date, as in previous editions, there has still been no decision made. However, there is speculation that, if the period is extended, there may need to be a rise in the MoT fees in order to replace the lost revenue. * Note the increase to 4,250 kg (above).*

Cars and light goods vehicles may be tested up to one month before the due date of their first test and the test certificate will extend for 13 months to expire on the anniversary of the first registration date.

Testing is carried out at garages displaying the blue and white MoT triple-triangle symbol, and application is made direct with the garage for a suitable appointment. Some centres claim to provide MoT testing 'while you wait'. There is no application form to be completed.

Computer systems installed in MoT testing stations facilitate checks on a vehicle's MoT status in order to reduce theft and forgery of MoT test certificates. Records of all MoT tests are held on a secure central database, which comprises the definitive proof of a valid test pass. MoT certificates are produced as A4-format receipts which have no value to thieves and there are no blank certificates to steal. With the new-type computerized test certificate a vehicle can be re-taxed online at www.gov.uk/tax-disc (archived at https://perma.cc/3NDE-28VU) as well as at a post office.

The maximum fees for the light vehicle test (as at September 2017) – payable to the garage at the time of the test – are as follows:

TABLE 15.1 Class IV & IVa (Class IVa includes seat belt installation check)

Vehicle type	Age first test certificate required (years)	Fee
Cars (up to 8 passenger seats)	3	£54.85
Motor caravans	3	£54.85
Dual purpose vehicles	3	£54.85
PSVs (up to 8 seats)	3	£54.85
Ambulances and taxis	1	£54.85
Private passenger vehicles and ambulances (9–12 passenger seats)	1	£57.30
Class IVa	–	£64.00

TABLE 15.2 Class V (with more than 13 passenger seats)

Vehicle type	Age first test certificate required (years)	Fee
13–16 passenger seats	1	£59.55
More than 16 passenger seats	1	£80.65

TABLE 15.3 Class Va (includes seat belt installation check)

Vehicle type	Age first test certificate required (years)	Fee
13–16 passenger seats	–	£80.50
More than 16 passenger seats	–	£124.50

TABLE 15.4 Class VII

Vehicle type	Age first test certificate required (years)	Fee
Goods vehicles (over 3,000 kg up to 3,500 kg DGW)	3	£58.60

Duplicate test certificates cost £10 or half of the above amounts.

NB: The term 'DGW' as used above means 'design gross weight'.

Vehicle Classes

Vehicles subject to the MoT test are classified as follows:

TABLE 15.5 Vehicle classes

Class I	Light motor bicycles not exceeding 200 cc cylinder capacity with or without sidecars.
Class II	All motor bicycles (including Class I) with or without sidecars.
Class III	Light motor vehicles with three or more wheels (excluding Classes I and II) not exceeding 450 kg unladen weight.
Class IV	Heavy motor cars and motor cars (excluding Classes III and V); ie any vehicle with an unladen weight of more than 450 kg which is: (a) a passenger vehicle (ie private car, taxi, vehicle licensed as private, with 12 passenger seats or fewer, or small public service vehicle with fewer than eight passenger seats); (b) a dual-purpose vehicle not exceeding 2,040 kg unladen weight (see p 252 for definition); (c) a goods vehicle not exceeding 3,000 kg gross weight; (d) a motor caravan irrespective of weight.
Class V	Large passenger-carrying vehicles; ie motor vehicles which are constructed or adapted to carry more than 12 seated passengers in addition to the driver, and which are not licensed as public service vehicles.
Class VI	Public service vehicles other than those in Class V above.
Class VII	Goods vehicles of 3,001 kg to 3,500 kg gross weight* (these vehicles may be tested at MoT garages – where the facility to test such vehicles is available – or at goods vehicle testing stations).

Exemptions

Public service vehicles with seats for eight or more passengers excluding the driver, track-laying vehicles, vehicles constructed or adapted to form part of an articulated vehicle, works trucks and all trailers are excluded from the above classes and the following vehicles are also exempted from the test:

- heavy locomotives;
- light locomotives;
- goods vehicles over 3.5 tonnes gross weight*;
- articulated vehicles other than articulated buses;
- vehicles exempt from duty under the Vehicle Excise and Registration Act 1994;
- works trucks;
- pedestrian-controlled vehicles;
- vehicles temporarily in Great Britain;
- vehicles proceeding to a port for export;
- some vehicles adapted for use by invalids supplied by the Department for Health or the Department for Social Security, the Scottish Office or the Welsh Office;
- vehicles provided for use by the police force;
- imported vehicles owned or in the service of HM navy, army or air force;
- vehicles which have Northern Ireland test certificates;
- certain hackney carriages.

Many of these vehicles are subject to the goods vehicle testing and plating scheme (see Chapter 14 for details). A full list of exemptions is available on form V112.

There is also an exemption which applies to vehicles which come within the MoT test scheme while they are being driven to a place by previous arrangement for a test or bringing it away, if it fails, to a place to have work done on it. This means that such vehicles can be driven on the road without a valid test certificate being in force, but only in the circumstances mentioned and no other.

* *Note the increase to 4,250 kg (above).*

The Test

Testing is carried out in accordance with *The MoT Tester's Manual* – copies are available from The Stationery Office, or it can be downloaded through the GOV.UK website. (Note: This publication should not be confused with *The Heavy Goods Vehicle Inspection Manual*, which relates solely to the goods vehicle annual test and which is also available from The Stationery Office or free to download.)

When presenting a vehicle for test the following conditions must be observed:

- The vehicle must be sufficiently clean so as not to make the test unreasonably difficult.

- The vehicle must have sufficient petrol and oil to enable the test to be completed.
- If the vehicle is presented for the test in a loaded condition (ie in the case of light goods vehicles) the load must be properly secured or removed.

Refusal and Discontinuance of Test

Failure to observe any of the above conditions can lead to a refusal to test the vehicle, and the test fee will be refunded. Furthermore, if the tester finds a defect of a serious nature which, in his opinion, makes it essential to discontinue the inspection on the grounds of risk to his own safety, risk to the test equipment or to the vehicle itself, he may do so and issue form VT30 showing the defects which caused the test to be discontinued.

Items Tested

The following items are tested and must meet the conditions specified in *The MoT Tester's Manual*:

TABLE 15.6 Items tested

Section I	Function of obligatory front and rear lamps Function of obligatory headlamps Function of stop lamps Obligatory rear reflectors Function of direction indicators Aim of headlamps
Section II	Steering wheel and column Steering mechanism Power steering Front wheel bearings Suspension All suspension types Suspension assemblies (springs, torsion bars, etc) Shock absorbers
Section III	Parking brake and operating lever Parking brake mechanism (under vehicle) Service brake operating pedal Service brake mechanism under vehicle Brake performance test
Section IV	Tyres Road wheels

TABLE 15.6 *continued*

Section V	Seat belts
Section VI	Function of windscreen washers Function of windscreen wipers Exhaust system Function of audible warning device Condition of the vehicle structure

Additional Test Items

Since 1 November 1991 the examination has covered additional items such as exhaust emissions (see below) – particularly in light goods vehicle tests; ABS (ie anti-lock braking system) warning lights; battery and battery wiring and security, rear wheel bearings; more extensive corrosion checks, including some pipework.

Since 1 January 1993 further additional items have been included in the MoT test in accordance with EU requirements. These include checks on the following vehicle components and systems:

- mirrors – a motor car must have a mirror on the driver's side and either an exterior mirror on the passenger side, or an interior mirror; they must be in good condition, capable of adjustment and secure;
- windscreens – damage (ie a crack) to a windscreen, exceeding 10 mm in zone A (an area 290 mm wide centred on a vertical line passing through the centre of the steering wheel and within the area swept by the windscreen wipers), will result in test failure as will obscuring clear vision with stickers or other obstructions;
- fuel tanks and feed pipes – must be in good condition and secure (including the tank filler cap);
- bodywork and body security – must be sound;
- seat fixings – must be secure and backrests lockable;
- security of doors and other openings – all doors must be capable of being opened from the inside and outside and they must latch securely;
- number (ie registration) plates – must be secure and in good condition and the letters and numbers must be correctly spaced (incorrect spacing of letters and numbers to make up names or other words will result in test failure);
- vehicle identification number (VIN) – must be present and capable of being clearly read;
- number plate lamps (at rear) – must be fitted and working correctly;
- rear fog lamps – vehicles first used after 1 April 1980 must have one and it must work and an interior warning light must be provided and must work;
- hazard warning devices – must work with the ignition on or off and there must be an interior warning light which works.

Exhaust Emission Checks

A check is made on emissions from diesel-engined vehicles subject to the test. These tests were reintroduced in 1994 after being temporarily suspended.

Cars, light goods vehicles and particularly goods vehicles within the weight range 3,001 kg to 3,500 kg gross weight which fall within the *Class VII* MoT test are subjected to additional exhaust emission checks during their annual roadworthiness test, as well as checks for excessively smoking exhausts. This involves measurement of the levels of carbon monoxide (CO) and hydrocarbons (HC) to ensure that engines are properly tuned.

Emission standards tests as described above do not apply to motorcycles or three-wheelers.

Regulations permit tests for exhaust emissions to be carried out on the roadside as well as at approved MoT test garages.

Seat Belt Checks

Additional seat belt checks have been included in the MoT scheme since 1 August 1998. From this date the condition of seat belts in all vehicles (whether required to be fitted mandatorily or fitted on a voluntary basis) will be examined to determine whether the belts are likely to fulfil their intended function in the event of an accident. The checks on seatbelts now include the warning light and the automatic pre-tensioner.

Similar checks on seat belts will be carried out during roadside and other enforcement spot checks.

NB: Clearly as technology drives the development of new vehicles the need to introduce additional items for test in the MoT test will continue. For example, airbag warning lights need to be working and LDWS and AEBS will soon be included as they are primarily safety features. However, at the time of writing they had still not been brought into the test.

Test Failure

If the vehicle fails to reach the required standard of mechanical condition a 'notification of refusal of a test certificate' (form VT30) is issued. This indicates the grounds on which the vehicle failed the test (ie it names the faulty components or component area and the actual fault).

Re-tests

If a vehicle fails the test, no further test fee is payable if it is left at the garage for the necessary repairs to be carried out before the end of the 10th working day from the day of the initial test. However, if the vehicle is taken away following the test failure, a three-tier system of re-tests and fees applies as follows:

- Tier 1 Full Test. Where a vehicle is presented for re-test more than 10 working days after the day of the initial test or if the original MoT tester is not available for a tier 2 test, a full test must be carried out and the full test fee is payable.

- Tier 2 Partial Re-test. Where a re-test is necessary that requires the use of a major piece of testing equipment (including hoist or pit, brake performance tester, exhaust gas analyser (EGA), diesel smoke meter (DSM) and headlamp aim equipment), or where a repair has been carried out by welding, or there has been a repair to the steering or braking system (excluding stop lamps), provided that the re-test is carried out by the same tester at the same MoT garage before the end of the 10th working day from the day of the initial test a partial re-test will be carried out and only half of the full test fee will be payable.
- Tier 3 Partial Re-test. Where a re-test does not require the use of a major piece of testing equipment, provided it is carried out at the same MoT garage before the end of the 10th working day from the day of the initial test, a half of the test fee will also be due.

Where any vehicle does not fall into tier 2 or 3 above, a full re-examination in accordance with tier 1 must be carried out. Only one partial re-examination is permissible per full examination.

Issue of Test Certificate

On completion of the test, if the vehicle is found to be in satisfactory condition and in compliance with the law, a plain paper test certificate (form VT20) is issued. Additionally, form VT20 is issued to indicate to the vehicle owner the general state of the vehicle and to point out components which may need attention in the future to keep it in good, safe working order. These points are referred to as 'advisory' points and do not require any immediate action to be taken, but should be noted by the owner. Comments on form VT20 are made against the following headings:

I Lighting equipment
II Steering and suspension
III Braking system
IV Tyres and wheels
V Seat belts
VI General items, including the start of any corrosion

Appeals

A vehicle owner can appeal if he is not satisfied with the result of the test. He must complete form VT17 and send it to the DVSA within 14 days of taking the test. Form VT17 is free to download from the GOV.UK website.

Production of Test Certificates

It may be necessary to produce a current, valid test certificate when taxing a vehicle to which the regulations apply, although most post offices can ascertain that the vehicle has a valid MoT electronically at the time of renewal, as can the DVLA when online renewals are requested. A police officer can still ask to see a vehicle test certificate. If the driver does not have it with him he can be asked to produce the certificate at a police station nominated by him within seven days. The police are also able to use a computerized system to electronically ascertain that the vehicle has a valid MoT.

Because MoT test certificates are now computerized and many people re-tax their cars and light vehicles online, the need for a paper copy of the MoT certificate is becoming less and less important.

Vehicle Defect Rectification Schemes

Operators of light vehicles (up to 3,500 kg gross weight) found on the road with non-endorsable minor vehicle defects (ie lights, wipers, speedometer, silencer, etc) in certain areas may be offered the VDRS procedure by the police force in that area who will issue a defect form but no prosecution will result if:

1. Arrangements are made for the repair of the defect within 14 days of the issue of the defect form.
2. The repaired vehicle and VDRS notice are presented to an MoT garage for examination and certification (usually by the use of a stamp) that the defects have been rectified.
3. The certificate is returned to the police within 14 days.

VDRS, which was introduced in 2012, is aimed at improving road safety and reducing the burden on the police of prosecuting motorists for minor offences that can be quickly rectified. However, failure to follow the procedure on receipt of a VDRS notice, or refusal to accept VDRS as a course of action, will result in prosecution and persistent offenders who are also operators will be reported to the Traffic Commissioner. Appeals are permitted under VDRS schemes.

NB: The Scottish VDRS Scheme allows 21 days for similar actions to be taken.

Vehicle Maintenance and Maintenance Records

16

The requirements of the Road Traffic Act 1988 for the annual testing of goods vehicles and trailers, the requirements of the current Construction and Use Regulations, and the parts of the Transport Act 1968 setting out the conditions relating to vehicle maintenance under which an 'O' licence will be granted create a situation whereby operators must ensure that their vehicles and trailers are always safe, are in a fit and roadworthy condition, and that their maintenance, vehicle inspection, daily checks and maintenance record systems meet the requirements laid down in the legislation.

In order for operators to meet these requirements they must maintain their vehicles and trailers (no matter how old they are) to a sufficiently high standard to enable them to pass the stringent annual goods vehicle test, which they should be able to do on the test day *and on every other day when they are on the road*. To be able to do this, an effective maintenance plan and ongoing maintenance regime needs to be in operation and, importantly, needs to work. It should be noted that operators applying for an O licence will be expected to demonstrate a maintenance plan in place for at least the coming six months, preferably 12 months. This plan can be a chart, graph or an electronic version but it is part of the application process and can also be checked during any subsequent visits by the DVSA and so it needs to be made available upon request.

The risk of the vehicle encountering a roadside check, or being on the operator's premises when DVSA examiners or the police decide to make an inspection, as they are empowered to do, is too great to take when the penalties for failure to maintain vehicles are so high. Besides the risk of heavy fines and adverse effects on the OCRS, there is the possibility that the operator may lose his 'O' licence since a satisfactory state of maintenance is one of the factors taken into account by the TC in considering applications and renewals for such licences.

Legislation, under EU Regulations 45/2014, 46/2014, and 47/2014, which came into force on 20 May 2014 (starting in 2017 and lasting until 2023) may further increase the requirements for satisfactory standards of roadworthiness, for UK vehicles, over the coming years, depending upon Brexit and whether or not the UK Government decides to adopt the later proposed changes. In addition, increasing standards of emissions controls are a factor for many cities and city areas.

Maintenance Advice

A DVSA team along with operator associations have produced a Code of Practice on vehicle maintenance for transport operators – *Guide to Maintaining Roadworthiness: Commercial Goods and Passenger Carrying Vehicles* – available from The Stationery Office, Traffic Area Offices and heavy goods vehicle testing stations and it can be freely downloaded from the DVSA or GOV.UK website or by simply typing 'DVSA Guide to Maintaining Roadworthiness' into a search engine. This was updated in November 2018. Additionally, there is the D*f*T's free guide *A Guide to Goods Vehicle Operators' Licensing* (reference GV74), which contains some specific advice on vehicle maintenance arrangements for licence applicants. The following notes are included as an appendix to the *Guide*.

There are two separate vehicle checks and inspections which should be carried out:

- daily/first use running checks;
- vehicle safety inspections and routine maintenance at set intervals, as determined by the TC, on items which affect vehicle safety, followed by repair of any faults.

Daily/first use running checks are normally carried out by drivers before a vehicle starts its daily journey or a driver first takes over a vehicle. They are checks on such basic items as engine oil, brakes, tyre pressures, warning instruments, lights, windscreen wipers and washers, and trailer coupling. These checks need to be comprehensive and effective and the types of check sheets required are available from trade associations and stationery suppliers.

Vehicle safety inspections and routine maintenance should be carried out at set intervals of either time and/or mileage, whichever occurs first. How often these inspections are done should be decided by the nature of the operator's business although the final decision or periodicity remains the prerogative of the Traffic Commissioners. A vehicle used on long-distance work will need inspecting at different intervals from one employed in heavy traffic on local work with frequent stops and starts. However, DVSA do recommend that trailers and vehicles over 12 years old should have a maximum period of six weeks between inspections irrespective of whether or not they have been used regularly since the last safety inspection or their annual mileage. In reality, six weeks is the normal periodicity. (This six-weekly period is the minimum period for trailers more than 12 years old.) That said, the *DVSA Guide to Maintaining Roadworthiness* does contain suggested set intervals and has a graph to help operators decide what intervals are most suitable for their own operation. The items inspected should include wheels, tyres, brakes, steering, suspension, lighting, and so on. More detailed information can be found in the DVSA's publication *The Heavy Goods Vehicle Inspection Manual* (available from The Stationery Office or online, see above). Vehicle checks and inspections are extra to a routine maintenance schedule. It is vital to the vehicle's safety that both types of checks and inspections are done.

Staff doing inspection checks must be competent and able to recognize faults they find, such as excessive wear of components. They should also be aware of the acceptable standard of performance and wear of parts. Trade associations offer regular inspections for their members' vehicles.

Records

Records must be kept of all safety inspections to show the history of each vehicle and made available to the authorities 'upon request'. These records must be kept for at least 15 months. If vehicles from several operating centres are inspected and repaired at a central depot, the records may be kept at that depot, although DVSA examiners are entitled to request inspection of records at the operating centres where vehicles are based.

If an outside garage does the inspections and repairs, you must still keep maintenance records and should make arrangements so that they can be made available, if required. You need to remember that, whoever inspects your fleet, you are responsible for the condition of any vehicle or trailer on your licence.

Maintenance records are now able to be kept in electronic form but, if they are, they must contain the same information as hard copy versions. Guidance can be found on trade association websites and at GOV.UK.

Facilities

These will depend on the number, size and types of vehicles to be inspected. It must be possible to have a covered area to inspect the underside of a vehicle with sufficient light and space to examine individual parts closely. Ramps, hoists or pits will usually be necessary, but may not be needed if the vehicles have enough ground clearance for a proper underside inspection to be made on hard-standing. Creeper boards, jacks, axle stands and small tools should be available.

As well as providing facilities for checking the underside of vehicles, operators should whenever possible use equipment for measuring braking efficiency and setting headlights. If many vehicles have to be inspected, it may be worthwhile providing a roller brake tester. Increasingly, where there may be problems with the maintenance standards relating to braking efficiency, the Traffic Commissioners will expect roller brake testing to become an integral part of future safety inspections.

Because of the need for suitable facilities, many small and medium-sized operators choose to have an external organization carry out the safety inspections. This decision has both positives and negatives in relation to sunken costs, downtime, prioritizing, etc, although safety inspections carried out as part of a dealership's 'fixed price' maintenance contract do allow operators some degree of certainty when costing future work (see below).

Drivers' Reports

Daily/first use checks require drivers to report vehicle faults to whoever is responsible for having them put right. The maintenance system should allow for these reports, which must be recorded in writing either by the driver himself or by the person responsible for maintaining the vehicle, to briefly describe the fault and contain a section to record who repaired the defect and when. Owner-drivers must note faults as they arise and keep these notes as part of their maintenance record. Defects recorded by drivers using vehicle check sheets must form a part of the vehicle's maintenance record and be retained for 15 months.

Nil returns, where the driver finds no faults during their daily check, need to be kept 'for as long as they are required'. DVSA recommend that this period should be the period between periodic safety inspections (usually six weeks).

Hired Vehicles and Trailers

In the case of hired, rented or borrowed vehicles or those belonging to other operators used in inter-working arrangements, it is the user who is responsible for their mechanical condition on the road. If disciplinary action is taken as a result of a mechanical fault, it is against the user's licence, not the company from whom the vehicle is hired, or the owner.

As a rule of thumb, if a vehicle is hired in with a driver then the company employing the driver is the 'user'. If a vehicle is hired in without a driver then the company hiring in the vehicle will be the 'user'.

The Choice: To Repair or Contract Out

The first decision an operator has to make when planning his vehicle maintenance is to determine whether it is to be carried out in his own workshops, by his own staff or whether it is to be contracted out to a repair garage. The size of the fleet and what existing facilities and premises he already has will usually determine the method to be used. It is unlikely to be an economic proposition for a very small operator with a fleet of fewer than five or six vehicles to establish his own workshop unless he actually does the work himself. On the other hand it is unlikely to be an economic proposition for a large operator to contract out the work. There are, however, many examples in industry where the opposites apply, and very successfully too; so it remains very much a matter for operators to assess their own requirements, balance out the costs of the alternatives and make arrangements accordingly.

Choice of Repairer

When choosing a repairer to do the work preference should be given to a garage which is a main distributor for the make of vehicle operated or an agent for that make of vehicle. The reason for this, in addition to this often forming a part of the warranty, is that such a firm, as part of its arrangement with the manufacturer it represents, will have had to send some of its mechanics to the factory for training in the repair and servicing of that particular make of vehicle. This ensures that skilled staff are working on the vehicle. Moreover, the distributors are also usually required by the manufacturer to hold considerable stocks of spare parts, with a predominance of fast-moving items. By using such a garage the risk of a vehicle being kept off the road waiting for spare parts is therefore considerably reduced, and since vehicle downtime is a heavy cost burden these days this is an important consideration. It is also true that many leasing agreements will insist that the vehicle is maintained by one of the dealer network facilities as a term of the lease, if not the actual manufacturer's warranty. If a garage of this type is not available locally and a second choice has to be made, this should be a firm which is experienced in heavy vehicle repair work and which has suitably trained staff and the necessary equipment. A garage which normally only handles motor car repair work should not be used, to ensure that work done is completed by staff with suitable heavy vehicle experience and knowledge.

There is a DVSA voluntary scheme which many repairers have signed up to. This scheme gives each repairer a 'repairer's identity number' and the numbers of passed and failed vehicles taken for annual test by that repairer are recorded as a percentage score. This allows good repairers to advertise higher than average scores in order to advertise their high standards. When considering a repairer it is good practice to ask if they have signed up to this scheme and, if so, for them to declare their percentage score.

Repair Arrangements

Any arrangements made with a repairer must be in writing. The 'O' licence application form requests that copies of any maintenance contract and copies of the inspection sheets to be used should be sent with the application but in any event the TC will want to know what arrangements have been made with a repairer and will need to see all the forms the repairer intends to use and all paperwork confirming that the maintainer in question will maintain the vehicles in question. All this paperwork will need to be submitted every time a maintainer is changed and a new maintainer takes over the fleet. Verbal arrangements or the practice of sending vehicles in for repair as necessary on an ad hoc basis are not acceptable to the TCs, some of whom have said that a verbal agreement for these purposes is no agreement at all.

Maintenance Agreements

The agreement should include provisions for the repairer to be responsible for supplying the operator with suitable records of the inspections and repair work carried out. The operator should ensure that he can escape reasonably quickly and easily from any agreement in the event of the standard of work deteriorating and thereby placing his 'O' licence at risk.

Care should be taken when discussing or making an agreement that the repairer is aware of the consequences of any negligent action on his part on the livelihood of the operator, remembering that it is the vehicle 'user' who remains responsible at all times for the safe and satisfactory mechanical condition of the vehicle, and it is he or she who is responsible for keeping and producing records of vehicle inspections and other maintenance work.

There is no standard or recommended form of maintenance agreement in universal use; it is left to the parties concerned to agree on terms.

NB: A suitable format for agreements is suggested by the DfT in its Guide to Maintaining Roadworthiness. *A copy of a suitable agreement is also included in the 'O' licence application pack and is available online on the GOV.UK website.*

The agreement should clearly set out in detail the work to be done, the intervals at which it is to be done, the responsibilities of the operator and the garage, the form which records should take and the action to be taken if defects are discovered or repairs over a certain value are found to be necessary.

Maintenance Contracts

In recent years there has been a proliferation of contract maintenance schemes, many of them offered by truck manufacturers who are looking to retain future business. However, the advice given in this chapter remains relevant even with such sophisticated schemes. It is worth pointing out here that no matter how good the contract scheme or how reputable and reliable the repairer, it remains the responsibility of the operator to ensure that vehicles are in a fit, serviceable and safe condition when on the road and that they comply fully with the law. (This is covered in more detail later in the chapter.)

Some of the prominent commercial vehicle repair specialists offer contract maintenance schemes. There are usually a number of options in such schemes which, for instance, give the operator a choice of having his vehicles inspected only at set intervals; inspected and serviced according to the manufacturer's recommendations; or inspected, serviced and all repair work carried out (excluding damage caused by the vehicle having been involved in an accident), including the supply of materials except for such things as tyres and batteries.

The charges (both labour and materials) for the various options are usually incorporated in the contracts and these remain fixed for the period of the contract with a clause which enables the garage to make additional charges if the vehicle exceeds, by a large margin, the mileage estimated by the operator at the time of negotiating the contract. The additional charges are usually based on the excess mileage at an agreed figure per mile.

In offering a fixed charge agreement to include all normal repair work, the garage is dependent to quite an extent on the good faith of the operator in using his vehicles in a manner which is not likely to involve the garage in excessive costs above what may be normally estimated in advance. Again, a clause may be included in the contract stating that additional charges will be raised for the repair of damage or defects because of misuse by the owner.

If a full maintenance contract under one of these schemes is negotiated, the garage usually accepts the responsibility for ensuring that the vehicle is always in a fully roadworthy condition, able to pass through DVSA roadside checks and pass its annual test without difficulty. In the event of a vehicle getting a PG9 prohibition for defects, the operator has some grounds for a claim against the garage but, unfortunately, he has no defence to present to the TC if he is called to explain why the vehicle was not maintained to the required standard because of the condition of 'O' licensing which makes the vehicle user totally responsible for the condition of his vehicles on the road (see below).

The garage offering a full fixed-price contract maintenance scheme will prefer, wherever possible, to negotiate a contract for a vehicle from the day it is new because, in addition to securing warranty conditions, it is much easier to plan and cost the amount of work likely to be necessary for an estimated annual mileage and the spare parts required.

The effective working of a contract agreement needs the cooperation of both parties if it is to be successful. Operators may feel that in return for paying the garage a fixed price for full maintenance they are left with little responsibility. But they must make it their business to ensure that whatever other considerations may be pressing, a vehicle is sent to the garage when it is required if the contract is one in which the garage calls the vehicle in at specified intervals for the work to be done.

Although armed with what appears to be a fair agreement with a reputable repairer, operators should not become complacent. It is strongly recommended that wherever possible they should arrange for a physical check of the work that the repairer claims to have carried out. While this is not to suggest that a repairer is likely to claim to have done work that he knows has not been done, it must be remembered what is at stake and an operator should therefore doubly check the quality of the work. Operators also need to be aware that, if they use a particularly busy facility and the regular safety inspections are not taking place exactly as stated for operator licensing purposes, it is the operator who may have to explain to the DVSA or Traffic Commissioner (TC) why things are not as they should be.

Operators must be aware that any change of repairer or maintenance provider is a notifiable change to the operator's licence and the TC must be informed 'as soon as possible'. The TC will want to see any new contract and the new forms to be used. In any event, failure to notify the TC, within 28 days of any change, may lead to disciplinary action being taken by the TC against the operating company.

Contract Maintenance Schemes

A number of package contract maintenance schemes are available to operators. Whichever they choose, if indeed they choose any, will depend on a number of considerations: the make of the vehicles they own, the trade association to which they belong, the availability of a suitable repairer, etc.

Freight Transport Association Maintenance Services

Under the FTA quality control maintenance inspection service member operators contract to have their vehicles inspected one or more times a year by Association inspectors (only skilled and highly experienced people are appointed) to see that they meet the requirements of the law. The inspections can be used by operators either as a second check on their own inspection and maintenance system, or as the sole means of inspection of their vehicles to comply with the law in this respect; the actual maintenance work being carried out by their own staff. Alternatively, the scheme can be used as a means of checking the standard of maintenance work carried out by a repair garage or agent. The FTA also provide ad hoc inspections should an operator require one for some reason, particularly where an operator may be in dispute with a maintenance provider.

The FTA vehicle check system is not purely a maintenance scheme as such. It is an inspection and maintenance advisory service available to Association members as a do-it-yourself scheme using the documents, checklists and advice provided.

It can include contract inspections of vehicles by a qualified inspector, although the company may need a suitable location for the inspections to be carried out.

After carrying out a vehicle check, the inspector completes a checklist indicating whether items are satisfactory, within reasonable tolerances, or whether attention is needed. When the inspector returns to carry out the next check on the vehicle he will expect to see that his previous recommendations have been followed. If they have not, the operator is told that there is little point in paying for a service which is not being used to its fullest advantage.

Following the experience of many operators who have received PG9s on brand new vehicles, the FTA also offers a service whereby it will conduct a full inspection of a brand new vehicle before it goes into service. One of the obvious advantages of this independent check is that it provides the operator with evidence to support claims to the vehicle supplier and manufacturer for new vehicles delivered in faulty condition.

Responsibility for Maintenance

The major point to remember when making any arrangements with a garage is that it is the operator (ie the vehicle 'user' – see p 17 for definition), not the repairer, who remains responsible for the mechanical condition of the vehicle, even where defects are due to negligence by the repairer. This point cannot be over-stated as it is extremely important and often causes problems for many operators who fail to appreciate it. *A Guide to Goods Vehicle Operators' Licensing (GV74)* is available on the GOV.UK website or from the Central Licensing Office, Hillcrest House, 386 Harehills Lane, Leeds LS9 6NF (email: enquiries@otc.gsi.gov.uk; tel: 0300 123 9000; fax: 0113 249 8142).

However the following warning is given:

> *Operators who contract out their inspections and maintenance work are still the legal 'users' of their vehicles and as such will be held fully responsible by the TC for the arrangements they make and the condition of their vehicles. If either are unsatisfactory it is the operator's licence and OCRS which will be placed in jeopardy.*

The same responsibility applies in the case of vehicles hired without drivers and trailers even if the hire company, as part of the agreement, carries out the inspection and repair work.

Responsibility for Records

As mentioned earlier, operators are also responsible for ensuring that proper records of maintenance work are kept. Even if the repairer makes the records and holds them on file it is up to the operator to ensure, first, that they are properly kept with all the necessary information recorded and, second, that they are retained on file and available for inspection, for a minimum period of 15 months. In completing the 'O' licence application 'undertakings' the vehicle operator promises to 'keep records'. This can be interpreted as meaning that the operator keeps the record rather than the repair garage keeping it on his behalf (see also Chapter 16). This point is often argued by maintainers who prefer to keep all documentation under their own control. However, in the event of a serious problem when the records are required 'immediately' by the police or DVSA officials, if they are some miles away at a closed facility there may be a problem relating to an inability to 'produce upon request'.

Negligence by Repairers

Unfortunately, however satisfactory the arrangements made with a garage may be in other ways, there is very little that operators can do contractually to protect themselves completely from negligence on the part of the repairer or the repairer's employees. This means that should action be taken by the Traffic Commissioner in relation to poor maintenance standards, the operator may be able to use an admission by the garage as 'mitigation' but it will not ensure that action is not taken against the operator. In any case, it is unlikely that the repairer would agree to be party to a contract in which he has fully to indemnify the operator against failure of his employees to carry out work to a required standard, even though he may agree that morally he should be held responsible (moral responsibility, incidentally, has no standing in law). Moreover, most small operators are not likely to be in a position to have sufficiently persuasive powers to get the repairer to agree to such terms.

Operators have no protection against poor workmanship other than relying on the reputation of the garage. However, if they are members of one of the trade associations (the FTA for own-account operators and the RHA for haulage contractors) they could try to enlist their help in pressing a claim.

In-House Repairs

The advantages of operators having their own workshop and being able to do their own safety inspections and repairs are many, provided that sufficient vehicles are operated to justify the overheads involved. Principal among them is that by employing the staff they become particularly familiar with the vehicles under their charge and the operator has direct control over the work carried out, the standard of the work and the record keeping which is so important.

If operators provide their own maintenance facilities they must be of a suitable standard, although once again no specific details are given in the regulations. The main requirement is for a covered area with hard-standing and facilities including adequate lighting for conveniently inspecting the underside of vehicles. Ideally this means that either a pit in the ground or a hydraulic lift should be provided. The former is the most commonly used and it is very much the cheaper of the two alternatives. Suitable lighting, either fixed in the pit shining upwards to the underside of the vehicles or by means of portable inspection lamps, is necessary.

The remainder of the tools and machines with which a workshop should be equipped are left entirely to the operator's choice, but such items as a 'rolling road' and beam-setter are useful to check that vehicles comply with the test requirements. There must also be some sort of system that ensures exhaust fumes are extracted from the building and that air quality is maintained. Where an operator does not have these facilities some elect to use 'rolling roads', etc at larger external maintenance facilities. Servicing equipment such as jacks, high-pressure greasing equipment, high-pressure washing or steam-cleaning equipment make maintenance work much less of a chore. Hand tools are, of course, essential and in general the better the equipment available (including the availability of the special tools and diagnostic equipment often needed to carry out work on today's sophisticated vehicles) the more likelihood there is of the work meeting the required standard.

Whilst there may be many advantages of in-house repairs, including prioritization of jobs, fleet familiarization, less downtime, overall control, etc, other issues in relation to the initial investment required, health and safety issues, training of staff, warranty validity, space taken for the facility and management and control of the facility all need to be factored in by any operator considering undertaking in-house repairs. Again, all forms used will need to be submitted when applying for an 'O' licence.

Vehicle Inspections

Vehicle inspections are an essential part of the maintenance programme, and legislation covers this aspect. Section 74 of the Road Traffic Act 1988 requires operators of goods vehicles to have them regularly inspected by a 'suitably qualified person' to ensure that they comply with Construction and Use Regulations (Chapter 12) and, of course, it is in the operator's best interests to have vehicles regularly inspected to ensure that they are kept in a fully safe and roadworthy mechanical condition.

Frequency of Inspection

Legislation does not specify the intervals at which vehicles should be inspected, what form the inspection should take or what is meant by a 'suitably qualified person'. In the case of the first-mentioned, it is very much a question of the type of operation on which the vehicle is used and a guide can be found in the *Guide to Maintaining Roadworthiness*. A tipping vehicle, for example, which spends much of its time on rough sites, with perhaps a fairly high mileage on the road as well, may need to be inspected at least every fortnight. The same applies to a vehicle which, although it remains on normal roads, is used on multi-shift work and does perhaps 1,500–2,000 miles a week. On the other hand, a six or, under rare circumstances, an eight-weekly inspection may be quite sufficient for a local delivery vehicle doing low weekly mileages on good roads and spending a great deal of its time standing while deliveries are being made, whilst older vehicles are bound by a six-week rule (see above).

An operator's own experience of their type of operation should indicate the intervals between which wear and tear takes place and defects become apparent. It has even been suggested that vehicles standing out of use in depots should be checked at least every six weeks. Although there is some suggestion that inspection intervals can be based on either a time or miles/km alternative it is clear that the TCs will not accept anything other than a time-based frequency from 'O' licence applicants. Traffic Commissioners will make the actual decision of the time between periodic inspections even though the operator suggests a time on the 'O' licence application form. The DVSA Code of Practice on vehicle maintenance also recommends that the normal maximum time interval between safety inspections should be six weeks with no mileage alternative. It also states that operators must have planning flow charts, either hard copy or electronic, covering at least the safety inspections due for the next six months, and preferably the next 12-monthly periods, to indicate when vehicle safety inspections are due. This requirement will be checked on any inspection carried out by either a DVSA official, or during a transport office audit check carried out by the FTA or an external consultant.

Items for Inspection

A full list of the items to be inspected at regular intervals is not laid down in regulations but it is obviously necessary that the inspection at the very least covers all the items set out in *The Heavy Goods Vehicle Inspection Manual* (see p 473), with particular emphasis on those items (eg brakes, steering, wheels, tyres, suspension systems and lights) that have special relevance to the safe operation of the vehicle. Tyres on vehicles used on site work or on local delivery work should receive particularly careful examination for damage.

The Inspector

There are no specified qualifications for a 'suitably qualified' vehicle inspector. Clearly, the most obvious one is wide experience in the repair of heavy commercial vehicles. A person with such experience would know where and how to look for wear and for defects and would recognize the symptoms of hidden faults, such as uneven tyre wear indicating that the steering is out of alignment or that kingpins or wheel bearings are worn.

It is possible, however, to train a person specifically as a vehicle inspector, and this is being done in the industry through schemes run by organizations such as the FTA and the Society of Operations Engineers (SOE) who offer IRTEC licensing schemes. The emphasis in training in such cases must be on following a predetermined list, such as *The Heavy Goods Vehicle Inspection Manual*, examining every individual item carefully and methodically, testing the wear in components and measuring the tolerances of moving parts accurately.

It is desirable, although not a legal requirement, that the person carrying out the vehicle inspection should not be expected to carry out repairs, however small, at the time of making the inspection. To have to do this would cause a lack of concentration and could lead to other items being missed if repairs took up too much of the inspector's time. In the case of an owner-driver carrying out his own inspections and repairs this can be a difficult situation and in such instances it is useful to have the work verified and an audit-type check carried out by an outside agency, such as the FTA, to ensure that the vehicle is kept up to a high standard.

Authority to Stop Use of Vehicles

The inspector, besides being suitably qualified and experienced to spot defects, should be given the authority to prevent a vehicle being taken on the road in the event of a serious or potentially dangerous defect being found. In order to prevent use the inspector may need to immobilize the vehicle or use an 'Out of Service' placard.

Vehicle Servicing

Regular servicing as opposed to specific inspections and repairs is another important part of vehicle maintenance and as such it should be carried out with unfailing regularity at predetermined intervals of time or mileage. The importance of servicing cannot be too highly emphasized for three reasons: first, because many warranties and leasing agreements insist on the service intervals; second, the vehicle must meet the requirements of the law; and third, because operators will benefit by always having their vehicles ready for work and able to carry out a job without breakdowns and delays. It also increases the life of the working parts and consequently of the whole vehicle as well as reducing downtime costs and disrupted delivery schedules.

The intervals at which servicing should be carried out are left to the owner's discretion (unless there are requirements under warranty terms, etc) depending on the work on which the vehicle is employed, in much the same way as the intervals for inspection are decided. To give owners some guidance, however, vehicle manufacturers usually provide a service schedule which owners can use in their own workshop or which their agent will use when vehicles are sent in for servicing. A useful guide to service intervals is 5,000/6,000-mile services carried out at least monthly with more extensive services at 15,000/20,000-mile/three-monthly intervals and 30,000/40,000-mile/six-monthly intervals. Progressively, service intervals are being extended with the use of longer-life components, sealed units and particularly improved filters and lubricating oils, which can go for very much longer periods these days without detriment to their lubricating properties.

In all cases, servicing should try to be aligned with safety inspections and the annual test, whenever possible, in order to reduce vehicle downtime and costs.

Cleaning of Vehicles

Particular reference is made in the instructions to operators submitting vehicles for DVSA heavy goods vehicle tests, that those which are not sufficiently clean will be refused the test. Again, it is difficult to specify a standard of cleanliness for the underside of a vehicle, but the main point is that all the components listed for the examination must be easily visible so that inspectors can see without difficulty if wear or damage exists. To achieve and keep a suitable standard of cleanliness it is desirable for vehicles to be washed with either a steam cleaner or a high-pressure water washer at regular intervals and certainly immediately before they are taken to the test station. The need to provide clean vehicles for test is further hampered during adverse weather conditions where snow, slush and salt spray may rapidly build up under the vehicle.

If the maintenance of the vehicles is contracted out to a garage on a maintenance scheme, the operator should arrange either for the garage to clean the vehicle before inspection or for one of the many specialist vehicle cleaners to do it. Where specialist cleaners are used, the operator may need to check to ensure that the 'run off' water is not acting as a pollutant in order to remove the risk of possible prosecution under environmental legislation.

Enforcement of Maintenance Standards

There has been increasing concern in recent times about the standards of vehicle maintenance. As a result of this concern, and through the use of the OCRS system, and the increasing numbers of foreign vehicles entering the UK, the DVSA has stepped up the levels of checking on vehicles by enforcement staff, particularly at night and at weekends. The purpose of these additional checks is to be able to check vehicles operating outside normal working hours – many legitimately but some possibly deliberately running the gauntlet – and to enforce the safe operation of foreign goods vehicles visiting the UK. The checks also allow the DVSA to take action against foreign operators and drivers who do not comply with the required standards, and through non-compliance, often seek to distort the transport market by unfair means.

Maintenance Records

There is a legal requirement under the Road Traffic Act 1988 for goods vehicle operators to keep records of maintenance work carried out on their vehicles. When completing form GV79, 'O' licence application, operators have to make the statutory 'declaration of intent' in which they promise to fulfil undertakings made at that time throughout the duration of the 'O' licence. A number of items in the declaration of intent relate to maintenance records. From this can be determined what records are needed by law.

In the declaration of intent the operator promises to ensure that the following records will be kept:

- safety inspections;
- routine maintenance;
- repairs to vehicles.

A promise is also made that drivers will report 'safety faults' in their vehicles 'as soon as possible' and the TCs insist that these reports should be in writing and therefore they become part of the vehicle record-keeping system. The operator promises to keep all these records, except daily check nil returns (as mentioned earlier), for a minimum period of 15 months and to make them available on request by DVSA examiners or the TC.

Driver Reports of Vehicle Faults

It is a specific requirement (and part of the declaration of intent on an 'O' licence application form) that arrangements must be made for drivers to have a proper means of reporting 'safety faults' (ie defects) in the vehicle they are driving as soon as possible. As already mentioned, the TCs expect these defect reports to be made in writing, not verbally. The trade associations (RHA and FTA) supply books which are in a format approved by the DVSA. Ideally, the report should be made either on an individual form which is completed and handed in by the driver, or in a defect book reserved for recording defects found on a vehicle which is kept in a convenient place where all drivers have easy access to it, and where whoever is responsible for ensuring that repair work is carried out can also easily reach it. To reiterate, it has been made abundantly clear that verbal reporting of defects is not in itself a system acceptable to the TCs.

Whichever written method is used it is important that the driver gives as much information and uses reasonable language about what is wrong in order to help the fitter make a repair as quickly as possible and that the repair of the defects is recorded on the form or in the book by a note of the work done and the signature of the person who has done it (see also under repair records). It is also important for operators to ensure that whatever system of defect reporting is used, they make regular checks on drivers and repair staff to see that the procedure is being followed correctly. This requirement has been pointed out by the TCs on a number of occasions. Using separate pads of defect sheets is the best alternative and where these can be made out in duplicate they provide the driver with his own copy of the report for future reference.

Systems of defect reporting which rely on a centrally located defect book are open to the risks of drivers forgetting to report defects when they return to base. If a driver's attention is distracted by his manager who wants to talk to him, for example, just as he is about to report a defect, the defect may not be reported and another driver may take the vehicle out the next day with a defect which could result in a prohibition notice being issued in a roadside check. A driver may also forget to report a defect when he returns late from a journey and is in a rush to get home or if he cannot find the defect book.

It is the operator's responsibility to make sure that the system used is infallible in all these circumstances, first because it is an offence to fail to cause the defect to be reported and second because the vehicle could be found on the road subsequently with a safety fault either not reported or not repaired. Many operators require drivers to hand in the daily check sheet book with the vehicle keys at the end of a shift and check all the books to ensure that no existing defects are overlooked. It is the control of vehicle keys which is an important element in an effective defect reporting scheme as vehicles carrying safety defects must be made inaccessible to drivers until the defect is cleared.

Where a driver checks the vehicle as part of a 'first use' or daily vehicle check and no defects are found, the check sheet still needs to be filled in and returned to the transport office for retention. However, 'nil returns' such as these are only required to be retained for 'as long as they are useful'. This term is generally accepted by the DVSA to be, as a minimum, the same time as the period between the vehicle's safety inspections (six weeks, etc).

Drivers' tachograph records should clearly indicate the time spent on their 'walk round' checks prior to taking a vehicle on the road. Where such records show drivers to have commenced driving immediately on starting their shift it will be interpreted by the DVSA that they have not carried out the 'walk round' check as required; or if they claim to have carried out the check:

- they have not made an accurate record; or
- they have falsified their record.

In any event, they will have committed one or more offences.

Defect Repair Sheets

Besides ensuring that proper records are kept of vehicle safety fault reports made by drivers and of regular safety inspections, the operator must also keep a record showing that any defects reported or found on inspection are rectified in order to keep the vehicle in a fit, serviceable and safe condition. Records of such repairs may be added to the driver defect report or the inspection report to provide combined records, or a separate repair or job sheet may be used. The important points about repair records are, first, that they should show comprehensive details of the actual repair work carried out, identifying components which were repaired or replaced and new parts added and who carried out the repair (printed name) and 'signed it off'. Secondly, there should be a matching repair sheet for every defect reported or found on inspection so that the vehicle examiners, when they visit to examine records, can see the report of the defect and then subsequently a report of the repair work carried out to rectify it. Reports of defects which do not have a corresponding repair record can arouse suspicion in the examiner's mind that perhaps the necessary repair has not been carried out and that the defect still exists. This is a good reason for him then to consider examining that vehicle, or perhaps the whole fleet.

Inspection Reports

The Road Traffic Act 1988 requires that records of regular periodic safety inspections to vehicles must be made. For this purpose the vehicle inspector (see p 482) should have a sheet on which are listed all the items to be inspected (preferably in accordance with the contents of *The Heavy Goods Vehicle Inspection Manual*).

The inspection sheet should identify the necessary items for inspection with a cross-check reference number to the *Inspection Manual* to enable, if necessary, full details of the method of inspection of that item – and the reason for its rejection as not being within acceptable limits – to be determined. The sheet should have provision for the inspector to mark against each item whether it is 'serviceable' or 'needs attention' and space to comment on defects for immediate rectification and other items for attention at a future date or on which a watch should be kept if attention is not required immediately. The form should contain space for the inspector to print and sign his name and add the date.

Service Records

In addition to the records of defects and vehicle inspections which have to be kept, a record should also be kept of all other work carried out on the vehicle, whether it is repair or replacement of working parts or normal servicing (oil changes and greasing, etc). These may be very useful in cases where the terms of warranty may be a factor.

Repair Records from Garages

When vehicle safety inspections, servicing and repair work are carried out for the operator by repair garages, the operator should obtain from the garage comprehensive documentation to enable him to meet the legal requirements detailed above. In many cases DVSA examiners are quite happy if the garage retains the records of inspection and repair, so long as they can be made available for examination when required. The operator must be certain, in these instances, that the garage is keeping proper records (for a period of 15 months) which satisfy the legal requirements and that they are being kept available for inspection, not bundled away out of easy reach in a store with thousands of others.

In the event of failure of the garage to keep records as required, the operator's licence would be at risk but there would be no penalty imposed on the garage. On the form GV79 undertaking the operator promised that he would 'make proper arrangements so that records are kept (for 15 months) of all driver defect reports, safety inspections, routine maintenance and repairs to vehicles and trailers and these are made available on request'.

It is important to note that in this respect, invoices, or copies of invoices from garages, for repair work are not in themselves sufficient to satisfy the record-keeping requirement. It is the actual inspection sheet and repair sheets, or photocopies of them, which are needed because of the greater and more precise detail which they contain.

Maintenance records and even forward maintenance planning are now increasingly being kept as computer records. This is deemed acceptable by the DVSA providing that full and detailed records are stored and can be made available 'upon request'.

Location of Records

Where companies hold operators' licences in a number of separate Traffic Areas the maintenance records for the vehicles under each licence should be kept in the area covered by the individual licence (preferably at the vehicle operating centre). With the sanction of the local TC, records may be kept centrally at a head office or central vehicle workshop, although the vehicle examiners may ask for them to be produced for inspection at the operating centre of the vehicles in the Traffic Area – probably giving three days' to one week's notice to enable the records to be obtained from the central files as opposed to producing 'upon request'.

Planning Charts

While it is not strictly a legal requirement, the DVSA like to see operators using wall planning charts (see note above about use of flow charts in accordance with the DVSA Code of Practice on vehicle maintenance) to provide a visual reminder of important dates such as:

- vehicle/trailer due for inspection;
- vehicle/trailer due for service;
- vehicle/trailer due for annual test;
- excise duty due.

Increasingly DVSA examiners now encounter the forward planning chart in an electronic version stored on a computer. In these cases the electronic chart must also be readily available if requested. Such charts, in either format, usually provide facilities for a whole year's recording of these items for the fleet (either shown by vehicle registration number or by fleet number). DVSA inspectors recommend that a minimum of six months' forward planning for vehicle inspections is available for them to see when carrying out site visits, but prefer to see 12 months' forward planning.

Vehicle History Files

A system of vehicle history files – one for each vehicle and trailer in the fleet – is a usual way of retaining a vehicle's records. They provide a facility for keeping all relevant records relating to individual vehicles and trailers together and in one place and a historic view that can highlight repeating problems and the numbers of problems and costs related to individual vehicles. Individual files can have all the important details of the vehicle/trailer on the front cover for easy reference. When a vehicle or trailer is sold, the vehicle history file (or copy) is normally required by the new owner but the seller needs to retain copies of the records even when vehicles are removed from the 'O' licence (as stated in the DVSA *Guide to Maintaining Roadworthiness*).

Safety – Vehicle, Loads and at Work

17

Transport operators, along with all other sectors of business and industry, are under constant pressure to become ever more conscious of the need for safety in their operations, in the provision of facilities for their employees, and in the way their employees work and conduct themselves on work premises. Predominantly, this is still influenced by the demands of the Health and Safety at Work Act 1974, and a subsequent barrage of legislation and the stringent requirements which it imposes on employers and employees alike covering all aspects of work and work related activities. But in transport, the requirements of the Road Vehicles (Construction and Use) Regulations 1986 (as amended) and the Road Traffic Act 1988, regarding the safety of vehicles and loads, place additional legal burdens on operators and drivers. The problems of safe loading and avoidance of vehicle overloading are not new, although there is new guidance on load safety and security within the D*f*T booklet, *Safety of Loads on Vehicles*, which is free to download from the GOV.UK website. This document is supported by increased enforcement activity, and the need for ever more efficient use of vehicles has accelerated concern in these areas. There is concern also on the wider front of safety in load handling and in the use of loading aids (forklift trucks for example) and with regard to vehicle manoeuvring in depots and works premises, which alone results in many workplace deaths and injuries annually. Further, whilst it is accepted that the UK will leave the EU, there is more detailed advice and best practice information in the EU publication *European Best Practices Guidelines on Cargo Securing for Road Transport*, which can be found on the EU publications website https://publications.europa.eu (archived at https://perma.cc/AFN3-5WU6).

According to the HSE, 147 workers were killed in 2018/19 which demonstrates far from satisfactory levels of safety at work. In addition, some 71,062 injuries were reported under The Reporting of Injuries, Diseases and Dangerous Occurrences Regulations 2013 (RIDDOR). Many other workers are forced to leave work each year and are unable to work again due to neglect of proper health and safety management procedures. According to the HSE, being struck by a moving vehicle is one of the most common causes of fatal injury among workers working where vehicles are used.

C&U Requirements

The Road Vehicles (Construction and Use) Regulations 1986 require that all vehicles and trailers, and all their parts and accessories, and the weight, distribution, packing and adjustment of their loads, shall be such that no danger is caused or likely to be caused to any person in or on the vehicle or trailer or on the road. Additionally, no motor vehicle or trailer must be used for any purpose for which it is so unsuited as to cause or be likely to cause danger or nuisance to any person in or on the vehicle or trailer or on the road.

Under the regulations, provisions relating particularly to bulk and loose loads make it an offence if a load causes a nuisance as well as a danger to other road users and such loads must be secured, if necessary by physical restraint, to stop them falling or being blown from a vehicle.

These regulations include two notable terms relating to load safety: one is the use of the term 'nuisance' in addition to the term 'danger' so that to commit an offence the operator does not have to go so far as causing danger; merely causing nuisance is sufficient to land him in trouble. The other term is 'physical restraint', which clearly implies the need for sheeting and roping or strapping any load, such as sand or grain, hay and straw and even builders' skips carrying rubble that may be blown from the vehicle.

The Road Traffic Act 1988 further states that 'it is an offence to use a goods vehicle, or cause or permit it to be used when overloaded'. The maximum fine for doing so is set at £5,000.

The Safety of Loads on Vehicles

Load Securing: Vehicle Operator Guidance, published by the DVSA in 2015 and the new code, *Safety of Loads on Vehicles*, referenced above, published in February 2017, are available to download from the GOV.UK website. They both set out general requirements in regard to who is responsible for load securing, the issues related to poor load securing and the way that the DVSA respond to poor load security. They give advice on loading and carrying different types of loads and explain what the DVSA look for when they stop a loaded vehicle and how different types of load restraints can be used. Neither guide is meant to contradict, undermine or replace the other but they do cover some different areas, and the new guide does update some aspects.

Of particular note is the basic principle on which both Codes are based, which is that 'the combined strength of the load restraint system must be sufficient to withstand a force not less than the total weight of the load forward and half the weight of the load backwards and sideways'.

In general terms the guides focus on subjects such as weight distribution, using the correct vehicle for the loads to be moved, the correct securing equipment and techniques for the load in question, overloading causes and prevention, risk assessment of loading and unloading activities using trained loading staff and drivers and actions to be taken when problems or concerns arise.

Distribution of Loads

When loading a vehicle, care must be taken to ensure that the load is evenly distributed to ensure stability of the vehicle and to conform to the vehicle's individual axle weights as well as the overall gross weight, and is secure so it cannot move or transfer its weight during transit. It is important on multi-delivery work to make sure that when part of the load has been removed in the course of a delivery, none of the axles have become overloaded because of the transfer of weight. This can happen even though the gross vehicle weight is still within permissible maximum limits and in such cases it is necessary for the driver to attempt to correct the situation by shifting the load, or part of it.

All loads should be securely and safely fixed, roped/strapped and sheeted, and chained or lashed if necessary. It is an offence to have an insecure load or a load which causes danger to other road users. Furthermore, it is a legal requirement of the C&U Regulations that loads must not cause or be likely to cause a danger or nuisance to other road users and that they should be physically restrained (ie roped/strapped and sheeted) if necessary to avoid parts of the load falling or being blown from the vehicle.

It should also be noted that drivers that need to climb onto, or into, a vehicle to secure, or sheet, a load are subject to the Working at Height Regulations 2005. These regulations apply to any person who, whilst at work, may fall from a position above ground level and suffer personal injury. This means that there is a duty on employers and work controllers to ensure that:

- all work at height is properly planned and organized;
- persons working at height are competent to do so;
- the risks from work at height are assessed, and appropriate equipment is selected and used;
- the risks of working on or near fragile surfaces are properly managed;
- the equipment used for work at height is properly inspected and maintained.

These duties mean that many companies have had to construct gantries for drivers to use to access vehicle bodies and that 'easy-sheet' systems, capable of being operated from ground level, are now commonplace. In fact, many loading sites will not allow drivers to enter a vehicle body, even to 'sheet-up', and some quarries, etc will ban drivers who attempt to do this or prevent access to any vehicle not fitted with a suitable 'easy-sheet' system.

NB: Tipping vehicles (and others), which carry loose loads that could emit dust into the atmosphere, must be sheeted before travelling on the road under the separate provisions of the Environmental Protection Act 1990.

It is also an offence for the securing ropes, straps or other devices and sheets to flap and cause nuisance or danger to other road users. Heavy penalties, with maximum fines of up to £5,000, can be imposed on conviction for offences relating to these matters.

Axle Load Calculations

Imposed axle loads can be calculated to determine whether a vehicle is operating legally in particular circumstances by using the following method:

- Determine the vehicle wheelbase.
- Determine the weight of the load (ie payload).
- Determine the centre of gravity of the load from the front or rear axle, depending upon which axle load you require.

Once you have these the formula is:

$$\frac{\text{Weight of the load} \times \text{Distance of the centre of gravity of the load from the axle}}{\text{Wheelbase of the vehicle}}$$

It must be said that this formula relies on the centre of gravity of the load being able to be determined, which in many cases is not possible. However, for some bulk loads and/or large single items of a regular shape, the formula is very useful.

$$\text{Weight on rear axle} = \frac{\text{front load base}}{\text{wheelbase}} \times \text{payload}$$

$$\text{Weight on front axle} = \text{payload} - \text{weight on rear axle}$$

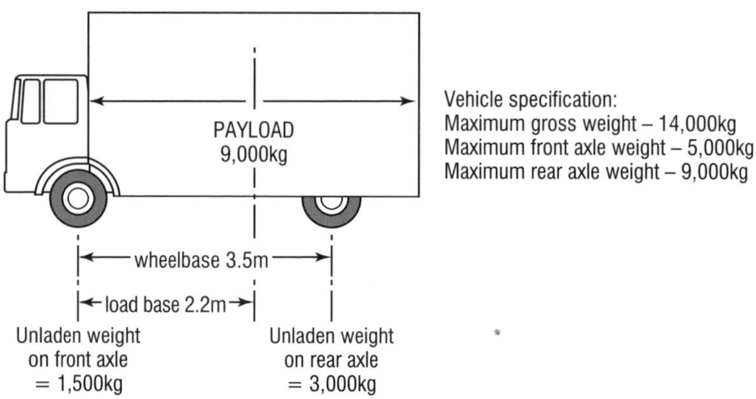

1. Rear axle weight calculation:

$$\frac{\text{front load base}}{\text{wheelbase}} \times \text{payload} = \text{payload weight on rear axle}$$

$$= \frac{2.2\text{m}}{3.5\text{m}} \times 9{,}000\text{kg} = 5{,}657\text{kg}$$

2. Front axle weight calculation:

Payload − rear axle weight = payload weight on front axle

9,000kg − 5,657kg = 3,343kg

3. Total vehicle weight distribution:

Rear axle: payload weight + rear axle unladen weight
= 5,657kg + 3,000kg = 8,657kg

Front axle: payload weight + front axle unladen weight
= 3,343kg + 1,500kg = 4,843kg

Road Safety

Government statistics show the following road casualties in Great Britain for the year ending June 2019: 1,782 people killed and 25,484 people seriously injured. In all, there were 160,378 casualties. The figures do not identify the numbers of goods vehicle driver or passenger casualties but do reflect an overall slight fall in all types of accidents.

Brake Campaigns

Vigorous campaigns to improve vehicle mechanical standards (especially in regard to heavy vehicle braking), reduce speed, improve safety awareness and reduce death on the road are being conducted by road safety charity Brake.

Brake has expanded its operations and work in recent years and now offers guidance and advice on a complete range of road safety issues. Brake also publishes a booklet called *Procedures Following a Death on the Road*, designed to help bereaved relatives and provide information on criminal prosecutions, claiming compensation and the way the police investigate a death on the road. Brake is particularly concerned about, and campaigning hard to eliminate, drivers using mobile phones and electronic devices whilst driving.

Brake can be contacted at brake@brake.org.uk or on 01484 559909.

Safety Reports

There are many work-related safety reports produced by the HSE based on studies of fatal accidents in industry indicating that motor vehicles are one of the biggest causes of industrial deaths. These motor vehicle-related deaths occur during vehicle loading, unloading, manoeuvring, maintenance and, of course, movement and are mainly caused by poor management, failure to provide safe working systems, 'corner cutting' and inadequate training.

Included in the reports are checklists which are intended to help transport operators and others to reduce unnecessary risks and dangers. The HSE also publish specific guides aimed at reducing risks and dangers in the workplace, which are free to download from the HSE website. Companies should use them to help examine their current practices and to institute new and safer procedures. The checklist (reproduced below with acknowledgement to the HSE) is only a general guide, and it is emphasized that safety requirements vary with different types of operation. *However, it is important to note that firms could face prosecution if they do not meet the minimum safety standards outlined in the list.*

This checklist is intended as a general guide only. It will not necessarily be comprehensive for every operation and all points will not be relevant for all work.

Organization, Systems and Training

- Have all health and safety aspects of the transport operation been assessed?
- Has an organization (and arrangements) for securing such safety been detailed in the safety policy?
- Has a person(s) been appointed to be responsible for the transport safety?
- Have risk assessments and safe systems of work been set up?
- Are all employees able to report safety incidents or issues?
- What monitoring is carried out to ensure that the systems are followed?
- Have all drivers been adequately trained and tested?
- Is there a satisfactory formal licensing or authorization system for drivers?
- Have all personnel been trained, informed and instructed about safe working practices where transport is involved?
- Is there an accident book and is it used?
- Are all accidents and near-misses reported?
- Is there sufficient supervision?
- What review procedures are in place?

External Roadways and Manoeuvring Areas

- Are they of adequate dimensions?
- Are they of good construction?
- Are they well maintained?
- Are they well drained?
- Are they scarified when smooth?
- Are they gritted, sanded, etc, when slippery?
- Are they kept free of debris and obstructions?
- Are they well illuminated?
- Are there sufficient and suitable road markings?
- Are there sufficient and suitable warning signs?
- Are there speed limits?
- Is there a one-way system (as far as possible)?
- Is there provision for vehicles to reverse where necessary?
- Is the area shared with cyclists?
- Are there pedestrian walkways and crossings?
- Are there barriers by exit doors leading on to roadways?
- Is there a separate vehicle parking area?
- Are there individual, clearly marked parking bays?

- Is there any storage positioned close to vehicle ways?
- Is the yard suitable for internal works transport, eg smooth surface, hard ground, no slopes?

Internal Transport

- Are internal roadways demarcated and separated where possible from pedestrian routes with crossings and priority signs?
- Are there separate internal doors for trucks and pedestrians? Have these vision panels?
- Are blind corners catered for by mirrors, etc?
- Are trucks kept apart from personnel where possible?
- Do the trucks use a satisfactory warning system?
- Are truck operators trained?
- Are trucks made unavailable for unauthorized use when not in use?

Vehicles

- Are all staff properly trained on new vehicles before being allowed to use them?
- Is there a maintenance programme for vehicles and mobile plant?
- Is there a fault reporting system?
- Are there regular checks to ensure that the vehicles are up to an acceptable standard?
- Are keys kept secure when vehicles and mobile plant are not in use?
- Are vehicles and mobile plant adequate and suitable for the work in hand?
- Is suitable access provided to elevated working places or vehicles?
- Are tractors and lift trucks equipped with protection to prevent the driver being hit by falling objects and from being thrown from his cab in the event of overturning?
- Are there any unfenced mechanical parts on vehicles, eg power take-offs?
- Are there fittings for earthing vehicles with highly flammable cargoes?
- Are loads correctly labelled (especially hazardous substances)?
- Are vehicles used to carry dangerous goods properly marked?
- Are the vehicles suitable for use in all the areas they enter?
- If passengers ride on vehicles, do they have a safe riding position?

NB: From 2020, vehicles entering London will need to meet 'Direct Vision' standards where nearside glass door panels will be required and improved all round vision will need to be available for the driver. There will be different 'star ratings' for vehicles depending upon the 'vision standard'. Operators who enter London should make themselves aware of dates for various requirements as these are fluid with the introduction currently planned to be phased in between 2020 and 2024.

Loading and Unloading

- Do loading positions obstruct other traffic? Do pedestrian ways need diverting?
- Are there special hazards, eg flammable liquid discharge? Do pedestrians need to be kept clear?
- Is there a yard manager to supervise the traffic operation, to control vehicular movement and to act as a banksman during reversing?
- Has he received satisfactory training? Does he use recognized signals, and has he cover during his absences?
- Are there loading docks? Will the layout prevent trucks falling off or colliding with objects or each other?
- Are there any mechanical hazards caused by dock levellers, etc?
- Are methods of loading and unloading assessed and drivers trained, as required?
- Are safe arrangements made for sheeting?
- Is there a pallet inspection scheme?
- Is PPE available, if required?

Motor Vehicle Repair

- Are appropriate arrangements made for tyre repair and inflation?
- Are arrangements made for draining and repair of fuel tanks?
- Is access available to elevated working positions?
- Are arrangements made to ensure brakes are applied and wheels checked?
- Is portable electrical equipment low voltage and properly earthed?
- Are moving vehicles in the workshop carefully controlled?
- Are vehicles supported on both jacks and axle stands where appropriate?
- Are engines only run with the brakes on and in neutral gear?
- Are raised bodies always propped?
- Are there systems in place for recycling/disposal?

As stated above, these points are general in nature but they may provide the basis for a company to begin to work up their own safety reports.

Health and Safety at Work

Stringent UK legislation on health and safety at work implements the EU's 'Framework Directive', namely EC Directive 391/1989. The overall objective of this Directive was to impose on employers a duty to encourage improvements in the health and safety of people at work.

The main legislation is contained in the Health and Safety at Work Act 1974, plus the regulations listed below – originally referred to as the 'six pack' – which were introduced to implement EC Directive 391/1989. Additionally, there are many other relevant provisions dealing with such matters as fire protection and safety signs. Collectively, this legislation largely replaced both the Factories Act 1961 and the Offices, Shops and Railway Premises Act 1963 which formerly applied.

- Management of Health and Safety at Work Regulations 1999;
- Workplace (Health, Safety and Welfare) Regulations 1992;
- Manual Handling Operations Regulations 1992;
- Health and Safety (Display Screen Equipment) Regulations 1992;
- Provision and Use of Work Equipment Regulations 1998;
- Personal Protective Equipment at Work Regulations 2002;
- Control of Substances Hazardous to Health (COSHH) Regulations 2002, 2003 and 2004;
- Reporting of Injuries, Diseases and Dangerous Occurrences Regulations 2013 (RIDDOR).

Additionally, there are others, including regulations such as the Lifting Operations and Lifting Equipment Regulations 1998, etc.

NB: A full list of all Statutory Instruments owned or enforced by the HSE is available on their website.

The Health and Safety at Work Act 1974

Since the original introduction of the Health and Safety at Work Act 1974 employers have had to take positive steps to draw up policy statements regarding health and safety at work, appoint safety representatives and establish safety committees in addition to ensuring that workplaces meet all the necessary safety requirements of the law. These responsibilities apply equally to employers in transport, and it should be remembered that here the requirements of the law apply to the transport operator's premises (ie offices, workshops, warehouses and yard) and to the vehicles which constitute the workplace of drivers.

The Act replaced certain parts of the Factories Act and the Offices, Shops and Railway Premises Act, and added other provisions. There are four parts to the Act:

- Part I relates to health, safety and welfare at work;
- Part II relates to the Employment Medical Advisory Service;

- Part III amends the law regarding building regulations;
- Part IV covers a range of general and miscellaneous provisions.

The main effects of the Act were:

- to maintain and improve standards of health and safety for people at work;
- to protect people other than those at work against risks to their health or safety arising from the work activities of others;
- to control the storage and use of explosives, highly flammable or dangerous substances, and to prevent their unlawful acquisition, possession and use;
- to control the emission into the atmosphere of noxious or offensive fumes or substances from work premises;
- to set up the Health and Safety Commission* and the Health and Safety Executive.

** The Health and Safety Commission no longer exists. The Health and Safety Executive is now the H&S controlling body.*

Duties of Employers

The Act prescribes the general duties of all employers towards their employees by obliging them to ensure their health, safety and welfare while at work. This duty requires that all plant (including vehicles) and methods of work provided are reasonably safe and without risks to health. A similar injunction relates to the use, handling, storage and transport of any articles or substances used in connection with the employer's work. Provisions contained in the Data Protection Act mean that employers are no longer permitted to design health questionnaires for completion by employees or to screen or interpret employees' medical data. Now, only qualified health professionals may carry out these functions.

Provision of Necessary Information

In order that employees are fully conversant with all health and safety matters, it is the duty of the employer to provide all necessary information and instruction by means of proper training and adequate supervision.

Employers must either: 1) display the 'Health and Safety Law' poster; or 2) distribute the 'Health and Safety Law' leaflet to employees. (Copies can be obtained from HSE Books: www.hse.gov.uk/pubns/books (archived at https://perma.cc/5FH2-P8CQ. Other leaflets and guides are free to download from this site.)

Condition of Premises

Workplaces generally, if under the employer's control, must be maintained in such a condition that they are safe and without risks to health, have adequate means of entrance and exit (again this applies equally to vehicles as it does to 'premises') and must provide a working environment that has satisfactory facilities and arrangements for the welfare of everybody employed in the premises. In addition, site visitors must also be free from risks to their health or safety and may need safety briefings before entering some parts of the site.

Statements of Safety Policy

It is necessary for an employer of five or more employees to draw up and bring to the notice of the workforce *a written statement of company policy* regarding their health and safety at work with all current arrangements detailed for the implementation of such a policy. Stress is laid on the necessity of updating the 'statement' as the occasion arises and of communicating all alterations to the personnel employed.

Appointment of Safety Representatives

Involvement of all employees in health and safety activities is envisaged by the appointment (by a recognized trade union) or election of safety representatives from among the workforce. A safety representative should be a person who has been employed in the firm for at least *two years* or who has had two years' similar employment 'so far as is reasonably practicable'. The broad duties of safety representatives are concerned with the inspection of workplaces, investigating possible hazards and examining the cause of accidents, investigating employees' complaints regarding health and safety matters, and making representations to their employer on health and safety at work matters.

Safety Committees

At the written request of at least two safety representatives employers must establish a safety committee, within a time limit of three months, to review health and safety at work matters. The establishment of a safety committee creates a joint responsibility with the employer for concern with all health and safety measures at the workplace, together with any other duties arising from regulations or codes of practice.

Duty to the Public

Employers and self-employed persons are required to ensure that their activities do not create any hazard to members of the general public. In certain circumstances, information must be made publicly available regarding the existence of possible hazards to health and safety.

Summary of Duties of Employers to their Employees

- It shall be the duty of every employer to ensure so far as is reasonably practicable the health, safety and welfare at work of all his employees. That duty includes, in particular:
  - the provision and maintenance of plant and systems of work that are so far as is reasonably practicable safe and without risks to health;
  - arrangements for ensuring so far as is reasonably practicable safety and absence of risks to health in connection with the use, handling, storage and transport of articles and substances;
  - the provision of such information, instruction, training and supervision as is necessary to ensure so far as is reasonably practicable the health and safety at work of employees;
  - so far as is reasonably practicable the maintenance of any place of work that is under the employer's control in a condition that is safe and without

risks to health, and the provision and maintenance of means of access to and egress from it that are safe and without such risks;
  - the provision and maintenance of a working environment for employees that is so far as is reasonably practicable safe and without risk to health and adequate as regards facilities and arrangements for their welfare at work.
- Except in such cases as may be prescribed it shall be the duty of all employers to prepare and as often as may be appropriate revise a written statement of their general policy with respect to the health and safety at work of their employees and the organization and arrangements for the time being in force for carrying out that policy, and to bring the statement and any revision of it to the notice of all employees.
- It shall be the duty of any person who erects or installs any article for use at work in any premises where the article is to be used by persons at work to ensure, so far as is reasonably practicable, that nothing about the way in which it is erected or installed makes it unsafe or a risk to health when properly used.
- No employer shall levy or permit to be levied on any employee any charge in respect of anything done or provided in pursuance of any specific requirement of the relevant statutory provisions.

As well as these statutory duties, employers have a common law duty of care. Where a breach of that care results in negligence (eg where careless conduct results in injury to a person), they may be liable to pay compensation, even if, in some cases, the injury was caused to a person who was acting illegally at the time.

Duties of Employees

The Act states in general terms the duty of employees to take reasonable care for their own safety and that of others who may be affected by their work activities and to cooperate with others in order to ensure that there is a compliance with statutory duties relating to health and safety at work. In this connection no person shall interfere with or misuse anything provided in the interests of health, safety or welfare either intentionally or recklessly.

Summary of Duties of Employees at Work

- It shall be the duty of all employees while at work:
  - to take reasonable care for their own health and safety and of other persons who may be affected by their acts or omissions at work; and
  - as regards any duty or requirement imposed on their employer or any other person, to cooperate with them so far as is necessary to enable that duty or requirement to be performed or complied with.
- No person shall intentionally or recklessly interfere with or misuse anything provided in the interests of health, safety or welfare.

General Duties of Employers and Self-Employed to Persons Other than Their Employees

- It shall be the duty of all employers and self-employed persons to conduct their undertaking in such a way as to ensure so far as is reasonably practicable that persons not in their employment are not thereby exposed to risks to their health and safety.
- It shall be the duty of all employers and self-employed persons to give to persons not in their employment, who may be affected, the prescribed information about such aspects of the way in which they conduct their undertaking as might affect such persons' health and safety.

Improvement and Prohibition Notices

Improvement Notice

An improvement notice may be served on a person by a health and safety inspector in cases where he believes (ie is of the opinion) that the person is contravening or has contravened, and is likely to continue so doing or will do so again, any of the relevant statutory provisions. Such a notice must give details of the inspector's reason for his belief and requires the person concerned to remedy the contravention within a stated period.

Prohibition Notice

A prohibition notice with immediate effect may be served on a person under whose control activities to which the relevant statutory provisions apply are being carried on, or are about to be carried on, by an inspector if he believes that such activities involve or could involve *a risk of serious personal injury*. A prohibition notice must specify those matters giving rise to such a risk, and the reason why the inspector believes the statutory provisions are, or are likely to be, contravened, if indeed he believes that such is the case. The notice must direct that the activities in question shall not be carried on unless those matters giving rise to the risk of serious personal injury, and any contravention of the regulations, are rectified.

Remedial Measures

Both improvement and prohibition notices may include directions as to necessary remedial measures and these may be framed by reference to an approved Code of Practice and may offer a choice of the actions to be taken. Reference must be made by the inspector to the fire authority before serving a notice requiring, or likely to lead to, measures affecting means of escape in case of fire.

Withdrawal of Notices and Appeals

A notice, other than a prohibition notice with immediate effect, may be withdrawn before the end of the period specified in the notice, or an appeal against it made. Alternatively, the period specified for remedial action may be extended at any time provided an appeal against the notice is not pending.

Penalties for Health and Safety Offences

Conviction for an offence under the Health and Safety at Work Act 1974 may lead to an unlimited fine (previously £20,000). However, it should be stressed that while generally the fine imposed is intended to reflect the gravity of the particular offence and the employer's attitude towards health and safety matters, the Court will also bear in mind the offender's resources and the effects of a heavy penalty on his business and may reduce the penalty accordingly.

NB: The Traffic Commissioners include health and safety prosecutions and penalties as factors when assessing the good repute of 'O' licence applicants and directors of companies applying for 'O' licences or holding 'O' licences.

Corporate Manslaughter

In a situation where a death is caused through the negligence of an employer, whether health and safety related or as a result of a road accident, the employer risks facing a charge of corporate manslaughter.

It has been ruled by the courts that for an indictment on such a charge to be sustained, three key issues must be established by the jury as follows:

- The defendant owed a duty of care to the person killed.
- The defendant had breached his duty of care and that breach of care led to the death.
- The defendant's negligence was so gross that a jury would consider it justified to bring in a criminal conviction.

In 2016 the *Health and Safety Offences, Corporate Manslaughter and Food Safety and Hygiene Offences Definitive Guide* came into force where a maximum fine of £20 million can be applied for the most serious corporate manslaughter offences.

The corporate manslaughter offence (or corporate homicide in Scotland) applies to both corporate organizations and Crown bodies such as government departments – which will be on the same footing as their private-sector counterparts when carrying out similar activities. The offence is focused on corporate liability and does not apply to individual directors or others. Prosecutions against individuals continue to be possible for existing offences – including manslaughter/culpable homicide and health and safety offences – where they themselves are personally at fault.

The Management of Health and Safety

The so-called 'management' regulations (p 497) are both wide-ranging and general in nature, overlapping with many existing regulations. They have to be viewed as a 'catch-all' regulation, sitting astride other more specific health and safety provisions (eg the COSHH regulations – see p 506). The HSE, in its Approved Code of Practice, advises that where legal requirements in these management regulations overlap with other provisions, compliance with duties imposed by the specific regulations will be sufficient to comply with the corresponding duty in the management regulations. However, the HSE says, where duties in the Management of Health and Safety at

Work Regulations 1999 go beyond those in the more specific regulations, additional measures will be needed to comply fully with the management regulations.

Specifically, these regulations cover:

- Requirements for employers (and self-employed persons) to make assessments of the risks to the health and safety of:
  - employees while they are at work;
  - other persons not in their employ, arising out of or in connection with their conduct or the conduct of their undertaking.
- Employers with five or more employees must record the significant findings of their risk assessment (ie make an effective statement of the hazards and risks which lead management to take relevant actions to protect health and safety).
- Employers and self-employed persons must make and give effect to such arrangements, as are appropriate to the nature of their activities and the size of their undertaking, for the effective planning, organization, control, monitoring and review of preventive and protective measures.
- Health surveillance must be provided for employees as appropriate to the risks to their health and safety as identified by the assessment.
- Employers must appoint one or more (competent) persons to assist them in undertaking the measures necessary to comply with the requirements and prohibitions of this legislation (see p 515 for more information on risk assessments).

The Workplace Regulations

These regulations (see second item in the list of new legislation on p 497) added further to existing legislation on workplaces. They applied to new workplaces as of 1 January 1993 and to any modifications or conversions to existing workplaces started after this date. Existing workplaces (ie which were unaltered) had to comply from 1 January 1996.

Specifically the regulations imposed requirements on the:

- maintenance of workplaces;
- ventilation of enclosed workplaces and temperatures of indoor workplaces and the provision of thermometers;
- lighting (including emergency lighting);
- cleanliness of the workplace, and of furniture, furnishings and fittings (also the ability to clean floors, walls and ceilings) and the removal of waste materials;
- room dimensions and unoccupied space;
- suitability of workstations (including those outside) and the provision of suitable seating;
- condition of floors, and the arrangement of routes for pedestrians or vehicles;
- protection from falling objects, and from persons falling from a height, or falling into dangerous substances;

- material of and protection of windows and other transparent or translucent walls, doors or gates, and to them being apparent;
- way in which windows, skylights or ventilators are opened and their position when left open and the ability to clean these items;
- construction of doors and gates (including the fitting of necessary safety devices), and escalators and moving walkways;
- provision of suitable sanitary conveniences, washing facilities and drinking water (including cups and drinking vessels);
- provision of suitable accommodation for clothing and for changing clothes, for rest and for eating meals.

Manual Handling

The Manual Handling Regulations 1992, amended and revised in 2002, 2007, 2015 and 2019 are intended to reduce back and other injuries suffered through the manual handling of loads and to ensure that manual handling operations are properly risk assessed. Employers must reduce the risk of injury to employees by using more mechanical aids, providing training in load handling, and providing precise information about load weights, centres of gravity and the heaviest side of eccentrically loaded packages.

Employers must avoid having employees undertake manual handling operations which involve risk of injury. Where it is not possible to avoid this, they have a duty to assess potential injury risks and take steps to reduce those risks to the absolute minimum or, better still, find an alternative way of achieving the same objective which does not involve manual handling, for example by mechanization of certain handling tasks or by eliminating some activities altogether.

Where such activities must take place, the employer should ensure that employees:

- are well trained in good handling techniques;
- understand how operations have been designed to ensure their safety; and
- make proper use of systems of work provided.

In particular, employees should understand:

- how potentially hazardous handling operations can be recognized;
- how to deal with unfamiliar operations;
- the proper use of handling aids;
- the proper use of personal protective equipment;
- features of the working environment that contribute to safety;
- the importance of good housekeeping;
- factors affecting individual capability; and
- good handling techniques.

Training in good handling techniques should be tailored to the particular handling operations likely to be undertaken, beginning with relatively simple examples and progressing to more specialized handling operations.

It is especially useful to train employees to:

- recognize loads whose weight as well as their shape and other features, and the circumstances in which they are handled, might cause injury;
- treat unfamiliar loads with caution and not assume that apparently empty drums or other closed containers are in fact empty;
- test loads first by attempting to raise one end; and
- apply force gradually when lifting or moving loads until either undue strain is felt, in which case an alternative method should be considered, or it is clear that the task can be accomplished without injury.

HSE booklets on manual handling are available from the HSE (hse.gov.uk/pubns (archived at https://perma.cc/4GA4-5532)) with many free to download as PDF files. They provide excellent guidance on the regulations and their application. Additionally, these notes will provide useful information to employers on many aspects of manual handling.

The Use of Display Screen Equipment

For the purposes of these regulations (fourth item in the list on p 497), a display screen is any form of alphanumeric or graphic display screen regardless of the process involved – generally termed visual display units (VDUs). Under the regulations employers are required to protect VDU users (ie those who habitually use VDUs for a significant part of their normal work) from the risks associated with habitual VDU use – mainly visual fatigue, mental stress, backache and upper limb pain. This must be done by controlling the design of workstations and time spent at the workstation and actual working conditions. Employers must make an assessment of the risks to which VDU users are exposed and reduce these to the lowest reasonably practicable level. Work at VDU screens must be periodically interrupted by breaks or a switch to other work and employers must provide eye and eyesight tests for relevant employees and, where necessary, also provide special corrective appliances (ie spectacles) where normal spectacles cannot be used. Both existing and new VDU users must be given health and safety information about, and training in the use of, the workstation.

Provision and Use of Work Equipment

The Provision and Use of Work Equipment Regulations 1998 (PUWER) require employers and the self-employed to ensure that equipment provided for use at work complies with the regulations. The law applies to owned, hired, leased and second-hand equipment and all machinery, appliances (including cranes, lift trucks and vehicle hoists), apparatus, tools or component assemblies so arranged as to function as a whole unit. Work equipment must be:

- suitable for its intended purpose;
- assessed as to any risks associated with the equipment;
- subject to a recorded inspection where such an inspection would assist in identifying health and safety risks; and

- maintained in efficient working order, in an efficient state and in good repair, and a maintenance log kept.

Personal Protective Equipment

Employers are required to provide suitable personal protective equipment (PPE) to employees where there are risks to their health and safety which cannot be adequately controlled by other means – it is a last-resort measure. Self-employed persons must provide their own protective equipment where necessary and employees must report defective PPE. PPE is not suitable unless:

- it is appropriate for the identified risks;
- account has been taken of the environment that it will be used in, ergonomic factors such as the nature of the job, the need for communication and the health of the wearer;
- it fits the wearer correctly and comfortably and is capable of being adjusted;
- it is effective, so far as is practicable, against the risks it is intended to control;
- it is serviceable and in good condition.

PPE is described as being any equipment designed to be worn or held by persons to protect them from one or more risks, including against extreme temperatures, poor visibility and adverse weather. Work clothing and uniforms, sports equipment and road safety protective wear such as crash helmets are excluded. PPE which is defective must be reported, exchanged or replaced and must not be used.

A fatal accident to a lorry driver on a motorway hard shoulder some years ago highlighted the need for drivers, and others, to wear high-visibility (high-viz) clothing when working in vulnerable situations. In this particular case the driver was criticized for being careless with his own safety in not wearing his reflective jacket. It should also be noted that in some EU countries it is an actual offence for a driver to leave a vehicle without wearing a high-viz jacket or tabard.

Further details on all the above areas of health and safety and many free guides are available on the HSE website.

The COSHH Regulations 2002 (as Amended)

These regulations are aimed at eliminating exposure, or controlling the degree of exposure, that workers were experiencing to hazardous substances. They do so by classifying the nature of the hazards as 'very toxic', 'toxic', 'harmful', 'corrosive', or 'irritant'.

Under the Act, employers are required to carry out adequate assessments before any employee is exposed to any hazardous substance, eliminate the use of the substance or, where this is not possible, to control the exposure by whatever means possible and to issue PPE as a last resort in that control, to monitor employees' exposure to hazardous substances, to keep records of such monitoring and to provide employees with information and training in relation to hazards.

The eight essential steps of COSHH as recommended by the HSE are:

Step 1 Assess the risks.
Step 2 Decide what precautions are needed.
Step 3 Prevent or adequately control exposure.
Step 4 Ensure that control measures are used and maintained.
Step 5 Monitor the exposure.
Step 6 Carry out appropriate health surveillance.
Step 7 Prepare plans and procedures to deal with accidents, incidents and emergencies.
Step 8 Ensure employees are properly informed, trained and supervised.

Acknowledgement: The above list is reproduced from the HSE Health and Safety Advice Sheet 14 and may be freely downloaded from the HSE website.

The Reporting of Injuries, Diseases and Dangerous Occurrences Regulations 2013 (RIDDOR)

RIDDOR covers certain accidents and incidents relating to the workplace and how these issues are reported and recorded.

RIDDOR is overseen by the HSE Incident Contact Centre (ICC) in South Wales and relates to accidents and incidents that occur in the workplace. These include:

- fatal accidents;
- accidents resulting in major injury (loss of a limb, fingers, or an eye and more than 24 hours' hospitalization);
- dangerous occurrences;
- accidents leading to seven consecutive days off work;
- some work-related diseases;
- most incidents relating to problems with natural gas and liquefied petroleum gas (LPG).

Where a report is required to be sent to the ICC, there are two different ways it can be done.

1. For accidents where there is a fatality or a major injury or a dangerous occurrence, the incident has to be reported immediately by phone to the ICC (0345 300 9923) or by using the link on the HSE website and subsequently supplying details electronically.
2. For accidents causing more than seven days' incapacity for work, there is no requirement to make an immediate telephone notification, but the electronic report is still required within 15 days. Reports should be made using the online forms that can be found on the HSE website at www.hse.gov.uk/riddor/report.htm (archived at https://perma.cc/3SKN-FMCJ)

In cases where the accident or incident involves vehicles on the public highway, the Traffic Commissioner must also be informed. In addition, records of all reportable accidents and incidents must be kept for a minimum period of three years whilst all minor accidents need to be recorded in an 'accident book'. Completed books also need to be kept for three years.

Full contact details for the ICC which is open 8.30am–5.00pm Monday–Friday, are as follows:

Telephone: 0345 300 9923 Email: riddor@natbrit.com
Website: www.hse.gov.uk/riddor (archived at https://perma.cc/GSU2-NA2H)

As there is no longer any 'paper' method of reporting under RIDDOR to the ICC, reports by post should be sent to:

RIDDOR Reports
Health and Safety Executive
Redgrave Court
Merton Road
Bootle
Merseyside
L20 7HS

Major Injury

For clarification, a 'major injury' is defined as follows:

- fracture of the skull, spine or pelvis;
- fracture of any bone:
  - in the arm other than a bone in the wrist or hand;
  - in the leg other than a bone in the ankle or foot;
- amputation of a hand or foot;
- the loss of sight of an eye; or
- any other injury which results in the person injured being admitted into hospital as an inpatient for more than 24 hours, unless that person was detained only for observation.

Dangerous Occurrences

The list of dangerous occurrences in the regulations is selective, the aim being to obtain information about incidents with a high potential for injury but with a low frequency of occurrence.

It is important to note that dangerous occurrences must be reported even though no injury was actually caused to any person.

Examples of incidents which constitute dangerous occurrences are as follows:

- failure, collapse or overturning of lifts, hoists, cranes, excavators, tail-lifts, etc;
- explosion of boiler or boiler tube;
- electrical short circuits followed by fire or explosion;
- explosion or fire which results in stoppage of work for more than 24 hours;

- release of flammable liquid or gas (ie over 1 tonne);
- collapse of scaffolding;
- collapse or partial collapse of any building;
- failure of a freight container while being lifted;
- a road tanker to which the Hazchem regulations apply either overturning or suffering serious damage to the tank while a hazardous substance is being carried.

Note 1: This list is abbreviated. Where appropriate the regulations themselves should be consulted.

Note 2: A useful leaflet on the subject is available to download through the HSE website.

Lifting Operations

The Lifting Operations and Lifting Equipment Regulations 1998 (LOLER) apply to all lifting equipment which is defined as 'work equipment for lifting and lowering loads and includes its attachments used for anchoring, fixing or supporting it'. These regulations obviously apply to forklift trucks and to automated goods storage and retrieval systems, and front-end loaders on tractors.

It is important to note that these regulations also apply to tipping vehicles. In this context it is important that the operator ensures he receives from the manufacturer adequate information about safe operation and correct methods of use and that such information is passed on to the driver, who should also be properly trained as per all health and safety requirements. All loading and unloading operations also need to be risk assessed.

The regulations make provisions regarding:

- the strength and stability of lifting equipment;
- the safety of lifting equipment for lifting persons;
- the way lifting equipment is positioned and installed;
- the marking of machinery and accessories for lifting, and lifting equipment which is designed for lifting persons or which might so be used in error;
- the organization of lifting operations;
- thorough examination and inspection of lifting equipment in specified circumstances;
- evidence of examination to accompany it (ie the lifting equipment) outside the firm's premises;
- exceptions for winding apparatus at mines;
- the making of reports of thorough examinations and records of inspections; and
- the keeping of information in the reports and records.

Additionally, according to the HSE *Simple Guide to the Lifting Operations and Lifting Equipment Regulations 1998*, operators must ensure that:

- Lifting operations are planned, supervised and carried out in a safe manner by people who are competent.
- Where equipment is used for lifting people it is marked accordingly, and it should be safe for such a purpose, eg all necessary precautions have been taken to eliminate or reduce any risk.
- Where appropriate, before lifting equipment (including accessories) is used for the first time, it is *thoroughly examined*. Lifting equipment may need to be thoroughly examined in use at periods specified in the regulations (ie usually at least six-monthly for accessories and equipment used for lifting people and, at a minimum, annually for all other equipment) or at intervals laid down in an examination scheme drawn up by a competent person. All examination work should be performed by a competent person.
- Following a thorough examination or inspection of any lifting equipment, a report is submitted by the competent person to the employer to take the appropriate action.

NB: ROSPA also produce a guide on these regulations. Both versions are free to download from the respective websites.

Work-Related Stress

All employers have a duty in law to ensure that their employees are not made ill by their work. Work-related stress is becoming recognized as a major cause of employee illness and absenteeism. Transport employers, in particular, need to recognize that stress can make their employees ill because the work involved, especially driving, is renowned as a stressful occupation.

Stress is a person's natural reaction to excessive pressure and thus it is not a disease. However, excessive and long-term stress can lead to mental and physical ill health causing, for example, high blood pressure, depression, a nervous breakdown and even heart disease. Stress in one person can also lead to stress in other people who have to cover their work.

The costs of stress can be high: high staff turnover, increased absence through sickness, reduced work performance, increased lateness and more customer complaints and we also need to consider the effects of depression and anxiety which can result from stress. An employer who ignores signs of stress among employees or who fails to take the necessary action to reduce stress may face claims for compensation from employees who have suffered ill health from work-related stress. During 2017/18, 595,000 people in Britain were diagnosed as suffering from stress, depression and anxiety, according to the HSE. In addition, during 2017/18, work-related stress accounted for 15.4 million lost working days in the UK alone. In general, these figures rise year on year at increasing levels and provide ammunition for anyone sceptical about the claims made in relation to stress at work.

Where stress has been caused in a workplace, or made worse by work, it is the employer's duty to assess the risks among employees, in particular:

- looking for pressures at work that could cause high and long-lasting levels of stress;

- judging which employees may be affected or harmed by stress;
- deciding whether sufficient measures are being taken to prevent harm from stress;
- determining what further measures can be taken to reduce the stress-inducing pressures of work.

Employers are not responsible for preventing ill health from stress caused by problems occurring outside work, but they should be able to recognize the effects of such stress, for example, people being unable to cope with their work, or performing below their normal standard. In such cases, adopting an understanding attitude would be helpful to the individual concerned and is in the employer's best interests.

Smoking in the Workplace

The Smoke-free (Premises and Enforcement) Regulations 2006 was the first step towards stopping smoking at work in order to protect non-smokers from 'secondary' smoke. Since its introduction many issues have been clarified, although some issues still remain.

What is firmly established is that legislation applies to virtually every 'enclosed' and 'substantially enclosed' public place and workplace, irrespective of whether or not it is a space in a temporary building or a permanent one. Because there are two definitions, 'enclosed' and 'substantially enclosed', we need to understand the difference between them.

Firstly, premises are considered 'enclosed' if they have a ceiling or roof and (except for doors, windows or passageways) are wholly enclosed. Secondly, premises are considered 'substantially enclosed' if they have a ceiling or roof, but have an 'opening' in the walls that is less than half the total area of the walls. (The area of the opening does not include any type of door, window, or fitting that is capable of being opened or closed.)

In reality, this means that it is now almost certainly an offence to smoke indoors in a public place or a place of work. As a result of this, 'No Smoking' signs must also be posted at prominent positions at the entrance to every building affected by this legislation.

In relation to transport, the regulations also apply to vehicles and vehicle cabs which are deemed to be 'places of work'. In order to fully comply with the regulations, 'No Smoking' signs need to be placed in every compartment where people may be carried in, or on, a vehicle. These signs must be the EU specified 'No Smoking' sign and be at least 70 mm in diameter.

Contravention of the regulations is dealt with under the Graduated Fixed Penalty Scheme. This means that the penalties vary according to the circumstances relating to the contravention. However, there are three principal ways that the regulations are enforced. These are:

- Fixed penalty notices for employees (including drivers) smoking in a place of work. However, if the person is taken to court and prosecuted, it can result in additional fines being levied.

- Fixed penalty notices being issued to employers who fail to post 'No Smoking' signs when and where they are required. This can also result in additional fines if taken to court.
- Fines being handed out to any person (director, manager, supervisor, etc) who is in a position to control smoke-free premises and fails to do so.

Note that since 1 October 2015, drivers who drive private cars in England and Wales and have children under the age of 18 as passengers can now also be fined £50 for smoking in the vehicle. Scotland introduced the same requirement in December 2016 but the fine in Scotland is £100.

Whilst considering smoking in the workplace, we must also consider e-cigarettes. These include both personal vaporizers (PVs) and electronic nicotine delivery systems (ENDS), which currently fall outside of the scope of the regulations above because nothing is actually 'burnt'. However, the Health and Safety Executive and ACAS strongly advise employers to develop a policy, in conjunction with worker representatives if possible, in relation to the use of e-cigarettes (vaping) at work in order to protect any employees who may have concerns about related health issues, whilst taking into account any possible benefits there may be for people trying to give up smoking. This advice was expected to change in 2016 when e-cigarettes were planned to become licensed medicines, and it is further expected that some sort of legislation will eventually accompany this change when it happens. In most cases, many organizations seem to have made decisions and/or have been advised to treat 'vaping' in the same way as smoking until official guidelines/regulations are announced and the delay 'appears' to be largely because most users of these devices are actually trying to give up smoking. More recently, there have been cases of employees demanding spaces where the fumes from vaping are not allowed to circulate freely.

Electric Storage Batteries

The HSE has issued guidance (INDG139, a pdf file that was updated in 2018) on the safe charging and use of electric storage batteries in motor vehicle repair and maintenance. This is to help reduce the number of injuries which occur annually when batteries explode through mishandling and improper use, generally causing acid burns to face, eyes and hands as well as other injuries.

The HSE warns of the dangers of charging batteries, particularly those described as maintenance-free but which still give off flammable hydrogen gas, which on contact with a naked flame will burn and cause the battery to explode. The advice it gives is as follows.

General Precautions

- Always wear goggles or a visor when working on batteries.
- Wherever possible, always use a properly designated and well-ventilated area for battery charging.
- Remove any metallic objects from hands, wrists and around the neck (eg rings, chains and watches) before working on a battery.

Disconnecting and Reconnecting Batteries

- Turn off the vehicle ignition switch and all other switches or otherwise isolate the battery from the electrical circuit.
- Always disconnect the earthed terminal first (often the negative terminal, but not always – CHECK) and reconnect it last using insulated tools.
- Do not rest tools or metallic objects on top of a battery.

Battery Charging

- Always observe the manufacturer's instructions for charging batteries.
- Charge in a well-ventilated area.
- Do not smoke or bring naked flames into the charging area.
- Make sure the battery is topped up to the correct level.
- Make sure the charger is switched off or disconnected from the power supply before connecting the charging leads, which should be connected positive to positive, negative to negative.
- Vent plugs may need to be adjusted before charging. Carefully follow the manufacturer's instructions.
- Do not exceed the recommended rate of charging.
- When charging is complete, switch off the charger before disconnecting the charging leads.

Jump Starting

Preparation:

- Before attempting to jump-start a vehicle always check to see if the vehicle is capable of being jump-started without causing any damage to the vehicle or any of its components.
- Always ensure that both batteries have the same voltage rating.
- If starting by using a battery on another vehicle, check the earth polarity on both vehicles.
- Ensure the vehicles are not touching.
- Turn off the ignition of both vehicles.
- Always use purpose-made, colour-coded jump leads with insulated handles – red for the positive cable and black for the negative cable.

Connection for vehicles with the *same earth* polarity:

- First connect the non-earthed terminal of the good battery to the non-earthed terminal of the flat battery.
- Connect one end of the second lead to the earthed terminal of the good battery.
- Connect the other end of the second lead to a suitable, substantial, unpainted point on the chassis or engine of the other vehicle, away from the battery, carburettor, fuel lines or brake pipes.

Connection for vehicles with *different* earth polarity:

> *The HSE warns that in view of the potential for confusion this should be attempted only by skilled and experienced personnel.*

- First connect the earthed terminal of the good battery to the non-earthed terminal of the flat battery.
- Connect one end of the second lead to the non-earthed terminal of the good battery.
- Connect the other end of the second lead to a suitable, substantial, unpainted point on the chassis or engine of the other vehicle, away from the battery, carburettor, fuel lines or brake pipes.

Starting

- Ensure the leads are well clear of moving parts.
- Start the engine of the 'good' vehicle and allow to run for about one minute.
- Start the engine of the 'dead' vehicle and allow to run for about one minute.

Disconnection

- Stop the engine of the 'good' vehicle.
- Disconnect the leads in the reverse order to which they were connected.
- Take great care in handling jump leads; do not allow the exposed metal parts to touch each other or the vehicle body.

Note 1: Because many modern vehicles include on-board engine and vehicle management systems, they should not be 'jump started' without professional advice on whether or not the electronic systems may be damaged or 'spiked' by doing so.

Note 2: Advice on risks when charging the main batteries fitted to electric cars is available on the HSE website.

The Batteries Directive

The EU's Batteries Directive (2006/66/EC) came into force in the UK on 5 May 2009 and was subsequently amended on 2013. It provides for controls of the environmental impacts of batteries, in particular setting limits for the content of certain heavy metals within batteries. Whereas the former directive on this issue applied to less than 10 per cent of batteries, the 2009 directive (as amended) applies to all types of battery and it also specifies tighter limits for the heavy metal content of batteries and sets targets for recovery, recycling, labelling and producer responsibility.

Two particular and connected environmental hazards are associated with batteries. First, they often contain heavy metals such as cadmium and mercury, which can pose a threat if released into the environment. Second, the disposal sources for many batteries are either landfill sites or incineration plants, the use of either being likely to lead to polluting releases into the environment.

The Directive includes all types of batteries and accumulators, and divides batteries into three main categories:

- Portable batteries: These include household batteries, such as those used to power portable electronic equipment and torches.
- Industrial batteries: These include lead-acid batteries used in heavy machinery and industrial power tools.
- Automotive batteries: All batteries used to power motor vehicles. These are commonly lead-acid batteries.

The main aims of the Directive include:

- restricting the use of mercury and cadmium in batteries;
- setting out labelling requirements for new batteries (to help consumers in choosing batteries and in deciding how to send them for recycling);
- setting targets for collecting waste portable batteries:
  - 45 per cent by September 2016 (figures of achievement or not were not available at the time of writing but in March 2018 there was a 57 tonne predicted shortfall announced, with the UK achieving a 28 per cent collection rate but with other European countries achieving 45 per cent);
- prohibiting the disposal by landfill or incineration of waste industrial and automotive batteries, which implies a 100 per cent collection and recycling target;
- introducing producer responsibilities.

So far as the UK is concerned, a significant increase in recycling is still needed to meet these proposed new limits, which poses a challenge – although progress has been made, current recycling facilities for batteries are still somewhat inadequate, especially for alkaline-manganese and zinc-carbon batteries, which make up about 80 per cent by weight of all portable batteries.

The Government legislation is contained in the Waste Batteries and Accumulators Regulations 2009, whilst the target collection figures were originally set in the EU's Batteries and Accumulators Directive.

Risk Management

Risk management may be defined as the process of measuring or assessing risks (ie in the workplace) and then developing strategies to manage those risks. Generally, the strategies adopted would include transferring the risk to another party, avoiding the risk, reducing the negative effect of a particular risk, or deciding to accept some or all of its consequences. Traditionally, risk management focuses on risks arising from physical or legal causes (eg natural disasters or fires, accidents, death and lawsuits) or malpractices in the workplace. Ideally, risk management should follow a prioritization process whereby the greatest risks (ie those likely to cause most harm to people or damage to equipment) are dealt with first, while those with a lower probability of occurrence and less likelihood to cause harm or damage are dealt with later. In practice, careful decisions need to be made about these issues. Most large companies have risk management teams, but even the smallest of firms and even one-man owner-driver businesses need to have focused risk management procedures.

Risk Management for Transport Operators

Running a safe operation is crucial in today's increasingly litigious world. When something goes wrong, particularly a serious accident or incident, it is increasingly the directors of a company that are held accountable, while the true costs of road traffic accidents are often overlooked when considering insured costs such as property damage and injury compensation. In any event, the impact on profitability of the following should not be underestimated:

- loss of revenue through vehicles being unavailable for use;
- the cost of replacement drivers following injury to regular drivers;
- loss of business through damage to customer relationships;
- damage to brand image if a liveried vehicle is involved in a fatal accident.

Risk Assessment

Many accidents could be prevented by simply examining what actually goes on in your business, removing and controlling hazards as far as possible and taking the necessary managerial and supervisory steps to make sure that what is supposed to happen does happen. For example:

STEP 1: Look for the hazards.
STEP 2: Decide who might be harmed and how.
STEP 3: Evaluate the risks and decide whether the existing precautions are adequate or whether more should be done.
STEP 4: Record your findings.
STEP 5: Review your assessment and revise it if necessary.

Source: HSE Guide to Risk Assessment.

NB: A hazard is simply something that can cause harm. Risk is the chance of anyone suffering harm from such a hazard.

Clearly, work activities need to be assessed for risk but it is not sufficient to 'assess and forget'. Risk assessments need to be ongoing and to change as activities change and new activities are introduced. In addition, workers undertaking the tasks need to be involved to give their feedback as to how risks can be reduced and eliminated. This is particularly important where the risk assessment is focused on technical tasks, complex tasks, specialized tasks, etc. Also note the new need for risk assessment when using tyres that are 10 years old, mentioned earlier in 'Construction and Use'.

Road Risk

Road risk is the new 'in' term for transport management to contend with. While knowledge of and compliance with the *Highway Code* is essential for both drivers and managers alike, the HSE free guideline publications *Driving at Work – Managing Work-Related Road Safety* and *Vehicles at Work: Driving at Work and Work-Related Road Safety* are now also essential reading for transport management and for anybody who drives on company business, ie managers and staff as well as commercial vehicle drivers, those who drive full-time and those who drive only occasionally and, of course, self-employed drivers. The late Dr Will Murray, who sadly passed away in December 2016, always said that the two documents went together 'like bacon and eggs'. The guidelines show how legal responsibilities under health and safety at work provisions must be complied with in addition to existing road traffic and vehicle construction and use provisions. They describe how to manage work-related road safety, assessing risks on the road and how to evaluate those risks. Overall, the aim is to cut the number of road accidents involving people at work in all sectors of industry.

Up to this point it is obvious that much of our safety at work regulation and standards stem from the EU and the UK Government has expressed the opinion that current standards will at least be maintained post-Brexit.

Fire Safety

All employers are required by law to carry out a fire risk assessment and introduce appropriate safety measures within their workplaces. This applies irrespective of whether the employer's premises are covered by a Fire Certificate or not, whereas previously this duty did not apply where a Fire Certificate was in force.

The Regulatory Reform (Fire Safety) Order 2005 which came into effect in England and Wales from 1 October 2006 (separate legislation applies to Scotland) revokes or repeals all previously existing fire legislation including the Fire Precautions Act 1971, the amended 1997 Fire Precautions (Workplace) Regulations, plus 100 other pieces of fire-related legislation. Fire certificates are no longer valid.

This regulatory Order is a fire risk assessment-based approach where the person responsible for the premises or area they control must decide how to address the risks identified, while meeting certain requirements. By adopting this fire risk assessment approach, the responsible person will need to consider how to prevent fire from occurring in the first place, by removing or reducing hazards and risks (such as ignition sources), then consider the precautions necessary to ensure that people are adequately protected if a fire were still to occur. The fire risk assessment must also take into consideration what effect a fire may have on any person in or around your premises plus in neighbouring property.

While the Order is intended to be less burdensome and clearer than former legal provisions, the main emphasis of the regulations remains in fire prevention so risk assessments will need to be kept under regular review.

The Order applies to all non-domestic properties, including those of voluntary organizations, and is subject to monitoring and where appropriate enforcement by the Local Authority Fire Service (LAFS).

Summary of the Order

- All existing fire legislation has now been repealed or revoked, which includes the Fire Precautions Act 1971, the amended 1997 Fire Precautions (Workplace) Regulations plus 100 other pieces of fire-related legislation.
- Fire certificates have been abolished and are no longer issued.
- A 'responsible person' is to be responsible for fire safety and they must conduct a fire risk assessment regardless of the size of the risk (see below).
- The identified responsible person(s) will carry full corporate liability.
- The Order extends the scope of consideration to include property safety, firefighter safety and the environment around the site. The responsible person has a duty to protect all risks.
- Unlike the previous legislation, this Order places emphasis on business continuity and containing and preventing the spread of small fires.

Protection is explicitly extended to occupants of all premises, including employees, visitors, contractors and passers-by, all of whom have to be considered in the fire risk.

The rules related to fire risk assessment and required actions are outlined below.

Employers and building owners and occupiers must carry out a fire risk assessment and keep it up to date. Based on the findings of the assessment adequate and appropriate fire safety measures must be put in place to minimize the risk of injury or death in the event of a fire.

The risk assessment needs to identify what could cause a fire (sources), substances that burn and people who may be at risk. The prime aim should be to eliminate risks but, where this is not possible, the risks need to be minimized and properly managed. Managing also includes considering how people at work can be protected if there is a fire.

General considerations include:

- keeping sources of ignition and flammable substances apart;
- avoiding accidental fires;
- ensuring good housekeeping practices;
- considering fire detection and fire warning measures;
- having sufficient fire-fighting resources and equipment;
- having appropriate, fully operational, fire-fighting equipment;
- ensuring staff are trained on actions to take in the event of a fire.

There is a whole range of fire prevention and risk guidance freely available on the GOV.UK and HSE websites covering many different work environments and requirements, depending upon the actual work sector.

First Aid

Regulations require employers to train members of their staff in first-aid techniques and to provide first-aid equipment and facilities under the Health and Safety (First Aid) Regulations 1981. An approved Code of Practice established by the Health and Safety Executive provides both employers and the self-employed with practical guidance on how they may meet the requirements of the regulations. Further, The Stationery Office has published a booklet in its health and safety series entitled *First Aid at Work* HS(R) 11 and the HSE produce a range of leaflets and guides on the subject.

The regulations state that 'an employer shall provide, or ensure that there are provided, such equipment, information and facilities as are adequate and appropriate in the circumstances for enabling first aid to be rendered to his employees if they are injured or become ill at work'.

Trained First-Aiders

The employer must, in some cases, provide suitable persons to administer first aid and these persons must have had specific training or hold appropriate qualifications. This usually requires attending periodic training and refresher courses run by the St John Ambulance service, although there are many private training providers. The numbers of first-aiders required depends upon the work activity and the number of employees but there are no actual statutory number requirements. However, HSE recommend that, generally speaking, one first-aider is required for every 50 workers in a company where there are no special risks or circumstances. Further advice is available on the HSE website.

First-Aid Boxes

First-aid boxes must be provided. These should be properly identified as first-aid containers, preferably with a white cross on a green background, and contain sufficient quantities of first-aid material *and nothing else*. In particular, the boxes should contain only material which a first-aider has been trained to use. The old style of contents list, according to the numbers of persons covered, has been scrapped in favour of a general specification. There is no mandatory list of items to put in a first-aid box. It depends on what you assess your needs to be. As a guide, the HSE suggest that where work activities involve low-level hazards, a minimum stock of first-aid items would be:

- a leaflet giving general guidance on first aid (eg HSE's leaflet *Basic Advice on First Aid at Work*);
- 20 individually wrapped sterile plasters (of assorted sizes), appropriate to the type of work (you can provide hypoallergenic plasters if necessary);
- two sterile eye pads;
- four individually wrapped triangular bandages, preferably sterile;

- six safety pins;
- two large, individually wrapped, sterile, unmedicated wound dressings;
- six medium-sized, individually wrapped, sterile, unmedicated wound dressings;
- at least three pairs of disposable gloves.

The HSE stress that this is a suggested contents list only and that the contents of any first-aid kit should reflect the outcome of your first aid needs assessment. They further recommend that tablets and medicines should not be kept in first-aid boxes.

Soap and water and disposable drying materials, or suitable equivalents, should also be available. Where tap water is not available, sterile water or sterile 9 per cent saline, in sealed disposable containers (refillable containers are banned) each holding at least 300 millilitres, should be kept easily accessible, and near to the first-aid box, for eye irrigation.

The contents of first-aid boxes should be replenished as soon as possible after use and items which deteriorate will need to be replaced from time to time. Items should not be used after the indicated expiry date on the packet. For this reason boxes and kits should be examined frequently to make sure they are fully equipped.

Travelling First-Aid Kits

An employer does not need to make first-aid provisions for employees working away from his establishment. However, where the work involves carrying passengers, travelling for long distances in remote areas, from which access to NHS accident and emergency facilities may be difficult, or where employees are using potentially dangerous tools or machinery, small travelling first-aid kits should be provided.

The contents of such kits may need to vary according to the circumstances in which they are likely to be used. The regulations suggest that in general the following items should be sufficient to comply with BSI-8599 minimum contents:

- one pair of rust proof, blunt-ended scissors;
- ten antiseptic wipes, foil packed;
- one conforming disposable bandage (not less than 7.5 cm wide);
- two triangular bandages;
- one packet of 24 assorted adhesive dressings;
- three large sterile un-medicated ambulance dressings (not less than 15 × 20 cm);
- two sterile eye pads, with attachments;
- assorted safety pins.

This contents list is not sufficient for some EU member states who may require contents in accordance with DIN-13416.

Today, many first-aid kit suppliers also include additional items for road kits and add items such as face masks, goggles, butterfly strips, gauze pads, eye irrigation fluid and eye pads, tweezers, scissors, irrigating syringes, torches, etc, which further highlights that every kit needs to reflect the intended risks and use but the list above is, as stated, a minimum requirement.

First Aid on the Road

Any help that a road user can give at the scene of an accident may just save a life, or may give much-needed comfort to a traumatized casualty. The following guidelines have been established for dealing with casualties at the scene of a road accident:

1 Assess the situation:
- What has happened?
- Is there any further danger to you or the casualty? (Remember, roadsides are particularly dangerous places to treat a casualty.)
- How many people are injured?
- Is anybody else able to help?

2 Assess the casualty:
- What is wrong with the casualty?
- Is it necessary to move the casualty, or can he/she be left safely in his/her current position?
- Remember, further injuries can be caused through unnecessary movement of the casualty.

3 Do you need assistance?
- Do you need assistance from the emergency services?
- Don't forget, other first-aiders/bystanders can help you.
- When you ask for help from the emergency services they will need to know:
  - the precise location of the incident;
  - what happened;
  - the injuries involved;
  - how many people are injured.

4 Make a diagnosis:
- What happened to the casualty? Did he or she fall, faint or have a bump on the head?
- Look for signs such as bleeding, swelling or unaligned limbs.
- If the casualty is conscious, ask him or her where he or she feels pain or if he or she went dizzy before the accident.

5 Priorities:

The priorities of first aid are usually referred to as the ABC of first aid:
- *Airway*: check inside the mouth and remove any visible obstruction. Put your fingertips under the point of the casualty's chin. Lift the chin to open the airway.
- *Breathing*: spend at least 10 seconds looking, listening and feeling for breathing. If the casualty is breathing, put him/her in the recovery position. Continue to monitor the patient's breathing.

- *Circulation*: look, listen and feel for normal breathing, coughing or movement by the victim. Only if you have been trained to do so, check the carotid pulse.

6 Priorities of general treatment (the three Bs):
- *Breathing* (see above).
- *Bleeding*: stop bleeding by raising the injured limb above the heart. Apply pressure to the wound with pad, bandage, clean handkerchief or towel.
- *Bones*: if necessary immobilize a broken arm in a sling. If a broken leg is suspected, keep the casualty still.

7 While you are waiting for the arrival of the emergency services:
- Look for changes in the casualty's condition, monitoring the vital signs.
- Check your treatment is adequate and successful.
- Cooperate with the emergency services when they arrive.

NB: It must be stated that guidance on the actual procedures to be administered change frequently and regular first-aid training should be undertaken.

Work-Based Safety Signs

At work, a safety sign is defined as one which combines geometrical shape, colour, and a pictorial symbol to provide specific health or safety information or an instruction as to whether or not any text is included on the sign. Regulations concerning the specification of safety signs in work premises have applied to all such signs since 1 January 1986. Specifications for various types of safety sign are given in BS 5378 (Part I). They are briefly described as follows:

- **Prohibition sign:** round in shape with a white background and a circular band and cross-bar in red. The symbol must be black and placed in the centre of the sign without obliterating the cross-bar. Typical examples of such signs are those prohibiting smoking, prohibiting pedestrians, or indicating the use of water for drinking purposes.
- **Warning sign:** triangular in shape with a yellow background and black triangular band. The symbol or words must be black and placed in the centre of the sign. Typical examples of such signs are those warning of the danger of fire, explosion, toxic substances, corrosive substances, radiation, overhead loads, industrial trucks, electric shocks, proximity of laser beams, etc.
- **Mandatory sign:** round in shape with a blue background, with the symbol or words placed centrally and in white. Typical examples of such signs are those advising that certain pieces of protective clothing must be worn (eg goggles, hard hats, breathing masks, gloves, etc).
- **Safety sign:** square in shape with a green background and white symbol or words centrally placed. Typical examples of such signs are those for fire exits, first-aid posts and rescue points.

Vehicle Reversing

Among the statistics of industrial accidents and road accidents, those resulting from vehicles reversing feature significantly. According to the HSE, nearly one-quarter of all deaths involving vehicles at work occur while vehicles are reversing. In a guide titled *Vehicles at Work – Reversing*, available from the HSE website, the HSE gives the following advice and information to those concerned:

- Remove the need for reversing altogether by setting up one-way systems, for example drive-through loading and unloading positions. Where reversing is unavoidable, routes should be organized to minimize the need for reversing.
- Ensure visiting drivers are familiar with the layout of the workplace, and with any site rules. Do drivers have to report to reception on arrival?

In locations where reversing cannot be avoided:

- 'Reversing areas and bays' should be planned out and clearly marked.
- People who do not need to be in reversing areas should be kept well clear.
- Consider employing a trained signaller (a banksman), both to keep the reversing area free of pedestrians and to guide drivers. Be aware: the use of signallers is not allowed in some industries due to the size of vehicles involved and the difficulty that drivers have in seeing them.
- A signaller:
  - will need to use a clear, agreed system of signalling;
  - will need to be visible to drivers at all times;
  - will need to stand in a safe position from which to guide the reversing vehicle without being in its way;
  - should wear very visible clothing, such as reflective vests, and ensure that any signals are clearly seen.
- If drivers lose sight of the signallers they should know to stop immediately.
- Consider whether portable radios or similar communication systems would be helpful.

The following steps might help to reduce the risk of reversing accidents. The following are examples, but it is unlikely that any single measure will be enough to ensure safety:

- Site layouts can be designed (or modified) to increase visibility for drivers and pedestrians, for example:
  - by increasing the area allowed for reversing;
  - by installing fixed mirrors in smaller areas.
- Reducing the dangers caused by 'blind-spots':
  - Install rear view cameras to vehicles and trailers.
  - Most vehicles already have external side-mounted and rear-view mirrors fitted. These need to be kept clean and in good repair.

- Refractive lenses fitted to rear windows or closed-circuit television systems can be used to help drivers to see behind the vehicle.
- If drivers cannot see behind the vehicle, they should leave their cab and check behind the vehicle before reversing.

- Reversing alarms can be fitted:
  - these should be kept in working order;
  - audible alarms should be loud and distinct enough that they do not become part of the background noise;
  - where an audible alarm might not stand out from the background noise, flashing warning lights can be used.
- Other safety devices can be fitted to vehicles:
  - For example, a number of 'sensing' and 'trip' systems are available, which either warn the driver or stop the vehicle when an obstruction is detected close to, or comes in contact with, the reversing vehicle.
- Stops such as barriers or buffers at loading bays can be used. They should be highly visible and sensibly positioned.
- Where vehicles reverse up to structures or edges, barriers or wheel stops can be used to warn drivers that they need to stop.
- White lines on the floor can help the driver position the vehicle accurately.

It is in consequence of the dangers of reversing that legislation permits the voluntary fitment of reversing bleepers on certain goods and passenger vehicles (see p 399 for full details). It should be remembered that the use of reversing alarms is subject to the same rules for sounding the horn of the vehicle after 11.30 pm and before 7.00 am. With the introduction of these voluntary provisions, there is the risk that any operator deciding not to fit such equipment on a voluntary basis, who then has one of his vehicles involved in a reversing accident, could face proceedings under the Health and Safety at Work Act for not taking sufficient care in safeguarding the health of others. A number of successful prosecutions on this account have been reported and in some cases very heavy fines were imposed.

Safe Tipping

Another area where concern has been expressed over safety measures involves the use of tipping vehicles (and vehicles with lorry-mounted cranes and suchlike) whereby elevated bodies (or crane jibs) come into contact with overhead power cables or are sufficiently close for arcing to occur in wet conditions. The specific danger lies in touching the vehicle body or tipping controls while in contact with the power cable. Drivers are safe when a cable is touched provided they remain in the cab, where the vehicle tyres prevent completion of an electrical circuit. This becomes difficult when many 'Hiab' systems are operated as the driver needs to be out of the cab and is therefore at a greatly increased risk. A spokesperson for the electricity supply industry advises drivers, where possible, to remain in their cabs and drive clear. If this is not possible they should jump from the cab and NOT touch any part of the vehicle, remaining well clear until an electricity engineer has been contacted and reports that it is safe to return to the vehicle.

Tipper operators should also advise drivers to ensure the ground is firm before tipping to prevent the vehicle sinking and overturning as the weight of the load shifts to the rear during tipping and to make sure the tipping gear is disengaged and the body is not in the raised position, or able to be raised, before driving off. Operators should also be aware of the provisions of the Lifting Operations and Lifting Equipment Regulations 1998 (LOLER) described on p 509.

Sheeting of Loads

A variety of load types need to be sheeted for both legal and operational reasons; particularly loads comprising waste skips, bricks, sand, gravel, ash, grain and various types of agricultural produce. Other loads need to be sheeted for weather protection and security reasons.

Many aspects of health and safety legislation and various Codes of Practice are relevant and should be carefully observed to avoid any breach of health and safety law. Also, specifically, it is an offence under C&U Regulations to allow loose loads of any type to cause nuisance or danger to other road users as a result of such material falling or being blown from the vehicle. These loads must be adequately restrained by sheeting or by covering with netting and 'auto-sheet' systems are now widely fitted to most tippers.

As we discussed earlier, 'working at height' legislation normally applies to these types of tasks and health and safety guidelines suggest that priority should be given to the use of closed vehicles or, where this is not feasible, to vehicles with mechanically operated sheeting systems or, at the very least, with mechanical systems that can be operated from ground level. Alternatively, consideration should be given to the provision of gantries from which operatives can sheet loads with minimal risk to their personal safety.

Useful guidance on safe sheeting methods is to be found on the HSE and GOV.UK websites and in a number of official publications (as earlier) and as follows:

- Health and Safety Executive publications:
  - *Workplace Transport Safety* – HS(G)136.
- Department for Transport:
  - *Safety of Loads on Vehicles: Code of Practice* (third edition, 2003).
- DVSA:
  - *Load Securing: Vehicle Operator Guidance* (2015).

Safe Parking

Many accidents occur with parked vehicles and trailers. In particular, within transport depots there should be proper procedures for parking, especially in regard to parking areas and level standing for detached semi-trailers. A common failing is not ensuring that semi-trailers are dropped onto hard and level ground, allowing the landing gear on one side to sink and the trailer to topple over to the side. Nose-diving is another common accident, where nose-heavy semi-trailers are not supported with trestles when left detached. Ground sinkage can also be a cause of difficulty when recoupling tractive units.

Cases have been reported (in *Commercial Motor*) of unsafe parking practices resulting in driver deaths related to the braking of parked semi-trailers. When recoupling tractive units, drivers insert the red air hose which releases the emergency brakes on the semi-trailer without checking that both the semi-trailer ratchet brake (if fitted) and the tractive-unit handbrake are fully applied. In such circumstances the vehicle combination can move while the driver is out of the cab. To counter this risk, alarms are available to warn the driver that the unit handbrake has not been applied. Other potential sources of accidents are when articulated combinations are coupled near to walls and loading bays, where there is always a danger of an unseen person walking behind the trailer. Again, if brakes are not properly set the semi-trailer is likely to shunt backwards as the tractive unit is driven under the coupling plate.

Work at Height

We have already discussed some elements of this set of regulations concerning health and safety matters, and the significant impact they have had on the road haulage industry. The Work at Height Regulations 2005 (SI 2005 No 735) came into effect from 6 April 2005. The regulations are intended to help prevent the many accidents involving falls from height. Falls from height remain the most common cause of workplace fatality. The HSE reports that they account for just over a quarter of fatalities at work and that in 2017/18 there were 35 fatalities due to a fall from height, and this figure rose to 40 fatalities for 2018/2019; in fact they are the biggest single cause of male workplace deaths and major injury. Replacing earlier regulations, the Work at Height Regulations consolidate previous legislation and implement EC Directive 2001/45/EC.

The new rules apply to most 'work at height' situations where there is a risk of a fall likely to cause injury to a person – as, for example, climbing into or out of a vehicle cab or the load area, or even being simply above ground level. The employer's duty is to ensure that current practices are risk assessed and safe and to take steps to prevent falls and ensure that relevant staff are trained, that work is planned accordingly and that work is suspended when weather conditions endanger health or safety. Provision in these regulations also relates to falling objects, which should be safeguarded against. In the context of this legislation, 'at height' means a place from which a person falling could be injured – and it also includes below ground level. Working means moving around at a place of work.

Noise at Work

According to Action on Hearing Loss (formerly the RNID), around 900,000 people in Britain actually suffer severe or acute deafness, tinnitus and other hearing problems, much of which stems from work activities. Hence, from April 2006 all workers in the transport industry were brought within the scope of the Control of Noise at Work Regulations 2005. As well as goods vehicle drivers, the regulations also include workers in garages, warehouses, and in bodybuilding, repair and paint shops, for example.

Where appropriate, employers are required to provide hearing protection (eg ear defenders) – and insist that employees use it – and regular hearing tests as well as training on minimizing the risk of hearing loss where the noise exceeds 80 dB. Noise control must be implemented where noise levels exceed 85 dB and there is an absolute maximum limit of 137 dB above which no employee should be subjected. Fines of up to £5,000 may be imposed for breaches of these regulations.

Further information can be obtained from the HSE website: www.hse.gov.uk/noise (archived at https://perma.cc/5LUM-TPKB) or from Action on Hearing Loss at informationline@hearingloss.org.uk.

Forklift Truck Safety

There has been much concern in recent years about the high level of industrial accidents which are caused by or which result from forklift truck misuse. In consequence of this a system of forklift truck driver licensing has been established in order to ensure a safe standard of operation. However, the HSE is keen to point out that there is no such thing as a statutory forklift truck driver's licence, but under the Provision and Use of Work Equipment Regulations 1998 (PUWER) there are certain requirements on employers and this has driven the need for both training and voluntary licensing of forklift truck operators.

PUWER states that employers must make sure that all people who use, supervise or manage the use of work equipment have received adequate training, which includes the correct use of the equipment, any risks from its use and the precautions to take. These requirements are the driving force that go to ensure employers can avoid conflict with the Health and Safety Inspectorate (HSI), who have powers to issue improvement notices and prohibition notices to employers to have drivers trained, ordering that the use of forklift trucks must be stopped immediately if they believe that danger is being caused and to take an employer to court if an untrained driver causes an accident with a forklift truck.

Further information can be downloaded from the HSE website or from publications such as:

- *Consulting Employees on Health and Safety: A brief guide to the law.* Leaflet INDG232 (rev2) HSE Books 2013, www.hse.gov.uk/pubns/indg232.pdf (archived at https://perma.cc/N9Z3-DBFB).
- *Rider-operated Lift Trucks: Operator training and safe use.* Approved Code of Practice and guidance L117 (third edition), HSE Books 2013 ISBN 978 0 7176 6441 2, www.hse.gov.uk/pubns/books/l117.htm (archived at https://perma.cc/5XXT-WSFS).
- *Use Lift Trucks Safely: Advice for operators.* Pocket card INDG457, HSE Books 2013, www.hse.gov.uk/pubns/indg457.htm (archived at https://perma.cc/CC57-6U3V).

Freight Container Safety Regulations

Owners and lessees and others in control of freight containers must ensure that they comply with the International Convention for Safe Containers – Geneva 1972. The Freight Containers (Safety Convention) Regulations 1984 apply to containers designed to facilitate the transport of goods by one or more modes of transport without intermediate reloading, designed to be secured or readily handled or both, having corner fittings for these purposes and which have top corner fittings and a bottom area of at least 7 square metres or, if they do not have top corner fittings, a bottom area of at least 14 square metres.

Containers must have a valid approval issued by the HSE or a body appointed by the HSE (or under the authority of a foreign government which has acceded to the Convention) for the purpose of confirming that they meet specified standards of design and construction and should be fitted with a safety approval plate to this effect. If they are marked with their gross weight such marking must be consistent with the maximum operating gross weight shown on the safety approval plate. Containers must be maintained in an efficient state, in efficient working order and in good repair. Details of the arrangements for the approval of containers in Great Britain are set out in a document *Freight Container Approval Arrangements in Great Britain*, which is free to download from the HSE website.

The safety approval plate (issued by the HSE) as described in the regulations must be permanently fitted to the container where it is clearly visible and not capable of being easily damaged and it must show the following information:

CSC SAFETY APPROVAL

- approval reference;
- date manufactured;
- identification number;
- maximum gross weight… kg… lb;
- allowable stacking weight for … g… kg… lb;
- racking test load value;
- next examination date.

NB: As mentioned earlier, freight containers now need to have their weight certified before being allowed to be loaded onto container ships, but this requirement does not apply to freight containers travelling by ro-ro ferries or on short sea crossings.

Operation of Lorry Loaders

The use of hydraulically operated lorry loaders or lorry-mounted cranes, as they are more commonly called (the name Hiab becoming perhaps the most used term for this equipment), has reduced the risk of accident from the arduous and potentially injurious manhandling of loads and they reserve the strength of the driver for safe conduct of the vehicle, according to the Association of Lorry Loader Manufacturers and Importers of Great Britain (ALLMI). But, the Association says, despite the inherent safety of a properly designed and installed lorry loader, accidents still occur through lack of knowledge and understanding. For this reason ALLMI has published an excellent book called *Code of Practice for the Safe Installation, Application and Operation of Lorry Loaders*. ALLMI also produces a range of other products including a training DVD to complement formal training as a visual aid. Copies are available from the Association (tel: 0844 8584334), by contacting ALLMI on www.allmi.com (archived at https://perma.cc/Y5XC-5F3G) or by writing to them at:

Unit 7b, Prince Maurice House
Cavalier Court
Bumpers Farm
Chippenham
Wiltshire
SN14 6LH

ALLMI also offer extensive training through a national network of approved training providers. Details of these training providers can also be found on the ALLMI website.

NB: See also Chapter 7 dealing with driver training for lorry-loader operatives.

Safety in Dock Premises

The Docks Regulations 1988 has now been repealed with new guidelines having been produced by the HSE (see below). The HSE guidelines still require many of the old regulations to be observed, such as goods vehicle drivers working in or visiting docks premises, including roll-on/roll-off ferry ports, being provided with high-visibility clothing to be worn when they leave the vehicle cab. The clothing may take the form of fluorescent jackets, waistcoats, belts or sashes and must be worn at all times when out of the cab on such premises, including when on the vehicle decks of ferries. Protective headgear (hard hats) must also be supplied and worn in such areas where there is likely to be danger of falling objects from above (eg where cranes are working). Other requirements include drivers leaving the vehicle cab when parked on a straddle-carrier grid or where containers are being lifted onto or off the vehicle.

In September 2019 the HSE has published an updated *Code of Practice: Safety in Docks: Approved Code of Practice L148*, which is free to download. This publication and further information relating to working in ports are available from the HSE website.

Loads – General, Livestock, Food, etc

18

In addition to the regulations referred to in Chapter 12 regarding the way in which vehicles are constructed and used, operators will find many more regulations imposed on them which depend on the types and sizes of load they carry. Some of these provisions are included in the Road Vehicles (Construction and Use) Regulations 1986, and its many amendments, but others are to be found elsewhere, particularly in the many EU Directives that have been put in place in order to make dimensions standard across most of Europe. This chapter deals with both the length and width of normal loads and also covers some of the special points applicable to carrying food, livestock, sand and ballast, solid fuel and containers.

Length and Width of Loads

Loads on normal goods vehicles (ie which come within the C&U Regulations) in excess of the actual vehicle dimensions of length and width may be carried provided that certain special conditions are met, as indicated here. Details of the requirements relating to abnormal and projecting loads are given in Chapter 19.

Length

When moving a vehicle, which complies with C&U Regulations, and its load, which is more than 18.75 metres long, the police must be notified two clear days in advance and/or the Electronic Service Delivery for Abnormal Loads (ESDAL) needs to be informed. If you have no password to log in to ESDAL you need to contact esdalenquiries@highwaysengland.co.uk or call 0300 470 3733. In addition to prior notification of the movement a statutory attendant must also be carried.

If a long load is carried on an articulated vehicle which is specially designed to carry long loads but in all other respects complies with the C&U Regulations, the

18.75-metre dimension is measured excluding the length of the tractive unit. Notice must also be given to the police and an attendant carried if the combination of a number of vehicles carrying one load is more than 25.9 metres long and if the load overhangs/projects from the vehicle by 2.0 m to the front and 3.05 m to the rear.

An overall limit of 27.4 metres is set for the length of a trailer and its load (the length of the towing vehicle is excluded from this dimension), above which movement can only be allowed by special order from the Secretary of State for Transport.

Further details of the requirements for dimensions, markers, police notification, escorts, highways, rail and bridge authority notification and attendants on long and projecting loads are given in Chapter 19.

Width

The overall width of a normal load (ie not an indivisible load) carried on a vehicle complying with the C&U Regulations must not be more than 2.9 metres. The load itself must not project more than 305 millimetres on either side of the vehicle. There is an exception to this requirement when loose agricultural produce is carried.

If an indivisible load is carried on a normal vehicle which complies in all respects with the C&U Regulations and the load is more than 2.9 metres wide, two days' notice must be given, as above. If such a load exceeds 3.5 metres, but not more than 4.3 metres, width then an attendant must be carried.

If the load on a vehicle is more than 4.3 but not more than 5 metres wide, five days' notice must be given, a statutory attendant must be carried and a Vehicle Special Order (VSO) must be obtained from the Vehicle Certification Agency (see below) using form VR1. If the load is more than 5 metres but not more than 6.1 metres wide, five days' notice must be given, a statutory attendant must be carried, a VSO must be obtained and speed limits apply (30 mph motorway, 25 mph dual carriageway and 20 mph single carriageway).

For loads exceeding 6.1 metres form BE16 must be used.

Details and further information are available from: vso@vca.gov.uk; or

VCA
No 1 The Eastgate Office Centre
Eastgate Road
Bristol
BS5 6XX (0300 330 5797)

Carriage of Livestock

A completely new set of rules concerning the welfare of animals during transit came into effect from 5 January 2007, replacing most of the former regulations. Council Regulation 1/2005/EC is a very long and detailed document for which the Department of Environment, Food and Rural Affairs (DEFRA) has provided a summary (latest version dated 2012 is available on the GOV.UK website) of the main requirements as follows.

The most important and overriding provision to note is that 'No animal shall be transported unless it is fit for the intended journey, and all animals shall be transported in conditions guaranteed not to cause them injury or unnecessary suffering' (source: Council Regulation 1/2005/EC on the protection of animals during transport and related operations and amending Directives).

All persons who take animals on a journey, whatever the length, should always apply the following good transport practice by ensuring that:

- the journey is properly planned and time is kept to a minimum and the animals are checked and their needs met during the journey;
- the animals are fit to travel;
- the vehicle and loading and unloading facilities are designed, constructed and maintained to avoid injury and suffering;
- the vehicle used is properly constructed, 'fit for purpose' and able to be cleaned effectively;
- those handling animals are trained or competent in the task and do not use violence or any methods likely to cause unnecessary fear, injury or suffering;
- water, feed and rest are given to the animals as needed, and sufficient floor space and height are allowed.

The Regulation applies to all those involved with the transport of live vertebrate animals in connection with an economic activity, for example:

- livestock and equine hauliers;
- farmers; and
- commercial pet breeders.

The Regulation also applies to those working at:

- markets;
- assembly centres; and
- slaughterhouses.

The Regulation does not apply to the transport of animals:

- where the transport is not in connection with an economic activity;
- to or from veterinary practices or clinics under veterinary advice, where the animal is an individual animal accompanied by its owner (or other responsible person) and is fit for the journey; or
- where animals are pet animals accompanied by their owner on a private journey.

Animals that Cannot Be Transported

It is illegal to transport an animal 'unfit for travel'. These groups include:

- very young animals, eg calves less than ten days old, pigs less than three weeks and lambs less than one week;
- calves less than 14 days old, for journeys over eight hours;
- cervine animals in velvet, ie deer with newly growing antlers;

- puppies and kittens less than eight weeks old, unless accompanied by their mother;
- newborn mammals where the navel hasn't completely healed;
- heavily pregnant females – where more than 90 per cent of the expected gestation period has passed – unless they are being transported for veterinary treatment;
- females who have given birth during the previous seven days;
- sick or injured animals where moving them would cause additional suffering, unless instructed by a vet;
- shorn sheep during cold weather particularly during November to March.

Transporter Requirements for Journeys up to 65 Kilometres

Transporters are not required to have vehicle authorization or training and certificates of competence. However, they must comply with the technical rules on fitness to travel, means of transport and transport practices as set out in Annex 1 of Council Regulation 1/2005/EC. Where these journeys do not include a market, there is no need to clean the vehicle between each load but this is required where any one point of the journey includes a market.

Transporter Authorization for Journeys Over 65 Kilometres and Under Eight Hours' Duration

A General Authorization will be granted by DEFRA, and will be valid for five years, if transporters can comply with the following:

- They have an established business or, in the case of businesses established outside the UK, are represented in the UK.
- They can demonstrate that they have appropriate staff, equipment and operational procedures to transport animals in compliance with the new Regulation.
- They have no record of serious infringements of animal welfare legislation in the three years preceding application.
- They have a driver who has undergone assessment and holds a certificate of competence to care for animals.
- Records of these journeys must be retained by the operator for a minimum of six months.

Transporter Authorization for Journeys of Over Eight Hours' Duration

A Special Authorization, issued by DEFRA, will be valid for five years. Authorization will be granted if transporters can comply with the following:

- They have an established business or, in the case of businesses established outside the UK, are represented in the UK.
- They can demonstrate that they have appropriate staff, equipment and operational procedures to transport animals in compliance with the new Regulation.
- They have no record of serious infringements of animal welfare legislation in the three years preceding their application.
- They have a driver who has undergone assessment and holds a certificate of competence to care for animals.

The transporter must provide:

- valid certificates of approval for vehicles and containers;
- a route plan which has been approved by the DEFRA Divisional Veterinary Manager (DVM);
- details of procedures enabling transporters to trace and record the movement of road vehicles under their responsibility and to contact the drivers at any time;
- contingency plans in the event of emergencies;
- from 2008, valid certificates of competence for drivers and attendants.

In addition:

- the animals must have sufficient bedding and food;
- the vehicle must have fittings for drinking water;
- the vehicle must be compartmentalized;
- the driver/crew must have access to each level.

NB: All cattle movements in Scotland require you to contact the British Cattle Movement Service usually at least three days before the cattle are moved. Other time limits do apply and further information is available from the BCMS at:

BCMS
Curwen Road
Workington
Cumbria
CA14 2DD
Tel: 0345 050 1234 (Mon–Fri 0830–1700)

Training and Competence for Drivers and Attendants and Assembly Centre Personnel

From 5 January 2008, drivers or attendants responsible for the transport of farmed animals, horses and poultry over distances greater than 65 km are required to hold a certificate of competence. Assembly centre staff are *not* required to obtain a certificate of competence but will need to have undergone training.

Training courses will cover the technical and administrative aspects of the rules and regulations that apply to the protection of animals during transport and cattle passports. These include:

- general conditions of transporting animals;
- the documents that are required;
- fitness for transport;
- journey planning;
- animal physiology and feed needs, animal behaviour and the concept of stress;
- practical aspects of handling animals;
- impact of driving behaviour on welfare of animals and on the quality of meat;
- emergency care for animals;
- safety of personnel handling animals.

The certificate of competence will be awarded once an independent assessment of knowledge of the above has been made.

Exporting of Animals

When animals are exported out of Great Britain the transporter must ensure that the journeys are properly planned and that a route plan is submitted to the Divisional Veterinary Manager at DEFRA for approval. Without this approval an export health certificate will not be issued. Operators based outside Great Britain will require an authorization from their own domestic authorities to transport animals.

Importing of Animals

When importing animals from the EU, every consignment must be accompanied by an Intra Trade Animal Health Certificate (ITAHC). In addition, if you import animals into the UK you must also ensure that the person you're importing the animals from has arranged the ITAHC in their own country. The importer is also legally required to send an importer notification form to the Animal and Plant Health Agency (APHA) who also provide the ITAHCs and advice on the import of animals. This must be sent at least 24 hours before any animals are due to arrive into the UK.

When you apply for an ITAHC you must nominate an official veterinarian (OV) who is authorized to sign trade documents and make sure a consignment meets requirements. For details on these issues contact APHA.

For animal movement licensing in England Tel: 03000 200 301 or
Email: customeradvice@apha.gsi.gov.uk.
(For enquiries in Wales and Scotland you must contact your local Field Services Office.)

For animal transport Tel: 03000 200 301 or Email: WIT@apha.gsi.gov.uk.

NB: After Brexit, if there is no deal it is expected that a system called The Trade Control and Expert System (TRACES) will operate. TRACES is an online system for tracking livestock consignments and health certification of animals coming into, and going out, of the UK. TRACES will allow Intra Trade Animal Health Certificates (ITAHCs) to be downloaded.

With 'no deal' ITAHCs could no longer be recognized by EU authorities and full Export Health Certificates (EHC) could be required for movements to the EU from the UK. In addition, consignments will need to pass through an EU Border Inspection Post. Transport authorizations, certificates of competence, and vehicle approval certificates will also no longer be recognized. The UK Government recommends that UK animal exporters should consider appointing representatives in EU member states in order to obtain journey logs for the member state concerned. Operators should use the animal movement contact details above or log on to the GOV.UK website for further details/updates. Further help can also be found by contacting the Animal and Plant Health Agency (APHA) on 03000 200 301.

Journey Logs (Over Eight Hours)

From 5 January 2007 anyone exporting farm livestock or unregistered horses is required to complete a journey log. This needs to be approved by the relevant DVM for the place of departure within 28 days of the journey being completed. Journey logs need to be retained by the carrier for a minimum of three years.

Animal Transport Certificates (Under Eight Hours)

Animal Transport Certificates (ATCs) are required for journeys of any species of animal over any distance or duration *except* journeys involving farm livestock and unregistered horses on export journeys of over eight hours, which require a journey log instead. The ATC is required to provide the following information:

- origin and ownership of animals;
- place of departure and destination;
- date and time of departure and expected duration of journey.

NB: Farmers transporting their own animals in their own means of transport on journeys of up to 50 km from their holding are exempt from this requirement.

The requirement for an ATC is not new and, as previously, there is no prescribed format in which the information required has to be presented. Any other document containing the required information – such as an Animal Movement Licence – may be used, if preferred. In all cases, the ATC needs to be retained by the carrier for six months following the movement.

Vehicle Inspection and Approval

From 5 January 2007 vehicles used for transporting farm livestock and horses on long journeys (those in excess of eight hours) must be inspected and approved by the competent authority of a member state or a body designated by a member state. In the UK this will include such organizations as the FTA, the European Food Safety Inspection Service (EFSIS) (Agriculture) and CMI Certification. In Scotland the approved authority was the Scottish Food Quality Certification Board, a private company formed in 1995 operating to ISO standards. This Board has now re-branded itself as Acoura and can be contacted by email at info@acoura.com or call 0330 024 0255.

Since 1 January 2009, all new cattle and horse transport vehicles need to be fitted with a satellite navigation system. Older vehicles used for transporting livestock and horses nationally on journeys in excess of 12 hours and internationally on journeys in excess of eight hours are subject to mandatory retro-fitting.

Food

The Food Standards Agency established under provisions contained in the Food Standards Act 1999 controls and regulates food safety and standards in the UK, particularly including such issues as the transport of livestock, fresh meat and other foods. It also has power to intervene if hauliers jeopardize food safety.

Special regulations (The Food Safety (General Food Hygiene) Regulations 1995) apply to vehicles used for the carriage of food, excluding milk and drugs. All mobile shops and food delivery vehicles and the equipment carried by such vehicles must be constructed and maintained so that the food carried can be kept clean and fresh.

The driver of a food vehicle should wear clean overalls and if meat or bacon sides are carried, which the driver has to carry over his shoulder, he should wear a hat and/or hairnet to prevent the meat touching his hair, and any cuts or abrasions on his hands must be covered with waterproof dressings.

If a driver or any other person concerned in the loading and unloading of food develops any infectious disease, his employer must notify the local authority health department immediately.

Food vehicles must have the name and address of the person carrying on the business shown on the nearside and the address at which the vehicle is garaged if this is a different address. If, however, a vehicle based in England or Wales has a fleet number clearly shown and is garaged at night on company premises, then the garage address is not required.

A wash hand basin and a supply of clean water must be provided on vehicles which carry uncovered food (except bread) unless the driver can wash his hands at both ends of his journey before he has to handle the food. When meat is carried, soap, clean towels and a nail brush must be provided on the vehicle. In Scotland all food-carrying vehicles must also be provided with these items.

Mobile shops and food delivery vehicles must not be garaged with food still inside unless it can be kept clean.

An authorized officer of a council may enter and detain (but not stop while it is in motion) any food-carrying vehicle except those owned by a rail company or vehicles operated by haulage contractors.

Perishable Foodstuffs

A whole range of legislation covers the carriage of food and particularly perishable food both in the UK and in Europe. When perishable foodstuffs are carried on international journeys to and through all EU member states and a further 17 non-EU and EFTA countries including, for example, countries such as Norway, Russia, Switzerland, Turkey and the Balkan states, the conditions of the United Nations

Economic Commission for Europe (UNECE) Agreement on the International Carriage of Perishable Foodstuffs (known as the ATP agreement) must be observed. ATP also applies on short sea crossings up to 150 km.

As a signatory to the agreement, the ATP agreement also applies in Britain and under its provisions vehicles used to carry perishable food must be constructed to design standards and tested for thermal efficiency (the initial test lasts for six years, thereafter three-yearly tests are required) to certain specified standards and must display an ATP approval plate, or carry an ATP certificate, to this effect. Details of where to get these tests can be obtained through the trade associations.

The principal requirement is that vehicles carrying certain specified perishable foodstuffs must comply with the body and temperature control equipment test standards and must be certified to this effect and that records of movements under ATP are properly monitored and, where thermographs are used, that records be retained for at least 12 months. The ATP agreement applies broadly to quick-frozen, deep-frozen, frozen and non-frozen foodstuffs but not fresh vegetables and soft fruit.

Information relating to food transport as well as codes of practice may be obtained from DEFRA.

Chilled Food Controls (ie Temperature-Controlled Food)

Following a series of food poisoning (salmonella and listeria) outbreaks in 1989 changes in legislation resulted in the introduction of the Food Hygiene (Amendment) Regulations 1990, which control the maximum temperature at which chilled food can be transported. The Regulations apply to goods vehicles exceeding 7.5 tonnes gross weight carrying 'relevant food' products (which are listed in the schedules to the regulations). Such vehicles must have equipment capable of maintaining the temperature of the food at or below the specified temperature (–5 °C for certain foods as listed in the schedules and –8 °C for other 'relevant' foods) or at or above 63 °C as appropriate and be fitted with either a thermograph or have a visible thermometer.

Vehicles up to 7.5 tonnes used for local deliveries must be capable of keeping relevant food at or below the specified temperature or at or above 63 °C as appropriate. However, in a case where the Regulations specify that food is to be kept at 5 °C, provided it is not kept in the vehicle for more than 12 hours, it may be at a higher temperature, not exceeding 8 °C.

There are exemptions to these requirements: where food is to be sold within two hours (ie if prepared at 63 °C or over) or four hours (ie if prepared below 63 °C). Other variations (ie not exceeding 2 °C for a maximum of two hours) may be permitted in certain specified circumstances such as variations in processing; while equipment is defrosted; during temporary breakdown of equipment; while moving food from one place or vehicle to another; or any other unavoidable reason.

Regulations (ie the Food Safety (Temperature Control) Regulations 1995 and the Food Safety (General Food Hygiene) Regulations 1995) which came into effect in September 1995 implement various provisions of EU Directive 43/93/EEC on these matters and parts of the so-called 'Water Directive' (EU Directive 778/80/EEC), which relates to the use of water for food production purposes. These regulations only marginally affect transport operations and for that reason they are not detailed here.

Quick-frozen Foodstuffs

The UK Quick-frozen Foodstuffs (QFF) Regulations 1990 are effective in setting general conditions for the quality and use of equipment for storing and transporting food labelled 'quick-frozen' (but not ice cream). These regulations require certain temperatures to be maintained within a percentage range of –18 °C, or colder, as follows:

- during transport (other than local distribution) a tolerance for brief periods of 3 °C (but not warmer than –15 °C);
- during local distribution 6 °C (but not warmer than –12 °C).

The Quick-frozen Foodstuffs (Amendment) Regulations 1994, which took effect from 1 September 1994, require refrigerated transport operators to fit temperature recorders to vehicles carrying frozen foodstuffs (but not chilled foods) and to keep the records for at least 12 months.

Waste Food

Vehicles used to collect unprocessed waste food must be drip-proof, covered and enclosed with material capable of being cleansed and disinfected.

Vehicles must be thoroughly cleansed and disinfected on the completion of unloading. No livestock or poultry or foodstuff or anything intended for use for any livestock or poultry may be carried in any vehicle which is carrying unprocessed waste food. Furthermore, processed and unprocessed waste food may not be carried in the same vehicle at the same time.

Grain Haulage

Grain hauliers are faced with rules banning them from using grain trailers for the carriage of other loads (such as glass, toxins, waste, bonemeal and manure) which may contaminate the trailer. Auditors from the Agricultural Industries Confederation (AIC) based in Peterborough which was formed in 2003 monitor standards and check hauliers' records and invoices to ensure they have not broken the Association's code, which is based on provisions in the Food Safety Act 1990. A 'grain passport' must be carried on vehicles, otherwise loads may be rejected by consignees if they are not satisfied as to the origin or standard under which loads have been carried.

Sand and Ballast Loads

The movement of sand and ballast comes under Schedule Four of the Weights and Measures Act 1985 and is subject to Trading Standards legislation, the latest update being published in July 2013 in 'Government Notice No 223'. These materials must be sold in weighed quantities (normally by volume in metric measures – in multiples of 0.2 cubic metres) and/or carried in calibrated vehicles which display a stamp placed on the body by the Trading Standards department of the local authority. In the cases where the vehicle is calibrated (although this is not often done nowadays) the load must be levelled off and 'evened out' to ensure that the full load is carried.

When sand and ballast (including shingle, ashes, clinker, etc) loads are carried, the driver must have a signed note (ie conveyance note) from the supplier indicating the following facts:

- the name and address of the sellers;
- the name of the buyer and the address for delivery of the load;
- a description of the type of ballast;
- the quantity by net weight or by volume;
- details of the vehicle;
- the date, time and place of loading the vehicle.

The document containing these details must be handed over to the buyer before unloading, or if he is not there it must be left at the delivery premises. Where a delivery is to be made to two or more buyers each must be given a separate document containing the details shown above. Similar requirements apply to the carriage of ready-mixed cement.

Aggregates Levy

From April 2002, in an effort to increase the use of alternative recycled materials, a 'quarry' tax (now called the Aggregates Levy) of £1.60 per tonne applied to all primary aggregates such as sand, gravel and crushed rock taken from quarries. In December 2014 this rate was raised to £2.00 per tonne and was still £2.00 in 2019. In effect this is a levy on aggregates excavated from the ground, dredged from the sea or imported. Some of the revenue earned from this tax goes into an environmental 'aggregates sustainability fund'.

Landfill Tax

Since 1996, this tax, brought in following the EU Landfill Directive, applies to most materials including wastes from construction, demolition, clay and coal extraction, etc, that go to landfill. The tax is levied at two rates and is linked to the RPI. From April 2019 the lower rate of £2.90 per tonne was applied to inert, or inactive, waste such as brick, concrete and glass, etc. This lower rate will rise to £3.00 per tonne on 1 April 2020. The higher rate of £91.35 will rise to £94.15 per tonne on 1 April 2020. This higher rate is levied on waste classified as 'active', which includes things like wood and plastics.

Solid Fuel Loads

When solid fuel is carried a document giving similar details to those mentioned above for sand and ballast carrying must be held by the driver of the vehicle. When solid fuel is carried for sale in open sacks a notice on the vehicle in letters at least 60 mm high must contain the following words: 'All open sacks on this vehicle contain 25 kg'.

Container Carrying

While there are no specific regulations on this subject apart from the general safety provisions of the C&U Regulations and the vehicle weight limitations, the authorities are concerned about the dangers arising from inadequate securing of containers. Containers, ideally, should be carried only on vehicles fitted with proper twist locks or, failing this, should be secured by chains of sufficient strength with tensioners for adjustment and taking account of the recommended strength of restraint systems given in the D*f*T and DVSA code of practice (see p 489).

The use of ropes for securing containers should be avoided, and would probably be judged to be illegal, because the corner castings through which they are passed are rough and will cut through the rope. Where possible, containers should be loaded against the headboard and directly on the platform of the vehicle, not on timber packing, which is liable to move.

Under the Freight Containers (Safety Convention) Regulations 1984 owners and lessees and others in control of freight containers used or supplied must ensure that they comply with the conditions of use as stated in the International Convention for Safe Containers 1972 (see also Chapter 17).

More recently however, following mis-declarations by organizations moving containers by sea, in 2016 the SOLAS Regulations were amended and unaccompanied containers being moved by sea (but not on ro-ro services) now need proof of their weight before they will be loaded onto container vessels.

Fly-Tipping

The Environmental Protection Act 1990 tightened up existing measures to prevent the illegal tipping (fly-tipping) of waste, demolition rubble and such materials including 'black bags', in unauthorized places. Among the specific measures legislated for under regulations called the Controlled Waste (Registration of Carriers and Seizure of Vehicles) Regulations 1991 are requirements for Waste Regulation Authorities (WRAs), the classification of different types of waste, the registration of waste transfer stations, registration of authorized waste transporters and tipper operators, the licensing of authorized operators, the retention for two years of waste transfer notes, restriction of tipping to authorized sites and further powers to impound (and possibly sell) vehicles belonging to operators who dump loads illegally (such powers also exist under the Criminal Justice Act 1988).

Offences such as fly-tipping can result in fines of up to £50,000 to companies and in-dividuals and a possible 12 months term of imprisonment for magistrate's court convictions. Where a case goes before a Crown Court, much higher penalties may be imposed, including unlimited fines and up to five years' imprisonment. In 2016 powers were also given to local authorities to issue fixed penalty notices of between £150.00 and £400.00 to anyone caught in the act of fly tipping.

NB: See Chapter 20 for more information on the carriage and disposal of waste materials.

Loads – Abnormal and Projecting

19

After a prolonged period of consultation, a set of rules on the carriage of abnormal indivisible loads on Special Types vehicles was made late in 2003 with the introduction of the Road Vehicles (Authorization of Special Types) (General) Order 2003 (STGO) under Section 44 of the Road Traffic Act 1988. These provisions are concerned primarily with:

- abnormal indivisible loads exceeding the weight and/or dimensions laid out in the C&U Regulations;
- vehicles unable to comply with C&U Regulations (such as engineering plant, etc).

Abnormal Indivisible Loads

For the purpose of regulations, abnormal indivisible loads (abbreviated to AILs) are loads which cannot, without undue expense or risk of damage, be divided into two or more loads for the purpose of carriage on the road and which cannot be carried on a vehicle operating within the limitations of the C&U Regulations as described in Chapter 12.

Number of Abnormal Loads

While normally the carriage of only one abnormal load is permitted, two such abnormal loads may be carried on one vehicle within Category 1 or Category 2 (see below) provided the loads are from the same place and are destined for the same delivery address.

Engineering Plant

In the case of engineering plant, such plant and parts dismantled from it may be carried on the same vehicle (ie to constitute more than one or two loads) provided that the carriage of the parts does not cause the overall dimensions of the vehicle and the main load to be exceeded and that the parts are loaded and discharged at the same place as the main load.

Escorts

Although there is no statutory requirement to have abnormal loads escorted highway authorities and most police authorities encourage the use of private or in-company escorts for such movement and anyone enquiring to the police about a forthcoming movement should enquire about the position relating to an escort being required.

Special Types Vehicles

Dimensions

Width Special Types vehicles, locomotives and trailers and their loads are normally permitted to be up to 2.9 metres wide but, if necessary to ensure the safe carriage of large loads, they may be up to a maximum of 6.1 metres wide.

Length The overall length of a Special Types vehicle and its load must not exceed 27.4 metres, which applies normally, but where the abnormal load is carried on a combination of vehicles and trailers or on a long articulated vehicle the dimension of 27.4 metres is measured excluding the drawing vehicle.

Weight The permissible maximum weight of a Special Types vehicle must not exceed 150,000 kg. There is a limit on the maximum weight which may be imposed on the road by any one wheel of the vehicle of 8,250 kg and the maximum weight imposed by any one axle must not exceed 16,500 kg. These limits may be exceeded only if authorization by Special Order is obtained from the Secretary of State for Transport (D*f*T).

NB: At the time of writing there is an overall 196 tonne weight limit imposed on the Forth Road Bridges in Scotland. Weigh in-motion sensors are now being used to prevent excessive weights being carried over the bridges, with supporting ANPR systems used to identify offenders. Operators with queries need to contact the bridge authorities for guidance and advice:

Forth Road Bridges
Administration Office
South Queensferry
West Lothian
EH30 9SF
Tel: 0800 042 0188
Email: OCCR.FBScotland@amey.co.uk

Vehicle Categories

The Special Types Order specifies three separate weight categories for abnormal load vehicles as follows:

Category 1 – up to 50 tonnes MAM
Category 2 – up to 80 tonnes MAM
Category 3 – up to 150 tonnes MAM

TABLE 19.1 Category 1 vehicles

Vehicles within this category will normally fall within the C&U Regulations in regard to permissible maximum weight, axle spacings and axle weights but where it is a five-axle articulated vehicle the weight may exceed 40 tonnes up to a maximum of 50,000 kg (ie 50 tonnes) provided the following minimum relevant axle spacings are observed:

Relevant axle spacing	Maximum weight
At least 6.5 metres	40,000 kg
At least 7.0 metres	42,000 kg
At least 7.5 metres	44,000 kg
At least 8.0 metres	50,000 kg

TABLE 19.2a and b Category 2 vehicles

Vehicles within this category may operate up to a maximum weight of 80,000 kg (ie 80 tonnes) but they must have a minimum of six axles with a maximum weight of 50,000 kg on any group of axles and they must meet the minimum axle spacing requirements specified below.

Individual wheel and axle weight limits are as follows:

Distance between adjacent axles	Maximum axle weight	Maximum wheel weight
At least 1.1 metres	12,000 kg	6,000 kg
At least 1.35 metres	12,500 kg	6,250 kg

Minimum axle spacings and applicable maximum weights are as follows:

Distance between foremost and rearmost axles	Maximum weight
5.07 metres	38,000 kg
5.33 metres	40,000 kg
6.00 metres	45,000 kg
6.67 metres	50,000 kg
7.33 metres	55,000 kg

TABLE 19.2b *continued*

Distance between foremost and rearmost axles	Maximum weight
8.00 metres	60,000 kg
8.67 metres	65,000 kg
9.33 metres	70,000 kg
10.00 metres	75,000 kg
10.67 metres	80,000 kg

TABLE 19.3a and b Category 3 vehicles

A minimum of six axles are needed on Category 3 vehicles operating up to a permissible maximum weight of 150,000 kg (ie 150 tonnes) with a limit of 100,000 kg on any group of axles or 90,000 kg on any group of axles where the distance between adjacent axles is less than 1.35 metres. Vehicles in this category must meet the minimum axle spacing requirements specified below. Individual wheel and axle weight limits are as follows:

Distance between adjacent axles	Maximum axle weight	Maximum wheel weight
At least 1.1 metres	15,000 kg	7,500 kg
At least 1.35 metres	16,500 kg	8,250 kg

Minimum axle spacings and applicable maximum weights are as follows:

Distance between foremost and rearmost axles	Maximum weight
5.77 metres	80,000 kg
6.23 metres	85,000 kg
6.68 metres	90,000 kg
7.14 metres	95,000 kg
7.59 metres	100,000 kg
8.05 metres	105,000 kg
8.50 metres	110,000 kg

TABLE 19.3b *continued*

Distance between foremost and rearmost axles	Maximum weight
8.95 metres	115,000 kg
9.41 metres	120,000 kg
9.86 metres	125,000 kg
10.32 metres	130,000 kg
10.77 metres	135,000 kg
11.23 metres	140,000 kg
11.68 metres	145,000 kg
12.14 metres	150,000 kg

VED for Special Types Vehicles

A separate VED taxation class applies to Special Types vehicles. They are also subject to the HGV Road User Levy – see Chapter 8 for details.

Braking Standards

Vehicles operating within Category 1 must meet the UK C&U regulation braking standard requirements and those operating within Categories 2 and 3 from 1 October 1989 must meet the EU braking standards (ie EC Directive 71/320). In cases of Category 2 and 3 vehicles, wheel chocks may be used along with the parking brake in order to improve braking efficiency to meet the required EC standard.

Identification Sign

Vehicles operating under the STGO must display an identification sign at the front. This sign, on a plate at least 250 mm × 400 mm, must have white letters on a black background as follows:

TABLE 19.4 Identification sign

STGO	letters 105 mm high
CAT ...	letters and figures 70 mm high

NB: A figure 1, 2 or 3 must follow the word 'CAT' as appropriate depending on the category of vehicle.

Special Types Plates

Vehicles falling within Category 2 and 3 which have been manufactured since 1 October 1988 must display Special Types plates (in a conspicuous and easily accessible position) showing the maximum operational weights recommended by the manufacturer when travelling on a road at varying speeds as follows: 12, 20, 25, 30, 35, 40 mph. The weights to be shown are the permissible maximum gross and train weights and the maximum weights for each individual axle. Plates on trailers (including semi-trailers) must show the permissible maximum weight for the trailer and the maximum weights for each individual axle. The plates must be marked with the words 'Special Types Use'.

Speed Limits

Maximum permitted speeds* are specified for Special Types vehicles as follows:

TABLE 19.5 Speed limits

Vehicle category	Motorways	Dual carriageways	Other roads
1. Up to 50 tonnes	60 mph	50 mph	40 mph
2. Up to 80 tonnes	40 mph	35 mph	30 mph
3. Up to 150 tonnes	40 mph	35 mph	30 mph

Speeds for Wide Loads

Vehicles carrying loads over 4.3 metres but not over 6.1 metres wide are restricted to 30 mph on motorways, 25 mph on dual carriageways and 20 mph on other roads.

** It is important to note that tyre equipment on vehicles and trailers must be compatible with both the gross weight of the vehicle and the authorized maximum speed of operation.*

Attendants

An attendant must be carried on Special Types vehicles:

- when the vehicle or its load is more than 3.5 metres wide;
- if the overall length of the vehicle is more than 18.75 metres (not including the length of the tractive unit in the case of articulated vehicles);
- if the length of a vehicle and trailer exceeds 25.9 metres;

- if the load projects more than 2.00 metres beyond the front of the vehicle;
- if the load projects more than 3.05 metres beyond the rear of the vehicle.

If three or more vehicles carrying abnormal loads or other loads of dimensions that require statutory attendants to be carried travel in convoy, attendants need only be carried on the first and last vehicles in the convoy.

Attendants must be at least 18 years of age and properly trained in their duties.

Police Notification

The police of every district through which a Special Types combination is to be moved must be given two clear days' notice excluding Saturdays, Sundays and bank holidays in the case of notification under the STGO, and excluding Sundays and bank holidays for notification under the C&U Regulations if:

- the vehicle and its load is more than 3.0 metres wide;
- the vehicle and its load (or trailer and load) is more than 18.75 metres long;
- a combination of vehicles and trailers carrying the load is more than 25.9 metres long;
- the load projects more than 3.05 metres to the front or rear of the vehicle;
- the gross weight of the vehicle and the load is more than 80,000 kg.

The notice given must include details of the vehicle and the weight and dimensions of the load, the dates and times of the movement through the police district and the proposed route to be followed through that district.

In the case where notice has been given to the police of the movement of an abnormal load, they have the power to delay the vehicle during its journey if it is holding up other traffic or in the interests of road safety.

Under the provisions of the STGO, which came into effect from 1 January 2004, responsibility for escorting abnormal loads has transferred to private escort companies (see below) or to in-company escorts.

It should be noted that despite these arrangements, notification about the movement of abnormal loads must still be made to the police, and that Chief Constables retain the right to escort vehicles 'where appropriate'.

Notification of Highway and Bridge Authorities

If a Special Types vehicle and its load weighs more than 80,000 kg, or the weight imposed on the road by the wheels of such a vehicle exceeds the maximum limit laid down in the C&U Regulations (see p 351), five clear days' notice must be given to the highway and bridge authorities for the areas through which the vehicle is to pass. Two days' notice is required when only the C&U axle weight limit is exceeded. The operator of such a vehicle is also required to indemnify the authorities against damage to any road or bridge over which it passes. These requirements also apply to vehicles which exceed the C&U gross weight limits and those which exceed their plated axle weight limits, plus mobile cranes and engineering plant which exceed the limits specified. The contact details of the actual person(s) who need to be contacted are available through ESDAL (see Appendix V).

Stopping on Bridges

The driver of a vehicle carrying an abnormal load must ensure that no other such vehicle and load are on a bridge before he drives onto the bridge and once on the bridge he must not stop unless forced to do so.

Where a vehicle weighing more than 44,000 kg gross has to stop on a bridge for any reason it must be moved off the bridge as soon as possible. If it has broken down, the advice of the bridge authority (usually the Highways Department of the local authority) must be sought before the vehicle is jacked up on the bridge. In the event of damage being caused to a road or bridge by the movement of a heavy or large load over it the highway authority can take steps to recover from the vehicle operator the costs of repairing the damage.

Notification to Network Rail

All movements of abnormal loads whether oversize or overweight over rail bridges must be notified to Network Rail at abnormalloadsenquiries@networkrail.co.uk Tel 01908 783 140. For operators using ESDAL (see below) it is somewhat easier as ESDAL will automatically notify Network Rail if the route is to use any of its bridges, etc.

Special Orders

Written approval has to be obtained from Highways England in cases where a Special Types vehicle and its load exceeds 5 metres in width. Application is made on form VR1 (ie the movement order) and a copy of this completed form must be carried on the vehicle. The route specified, and the date and timings for the journey notified in the application, must be adhered to, otherwise further approval will have to be sought.

Dump Trucks

When dump trucks (ie vehicles designed for moving excavated material) are used on the road the maximum permissible gross weight is limited to 55,000 kg and the maximum axle weight allowed for such vehicles is 22,860 kg. They must not exceed a speed of 12 mph on normal roads and an attendant must be carried if the width exceeds 3.5 metres. If a dump truck is more than 4.3 metres wide, permission in the form of a Special Order from the Secretary of State is required before it is moved. Where three or more such vehicles over 3.5 metres wide travel in convoy only the first and last vehicles need carry attendants.

Other Plant

The Special Types General Order also makes special provision for other items of plant such as grass-cutting machines and hedge trimmers, track-laying vehicles, pedestrian-controlled road maintenance vehicles, vehicles used for experimental trials, straddle carriers, land tractors used for harvesting, mechanically propelled hay and straw balers, vehicles fitted with movable platforms and engineering plant. Any person proposing to move such items on public roads is advised to check that the appropriate legal requirements are met.

Internet Notifications for Abnormal Loads (ESDAL)

The Highways authorities, together with their agent SERCO, have launched a free website called ESDAL (Electronic Service Delivery for Abnormal Loads) which is designed to ease the complex statutory notifications which operators must make when planning to move abnormal loads. The scheme is said to 'cut bureaucracy' by making it easier for operators to find out who they must contact in both the police and the highway authorities in order to make these notifications.

Where ESDAL is used the authorities will normally expect an escort vehicle to be provided and that the escort staff will be properly trained and at least 18 years of age.

The helpdesk address for operators to register their details and obtain more information on this topic is: esdalenquiries@highwaysengland.co.uk or call 0300 470 3733. (See also contact details in Appendix V.)

Escorts for AILs

Although not normally mandatory, the police and/or private escorts may be used to escort AILs and some vehicles with projecting loads. In these cases the police have laid down procedures and need to risk assess every movement they will be expected to be involved with. Their priority is the safety of road users and the guidelines have been prepared for them by the Association of Chief Police Officers (ACPO). Although many companies do now provide their own escorts, where there may be a requirement for the escort to stop other traffic the police do have this power and may be the preferred option.

Where the haulage company, or private escort company, escort the load the vehicle(s) used need to be of a specification recommended in the Code of Practice published by Highways England and approved by the police. The rules state that the escort motor vehicle shall have a minimum of four wheels, enable the driver to have good visibility, be fitted with mirrors and have no open cargo space. It must be made conspicuous to other road users and be of a uniform bright colour such as white or orange.

In addition to the obligatory vehicle lighting flashing warning beacons need to be fitted to the roof, but only be used whilst the vehicle is actually escorting an abnormal load.

The vehicle needs to be marked clearly identify it is an escort vehicle by marking 'Escort Vehicle' or 'Escort' on the front along with ABNORMAL LOAD or WIDE

LOAD or SLOW LORRY or LONG LOAD, etc. either mounted on the roof or also on the front. A rear sign with the same information also needs to be fitted.

The name of the vehicle operator and/or owner may be displayed upon the side of the vehicle but no company livery can be displayed on the front or rear. To help alert other road users approaching the escort vehicle from the rear, high visibility 'chevron' markings need to be applied to the rear of the vehicle. As much of the rear of the vehicle as possible should be marked in this way. To maintain high vehicle visibility from different angles, the red and yellow chevron markings need to be continued in an unbroken pattern onto the side of the vehicle body.

Full detailed information on the exact format of these markings and positioning can be downloaded from the Government website: www.gov.uk/government/collections/abnormal-loads-forms-and-guidance (archived at https://perma.cc/6M7X-C73Q).

(Highways England is the body that replaced the Highways Agency when the Infrastructure Act became law in February 2015.)

High Loads

While there are no general legal height restrictions on vehicles or loads within the UK (except those specific instances mentioned on p 349), clearly vehicles must be loaded so that they can pass under bridges on the routes to be used.

In particular it should be noted that motorway bridges are built to give a clearance of 16 ft to 16 ft 6 ins and overhead power cables crossing roads are set at a minimum height of 19 ft (5.8 metres) where the voltage carried does not exceed 33,000 volts and at 6.0 metres where this voltage is exceeded (see also the note on p 524 about tipping vehicle dangers in regard to contact with overhead power cables). When planning to move loads above 19 ft it is a legal requirement to make contact with the National Grid or the appropriate regional electricity distribution company (ie previously the regional electricity boards) beforehand. It is also recommended that contact should be made with British Telecom (BT) regarding the presence of its overhead lines on the routes to be used. Some police forces now report that they will not action notification of abnormal load movements until both the electrical distributors and BT have been notified. (It should also be noted that at times of festivals, eg Christmas and carnivals, some local authorities erect overhead decorations and lights and extra care, and information, may be required if moving high loads at these times.)

Projecting Loads

Projecting loads may be carried on normal C&U regulation vehicles as well as on Special Types vehicles as described above. A projecting load is one that projects beyond the foremost or rearmost points or the side of the vehicle and, depending on the length or width of the projection, certain conditions apply when such loads are carried on normal vehicles, including requirements for lighting and marking.

Side Projections

Loads more than 4.3 metres wide cannot be moved legally under the C&U Regulations although they can be carried on vehicles which comply with those regulations. In such cases the provisions of the Special Types General Order apply (see above).

The normal width limit for loads is 2.9 metres overall or 305 mm on either side of the vehicle except in the case of loose agricultural produce and indivisible loads. Where an indivisible wide load extends 305 mm or more on one or both sides of the vehicle or exceeds 2.9 metres overall, the police must be given two clear days' notice in advance and end marker boards must be displayed front and rear (fitted within 50 mm of the edge of the load), and if it exceeds 3.5 metres, police notification, end marker boards and an attendant are required.

Forward Projections

A load projecting more than 2.0 metres beyond the foremost part of the vehicle (on C&U vehicles) must be indicated by an approved side and end marker board (Figure 19.1) and an attendant must be carried. On Special Types vehicles only, where the load projects more than 1.83 metres to the front, an end marker must be displayed and an attendant carried.

If a load projects more than 3.05 metres beyond the front (on both C&U and Special Types vehicles), the police must be given two days' notice of its movement, both side and end approved marker boards must be displayed and an attendant must be carried.

If a load projects more than 4.5 metres beyond the front of the vehicle the provisions mentioned above must be observed and additional side marker boards must be carried within 2.5 metres of the first set of side markers.

Rearward Projections

Where a load projects more than 1.0 metre beyond the rear of a C&U vehicle (1.07 metres on Special Types vehicles) it must clearly be marked (the form which this must take is not specified, but a piece of rag tied to the end is usually sufficient). If the rear projection is more than 2.0 metres on C&U vehicles (1.83 metres on Special Types vehicles) an end marker board must be displayed.

Where the rearward projection is more than 3.05 metres the police must be notified, an attendant carried and approved side and end marker boards displayed. An end marker is not required if the projecting load is fitted with a rear reflective marker. If the rearward projection exceeds 5.0 metres additional side marker boards must be carried within 3.5 metres of the first set of side markers.

Marker Boards

Marker boards carried in accordance with the requirements described above must conform to the dimensions and colours shown in Figure 19.1 and they must be indirectly illuminated at night.

FIGURE 19.1 The approved-type marker boards which must be displayed when projecting loads are carried

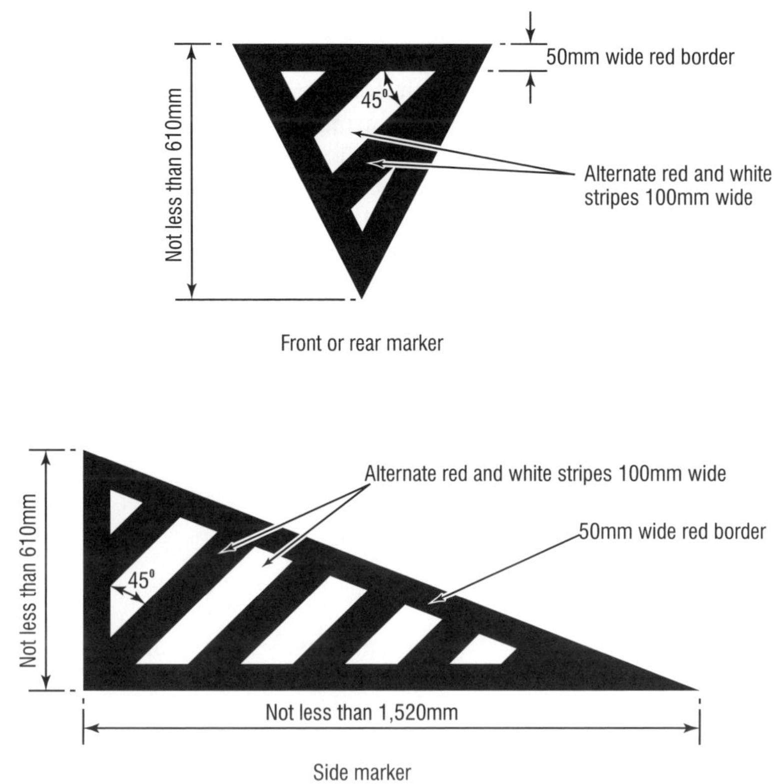

Lighting on Projecting and Long Loads

Rearward Projections

When carrying a load projecting more than 1.0 metre beyond the rear end of the vehicle an additional red rear position light must be carried within 1.0 metre of the end of the load or if the projecting load covers the rear lights and reflectors of the vehicle, additional lights and reflectors must be fixed to the load. This is usually best accomplished by having a complete lighting set and reflectors fitted to a board which can be fixed to the load.

Side Projections

When a load projects sideways more than 400 mm beyond the front and rear position lights of a vehicle, front position lights must be carried within 400 mm of the outer edges of the load and additional rear lights must also be carried within

400 mm of the outer edges of the load. White front and red rear reflectors must also be carried within 400 mm of the outer edges of the load.

Long Vehicles

A vehicle or combination of vehicles which, together with their load, are more than 18.75 metres long must, when on the road during the hours of darkness, carry side marker lights on each side positioned within 9.15 metres of the front of the vehicle or load and within 3.05 metres of the rear of the vehicle or load and other lights positioned between these at not more than 3.05-metre intervals. These requirements do not apply if approved illuminated marker boards are carried or if the combination is formed of a towing vehicle and a broken-down vehicle.

In the case of a combination of vehicles carrying a supported load (a load not resting on a vehicle except at each end) when the total length of the combination exceeds 12.2 metres but not 18.75 metres, side marker lights must be carried when on the road during the hours of darkness, positioned not more than 1.53 metres behind the rear of the drawing vehicle, and if the load extends more than 9.15 metres beyond the drawing vehicle an additional side marker light must be carried not more than 1.53 metres behind the centre line of the load.

All Vehicles

Where any projecting load or part load obscures, either completely or partially, an obligatory vehicle light or the vehicle registration plate, a replacement light or plate, fixed to the projection must be used. This is normally achieved by attaching a trailer board to the end of the projection.

Loads – Dangerous, Explosive and Waste

20

Many millions of tonnes of all types of dangerous goods are transported annually on British roads. Legislation on the carriage of dangerous goods is largely EU-driven and will continue to apply after Brexit. It is extensive and complex, and should be studied in detail by those responsible for such operations. Failure to comply with the strict provisions of the law can lead to harsh penalties. It could also result in risk to health and human life and cause serious environmental pollution. Clearly, EU standards will need to be maintained by UK visiting vehicles intending to carry dangerous goods there and the international standards currently in force, under what are known as ADR Regulations, will remain in force in any event.

Legislation Summary

The principal piece of dangerous goods legislation is known by the name of REACH. This is European Community Regulation EC 1907/2006 on chemicals and their safe use. In the UK the overseeing body is known as REACHReady with offices in Westminster, London. It deals with the registration, evaluation, training, authorization and restriction of chemical substances. The regulation originally came into force on 1 June 2007 and its aim was to improve the protection of human health and the environment through the better and earlier identification of the intrinsic properties of chemical substances. REACH has been amended and updated since 2007 and further information is available on 0207 901 1444 or enquiries@reachready.co.uk or on the HSE website.

The REACH Regulation gives greater responsibility to industry to manage the risks from chemicals and to provide safety information on the substances. Manufacturers and importers will be required to gather information on the properties of their chemical substances that will allow their safe handling, and to register the information in a central database run by the European Chemicals Agency (ECHA) in Helsinki.

UK national legislation on the carriage of dangerous goods by road is now aligned with the European Agreement Concerning the International Carriage of Dangerous Goods by Road (ADR) under Council Directive 94/55/EC, which harmonizes the law throughout the European Union. A so-called consolidated 'restructured' edition of ADR was published for 2005, taking effect from 1 January 2005, but the latest edition was published as late as 2019. The main changes are listed in the following text in summary form on a part-by-part basis. The current edition of ADR is described further below.

UK Carriage by Road Regulations

The current dangerous goods regulations, namely the Carriage of Dangerous Goods and Use of Transportable Pressure Equipment Regulations 2009 (SI 2009 No 1348), generally referred to as the Carriage Regulations, deal with the carriage by road and rail of dangerous goods (other than explosives and radioactive material) in packages or in bulk in any container, tank or vehicle. However, unlike former UK domestic dangerous goods legislation, these regulations implement ADR in the UK and cross-reference to the provisions set out in the Agreement.

These regulations, in Part 2(5), state that no person may carry dangerous goods, or cause or permit dangerous goods to be carried, where that carriage is prohibited by ADR or where that carriage does not comply with any applicable requirement of ADR. In other words, all carriage of dangerous goods by road must be in accordance with the ADR Agreement as described in this chapter, meaning that most domestic movements within the UK are now carried out to the same standards as ADR movements.

The ADR Convention

The international carriage of dangerous goods by road within Europe is governed by the United Nations Economic Commission for Europe (UNECE) European Agreement concerning the International Carriage of Dangerous Goods by Road (known conveniently as 'the ADR Convention' or 'the ADR Agreement') and most European countries are contracting parties to it. All EU member states are signatories to it and their respective domestic legislation on dangerous goods carriage is based on this Convention, which is regularly updated. It is an agreement between member states with no overall enforcing authority – the relevant authorities in contracting countries prosecute contravention of the ADR requirements under their own domestic legislation. The Agreement is a substantial document, and as previously mentioned it was updated in 2019. The Agreement and information relating to domestic carriage of dangerous goods are available and free to download at www.hse.gov.uk/cdg/manual/adrcarriage.htm (archived at https://perma.cc/5QSX-5AEV).

ADR is published in two volumes and is also available in hard-copy book form or is available on CD from The Stationery Office and is consistent with the United Nations' Model Regulations on the Transport of Dangerous Goods, the International Maritime Dangerous Goods Code and the International Civil Aviation's Technical

Instructions for the Safe Carriage of Dangerous Goods by Air, and is fully harmonized with the Regulations concerning the International Carriage of Dangerous Goods by Rail (RID). It is also available to download as PDF files from the UNECE website.

Volume 1 of this edition contains the text of the actual ADR Agreement, the Protocol of Signature and Parts 1 to 3 of Annex A, which cover the general provisions and provisions concerning dangerous substances and articles as follows:

- Part 1 deals with the scope of the Agreement, definitions and units of measure, training of persons involved in the carriage of dangerous goods, safety obligations of the participants in the carriage of such goods, various derogations and transitional measures, the general requirements for the carriage of Class 7 goods (ie radioactive material), checks and other measures to ensure compliance with safety requirements, the rights of Contracting Parties to the Agreement to restrict or prohibit the carriage of certain dangerous goods for reasons other than safety, and it lists in an Appendix to Part 1 the competent authorities in each of the signatory states. In the UK this is the D*f*T.
- Part 2 deals with the general provisions concerning the classification of dangerous goods and lists the nine main classes and sub-classes. It also describes the test methods to be used for the classification of dangerous goods and cross-references the procedures to the United Nations' *Manual of Tests and Criteria*.
- Part 3 is taken up with the actual Dangerous Goods List in which all relevant substances are classified across 20 column headings under their UN Number and also by their names in alphabetical order.

Volume 2 contains:

- continuations of Annex A and Part 3 from volume 1;
- Part 4 dealing with packing and tank provisions;
- Part 5 dealing with consignment procedures;
- Part 6 dealing with the construction and testing of packagings and IBCs;
- Part 7 dealing with carriage by road, loading and handling of dangerous goods;
- Part 8 dealing with vehicle crews and equipment;
- Part 9 dealing with the construction and approval of dangerous goods carrying vehicles.

Definition and Classification of Dangerous Goods

Definition

Dangerous goods are defined as being those substances and articles the carriage of which is prohibited by ADR (or RID in the case of carriage by rail), or authorized only under the conditions prescribed in these Agreements.

In general terms the following types of article and substance would be defined as dangerous goods:

- goods named in the ADR classification list as set out in ADR Part 2 (see also SI 2004/568, regulation 15);
- other goods which have one or more hazardous properties;
- explosives; or
- radioactive material.

Dangerous articles or substances falling within the scope of the legal requirements may range from:

- quite small quantities of individually packaged goods such as domestic cleaning products;
- tanker loads of acids and corrosive substances;
- explosives (both substances and explosive articles – eg detonators, etc);
- radioactive substances.

Identification

The purpose of, and legal necessity for, identifying dangerous goods is to determine their classification and identify their most hazardous properties and the dangers which may arise or be created when they are loaded, transported and unloaded. In many cases such goods have a number of hazards, not all of which may be immediately apparent.

It is for the manufacturer or consignor initially to determine the classification for dangerous goods intended to be consigned for carriage by deciding whether they are:

- explosives;
- radioactive material;
- named individually in the ADR Chapter 2;
- not named individually in the ADR Chapter 2.

Dangerous Goods Named Individually in the ADR Dangerous Goods List

Most of the commonly transported dangerous goods are named individually in ADR under their proper name, in alphabetical order and with their UN number. If the goods comprise a mixture or preparation of substances these too may be listed, as many dangerous goods have a generic name. This 'dangerous goods list' is to be found in ADR Chapter 3.2.

Dangerous Goods Not Named Individually in the ADR Dangerous Goods List

Where the dangerous goods are not 'named individually' the most appropriate generic entry (where the goods are of one chemical family) must be established or, alternatively, the relevant 'Not Otherwise Specified' (NOS) entry should be used for those goods. This is done by first establishing the hazardous properties of the goods and then checking to see whether any alternative name can be found in the list that could be used to classify the goods.

Classification

It is important to note that the carriage of dangerous goods is prohibited unless their classification, packing group and any subsidiary hazards have been determined. An established classification system applies to the carriage of dangerous goods as set out in the United Nations' so-called *Orange Book** and in ADR Part 2.

**The internationally recognized recommendations for the classification, package testing and marking requirements for the transport of dangerous goods. It is in two volumes comprising a set of model regulations (volume I) and tests and criteria (volume II).*

The UN system classifies dangerous goods into:

- classes (of which there are nine);
- divisions;
- packing groups.

The nine classes cover the main types of dangerous goods (eg explosives, gases, flammable and oxidizing substances, etc) – see full list below. Each of these classes is further subdivided into a number of divisions which more specifically identify dangerous goods falling within each of the classes. A further degree of classification is achieved by assigning goods to a packing group according to the degree of danger they present.

Classes and Divisions

The following list shows the classes and divisions for dangerous goods:

- Class 1: Explosive substances and articles.
  - Division 1.1: Substances and articles which have a mass explosion hazard.
  - Division 1.2: Substances and articles which have a projection hazard, but not a mass explosion hazard.
  - Division 1.3: Substances and articles which have a fire hazard and either a minor blast hazard or a minor projection hazard or both, but not a mass explosion hazard.
  - Division 1.4: Substances and articles which present no significant hazard.
  - Division 1.5: Very insensitive substances that have a mass explosion hazard.
  - Division 1.6: Extremely insensitive articles that do not have a mass explosion hazard.

- Class 2: Gases.
  - Division 2.1: Flammable gases.
  - Division 2.2: Non-flammable, non-toxic gases.
  - Division 2.3: Toxic gases.
- Class 3: Flammable liquids.
- Class 4: Flammable solids, substances liable to spontaneous combustion and substances which, on contact with water, emit flammable gases.
  - Division 4.1: Flammable solids, self-reactive and related substances and desensitized explosives.
  - Division 4.2: Substances liable to spontaneous combustion.
  - Division 4.3: Substances which, in contact with water, emit flammable gases.
- Class 5: Oxidizing substances and organic peroxides.
  - Division 5.1: Oxidizing substance.
  - Division 5.2: Organic peroxides.
- Class 6: Toxic and infectious substances.
  - Division 6.1: Toxic substances.
  - Division 6.2: Infectious substances.
- Class 7: Radioactive material.
- Class 8: Corrosive substances.
- Class 9: Miscellaneous dangerous substances and articles.

UN Numbers and Proper Names

Besides the system of classification described above, dangerous goods are assigned a UN number comprising four digits which are used in conjunction with the letters 'UN' (eg UN 2426, which identifies ammonium nitrate liquid in a hot concentrated solution); and a proper shipping name according to their hazard classification and depending on their composition (eg as above).

UN Packing Groups

Dangerous substances are also allocated UN packing groups as follows:

- Packing group I: for goods presenting high danger.
- Packing group II: for goods presenting medium danger.
- Packing group III: for goods presenting low danger.

UN Table of Precedence

The UN *Orange Book* sets out a table of precedence to take account of situations where dangerous goods not specifically identified in the Dangerous Goods List (in ADR Chapter 3.2) have more than one risk, or where dangerous goods have multiple risks. In such cases the most stringent packing group (ie Packing group I) takes precedence over other packing groups.

The following tables indicate the relevant classifications for dangerous goods, along with their packing group number (ie I, II or III), their class number and any optional lettering to be shown on packages (Table 20.1) and the relevant danger signs for dangerous goods indicating the symbol to be used and the colouring of the lettering and background (Table 20.2).

TABLE 20.1

Classification	Packing group	Class no	Optional lettering
Non-flammable, non-toxic gas	–	2.2	Compressed gas
Toxic gas	–	2.3	Toxic gas
Flammable gas	–	2.1	Flammable gas
Flammable liquid	I, II or III*	3	Flammable liquid
Flammable solid	I, II or III*	4.1	Flammable solid
Spontaneously combustible substance	I, II or III*	4.2	Spontaneously combustible
Substance which in contact with water emits flammable gas	I, II or III*	4.3	Dangerous when wet
Oxidizing substance	I, II or III*	5.1	Oxidizing agent
Organic peroxide	II	5.2	Organic peroxide
Toxic substance	I, II or III*	6.1	Toxic
Infectious substance	–	6.2	Infectious substance
Corrosive substance	I, II or III*	8	Corrosive
Miscellaneous dangerous goods	–	9	–

* Depending on its relevant properties.

TABLE 20.2

Description of sign	Symbol	Lettering	Background
Non-flammable, non-toxic gas	Black gas cylinder	Black or white	Green
Toxic gas	Black skull & crossbones	Black	White
Flammable gas	Black flame	Black or white	Red
Flammable liquid	Black flame	Black or white	Red
Flammable solid	Black flame	Black	Vertical white/ red stripes
Spontaneously combustible substance	Black flame	Black or white	White top/red bottom
Substance which in contact with water emits flammable gas	Black flame	Black or white	Blue
Oxidizing substance	Black 'O' & flame	Black (5.1)	Yellow
Organic peroxide	Black 'O' & flame	Black (5.2)	Red top/yellow bottom
Toxic substance	Black skull & crossbones	Black	White
Infectious substance	Black symbol	Black	White
Corrosive substance	Black symbol	White	White top/ black bottom
Miscellaneous			Vertical white/ black stripes at top
Limited quantity	Plain	None	Horizontal black (2) and white (1) stripes
Environmentally hazardous substance	Black	None	White with picture of black fish and black tree

Dangerous goods being moved throughout the UK, and from the UK to mainland Europe, will also require 'tunnel codes'. Tunnel codes are a two-part code where one letter code (A–E), with A being the least restrictive, identifies the tunnel concerned and what restrictions apply. The other part of the code refers to the substances covered by the A–E grading of the tunnel. The codes were introduced as a precaution against 'fire, explosion and the release of toxic gases or liquids' in road tunnels through Europe. All road tunnels are risk assessed and then classified and given codes which relate to any potential danger posed as well as any available or alternative routes in order to avoid them.

The tunnels are categorized as follows:

- Category A – no restrictions;
- Category B – risk of a large explosion;
- Category C – risk of a large or very large explosion or a large toxic release;
- Category D – risk of a large or very large explosion, a large toxic release or a large fire;
- Category E – restriction on the carriage of all dangerous goods in consignments of more than 8 tonnes.

The coding system works by the different UN classes of dangerous goods being given different code ratings so that the driver is aware of the code rating of the goods and the associated potential risks. Along the tunnel routes, signs bearing the appropriate tunnel code (B, C, D, or E) are placed at locations which allow the driver to divert and/or find a different route.

There are no signs for tunnels in Category A because there are no restrictions and the driver is able to use the tunnel.

Further information can be found at www.gov.uk/government/publications/adr (archived at https://perma.cc/ZC29-MJZD).

Responsibilities

Responsibility for Classification of Dangerous Goods

Responsibility for the classification of dangerous goods rests with:

- the appropriate competent authority (eg the United Nations) in publishing the classification system; and
- the manufacturer of the goods and the consignor (ie the sender) – these may be one and the same or separate entities who must:
  - identify their hazards;
  - determine the most appropriate description for them; and
  - establish their correct UN identification number (ie a four-digit number) by reference to the ADR Dangerous Goods List and their packing group.

Responsibility for Ensuring that Legal Requirements are Met

Responsibility for ensuring that relevant legal requirements are met (including the task of correctly identifying and classifying dangerous goods) rests with:

- the competent national authority, which in the UK is the D*f*T;
- HSE and the police;
- consignors of dangerous goods; and
- those who load, unload and transport such goods, namely:
  - employers/carriers;
  - dangerous goods safety advisers (DGSAs);
  - drivers of dangerous goods carrying vehicles;
  - employees and other people.

Employer Responsibilities

Firms (described in the legislation as undertakings) or individuals involved in the loading, unloading or transport (ie carriage) of dangerous goods by road must comply with statutory requirements on the prevention of risks to the health and safety of persons, or to damage of property or the environment. They also need to appoint a qualified safety adviser (DGSA) (SI 2004 No 568, regulation [12] and ADR 1.8.3). An 'undertaking' is any legal body (eg limited liability company), association or group (eg voluntary and charitable organizations), or any official body that transports, loads or unloads dangerous goods.

Employers are responsible for ensuring that:

- a qualified DGSA is appointed, where relevant; and
- dangerous goods vehicle drivers:
  - hold vocational training certificates;
  - are trained in emergency action procedures; and
  - vehicles used are approved and carry the correct emergency equipment.

Rules for Drivers

Drivers must not:

- carry unauthorized passengers on vehicles transporting dangerous goods (ADR 8.3.1);
- open any package containing dangerous goods unless authorized to do so (ADR 8.3.3);
- carry matches or lighters (or anything else capable of producing a flame or sparks) on vehicles carrying dangerous goods (except where the only goods on the vehicle are infectious substances), nor must the vehicle crew smoke during handling operations inside or in the vicinity of the vehicle (ADR 8.3.4 and 8.3.5).

Responsibility for Safety

Responsibility for compliance with the dangerous goods regulations, in particular in relation to safety issues, rests with the participants, who are defined in ADR 1.4 as the consignor, the carrier and the consignee together with other personnel such as loaders, fillers, packers, etc (ADR 7.5.1 and SI 2004 No 568, regulation 23[5]). In particular, these participants must take appropriate measures according to the nature and extent of foreseeable dangers, so as to avoid damage or injury and, if necessary, to minimize their effects. Where there is an immediate risk that public safety may be jeopardized, the participants must immediately notify the emergency services and make available to them the information they need to take appropriate action. Chapter 1.4 of ADR specifies the individual responsibilities of the three main participants as outlined below.

The Consignor

The consignor must ensure, when handing over dangerous goods for carriage, that consignments conform to the requirements of ADR, in particular by:

- ensuring that the goods are classified and authorized for carriage in accordance with ADR;
- giving the carrier relevant information, data and the required transport documents;
- using only packaging, intermediate bulk containers (IBCs) and tanks (ie tank vehicles, demountable tanks, battery vehicles, MEM, portable tanks and tank containers) approved for and suited to the carriage of the substances concerned and displaying the markings prescribed by ADR;
- complying with the requirements on the means of dispatch and on forwarding restrictions.

Where he uses the services of other participants (packers, loaders, fillers, etc), he must still ensure that the consignment meets the requirements of ADR.

The Carrier

The carrier must ascertain that:

- the dangerous goods to be carried are authorized for carriage in accordance with ADR;
- the next due test date for tank vehicles, portable tanks and tank containers has not passed;
- vehicles are not overloaded;
- visually, vehicles and loads have no obvious defects such as leakages, cracks or missing equipment, etc;
- appropriate danger labels and prescribed markings have been affixed to the vehicle;
- prescribed documentation is being carried on board the vehicle; and
- the equipment prescribed in the driver's written instructions is on board the vehicle.

If, in carrying out the above checks, the carrier observes any infringement of the ADR requirements, he must not allow the consignment to be shipped until the matter has been rectified. Similarly, if during the journey an infringement is detected which could jeopardize the safety of the operation, the consignment must be stopped as soon as possible bearing in mind the requirements of traffic safety, the safe immobilization of the consignment and of public safety.

The Consignee

Consignees may not defer acceptance of a consignment of dangerous goods without compelling reasons. They must also, after unloading, verify that the requirements of ADR have been complied with.

Other Participants/DGSAs

Other participants may be involved with the carriage of dangerous goods consignments, such as employees described as tanker operators, loaders, packers, fillers, etc. Broadly, such employees have a duty to ensure that their actions and the loads they deal with comply in all relevant respects with the requirements of ADR.

In particular, a Dangerous Goods Safety Advisor (DGSA) may be required. The DGSA needs to be qualified and able to provide advice and assistance, and an annual report relating to the types of dangerous goods carried (see below).

Duty of Care

Employers have a general duty of care towards their employees under the Health and Safety at Work Act 1974, to ensure their health, safety and welfare. They also have a duty to ensure that their premises are safe and without risk to the health of those who are not employees but who use the premises as a place of work. Employees must take reasonable care for their own health while at work. Employers and self-employed persons must ensure that their work activities do not expose other persons (ie not in their employ) to risks to their health and safety through their work activities.

Exemptions

A number of exemptions to ADR are specified in Chapter 1.1 (ie 1.1.3) and in SI 2004 No 568, regulation 7 and are set out in simplified form in the publication *Working with ADR* as follows:

- the carriage of dangerous goods by private individuals where the goods are packaged for retail sale and are intended for their personal or domestic use or for their leisure or sporting activities;
- the carriage of machinery or equipment not specifically listed in the Dangerous Goods List and which contain dangerous goods in their internal or operational equipment;

- carriage undertaken by enterprises which is ancillary to their main activity;
- carriage by, or under the supervision of, the emergency services, in particular by breakdown vehicles carrying vehicles which have been involved in accidents or have broken down and contain dangerous goods;
- emergency transport intended to save human lives or protect the environment.

Special Provisions Exemptions

Certain special provisions of the ADR (ie Chapter 3.3) exempt, either partially or totally, the carriage of specific dangerous goods from the requirements of ADR, as identified in column 6 of the Dangerous Goods List (Chapter 3.2, Table A), against the appropriate entry for that article or substance.

Limited Quantities Exemptions

Exemptions also relate to dangerous goods packed in limited quantities where a 'limited quantity' code Q1–Q29 (see table at ADR 3.4.6) appears in column 7 of the appropriate entry of the Dangerous Goods List, in which case that article or substance is exempted from the requirements of ADR, but only if it meets packaging and marking requirements; and the prescribed maximum quantities per inner packaging, and per package, are not exceeded.

When the code LQ0 appears in column 7 of the Dangerous Goods List (ADR 3.2), the substance or article is not exempted from any of the requirements of ADR (unless otherwise specified).

ADR 2011 introduced some changes relating to the carriage of dangerous goods in Limited Quantity (LQ) packages in regard to training requirements for consignors, packers, carriers, drivers, loaders and unloaders. Basically, these provisions mean that anyone involved in the carriage of LQ packages must either already have been trained in the carriage of dangerous goods, or must be given suitable and appropriate training as required by ADR Chapter 1.3. Those who have already been trained in the carriage of dangerous goods under the provisions of ADR 1.3.2.4 may need to receive supplementary refresher training in order to understand the new provisions.

The training provisions will have to be complied with, for example, by those who simply place the goods on pallets ready for shipment (so that those people are aware of the obligations to ensure the LQ marks are visible or repeated on the overpackage and marked also with the word 'OVERPACK') or those who drive vehicles that are delivering LQ packages.

NB: This requirement even includes drivers who deliver shopping from supermarkets to customers' homes, because such orders may include 'products' subject to the LQ provisions, and perhaps even unpackaged goods under the Dangerous Goods: Approved Derogations and Transitional Provisions Road Derogation 4 provision for end of supply chain deliveries.

TABLE 20.3 Transport categories and maximum quantities per transport unit

Transport category	Max total quantity per transport unit*
0	0
1	20
1A	50
2	333
2A	500
3	1,000
4	unlimited

* For articles, gross mass in kg (for articles of Class 1, net mass in kg of the explosive substance); for solids, liquefied gases, refrigerated liquefied gases and dissolved gases, net mass in kg; for liquids and compressed gases, nominal capacity of receptacles (see definition in ADR 1.2.1) in litres.

Transport Unit Exemptions

This class of exemptions is sometimes also referred to as being a 'limited quantities exemption', but it should not be confused with the limited quantities exemption described above. In this case, the exemption applies where:

- a specified maximum total quantity per transport unit, depending on its transport category (ADR 1.1.3.6) is not exceeded; or
- where the dangerous goods carried in the transport unit are in more than one transport category and the total quantity carried does not exceed the value calculated in accordance with ADR 1.1.3.6.4.

If either of the two bullet point conditions (above) applies, the dangerous goods may be carried in packages in a single transport unit and the following requirements of ADR will not apply.

Other Exemptions

ADR also includes other exemptions relating to:

- the carriage of gases;
- the carriage of liquid fuels;
- empty uncleaned packaging;
- carriage in a transport chain including maritime or air carriage;

TABLE 20.4 Other exemptions

ADR	Covering
5.3	Placarding and marking of containers, etc
5.4.3	Documentation – instructions in writing
7.2 except for V5, V7 and V8 of 7.2.4	Carriage in packages
CV1 of 7.5.11	Prohibitions on loading and unloading in public places
Part 8, except for 8.1.4.2–8.1.4.5, 8.2.3, 8.3.4, 8.4 and S1(3), S1(6), S2(1), S4, S14–S21 of 8.5	Vehicle crews, equipment operation and documentation
Part 9	Construction and approval of vehicles

- the use of portable tanks approved for maritime transport; and
- carriage other than by road.

A full list of exemptions can be found in the current version of ADR.

Transport Information and Documentation

Information to Be Provided

Consignors of dangerous goods must provide the transport operator (ie carrier) with a transport document (often referred to as the ADR note) showing:

- the designation, classification code, UN number and proper name for the goods;
- any additional information needed to determine their transport category and their control and emergency temperatures;
- the hazard class of the goods and any additional/associated hazards;
- the tunnel code for the goods;
- for packaged goods, the number and weight or volume of individual packages, or the total mass or volume in each transport category;
- for bulk loads, the weight or volume in each tank or container and the number of tanks or containers;

- the name and address of both consignor and consignee;
- any other information which the operator must give to the driver;
- a 'consignor's declaration' that the goods may be carried as presented, that they, their packaging and any container or tank in which they are contained is fit for carriage and is properly labelled.

It is an offence to provide false or misleading information and where one transport operator sub-contracts a dangerous goods consignment to another operator he must, by law, pass on the information provided by the consignor.

Documentation to Be Carried during Carriage

Drivers and crew members of vehicles carrying dangerous goods must be provided with the following 'transport documentation', in writing:

- the information provided by the consignor (see above);
- details of the weight or volume of the load;
- the relevant hazard identification number, tunnel code (if applicable) or the emergency action code (where appropriate);
- emergency information comprising:
  - the dangers inherent in the goods and safety measures;
  - what to do and the treatment to be given should any person come into contact with the goods;
  - what to do in the event of fire and what fire-fighting appliances or equipment must not be used;
  - what to do in case of breakage or deterioration of packaging or of the goods, particularly where this results in a spillage onto the road;
  - what to do to avoid or minimize damage in the event of spillage of goods likely to pollute water supplies;
- any relevant additional information about the particular type of dangerous goods being carried.

It is an offence to provide false or misleading information to drivers about the particular type of dangerous goods being carried.

Drivers must keep the transport documentation readily available during dangerous goods journeys and produce it on request by the police or a DVSA goods vehicle examiner. Where a dangerous goods carrying trailer is detached from the towing vehicle the transport documentation (or an authenticated copy) must be given to the owner or manager of the premises where it is parked, or attached to the trailer in a readily visible position.

Documentation relating to dangerous goods no longer carried on a vehicle must be either removed completely, or placed in a securely closed container clearly marked to show that it does not relate to dangerous goods still on the vehicle.

Operators must keep a record of journey transport documentation for at least three months (SI 2004 No 568, regulation 54).

Note: vehicles using ferry services may need additional documentation to meet the International Maritime Dangerous Goods (IMDG) requirements and operators are advised to either contact their trade association or contact the shipping line to clarify any additional requirements.

Instructions in Writing

Since 2009 operators have had a responsibility to also give drivers 'instructions in writing' to help them with any emergency that may arise. The key features are:

- they are to be issued by the carrier not the consignor;
- they must be in a language that the driver and/or crew members can read and understand before starting their journey and in the language of the country(ies) of origin, transit and destination (particularly for use by the emergency services);
- vehicle crews are required to familiarize themselves with the emergency arrangements for the dangerous goods loaded *before* commencing a journey;
- a new four-page model of the revised instructions in writing consists of:
  - action to be taken in the event of an emergency;
  - guidance on the hazards and actions to be taken for each class of dangerous goods.

In addition to an instruction that smoking is not permitted in the guidance to drivers, new instructions in writing have been amended to include not using 'e-cigarettes'. Old versions of the instructions without this addition could only be used until 1 July 2017 when the new versions became mandatory.

Information to be Displayed on Containers, Tanks and Vehicles

Containers, tanks and vehicles used for carrying dangerous goods must display information as described below. All panels and danger signs must be kept clean and free from obstruction.

It is an offence to display information when the container, tank or vehicle is not carrying dangerous goods, and to cause or permit the display of any information likely to confuse the emergency services.

Signs and panels relating to dangerous goods no longer being carried must be covered or removed. Where an orange-coloured panel is covered, the covering material must remain effective after 15 minutes' engulfment in fire. Danger signs, hazard warning panels, orange-coloured panels or subsidiary hazard signs need not be covered or removed if the mass or volume of dangerous goods in packages falls below the following limits:

TABLE 20.5

Transport category	Total mass/volume (kg/litres)
0	0
1	20
2	200
3	500
4	unlimited

It is an offence to remove panels or signs from a container, tank or vehicle carrying dangerous goods (except for updating the information) and to falsify information on any panel or sign.

Danger Signs and Panels

A reflective orange-coloured, black-bordered panel (plain with no letters or figures) must be displayed at the front of vehicles carrying dangerous goods. A similar panel must be attached to the rear of vehicles carrying dangerous goods in packages. If the vehicle, exceeding 12 tonnes unladen, is carrying more than 8 tonnes of packaged dangerous goods that are being carried as limited quantity goods, the orange panels can be used or they can be replaced with black and white diamond-shaped limited quantity plates.

Single Load Labelling

Where a *single load* of dangerous goods is carried in a container, tank or vehicle an orange-coloured panel showing the appropriate UN number and emergency action code (see Figure 20.1) must be displayed:

- one at the rear of the vehicle;
- one on each side of the vehicle or the tank;
- one on each side, one at the rear and one at the front of a tank container;*
- and, in the case of a tank, one on each side of the frame of the tank, or on the vehicle positioned immediately below the tank.

**Containers are marked on all four sides and not just on the sides and the rear.*

Multi-Load Labelling

Where a vehicle is carrying a *multi-load* in tanks, or in bulk in separate compartments of the vehicle, or in separate containers, an orange-coloured panel showing

FIGURE 20.1 Orange panel showing the emergency action code and the UN number identifying the dangerous substance being carried

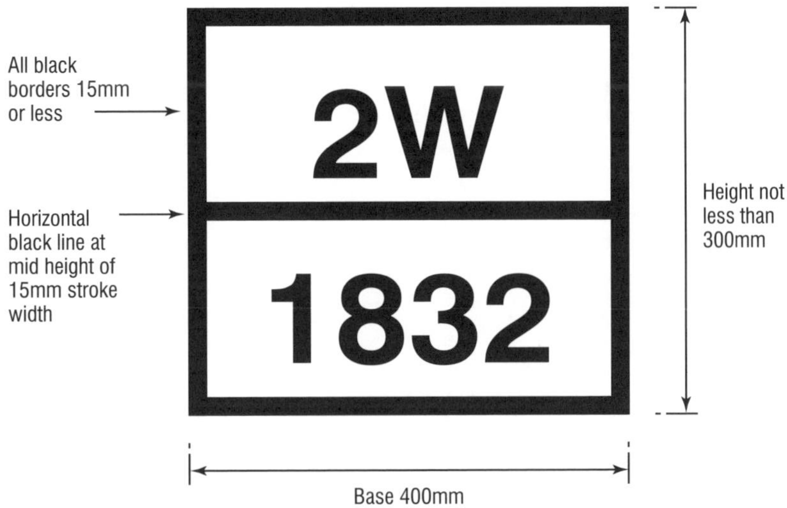

the appropriate emergency action code only (see below) must be displayed at the rear of the vehicle.

Additionally, orange-coloured panels as follows are required on both sides of each tank (or, if it has multiple compartments, on each compartment), on each compartment of the vehicle or on each container on the vehicle:

- at least one on each side showing the appropriate UN number and emergency action code (Figure 20.1); and
- the remainder showing only the appropriate UN number.

Alternatively, for dangerous goods carried in a tank, the panels may be displayed on both sides of the frame of each tank, or on the vehicle positioned immediately below the tank or tank compartment concerned.

Where diesel fuel, gas oil or heating oil (UN 1202), petrol, motor spirit or gasoline (UN 1203), or kerosene (UN 1223) is carried in a multi-compartment road tanker it may be labelled as a single load only, showing the UN number and emergency action code for the most hazardous of the products carried.

Detail of Panels

The orange-coloured panels must be either:

- a rigid plate fitted as near vertical as possible; or
- in the case of a vehicle carrying dangerous goods in a tank container or in bulk in a container:

- orange-coloured self-adhesive sheets; or
- orange-coloured paint (or equivalent), provided the material is weather-resistant and ensures durable marking.

UN numbers and emergency action codes must be shown in black, at least 100 mm high and 15 mm wide – but where the emergency action code is white on a black background, it must appear as orange on a black rectangle at least 10 mm greater than the height and width of the letter. Except where panels comprise self-adhesive sheets or are applied by paint, UN numbers and emergency action codes must be indelible and remain legible after 15 minutes' engulfment in fire (not applicable to tanks constructed before 1 January 1999).

Where there is insufficient space for full-sized panels, these may be reduced to 300 mm wide by 120 mm high with a 10 mm black border.

Emergency Action Codes

The emergency action codes are as follows:

1. By numbers 1 to 4 indicating the equipment suitable for fire-fighting and for dispersing spillages (ie 1 = water jets, 2 = water fog, 3 = foam, 4 = dry agent).
2. By letters indicating the appropriate precautions to take (as shown in Table 20.6).

Where a letter 'E' is shown at the end of an emergency action code this means that consideration should be given to evacuating people from the neighbourhood of an incident.

Display of Telephone Number

The Carriage of Dangerous Goods Regulations (CDG2009) allow a contact telephone number as a concession, comprising black digits at least 30 mm high on an orange background, which must be shown on vehicles carrying single or multi-loads of dangerous goods in tanks, within the UK, positioned:

- at the rear of the vehicle;
- on both sides of the tank (or each tank if more than one), the frame of each tank or the vehicle; and
- located in the immediate vicinity of the orange-coloured panels.

Instead of a telephone number, the words 'consult local depot' or 'contact local depot' may be substituted, but only if:

- the name of the operator is clearly marked on the tank or the vehicle; and
- the fire chief for every area in which the vehicle will operate has been notified in writing of the address and telephone number of that local depot, and has confirmed in writing that he is satisfied with the arrangements.

TABLE 20.6 Emergency action codes

Letter	Danger of violent reaction	Protective clothing and breathing apparatus	Measures to be taken
P	Yes	Full protective clothing	Dilute
R	No	Full protective clothing	Dilute
S	Yes	Breathing apparatus	Dilute
S*	Yes	Breathing apparatus for fire	Dilute
T	No	Breathing apparatus	Dilute
T*	No	Breathing apparatus for fire	Dilute
W	Yes	Full protective clothing	Contain
X	No	Full protective clothing	Contain
Y	Yes	Breathing apparatus	Contain
Y*	Yes	Breathing apparatus for fire	Contain
Z	No	Breathing apparatus	Contain
Z*	No	Breathing apparatus for fire	Contain

* These symbols, shown as orange (or can be white) letters reversed out of a black background, remain valid but are not included in the latest versions of the EAC.

Display of Danger Signs and Subsidiary Hazard Signs

Where a vehicle is carrying:

- packaged dangerous goods in a container:

  any danger sign or subsidiary hazard sign required on the packages must also be displayed on at least one side of the container;
- dangerous goods in a tank container or in bulk in a container:
  - any danger sign or subsidiary hazard sign required on the packages containing such goods must be displayed on each side of the tank container or container, and where such signs are not visible from outside the carrying vehicle, the same signs must also be shown on each side of and at the rear of the vehicle;
- dangerous goods in a tank, other than a tank container, or in bulk in a vehicle, but not in bulk in a container on a vehicle:

- any danger sign or subsidiary hazard sign required on the packages containing such goods must be displayed on each side of and at the rear of the vehicle.

Danger signs for a particular classification, or subsidiary hazard signs, need not be shown more than once on the sides or rear of any container, tank or vehicle.

Danger signs and subsidiary hazard signs must have sides at least 250 mm long; have a line the same colour as the symbol 12.5 mm inside the edge and running parallel to it; and be displayed adjacent to one another and in the same horizontal plane.

Display of Hazard Warning Panels

Despite the requirements described above for the display of orange-coloured panels the regulations permit, wherever such a panel is required on the sides or rear of a container, tank or vehicle, the alternative use of existing-type combined hazard warning panels (see Figure 20.2) on vehicles operating within the UK.

These are mainly orange with black borders and lettering – except for the white background where a reduced-size (ie 200 mm sides) danger sign is located and any subsidiary hazard sign must be the same size and displayed adjacent to it and in the same horizontal plane.

All danger panels and signs required on the front or rear of a vehicle must be positioned at right angles across its width, and those on the sides of a container, tank or vehicle at right angles along its length. All signs must be clearly visible.

Vehicles operating internationally under ADR may display a similar orange board with a three-digit ADR Kemler Code instead of an Emergency Action Code – as with most European dangerous goods vehicles. The UN number is shown in the lower half of the panel, as with UK transport. Foreign vehicles running under ADR tend not to have integrated Hazchem boards (as shown in Figure 20.2), with the class diamonds (referred to as 'placards' in the ADR regulations) being displayed separately.

Emergency Procedures

Vehicles carrying dangerous goods must be equipped so that the driver can take emergency measures, as follows:

- Vehicles up to 3.5 tonnes must have a minimum total of 4 kg of fire extinguishers with a minimum 2 kg cab extinguisher plus one other 2 kg extinguisher.
- Vehicles exceeding 3.5 tonnes but not exceeding 7.5 tonnes gvw must have a minimum 2 kg cab extinguisher, and one other extinguisher which must have a minimum capacity of 6 kg (totalling 8 kg).
- Vehicles exceeding 7.5 tonnes must carry a total capacity of 12 kg of fire extinguishers. This must include a minimum of a 2 kg cab extinguisher and at least one of the others must have a minimum capacity of 6 kg (totalling 12 kg).
- In all cases the vehicle crew must be trained to use the extinguishers carried and the extinguishers must be capable for use on classes A, B and C fires as defined in Standard EN2-1992, 'Classification of Fires'.

FIGURE 20.2 Existing UK-type combined hazard warning panel which may be used on the sides and rear of a bulk chemical tanker vehicle or container

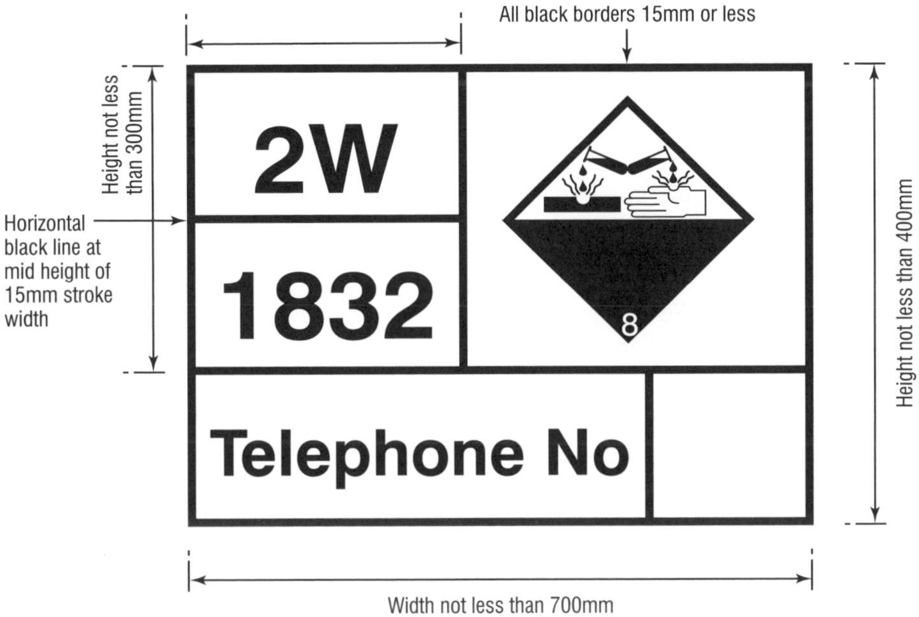

Portable fire extinguishers must not be liable to release toxic gases into the driver's cab, or under the heat of a fire. They must be marked in compliance with a recognized standard; fitted with a seal verifying they have not been used; and be inscribed with the date for their next inspection – it is an offence to carry an extinguisher with an overdue inspection date.

A fire extinguisher is not needed where only infectious substances are carried.

Where toxic gases are carried, vehicles must carry respiratory equipment to enable the crew to escape safely.

Other equipment to be carried includes:

- a shovel and a plastic collecting container (eg a 9-litre bucket with lid);
- non-sparking torch;
- protective gloves;
- eye protection and eye-rinsing liquid;
- high-visibility clothing;
- two warning cones, triangles or flashing amber lights;
- at least one wheel chock for the unit or prime mover and at least one for any semi-trailer or trailer being drawn;
- any tools or equipment required for dealing with a spillage.

In addition, vehicles exceeding 16 tonnes mpw and trailers exceeding 10 tonnes mpw that are tankers or carrying tank containers must have anti-lock and endurance braking systems. There are also more stringent requirements relating to the vehicle batteries and wiring for these types of vehicles and trailers and vehicle engine screening requirements for some tankers and vehicles pulling tank trailers where the contents of the tank are highly flammable.

Accidents and Emergencies

In accident or emergency situations drivers must comply with the emergency information given to them and apply the emergency procedures for which they are trained and which are stated on the emergency action information given to them (eg on the instructions in writing), including:

- notifying the relevant emergency services by the quickest practical means;
- taking steps to prevent chemical contamination of the environment (eg watercourses);
- taking steps to prevent the risk of fire;
- keeping the public away from the scene;
- applying first aid where necessary.

Accident Investigation and Reports

All accidents and dangerous goods incidents must be reported and investigated to determine how and why they were caused and how any such event may be prevented in the future – possibly by changing procedures and the issue of fresh safety instructions.

Dangerous goods safety advisers (DGSAs) have a statutory duty to prepare reports on serious accidents, incidents or legal infringements occurring during the loading, unloading and transport of dangerous goods and to implement appropriate measures to avoid recurrence of such events.

Reporting to the Health and Safety Executive

Accidents and serious incidents involving dangerous goods must be reported to the HSE at the Incident Control Centre (ICC) as required under the Reporting of Injuries, Diseases and Dangerous Occurrences Regulations 1995 (SI 1995/3163 – commonly known as RIDDOR). The report must be made to the ICC both immediately by telephone and also electronically using forms available from the HSE website. As discussed, postal notification is not now allowed to be sent to the ICC but, if it is sent, it needs to be sent to:

RIDDOR Reports
Health and Safety Executive
Redgrave Court
Merton Road
Bootle
Merseyside
L20 7HS

Notification is required for any occurrence causing:

- death or major injury to an employee;
- any injury occasioning an employee to be away from work for more than seven days;
- any work-related disease.

Any dangerous occurrence (even if it does not result in less than seven days' absence from work or personal injury to any person) must also be reported within 15 days including:

- splitting or collapse of a tank or tank container;
- failure of pipework or valves resulting in spillage;
- overturning of a dangerous goods carrying vehicle;
- a dangerous goods carrying vehicle catching fire; or
- a fire in the loading or unloading premises.

In Northern Ireland the relevant legislation is the Reporting of Injuries Diseases and Dangerous Occurrences Regulations (Northern Ireland) 1997 (SR No 455). Details can be found on the HSENI website.

Road Traffic Accidents

The procedures to be followed in the event of a road traffic accident, apart from the special considerations relating to the carriage of dangerous goods as set out above, are those described on pp 326–27 of this *Handbook*.

Security Provisions

On 22 July 2005, in response to new measures included in the revised ADR 2005, the Government introduced new security provisions relating to the carriage of all dangerous goods except nuclear materials. The requirements fall into four groups as shown below; namely, general provisions, provisions relating to high consequence dangerous goods, training requirements and the need to implement security plans. The overseeing body for these requirements is the Department for Transport.

General Provisions

These require that:

- All persons engaged in the carriage of dangerous goods must consider the security requirements for the carriage of dangerous goods commensurate with their responsibilities.
- Dangerous goods may only be offered to carriers that have been appropriately identified.

- Areas within temporary storage terminals, temporary storage sites, vehicle depots, berthing areas and marshalling yards used for temporary storage during carriage of dangerous goods must be properly secured, well lit and, where possible and appropriate, not accessible to the general public.
- Each crew member of a vehicle carrying dangerous goods must carry with them means of photographic identification.
- Safety inspections must cover appropriate security measures.

High Consequence Dangerous Goods

High consequence goods are those goods that may be used in a terrorist incident where there is a serious risk of danger, such as explosives, some flammable liquids and solids and some toxic, corrosive and infectious substances. These goods now require a security plan to be drawn up when they are moved by road. Plan contents and a list of such 'high consequence' goods are below.

Full details, instructions and a template to draw up a plan are available on the GOV.UK website.

Training Requirements

Additional provisions relating to training require that up-to-date registers of all valid training certificates must be maintained by the competent authorities and that relevant training, and refresher training, must include elements of security awareness, in particular addressing the following issues:

- the nature of security risks;
- how to recognize security risks;
- how to address and reduce such risks;
- what actions to take in the event of a breach of security.

NB: Recent changes to the rules now mean that personnel who only move 'limited quantities' are no longer exempted from a requirement that they receive adequate training in the handling and storage of dangerous goods. Training is now required by ALL personnel involved in moving or storing dangerous goods.

Security Planning

Another key provision is that all carriers (eg road hauliers), consignors and other participants engaged in the carriage of high consequence dangerous goods (as listed below) must formulate, implement and comply with a security plan that covers at least all the requirements specified below:

- The plan must specifically allocate responsibility for security to competent and qualified persons with appropriate authority to carry out their responsibilities.

- Records must be kept of the dangerous goods or types of dangerous goods involved in the carriage.
- A review must be undertaken of current operations and assessment of security risks, including at any stops necessary to the transport operation, the keeping of dangerous goods in the vehicle, tank or container before, during and after the journey and the temporary storage of dangerous goods during the course of intermodal transfer or transhipment between units.
- A clear statement must be made of the measures that are to be taken to reduce security risks, commensurate with the responsibilities and duties of the participant, including:
  - training matters;
  - security policies;
  - operating practices;
  - equipment and resource use to reduce security risks.
- Effective and up-to-date procedures must be established for reporting and dealing with security threats, breaches of security or security incidents.
- Procedures must be put in place for the evaluation and testing of security plans and actions.
- Measures must be taken to ensure the physical security of transport information contained in the security plan.
- Measures must be taken to ensure that the distribution of information relating to the transport operation contained in the security plan is limited to those who need to have it.
- A process needs to be established to cooperate in the exchange of security threat information, to apply appropriate security measures and to respond to security incidents.
- Steps must be taken to prevent the theft of vehicles carrying high consequence dangerous goods or their cargo by means of suitable security devices, equipment or arrangements. These must be kept operational and effective at all times, but must not jeopardize any emergency response.
- Transport telemetry or other tracking methods or devices should be used to monitor the movement of high consequence dangerous goods, when it is appropriate to do so and when such systems are already fitted.

The D*f*T has produced a guide on the security of high consequence dangerous goods and also produces guidance on licensing and other issues. They also produce a sample laminated HCDG card for use by drivers. These are all free to download from the D*f*T and GOV.UK website.

High consequence dangerous goods are those listed in Table 20.7 and carried in quantities greater than shown. Further information can be found in the booklet *ADR – A Guide for Business*, published by the HSE.

TABLE 20.7

Class	Division	Substance or article	Quantity		
			Tank (ltrs)	Bulk (kg)	Packages (kg)
1	1.1	Explosives	a	a	0
	1.2	Explosives	a	a	0
	1.3	Compatibility group C explosives	a	a	0
	1.5	Explosives	0	a	0
2	2.1	Flammable gases (classification codes including only the letter F)	3,000	a	b
	2.2	Toxic gases (classification codes containing the letters T, TF, TC, TO, TFC or TOC) excluding aerosols	0	a	0
3		Flammable liquids of packing groups I and II	3,000	a	b
		Desensitized explosives	a	a	0
4	4.1	Desensitized explosives	a	a	0
	4.2	Packing group I substances	3,000	a	b
	4.3	Packing group II substances	3,000	a	b
5	5.1	Oxidizing liquids of packing group I	3,000	a	b
		Perchlorates, ammonium nitrate and ammonium nitrate fertilizers	3,000	3,000	b
6	6.1	Toxic substances of packing group I	0	a	0
	6.2	Infectious substances of Category A	a	a	0
7		Radioactive material	3,000 A1 (special form) or 3,000 A2, as applicable, in Type B or Type C packages		
8		Corrosive substances of packing group I	3,000	a	b

Enforcement

In the interests of public safety, the police and authorized DVSA examiners are given wide-ranging powers to ensure compliance with the law on dangerous goods carriage. For example, they can demand production of the statutory information which drivers must carry when on a dangerous goods journey as well as production of the driver's own Vocational Training or ADR Certificate, which he must carry at all times during such journeys.

The DVSA is empowered to enforce certain aspects of dangerous goods law relating solely to vehicles (the HSE retains its responsibility for premises-based inspections). DVSA inspectors are authorized to serve Prohibition Notices and prosecute offenders for breaches of the law, but they *will not* serve Improvement Notices as these are not normally appropriate for on-the-road work.

Offences and Penalties

Dangerous goods legislation is complex and extensive with a large number of potential offences which may be committed, either singly or in conjunction with other offences. Offenders can expect to be prosecuted and dealt with severely by the courts on conviction.

On summary conviction in the magistrate's court (sheriff's court in Scotland) for an offence under the HSWA 1974, currently a fine of up to £5,000 may be imposed, while in more serious cases indictment by the Crown Court for an offence may lead to an unlimited fine and/or a two-year prison sentence.

Obstruction of an inspector who is fulfilling his statutory duties is a serious offence carrying a fine of up to £5,000 on conviction while breach of any notice served by an inspector can result in a fine up to £20,000 on conviction or in either case an unlimited fine on indictment.

Defence

A person charged under these regulations can, in his own defence, prove that the offence was due to the act or default of another person (other than his own employees), and that he had tried to avoid committing the offence, but he must give the prosecutor, in writing, at least seven days before the court hearing and to the best of his knowledge, information identifying or assisting in the identification of that other person.

Carriage of Explosives

Since 1983, GB explosives transport legislation has followed the UN Recommendations on the Transport of Dangerous Goods (UN Orange Book) concerning classification of explosives as presented for transport (CLER), their packaging (PEC), and requirements during transport (CER).

GB regulations are supported by Approved Codes of Practice (ACoPs), Approved Documents, HSE Guidance papers and Industry/HSE guides. Where relevant these are consistent with ADR.

The regulations cover existing legislation in relation to DGSAs, driver vocational training, the specification of explosives and their packaging but they also cover the design specification for vehicles used to carry different types of explosives.

Although the majority of GB explosive transport legislation applies to transport under the control of the armed forces, both for national and international movements, the armed forces are exempt from compliance with ADR. This is also true when explosives are carried in limited quantities for private use or when they are carried during emergency circumstances.

For non-armed forces movements and other non-exempted movements European Regulation (EC) No 1272/2008 on classification, labelling and packaging of substances and mixtures (the CLP Regulation or CLP), which was updated in 2015, and the European Registration, Evaluation, Authorisation & Restriction of Chemicals Regulation (REACH) are the relevant legislative guides. This also means that ADR does cross into the carriage of explosives and operators are advised to seek specialist advice or visit the GOV.UK website for more detailed advice or to access the ADR regulations.

Radioactive Substances

Complex legislation controls the carriage of radioactive substances. In particular, the Radioactive Material (Road Transport) Regulations 2002 (amended 2018) made under the provisions of the Radioactive Material (Road Transport) Act 1991 apply to the carriage of such materials, while the Ionising Radiations Regulations 1985 and the Ionising Radiations (Outside Workers) Regulations 1993 cover controls on radiation doses received by persons working with such materials. Further, *A Code of Practice for the Carriage of Radioactive Materials by Road* is available from the Office for Nuclear Regulation (ONR). This guide sets out the law and gives advice on all aspects of transporting these materials. Advice on the requirements for transporting radioactive material can be accessed by contacting the ONR's Radioactive Materials Transport Team at **onr.org.uk**. They produced new guidelines in 2017 in relation to carriage by road, controlling dose rates and some emergency procedures. The team also summarized the relevant changes from ADR 2015, ADR 2017 and ADR 2019 and can help and advise with general health and safety issues related to the carriage of radioactive materials.

Driver Training

Drivers of vehicles carrying dangerous goods must be instructed and trained so they understand the dangers of the particular goods being carried and the emergency action to be taken, as well as their duties under the Health and Safety at Work Act 1974, and current dangerous goods legislation. Operators must keep training records.

The driver training specified in ADR 8.2 applies (from the time of loading until the goods have been unloaded and, where appropriate, the compartment has been cleaned or purged) to drivers of the following dangerous goods vehicles:

- road tankers exceeding 1 m^3 capacity;
- those carrying tank containers exceeding 3 m^3 capacity;

- those carrying dangerous goods:
  - in bulk;
  - in a road tanker with a capacity not exceeding 1,000 litres;
  - in a tank container with a capacity not exceeding 3,000 litres;
  - where any of the goods are in transport category 0;
  - comprising more than 20 kg/litres* of category 1 goods in packages;
  - comprising more than 200 kg/litres* of category 2 goods in packages;
  - comprising more than 500 kg/litres* of category 3 goods in packages;
- those carrying explosives;
- those carrying radioactive materials.

** This refers to 'total mass or volume' (ie as measured in kg or litres).*

Vocational Training Certificates

Transport operators must ensure their drivers hold valid 'vocational training certificates' appropriate to the dangerous goods work they are employed in. This includes drivers of all vans as well as larger vehicles and is necessary irrespective of how short the journey.

These certificates, issued under the auspices of the D*f*T through the Scottish Qualifications Authority adr@sqa.org.uk (Tel: 0345 279 1000), are granted to drivers on successful completion of an approved course of theoretical study and practical exercises and passing an approved examination. Certificates are valid for five years and may be extended for further five-yearly periods if in the 12 months preceding their expiry the holder has successfully completed a refresher course and passed the examination.

Current driver ADR certificates (if valid for the type of operation engaged in) are accepted as vocational training certificates for these purposes.

NB: Importantly, ADR training for drivers can now count towards their 35 hour Driver CPC periodic training requirement.

Certificates to be Carried and Produced to the Police

Drivers must carry their vocational training certificates on all dangerous goods journeys and produce them on request by the police or a goods vehicle examiner.

Minimum Training Requirements for Issue of Vocational Training Certificates

Approved training for drivers must cover at least:

- general requirements on dangerous goods carriage;
- main types of hazard;
- environmental protection in the control of the transfer of wastes;
- preventive and safety measures appropriate to various types of hazard;

- what to do after an accident (first aid, road safety, the use of protective equipment, etc);
- labelling and marking to indicate danger;
- what to do and not do when carrying dangerous goods;
- the purpose and operation of technical equipment on vehicles used for carrying dangerous goods;
- prohibitions on mixed loading in the same vehicle or container;
- precautions during loading and unloading of dangerous goods;
- civil liability;
- multi-modal transport operations.

For drivers of vehicles carrying packaged dangerous goods, training must also cover the handling and stowage of packages, and for road tanker or tank container drivers training must cover the behaviour of such vehicles on the road, including load movement during transit.

Dangerous Goods Safety Advisers (DGSAs)

From 31 December 1999, firms which load, unload or carry dangerous goods by road (and by rail and inland waterway) must appoint a qualified dangerous goods safety adviser (DGSA) under provisions contained in EU Directive 96/35/EC. This also applies to self-employed persons, who must become qualified and appoint themselves. The person appointed must hold a valid vocational training certificate confirming they have passed the official DGSA examination conducted by the Scottish Qualifications Agency (SQA – appointed by the D*f*T to conduct all UK DGSA examinations). *Details of the examination system and a copy of the syllabus may be obtained from the SQA, Customer Contact Centre, as detailed previously.*

To qualify as a DGSA it is necessary to study the subject material contained in the official syllabus, sit the relevant examinations and pass in at least three of the following subjects:

- the core examination, which is compulsory for all candidates;
- one modal paper covering either road, rail or inland waterways;
- at least one dangerous goods class paper covering either:
  - Class 1;
  - Class 2;
  - Class 3 (specifically UN 1202, 1203 and 1223 – ie mineral oils);
  - Class 7;
  - General Chemical Classes (3, 4.1, 4.2, 4.3, 5.1, 5.2, 6.1, 6.2, 8 and 9); or
  - all classes.

It has been illegal to carry on a business in which dangerous goods are loaded, unloaded or transported since 31 December 1999 unless a qualified DGSA has been appointed and taken up his duties as outlined below.

Tasks and Functions of DGSAs

Appointed DGSAs must effectively carry out the legal duties and bear the responsibilities set out in law as follows:

- monitor compliance with the law on the transport of dangerous goods;
- advise their employer on the transport of dangerous goods;
- prepare reports on any accidents involving dangerous goods;
- prepare an annual report to their employer on the firm's activities in transporting dangerous goods (to be kept for five years and made available to the authorities on request).

The DGSA must also monitor:

- procedures for identifying dangerous goods being transported;
- practices for taking account of any special requirements in connection with dangerous goods being transported;
- procedures for checking equipment used in the transport, loading or unloading of dangerous goods;
- employee training and maintenance of training records;
- emergency procedures to be taken in the event of accidents that may affect safety during the transport, loading or unloading of dangerous goods;
- investigation and preparation of reports on serious accidents or legal infringements during the transport, loading or unloading of dangerous goods;
- implementation of steps to avoid the recurrence of accidents, incidents or serious legal infringements;
- account taken of the legal requirements in the choice and use of sub-contractors;
- operational procedures and instructions that employees must follow;
- introduction of measures to increase awareness of the risks inherent in the transport, loading and unloading of dangerous goods;
- verification procedures to ensure that vehicles carry the documents and safety equipment required and that they comply with the law;
- verification procedures to ensure that the law on loading and unloading is complied with.

NB: Because ADR is a UN controlled regulation it is expected that the UK DGSA qualification will not be challenged or invalidated when we leave the EU. That said, this issue should be closely monitored as individual EU member states may decide that there is a need for some sort of additional/alternative qualification for UK businesses exporting dangerous goods through, or to, their territories.

Controlled and Hazardous Waste

Many own-account operators and transport operators (and skip-hire firms) are concerned with the disposal of 'waste' (especially waste packaging) and, as such, they are affected by strictly enforced legislation. Controlled waste is classified as three types, domestic, commercial and industrial, but for disposal waste may be considered in two forms:

- controlled waste which comprises 'household, industrial and commercial waste or any such waste' (ie including waste paper, scrap metal and recyclable scrap);
- hazardous waste which is material defined as 'special waste' in the controlled waste legislation, or material which falls within the classification of dangerous substances for the purposes of the road tanker or packaged dangerous goods legislation described earlier in this chapter.

A range of legislation applies in this area of activity including the Disposal of Poisonous Waste Act 1972 (which makes it an offence to dispose of poisonous waste in an irresponsible way), the Criminal Justice Act 1988 (which provides powers for the authorities to impound vehicles engaged in illegal fly-tipping) and the Control of Pollution (Amendment) Act 1989, the Controlled Waste (Registration of Carriers and Seizure of Vehicles) Regulations 1991 and the Controlled Waste Regulations 2012. Other sets of regulations are also important including the Environmental Protection Act 1994, the Waste Management Licensing Regulations 2011 and the Hazardous Waste Regulations 2016.

Controlled Waste

Controlled waste should not be disposed of, or transported away by, a person or firm not legally authorized for this purpose.

Registration of Operators

The 1990 Environmental Act Protection requires operators who transport controlled waste within Great Britain to register with the appropriate waste regulation authority (WRA) ie in the area in which they have their business. The relevant authorities are:

- the Environment Agency (EA) – England and Wales;
- the Scottish Environmental Protection Agency (SEPA) – Scotland;
- the Northern Ireland Environment Agency (NIEA) – Northern Ireland.

All the WRAs above can be contacted on their websites for advice and guidance on registration, licensing and the carriage of waste of any description.

It is an offence to fail to register or to carry controlled waste when not registered. Besides fines following prosecution and conviction for such offences, legislation provides powers for the seizure and disposal of vehicles used for such illegal purposes.

There are two tiers of licensing: 'upper tier' licences which are valid for three years and 'lower tier' licences which renew automatically.

Exemptions are provided for charities, voluntary organizations, domestic householders disposing of their own waste, waste collection authorities and producers of controlled waste. Builders and demolition companies are not exempt and must register and otherwise comply with the legislation.

A new, and quite complex, charging scheme has been instituted by the Environment Agency from 2008. Full details can be viewed at: www.gov.uk/government/organisations/environment-agency (archived at https://perma.cc/DML3-5TDC). It should also be noted that, due to the structures of regional governments, some definitions used within the overarching legislation do differ in different regions of the UK.

Duty of Care

Under the Environmental Protection Act 1990 firms and individuals that produce, import, store, treat, process, recycle, dispose of or transport controlled waste (see above for definition) have a statutory 'duty of care'. This places responsibility for the completion of paperwork (ie 'waste transfer notes'), taking all reasonable steps to stop waste escaping and ensuring its safety and security, recording all involved parties, taking waste to authorized sites and keeping records of waste transfers on parties involved with the carriage of controlled waste.

Waste Transfer Notes

Waste transfer notes comprise written descriptions of waste handed over to other persons to transport and/or dispose of, and a transfer note signed by both parties (allowable as a single document) containing the following details:

- what the waste is and the quantity;
- the type of container in which it is carried;
- the time and date of transfer;
- the place where the transfer took place;
- the names and addresses of both parties (ie consignor and recipient);
- detail as to which category each falls into (eg producer and registered waste carrier);
- a certificate number if either or both parties hold waste licences and the name of the authority from whom it/they was/were issued;
- reasons for any exemption from registration or waste licensing.

Copies of documents (ie descriptions of waste and/or transfer notes) given and received must be retained by carriers for at least one year and by waste dealers and brokers for at least three years. Both or either party may be required to produce these and prove in court where particular consignments of controlled waste originated. Alternatively, waste transfer notes can be downloaded and completed electronically if registered carriers register with the national Electronic Duty of Care system (EDOC). Details about this can be obtained from the relevant WRA.

Seizure of Vehicles

The law gives powers to waste regulation authorities to seize the vehicles of offenders, remove and separately store or dispose of loads as necessary, and dispose of (or destroy) vehicles following set procedures to publicize details of the seizure in local newspapers. Attempts will be made to seek out legitimate owners, who may reclaim their vehicles on satisfactory proof of entitlement and identification.

Hazardous Waste Disposal

Broadly, the law on hazardous and toxic waste requires that waste which is poisonous, noxious or polluting is not deposited on land where its presence is liable to give rise to an environmental hazard. And it is necessary for anyone removing or depositing poisonous material to notify both the local authority and the river authority before doing so.

An environmental hazard is defined as waste that is deposited in a manner or in such quantity that it would subject persons or animals to material risk of death, injury or impairment of health or threaten the pollution or contamination of any water supply. The European Commission has also produced a booklet on this subject for local authorities in EU member states.

There are additional controls over the carriage and disposal of particularly hazardous waste. The Control of Pollution (Special Waste) Regulations 1980 (amended in 1996) were introduced in order to comply with EU Directives and we also have the Hazardous Waste Regulations 2005 (amended in 2018).

The main requirements of these regulations are outlined below:

- Certain types of waste are to be regarded as special waste and subject to the additional controls. These are wastes that are regarded as dangerous to life as set out in the regulations.
- Waste producers have to give not less than three days' and not more than one month's prior notice to waste disposal authorities of their intention to dispose of a consignment of special waste.
- A set of consignment notes must be completed when special wastes are transported. This means that a consignment of special waste can be transported from the producer to the disposal site only if each person has signed for it and taken on responsibility for it. This is to ensure that waste disposal authorities know who is carrying the waste and they have to be informed within 24 hours of when it reaches the disposal site. Waste producers should take particular note of the requirement that all notices must be made on the statutory forms. Each form contains a unique reference number to assist an authority in making sure that waste is safely disposed of.
- A record of the location of the point of disposal on site of all special wastes must be kept in perpetuity. This is to ensure that proper arrangements can be made to bring the site back into use after the waste disposal operation has ceased.
- Proper registers of consignments must be kept by the producers, carriers and disposers.
- There will be a 'season ticket' arrangement for regular consignments of special wastes of similar composition disposed of at the same site. The waste disposal authorities will decide which producers and disposers in their areas qualify.
- The Secretary of State will have emergency powers to direct receipt of special wastes at a particular site. This is likely to be rarely used.
- Radioactive waste which also has the characteristics of special waste will be subject to the new controls.

Failure to comply with any of the requirements of the regulations is an offence.

Advice on particular problems can be obtained from waste regulation authorities (see below) and details about the 2005 regulations are free to download from the GOV.UK website.

Waste Site Licensing

Waste regulation authorities must inspect sites regularly and make sure the operators are following the conditions of the licence. Failure to comply with licence conditions is a criminal offence carrying a fine of up to £20,000. This can be increased to five years' imprisonment where special waste rules are broken. In addition to prosecution, a WRA can amend or even revoke the licence. See also the section dealing with unauthorized tipping of waste (ie fly-tipping) on p 541.

Packaging Waste

Waste Packaging

The Directive on Packaging Waste 94/62 EC sets out the definition of the materials covered and the target recycling percentages for producers of waste packaging. Registered businesses with a turnover of more than £2 million or who deal with more than 50 tonnes of packaging a year need to provide details of annual tonnages to be recycled or disposed of and to prove that they have achieved a target percentage. Under this scheme waste producers are classed as 'large' or 'small' and pay fees accordingly.

Proof of packaging recycling and recovery is done by producing packaging recovery notes issued by the recycling/disposal organization. The UK itself has targets of recycling all types of packaging with some targets changing year on year. Below is the latest UK target table which was released in 2018:

TABLE 20.8

Material	2017 (%)	2018 (%)	2019 (%)	2020 (%)
Aluminium	55	58	61	64
General recovery	79	80	81	82
General recycling	92	92	92	92
Steel	76	79	82	85
Paper/ board	69.5	71	73	75
Plastic	51	53	55	57
Wood	22	38	43	48
Glass	77	78	79	80

Further information on waste packaging is available from the WRAs or from NetRegs, which is able to advise on matters concerning all the WRAs. They can be found on www.netregs.org.uk (archived at https://perma.cc/LC9W-JM9G).

Fleet Car and Light Vehicle Operations

21

Transport managers and other staff responsible for the operation of large goods vehicles within companies frequently have additional responsibilities for the operation of company-owned cars used by management, sales and service personnel, and light commercial vehicles, which are outside the general scope of much of the legislation explained in this book. It is equally important that such vehicles should be operated strictly within the law. Most of the offences and penalties described in earlier chapters apply when operating such vehicles and the consequences of operating illegally can be serious. As already mentioned, for example, TCs will take account of failure to operate light vehicles safely and within the law when deciding whether an applicant is fit or is of sufficient good repute to hold an 'O' licence for larger vehicles. In addition, the HSE may consider that safety, risk assessment or duty of care issues may be relevant in cases of these vehicles being involved in road traffic accidents or collisions or found to be unroadworthy.

For the purposes of this chapter, light goods vehicles are vehicles with a gross plated weight not exceeding 3.5 tonnes (ie currently below the 'O' licensing, LGV plating and testing and the EU drivers' hours and tachograph requirement thresholds). However, there are currently discussions as to whether or not some of these light vehicles (2,400 kg–3,500 kg) should be subject to some, or all, of the regulations that apply to LGVs, including 'O' licensing, drivers' hours and tachograph regulations, or some other bespoke scheme as some enforcement authorities feel that these types of vehicles have often abused the lower levels of enforcement levelled at them. It should also be noted that the 3,500 kg weight limit has been raised to 4,250 kg for vehicles powered by alternative fuels and electricity in order for them to carry the same payload as a current 3,500 kg vehicle. However, in order to drive at this higher weight the driver will need to undergo at least five hours of approved training.

Much of the legislation applicable to the use of private motor cars and light goods vehicles has already been dealt with under such headings as excise duty, insurance and traffic regulations. The same system as described previously in Chapter 8 applies to the registration and excise licensing of such vehicles and the legal requirements for insurance cover have been outlined in Chapter 9.

Most of the traffic restrictions, particularly with regard to parking and waiting, road signs, motorway lights, seat belts, breath and drug tests, smoking in vehicles and zebra crossings, which apply equally to the business car and light vehicle driver and to the large goods vehicle driver, have been dealt with in Chapter 10. Nevertheless, some of these items of legislation are worth emphasizing here for the benefit of the light vehicle fleet manager along with other matters applicable to such operations within firms.

Excise Duty

Private-type motor cars owned by firms and used for business purposes can be licensed at the private/light goods (PLG) rate of duty. See Chapter 8 for details of VED rates. If a private car is adapted for carrying goods, or an estate car is used for carrying goods, tools or samples, the appropriate goods rate of duty must be paid if the permissible maximum weight exceeds 3,500 kg.

In determining whether an estate car or dual-purpose vehicle (see p 252 for definition) is subject to the goods vehicle rate of duty, if its permissible maximum weight exceeds 3,500 kg then consideration has to be given to the nature of the goods or burden carried. No specific guidelines are laid down but the DVLA takes the view that if any goods or samples, service equipment or spare parts are carried in connection with a business from which profit may result, then the vehicle should be taxed as a goods vehicle. Samples which can be accommodated in a normal briefcase would not generally constitute goods for this purpose.

In respect of 'double-cab' pick-ups HMRC have made a ruling that if the vehicle is capable of carrying a payload of 1.0 tonne then it will be classed as a van in relation to vehicle tax. This is important because if the vehicle has a removable hard top it is classed as a part of the vehicle, with the usual weight allowed for an 'ex-works' hard-top being 45 kg. This 45 kg figure may bring the payload down to under 1.0 tonne in which case the vehicle can then be taxed as a car and not a van.

In addition, vans with side and rear windows are classed as car-derived vans for road tax, speed limits and toll purposes and not as light commercial vehicles which can lead to serious savings especially if toll bridges and/or toll tunnels are used frequently. Advice on the required specification for anyone considering such modifications is available on the GOV.UK website.

Registration and Licensing of Foreign Vehicles

Foreign-registered cars and light vehicles brought into Great Britain temporarily by overseas residents are exempt from UK registration and licensing.

A vehicle which is properly registered and taxed in its home country may be used by a visitor for up to six months in 12 without being subject to domestic registration and licensing. To qualify for this, a visitor must have his normal residence outside the country he is visiting. Any vehicle used in the UK for more than six months has to be registered and licensed by the DVLA in the normal way.

If a vehicle displaying foreign registration plates is stopped by the police, the keeper must demonstrate that he is eligible to use it in Britain without registering and licensing it here.

Insurance

Private-type motor cars and light goods vehicles, like all other vehicles, are required by law to be covered for third-party insurance risks as a minimum, but clearly in the case of fleet cars additional cover would be taken out, and in most instances comprehensive cover is advisable. Most insurance policies contain a variety of option clauses, some of which are included in the basic premium and others are available at extra cost.

Correct Cover

Of importance to the fleet manager is the need to ensure that company cars are fully insured for business use by employees of the company. The difference in insurance classification for business cars used for commercial travelling and for those which are not used for this purpose is an important point for the fleet manager to consider. Most policies differentiate between such use, and in a car fleet where vehicles are used by both salesmen and other staff and management, it is essential to ensure that either the policy covers the whole of the car fleet for commercial travelling or, if it does not do so, the sales force should be restricted to driving only those cars which have this cover. If a salesman, or indeed any other staff member, uses a car for a purpose which can in any way be described as soliciting an order, then in insurance terms this use is classed as commercial travelling and the cover on the car must include this clause.

In addition, cars that are used abroad may not be insured to the same level as when they are used within the UK and fleet managers should check that the insurance cover offered for a vehicle in the UK is the same when the vehicle is driven outside the UK. Additional cover may be required even if a Green Card is used as this card only provides proof of third-party liability cover and most UK insurance policies also only grant third-party cover when the vehicle is abroad, unless requested to do otherwise by the owner/driver.

Dual-purpose vehicles registered and licensed as goods vehicles must be insured with cover permitting goods to be carried for business purposes. Post-Brexit this may mean that the goods carried will require CMR insurance if the vehicle is to travel to an EU member state and operators are advised to contact their insurers for advice on individual cases. Fleet managers also need to check with their insurers the definition of 'business use' for cars on fleet, including 'pool cars' or 'company cars' that are issued as a part of the job, as travelling to and from the workplace 'may' be deemed to be business use (also see below).

Cover for Special Cars

There can be problems in a fleet with certain individual cars on insurance cover which may not be driven by certain employees. For example, if the managing director has a high-powered sports-type car it is likely that the insurers would impose severe restrictions on the driving of that car, for whatever purpose (chauffeuring, ferrying back and forth for service or repairs, for example), by relatively inexperienced drivers or by, say, young drivers under 25 years of age. There are also issues relating to where the vehicle is normally parked overnight and at weekends. Alternatively, such cars may be restricted to named drivers and specific uses only.

Private Use of Company Cars and Light Vehicles

A further point which needs consideration is cover for the employee's use of a company car or light vehicle for private purposes. It is general practice for firms to allow their employees this concession both for commuting to work and, in the use of cars, also for family motoring at the weekends and for holidays. The cover taken out for fleet vehicles where this is the case should specifically include this provision if such use is permitted, otherwise the vehicle owner (the firm) may be guilty of permitting the use of an uninsured vehicle. In addition, the company may need to include family members (husband, wife, partner, etc) on the insurance if the company allows them to drive the vehicle, in spite of them not being actual employees. In these circumstances, if an accident and claim were to result, the consequences for the employee could be very serious in terms of meeting damage claims and in prosecution for using an uninsured car. The same provisions should be applied if the firm permits the employee's wife (or husband) or even his children (if they are qualified drivers) to drive a company car at any time.

Please also note the rules relating to no smoking in the workplace, which covers no smoking in fleet vehicles and no smoking when carrying young people under the age of 18 in a 'private' car in England and Wales. This rule also applies to any driver who fails to get a smoker to extinguish their cigarette in a vehicle where children under the age of 18 are being carried. Contravention carries a £50.00 fine. Scotland has its own Smoking Prohibition (Children in Motor Vehicles) (Scotland) Act 2016 which also covers young people under the age of 18.

In relation to 'vaping' in cars it is still allowed but drivers can be fined if the smoke is deemed to be a 'distraction'. It is also proposed to introduce a ban on 'vaping' in cars where children are present but no date has been set for this.

Employees' Use of Own Cars

If employees are ever required, or likely to be required, to use their own private car for business purposes, even for only the occasional errand, the fleet manager should ensure that they have adequate insurance cover on their own vehicle for such purpose. This usually means that employees' own policies must include provision for their car to be used in connection with the business of their employer.

The fleet manager, confronted with this type of situation, should ask to see evidence of the cover (ie a valid Certificate of Insurance or a temporary cover note showing the conditions for use covered by the policy) and not just rely on the word of the employee. Evidence should be checked periodically (perhaps at the time of annual insurance renewal) to ensure that cover is still effective over prolonged periods. Similarly, the fleet manager would be wise to inform all other persons in the firm, management and staff alike, that employees should not use, or be requested to use, their own car on company business without first having the insurance cover verified.

To avoid the dangers which could arise from an employee using his own private car for business purposes when it was not covered for such use, when the policy was not in force at all because the premium had not been paid or because the policy was invalid as a result of the employee giving incorrect information at the time of completing the policy application, the company can take out a motor contingency policy which will indemnify it against any claims arising from an accident involving an employee undertaking company business in his own uninsured car. This type of policy is very cheap to obtain and well worth the cost when considered against the risks. For example, if the employee had an accident causing serious injury to one or more third parties and his own insurance proved to be void, the third parties would look to the employer on whose business the employee was engaged at the time of the accident to meet their claims.

Dual Car Use

When an employee who is provided with a company car also owns a car which his wife uses, an anomalous situation on insurance cover can arise if his own car is insured in his, and not his wife's, name. This problem occurs because the cover provided on his own car automatically provides him with third-party cover while driving any other car not belonging to him but this third-party cover will not apply to his wife, unless she is named as a named driver to drive the other car. Consequently, when driving the firm's car for pleasure purposes he has the double cover provided by both the firm's policy and his own policy. If he should then be involved in an accident resulting in a third-party claim, his own insurers could be held partially liable for the damages arising out of the claim.

In order to overcome this particular problem the major insurance companies have made an undertaking indicating that it is not their intention to take advantage of the cover provided by the driver's own personal insurance policy in such circumstances. However, not all insurance companies are party to this undertaking and drivers/fleet managers who feel they may be affected by this need to check with their fleet insurers.

Electric Cars

Many companies and organizations are now seeking to use, or are using, electric cars as fleet vehicles and/or offering them as options for staff where a car is a part of the overall work package. In these cases, it may be that the insurance company will require some sort of familiarization training or assessment before granting cover as some techniques and vehicle responses can be different from those when driving a conventional vehicle. In these cases it is important to verify everything with the insurers. (As a note, there may also be a need to risk assess these new vehicles, especially for charging the batteries safely.)

Payment by Passengers

Payment by passengers towards the cost of fuel consumed on a journey no longer infringes the 'hiring' exclusion clause on insurance cover. However, payment towards other motoring expenses such as parking fees or depreciation, could still fall within the 'prohibition of hiring' clause in most insurance policies. In cases where this situation arises a check should be made with insurers to ascertain the current position.

When an employer makes a company car available for the private use of an employee a 'benefit in kind' value has to be calculated in relation to the car, and the fuel if that is also provided for private use:

- it allows the 'benefit in kind' value of a company car to be calculated and, if appropriate, the car fuel benefit;
- it provides an indication of the income tax liability for the provision of the company car and car fuel benefit.

The calculator is updated annually to allow calculations for current tax years.

Further information for employees can be found in HMRC Booklet 480 for employers, available on the GOV.UK website. The GOV.UK website also provides links to proposed changes for the coming years.

Changes to the Car Benefit Rules

The car benefit charge is levied to employees with conventionally powered and electric cars. (Up to 2015 there was no car benefit charge for electric cars as HM Government did not class electricity as 'fuel'.) For a full year the amount is obtained by multiplying the price of the car for tax purposes (in most cases, its list price plus accessories less capital contributions) by the 'appropriate percentage' according to the level of the car's CO_2 emissions. More detailed guidance is available for employees and for employers in the free HMRC booklet available via the website, but the percentage rates for 2019–2020 vary from a 16 per cent charge for a vehicle with zero CO_2 emissions to a 37 per cent charge for a vehicle with over 220 g/km emissions.

From 2015 onwards the lower threshold (ie the CO_2 emissions figure which sets the 15 per cent rate for petrol engines and 18 per cent rate for diesel engines) was reduced to 104 to 100 g/km. For 2016–17 this was further reduced to 94 to 76 g/km but with the levels being re-calculated, for 2019–2020 if not set at zero, it stands at the lowest possible rate of 1–50 g/km.

Fuel Benefit Charge

HMRC holds that free fuel 'incentivizes unnecessary motoring, which is contrary to the Government's environmental objectives. Taxing the benefit-in-kind represented by free fuel therefore serves to discourage unnecessary driving.'

The system for valuing the benefit for cars from free fuel, based on the multiplier and the appropriate percentage, was originally introduced by the Finance Act 2002. The benefit charge was intended to reflect a notional value for the fuel received. The system is still functioning and benefits can be calculated using HMRC's 'Company car and car fuel benefit calculator'. The benefit can also be calculated manually on a P11D working sheet 2. The threshold is based on the CO_2 emissions of the vehicle and changes annually. Details of current, and planned future, rates are available on the GOV.UK website but are 60 per cent for 2019–20.

Private Use of Vans

Legislation introducing a flat-rate fuel charge for the use of vans was introduced by the Finance Act 2004. The Van Benefit and Car and Van Fuel Benefit Order 2015 set the van benefit charge at £3,430 for 2019 to 2020 and the flat van fuel benefit at £655. For vans that do not emit CO_2 when driven, the cash equivalent is calculated based on the tapered appropriate percentage rate, which is 60 per cent for 2019 to 2020.

Where a van is used solely for business travel to and from work, with only occasional private use, the benefit in kind rules do not apply.

National Insurance on Private Fuel Usage

Where employees are provided with free fuel for private use there is a liability to pay National Insurance contributions on the value of the benefit to the employee. Where such value has not been taken into account by the employer there is a risk of claims by HMRC for retrospective payment of contributions going back one year. This charge does not apply if the vehicle is not used privately but the employer needs to check that this is the case.

Construction and Use Regulations

Apart from the sections of the C&U Regulations which apply to private cars concerning their construction, lighting, noise, silencing and all the provisions which require the motor car to be maintained in accordance with the regulations, they are not involved in the special requirements relating to goods vehicles, unless the car has in any way been adapted to carry goods, for example, by removing seats or fitting racks on which goods can be carried. In this case the goods vehicle rate of excise duty applies and the vehicles become subject to certain aspects of the C&U Regulations regarding goods vehicles (see Chapter 12).

It should be noted that 'double-cab' type pick-up vehicles are treated as vans for tax purposes where they are capable of carrying a payload of at least one tonne. In addition fitting a side window or windows, behind the driver's seat, into a van, removing seats from a vehicle originally with 12 seats and fitting a rear seat(s) into a van to convert the van into a car, in relation to speed limits, some tolls and VAT and, where the VAT has been reclaimed when the van was purchased, the VAT to be repaid is only that on the value of the van at the time of the conversion to a car.

It should be remembered that the overriding requirement of the C&U Regulations – for all vehicles to be maintained at all times in such a condition that they shall not cause danger to people carried on the vehicle and other road users – applies equally to private cars and to goods vehicles, irrespective of their size or weight.

Towing

From 1 August 1998, all tow bars fitted to new cars must be EU Type Approved and marked accordingly. It is an offence to fit – or have fitted – a tow bar which does not comply with Euro-legislation contained in Directive 94/20/EC. This type approval standard is expected to be adopted by the UK if the UK has to develop its own type approval system and standards following Brexit.

Local Authority Emissions Testing

Local authorities throughout England who have declared an Air Quality Management Area (AQMA) and all local authorities in Scotland are operating their own schemes of roadside emissions testing. Drivers of vehicles which fail the test will be issued with a fixed penalty notice usually requiring payment of £60, rising to £90 if unpaid within 28 days, although these figures do change depending upon individual authorities. The test levels are the same as those that vehicles would be expected to meet at the annual test. Commercial vehicles that fail an emission test invariably have poorly maintained engines. The scheme covers all types of vehicles, including commercial vehicles.

NB: Failing emissions tests during an annual MOT can now lead to a fine of up to £2,500.

Safe Use of Mobile Phones, etc

Mobile telephones emit electrical energy when transmitting and should be switched off before entering a filling station. Receiving incoming calls presents the same hazards as when making outgoing calls. A number of serious fires have resulted from mobile phone use in filling stations which is why there is always signage banning their use at fuelling stations.

The *Highway Code* prohibits the use of hand-held mobile phones or microphones while driving. It also says that using hands-free equipment may distract a driver's attention from the road. It is an offence to fail to exercise proper control of a vehicle at all times. If a driver is caught using a hand-held mobile phone whilst driving there is a £100 fixed penalty and three points added to the drivers' licence. This fine is £200 with six penalty points, if the driver is driving a vehicle which requires a vocational licence to be held, such as Category C1, C, etc. Larger fines can be imposed if the offender goes to court (up to £2,500 for drivers of goods vehicles).

A similar injunction applies in regard to in-vehicle (or on-board) systems such as those used for route guidance, navigation and congestion warning, and the use of laptop or hand-held PCs and multi-media, etc.

In all instances, when it is necessary to use such equipment the driver should stop the vehicle in a safe place (ie not on the hard shoulder of a motorway except in an emergency), apply the handbrake, switch off the engine and remove the key from the ignition to avoid any possibility of a prosecution for using the equipment or telephone whilst 'driving'. This may seem somewhat 'extreme' but there have been a number of prosecutions where the driver has been deemed to be driving because 'they were at the controls of the vehicle for the purpose of controlling the motion' despite the vehicle being stopped.

Carrying Dangerous Goods in Cars

According to the National Chemical Emergency Centre (NCEC), the carrying of small quantities of dangerous goods, such as samples, in company cars can present both legal problems and safety risks.

The legal situation is determined by the type of goods carried, the size of the receptacles in which they are carried and the total size of the load. The quantity thresholds for UK carriage are shown in the CDG Road Regulations (Schedule 1, Table 2 – see p 568 for further details).

For the most part, it is unlikely that sufficient quantities of such goods in Class 3 (Flammable), Packing Group III (Transport Category 3) would be carried in a private car to require the full legal gamut of vehicle placarding, the provision of Instructions in Writing and the need for driver training. Provided these goods are in receptacles with a volume of 25 litres or less it would be difficult to exceed the quantity threshold of 500 litres above which these legal requirements apply.

However, should the samples fall within the requirements for Packing Group I substances (Transport Category 1), goods must then be in a receptacle with a capacity of 1 litre or less, with a total volume of 20 litres or less, to avoid these requirements.

So far as the risk element is concerned, it is necessary to consider what would happen in the event of a road accident. With no Instructions in Writing on the vehicle, there is no emergency information available for either the driver or the emergency services, nor, invariably, is there likely to be any emergency equipment such as the appropriate fire extinguishers, first-aid kit, respirator, gloves, spill kit or emergency warning triangle to place on the road.

Besides all the dangers implicit in the carrying of dangerous samples, there is the question of the vehicle insurance to consider. Generally, it may be expected that an insurance company would repudiate any claim if they were not advised beforehand of the carriage of such goods, especially if legal requirements were not being met at the time.

Advice and information can be obtained from the NCEC at:

National Chemical Emergency Centre (NCEC)
The Gemini Building
Fermi Avenue
Harwell
Didcot
Oxfordshire
OX11 0QR
United Kingdom (Tel: 01235 753654)
Email: ncec@ricardo-aea.com

Drivers' Hours and Records

Light goods vehicle drivers (ie of vehicles not exceeding 3.5 tonnes gross weight*) coming within the scope of this chapter and employees driving company-owned private-type motor cars are exempt from the EU driving hours regulations – consequently, only the relevant British provisions apply in certain cases.

**Note the increase to 4,250 kg for alternative fuel and electric vehicles, covered earlier.*

The applicable limits for drivers of goods vehicles not exceeding 3.5 tonnes gvw are as follows:

- maximum daily driving time 10 hours;
- maximum daily duty time 11 hours.

There are no specified break or daily or weekly rest period requirements; no limits on continuous duty or weekly limits on duty or driving. However, Working Time Regulations breaks are required (see Chapter 3) and the *Highway Code* does state that drivers should take a break from driving every two hours.

Drivers of light goods vehicles of not more than 3.5 tonnes gross plated weight and dual-purpose vehicles (see p 252 for definition) of any weight used for certain specialized duties are required to observe only a daily maximum driving time of 10 hours. This applies to light goods vehicles used:

- by doctors, dentists, nurses, midwives or vets;
- for any service of inspection, cleaning, maintenance, repair, installation or fitting;
- by a commercial traveller and carrying only goods used for soliciting orders;
- by an employee of the AA, the RAC or the RASC;
- for business of cinematography or of radio or television broadcasting.

Record Keeping

Light goods vehicle drivers (ie vehicles under 3.5 tonnes gross weight) and drivers of dual-purpose vehicles in the UK are exempt from the requirements to keep records of their driving, duty and rest periods. Drivers of these vehicles driving in mainland Europe are advised to check whether or not this is the case in any of the countries they intend to visit or transit, as Germany requires records to be kept for goods vehicles between 2,800 and 3,500 kg.

Employees driving vehicles in this category currently remain exempt from the requirements of the goods vehicle drivers' hours and record requirements, but only so long as they do not drive vehicles to which these requirements do apply. If at any time an employee who normally drives only light goods vehicles or motor cars also as part of his work needs to drive a goods vehicle to which the drivers' hours regulations do apply then any time spent driving a van or a private car (his own or the company's) for his firm's business must be counted within his total daily working time (ie duty time). If the goods vehicle exceeds 3.5 tonnes gross weight the driving of the car should be shown on his record sheet (ie tachograph chart) for the day on which he drives a goods vehicle as 'other work'.

Full details of the goods vehicle drivers' hours and records are given in Chapters 3 and 4.

Tachographs

Light goods vehicles of not more than 3.5 tonnes gross plated weight are currently exempt from the EU tachograph regulations requiring tachograph fitment and use, but if such a vehicle is coupled to a goods-carrying trailer exceeding 750 kg in weight, so that the total of the combined gross weights exceeds 4.25 tonnes, then the vehicle will come within the scope of the EU tachograph regulations, unless it is otherwise exempt due to special use. This means that a fully calibrated tachograph must be fitted and must be used by the driver when the trailer is drawn (see Chapter 5 for full details of the tachograph regulations) and the EU drivers' hours rules must be followed (see Chapter 3 for details).

NB: If light commercial vehicles from 2,400 kg to 3,500 kg are required to be 'O' licensed for international hire and reward operations, as the EU intends, then EU/ AETR drivers' hours and tachographs will apply.

Speed Limits

Private cars and dual-purpose vehicles not drawing trailers are restricted to maximum permitted speeds on certain roads in accordance with the restriction signposted on the section of road and to overall maximum speeds of 60 mph on single-carriageway roads and 70 mph on dual carriageways and motorways.

Speed limits for cars and light goods vehicles are as follows:

FIGURE 21.1

	Motorways	Dual carriageways	Other roads
Cars and car-derived vans	70	70	60
Cars and car-derived vans towing trailer	60	60	50
Rigid goods vehicles not exceeding 7.5 tonnes	70	60	50
Articulated vehicles and rigid goods vehicles not exceeding 7.5 tonnes drawing trailer	60	60*	50

In all cases of speed restrictions mentioned above, if specific lower limits are in force on any section of road, then it is the lower limit which must be observed. Lower limits also apply when towing trailers.

* In Northern Ireland the limit for this category of vehicle is 50 mph.

NB: Many smaller vans are now fitted with side windows and at least one seat fixed behind the driving seat position. This allows those types of vehicles to travel at the same speeds as cars and car-derived vans and to pay lower tolls at crossings.

Speed Limiters for Vans

Since 1 January 2007 all goods vehicles over 3,500 kg gvw fitted with Euro-III, or above, engines should have been fitted with a speed limiter calibrated to a maximum speed not exceeding 56 mph (90 kph).

Euro-III, and above, vehicles have the facility to have a top speed limiter already built into the engine electronic control unit, thus ensuring that the calibration procedure does not involve the fitment of brackets, air cylinders or piping.

From the same date, 1 January 2007, vans over 3.5 tonnes gross weight have been prohibited from using the outside lane of a three-, or more, lane motorway.

Many fleet operators are now also fitting speed limiters to vans not exceeding 3,500 kg gross weight in order to reduce fuel usage and to improve the image of the 'white van man'.

Seat Belts

Compulsory fitment of seat belts applies in the case of the following light vehicles (see also pp 328–31):

- goods vehicles not exceeding 1,525 kg unladen (first registered since April 1967);
- goods vehicles not exceeding 3,500 kg maximum gross weight (first registered since 1 April 1980);
- dual-purpose vehicles first registered since 1 January 1965;
- private cars first registered since 1 January 1965.

Vehicles to which the regulations apply, first used since 1 April 1973, must be fitted with belts which can be secured and released with one hand only and must also be fitted with a device to enable the belts to be stowed in a position where they do not touch the floor. The belts must be maintained in a fit and serviceable condition and kept free from permanent or temporary obstruction which would prevent their being used by a person sitting in the seat for which the belt is provided. Failure to comply with these requirements is an offence and can lead to failure of the MoT test.

In cases where the regulations apply, as above, belts must be provided for the driver and one front seat passenger.

Wearing of Seat Belts

The wearing of front seat belts in vehicles fitted with them by law has been compulsory since 1 January 1983.

Since 1 September 1989 children up to 14 years of age riding in the back seats of motor cars fitted with rear seat belts or child restraints must wear those belts or restraints.

Since 1 July 1991 adult rear seat passengers travelling in cars or taxis fitted with rear seat belts must wear the belts provided, irrespective of the age of the vehicle.

Certain exemptions to the wearing of belts have been included in the regulations (see pp 330–31 for list of exemptions).

Heavy fines may be imposed on conviction for failing to wear a seat belt as required by law. The responsibility for seat belt wearing rests with the person sitting in the seat for which the belt is provided except that responsibility for ensuring that children wear seat belts as required by law either in the front or rear seats rests with the driver of the vehicle (ie not the parent or guardian who may be accompanying the child).

Fuel Consumption Tests

Concern about energy conservation led to the Energy Act 1976 and the Passenger Car Fuel Consumption Order 1977 being enacted. Because of interest among readers of the *Handbook* in this subject, details of the legal requirements and the scheme are outlined here.

Since 1 April 1978 new cars on display in showrooms and on forecourts must carry a label showing official fuel consumption figures for that model of car. Every dealer must have details of officially approved fuel consumption tests for all cars listed in a booklet available in his showroom for buyers to consult on request. In addition, where reference is made in promotional literature, such as advertisements, technical specifications and sales brochures, to the petrol consumption of a new car the test results must be included. In all such cases the results of all tests carried out must be quoted (urban cycle, 90 kph – and 120 kph where appropriate) in both miles per gallon and kilometres per litre. These requirements do not apply in the Channel Islands or the Isle of Man.

Official Tests

The official tests are carried out in approved laboratories or on test tracks. They have been designed to be representative of real-life driving situations and the results achieved provide a guide to the models which are likely to be more economical in their fuel use.

The test results do not guarantee the fuel consumption of any particular car. Each new car has not itself been tested and there will inevitably be differences between cars of the same model. The driver's style, the loading of the car, road, weather and traffic conditions, the overall mileage of the car and its standard of maintenance will all affect its fuel consumption. For all these reasons the fuel consumption achieved on the road will not necessarily accord with the test results.

The Standard Test

The tests follow an internationally agreed procedure and consist of two compulsory parts:

Part 1. A cycle simulating urban driving.
Part 2. A constant speed test at 56 mph (90 kph).

Models Included in the Tests

Almost all types of new passenger cars are covered by the tests. However, certain types are excluded as follows:

- Cars manufactured before 1 January 1978.
- Second-hand cars.
- Cars adapted to carry more than eight passengers (excluding the driver).
- Three-wheelers.
- Invalid carriages.
- Van-derived passenger cars.
- Cars built specially for export.
- Cars operating on four-wheel drive only.
- Cars whose engines run on diesel, liquefied petroleum gas or other such fuels.

These vehicles will not, therefore, be labelled in the showrooms. Heavy goods vehicles, vans and motorcycles are also excluded from these tests. Also, a small number of manufacturers and importers have been granted exemption from testing because of the low volume of production involved. Consequently, these particular makes and models are not likely to be of significant interest or concern to the fleet user.

Urban Test Cycle

The urban test cycle is carried out in a laboratory where equipment simulates the loads experienced under normal driving conditions and the standard patterns of urban driving. The car is driven from a fully warmed-up start and is taken through a cycle of acceleration, deceleration and idling with a maximum speed not exceeding 31 mph (50 kph).

Constant Speed Test

The constant speed test at 56 mph (90 kph) is intended to be representative of open-road driving. It may be carried out in the laboratory or on a test track (under strictly controlled road and weather conditions).

Optional Constant Speed Test

This test is carried out at 75 mph (120 kph) in a laboratory or on a test track. Although it is recognized that this test exceeds the UK maximum speed limit, it is included to illustrate to car drivers the worsening fuel consumption at higher speeds. It may also be useful to manufacturers exporting to some parts of Europe where speed limits are higher.

Only one production car is tested as a representative of each model. It must have been run in and have been driven for at least 1,800 miles (3,000 km) before testing. In some cases several models which do not differ significantly in certain technical characteristics thought to be important in determining fuel consumption may be grouped together into a 'class'. Only one car in the class needs to be tested.

Testing

The responsibility for testing lies with the manufacturers and importers themselves. They must either carry out the tests themselves or arrange for them to be carried out on their behalf. DfT officials have the right to inspect the test laboratories and to witness tests in progress to ensure that they are being carried out correctly.

Manufacturers must submit their fuel consumption test results to the DfT, who record the results in an official fuel economy certificate.

In spite of these requirements and standards there has clearly been some 'massaging' of actual emission standards: road tests have not been representative of actual road conditions, vehicle engine management systems have been modified for testing purposes and emissions data from some vehicle manufacturers has become almost completely unreliable, leading to the current position where several motor manufacturers are now faced with the costs of corrective action, compensation and legal action.

SAFED Training for Van Drivers

In addition to a safe urban driving scheme for LGV drivers, a DfT SAFED scheme launched in mid-2006 offers free driver training under its SAFED (Safe and Fuel Efficient Driving Standard) initiative for van drivers (ie drivers who fall below the 7.5-tonne threshold for LGV licensing).

NB: Professional drivers driving vans exceeding 3,500 kg gross weight but not exceeding 7,500 kg gross weight (Category C1) are now classed as vocational drivers and additional Driver CPC requirements apply.

SAFED for vans is a one-day course and the acclaimed benefits for drivers are as follows:

- reduced risk of accidents while driving;
- reduced stress levels and enhanced satisfaction of driving;
- increased confidence in vehicle control and driving technique;
- enhanced job efficiency and professionalism;
- potential financial incentives.

There are also many benefits for employers (ie owner-drivers and fleet operators), such as:

- reduced accidents;
- less vehicle downtime due to a reduction in accidents;
- reduced fuel bills;
- increased productivity and vehicle utilization;
- improved resale value of vehicles;
- reduced running costs (particularly relating to maintenance and tyres);

- potential reductions in insurance premiums;
- reduced environmental impact.

The SAFED training offered in the UK is predominantly provided by private driver training companies. Further details of the scheme can be obtained by visiting local providers' websites.

In 2013 the then VOSA produced a best practice guide for van drivers and van fleet operators. This guide (*Your Van: Best Practice Guide*) is still available and free to download from the DVSA website. There are also guides relating to 'running a fleet of vans' on the GOV.UK website.

Daily Walkaround Checks for Van Drivers

In July 2015 the DVSA issued a new guide on the daily checks that should be carried out by van drivers. It was issued as a guide to help light-vehicle fleet operators to improve the overall maintenance and safety standards of their fleets. It is available and free to download from the GOV.UK website. It is in the same format as the guides for LGV and coach drivers which can be found in the DVSA's *Guide to Maintaining Roadworthiness*. The FTA also offer DVDs and poster guides covering walkaround checks.

Vehicle Fuel Efficiency

22

Next to wage costs (and sometimes even higher than wage costs), fuel is normally the most expensive goods vehicle operating cost item, accounting for an average of around 40 per cent of road transport operating costs for an articulated LGV. It is a high-cost commodity which is a major budget feature of all vehicle fleet operations. It is also subject to occasional and dramatic shortages and cost fluctuation as a result of political unrest and economic conditions in some of the major oil-producing countries. Scientists predict total extinction as world supplies of crude oil are consumed ever more rapidly by developed nations, which have become increasingly dependent on transportation systems powered by oil-based fuels and emissions are also a major factor associated with fuel usage. This has led to the rapid development of aerodynamic body shapes, alternative fuels, fuel additives, 'dual fuel' and electric vehicles, improved fuel efficiency, EGR and SCR systems, etc and innovative solutions aimed at reducing our reliance on traditional fuel sources. It has also led to the introduction of 'fracking' for shale oil and gas and continued searches for oil and gas in traditional locations and the more remote areas of the globe.

While the search for and research into acceptable alternative fuels and power units goes on, it is important to take steps to minimize consumption of our present fuel supplies. As well as being a problem for nations, this is a problem which concerns all fleet operators, whatever their size. Besides any conscience they may have about energy conservation they will readily appreciate that fuel consumption must be reduced in the campaign to keep vehicle operating costs down. There are other, wider considerations including emissions, company image and the environment, etc and many of these are covered in other areas of this *Handbook*.

Fuel and Vehicle

Fuel consumption is substantially related to the type of vehicle, its power unit and drive line, its mechanical condition, the use to which it is put and how it is driven. In recent times manufacturers have offered fuel economy models within their ranges so the cost-conscious operator can choose between economy or outright performance with some operators claiming to get better/cheaper fuel returns by using larger engines, which don't need to operate at maximum load, in their vehicles instead of smaller engine vehicles which need to work harder on a daily basis, but this debate will probably never be concluded, not least because it does nothing to reduce sales by the major manufacturers.

The fuel-conscious operator who is in a position to buy new vehicles will almost undoubtedly choose fuel economy models where these are suited to his particular needs and, in particular, where there is a need for vehicles to enter cities where poor emissions standards may attract surcharges and actually ban access or restrict it to certain times of the day. However, for the most part, fleet operators have to stick with the vehicles they already have in their fleets and are faced with the need to consider how improved fuel economy can be achieved with existing vehicles. Three principal areas exist for improvement in the vehicle itself. These are as follows:

- mechanical condition;
- efficient use;
- addition of fuel economy aids.

Mechanical Condition

A vehicle which is poorly maintained will inevitably consume more fuel. Particular attention should be paid to efficient maintenance of the following items:

- Fuel system (fuel tank, pipe lines, filters, pump and injectors). There should be no leaks and the vehicle should not emit black smoke. Both of these are causes or consequences of excessive consumption as well as matters which could result in test failure and prosecution. Drivers need to be trained to ensure that they check the fuel cap is in place and the seal in good condition as one of their daily walkaround check items. Fuel pumps and injectors should be properly serviced as recommended by the manufacturers. There are also options on 'dual-fuel' engines and the use of supplements such as AdBlue but this can be difficult to source when out on the road and has become less popular in recent years.
- Wheels and brakes. Wheels should turn freely and without any brake binding. Front wheels should be correctly aligned. Brake binding and misalignment cause unnecessary friction which is only overcome by the use of more fuel. Axles on bogies should be correctly aligned because tyres running at slip angles have a high rolling resistance and therefore are a source of increased fuel consumption. Some operators also elect to fit lifting axles and 'low running resistance' tyres which are specially designed with fuel efficiency in mind. In addition, many vehicles are now fitted with automatic exhaust brakes which effectively shut the fuel off when the vehicle is decelerating.
- Driving controls. Throttle, clutch and brake pedals should be correctly adjusted so the driver has efficient control over the vehicle. In particular, engine tick over should be accurately adjusted to save throttle 'blipping' to keep it running when the vehicle is stationary. Stop–start technology may also be considered and is becoming more and more common on new vehicles.
- Where the controls are governed by one or more on-board engine management computers, these need to be checked regularly in order to ensure the controls are set for optimum performance. Effective use of driver-controlled exhaust

brakes (where fitted), gear box/changing techniques and speed limiters, especially when set to a slightly lower than maximum permitted speed, also increase fuel efficiency.

Efficient Use

Inefficient use of vehicles constitutes the greatest waste of fuel. The following activities should be avoided by careful route planning, scheduling and prior thought about the cost consequences:

- vehicles running long distances when only partially loaded;
- vehicles covering excessive distances to reach their destination;
- large vehicles being used for running errands or making small-item deliveries which could be accomplished more efficiently, and certainly more economically, by other means;
- unnecessary detours and extended, but preferred, routes taken by drivers;
- engines idling excessively;
- compliance with speed limits;
- vehicles running empty.

It used to be frequently argued that traffic office staff had little control over these matters, since customer demands for orders and the need to give drivers freedom to choose routes are dictates which overrule efficient planning. Nevertheless, modern IT applications and trackers have gone a long way towards improving office control of the fleet and attempts should be made to persuade those concerned of the need for restraint, in the quest for saving fuel and thereby reducing costs. Indeed, some companies offer drivers' incentive schemes for those drivers able to meet fuel economy targets. It should also be noted that the new era of smart tachographs have a GPS facility and are able to detect excessive speed and a range of driver activities throughout the day.

Where possible, tracker systems can also be used to enforce speed limits, route and schedule compliance, inform customers of expected delivery times and reduce the 'subjective' preferences of routes and drop sequences by some drivers.

Fuel Economy Aids

The quest for fuel saving has led to a market for economy aids which can be added to existing vehicles. These aids fall into six general categories:

- streamlining devices such as skirts, cab-top air deflectors, 'banana trailers', under-bumper air dams, front corner deflectors for high trailers and box vans, in-fill pieces for lorry and trailer combinations, and shaped cones for addition to the front of van bodies – radiusing or chamfering the front edges of the body is perhaps the simplest means of reducing air drag;
- road speed governors which restrict maximum speed – high speed is one of the greatest causes of excessive fuel consumption – can be set at slightly lower than the maximum permitted speed for the vehicle;

- engine fans and radiator shutters which are designed to ensure that diesel engines are always operating at the correct temperature to give the most efficient performance and fuel economy;
- exhaust gas recycling (EGR) and selective catalytic reduction (SCR) systems also help with fuel economy as well as reducing emissions whilst hybrid engines and improving technologies continue to reduce fuel usage;
- 'stop–start' technology to reduce fuel usage when the vehicle is stationary. This technology is increasingly required in many London boroughs and other towns and cities where local fines can be levied when engines are left idling while the vehicle is at rest;
- duel-fuel, alternative fuel and electric power to reduce conventional carbon-based fuel and emissions and, in some cases, engine noise and even maintenance costs.

Note: Since 2017 some large rigid vehicles which have alternative means of power such as an electric motor or lpg are allowed to operate at up to 1 tonne in excess of their maximum weight in order to accommodate the additional weight of the alternative propulsion equipment. This was followed by the Government agreeing to allow vehicles to exceed their maximum authorized length where this was due to the fitting of aerodynamic crumple zones. No firm date has been announced for the introduction of all of these measures but the increase up to 4,250 kg for electrically and alternatively powered vans has been drafted into law.

All these types of devices can be economically justified to a varying degree, but it is important to note that fitting streamlining devices in isolation only reduces fuel consumption if vehicle speeds are kept down. If the driver is able to use the few extra miles per hour which these devices provide – which he will do unless otherwise restricted – then there will be little fuel saving and the cost of fitting would not be wholly justified. In addition, efficient scheduling, so as to avoid congestion and reduce idling time, etc can also play a major part in reducing fuel usage. It is also worth remembering that in the future, as in the note above, it is planned that vehicles will be permitted to operate above some dimensional limits if these limits are due to the vehicle being fitted with aerodynamic equipment.

Operators considering fuel reduction measures which may impact upon a vehicle's dimensions or weight, etc, should check with the D*f*T before assuming they will be allowed to operate the vehicle once the modifications have been made.

Fuel and Tyres

The type and condition of tyres on a vehicle play a significant part in its fuel consumption. It is a proven fact that the lower rolling resistance inherent in radial-ply tyres adds considerably to the fuel economy of the vehicle compared to the greater resistance of cross-ply tyres.

Tyre manufacturers claim that improvements in fuel consumption of 5 to 10 per cent can be expected from the use of radial-ply tyres. Low-profile tyres which offer a number of operational benefits over conventional radial tyres – such as reduced platform height and reduced overall height – also offer further possibilities for fuel saving. It is also possible to purchase 'low-resistance' tyres designed to reduce the level of friction between the tyres and the road surface.

The savings mentioned will only be achieved if the tyres are in good condition, are correctly inflated to the manufacturer's recommended pressures and are properly matched, especially when used in twin-wheel combinations. Neglect of tyre pressures is common in fleets and under-inflation is one of the major causes of tyre failure. It is also a major contributor to excessive fuel consumption.

Vehicles with steering axle and lift axle options can also reduce fuel consumption as they drastically reduce scrub and reduce resistance/friction between the vehicle and the road surface.

Fuel and the Driver

Driving techniques, above all else, influence the overall fuel consumption of vehicles. A driver with a heavy right foot will negate all fuel-saving measures and devices and destroy any expectations of acceptable fuel consumption. Many drivers may also need to be made aware of the engine tachometer in front of them and to realize that the amber, green and red sectors all relate to engine performance and the use of fuel. In addition, tracking drivers and monitoring distances run is seen to deter some of them from using preferred routes instead of more direct routes, whilst lockable fuel tanks and 'sensible' overnight parking locations can also avoid/reduce the theft of fuel. In larger vehicles efficient and effective use of the exhaust brake also helps reduce fuel usage as does the purchase of the most up-to-date vehicles with features such as stop–start technology, improved engine efficiency and alternative fuel and fuel additive technology. Poor driving falls into two categories:

- high-speed driving;
- erratic, stop–go driving.

Fast driving, including over-revving when changing gear, consumes excessive fuel: this fact is beyond question but the extent of the extra consumption is difficult to assess accurately. Tests carried out some time ago (but still making a valid point) on an articulated vehicle on motorway operation indicated that fuel consumption increased quite dramatically when the vehicle was travelling at over 40 mph. In the tests, at 40 mph the fuel consumption was 10.5 mpg, but at 50 mph this reduced by 2.6 mpg to 7.9 mpg. This represents a 24.76 per cent increase in fuel consumption. The real significance of these figures will be fully appreciated when annual motorway travel is calculated and this is multiplied by the increase in consumption, by the number of vehicles in the fleet and by the cost per gallon of diesel fuel. It is also a fact that in 2015 the speed limits were raised for LGVs on single and dual carriageways in England and Wales and this too will have had an impact on fuel usage which operators may need to counter. (Scotland is still evaluating the effects of this increase, and has a pilot scheme running on the A9, and may follow suit at some later date.)

The effects of erratic driving are more difficult to determine in quantitative terms, but it is sufficient to say that it results in abnormally high fuel consumption as well as causing excessive wear and tear on vehicle components. Impatience behind the wheel and an inability to assess in time what is happening on the road ahead leads the driver to see-saw between fierce acceleration to keep up with the traffic and violent braking to avoid running into the vehicle in front – hence the excessive use of fuel.

More economical driving is achieved by concentration on the road and traffic conditions ahead, anticipating well in advance how the traffic flow will move and what is happening in front, so that acceleration and braking can be more progressive and a smooth passage assured.

One other fuel-saving practice which the driver can adopt, if they do not have stop–start fitted, is to stop the engine while the vehicle is stationary rather than letting it tick over for unnecessarily long periods. If he feels this is necessary because his battery is in poor condition, then it is much cheaper to deal with the battery and charging problems than pay for the extra fuel to compensate.

It is also a fact that many fleet operators are now electing to buy vehicles with automatic gear boxes in an attempt to cut out poor practices such as 'over-revving' and unnecessary gear changing and although some operators see 'automatics' as using more fuel others feel that the savings made are a real advantage in relation to fuel usage and reduced vehicle abuse.

Fuel and Fleet Management

Fleet operators can take a number of basic steps to reduce fuel consumption besides ensuring that the measures already mentioned are implemented.

Bulk Supplies/Buying

Control over the buying of bulk supplies and bulk issues and over the buying of supplies from outside filling stations at the higher pump prices are important aspects requiring management attention. So too is accurate record keeping, without which it is impossible to compare the fuel consumption of vehicles or to see which vehicles are consuming excessive amounts of fuel. Without records to identify these problems, there is no hope of remedying high fuel costs. Fuel agency cards are also a good way to monitor fuel usage by driver and vehicle. (The invoices issued by the fuel agencies are also seen as acceptable proof for re-claiming the VAT on fuel, especially when operating abroad.)

Recording Issues

Overfilling of vehicle tanks, causing spillage, is a common occurrence which wastes fuel and prevents accurate consumption records being obtained, as well as causing a mess and a health hazard. Accurate recording of issues against individual vehicles and/or drivers is another area which demands close attention. Modern electronic and computerized fuel-dispensing systems are available which ensure security of bulk supplies by preventing access except with a known key or card. This stops unauthorized drawing of fuel and it monitors issues to identified vehicles or keyholders. The cost of such systems can be quickly recouped through savings in missing or unaccounted fuel and through better record keeping, which enables high vehicle consumption to be quickly identified and investigated.

Buying Away from Base

Where bulk supplies are available at base, drivers should be discouraged from buying supplies from outside sources at higher prices except when absolutely necessary and even then they should buy only sufficient to get them home. Commonly, drivers fill tanks to the top, which is enough to cover the trip home and to do further journeys as well on fuel which cost much more than that which they could have drawn once they got back to base. It is important to keep watch on the purchase of outside fuel supplies, especially for cash, because of the incentives (including free gifts, refreshments or loyalty points) which are offered to drivers to fill to the top. If outside fuel drawings are necessary then recognized bunkering card systems should be established. Buying away from base can also lead drivers to travel to preferred fuelling sites incurring additional mileage in doing so and this too needs monitoring.

Long-Range Tanks

In the case of vehicles which operate regularly on long distances – on international work, for example – the fitting of long-range tanks is an economic proposition because of the savings achieved by using bulk-purchased supplies. A word of caution though: the extra fuel carried should not be at the expense of payload unless this can be justified, and on international work there is also the cost of fuel levies or taxes to be borne in mind. These are chargeable when entering some countries (notably Norway) and are based on the amount of fuel in the tank. British hauliers returning to the UK may also find they have to pay an excess fuel tax on supplies bought outside the UK. However, long-range tanks do allow drivers to fill up in countries where fuel is cheaper and, in some cases, this can be an advantage.

Following a number of cases where road hauliers have been stopped for using overlarge diesel fuel tanks on vehicles, the RHA has reminded its members of the official definition for 'standard' fuel tanks.

Under Article 8a of Council Directive 92/81/EEC, the diesel tanks fitted to new vehicles are defined as follows:

> The tanks permanently fixed by the manufacturer to all motor vehicles of the same type as the vehicle in question and whose permanent fitting enables fuel to be used directly, both for the purpose of propulsion and, where appropriate, for the operation, during transport, of refrigeration and other systems.

In the case of used vehicles, the RHA advice is that:

> any tank already fitted to such a vehicle when purchased by its current owner, would satisfy the 'standard tank' criteria. This means that should the original tank have been replaced by a new, larger tank prior to purchase by a subsequent owner, then that larger tank would be regarded as having been fitted by the manufacturer for the purpose of the legal definition.

HM Revenue & Customs has warned that the focus of attention on fuel import issues is on the misuse of duty relief and has emphasized that fuel brought into the UK may only be used by the particular vehicle carrying it and should not be offloaded from that vehicle for use by other vehicles or for transfer to a bulk fuel installation.

Operators should also be aware that some European countries do not recognize rebated fuel such as 'Red Diesel' and, if it is detected, perhaps in a trailer tank to supply a refrigeration motor, the driver may be subject to pay a penalty based upon the loss of duty.

Route Planning/Scheduling

Better planning of vehicle schedules and routes and maximizing 'backloading' and cabotage possibilities offer the prospect of quite considerable fuel savings, besides other savings which may also result from actions such as fuelling in countries where fuel is cheaper when on international journeys. A reduction in the miles travelled to fulfil particular delivery schedules will inevitably result in fuel savings. If the schedules can be planned so that fewer vehicles are needed to carry out the operation then, besides the broader savings in vehicle costs, the fleet as a whole will use less fuel. Therefore, the elimination of unnecessary trips or trips where vehicles are only partly loaded is a major priority in the search for fuel cost savings.

Scheduling vehicles so that they are on roads such as the M25, and operating in city centres, at peak traffic times should also be avoided wherever possible.

The future for cabotage for UK vehicles operating in Europe and for European vehicles operating in the UK is uncertain and will depend upon the terms of the UK leaving the EU or agreements between the UK and individual European countries.

Tachographs and Fuel Saving

The use of tachographs in vehicles and detailed analysis of tachograph records are steps which have also provided many fleet operators with fuel savings and fuel consumption comparisons if nothing else. The value of recordings in this connection should not be overlooked. In addition, data collection from the new fourth generation tachographs will enable operators to better analyse routes and journeys with a view to reducing fuel usage.

Agency Cards

There are a number of agency and fuel cards available to fleet operators. Generally they can be categorized between those from the major oil companies (eg Shell, Esso, BP) and those from other commercial organizations such as Allstar and Keyfuels.

Principally these systems offer the opportunity to buy fuel at pump prices, paying only when fuel is actually purchased. The difference in the various schemes is in the levels of service which they offer. Operators may also need to consider availability when deciding on which card to select, as some cards may need the driver to divert in order to find a suitable place to purchase fuel if the card he has is not widely accepted.

Fuel Economy Checklist

Check

- Fuel systems (including filler cap) free from leaks.
- Filler cap lock fitted and operational.

- Fuel pump and injectors serviced and correctly adjusted.
- Exhaust not emitting black smoke.
- Air cleaners not blocked.
- Engine operating at correct temperature.
- Wheels turning freely.
- Controls properly adjusted and lubricated.

Tyres

- Condition and inflation pressures.
- Possibility of changing to low resistance radials on all vehicles.
- Lifting/steering axle considerations.

Drivers

- Speed limits not being exceeded.
- Driving methods smooth and gentle.
- Engines stopped when vehicle standing.
- Authorized routes used.

Management

- Control over supplies and issues.
- Avoidance of spillage, loss and unauthorized use.
- Purchases from outside suppliers kept to a minimum.
- Record systems accurate and up to date.
- Possibility of installing fuel issue and monitoring systems.
- Use of vehicle trackers.
- Possibility of fitting fuel economy aids (alternative fuels, deflectors, engine fans, etc).
- Possibility of using long-range fuel tanks on vehicles.
- Routeing and scheduling practices to reduce wasted journeys and unnecessary mileage.
- Fuel economy programme/training to ensure all possible steps being implemented efficiently and recorded accurately.

Energy Efficiency Best Practice Programme

The Government has produced a comprehensive guide outlining its energy efficiency strategy and various sustainable transport bodies, including the respected Energy Saving Trust, produce guides and help. The guides cover many aspects of best practice in fuel efficiency, including easy methods of capturing and monitoring of data, vehicle specification and maintenance as well as driver training. The Trust can be contacted at:

England
EST England
30, North Colonnade
Canary Wharf
London E14 5GP
Tel: 020 7222 0101

Northern Ireland
EST Northern Ireland
Titanic Suites, 55/59
Adelaide Street
Belfast BT2 8FE
Tel: 028 9072 6006

Scotland
EST Scotland
Second Floor, Ocean Point 1
94, Ocean Drive
Edinburgh EH6 6JH
Tel: 0131 555 7900

Wales
EST Wales
33, Cathedral Road
Cardiff CF11 9HB
Tel: 029 2046 8340

Freight Best Practice

This scheme is no longer funded by the D*f*T and is now termed Freight Best Practice-Transport Business. It still promotes operational efficiency within UK road freight transport operations, and it offers essential information, free of charge, for the freight transport industry right across the UK covering topics such as fuel saving, skills development, the use of efficient equipment and systems, operational efficiency and performance management.

Contact and guidance, publications and brochures are available from: www.transportbusiness.net (archived at https://perma.cc/275K-TC6E).

Reducing Fuel Bills

The University of Huddersfield published a 20-point plan to help transport and distribution companies reduce their fuel bills following recent increases in fuel duty. It says the following aspects are key to improving fuel efficiency:

- Ensure that you have accurate fuel consumption figures.
- Get the best from your present fleet.
- Make fuel-efficient purchasing decisions when buying new or second-hand equipment.

It also suggests following the points listed below:

- Check that weekly or monthly averages are produced by total distance divided by total fuel used rather than average of the daily averages. Quarterly summaries (using average of the daily averages) have been found to be inaccurate by as much as half a mile per gallon (mpg).
- In most cases there is a seasonal pattern to mpg, which peaks in July and August and bottoms out in December and February. It is very important to know this if you are going to test products that claim to improve mpg.
- When you find a large discrepancy in daily mpg, investigate it. Don't just average it or ignore it. Take measures to prevent it from happening again.
- Driver training/assessment consistently achieves better miles per gallon (mpg), but it needs a reinforcement mechanism otherwise it will fail.
- Reinforcement mechanisms for fuel efficient driving can be:
  - simple feedback on a noticeboard;
  - individual letters to drivers; or
  - a fuel bonus; however, while an annual bonus can be based on the annual average mpg, shorter-term bonus systems (eg weekly or monthly) should not use the annual average mpg (and remember too that bonuses must not endanger road safety).
- The most senior person with an LGV licence should be trained first.
- Identify the most fuel-efficient vehicles and, if possible, bearing in mind other operational factors, place them on the operations or routes that use the most fuel.
- Think of aerodynamics. For example, ensure that the gap between the back of the cab and the front of the trailer is minimized to reduce aerodynamic resistance. Tippers with easy sheets should have them closed when empty to prevent the airflow hitting the inside of the tailboard.
- If adjustable air deflectors are fitted, get the drivers to adjust them for maximum effect. If the deflector is too low, you will see a tidemark on the front of the trailer.
- Specify the correct bodywork – it should be no higher or wider than the job requires.
- Monitor maintenance records – poor mpg and short brake-lining life are good indicators of a driving style that wastes fuel.
- When buying new vehicles, calculate which is best over the life of the vehicle. Is there a better residual at the end of the vehicle's life from a larger engine, or are there reduced fuel costs from a smaller engine that is just as capable of doing the job?

- Specify trailers or bodywork with rounded leading edges (minimum 200 mm radius) or with curved roofs.
- Aerodynamic aids may not be cost-effective on vehicles that do not undertake long, high-speed journeys as part of their regular work.
- Beware of claims made for aerodynamic equipment tested at 56 mph and translating the saving to your vehicle(s). Aerodynamics are highly sensitive to speed. As a rough guide, calculate the average speed of your vehicle(s) and ask for test results conducted at that speed.
- Specify and activate an engine speed limiter. (In some vehicles these are a legal requirement.)
- When buying a second-hand vehicle, take it for a test drive and note the engine speed at 56 mph. If the vehicle is being purchased for medium- or long-distance work, you do not want to purchase a vehicle that is geared for local work. If you get this wrong, you will end up cruising at too high an engine speed and subsequently wasting a lot of fuel.
- When purchasing a new vehicle, get the manufacturer to provide free driver training. Most do, so take advantage of it.

NB: Much of this valuable research was led by the highly respected Dr Will Murray who sadly passed away after an illness in December 2016.

Gas-Powered Heavy Trucks

Increasingly, environment-conscious transport operators are looking to natural gas for powering heavy vehicles. Among the early key players were Marks and Spencer and the Somerfield supermarket group, which originally put 300 compressed natural gas-powered, Detroit-engined ERF vehicles into service. Iveco, Scania and Volvo are also leading names in gas truck production. Gas power is now used by other names in in the UK such as BOC, DHL, Waitrose and Calor. These trucks have also been trialled and used by Kuehne + Nagel, Wincanton, ASDA, Brit European, Howard Tenens, Great Bear and many others. Besides the savings in fuel costs, these vehicles are much quieter than conventional diesel-powered vehicles – quieter than a saloon car, it is said, thus allowing night-time deliveries to stores without upsetting local residents.

There are three main types of gaseous fuels in use in the UK:

1. liquefied petroleum gas (LPG);
2. compressed natural gas (CNG);
3. liquefied natural gas (LNG).

All these three types of gas are used by both van and truck operators due to their environmental benefits, particularly:

- clean exhaust emissions;
- reduced engine noise;
- favourable duty treatment reducing fuel costs.

The Government's National Air Quality Strategy requires the monitoring of airborne pollutants such as NOx (nitrogen oxide) and particulates while the Air Quality Regulations 1997 oblige local authorities to assess air quality. As a result of this, a number of councils are now running gas-fuelled vehicles.

It has to be noted that gas can be difficult to obtain in some parts of the UK, although it is more readily available in Europe. This problem has led to many operators choosing dual-fuel options (gas and diesel) in order to reduce problems caused by lack of gas-fuelling facilities when the vehicle is away from base.

Further details on saving energy can be obtained from the Energy Saving Trust (see above). See also the website: www.energysavingtrust.org.uk (archived at https://perma.cc/2RJH-HRDS).

Low-Sulphur Diesel

The International Road Transport Union (IRU) called for supplies of low-sulphur diesel fuel to be made readily available throughout Europe long before the EU's proposal for universal supplies from 2009. With legislation requiring all new heavy vehicles from October 2006 to meet at least Euro-IV exhaust emission standards, this fuel is essential since these engines need fuel that does not exceed a sulphur content of 10 parts per million (ppm) whereas some current diesel supplies have a sulphur content of up to 50 ppm. Ultra-Low Sulphur Diesel (ULSD) is also available. This fuel has a maximum sulphur content of 50 parts per million but produces quite a low energy output which can lead to reduced fuel efficiency in some circumstances. This dilemma is being addressed by engine manufacturers but it remains a fact that improved emission standards do generally mean higher fuel usage, except where emissions are reduced by a dual-fuel, diesel and electric powered engine.

Biodiesel

Biodiesel is a diesel-equivalent, clean-burning processed fuel derived from biological sources (such as vegetable oils), which can be used in unmodified diesel-engined vehicles. It differs from straight vegetable oils (SVO) or waste vegetable oils (WVO), used as fuels in some diesel vehicles. It is biodegradable and non-toxic – in fact, it is said to biodegrade as fast as sugar and be less toxic than table salt. It typically produces about 60 per cent less net CO_2 emissions than petroleum-based diesel, as it is itself produced from atmospheric CO_2 via photosynthesis in plants.

Biodiesel is claimed to be better for the environment because it is made from renewable sources which can be grown in the UK and elsewhere, which consequently decreases Britain's dependence on foreign oil supplies and contributes to our own national economy.

Some vehicle manufacturers are positive about the use of biodiesel, citing lower engine wear as one of its benefits. However, as biodiesel is a better solvent than standard diesel, it 'cleans' the engine, removing deposits in the fuel lines, and this may cause blockages in the fuel injectors. For this reason, manufacturers recommend that the fuel filter be changed a few months after switching to biodiesel (this part is often replaced anyway in regular servicing). Other vehicle manufacturers remain cautious over its use. For example, in the UK many only maintain engine warranties for use with maximum 5 per cent biodiesel, blended in with 95 per cent conventional diesel – which is generally considered to be overly cautious. Peugeot and Citroën are exceptions in that they have both announced that their HDI diesel engines can run on 30 per cent biodiesel. Scania and Volkswagen are other exceptions, allowing most of their engines to operate on 100 per cent biodiesel.

Some operators have claimed to have experienced some problems with biodiesel when it is used during very low temperatures as it becomes 'thicker' and has a higher viscosity and it has to be noted that it can be more difficult to source than conventional diesel.

Electricity and Other Options

Increasingly, the use of low emission vehicles, especially in the urban cycle, is being seen as necessary. This has led to an increase in dual-fuel vehicles which may be diesel-electric or diesel-gas, etc or solely powered by electricity. Whilst, at this current time, electricity may not be suitable for some large goods vehicles it is a viable option for many van and lighter vehicle operators. That said, an all-electric 40 tonne LGV has been developed by BMW and there is a 'trolley bus' type articulated vehicle on trial in Norway. In addition, major manufacturers have dual electric and diesel truck options but they are still some way off becoming seen in any numbers other than trials.

We are now seeing bio-fuelled buses, electric buses, hydrogen cell buses and smaller vehicles and so it is not unreasonable to expect these developments to transfer across into the general freight sector in time and the proposed increased weights for dual fuel vehicles mentioned earlier are a witness to this. In addition, the UK Government is funding trials on some major roads that will evaluate technology aimed at enabling electric powered vehicles to be charged as they travel without the need for stopping to recharge.

Mobile Communications and Information Technology in Transport

23

Technological developments in mobile communications have, over recent years seen the introduction of systems that many drivers now consider standard, and it is now commonplace for vehicle drivers to be in almost constant touch with their office, customers, collection and delivery sites and home base by mobile, or smartphone, sending live information from trackers on the vehicle and being directed to their exact destination by a satellite navigation (sat nav/TomTom) system. Trackers also mean that base is in constant touch with the driver and able to supply live information relating to any difficulties en route or required changes to the route or schedule, etc. Trackers also give live feedback to base on driving issues such as speed and any breaks taken, etc.

The new fourth generation digital tachographs are all fitted with GPS systems enabling the vehicle position to be known at the start, during and end of the working day. Whilst positioning is probably of more interest to the operator the information will be available to enforcement authorities who can download data even from passing vehicles whilst they are in motion. That said, the UK authorities have stated that they do not intend to begin this type of data collection/enforcement activity until there are sufficient numbers of the new tachographs in operation, which may take several years. Later fifth generation tachographs are expected to provide even more detailed positioning information for both operators and drivers but again it is expected that there will not be immediate enforcement activity after first introduction.

It used to be a common experience in transport operations for considerable cost to be wasted through late, changed, redirected and cancelled orders and instructions. Try as they might, transport or fleet managers could rarely avoid their share of these annoying frustrations and there was nothing that they could do, usually because they could not contact the driver while he was travelling. Vehicle-based mobile communications at today's level of sophistication have changed all this and the wasted costs of the past can be turned into savings and even into profit quite simply by being able to contact the driver, relay details of the changed plans and generally divert vehicles to meet the current needs of the business. These systems also allow the driver to feed back live information to his base where he makes a successful delivery, encounters a problem, such as a breakdown, or gets otherwise delayed, enabling the depot to give suppliers and customers details of any unplanned delay of collections or deliveries. They also allow the driver to notify of any problems with deliveries in relation to missing or incorrect items.

As communications allow changes to schedules they also allow base to arrange back-hauls or return loads. The savings in wasted time and miles, the avoidance of heavy vehicles returning home empty, because they can be directed to pick up return loads, and the response to last-minute customer demands are significant benefits which in themselves, or with other benefits, add up to offset the capital costs of buying and installing communications equipment and the ongoing costs of rentals and call charges.

Mobile/Smartphones

The advent of the mobile phone system has revolutionized mobile communications. A telephone can now be interconnected to the national and international telephone networks from a vehicle-based (ie mobile) installation or from a unit or telephone carried by a driver. Such systems provide the user with the facility to dial direct and/or text almost any telephone number in the UK and internationally. Similarly, any telephone user can dial direct to a mobile cell-phone number.

The increasing number of 'apps' available to mobile phone and 'tablet' users also enables drivers and fleet controllers to access almost any information relating to weather conditions, road conditions, roadworks, hold ups, ferry schedules, tunnel closures, industrial action, etc, and so, in reality, the driver today is supported by an array of technology all aimed at making him aware of issues which may affect his ability to do his job as planned and all enabling more efficient and effective use of the vehicle fleet.

It must be noted, however, that an increasing number of commercial vehicle drivers are being prosecuted for using mobile phones whilst driving and that the penalties have been increased to a fine of up to £200 with six penalty points, with the police using unmarked vehicles, including large vehicles, to enforce the rules on motorways and primary routes. It should also be noted that a driver using a mobile phone can be considered to be driving if the keys are in the ignition and they are at the controls of the vehicle (in the driving seat) even though the vehicle may be stopped.

In addition to mobile phones, there is now an increase in the use of laptop computers in commercial vehicles, enabling not only contact with the driver but also allowing the driver to email a completed delivery or email any problems back to base.

Safety

The *Highway Code* includes a special section on the use of microphones and in-vehicle telephones. It prohibits using a hand-held microphone or telephone handset while driving, except in an emergency. It says the driver should only speak into a fixed, neck-slung or clipped-on microphone when it would not distract attention from the road. Importantly, drivers should not stop on the hard shoulder of a motorway to answer or make a call, no matter how urgent, other than to summon the emergency services in the event of an accident. Rules relating to the use of mobile phones in vehicles have also been discussed in earlier sections of this *Handbook*.

Satellite-Based Communications Systems

The Global Positioning System

The Global Positioning System (GPS), originally devised by the US military to assist navigation of both ground and air crew, incorporates satellites orbiting the earth. As the system developed, it has been utilized for civilian purposes, in particular the marine, small aircraft, leisure and commercial markets, for vehicle navigation and for use by the emergency and security services.

The nature of the satellite signal enables the GPS receiver, ranging in size from those fitted into smartphones to some the size of a small television set, to track vehicles and craft accurately and efficiently. At least three satellites are in view of the receiver at any one time, and this decodes the information to display global position in longitude and latitude, and a number of different coordinate formats. Because it does not rely on radio signals GPS can be used anywhere in the world.

'In-vehicle GPS systems' are capable of incorporating DVD, radio and GPS in a single unit. For navigation purposes, it is just a case of entering a destination (such as a postcode or the name of a road) and within seconds the distance, route and travel time is calculated and displayed. A voice gives commands for turning at the correct junctions, while a map on the screen is a useful navigation aid.

The main problem with these systems can be that they have largely been designed for use by car drivers, and large vehicles can be directed along prohibited, or otherwise impossible, routes, as widely publicized on several occasions. Operators considering GPS systems should ensure that the equipment selected is appropriate for use by large vehicles. This is becoming less of a problem as more and more LGV GPS systems come onto the market but it has been the cause of many 'high profile' incidents.

Another problem 'can' be that, because the systems were originally developed for military use, when the US forces are planning some sort of military activity/action they are able to put set 'errors' or variances onto the system, which their forces can allow for but which distort the information for other, non-military users.

The same technology, based on satellite positioning, is used in vehicle tracker systems (see below).

Siemens VDO System and TMC

Siemens VDO Automotive was the first company in the UK to incorporate and introduce a Traffic Message Channel service (TMC) (now known as the Radio Data Systems Traffic Message Channel (RDS-TMC)) into its aftermarket satellite navigation systems, enabling it to combine satellite navigation with real-time traffic information. Since the early days, TMC has been expanded to transmit via FM and DAB radios to vehicles fitted with on-board navigation systems, such as TomTom. TMC is actually a coded signal and not the voice message systems that interrupt radio programmes to give live traffic updates. In 2011 the Government produced a plan that included the phasing out of TMC and all new vehicles using DAB systems, using TPEG by 2020 because of poor TMC coverage. It did however appreciate that there may be a considerable 'changeover' period as many existing vehicles will still be fitted with the old TMC systems and, to date, the changeover is incomplete. The digital data stream carried by TMC was originally sent by radio broadcaster Classic FM, although this has now expanded with many more FM service providers coming onto the market. Many motorway service areas and some hotels, etc also use similar TMC systems to provide live information for travellers. Data is gathered from a wide variety of sources, including real-time information from vehicles actually out on the road and the telemetry systems used on motorways and trunk roads. The system is also 'intelligent', being capable of differentiating between different types of delays, for example slow-moving traffic, accidents, fog or roadworks.

TMC data can also be used by the navigation system to automatically plan alternative routes around incidents or congested areas and to predict arrival times. This form of real-time traffic information significantly adds to the usefulness of on-board navigation systems, now fitted as standard to most new vehicles with touch-screen and even voice-activated technology available, turning it into a driving aid that has reduced the need for stopping and reading maps or asking for instructions or directions; it can assist in reducing journey times, even for drivers travelling on routes they use regularly.

New RDS-TMC providers use radio data location codes to improve coverage and Digital Audio Broadcasting (DAB) applications are also in use as the industry tries to improve coverage to a whole range of technologically different receivers.

Information Technology in Transport

Information technology (IT) is quite simply the means by which information is collected accurately, fully analysed, transmitted to all relevant functions within and without an organization, and disseminated by those charged with decision making. Many efficient transport and distribution operations these days are totally dependent on reliable IT systems (for example, 'just-in-time' stocking principles hinge on rapid and efficient communications) for communication with customers, suppliers and contractors. Other applications include automated order picking, electronic point of sale (EPOS) applications, electronic data interchange (EDI) systems, and warehouse management systems (WMS).

Radio frequency identification (RFID) is used in warehouses and distribution centres to locate stock and 'track and trace' applications which can locate goods in transit and record final delivery and many, many more. Fuel and vehicle engine and maintenance monitoring systems, 'Trafficmaster/Navmaster', the operator licence VOL system, online vehicle records and taxation, online licence checking, DCPC records, vehicle engine management systems and even digital tachographs and trackers are also all examples of information technology in transport and it is probably true to say that we rarely consider it in our everyday working lives as it has become integral in most of what we do, manage, monitor and record.

The GOV.UK website is clearly a good example of the IT revolution as almost everything an operator and/or driver may need is available online through this most comprehensive database of information and its use cannot be underestimated and is to be encouraged.

Within IT systems, one of the fastest-growing areas is that of electronic data interchange (EDI), whereby transport and distributor firms receive orders, delivery documentation and invoices direct from their customers' computers into their own (compatible) systems via direct communications links, completely eliminating the delays, errors and other difficulties associated with the creating and movement of paper documents via postal and courier systems. EDI systems provide the benefits of rapid and accurate order passing and processing (at less direct cost) with the potential for reducing stock levels and give an opportunity to develop systems of cross-docking which reduces the delays in customer service time and reduces handling and storage costs.

More recently, systems such as automatic emergency braking systems (AEBS) and lane departure warning systems (LDWS) have been introduced as standard on new vehicles. These safety applications show the continuing progress of IT in transport and it is surely only a matter of time before 'driverless vehicle technology' becomes a reality although following publicity of 'convoy' applications of this technology in 2018 there seems to be something of a lull in its progress towards becoming generally accepted.

HM Revenue & Customs

Widescale computerization in the road freight, shipping and export/import industries and by HM Revenue & Customs in their New Computerized Transit System (NCTS) used for international movements of goods has led to the introduction of modern systems for passing shipping and export/import data between traders, shippers and Customs authorities. This is now done via direct or indirect computer links between the Customs offices of departure and offices of transit, enabling consignments to be tracked along the entire route of an international journey after leaving the country of origin, without the need for paper documents to pass or confirm information. The whole concept of EDI, sometimes called a paperless system of trading, and its use results in automatic handling and actioning of data. To ensure uniformity in this method of trading the United Nations has set a standard for EDI known as EDIFACT (an acronym for Electronic Data Interchange for Administration, Commerce and Transport), under which there are standard procedures and messages for passing such matter as shipping instructions.

It is obvious that when the UK leaves the EU there will need to be major changes made to NCTS because our status as an EU member state will change and the status of our goods will also change. This may require different import and export procedures and operators should try to keep abreast of proposals in these areas as the UK moves towards new trading regimes, although if the UK remains as a member of the European Free Trade Association (EFTA) this may limit the need for changes as we would retain certain rights and status under EU legislation. Of course, it will all depend upon the final deal (or no deal) situation when we leave but HMRC are working on new procedures and IT applications aimed at minimizing problems and time wasted for getting UK goods out of the country and EU goods into the country. This led to eCMR consignment notes being introduced in 2019. Operators moving goods internationally are strongly advised to contact their trade association and to monitor HMRC press releases in order to ensure that they are able to manage any new systems and procedures that may be introduced, post-Brexit.

Computerization in Transport

Computerization provides many facilities of value to the transport industry, especially vehicle routeing and load scheduling systems which determine the most cost-effective and load-efficient delivery routes and schedules. It also allows the use of on-board vehicle and axle weighing which reduces the risks of prosecutions for operators and drivers collecting bulk, or otherwise un-weighed, consignments.

In addition, bar coding systems allow packages to be scanned for data in the warehouse, at hubs and on the vehicle, allowing data to be transferred back to base in relation to the progress of the consignment or as soon as a consignment has been delivered to its destination. In the office, all manner of data can be held on file, readily accessible by staff, to give information about employees, vehicles, customers, suppliers, loads, etc.

Additionally, whilst digital tachograph analytical systems allow operators to meet their legal obligation to check drivers' tachograph records on a regular basis and to bring to a driver's attention any relevant issues, a full range of data recording, information and analysis operations, including accident records, fuel usage accounting, staff records and vehicle maintenance records, can be accessed by all relevant staff and management, both in the office and away from base on laptop or hand-held computers via an internet connection.

The use of email and the internet has led to enormous improvements in business efficiency and information, providing rapid person-to-person, business-to-business (B2B) and business-to-customer (B2C) communication and access to unlimited data on just about every subject under the sun.

We also need to remember that engine management systems fitted to all modern vehicles are also computer controlled and, in a similar vein, that vehicle repairers and maintainers need computer programs to diagnose and correct or clear faults on vehicles.

Intelligent Transport Systems

Intelligent transport systems (ITS) that use telematics and telemetry (ie the combination of information technology and telecommunications which allows the transfer of data from instruments) provide online (electronic) information and control systems for all modes of transport, including vehicle-based systems used to record thermograph readings or engine management information. Typical of these systems used in road transport are also those that operate:

- variable message signs (VMS) for use on, for example, motorways;
- on-board route and traffic information, such as Trafficmaster/Navmaster;
- traffic control and enforcement signs, such as the digital speed and average speed cameras and variable speed limit technology;
- electronic road charging;
- traffic monitoring;
- vehicle-to-base communications;
- electronic ticketing.

NaviTrans is a rapidly expanding company which specializes in IT transport and logistics solutions and offers help and advice in this sector. NaviTrans can be contacted at info@navitrans.eu.

Teleroute

Teleroute is a leading European online matching service for freight and vehicle space, operated by the Walters Kluwer group, providing freight forwarders and road hauliers with opportunities to maximize efficiency and increase profits. Established in 1985, the system is now known as the Teleroute Freight Exchange and has over 200,000 freight offers posted and consulted online daily by more than 70,000 subscribers in 16 European countries. Each year more than 120 million tonnes of freight are efficiently transacted in 40 different countries.

Teleroute claims to provide:

- secure transactions;
- more efficient and strategic transport planning and the ability to reduce empty running by 25 per cent;
- flexible reaction to customers' needs;
- better load combinations;
- new UK and international contacts;
- improved planning and time management;
- immediate results with only data that really matter;
- increased profitability through optimized efficiency;
- lower communication costs.

Teleroute is an Alpega application and Transwide is a later sister application which specializes in freight and logistics software solutions.

Contact: www.teleroute.com (archived at https://perma.cc/Y3V4-G8RX) for details.

General Data Protection Regulation (GDPR) and the Data Protection Act (2018)

Below is a summary of the GDPR as it applies to the UK. It should also be noted that the Data Protection Act 2018 came into law on 23 May 2018 and was formatted using the bulk of the GDPR in order that the UK will be able to comply with EU standards of data protection post-Brexit as the GDPR is an EU instrument and will not apply to the UK following our exit.

Changes in the Act were largely made to protect cyber researchers who work to bring to light incidents where personal data is misused and to ensure that individuals have stronger rights over their own personal data.

The Information Commissioner's Office (ICO) recommend that organizations should consider the following '12 step approach' to data protection in light of these new requirements.

Step One: Awareness

This focuses on the need for decision makers within organizations to be aware of the changes in order to properly assess their impact.

Step Two: Holding Information

The new rules require organizations to hold accurate files on personal data held and that these files and the way in which they are compiled should be properly recorded as company policy.

Step Three: Communication

When collecting personal data, organizations need to make sure that they explain who they are, what they want the data for and how long they intend to hold it. This ensures legality and gives individuals the right to make complaints to the ICO.

Step Four: Individuals' Rights

Individuals have the right to know the format of the data, a right to access it, a right to have it amended or deleted and a right to object to how it may be used.

Step Five: Access

Organizations holding personal data cannot charge a fee for access and have one month to comply with a request for access. If a request is not granted they have one month to explain to the individual concerned why this is so.

Step Six: Data Processing

Processing must be lawful and only done with consent of the individual, to do otherwise is illegal. Organizations also need to ensure that their data processing procedures comply with the GDPR.

Step Seven: Consent

Organizations must gain and manage consent to hold personal data. Consent must be given freely and openly.

Step Eight: Children

Under GDPR rules a child of 16 can give consent. This is reduced to 13 in the UK. This may not apply often but could apply where temporary employment is offered over school holidays, etc.

Step Nine: Data Protection Breaches

Breaches must be detected, reported and investigated and notice given to the ICO, within 72 hours, of any breach where a risk to the 'rights and freedoms of individuals' is possible. The individuals concerned must also be notified. Fines are levelled for both breaches and failure to report them.

Step Ten: Data Protection and Data Protection Impact Assessments (DPIA)

Whilst data protection is a legal requirement under GDPR, impact assessments are also mandatory. Organizations with 'high risk' data being protected may need to contact the ICO for advice on DPIAs.

Step Eleven: Data Protection Officers (DPO)

In organizations where high levels of data are held there should be a DPO nominated to have overall responsibility for data protection. This person can be either an employee or an external consultant.

Step Twelve: International Aspects

Organizations operating in more than one EU member state must appoint a lead authority where they have their main activity.

Clearly, this is only a summary of the new requirements under GDPR but they are a significant step towards preventing data protection abuse which was possible under the old Act of 1998.

Whilst overall responsibility for data protection is given to the Department for Digital, Culture, Media and Sport, detailed information can be obtained by contacting the ICO at 0303 123 1113 or emailing casework@ico.org.uk.

Freedom of Information Act 2000

In addition to the Data Protection Act, the Freedom of Information Act 2000 applies to all recorded personal data held by data controllers who are also public authorities for the purposes of the 2000 Act.

The Freedom of Information Act 2000 is overseen by the Information Commissioner's Office (ICO) and applies to all public authorities. These authorities include central and local government, schools and colleges, the police, the NHS and many other public and advisory bodies in England, Wales and Northern Ireland and those nationwide public authorities based in Scotland. Scotland has its own Freedom of Information Act 2002, which is very similar to the 2000 Act.

The 2000 Act allows any individuals to request to be given the information held by the public authority which relates to that individual. The public authority concerned then has 20 days in which to supply the information requested. Should the information not be supplied or be withheld for some reason the individual concerned must be told why.

CCTV

Because rules relating to CCTV are directly linked to data protection the scales of fees are the same as for registering under that Act. Therefore, a registration fee of £40 is legally due under the Act, if the company employs no more than 10 people and has an annual turnover not exceeding £632,000. If the company is larger and has a maximum turnover of up to £36 million and no more than 250 employees the fee is £60 and if it is a large company with figures above 250 employees and £36 million then the fee is £2,900. All fees are payable direct to the Information Commissioner. Public sector organizations, charities and small occupational pension schemes are all subject to discounts and some exemptions.

All CCTV systems need to be accompanied with signs clearly stating that they are fitted and in operation and you should also note that if a person who has been filmed on CCTV requests to see the footage that was taken you must show it to them within 40 days, but you are able to charge up to £10 for doing so. However, this charge seems to be being ignored by many local authorities who charge much higher fees, some well over £100.

Warning

Road hauliers could face fines of up to £5,000 for operating unregistered CCTV systems in their premises for security purposes. Such systems must be registered under the Act and the fee paid to the Information Commissioner in order to satisfy the terms of the Act.

Transport and the Environment

24

One of the most important and widely discussed issues in transport continues to be the impact which the industry as a whole, and heavy lorries in particular, have on the environment. So-called 'green' issues feature in every aspect of transport operation, from the siting of vehicle depots to the routeing of heavy goods traffic, access to some cities and areas and the disposal or recyclability of vehicles and certain loads, especially waste.

The drive towards 'Low Emission Clean Air Zones' continues apace with the London 'Ultra-Low Emission/Clean Air Zone'. In a road safety matter more than an environmental issue, the London Safer Lorry Scheme has also now been introduced. When visiting London operators are strongly advised to use the Transport for London (T*f*L) website to ensure that they are up to date with any changes or requirements for driving commercial vehicles in the capital. It is also worth noting that individual London boroughs are introducing their own 'clean air' requirements with Hackney and Islington having introduced total bans on some commercial vehicles at certain times of the day and so operators who may be unfamiliar with the areas should check if they need to enter the areas concerned.

It is widely expected and planned that cities such as Southampton, Birmingham, Nottingham, Derby, Leeds, Glasgow, Edinburgh, Dundee and Aberdeen could have emission zones by 2020 and that up to 30 zones could be in force before the start of 2022. Again advice is the same as for operators visiting London – operators need to keep abreast of intended changes all across the UK.

Although quite demanding, these initiatives are actually minor issues when we think about the announcement last year that all new petrol, diesel and hybrid cars are to be banned in the UK from 2040. This issue will surely create more legislative changes and see a new 'drive' (excuse the pun) towards new technology and investment.

This *Handbook* charts in earlier chapters the legal requirements regarding choice of vehicle operating centres to satisfy 'O' licensing requirements, and the need for licence applicants to advertise their proposals in this regard and defend their premises against potential environmental representations from local residents. In the technical section, legal requirements concerning the emission of noise, smoke, fumes, fuel storage and exhaust pollutants are detailed, and in Chapter 20 the subject of waste carriage is covered with descriptions of the legal requirements regarding hazardous waste and the more recent legislation on 'controlled' waste – which is basically everyday waste emanating from commercial and industrial premises and is now subject to stringent control as to its carriage and disposal.

Many of the UK's major transport groups have developed clear environmental policies. These initiatives are concentrated mainly on fuel conservation and emissions standards at this stage, which has a direct payback benefit by way of cost savings and an indirect benefit in the shape of an improved company 'image', as well as achieving actual reductions in the amount of CO_2 which their respective company vehicles discharge into the atmosphere. This in turn helps to reduce global warming, which scientists have identified as being a problem of catastrophic proportions. However, there are many other ways in which these and other firms are contributing to the environmental effort, even down to the use of recycled paper for routine stationery needs and using 'paperless' systems for example.

It is a fact that organizations now use their 'green credentials' to maximize their commitment to the environment for marketing and business purposes, such is the focus on environmental issues and sustainability.

Major steps towards tackling the environment 'problem' have been taken with reports by the Royal Commission and more recently the Government's consultation documents on roads and on developing an integrated transport policy – both aiming to find ways of reducing traffic congestion and the adverse effects of air pollution from road traffic. It should also be noted that HM Government has made £15 million available under a 'Green Truck Fund' to the Office for Low Emission Vehicles (OLEV) for research into this area and a further £4 million for research into infrastructure, as well as the £8.1 million put into the convoy truck programme and the launching of the Low Carbon Accreditation Scheme aimed at improving the efficiency of, and the technology used in, goods vehicles. Whilst the schemes and initiatives above remain 'live', it must be accepted that they have taken something of a 'back seat' during the Brexit negotiations.

There are also the issues of dual-fuel, alternative fuel, the continuing trial of longer trailers which is also aimed directly at reducing vehicle movements and thereby reducing emissions, allowing vehicles fitted with equipment aimed at reducing fuel consumption to operate at higher weights and the trialling of 'on the move' electric vehicle charging technology.

Originally, many consultation exercises came to fruition as early as 1998 with a White Paper in which positive and sustainable solutions were put forward. It must be said, however, that many of the proposed solutions were never taken up, as has been the case since, where what are seen as 'unpopular' measures are avoided by some politicians with their eye on another term in office. To that end it could be argued that some things never change, as we see goods vehicles continually demonized whenever possible and whenever it can be done in order to allow a politician to show off his environmental credentials.

In another initiative, the CILT also promotes its Fleet Operator Recognition Scheme (FORS) which was initially trialled in London but has now been rolled out nationwide.

FORS is a voluntary scheme covering fuel efficiency, vehicle emissions, improved operations and all aspects of safety. FORS aims to help fleet operators monitor and measure performance and to change their ways of working in order to demonstrate 'best practice'. The potential benefits of FORS include improved road safety, reduced incidences of fines and other charges, reduced fuel emissions and improved fuel efficiency, greater industry intelligence and networking opportunities and enabling operators to stand out from the crowd. FORS has enjoyed strong support and good take up within the industry and is now permitted as part of periodic DCPC training. It should be viewed positively by operators seeking ways of improving both margins and image and encouraged unreservedly.

As a supplement to FORS there is also the Construction Logistics and Community Safety (CLOCS) scheme which requires operators using vehicles in the construction industry to consider vulnerable road users, such as cyclists, and requires FORS Bronze level achievement and vehicles to be fitted with certain safety equipment and signage.

Further information on both schemes can be obtained at www.cilt.org.uk (archived at https://perma.cc/R9CD-ZAY3) or at www.fors-online.org.uk (archived at https://perma.cc/U3RL-5UEU).

Energy Savings Opportunity Scheme (ESOS)

From 5 December 2015, in order to comply with the EU Energy Directive, all large companies with more than 250 employees or an annual turnover exceeding €50 million and a balance sheet exceeding €43 million, are required to conduct energy saving audits every four years that cover buildings, transport and industrial operations. Many public sector operations will not be covered by this and many organizations with ISO 50001 accreditation may also be exempt. Information on compliance and a general guide to ESOS can be obtained from the Carbon Trust at info@carbontrust.com who will be able to provide guidance and who offer webinars for interested parties. The FTA and RHA are also able to offer guidance and advice.

Businesses affected by this need to appoint an ESOS Energy Assessor who will be responsible for conducting, controlling and 'signing off' the audit. The audit will need to address the following:

- Measure the total energy consumption of building, transport and industrial operations.
- Identify areas of significant energy consumption, amounting to at least 90 per cent of the total energy consumption.
- Identify cost and energy efficient recommendations for areas of significant energy consumption.
- Report compliance to the Environment Agency.

The ESOS legislation is seen as a first step towards an ongoing approach to reducing energy consumption and operators are advised not to avoid or delay compliance and to keep informed of new environmental legislative requirements.

ESOS is being further advanced with ESOS2 being phased in by December 2019. The main thrust of ESOS2 is to enable compliant operators to take full advantage of the opportunities available through energy saving. The Carbon Trust should be contacted for full details.

Impact of Transport

Transport impacts on the environment in a variety of ways; some are more distinctly controllable by fleet operators than others; some produce more tangible benefits both to the vehicle operator and to the community than others; but it has to be remembered that, inevitably, any form of transport, serving any and every need imaginable, has an adverse impact on the environment. There is no such thing as a totally environmentally acceptable form or means of transport. What there can be, however, are means and systems of transport which are more 'friendly' towards the environment, and which can be controlled and managed in such a way that the environmental impact is minimized.

So far as transport operations are concerned the following list identifies some of the main areas of environmental impact which can be, and should be, challenged by management.

Vehicle Depots

- Size, siting, access and egress;
- noise, fumes, vibration and light emitted;
- obstruction;
- disposal of waste;
- recycling levels;
- energy use;
- pollution;
- MHE operation;
- times of operation.

Vehicle Operations

- Engine, exhaust, tyre, body and loading/unloading noise;
- smoke, fumes, gases, spray emitted;
- fuel/oil consumption;
- visual impact;
- driver standards;
- routes and schedules;
- load and vehicle utilization;
- waste and general recycling;
- vehicle and component recyclability.

Oil Storage

Regulations, which came into effect from 1 September 2005 to protect against water pollution, will apply to road hauliers who store more than 200 litres of oil on any site that is located near to a river, waterway, borehole or even close to the water table. These regulations, the Control of Pollution (Oil Storage) Regulations 2001, require the person with custody of the oil to carry out such works or to take such precautions or actions as are necessary to minimize the risk of oil-related water pollution. The regulations specify technical details relating to the storage facility, particularly its bund base and wall, which must have a capacity of 110 per cent of the capacity of the tank and be checked regularly, along with the pipework, valves and gauges. It is essential that the tank or its pipework is not positioned where there is a risk from vehicle impact, especially when reversing.

To prevent oil-contaminated water entering the public surface water sewer, an 'interceptor' should be incorporated into the operating centre's internal drainage system. This interceptor will separate the oil from the remainder of the surface water run-off. The unpolluted surface water will be allowed to leave the site and enter the public sewer, and the collected oil will be retained for safe collection and disposal by a waste-processing company. Other products, such as fuel or chemicals, such as those used in lorry cleaning/wash bays and systems, and any oils or lubricants used for vehicle maintenance that might be spilled or drained off, should also be prevented from entering the main drainage system. Spill kits containing items such as retaining booms, absorbent granules and waste bags should be used to retain and mop up any spillages and interceptors are required on fixed vehicle washing installations. The resultant polluted waste would have to be removed by a specialist waste-processing organization. In such cases the principle of 'the polluter pays' will apply. The need for such equipment and the risk of prosecution have led to many smaller companies now using external vehicle cleaning contractors in order to avoid the costs of fitting and maintaining the required equipment.

In addition to these more environmentally controllable aspects of transport, there are other aspects which have a powerful impact, but over which the transport manager has virtually no control, namely vehicle design and manufacture, road planning and building, legislative controls which are not necessarily environmentally oriented and customer demand, which is influenced more by commercial pressure and financial consideration than by the vehicle operator's quest to, among other things, reduce fuel consumption, deliver during non-congested times or combine loads to improve vehicle efficiency and which is increasingly calling for smaller, more frequent deliveries and collections in an attempt to reduce levels of inventory.

Possible Solutions

Transport managers and small fleet operators are undoubtedly limited in the steps they can individually take towards improving the environment, but this does not mean they should take no steps at all. Simple measures are available to them which will make a valuable contribution. The following list provides just a few examples.

In the Depot

- Examine the way that waste material is stored, recycled and disposed of.
- Ensure that controlled waste (see Chapter 20) is correctly and safely stored on site and then handed over to licensed disposal contractors.
- Avoid burning of waste, which can cause pollution and lead to complaints.
- Ensure that recyclable material is identified and saved for proper disposal – including waste paper and packing materials from office and stores.
- Take steps to ensure that vehicle washing does not result in dirty (ie grease-laden) water draining on to neighbouring properties as well as into sewage systems.
- Ensure that oil and fuel spillages do not pollute drains and are cleaned up immediately.
- Consider the use of recycled products such as paper for administrative uses and packing.
- Undertake regular depot clean-up campaigns (in particular, ensuring that the outside appearance of the depot is 'environmentally friendly' to local residents, business visitors and others).
- Consider involving customers and suppliers in developing more environmentally acceptable ways of working.
- Ensure noise from reversing alarms, site music and tannoy systems and vehicle in-cab radios, etc, is not excessive or generated during out of normal working hours.
- If possible, also try to engage local residents and businesses and develop discourse.

On the Vehicle

- Ensure that legal requirements regarding noise, smoke, exhaust emissions and spray suppression are fully complied with.
- Take steps to economize on fuel consumption (see Chapter 22).
- Invest in the latest Euro emissions, dual fuel, alternative fuel technology.
- Provide driver training to ensure courtesy and consideration on the road and the use of defensive driving methods* (which saves on wear costs).
- Fit speed limiters (now a legal requirement on certain vehicles – see Chapter 12).
- Fit body skirts and air deflectors and use aerodynamic 'curve top' trailers and bodies.
- Specify lifting and/or steering axles, where possible.
- Ensure that drivers obey rules about parking and causing obstruction with their vehicles, and are aware of the problem of visual intrusion, noise and vibration on domestic properties (contravention of these matters can jeopardize 'O' licences – see Chapter 1).

- Route vehicles and plan journeys to avoid congestion – ensure full utilization of vehicles to avoid extra or unnecessary journeys (which add to congestion, air pollution and the operator's own costs).
- Fit rubber 'buffers' to tail-lifts and roller doors and switches to reversing alarms to reduce noise during the 'silent hours'.
- Consider the visual impact of vehicles in terms of their general appearance and livery (change aggressive liveries to present a 'softer' image).

In the Community

- Consider the sponsorship of local community efforts to improve the environment and encourage staff to undertake environmental protection projects.
- Make it known that local residents are able and welcome to discuss issues with management.

The International Organization for Standardization (ISO) has developed a set of internationally recognized standards so that businesses can monitor and control the environmental effects of their activities. The key stages in developing an environmental management system in compliance with the ISO 14001 standard are as follows:

- Draw up an environmental policy.
- Carry out environmental impact assessments (EIAs) as a part of expansion and new-build projects.
- Set targets and make plans to achieve those targets.
- Implement the plans and ensure that information is communicated to all relevant staff.
- Measure results and compare these to the set targets, take corrective action where necessary and implement a system for regular reviews of the policy.
- Invite local community members to visit the depot and discuss their concerns (work with them, not in isolation).

Natural Gas Vehicles

In an effort to make towns and cities cleaner and quieter places in which to live and work, the Government is making progress in cutting vehicle emissions and noise by encouraging greater use of cleaner vehicles.

A Government Minister speaking at a commercial vehicle show at the NEC in Birmingham said that natural gas vehicles are part of the solution, offering transport operators an opportunity to contribute to a cleaner, quieter environment as well as save money on their fuel bills. The Government is encouraging the wider availability of natural gas vehicles and electric vehicles by offering grant funding through the Energy Saving Trust for carbon reduction initiatives and electric vehicle plug-in points.

Vehicles powered by natural gas – essentially the same product as used for domestic cooking and heating – can offer substantial environmental benefits, in particular compared with equivalent diesel vehicles. They are much quieter than diesel vehicles and emit lower levels of the two air pollutants of most concern in the UK – particulates and oxides of nitrogen. Development of larger vehicles powered by natural gas could be said to have been led by IVECO who produced the first 40 tonne long range gas truck in 2016 and won the Green Truck of the Year Award for it in 2017.

In addition, they are subject to lower VED rates due to lower emissions although these discounts have tended to be eroded where large numbers of less pollutive vehicles are brought onto the UK's roads.

Electric Vehicles

Whilst the use of natural gas vehicles is still in relative infancy, the use of electric vehicles is increasing. In reality, at the present time, their use is somewhat limited to smaller vehicles and vans but it is seen as a cheap and clean alternative for collections and deliveries in the urban cycle. As mentioned earlier, there are now electric buses in use (with more to come) and many public sector operators and local authorities have invested in electric vehicles. The first all electric LGVs have also been developed although they are still in the development stage. With the progression towards powering larger vehicles by electricity, the Government has permitted Highways England to undertake trials on some major motorways and trunk roads to evaluate the technology that will allow electric vehicles (and some hybrid vehicles) to be powered as they travel along these routes and thereby not have to keep stopping to recharge the batteries. It should really be remembered that electric powered 'milk floats' capable of carrying up to about 2 tonnes were a common feature on our roads and streets making 'urban deliveries', before the 'supermarket era' priced them out of business.

Dual Fuel and Other Vehicles

Dual fuel vehicles generally use a diesel engine for the stem mileage of a journey and then switch to either gas or electric propulsion for the urban cycle. They are perhaps most commonly used as buses although some freight vehicles are used in limited circumstances. In addition to dual fuel there are fuel additives such as 'AdBlue', which is an ammonia-based additive mixed with the fuel to improve fuel economy, and even vehicles such as hydrogen cell vehicles, although these are still in the experimental and evaluation stage of development. It must be accepted that the use of alternative fuels and innovation in engine design will continue to grow as the need to reduce emissions and to reduce the use of carbon-based fuel becomes increasingly important and carbon-based fuels become more expensive and increasingly scarce.

Reverse Logistics

The term 'reverse logistics' applies to activities aimed at moving items back from the end user (customer) as opposed to moving items towards the customer. In this respect, the repatriation of pallets, roll cages, tubs and totes back to the depot for re-use would be classed as reverse logistics, as would the carriage of waste packaging back for recycling and returns and damages from shops. These types of activities are widespread in the retail sector and are usually carried out by the driver and vehicle on completion of a delivery.

Clearly, re-using items such as pallets has an impact on the environment as does the recycling of packaging. These types of activities also improve vehicle utilization and reduce overall fuel usage as no/fewer outside contractors are required to move the items for disposal, recycling or re-use.

Cooperative and 3PL Initiatives

In cases where it is possible, more and more companies are seeking opportunities to enter into cooperative arrangements for the supply and distribution of goods. Many of these arrangements see companies sharing vehicles with competitors to reduce the numbers of vehicles used, reduce fuel usage, reduce emissions, improve vehicle utilization and reduce costs. Operators are urged to try to develop these types of initiatives as part of their environmental strategy. In a similar manner, many operators choose to use third party logistics providers (3PL) to distribute some, or all, of their goods. By doing so, the 3PL can often make up loads from several operators seeking to deliver goods to certain, perhaps remote, areas or regions. This type of 'groupage' clearly has environmental advantages as opposed to each operator using their own vehicles to deliver small, often uneconomic, consignments.

Cabotage

Another activity aimed at environmental improvement and protection is the EU's cabotage activities. Cabotage is defined as 'haulage for hire and reward in one member state by an operator from another member state'. This is specifically aimed at reducing long homeward runs by empty vehicles when loads could be carried. The future for UK operators to engage in cabotage whilst in Europe and for European operators to engage in cabotage whilst in the UK post-Brexit will certainly depend upon the deal or no deal situation.

Business Management in Transport

25

Quality Management

Increasingly, road hauliers are facing demands from customers, and from principal contractors, to meet recognized standards of quality assurance in the form of certification to the ISO 9001, 14001, 27001 or 45001 standards covering not only quality assurance but environmental standards, information security management and occupational health and safety in the United Kingdom. However, this chapter outlines the basic requirements for meeting quality assurance standards to achieve recognized certification to those standards which allows organizations to have the necessary quality infrastructure to move towards other ISO standards. It should be noted that the quality standards criteria in this chapter are largely generic for all ISO standards qualification but differ in relation to the subject matter.

A great deal has been written about the subject of 'quality', and many myths have been spread, but it is quite simply the concept of doing things right first time, and right every time and documenting actions taken in order to create a full set of operational procedures and standards. This saves having to repeat operations at extra cost, and annoyance to both suppliers and, most importantly, the customer, whether in production of goods or the provision of a service – road haulage for example. It means supplying customers with the service they need, not what suppliers think they can best provide in order to simply maximize profit. In haulage, it means, particularly, providing cost-effective deliveries – on time – in full (OTIF), to the right address, with the load intact and undamaged and delivered by a courteous and reasonably presented driver in a presentable vehicle at an agreed or appropriate time. It does not mean a service which causes customer complaint which in turn incurs additional, avoidable cost.

The concept of 'quality' is not new. It has been applied to production for many years, especially by the Japanese, who have captured world markets for cars, motorcycles, electronics and cameras due to the inherent quality, reliability, durability and desirability of their products. Only more recently has the quality concept been applied to service industries, and particularly to road haulage. Achieving quality assurance (QA) certification involves complex steps, changed ideas, new thinking and acceptance that 'old ways' must be replaced by new methods, despite extra paperwork, form filling, writing of manuals, checking and rechecking of standards, and visits from inspectors. What are quality systems and quality management? A quality system is one where problems, queries, faults, and anything which could give rise to customer dissatisfaction or complaint is identified and eliminated. Every aspect of operating procedure is critically examined to ensure that nothing unexpected (short of pure accident, and contingencies can even be established for these) can arise to jeopardize service to the customer. Quality management is the management of quality systems – a totally new way of doing business, hence the expression 'total quality management' (TQM). It is true to say that TQM is more and more an integral part of successful organizations seeking to develop competitive advantage over their rivals.

In assessing quality it must be appreciated that 'deluxe' or 'expensive' are not necessary 'quality' and that some contracts will involve providing a low-cost service without the requirement for performance to the high standards of contracts involving a JIT system for instance. Other contracts may demand dedicated distribution which does not normally see particularly good vehicle utilization levels but, if that is agreed, then that is what must be supplied. In short, whatever customer service and performance levels are agreed these levels must always be met, documented, constantly monitored and changes introduced where necessary, if a quality service is to be delivered.

Quality Assessment and Accreditation

Quality assessment and accreditation is the process by which a firm demonstrates to an accredited certification body, such as the ISO or the British Standards Institution, that its services meet pre-established quality standards, followed by certification of this fact.

Accreditation

The British Standards Institution (BSI) standard for quality management systems is designated BS5750. It uses the nationally recognized 'kite' symbol and the Institute is the UK's national body for setting standards across industry. Today, BSI standards are largely built up from the ISO quality standards ISO 9001. This incorporates the provisions of both the international and European standards (EN 2900/2901) and is fully accepted in the member states of the EU and the four EFTA members – Norway, Iceland, Switzerland and Liechtenstein. As mentioned many times in this year's *Handbook*, the future direction the UK takes will depend on Brexit, but as the standards are accepted by the EU it would seem logical to maintain them for EU trade purposes in spite of Brexit. It seems probable that the EU member states will be more likely to accept ISO standards than those of the BSI because, as international standards, both the EU and the UK will be able to demonstrate parity in relation to them.

Firms whose quality systems meet specified standards may register with an approved body and, on satisfactory completion of the formalities, receive accreditation 'Registered Firm' status when they may use the accreditation body's symbol of approval on their company literature (ie letterheads, brochures) and on vehicles. A road haulier or distribution organization quality accredited in the UK is additionally accepted as meeting both European and international quality standards, an essential ingredient for trading in the European market. Once accredited, companies will be required to prove continued compliance in order for the registration to be renewed.

Standards

The essence of a quality haulage/distribution service is that every step in fulfilling customer orders is undertaken in accordance with a documented standard – a set of rules governing the best way to operate and against which day-to-day operations are compared. This compliance to meet the documented standard must be continual and repeated every time the documented activities are carried out. Any non-conformance must be documented and recorded in a non-compliance log and actions taken to prevent any recurrence. The act of recording non-compliance and any other problems encountered can prove valuable should an organization wish to introduce BSI into other depots as it can help avoid problems when they are working towards accreditation.

Performing to standard means performing as set out in the rules. BS 5750 is a standard for quality systems which identifies the basic disciplines and specifies the procedures and criteria to be applied to ensure that services are of a quality that will always meet specified customer requirements.

Assessment by Accreditation Certification Bodies

Assessment for accreditation involves a number of stages. Among these, one is the need to establish, document, maintain and improve, if required, a quality system demonstrating a commitment to quality and to meeting customer service needs. Another is the selection of an appropriate accreditation body to which application for registration is made. This involves providing information about the business, its size and scope, the number of employees, how many locations are involved, the particular nature and manner of its operation and the services provided. Applicants must submit their documented quality system for examination and approval. The accreditation body checks this to ensure it covers all aspects of the quality system standard and then follows up with site visits to thoroughly review the operation in practice. These inspections – made by specialists in quality assessment – are a key element in quality assurance. Documented procedures are examined in detail and systems observed in operation to ensure that day-to-day procedures follow the documented quality system in every respect and comply with the laid-down standards of the accreditation body. Where shortfalls are found there may be a follow-up assessment, or series of assessments, required.

Monitoring

A process of continuous monitoring for compliance with standards is maintained through inspectors from the accreditation body making regular visits – up to four times each year. Any drop in performance will require renewed efforts to bring procedures back to standard. Continued failure to meet the standard will result in withdrawal of registration. In addition, the company itself needs to monitor compliance as an ongoing issue and, if changes are required in order to address a non-compliance, then the change must be documented and recorded and also monitored in order to ensure that it succeeds in addressing the problem. Records are required to be kept of any changes as these not only document the change but can be used in the future to indicate improvement activity that may be required in similar circumstances. Every company needs to have at least one individual who is capable of monitoring compliance and monitoring the need for new or amended working practices.

Establishing a Quality System

To establish a quality system within an organization, it is necessary to identify key aspects of the business where quality principles are to be applied and record precisely how these should be carried out. This is achieved by translating individual tasks into descriptive text in manual form, and by making step-by-step checklists or by establishing codes of practice. The key aspects will include:

- setting company policy and objectives for quality systems;
- determining the structure of the organization and responsibilities;
- ensuring all departments and functions are informed and 'fully onboard';
- preparing instructions and codes of practice for quality work standards;
- monitoring sub-contracted supplies and services for quality;
- establishing operational methods and controls to meet specified standards;
- inspection and monitoring of the transport service;
- controlling defective work;
- determining corrective actions before problems arise;
- measuring and recording quality performance;
- determining training requirements;
- establishing quality audit and review procedures.

Determining Customer Needs

Quality starts with the customer; the need to determine exactly what every customer wants not what we want them to want. Never *assume* that one customer's service requirements are identical, or even remotely similar, to those of another. Each must be asked individually about their precise expectations when making enquiries and placing orders. They will differ widely: a customer may even have differing service requirements in differing circumstances. These requirements, whether few or many, whether standard in all circumstances or varying widely for individual consignments, must be clearly understood, leaving no doubt whatsoever as to what is needed and expected in all circumstances. This information should be carefully recorded (and regularly updated) to form the basis for the quality system. It will become the standard against which all future responses to each customer's demands will be measured to ensure satisfaction.

The next step is to consider internal workings of the operation to determine how these relate to the provision of a quality service. This task should be split into individual components or identifiable activities and for each there should be a documented set of procedures to be followed. The following are some examples of such activities and include some distribution activities:

- receipt of customer orders;
- receipt of goods-in;
- 'put away';
- order picking and packing;
- planning daily work schedules;
- allocation of work to various sections of the operation;
- allocation of work to vehicles and drivers;
- preparation of collection/delivery note sets;
- instruction of drivers;
- preparation of vehicles;
- condition of vehicles;
- confirmations to customers;
- driver conduct on arrival;
- returns and waste retrieval;
- reverse logistics;
- driver debriefing on completion of deliveries;
- recording/confirmation of work completed;
- recording of shortage and damages;
- invoicing.

Where vehicles may travel in a customer's livery this may not be defaced or blurred by stickers or flags, etc. The drivers' performance and dress code may also be included in order to ensure that drivers do not give the public a negative impression of the customer company by appearing unkempt or by erratic or aggressive driving, for example.

Documenting the System

The individual tasks mentioned above – and many more if appropriate – should be written down in the form of checklists to ensure that no matter who takes the order, who prepares the loads, who allocates the vehicle or driver, who prepares the delivery notes or who carries out any other of these functions, the established step-by-step procedure is followed and no key element is missed which could lead to customer dissatisfaction. Documenting the system fully and effectively means preparation of a 'quality manual'. These documents must be reviewed periodically to ensure that they are still relevant and updated if any task changes or is altered in any way.

Quality Procedures Manual

A quality procedures manual is a statement of the firm's commitment to quality, a constant reminder to management of their obligation to the firm's customers based on these documented procedures. It becomes the bible of operating practice for the staff, which has to be followed from when a customer first rings with an enquiry to when the job papers are finally filed away. It should detail:

- the organizational structure of the company;
- relationships between, and the responsibilities of, individual operating departments and functional managers;
- how the company's quality system is to work in practice:
  - every day;
  - every time an order is received;
  - every time an order is assembled;
  - every time a customer rings up;
  - every time a load is scheduled;
  - every time a driver/vehicle is allocated to a job;
  - every time a delivery is made.

No matter what process or function is carried out, the manual should define it, who does it, how he does it, when, where and in what sequence, what follow-up action is carried out, by whom, to whom everyone reports in the event of difficulties or potential problems, what records are kept and so on. It is the ultimate guidebook to the firm: every single company operation is described, and cross-referenced to every other related function.

Mistakes may still be made, but the procedures manual should take account of such possibilities by detailing the action to be taken when errors are discovered (or pointed out by customers), and by whom, as well as to whom in the firm such matters should be reported, what reports should be written and to whom they are to be submitted. These 'failure reports' should be acted upon promptly, and details of the corrective action taken should also be recorded for future reference. By documenting failures and capturing corrective actions, they should progressively be eliminated from the system. This also helps to create a log of 'lessons learned' which, as stated, may be useful in the future.

Manuals within Manuals

A simple manual would have an opening section containing basic reference material as follows:

- firm's name;
- description of the business in which it is engaged (eg haulage of aggregates and excavated materials, distribution of FMCG, also contract haulier to, etc...);
- number of locations (eg one only or head office and vehicle base at...);
- general description of resources (eg 'x' number of vehicles/plant/resources);
- names/functions of key departments (eg traffic/warehouse/administration/workshop);
- names/titles of key managers/personnel;
- job descriptions for key positions (eg operations manager/fleet engineer/company accountant/marketing manager);
- date(s) and name(s) of person(s) compiling manual;
- names of persons issued with the quality manual and those responsible for keeping it up to date;
- statement of firm's quality policy;
- name(s) of person(s) with ultimate responsibility for compliance with quality policy.

From this point, the manual could divide into sections covering each functional department (eg traffic operations/warehouse/accounts and administration/workshop). For each there could be a general statement of departmental responsibility; the names, positions and individual responsibilities of key personnel; and the lines of reporting and communication (ie upwards to the company's top management or board of directors, downwards to supervisors, shift leaders, etc, and sideways by liaison with other departmental heads). Information on staff needs to be closely monitored and adjusted as staff gain qualifications, move positions, get promoted or leave.

To compile the procedures manual, the work of each department must be examined in detail to see what current practices exist, who does what job (routine ones, special ones, urgent ones, etc), what controls are imposed and what safety procedures, if any, are followed to avoid failures (eg orders not filled correctly, loads missed, jobs not invoiced, vehicles missing out on services, etc). Every step should be categorized within a functional heading (eg receipt of customer orders, recording orders on daily work sheets, allocating orders to vehicles, planning vehicle loads and so on) and the correct procedure for carrying out each step needs to be recorded. It is necessary to describe how details relating to the job should be entered, in what form or sequence, and the safety measures necessary to ensure that no essential information (eg a customer's special instructions) is missed.

The manual must be capable of being read – and the procedures understood and followed – by any member of the firm and by the inspector from the quality accreditation organization which checks the procedures. If the wording is tortuous and the manual littered with technical terms and unexplained abbreviations its point will be lost. For this reason, manual writing demands the use of clear, concise and simple language. Jargon should be avoided and technical terms kept to a minimum. When they are essential they should be defined or explained. Essential legal obligations (such as goods vehicle drivers' hours, tachographs, safe loading, etc) must be explained or cross-referenced to a source of detailed legal information. It may be appropriate to consider producing manuals in languages other than English where foreign workers form a sizeable proportion of the workforce.

Manuals in a form other than full-size pages in ring binders (eg pocket-size handbooks) may be more appropriate for drivers. These should detail the rules to be followed on drivers' hours, the correct use of tachographs, safe loading, dangerous load procedures, routine daily vehicle inspections, what to do in an emergency or the event of an accident and many other instructions. Workshop staff could have their own handbooks concentrating on safety procedures, what to do in the event of injury or accident, use of tools and equipment, procedures for drawing spare parts and consumable supplies and so on. Fitters who are required to road-test vehicles and 'shunters' should also be issued with a copy of the driver's handbook. It is important to make sure that every department has its own instructions/guides that cover specific tasks and safety issues and that these are updated to reflect new technologies and working practices.

The key point about any manuals that are produced is that they are regularly reviewed as the law changes, work practices change, different types of equipment or vehicles are used, new products are handled and new routes are developed, etc. And it is vital that these types of changes are made to the exacting standards required. Changes, as mentioned above, obviously rely on a rigid system of version control in order to ensure that everybody is using the latest version of a handbook.

Other Documentation

Besides the main manual, other documentation systems are needed – a 'day book' in which to record customer orders, collection notes, delivery notes, receipt notes or combined consignment note sets, invoices, statements and suchlike. Many of the forms may relate to ongoing or periodic events such as the periodic examination of employee driving licences, driver assessment, driver periodic CPC (DCPC) training, annual medical examinations and eyesight tests, inspections of safety equipment and safety signs, workshop equipment, MHE inspections, fire-fighting equipment and first-aid kits, etc. Other forms would record company meetings with staff, drivers, workshop staff, and training sessions on new procedures or new legislation. Examples of all forms used should be included in the procedures manual to show which form to complete in any particular set of circumstances, where supplies of the form can be found, how it should be completed and what to do with it following completion.

Training to Achieve Quality Standards

All staff within a firm seeking quality accreditation should be properly trained to operate in accordance with specified quality procedures (ie to perform to standard). Management, staff and workers should be updated on the latest techniques and new developments. For example, goods vehicle drivers may need refresher courses or assessments in driving skills to eradicate bad habits and training in efficient and economical driving techniques for new vehicles, or vehicle equipment such as new types of fuel, gearbox, mounted crane or tail-lift; they need reminders and updating on essential safety procedures and the use of safety equipment, on legal requirements (such as on drivers' hours rules and tachograph use) and on the use of mechanical loading aids. Often, some of these training or refresher subjects can be incorporated into DCPC sessions (JAUPT can advise on whether or not particular subjects will be accepted for DCPC training at enquiries@jaupt.org.uk).

At all levels from management to driver/operative, training improves job skills, contributes to the individual's motivation and job interest and provides an incentive to do that job better and take more of an interest in the firm's overall objectives – namely, to provide a quality service. The following list shows examples of training from which various grades of management and staff may benefit:

Top management

Strategic management techniques.
Sales/marketing/public relations.
Leadership.
People management.
Motivational skills.
Communication skills.
Employment legislation.
Marketing.
Financial controls.
Taxation matters.

Middle management

Operational management techniques.
Administrative controls.
Business systems.
Computer familiarization.
Management techniques.
Team building.
Budgeting.
Motivational skills.
Communication skills.
Health and safety law.

Functional management

Functional management techniques.
Team building.
Transport legislation.
Safety systems.
Engineering skills.
Computer techniques.
Accounting practices.
Data protection.

Goods vehicle drivers

Vehicle sympathy.
Economic driving.
Courteous driving.
Safety procedures.
Legal requirements.
Driver CPC.
Product awareness.
Dealing with customers.
Road accident/incident procedures.
Dangerous loads requirements.
Temperature control requirements.
Livestock carriage requirements.
Ancillary equipment operation.

Loaders

Safety matters.
Manual handling techniques.
Loading principles.
Load security.
Product features.

Forklift truck drivers

Driver training.
Company policy.
Safety procedures.
Truck maintenance.

Vehicle workshop staff

Safety procedures.
Legal requirements.
Equipment training.
Breakdown procedures.
Health and safety.
Vehicle manufacturer training.
Component training.
First aid.

Administrative and secretarial staff

Office procedures.
Computer skills.
Customer contact techniques.
Order and complaints procedures.
Telephone techniques.
Emergency procedures.
Use of office equipment (photocopiers/fax machines, etc).
First aid.

The lists above are not meant to be exhaustive as every company will be different but they are 'generic' examples. While the range of courses and training opportunities is endless, there is a need to identify activities which demand acquired skills; for example, where special competence is legally required such as for goods vehicle vocational driving licences and dangerous goods training. These require priority over other training because failure could result in prosecution, or loss of operating licences.

Training Records

All training should be carefully recorded, especially statutory training such as for DCPC or ADR, whether it is a 30-minute in-company explanation of new legislation or the desired telephone answering techniques, or a longer external training course for management. This should show dates, who attended, who presented the training session, the duration, the location, the facilities/aids used, the objectives of the session, the results achieved and any other relevant data, including any follow-up action necessary. Recording training can also mitigate a company when an employee or driver commits an offence or breach of any regulation because it removes the 'nobody told me' excuse. Similarly, where staff achieve other qualifying standards as a result of company-sponsored incentives (eg attendance at evening or day-release classes or by home-study learning), or on a voluntary basis, these should be recorded.

Monitoring of Quality Standards

Successful operation of quality management systems involves a continuous monitoring process to ensure quality procedures are maintained and do not slip back into old inferior methods. A variety of monitoring methods may be employed. The establishment of quality circles is one, with groups or teams of volunteer employees meeting to discuss the application of quality, particularly in relation to their own departments or work sections. They identify quality 'problem' areas and put forward suggestions as to possible solutions. They also serve as opportunities for internal benchmarking where 'best practice' in one department might be able to be adopted by other departments.

In small firms, where the cost structure does not warrant full-time monitoring, two methods in particular will ensure that standards are maintained. The first is regular monitoring of customers' perception of the quality of service they are receiving; customers should be asked to point out any deficiencies and their answers noted, analysed and corrective action taken. Second, maintaining full and clear communication in the firm will ensure that everybody, from top to bottom, is on the same quality wavelength and working towards the same goals. In this way the whole firm will feel united in the quest for total quality management.

Further Information

Further information on the establishment of quality systems in road haulage may be obtained from:

The BSI
389 Chiswick High Road
London
W4 4AL
Tel: 020 8996 7001
www.bsigroup.com (archived at https://perma.cc/Y7DG-PYT4)
(The BSI also have offices in Hemel Hempstead, Lancaster, Loughborough and Milton Keynes)

The Department for Business, Energy and Industrial Strategy (BEIS)
1 Victoria Street
London
SW1H 0ET
Email: enquiries@beis.gov.uk
Tel: 020 7215 5000

BEIS Aberdeen office:
AB1 Building
Crimon Place
Aberdeen
AB10 1BJ

Debt Collection

The Late Payment of Commercial Debts Regulations 2013 allows small businesses to claim interest on commercial debts from large businesses that relate to the supply of goods and services that are paid late. It does not apply to consumer debt. In effect, interest becomes chargeable from the day after the agreed date for payment. The term 'late' means later than 60 days in respect of business-to-business transactions and 30 days in relation to business-to-public authority transactions. Compensation for the costs of recovery can be charged under these regulations at £40 for a debt of up to £1,000, £70 for a debt between £1,000–£10,000 and £100 for debts over £10,000 and claims can also be made for any additional costs incurred.

The payment of the debt itself is also subject to interest. The rate of interest chargeable is the bank base rate plus 8 per cent.

The Regulations were implemented in 2014 and updated in 2016 and 2018. They are overseen by BEIS, and the figures above were correct in late 2019.

Further guidance is available on the GOV.UK website.

Insolvency

People often refer to a company being insolvent, but what does that actually mean? It is important at the outset to establish exactly what form of insolvency you are dealing with. Each type of insolvency has its own specific office holder, who has differing obligations, duties and powers. This will undoubtedly affect how you act, and whether or not you have any chance of recovery of a debt from that company. This is important because when dealing with limited companies their assets are only those of the company itself and not any personal wealth created by any of the company directors.

Administration

The holder of office is called 'the administrator' and is appointed by the court following a petition. His aim is either to achieve the survival of the company and the realization of assets and liquidation, or to enable a Company Voluntary Arrange ment (CVA). In a similar manner, sole traders may select to use an Individual Voluntary Arrangement (IVA). The effect is a moratorium preventing any creditor action. While the administrator owes a duty to creditors in general, he will not agree creditors' claims, nor has he the power to distribute funds to the creditors. Both a CVA and an IVA require the engagement of an insolvency practitioner.

Administrative Receivership

The holder of office is called 'the receiver' and is appointed by someone holding a debenture over (substantially) all the assets and undertaking of the company. The receiver's aim is to continue trade with a view to sale of the business as a going concern. The directors remain in office, albeit the receiver has day-to-day control of the business. There is no moratorium preventing creditor action, but the administrative receiver's duty is solely to get in and realize the assets of the company, sufficient to repay the indebtedness of the debenture holder.

Liquidation

There are different types of liquidation. These are:

- compulsory liquidation;
- creditors' voluntary liquidation;
- members' voluntary liquidation; and
- pre-pack administration.

In the first three cases the office holder is called 'the liquidator', but his/her appointment is different, depending on what type of liquidation it is.

- In the case of compulsory liquidation the company is placed in liquidation by the court following the making of a winding-up order.
- In the case of creditors' voluntary liquidation, the liquidator is appointed by the directors/shareholders where the company is insolvent and unable to pay its debts.
- In the case of members' voluntary liquidation, the liquidator is appointed by the directors/shareholders where the directors have sworn a statutory declaration of insolvency. The aim of the liquidation is to realize assets, shut

down the company and distribute the assets in accordance with a strict order of priority.

With CVA, the office holder is called 'the supervisor' and their rights and powers are set out in a document entitled *the proposal*, which is put to and voted upon by the company's creditors. The company can, and invariably will, trade under the auspices of a CVA, which is often used to effect a reconstruction or reorganization of the company's trading enterprise. The proposal that leads to the making of the CVA forms a private contract between the company and its creditors and is normally aimed at the creditors receiving at least some of the money owed to them over a given period. If the proposal is approved, creditors are bound to accept the terms in full and final settlement of their indebtedness.

Insolvency Pre-Pack Administration

An insolvency pre-pack is a deal whereby an insolvent company's assets are sold, or a deal for their sale is negotiated, before the company actually goes into formal insolvency. The deal to sell the business (eg to the management, the staff or others), usually as a going concern, will have invariably been agreed before the Insolvency Practitioner is appointed, but it will be executed by the Insolvency Practitioner shortly after his appointment. If the conditions are appropriate, a pre-pack can be advantageous for all involved, and can be the best way of extracting value from a dire situation.

Pre-packs mean a business can be sold without negative publicity, which could destroy the value of the business and lead to loss of customers and staff. This is often the case with haulage companies which are owner-managed businesses and where most of the value is in key staff who may leave, or assets that may lose considerable value once the administration or liquidation process is announced. Hence, the business is usually sold with little or no open market promotion. Unsecured creditors are normally only informed of the pre-pack after it has been completed. By contrast secured creditors are often aware of the transaction ahead of the formalized deal as it will generally require them to release their security.

The main advantage of pre-pack insolvency is that the debts of the business remain with the old company and therefore the new (often called a 'phoenix') company can start again with a clean slate. At the point when the sale is agreed the existing company will move into administration or liquidation and the new company will start trading immediately. Therefore, the whole process will be seamless to the business, the staff and the customers.

The Competition Act

The Competition Act 1998 (as amended), which came into force on 1 March 2000, is designed to ensure that UK businesses remain competitive. It applies to all businesses irrespective of the trade in which they are engaged and their size. It even applies to sole traders such as owner-driver road hauliers.

Principally, the Act prohibits anti-competitive agreements, monopolies, cartels and abuse of a dominant position in the market. It is overseen by the Competition and Markets Authority (CMA) (see below).

Anti-Competitive Agreements

The prohibition on anti-competitive agreements covers agreements and practices that prevent, restrict or distort competition, or are intended to do so. These can be formal or informal, written or not. In particular, they include agreements to:

- fix purchase or selling prices or other trading conditions;
- limit or control production, markets, technical development or investment;
- share markets or sources of supply;
- apply different trading conditions to equivalent transactions, which will put some parties at a competitive disadvantage;
- make contracts subject to unrelated supplementary conditions.

The effect of an agreement must be 'appreciable' to be caught by the Act. There are certain exemptions and exclusions.

Abuse of a Dominant Position

Whether a business is in a dominant position will depend on how much it can act independently of its competitors and customers. As a general rule, a dominant position is unlikely if its market share is less than 40 per cent. This will, however, depend on the structure of the market. Examples of abuse are:

- imposing unfair purchase or selling prices or other unfair trading conditions;
- limiting production, markets or technical development to the prejudice of consumers;
- applying different trading conditions to equivalent transactions, which will put some parties at a competitive disadvantage;
- making contracts subject to unrelated supplementary conditions.

Since the closure of the Office of Fair Trading in 2014, the Competition and Markets Authority (CMA) and the Financial Conduct Authority (FCA) have wide-ranging powers to investigate suspected breaches of the law. Officials can enter premises and demand relevant documents, and may even get a warrant to make a search. They can order offending agreements or conduct to be terminated. Businesses can be fined up to 10 per cent of their UK turnover; prohibited agreements will be made void and unenforceable; and any third party harmed by an unlawful agreement or conduct may be able to sue for damages.

If Your Business is a Victim of Unfair Competition

A complaint may be made to the CMA or FCA by anyone who suspects that the competition rules are being broken. Further advice is also available through Citizens Advice. Complaints may be in writing or by telephone and the complainant's identity may be protected although evidence will be needed to back up any such complaint. The CMA/FCA may launch a formal investigation if there are reasonable grounds for suspecting that an offence is being, or has been, committed.

Where a business finds that it is part of an illegal cartel and provides information voluntarily, it may receive a significant reduction in any financial penalty imposed or, if it is the first to notify the authorities of the situation, it may gain complete immunity from financial penalty.

Further information is available from:

Competition and Markets Authority
The Cabot
25, Cabot Square
London
E14 4QZ
General enquiries: 020 3738 6000
Email: general.enquiries@cma.gov.uk

The CMA also have offices in the other countries of the UK: Sheila Scobie (Scotland) sheila.scobie@cma.gov.uk; Simon Harris (Wales) simon.harris@cma.gov.uk; Robert Stewart (Northern Ireland) robert.stewart@cma.gov.uk

FCA Head Office
12, Endeavour Square
London
E20 1JN
Tel: 020 7066 1000
Email: firm.queries@fca.org.uk

International Haulage

26

Since the removal of barriers to inter-Community trading from January 1993, UK road hauliers have been largely free to operate, uninhibited, across the whole of the EU, which (prior to our eventual departure) was comprised of 28 countries and a consumer market of some 513.5+ million people. In addition, it has become much more straightforward to operate in, and transit, the EFTA countries and countries in the Balkans region and some of the ex-USSR independent states as trading patterns change and developing economies seek to increase trade with EU member states. The UK referendum result of 2016 has had some major effects on the way the UK has operated internationally for the past years and 2020 'may' (depending upon the deal or no-deal Brexit situation) be a year that sees almost total change in the way the UK's international transport sector operates within the EU.

This section is being written in late 2019. Because of political issues, we are currently in a state of limbo and the way we trade today may well continue in the same manner for some time to come. Because of this, this chapter remains in situ but Appendix X has been written to supply the latest picture for both a deal and a no-deal Brexit.

Certainly, all international road freight operators need to keep abreast of intended changes and be prepared for new ways of working. However, some older transport professionals may recognize the new procedures, should they be implemented, and operators moving goods to non-EU countries will certainly recognize the procedures in this case.

In any case, the UK will be seen as a non-EU country and so our drivers' licences will require supporting by International Driving Permits (IDPs), a passport that has at least six months' validity upon the driver's arrival back in the UK and a Green Card for insurance purposes; the UK DCPC is stated to be recognized at least through a 'honeymoon' period, although holders of UK DCPCs who work for EU-based companies are advised to exchange their UK DCPC for an EU equivalent. The 'honeymoon' period is based on the fact that the DCPC is founded on an EU Directive. Current UK type approved vehicles may need to be re-approved by the Vehicle Certification Agency (VCA) and our trailers require registering (mentioned earlier in the *Handbook*) and to be accompanied by their registration certificate.

In the 'what if' scenarios mentioned in the Appendix we note that the T1 and T2 status of UK goods may change, Customs procedures may require permits and

Economic Operator Registration Identification (EORI) numbers may have to be used, permits will be required and procedures either side of the channel will change and the subject of cabotage could be one to cause specific problems for both UK and EU operators. These are just some of the UK-centred 'what-if' considerations which will become clearer as time passes and the impact of Brexit becomes a lot clearer. Of course, many of the issues affecting UK operators and drivers will also affect EU operators and drivers and they are by no means to be seen as 'one-sided' issues. At the time of writing there are still innumerable issues to be resolved and I can only apologize if any of the suggested changes/requirements in this chapter turn out to not actually happen or be required.

I have left previous content in the text because of the uncertainty as it too 'could' remain a reality and be largely unchanged if a 'soft' Brexit is accepted.

Transport Implications

The transport implications of the Single European Market (SEM) were very significant and whole new horizons were opened up for the UK. In the past, road freighting across Europe was impeded by restrictive Customs procedures and road haulage permit requirements resulting in excessive administrative burdens, frustrating delays and inhibiting costs. In the wider arena of distribution, past inhibition has been rather more to do with the inability to trade across frontiers. Certainly, ECMT permits have been re-introduced and these are limited in numbers, but the modern IT systems available to Customs authorities should mean that the 'bad old days' remain as such, and HMRC is working very hard to ensure there are sufficient permits for the UK's needs. However, if there is a shortage HMRC recommends that exporters consider alternative methods for moving freight into Europe, such as increased use of container traffic.

Now, since the introduction of the Single Market Acts I (April 2011) and II (October 2012) and with all these constraints swept away, road freighting into Europe and the setting up of Euro-wide distribution networks is basically no more complex and no more fraught with bureaucracy than operating in the domestic marketplace. Our concepts of what is 'local' and what is 'regional' in terms of distribution are undergoing considerable change. However, it must also be accepted that the continual drive towards saving energy has been, and is, promoting different modes of transport other than road to be used wherever and whenever this is possible, and it cannot be ignored that some EU member states have begun to impose domestic sanctions and legislative requirements in spite of the Single Market, in what many believe to be attempts at protecting domestic interests (not least minimum wage requirements).

NB: The results of the EU referendum have distorted traditional patterns of trade and data is likewise distorted, making it unrealistic to give actual figures of import/export levels. However, the UK continues to import more goods than it exports, which, some trade professionals believe, is a positive sign for 'post-Brexit' as the UK is a valuable customer for many EU member states and our financial institutions are also globally accepted as superior to those within the EU.

Entry to the International Road Haulage Market

The sections below, relating to EU standards, etc, are likely to remain much as they are irrespective of the type of Brexit as they are in place and accepted by our EU customers and domestic operators alike, but individual EU member states will have much more freedom to treat the UK as a 'third party' country and require individual standards of compliance.

Currently, access to the European haulage market is governed solely by a system of quality licences much on the lines of the present UK scheme of operators' licensing – which has been amended to align with many of the EU requirements, many found in Regulation 1071/2009/EC for establishment of a professional competence qualification for those wanting access to the road haulage industry. That said, holders of UK CPCs are being advised to exchange their CPC for one issued within an EU member state, if they intend to work in that state, in order to avoid any possible 'loss of competence' issue if the EU member state in question decides not to recognise the UK version. The EU also influences and standardizes entrants to the haulage business insofar that it sets standards of good repute, financial standing and professional competence, and the granting of licences is dependent on satisfactory proof that these standards are met. Past convictions, mainly, but not exclusively, for transport- and vehicle-related offences will result in licence penalty – even revocation – and inability to sustain adequate finances will have a similar effect. Licence holders have to prove resources or provide financial guarantees (this topic is dealt with in detail in Chapter 1) although, due to the fluctuating value of the euro, the UK Traffic Commissioners now set the required levels of financial resources annually in GBP. Further details on international 'O' licensing can be found in the DVSA Goods Vehicle Operating Guide (GV74) which is free to download from the GOV.UK website.

NB: The CPC qualifications offered by the CILT, OCR and City & Guilds all give competence for national and international operations and are no longer split into 'national' and 'international' individual qualifications.

Community Licensing/Licences for the Community

A system of 'Community Licensing' was implemented from 1 January 1993 (then termed 'Community Authorizations') enabling EU road hauliers to operate freely (ie to undertake as many journeys as they wish) *between* member states* – the old term 'authorization' in this respect was often confused with the quite separate cabotage authorizations which are needed by hauliers wishing to collect and deliver goods *within* EU member states other than their own (see below). International hauliers operating within the EU (apart from when operating domestically within their own state) must hold a Community Licence/Licence for the Community issued by the transport authority in their own member state.

Very importantly, the status of the Community Licence/Licence for the Community for UK operators visiting the EU and EU operators visiting the UK is unclear and it may, or may not, remain a valid licence post-Brexit. Certainly, a 'hard' Brexit will make the UK's Licence/Licence for the Community invalid for EU operation and, if this is so, 'third party' processing and standards will apply. In addition, it has been declared that cabotage will almost certainly cease for UK operators, following some sort of 'honeymoon' period, as we will no longer be an EU member. This will, however, depend upon any terms of leaving the UK may negotiate. If it is not allowed, then it will mean that cabotage within the UK will not be able to be performed by EU operators although individual arrangements between individual countries could be made.

** Valid Licences/Licences for the Community also permit cross-border operations into four European Free Trade Association (EFTA) states – namely, Liechtenstein, Norway, Iceland and Switzerland.*

It is important to note the continuing requirement for bilateral and ECMT permits (see p 667) for road haulage journeys *outside* the EU and some dangerous and/or specialized goods. It is these types of permits which UK operators may need to trade with EU customers and their numbers are extremely limited.

Regulation 881/92/EEC (as amended)

The system of Community Licences for intra-EU road haulage operations is established under Council Regulation (EEC) 881/92 and implemented in the UK by the Goods Vehicles (Community Authorizations, now Community Licences) Regulations 1992 (SI 1992 No 3077). Regulation 881/92 amended earlier legislation (ie Council Regulation (EEC) 3164/76 as amended by Council Regulations (EEC) 1841/88 on Access to the Market in the International Carriage of Goods by Road) by effectively introducing qualitative criteria in place of the previous system of quantitative restriction. The qualitative criteria are as specified in Council Regulation (EEC) 561/74 as amended by Council Regulation (EEC) 438/89, namely a requirement that the road haulage operator be of good repute, of adequate financial standing and professionally competent in road haulage operations. Various amendments have been made to this regulation, including the change of term from 'Authorization' to 'Licence' and the inclusion and involvement of the EFTA countries. The UK 'could' gain a very similar status to EFTA countries and this may mean that Community Licensing/ Licensing for the Community remains a reality but this is another issue that remains unclear.

Issue of Community Licences

Community Licences are issued in the UK by the TCs on an automatic basis to all standard international operator ('O') licence holders (ie there is no need for UK operators to make a separate application for these licences). It should be noted that such 'O' licences are granted only to those applicants who fully satisfy the qualitative standards of the EU, in other words the legal requirements for good repute, adequate financial standing and professional competence in road haulage operations. In effect, the Community Licence/Licence for the Community acts as a permit for UK operators to trade in any of the EU and EFTA countries. The general opinion is that because of EU influence over the UK Community Licensing/Licensing for the Community standards the EU will continue to recognize them as equivalent and acceptable to allow UK operators to operate within EU member states. This was at least until 1 November 2019, after which date a current EU Community Licence was supposed to be termed a UK Licence for the Community. Again, delays to Brexit make the actual date for re-titling unclear. What is clear is that there will be at least a short period of grace if the EU recognition of our licensing is to be withdrawn.

Currently, the licence comprises an original document to be retained safely at the licence holder's main place of business, and a number of certified true copies equalling the total number of vehicles authorized on the operator's licence. One of the certified true copies of the licence must be carried in each vehicle undertaking international journeys within the EU. Community Licences/Licences for the Community and the certified true copies carried on vehicles must be produced for inspection on request. Failure to do so, and not to carry the certified true copy on a vehicle while on an international journey within the EU, is an offence. This situation will remain as it is until Brexit and until any agreed transition period expires. A two year transition period is largely being proposed but this too may, or may not, come to fruition.

Penalties for Infringement of the Law

UK-based international hauliers who jeopardize their 'O' licences by failing to meet the requirements of good repute, financial standing or professional competence also jeopardize their Community Licence/Licence for the Community. In other words, where circumstances arise which, as a result of infringement of the law or failure to meet the qualitative requirements of good repute, financial standing and professional competence, require the TC to suspend, curtail or revoke an 'O' licence, the Community Licence/Licence for the Community will also be automatically suspended, curtailed or withdrawn (ie revoked). The precise action taken by the TC will depend on the seriousness of the offence or offences. Serious or repeated minor infringement of carriage regulations (ie the Community Licensing Regulation itself) will result in temporary or partial suspension of the certified true copies of the licence.

In member states where 'O' licences of the type issued in the UK or its equivalent are not used, failure by international hauliers based in those states to meet (or maintain) the standards of good repute, financial standing and professional competence required under the EU regulation will, nevertheless, result in jeopardy of the Community Licence/Licence for the Community. Post-Brexit, such transgressions by UK operators will most probably lead to sanctions, up to and including a ban from entering, by the state concerned.

It is a specific requirement of the regulation that where one member state becomes aware of infringement of Community Licence/Licence for the Community legislation by a haulier from another member state, it shall inform the authorities in that member state and may ask that state to impose sanctions on the haulier in accordance with the regulations (ie for temporary or partial suspension of certified copies or withdrawal of the Community Licence/Licence for the Community).

Validity and Duration of Licences

Community Licences/Licences for the Community are made out in the original licence holder's name and are not transferable to any third party and remain valid while the 'O' licence is in force unless otherwise revoked. Certified copies, as mentioned above, must be carried on the relevant vehicle when on an international journey and must be produced by the driver for examination whenever he is required to do so by an authorized inspecting officer.

On the expiry of a Community Licences/Licences for the Community after five years, it is a requirement that the issuing authority (ie in the UK, the TC) must verify whether the operator still satisfies the legal conditions for its issue. Since these conditions are identical to those on which renewal of the haulier's 'O' licence depends, namely good repute, financial standing and professional competence, in the UK at least, operators whose 'O' licences are renewed can rest assured that their Community Licences/Licences for the Community will be automatically renewed at the same time. The five year cycle for 'international licences' is likely to continue as it is a logical and accepted timescale.

Community Licence Documents

Annex I to EU Regulation (EEC) 881/92 specifies a model for the Community Licences/Licences for the Community, the front page of which contains details of the haulier (ie name and full address), the date from which it is valid, the name of the authority by whom it is issued and the date of issue; on the rear are printed the general provisions for the use of such licences, in particular that while within the territory of any member state the holder (ie both the road haulage operator and the vehicle driver) must comply with the 'laws, regulations and administrative provisions in force in that state', especially in regard to transport and traffic.

Exemptions from Community Licensing/Licence for the Community Procedure

Certain transport operations are specifically exempt from the requirement for Community Licences/Licences for the Community in accordance with Annex II to the EU regulation as follows:

- carriage of mail as a public service;
- carriage of vehicles which have suffered damage or breakdown;
- carriage of goods in vehicles with a permissible gross weight exceeding 3.5 tonnes;
- carriage of goods* in vehicles owned (including hired) by an own-account firm solely for its own purposes and where the transport is no more than ancillary to its overall activities and where the vehicle is driven only by an employee of the firm;
- carriage of medicinal products, appliances, equipment and other articles required for medicinal care in emergency relief, in particular for natural disasters.

As discussed earlier, the list of exempted vehicles and operations may remain, at least in the short term, during any early transition period.

** The goods concerned may be the property of the firm, or have been sold, bought, let out on hire or hired, produced, extracted, processed or repaired by the firm. Although exempt the company may need to carry 'own-account' documentation in order to prove the status of the goods in question.*

Road Haulage Cabotage

Cabotage operation is provided for under the Treaty of Rome. We will still discuss it, as it may be a transport option post-Brexit in some form or another, although this looks increasingly unlikely. That said, it has been proposed it may be permitted in individual EU member states post-Brexit for similar permission being granted to those states' operators.

Cabotage is quite simply internal haulage by foreign transport operators – the collection and delivery of goods by road within a country by a road haulier whose business is established in another country. The significance of cabotage, of course, is that it protects internal haulage markets against incursion – or in this case the abstraction of domestic traffics – by outsiders (see below). Hence the reason why, hitherto, it has always been an illegal practice, but now, with the liberalization policies of the Single European Market, such restrictive practices have been swept away and road freight cabotage within EU member states is permitted by regulation.

Cabotage by EU own-account road transport operators is permitted, but only on the same basis as defined above (ie the fourth item under exemptions from Community Licensing requirements). As noted above, when the UK becomes a non-EU country cabotage by UK operators 'should' become illegal as it is a Single Market regime unless the EU grants a concession in the hope that, as they send proportionately more vehicles to the UK than we have visiting the EU, it may well be in the EU's interests to allow it to continue.

The Cabotage Regime

As Brexit drags on we must still discuss cabotage in its present form. The current EU rules on road haulage cabotage came into effect from 14 May 2010 in accordance with articles 8 and 9 of Regulation 1072/2009/EC. This followed many years of discussion within the EU and much uncertainty for international road hauliers who often did not known what, precisely, the cabotage rules allowed and prohibited.

For the purposes of this regulation, cabotage is defined as 'national carriage for hire or reward carried out on a temporary basis in a host member state in conformity with this regulation'.

Under the regulations, international road hauliers holding a Community Licence/Licence for the Community (issued by TCs to UK-based hauliers who are holders of international 'O' licences), and whose driver, if he is a national of a third country, holds a Driver Attestation document in accordance with the same regulation (ie Article 5 of 1072/2009/EC), is permitted to undertake cabotage operations. This means that they may carry out national road haulage for hire or reward on a temporary basis (ie not regularly) within a member state other than the one in which they are registered. But in so doing they must comply with the legal requirements on road traffic applicable in the host country. It should also be noted that the 'three loads in seven days' provision is constantly being reviewed as some member states feel this is acting against their domestic road haulage industry.

Within a period of seven days following on from the delivery of an incoming loaded international journey into the member state, road hauliers may undertake three loaded domestic journeys within that other member state, using the same vehicle, provided the work is not permanent or continuous. It is emphasized that the last unloading in the course of a cabotage operation before the haulier leaves the host country must take place within seven days from the last unloading of goods comprising the incoming international journey.

It should be noted that cabotage work is not permissible if:

- the activity is permanent and exercised continually and regularly;
- the activity is carried out systematically and not just on an ad hoc basis;
- the activity involves a vehicle belonging to a non-resident haulier, where the vehicle in question never left the territory of the host state.

Hauliers are required to be able to provide suitable clear evidence of their compliance with the rules – ie of the incoming international journey and of the subsequent cabotage journeys carried out. For these purposes the following information is required as evidence:

(a) the name, address and signature of the sender;

(b) the name, address and signature of the haulier;

(c) the name and address of the consignee as well as his signature and the date of delivery once the goods have been delivered;

(d) the place and the date of taking over of the goods and the place designated for delivery;

(e) the description in common use of the nature of the goods and the method of packing, and, in the case of dangerous goods, their generally recognized description, as well as the number of packages and their special marks and numbers;

(f) the gross mass of the goods or their quantity otherwise expressed;

(g) the number plates of the motor vehicle and trailer.

Additionally, hauliers engaging in cabotage operations must observe the law and administrative provisions in force in host member states relating to, among other things:

- the conditions governing transport contracts (these should be checked to see if any particular conditions apply);
- the maximum weights and dimensions of road vehicles permitted in host states for national traffic – these limits must not be exceeded even if limits in the haulier's home country are greater;

- the requirements relating to the carriage of certain categories of goods, in particular dangerous goods, perishable foodstuffs and live animals;
- drivers' hours law and tachograph records;
- driver CPC requirements;
- VAT on transport services (VAT normally has to be charged at the rate applicable in the country of operation (ie the host country).

The latest information at the time of writing is that cabotage will initially be restricted for UK operators down to two movements in any seven days and then be finally banned from February 2020. Clearly, this date may well also change as Brexit continues to be delayed.

VAT on Cabotage Operations

Internal transport operations under cabotage authorization require operators to comply with national VAT regulations. For this purpose, if cabotage is permitted in any EU member state post-Brexit, operators may need to register in the member states in which they are operating or appoint a suitable VAT agent or fiscal representative to handle these matters on their behalf. Detailed advice on this matter is available through the trade associations (RHA and FTA).

Road Haulage Permits

Certain road haulage operations from the UK and EU member states to non-EU member states still require the issue of a bilateral road haulage permit. At the present time road haulage journeys to or through Belarus, Georgia, Kazakhstan, Morocco, Russia, Tunisia and Ukraine require such permits for specified transport operations. A bilateral permit is not required for journeys to Turkey but is required for journeys that transit Turkey for a destination in another country. Bilateral permits are not required for some humanitarian aid consignments but the situation requires clarification from the International Road Freight Office (IRFO) (details below).

Bilateral road haulage permits are not currently required for transport operations within the EU. However, hauliers on transit journeys across Community territory to non-EU destinations using a bilateral permit will need an ECMT permit to transit the EU if there is a no-deal Brexit. They must also be in possession of a Community Licence. It is permits that are currently a major concern to most UK international hauliers because of their scarcity and because of the associated costs.

Permits are available from the International Road Freight Office (IRFO) which is a part of the DVSA:

International Road Freight Office
Hillcrest House
386 Harehills Lane
Leeds
LS9 6NF
Tel: 0113 305 1115
Website: www.gov.uk/government/publications/general-quota-application (archived at https://perma.cc/YLN5-XQUN).

Post-Brexit ECMT* permits may become available through the VOL system but the costs are £10.00 per application and a further £123.00 per each permit issued. ECMT permits come in two types. Unrestricted permits are granted on a 'first come first served basis', whilst restricted permits are based on Euro emissions, etc. Bilateral permits cost £2.00 per application and £6.00 per permit issued. In reality, it is unlikely that permit restrictions will apply to vehicles visiting the UK from the EU but this is also unclear.

As the UK approaches Brexit and permit requirements become a major concern to many international operators, it is worthy of note that goods in containers and on unaccompanied trailers are currently not required to use permits and moving goods in these ways may be an alternative for some UK operators.

* Full details on the latest position regarding ECMT permits are below and in Appendix X.

Validity of Permits

Where bilateral road haulage permits are required as described above, such permits are available covering single journeys only, allowing just *one* return journey to be undertaken between the UK and the nominated country on the dates shown on the permit. Outside of these dates the permit is invalid and it would be illegal to commence or continue the journey. These are usually valid for one month. Annual permits (quota) relate to Euro emissions and are extremely limited with fewer than 1,000 being issued annually (at the time of writing).

Third-Country Traffic

Third-country traffic, which is the carriage of goods between two countries other than the country in which the vehicle is registered, is permissible in certain cases (ie between any EU country) but not in many non-EU countries. For UK hauliers, journeys are currently permissible between any two EU countries.

NB: Permits valid for third-country traffic involving a country outside the EU are available and full details can be obtained from the IRFO but ECMT permits will be required to transit the EU in order to get to the country concerned.

Issue of Permits

Road haulage permits where necessary as described above are issued by the relevant authority in each member state. Normally, this involves completion of application forms, advance payment of the relevant fee and submission by the applicant of a copy of his authority to operate (eg his Community Licence). Application needs to be made 7–10 days before the permit is required.

Permits may be quota (limited numbers issued) or non-quota (unlimited issue). Where quota permits are issued but not used, operators may have the number requested on their next request reduced as quota permits are often in short supply. The issue of non-quota permits is a role of VOL, and applicants must use VOL when applying.

Return of Used Permits

Used and expired bilateral permits must be returned to the issuing authority not later than 15 days after the relevant journey has been completed as they are 'single journey' permits.

European Conference of Ministers of Transport (ECMT) permits (see below), used for tramping operations and EU transit, are valid for 12 months and must be returned to IRFO within 15 days of the expiry date. The terms of these permits also require the haulier to use log books and submit monthly returns to IRFO giving details of work carried out under the permit.

Lost or Stolen Permits

Road haulage permits are valuable transit documents and as such should be treated with care and appropriate security. They are not transferable to another operator and such misuse is illegal throughout the Community, with harsh penalties imposed on offenders (see also below). Replacement of lost or stolen permits is not normally automatic, and in any case a full written explanation of the circumstances surrounding the loss or theft is required, together with a copy of the police report.

Journeys to or through Non-Agreement Countries

If vehicles are to travel to or through a country with which an EU member state has no agreement, permission to operate in that country has to be sought direct from its transport authority. Application should be made well before the journey is due and full details of the vehicle, the load and the route should be given. Advice is available through the trade associations, IRFO or embassies of the countries concerned.

ECMT Multilateral Permits

NB: The former European Conference of Ministers of Transport (ECMT), which had existed since 1953, has been transformed into a new intergovernmental organization called the International Transport Forum (ITF). Its principal aim is to help both policymakers and the general public gain a deeper understanding of the essential role played by transport. However, the acronym ECMT is still used in relation to these types of permits.

It is these permits which, post-Brexit, will form the 'lion's share' required by UK-based international haulage operators seeking to move goods out of the UK into the EU member states.

Currently, a number of ECMT permits are allocated to the UK for EU transit and haulage journeys between ECMT member countries (ie all EU member states plus, as at 1 January 2009: Albania, Armenia, Azerbaijan, Belarus, Bosnia and Herzegovina, FYR Macedonia, Georgia, Moldova, Montenegro, Russian Federation, Serbia and Turkey (transit)). A full list is included in Appendix X.

These ECMT permits allow journeys between member countries, including laden or empty transit journeys and third-country journeys to other ECMT countries which are prohibited by certain bilateral agreements. However, they cannot be used for transit of ECMT countries on journeys to non-ECMT states or for cabotage. The normal permits are for hire or reward journeys only and may not be used by unaccompanied trailers or semi-trailers. They are valid for one calendar year (Dec–Jan) and allow an unlimited number of journeys within that period, but they may be used with only one vehicle at a time. Journey logs are required when operating under ECMT permits. They need to be sent to the IRFO on a monthly basis while the permit is valid. The permits and any outstanding logs have to be returned to the IRFO within 15 days of expiry of the permit. The quota for their issue is limited, so these permits are allocated before the beginning of the year in which they are issued. Usually no further supplies are available during the course of the year, but should the quota be increased an announcement is made in the trade press.

ECMT Removals Permits

These permits are quota-free and can be used for international removals between, or crossing, ECMT member countries. They are available only to firms employing the specialized equipment and staff needed to undertake such operations and are valid for one year from the date of issue.

Details available from www.gov.uk/government/publications/ecmt-international-removal-permit (archived at https://perma.cc/X2VP-Z3FN).

Permit Checks

As a result of the exposure of a number of cases of permit frauds, stringent regulations exist to prevent vehicles on international journeys travelling without valid permits (where relevant – see above) and checks are made on vehicles to ensure that these regulations are complied with. A vehicle will be prevented from continuing its journey if it does not carry a valid permit. In the UK it is an offence to forge or alter permits, to make a false statement to obtain a permit or to allow one to be used by another person.

Own-Account Transport Operations

Own-account transport operations within Community territory (including cabotage as defined above) were free from all bilateral permit requirements (under the provisions of EU Regulation 881/92 Annex II) provided that goods are carried solely in connection with the trade or business of the vehicle user and were not carried for hire or reward, and that the following conditions are also met:

- The goods carried must be the property of the business (of the vehicle user) or must have been sold, bought, let out or hired, produced, extracted, processed or repaired by the business.
- The purpose of the journey must be to carry the goods to or from the business or to move them, either within the business or outside for its own needs.
- Motor vehicles used for the carriage must be driven by employees of the business.

- The vehicles carrying the goods must be owned by the business, bought on deferred terms or hired by it (this does not apply where a replacement vehicle is used during a short breakdown of the vehicle normally used).
- Road haulage must not be the major activity of the business.

Own-account operations between the UK and mainland Europe (EU and EFTA) were generally free from permit requirements but in the case of such journeys permits may be required in the future and drivers should carry on the vehicle an 'own-account' document containing the following information to confirm that the operation is solely for own-account purposes:

- the name and address of the vehicle operator (ie user);
- the nature of the operator's trade or business;
- the nature of the goods being carried;
- the location of the loading and unloading points;
- the registration number of the vehicle on which the goods are carried;
- details of the route to be followed.

In all cases, own-account vehicle operators (and their drivers) should be aware that they may be asked to provide satisfactory evidence to help the authorities to determine the ownership of the goods and that they are being carried solely for own-account purposes. Drivers may also now need proof that their earnings are at, or above, the minimum wage rates of the countries they visit. Own-account documentation and proof of minimum wage requirements can be prepared/supplied by the FTA, upon request.

Below is a summary of the RHA advice to operators relating to future permit operation and largely focuses on a no-deal situation. This advice is still seen as reasonable.

Legislation provides powers for the Government to issue and allocate permits to UK operators for the operation of international road haulage if it is required to do so but it remains the hope that no permits will be required for UK vehicles from Northern Ireland travelling to the Irish Republic.

Something as yet unclear is the continuation of the EU Community Licence/ Licence for the Community. However, the UK Government is preparing a new allocation scheme for international road haulage permits if the Community Licence/Licence for the Community does become invalid. In this case, it is expected that non-quota bilateral schemes will continue to allow operators to obtain as many permits as they need although future bilateral permits with the states currently covered by Community Licence/Licence for the Community arrangements are uncertain. Some may not even require a permit if they adopt the system currently operated between the UK and Turkey. However, future bilateral agreements could be trip based, multi-trip, annual or even multi-year.

Where an EU member state does not introduce a bilateral permit scheme for UK operators, ECMT permits will be made available for affected UK operators although only a limited number of these permits are allowed to be issued by the UK authorities but EURO emission standards apply. In these cases the UK Government will decide which operators will be allowed to work internationally.

There is currently no information on transit through intermediate countries and it is not known if separate 'transit' permits will be required.

It is also noted that to try to predict future requirements post-Brexit given the different attitudes towards the UK by different EU member states makes these notes little more than a 'best-guess' or a 'likely outcome' and not hard fact.

International Carriage of Goods by Road – CMR

Transport operators – whether just a one-man haulage business (ie owner-driver) or a large firm – carrying goods for reward on international road haulage journeys must comply* with the Convention on the Contract for the International Carriage of Goods by Road 1956 (*Convention Relative au Contrat de Transport International de Marchandises par Route* – commonly referred to as the CMR Convention). This Convention is applied in the UK by the provisions of the Carriage of Goods by Road Act 1965. The Convention defines the carriers' liability and the documents to be carried on vehicles engaged in the international movement of goods between different countries, of which at least one is a party to the CMR Convention.

In an attempt to modernise CMR and reduce the amount of paperwork eCMR has been trialled where multiple border crossings were a factor. This new development allows electronic data input and transfer and is seen as the future for cross-border freight movements.

In any case, it has been declared that CMR will remain in place and in its current form irrespective of the UK's eventual position in relation to international operations.

** Since, in effect, CMR applies automatically when moving goods between over 45 countries, the haulier has no choice in the matter – but may be carrying out the operation in ignorance of this fact.*

Applicable Law

International conventions such as CMR override the relevant provisions of national law but only insofar as they cover the point at issue. However, not all points of issue that may arise by way of dispute or claim out of a contract for international carriage are covered by the CMR Convention, in which case relevant national law would apply (basically this means the law of the country in which the dispute or claim arose and to whose courts the matter is referred). In deciding the outcome of any dispute or claim, the courts may refer to either the French or English language texts of the Convention although the French text is not reproduced in the schedule to the Carriage of Goods by Road Act 1965. When referring to this Act, a court is still free to consider the French language version of the Convention for clarification should difficulty be found in determining the precise meaning of any aspect of the English text.

Non-CMR Operations and Journeys

For the CMR Convention to apply there must be clear evidence of a contract for the international carriage of goods for reward. In other words, the carriage of goods on an international journey at no charge, and therefore outside of a contract for carriage as specified in the Convention, would not be covered by CMR. Furthermore, the carriage must be of *goods* to allow the Convention to apply.

Besides these exclusions arising from defining the precise terms of applicability, the Convention has a number of more specific exemptions. Namely, its terms do not apply to:

- own-account* operations which involve international journeys;
- furniture removals;
- funeral consignments which are transported abroad;
- carriage under an International Postal Convention.

** The position about individual EU member states agreeing that 'own-account' movements by UK businesses will be permitted outside of CMR post-Brexit is, as yet, unclear.*

The Convention is also *not* applicable in respect of international haulage operations between the United Kingdom (including Northern Ireland) and the Republic of Ireland,** or to contracts for the carriage of goods between the UK mainland and the Channel Islands (ie Guernsey, Jersey, Alderney, Sark and Herm), such operations not being legally classed as international journeys. Cabotage journeys (ie internal journeys within a country by a road haulier from another country) are also outside the provisions of the CMR.

*** This 'could' change post-Brexit depending upon the final outcome of the UK leaving the Union.*

Basic Requirements of CMR

The CMR Convention automatically applies to every contract for the international carriage of goods by road in vehicles for reward, even when the vehicle containing the goods is carried over part of its journey by sea, rail or inland waterway, providing that the goods concerned are not unloaded from the vehicle in transit at any point. Other conventions may also apply and take precedence over CMR. A CMR-type consignment note must be completed for the journey. There is no escape from the Convention's provisions and road hauliers may not opt out (by agreement with consignors or otherwise) from its legal (ie liability) requirements. Thus, for example, if a road haulier was induced to carry goods for reward on an international journey knowing nothing of the CMR and its provisions and his consequential liability responsibilities, and even without a CMR consignment note in force, the provisions of the Convention would still apply. Should a legal dispute or claim subsequently arise he could be liable to pay substantial compensation not covered by his domestic Goods in Transit insurance policy. This kind of unfortunate circumstance is referred to as 'unwitting CMR'.

Even in circumstances where a road haulier may not be aware that a load being carried on one of his vehicles is destined to continue on, or has previously been moved on, an international journey, and where he is not aware of the conditions and implications of CMR, the Convention's provisions still apply. This is particularly relevant where loaded, unaccompanied articulated semi-trailers are collected or delivered – it is the load and that part of the vehicle which are together at the time of crossing national boundaries which determines that a particular journey is legally an international journey to which CMR applies. The Convention is not relevant where containers are carried domestically after having been transferred from the vehicle or rail wagon which crossed national boundaries; or where loads are trans-shipped between the vehicle which undertook the international part of the journey (to which CMR did apply), and local delivery vehicles (to which CMR did not apply).

CMR Conditions for International Road Haulage Journeys

An outline of the principal conditions of the Convention is given here:

1. The Convention applies to every contract for carriage of goods, whether wholly by road or partly by road and partly by rail, sea or inland waterway, as long as the goods remain in the original vehicle, on a journey from one country to another, one of which is a contracting party to the Convention (with the exception of UK–Eire (see note above) and UK mainland–Channel Islands journeys which are ruled not to be international journeys for this purpose). Exemptions to CMR apply to carriage under international postal conventions, funeral consignments and furniture removals.
2. The carrier (ie road haulier) is responsible under the Convention for the actions and omissions of his agents and any other persons whose services are used in carrying out the movement. Even if the original road haulier contracted to undertake the movement sub-contracts the whole of the operation to another road haulier (whose name appears on the CMR consignment note) the first (original) haulier remains fully liable under CMR should a dispute or claim arise. This can present problems in a case where, for example, the first (original) haulier operates only in domestic transport and thus is covered only by, say, Road Haulage Association Conditions of Carriage and is insured accordingly – not being insured to the much higher CMR level of liability.
3. A contract for the international carriage of goods for reward is confirmed by making out a CMR consignment note in at least four original copies which should be signed by the sender and carrier. Each keeps a copy, a copy travels on the vehicle with the goods and the final copy is retained by the carrier at base. While a CMR consignment note confirms that a contract exists, the absence of, or failure to raise, such a note does not invalidate the contract or dis-apply the terms of the Convention.
4. If the goods are carried under a single contract in different vehicles or are divided owing to their different nature, the carrier or the sender can specify that a separate consignment note should be made out for each vehicle or each load of goods.
5. The consignment note must contain certain specified details and may also contain additional information of use to the parties to the contract. It must state that the carriage is subject to CMR. Although not a 'title' to the goods, the consignment note is evidence of the facts it contains (ie the details shown

are presumed to be correct), such as the number of packages, etc, and any claim which disputes such facts would have to be backed by substantial independent evidence to the contrary. Normally a standard note such as that available from the International Road Transport Union (IRU) is used (or in the UK from the Road Haulage Association or the Freight Transport Association – both IRU members).

6 The sender is responsible for all expenses, loss and damage sustained by the carrier as a result of inaccuracies in completion of the consignment note in relation to information supplied by him – even if the road haulier completes the note from information given to him by the sender.

7 On receipt of the goods, the carrier must check the accuracy of the details shown in the consignment note, particularly, for example, as to the number of packages, the apparent condition of the goods, their packaging and how they are marked. Any discrepancies or comments about other relevant matters such as the condition of the goods or packages or not being able to physically check the goods should be noted by a 'reservation' on the note. Should the sender request the carrier to check the contents of packages or to have the consignment weighed he must reimburse the carrier any costs incurred in doing so.

8 The sender is liable to the carrier for damage and expenses due to defective packing of the goods unless the defects were known to the carrier when taking over the goods and he indicated this fact by way of a 'reservation' on the note. The absence of such a reservation means that the carrier, if he was aware of the damage, accepted any likely risks of subsequent claims.

9 The sender must attach to the consignment note or make available to the carrier the necessary documents to complete Customs formalities. The sender is liable to the carrier for any damage caused by the absence, inadequacy or irregularity of such documents.

10 The sender has the right of disposal of the goods and may stop transit of the goods or change the delivery address up to the time of delivery to the consignee unless he has stated on the consignment note that the consignee has this right. Once the goods are delivered to the address on the consignment note, the consignee has the right of disposal.

11 A carrier who fails to follow the instructions on the consignment note or who has followed them without requesting the first copy of the consignment note to be produced is liable for loss or damage caused by such failure.

12 The carrier must provide the consignee with a second copy of the consignment note at the time of delivering the goods.

13 If the carrier cannot follow the instructions on the consignment note for any reason, he must ask the sender or the consignee, depending on who has the right of disposal (see item 10 above), for further instructions.

14 The carrier is liable for the total or partial loss of the goods and for any damage to them occurring between the time when he takes over the goods and the time of their delivery unless the loss, damage or delay was caused by a wrongful act or neglect of the claimant. The burden of proof in this case rests with the carrier. However, the carrier is not bound to pay any

compensation for delay where they do not receive a 'reservation' from the consignee within 21 days of the date of delivery.

15 Failure to deliver goods within 30 days of a specified time limit, or within 60 days from the time when the first carrier took them over if there is no time limit for delivery, results in the goods being considered to be lost.

16 When goods of a dangerous nature are consigned, the carrier must be informed of the nature of the danger and the precautions to be taken.

17 Calculation of compensation in the event of loss or damage is related to the value of the goods at the place and time they were accepted for carriage but will not exceed a set value (ie related to SDR – see p 675 for explanation).

18 Carriage charges, Customs duties and other charges in respect of the carriage are refunded in the case of total loss of the goods and proportionately in the case of partial loss.

19 Higher levels of compensation may be claimed where the value or a special interest in delivery has been declared or where a surcharge has been paid in respect of a declared value exceeding the limit mentioned in item 17 above.

20 In the case of damage the carrier is liable for the amount by which the value of the goods has diminished.

21 The claimant may demand interest in respect of the amount of any claim at 5 per cent per annum from the date on which the claim was sent to the carrier.

22 A carrier cannot avail himself of exclusions or limiting clauses if damage to goods was caused by his wilful misconduct or default which constitutes wilful misconduct.

23 The consignee is considered to have accepted the goods in a satisfactory condition if he does not indicate his reservations at the time of delivery or within seven days (excluding Sundays and public holidays).

24 In legal proceedings, the plaintiff may bring an action in any court or tribunal of a contracting (ie CMR contracting) country, or of a country in which the defendant is normally resident or has his principal place of business, or of a country where the goods were taken over by the carrier or where they were designated for delivery, and in no other courts or tribunals.

25 The period of limitation for an action under the Convention is one year, or three years in the case of wilful misconduct.

26 Where successive road carriers are involved in a contract under the Convention, each one of them is responsible for the whole operation as a party to the contract. Each successive carrier must give the previous carrier a dated receipt and must enter his name and address on the second copy of the consignment note.

27 A carrier who has paid compensation arising from a claim may recover the compensation plus interest, costs and expenses from other carriers who were parties to the contract subject to:

(a) the carrier responsible for the loss or damage paying the compensation;

(b) each carrier responsible for loss or damage jointly caused shall be liable to pay proportionate compensation, or compensation proportionate to their share of the carriage charges, if responsibility cannot be apportioned.

28 If a carrier who is due to pay compensation is insolvent, his share must be paid by the other carriers who are party to the contract.

In particular, road hauliers should note that the terms of the carriage contract require the carrier taking over the goods to check the accuracy of the statements in the consignment note as to the number of packages, their marks and numbers, the apparent condition of the goods and their packaging – and they should obviously do so for their own protection in the event of later disputes or claims. Under the Convention the carrier is responsible for loss, damage or delay from the time of taking over the goods until the time of their delivery.

Furthermore, where goods are handled by a number of carriers on an international journey (eg by transferring a loaded articulated semi-trailer from one to another), provisions are contained in CMR to apportion the liability for loss or damage between all the carriers (based on the relative proportions of the total carriage cost charged by each one of them). This is because of the difficulties which may arise in pinpointing the exact time and place when the damage occurred (unless specific responsibility can be determined), but should one or more of the carriers in this situation default (ie through insolvency) in meeting their share of any claim for damage to or loss of the goods then the remaining carrier or carriers will have to meet the share of those defaulting.

CMR Liability

As stated above, in international road haulage operations (but not own-account road transport operations) the carriage automatically comes within the terms of the CMR Convention under which the carrier's liability for claims resulting from loss of or damage to the goods carried is determined by comparison with a measure known as 'Special Drawing Rights' (SDRs), whereby compensation must not exceed 8.33 units of account per kg of gws (gross weight short). SDRs are defined by the International Monetary Fund (IMF) as being a unit for converting currency values based on a 'basket' of the currencies of the key member states of the IMF and are converted to the national currency of the country in which any claim is dealt with in court, and is assessed as to value on the date of the judgment, or on a date agreed to by the parties. A treasury certificate stating the value for that day is taken to be conclusive proof of that fact.

Note: In 2018 changes were made that now make it compulsory for claim management companies (CMCs) working on CMR claims to ensure that they only charge what is 'reasonable' in relation to a claim and provide the client with an itemized bill explaining where costs have arisen before any payment is to be made.

SDR Conversion Rate

The daily conversion rate for SDR to national currencies can be found in the financial newspapers or on the internet. With changing values it is essential that the current value should be established at any particular point in time, and adequate insurance cover to at least this level of liability should be carried. To give an approximate idea of what this value represents, in September 2019 a conversion of SDR to sterling at a rate of £1.00 = 1.13* SDRs per kilogram represented a value of £7,371.68 per tonne (ie calculated as £1.00 divided by 1.13 = £0.8849557 × 8.33 × 1,000 kg).

** It is important to note that the SDR rate changes daily. This is important to remember when major currencies such as the euro and USD are somewhat volatile and exchange rates vary from day to day.*

CMR Consignment Notes for International Haulage Journeys

Road hauliers carrying goods for hire and reward on international journeys under the provisions of the CMR Convention as described above must complete special CMR consignment notes to be carried on the vehicle. These consignment notes confirm that the carriage is being conducted under a contract subject to the terms of the CMR Convention, but even in the absence of a CMR note, the carriage will still be subject, under international law, to the terms of the Convention although the carrier may not have been aware of this fact.

As mentioned above, the consignment note is made out in four original copies all of which should be signed by both the carrier and the consignor of the goods. One copy of the note (with red lines) is retained by the consignor, the second copy (with blue lines) is for the consignee and the third copy (with green lines) is for the carrier and must travel forward with the vehicle and remain with it while the goods are on board – the fourth copy (with black lines) may be retained on file by the originator of the document.

Where a consignment is divided to travel by different vehicles or by separate means, separate CMR consignment notes can be made out for each individual part of the consignment.

The following details must be entered on CMR consignment notes:

Box 1	Sender (name, address, country)
Box 2	Customs reference/status
Box 3	Sender's/agent's reference
Box 4	Consignee (name, address, country)
Box 5	Carrier (name, address, country)
Box 6	Place and date of taking over the goods
Box 7	Successive carriers
Box 8	Place designated for delivery of goods
Box 9	Marks and numbers; number and kind of packages; description of goods*
Box 10	Gross weight (kg)
Box 11	Volume (m^3)
Box 12	Carriage charges
Box 13	Sender's instructions for Customs
Box 14	Reservations
Box 15	Documents attached
Box 16	Special agreements
Box 17	Goods received

Box 18 Signature of carrier
Box 19 Company completing the note
Box 20 Place, date, signature
Box 21 Copies to:

(i) Sender
(ii) Consignee
(iii) Carrier

**For dangerous goods indicate:*

(i) *correct technical name (ie proper shipping name);*
(ii) *Hazchem class;*
(iii) *UN number;*
(iv) *flashpoint (°C), if applicable.*

Box 14 (Reservations) is required so that the driver/haulier can make a statement that they could not check or confirm some item of detail (condition, volume, shortages, etc) relating to the consignment at the time of taking over the consignment. This can be a very important element of CMR when claims are made against the carrier.

Where applicable, the consignment note must also contain the following particulars:

- a statement that transhipment to another vehicle is not allowed;
- the charges which the sender undertakes to pay;
- the amount of 'cash on delivery' charges;
- a declaration of the value of the goods and the amount representing special interest in delivery;
- the sender's instructions to the carrier regarding insurance of the goods;
- the agreed time limit within which the carriage is to be carried out;
- a list of documents handed to the carrier.

The consignor or consignee can also add to the consignment note any other particulars which may be useful to the road haulier.

Consignment Notes for Own-Account Carriage by Road

Own-account operators are not required to use the CMR consignment note for international journeys. For most journeys a simple consignment note is all that is necessary to prove that the journey is on own-account (ie not for hire or reward). It should contain details of the following:

- the vehicle operator;
- his trade or business;
- the goods being carried;
- their loading and delivery points;
- the vehicle being used (ie by registration number, etc);
- the route to be followed.

As stated above, the FTA will prepare own-account documents. For further information call the FTA on 01892 526171 and ask for the International Department.

Authorized Economic Operators

The horrific events around the world, which are generally acts of terrorism, have significantly raised the profile of international security issues, not only for counter-terrorism purposes, but also in the fight against organized crime and other threats to society. Among a number of subsequent initiatives was the introduction of the concept of Authorized Economic Operator (AEO). EU member states successfully voted on the detailed legal provisions to implement the concept, effective from 1 January 2008. The Security Amendment (Council Regulation 648/2005/EC) and its implementing provisions (Commission Regulation 1875/2006/EC) are available on the Commission's Europa website.

The aim of the AEO concept is to provide business with an internationally recognized quality mark that will demonstrate that they operate within a secure supply chain and that their internal Customs controls and procedures are sufficiently efficient and compliant for them to conduct 'self-clearance' for customs purposes. Under the legislation, businesses that satisfy certain EU-wide criteria may apply for, and be granted, the status of AEO by HMRC. When a member state has granted a business AEO status, this status is currently recognized across all member states. AEOs will be able to benefit from facilitation of Customs controls or simplifications of Customs rules or both, depending on the type of AEO certificate.

Application packs for AEO status and further details on the benefits and criteria are available on the HMRC or GOV.UK websites. There are also grants available until 31 January 2020 (unless extended) to enable organizations to train and recruit staff with AEO skills.

However, although this was originally an EU scheme, the UK AEO scheme allows self-assessment, unlike the scheme in the EU, although as it otherwise 'mirrors' that of the EU it is recognized and enables UK operators to reduce delays and inspection rates at borders through 'mutual recognition' of both schemes. Again, the picture post-Brexit is unclear but it does seem that there will at least be some sort of 'honeymoon' period, although it is hoped that the UK scheme will continue to be recognized.

Community (EU) Transit

In recent years, many former complicated document systems have been replaced with simplified paperwork and electronic systems and the term 'export' no longer applies to shipments within the territories of the EU. Clearly, UK operators may, or may not, be permitted to conduct Community Transit depending upon any terms of our departure from the EU, although if UK operators establish businesses within the EU then it will be permitted, providing the terms and details below are satisfied.

The EU's key procedures for dealing with this trade are known as Community Transit and Common Transit. These are both Customs procedures that allow respectively:

- goods that are not in free circulation, and in certain cases EU goods, to move between two points in the EU, including two points in a single member state, with the duties and other charges suspended. The procedure is also used to control the movement of goods to and from Andorra, San Marino and the 'special territories' of the Community (such as the Channel Islands) – Community Transit;

- the movement of both Community and 'non free circulation' goods to, from and through EFTA countries such as Iceland, Norway, Liechtenstein and Switzerland – Common Transit.

For Community Transit (CT) purposes goods are said to have a particular Customs 'status' which is based on their liability to Customs duty and other charges (eg excise duty and VAT) or claims to Common Agricultural Policy (CAP) refunds. Goods are divided into two distinct categories as follows:

1. Goods which have EU status (ie EU goods). These are goods which:
   - originate in the EU;
   - have been imported from a non-EU country and have been put into free circulation (see below) in the EU; or
   - have been manufactured in the EU from materials or parts imported from a non-EU country provided the imported materials or parts are in free circulation.

   The term 'free circulation' is used to describe imported goods on which all import formalities have been complied with and any Customs duties or equivalent charges which are payable have been paid and not repaid in whole or in part. Goods originating in the EU are also in free circulation unless a CAP export refund or other refund has been claimed on them. Consequently, as a general rule, EU goods can move within the EU without any Customs controls and have what is called T2 status.
2. Goods without EU status (ie 'non-EU goods') with duty to pay or not yet cleared by Customs are said to be 'not in free circulation' and have what is called T1 status.

As may be appreciated, Community Transit arrangements for UK goods are yet to be finalized and permits may be required for goods passing through individual EU member states post-Brexit. What has transpired is that, due to the general updating/ modernizing of Customs procedures, the status of T1 or T2 is now an element of the Transit Advice Document (TAD) barcode and, as a part of the modernization, the TAD is now produced on green paper.

The Tariff

All the information and advice needed to help with importing and exporting procedures is to be found in 'The Tariff' (ie *The Integrated Tariff of the United Kingdom*). This document, published in three volumes and to the same format in the EU member states, contains all the relevant commodity codes (more than 65,000 of them); duty rates; procedures, including a box-by-box completion guide for C88 Single Administrative (SAD) documents (see below); as well as references to the legal provisions.

Customs Documentation

An eight-part Customs document (C88), which actually replaced a total of 27 other documents, is known as the 'Single Administrative Document' (SAD), and is used throughout the EU and EFTA countries for the purposes of non-NCTS (see below) import, export and transit controls. A CT declaration comprises completed copies of pages 1, 4 and 5 of the SAD. In certain circumstances a Community status document (T2L) may be used where required to provide evidence to Customs of EU status. A T2L can be either a copy of page 4 of the SAD, or a commercial document such as an invoice, a transport document or a manifest.

The SAD (form C88) comprises an eight-part document set, but not all of it is used since the opening of the SEM. Only the following copies are now required:

Copy 1	Copy for the Customs office of departure.
Copy 3	Consignor/exporter's copy.
Copy 4	For Customs office of destination, or T2L declaration.
Copy 5	Return copy from Customs office of destination to prove that the goods arrived intact.
Copy 7	Statistical copy for Customs in the country of destination.

Copies 1 and 3 remain in the country of origination (ie export) and copies 4, 5 and 7 travel forward with the goods, copy 5 eventually being returned to the office of departure.

The SAD currently acts as a Customs document for goods being exported from the UK to any non-EU countries and it is likely that the SAD will be the main non-electronic form to be used for EU exports post-Brexit. If this is the case, the SAD will need to be supported by the CMR document and possibly even certificates of origin. What is certain is that HMRC are modernizing their procedures in such ways that the SAD will become much less used or required, in favour of electronic processing.

NB: Whilst the term 'community transit' is used throughout this section, the European Community (EC) is now almost exclusively referred to as the European Union (EU).

Community Transit Movements

There are two types of CT procedure:

1. The external CT procedure. This is mainly used to control the movement of non-EU goods and to control the movement of EU goods which are subject to EU measures involving their export to a third country, eg CAP goods which are liable to an export refund. This procedure is also known as the 'T1' procedure.
2. The internal CT procedure. This procedure controls the movement of free circulation goods to or from the special territories, to or via the EFTA countries and between the EFTA countries. This procedure is also known as the 'T2' procedure (or the 'T2F' procedure for goods moving to or from the special territories).

These status classifications could be subject to change for UK goods post-Brexit, but it seems likely that T1 and T2 status may actually largely remain in their current formats although, as noted above, declared differently.

Control Procedures

All transit movements are the responsibility of a 'principal', who is the person or company who undertakes to ensure that the goods are delivered to the office of destination within the prescribed time limit. The principal must put up a guarantee to secure the relevant duties and other charges in case the goods do not arrive intact at the office of destination. The guarantee can be cash (lodged at the office of departure), vouchers (purchased from a guaranteeing association) or a guarantee undertaking (provided by a guarantor).

To start a CT movement the completed declaration must be presented to Customs at an 'office of departure' where it will be authenticated and a time limit for completing the movement will be set. The goods may also be sealed and an itinerary set. Copies 4 and 5 of the CT declaration (ie the SAD) must travel together with the goods until they reach the EU member state or EFTA country where the movement is to end. Here the declaration and goods must be presented to the appropriate Customs at the 'office of destination'. This office will then stamp copy 5 of the SAD and return it to the office of departure so that the movement can be discharged. If copy 5 is not received within two months the principal is contacted and asked to provide proof that the procedure has ended correctly. If proof is not provided within four months, the enquiry procedure is initiated to recover the potential debt.

There are a range of transit simplifications available for use by compliant and reliable traders. These include the use of comprehensive and reduced guarantees or waivers, becoming authorized consignors and consignees, using trader seals on vehicles, special loading lists, having an exemption from prescribed itineraries, goods moved by pipeline, use of other simplified procedures and being able to use commercial documentation instead of the SAD in the case of air, rail and sea environments. All of these simplifications are subject to authorization by the Customs authorities.

NCTS

The New Computerized Transit System (NCTS) is a European-wide system, based on the concept of electronic declaration and processing, and is designed to replace the old, paper-based CT system and to provide better management and control of CT (NCTS is supposed to remain in its current form post-Brexit with no change). However, many exports from minor ports will still require the old CT (C88) procedure. NCTS involves exporters registering their consignments at a Customs 'office of departure' which will generate a Movement Reference Number for the consignment concerned. The 'office of departure' will also give the exporter a Transit Accompanying Document (TAD) (similar to a SAD) which will need to travel with the consignment. All the details are then transmitted to a Customs 'office of destination', in the country, or at the border of the country, concerned giving that office notification of expected arrival. Upon arrival the details are checked and arrival at the 'office of destination' confirmed. NCTS involves all EU member states and the EFTA countries, 32 countries in all. Each country develops its own NCTS processing system, according to centrally defined architecture and these systems are connected, through a central domain in Brussels, to all of the other countries – some 3,000+ European Customs offices.

The UK, in common with many other participating countries, is using the Minimal Common Core (MCC) software developed by the European Commission, which provides all of the basic data capture and messaging functionality for effective connection to the European network. It is important to note that UK NCTS is a completely separate system from Customs Handling of Import and Export Freight (CHIEF) (see below) and is not interconnected to it in any way, and separate declarations for transit will continue to be required. Again, it is expected that the UK NCTS will cease to be available to be used by UK exporters, who should try to keep fully up to date as proposed changes are announced.

Customs Handling of Import and Export Freight

CHIEF is one of the largest Customs declaration processing systems in the world, providing a sound technological platform for Customs & Excise and international trade. Its sophisticated computer software controls and records the UK's international trade movements, whether by land, sea or air, and links with several thousand businesses. It uses the latest technology and is designed to cope with continuous growth in international trade. While it enhances Customs & Excise control of imports and exports, it is also claimed to improve the service provided to the international trade community and reduce overall administrative costs.

CHIEF is now being replaced by a system known as the Customs Declaration Service (CDS). However, HMRC state that everything currently done by CHIEF will continue to be done by CDS although there will be some changes. These include the fact that CDS needs to be accessed from the GOV.UK website using a Government Gateway account and that CDS offers a single access point for a wider range of services and also offers guides and online help.

In order to offer the increased range of services additional information will be required for some declarations in order to align with the World Customs Organization requirements to which the UK is committed.

The additional information includes:

- location of goods identification (based on UNLOCODE);
- the warehouse type code list;
- item tax lines, including method of payment codes;
- unit of quantity codes (ISO);
- the way customs procedures are quoted;
- the number of items on a declaration – CDS allows a maximum of 999 items on a customs declaration instead of the 99 items on CHIEF.

CDS has been tested, especially with Community System Providers (CSPs) as CSPs operate computerized inventory systems that control the physical movement of import and export freight at UK ports and airports. It was originally hoped for CDS to be fully functioning by the end of 2019 but the actual date has been put back. Progress on CDS can be monitored by registering for the HMRC Business Help and Education email service, where CDS updates can be found 'trading with other countries'. Progress reports are also available through different trade associations.

Further details of the extensive CT procedures can be found in *The Transit Manual* on the European Commission website at http://ec.europa.eu/taxation_customs/sites/taxation/files/transit_manual_en.pdf (archived at https://perma.cc/WNG3-YTBP) or customs.bg/wps/portal/3165/ (archived at https://perma.cc/24AK-FUCG) for information for freight forwarders.

Information on UK Customs procedures and a UK supplement to *The Transit Manual* can be found on the GOV.UK website and international hauliers and operators need to ensure that they get up to the minute information on any new requirements to avoid delays registering for new procedures or having paperwork delayed or returned due to errors being made.

The TIR Convention

The TIR Convention system applies to road journeys to all countries (except for journeys between member states of the EU and EFTA made by EU and EFTA operators) which are party to the Convention but only where the haulier elects to conform to the Convention's requirements. TIR is being seen as a good 'backstop' for UK hauliers to use post-Brexit in order to reduce delays at borders as it is a UNECE Convention and not an EU Convention and it is expected that many UK operators will select TIR as a preferred way forward post-Brexit.

Under the Customs Convention on the International Transport of Goods by Road (TIR Carnets) 1959, to which the UK is party, goods in Customs-sealed vehicles or containers may travel through intermediate countries en route to their final destination with the minimum of Customs formalities provided a TIR Carnet has been issued in respect of the journey (UK vehicles may currently operate on international haulage journeys outside the EU without the protection of TIR but in this case they will be subject to the full weight of Customs formality and bureaucracy (and delay) at each border crossing and on arrival at destination – see also below).

The Carnet is a recognized international Customs document intended purely to simplify Customs procedures; it is not a substitute for other documents, nor is it mandatory for any operator to use it; it does not give any operator the right to run vehicles in any European country. Use of a Carnet frees the operator from the need to place a deposit of duty in respect of the load he is carrying in each country through which the vehicle is to pass.

The issuing authorities for the Carnets (in this country the FTA and the RHA – see Appendix I for addresses) act as guarantors on behalf of the IRU (International Road Transport Union) – the international guarantor, and for this reason Carnets are issued only to bona fide members of these two associations.

Goods may only be carried under a TIR Carnet provided the vehicle in which they are carried has been specifically approved by the Driver and Vehicle Services Agency (DVSA). This means complying with constructional requirements so that the load-carrying space can be sealed by Customs, after which it must not be possible for any goods to be removed from or added to the load without the seals being broken, and there must be no concealed spaces where goods may be hidden.

Detailed requirements are laid down concerning the structure of the body, particularly regarding the manner in which it is assembled, so that there is no possibility of panels being removed by releasing nuts and bolts and so on. The manner in which doors and roller shutters are secured must also meet stringent specifications. Sheeted vehicles or containers may be used provided conditions relating to the construction of the sheet are observed and as long as when the closing device has been secured it becomes impossible to gain access to the load without leaving obvious traces.

The DVSA examines vehicles (by appointment at Goods Vehicle Test Stations) to ensure that they meet the technical requirements for operation under the TIR Convention and issues a certificate of approval (GV 60), which must be renewed every two years and must be carried on the vehicle when it is operating under a TIR Carnet. This point is particularly important as Customs authorities carry out checks on vehicles leaving the UK to ensure that this certificate is being carried where necessary.

Application for TIR Certification

Application for the examination of vehicles or containers must be made as early as possible and in any case not less than one month before inspection is required. The application form (GV62) can be downloaded from the GOV.UK website. The application should be forwarded to the Test Station for the area in which the vehicle is available for inspection and postage must be prepaid. A separate application must be submitted for each vehicle/trailer.

If there is a GV60 test certificate already in existence that simply requires renewing, has not been laminated over and has photographs of the vehicle in its current livery and condition, no photographs are required. If it is a first test or otherwise does not qualify for the above, two 'Polaroid' or similar colour photographs approximately 75 mm (3″) square should be provided of the vehicle in its current livery, one showing the front and one side of the vehicle and another showing the rear and the other side. These will be glued to the certificate and endorsed by the station as accurately portraying the vehicle. Digital photographs are acceptable provided they are of good resolution and are printed on photograph paper. If a TIR-approved vehicle is sold to another operator, the TIR certificate (form GV60) is not transferable and the new owner must have the vehicle re-certified if he wishes to use it for TIR operations.

The fee for examination of a vehicle for TIR purposes is £106.00, unless it is not of a previously approved TIR design type, in which case the fee is £644.00. The fee for a TIR certificate is £14.00. For a re-inspection of a failed vehicle, the fee is £70.00.

TIR Plates

When a vehicle has been approved it must display at the front and the rear a plate showing the letters 'TIR' in white on a blue background. Such plates are obtainable from the FTA and RHA. They should be removed or covered when the vehicle is no longer operating under TIR.

NB: The UK authorities are aware of the likely increase in vehicles applying for TIR status and state that they have taken steps to increase inspection and testing facilities and capability.

TIR Carnets

TIR Carnets are internationally recognized Customs documents. Carnets are in pairs and have counterfoils in a bound cover. They are in four parts and contain 6, 14 or 20 pages (ie *volets* in French). A six-page Carnet is valid only for a journey between the UK and one other country. Journeys to more than one other country require 14- or 20-page Carnets, which are valid for two months and three months respectively. A Carnet covers only one load and if a return load is to be collected, a separate Carnet is needed (each individual voucher covers one frontier crossing) and the driver should take this with him on the outward journey. At each Customs point en route a voucher is detached and the counterfoil is stamped. Careful attention must be paid to the completion of the Carnet if delays and difficulties are to be avoided during the journey.

Carnets are valid for limited periods only (see above), and if not used they must be returned to the issuing authority for cancellation. Those which are used and which bear all the official stampings acquired en route must also be returned within 10 days of the vehicle's return.

Strict instructions regarding the use of Carnets are supplied by the issuing authorities for both the operator and the driver. For example, the driver should never leave the Carnet with any Customs authority without first obtaining a signed, stamped and dated declaration quoting the Carnet number and certifying that the goods on the vehicle conform with the details contained in the Carnet. Drivers should also ensure that the Customs officials at each departure office, transit office and arrival office take out a voucher from the Carnet and stamp and sign the counterfoil accordingly.

The four parts of the Carnet comprise the following:

1. Details of the issuing authority, the Carnet holder, the country of departure, the country of destination, the vehicle, the weight and the value of the goods as shown in the manifest (see 3 below).
2. A declaration that the goods specified have been loaded for the country stated, that they will be carried to their destination with the Customs seals intact and that the Customs regulations of the countries through which the goods are to be carried will be observed.
3. A goods manifest giving precise details of the goods, the way in which they are packed (the number of parcels or cartons) and their value.
4. Vouchers which Customs officials at frontier posts will remove, stamping the counterfoil section which remains in the Carnet.

Before obtaining a Carnet the applicant must sign a form of contract with the issuing authority, agreeing to abide by all the necessary legal and administrative requirements. A financial guarantee is required to ensure that any claims which may be made against the applicant will be met. The FTA and RHA both act as guarantors for members.

Seal Breakage

If a Customs seal on a TIR vehicle is broken during transit as a result of an accident or for any other reason, Customs or the police must be contacted immediately to endorse the Carnet to this effect and to re-seal the vehicle and, if required, amend the load documentation.

Non-TIR Journeys

Goods may be sent abroad in vehicles without TIR cover and no Carnet is required. In this case, however, it is necessary to comply with the individual Customs requirements of each country through which the vehicle passes. A guarantee in lieu of import duty, or a deposit against such duty, will have to be paid before the vehicle is allowed to enter the country to which it is travelling, or any country through which it needs to pass, and the vehicle will be subject to stringent Customs scrutiny not only at the port of exit from the UK and the port of entry to the Continent, but at all further frontier crossings during the journey.

Further information is available on the TIR website at: www.unece.org (archived at https://perma.cc/TMY4-6E33).

The ADR Agreement

When dangerous goods are transported on international road journeys the provisions apply of the European Agreement concerning the International Carriage of Dangerous Goods (the ADR Convention). The current edition is that for 2019. The ADR is normally updated annually or bi-annually. This is a long and complex document contained in two large volumes (details are: ECE/TRANS/242, Vol I and II (ADR 2019)). However, for most general purposes, if the reader refers to the provisions of our dangerous goods legislation in Chapter 20 of this *Handbook* he will find all the information he needs, since UK rules are based on the international ADR requirements.

Carnets de Passage en Douane

Most countries to which vehicles are likely to travel permit the temporary importation and re-exportation of foreign vehicles and containers (not to be confused with the loads they carry) free of duty or deposit and without guaranteed Customs documents.

However, a Customs document known as a *Carnet de Passage en Douane* is required for vehicles and trailers intending to transit or visit most countries in the Middle East.

Where *Carnets de Passage* are needed for travel they can be obtained from the Royal Automobile Club (RAC) and the Royal Scottish Automobile Club (RSAC).

ATA Carnets

Goods that are being imported only temporarily into certain countries, such as samples, professional equipment and items for display at exhibitions and fairs, and which, eventually, will be returned to the UK can be moved, and will be allowed to be moved post-Brexit, under an international Customs clearance document known as an ATA Carnet. These documents, valid for 12 months from the date of issue, are issued by chambers of commerce to members without the need for payments of, or deposits against, duty. They can be used any number of times provided that the same goods are carried. It should be noted, however, that holding an ATA Carnet does not relieve the operator from observing Customs requirements in each individual country.

Further information is available at the following website: www.londonchamber.co.uk (archived at https://perma.cc/5MYX-TKN5).

'De Suivi' Document

Drivers of UK haulage and own-account vehicles entering France must be able to produce a 'de suivi' document in addition to the normal CMR or own-account consignment note.

There is no official or formal layout for this additional document, it being left to operators to determine how they present the relevant information which can be added to the existing CMR document if space permits. The relevant information required is as follows:

- date the consignment was drawn up;
- transport operator's name and address;
- transport operator's VAT number;
- date when goods were taken into charge;
- nature, weight and volume of goods;
- name of the consignor;
- address of loading point;
- name of consignee;
- address of unloading point.

Space must be provided on the note for entering of the following information:

- time of vehicle arrival at loading point;
- time of departure of loaded vehicle;
- required time of arrival at destination.

A separate document must also be made out to show:

- date and time of arrival at destination;
- date and time of departure of unloaded vehicle.

On all international journeys the driver must (or should) also carry a further document showing the relationship between the transport operator and the driver (ie whether he is a direct employee, an owner-driver or an employee of a sub-contractor). This is known as a letter of authorization and should be on company headed paper and signed by a senior manager or director in order to prove to any enforcement staff that the driver is authorized by the company to drive the vehicle on the journey concerned.

NB: Some EU member states are now also calling for drivers of foreign registered vehicles to provide proof that they are paid at a rate which exceeds the minimum wage in the member state concerned. This is becoming the norm for countries such as France, Austria, the Netherlands and Germany and appears to be gaining popularity across several other EU member states. The German authorities only require this information if the vehicle is either delivering or collecting within the country and not if the vehicle is simply in transit.

Road Tolls

The Austrian 'Maut' System

The former Austrian Eco-points system described in some earlier editions of this *Handbook* has been completely abolished and replaced by a new 'Maut' (toll) 'per mile' system for trucks over 3.5 tonnes gross weight similar in concept to the German LKW-Maut system mentioned below. This system is based on day and night charges and varies according to certain zones within the country. The previous Austrian 'Vignette' sticker system has also been replaced. The system requires relevant vehicles to be fitted with an easy-to-install DSRC-TAG electronic (microwave) transponder, colloquially called a 'GO-Box', and payment is via the internet (www.go-maut.at (archived at https://perma.cc/2LZT-XAC5)) or at point-of-sale terminals, located mainly at roadside fuel-filling stations.

All 2,000 km of Austria's motorways are wired for DSRC (short-range electronic tolling) to operate the nationwide toll system, which is achieved with the aid of an electronic transponder or by off-road payment, normally by internet or at one of 200-odd point-of-sale terminals, mostly located at fuel-filling stations. When paying the toll the truck driver enters his registration number, which is recorded on a list of payers. When the vehicle is seen on the road by cameras mounted on some 400 overhead gantries, it is matched against the so-called 'white' payment list.

A higher toll rate is charged for use of a number of special road sections on the A9, A10, A11, A13 (the Brenner Pass) and A16 motorways. VAT at the local rate is added to the tolls.

The German LKW-Maut System

Germany's distance-based LKW-Maut road toll system, operated by Toll Collect, changed in 2019. It now applies to all trucks, domestic and foreign, of 7.5 tonnes gross weight and above. It was also expanded so that from 1 July 2018 the toll system now covers all federal trunk roads.

TABLE 26.1

Tariff group	Category 2 2 axles		Category 3 3 axles		Category 4+ 4 & more axles	
	Day	Night*	Day	Night*	Day	Night*
A EURO emission class EURO VI	0.18820	0.18860	0.26411	0.26503	0.39443	0.39559
B EURO emission classes EURO V and EEV	0.20240	0.20280	0.28399	0.28491	0.41875	0.41991
C EURO emission class EURO IV	0.20870	0.20910	0.29281	0.29373	0.42883	0.42999
D EURO emission classes EURO 0 to III	0.22870	0.22910	0.32081	0.32173	0.46083	0.46199

Prices in euros per kilometre, excluding 20 per cent VAT.
* The night tariff applies between 2200 and 0500.

Toll payments can be made in several alternative ways as follows:

- LogPay plan (direct debit);
- Road Account;
- fuel card payment;
- credit account payment;
- EC card payment;
- credit card payment;
- cash payment.

The charges for 2020 remain at 2019 levels and will not rise until December 2020.

The total cost is broken down into infrastructure, pollution and noise. Details are below:

Infrastructure

GVW 7.5 t–12 t	8.0 cents per km
GVW 12 t–18 t	11.5 cents per km
GVW less than 4 axles and less than 18 t	16.0 cents per km
GVW with more than 4 axles and more than 18 t	17.4 cents per km

Pollution

Euro 0, 1	8.5 cents per km
Euro 2	7.4 cents per km
Euro 3	6.4 cents per km
Euro 4	3.2 cents per km
Euro 5	2.2 cents per km
Euro 6	1.1 cent per km

Noise

0.2 cents per km for all vehicles.

Eurovignettes

Motorway charges (ie tax) must be paid (in accordance with EC Directive 1999/62 EC – the so-called Eurovignette Directive) for goods vehicles of 12 tonnes maximum weight and over, including those towing trailers where the combined maximum weight is 12 tonnes or more, when travelling in or through the Netherlands, Luxembourg, Denmark and Sweden. The tax is charged in euros (a), payable in advance, and is based on a sliding scale according to the pollution emission rating of the vehicle engine (ie Euro-0, Euro-I or Euro-II/III – see Chapter 11), the number of axles and the amount of time during which the motorways will be used (eg day, week, month, etc), as per the following table. Payment covers journeys in all four countries.

Eurovignette charges in euros apply as follows:

TABLE 26.2

Annual tariff emission group	1–3 axles	4 or more axles
Euro 0	1,407.00	2,359.00
Euro 1	1,223.00	2,042.00
Euro 2	1,065.00	1,776.00
Euro 3	926.00	1,543.00
Euro 4	842.00	1,404.00
Euro 5	750.00	1,250.00
Euro 6	750.00	1,250.00
Monthly tariff emission group	**1–3 axles**	**4 or more axles**
Euro 0	140.00	235.00
Euro 1	122.00	204.00
Euro 2	106.00	177.00
Euro 3	92.00	154.00
Euro 4	84.00	140.00
Euro 5	75.00	125.00
Euro 6	75.00	125.00
Weekly tariff emission group	**1–3 axles**	**4 or more axles**
Euro 0	37.00	62.00
Euro 1	32.00	54.00
Euro 2	28.00	47.00
Euro 3	24.00	41.00
Euro 4	22.00	37.00
Euro 5	20.00	33.00
Euro 6	20.00	33.00

TABLE 26.2 *continued*

Daily tariff emission group	1–3 axles	4 or more axles
Euro 0	12.00	12.00
Euro 1	12.00	12.00
Euro 2	12.00	12.00
Euro 3	12.00	12.00
Euro 4	12.00	12.00
Euro 5	12.00	12.00
Euro 6	12.00	12.00

These fees are set to rise again in early 2020 but these are the latest available at the time of writing.

When the tax is paid, a certificate/receipt called a Eurovignette is issued, showing the vehicle registration number, the date and period of validity, and the amount paid. The Eurovignette must be carried on the vehicle at all times as proof of payment. Failure to obtain a Eurovignette or to be able to produce it on request can result in a fine of up to £5,000.

Eurovignettes should be purchased online by going to the Eurovignette home website (www.eurovignettes.eu (archived at https://perma.cc/57SM-WMC3)) and following a link to 'AGES', the service provider responsible for selling Eurovignettes.

Other Motorway Tolls in Europe

Belgium has now left the Eurovignette scheme and from 1 April 2016 all goods vehicles over 3,500 kg gvw travelling in Belgium need to have an On Board Unit (OBU) which operates through a system using ANPR cameras and mobile enforcement. Penalties of up to €1,000 can be levied for non-compliance and drivers without OBUs can be made to obtain one within three hours. The toll charges are based on the gross weight of the vehicle, the vehicle's emissions and the type of road.

Hungary introduced in 2008 an electronic payment toll system for trucks weighing more than 7.5 tonnes on all its main roads (mostly trans-border routes). France, too, has an e-Toll system ('TIS PL') for trucks over 3.5 tonnes using its motorways, with automatic billing via an electronic box system. The TIS PL system in France is also valid for use on Spanish motorways by some LGVs. Contact www.servitir.co.uk (archived at https://perma.cc/DYG5-VEQE) for more details. However, use of the system is not compulsory, although frequent users who sign up to the system will be eligible for rebates.

In 2014, the French Government introduced an HGV transit tax. This tax, called the '*peage de transit poids lourds*', is charged on major transit routes that carry more than 2,500 lorries a day and is applied to vehicles exceeding 3,500 kg.

In January 2015 the Norwegian Government replaced their Autopass system with a new device known as a 'bar-tag'. It is required by vehicles over 3.5 tonnes and applies to most of the roads in Norway and not just the main routes. It was introduced in order to counter non-payment of tolls on the primary routes.

There are also automated billing arrangements across most of the EU, including Autopass in Italy and even the Heavy Goods Vehicle Road User Levy and some estuarial crossing charges in the UK and péage, autobahn and Autostrada charges throughout Europe and so it is important that when travelling abroad to check the requirements for every country you may want to enter or transit.

European Lorry Bans

Many European countries impose restrictions on the movement of goods vehicles on certain routes and at certain times. Usually these apply at weekends, during public and annual holiday times, at religious or traditional festival times, and when and where severe weather conditions may be expected. Some countries also restrict the movement of some hazardous goods in some urban areas and through some road tunnels. Severe penalties may be imposed on drivers who flout these restrictions. Operators are advised to check the current position via the internet or with the RHA or the FTA before scheduling vehicles for weekend and holiday working.

Environmental Plaques on Heavy Lorries

The International Transport Forum European Conference of Ministers of Transport (ITF/ECMT) scheme (see above), for the issue of multilateral quota road haulage permits, allows for an additional quota of permits for those countries participating in the so-called 'green lorry' scheme. In order to gain the additional quota the vehicles used on ECMT multilateral permit journeys must comply with specified minimum standards for noise emissions and chemical exhaust emissions for diesel engines as well as certain other safety requirements. Compliance with these standards is confirmed by the issue of an environmental certificate of conformity, which must be carried on the vehicles during relevant journeys, and by the display of an environmental plaque – usually stuck in a prominent place on the vehicle front bumper or cab front. These plaques and certificates indicate to the relevant authorities, while in cross-border and internal transit, that the vehicle in question meets ECMT standards for either 'green' or 'greener and safe' lorries with Euro-IV, V or VI specification engines. The plaques are green with white numbers and need to be circular and 200 mm diameter with a 20 mm white border.

These requirements are set out in the ECMT's document *Guide for Government Officials and Carriers on the Use of the ECMT Multilateral Quota*. UK operators granted ECMT permits may need to display these once the UK leaves the EU, but this is yet another issue that remains unresolved.

Austria and Germany also have their own certification and vehicle plaques relating to low noise as follows:

- 'L' – denoting *Lärmarm Fahrzeug* (ie low-noise vehicle): Austrian version of the symbol for 'quiet' diesel vehicles, which are:

  - small and medium-sized lorries of no more than 150 kW producing noise levels no greater than 78 dB; and
  - heavy lorries exceeding 150 kW with noise levels no greater than 80 dB.
- 'G' – denoting *Geräuscharm Fahrzeug* (ie noiseless/quiet vehicle): German version of the Austrian 'L' plate for use only on diesel vehicles meeting German low-noise requirements – similar to those for Austria as above.

Other Vehicle Markers

In some European countries, particularly Germany and Austria for example, vehicles may also be seen displaying other plaques such as the following:

- 'A' – required in Germany on all vehicles carrying waste;
- 'K' – required in Germany for vehicles making use of exceptions to the Motor Tax Law.

In Italy the following plaques (displayed on the rear and on both sides of the vehicle) are used to indicate vehicles carrying special products and which are therefore exempt from weekend driving bans as follows:

- 'a' – for vehicles carrying easily perishable foodstuffs;
- 'd' – for vehicles carrying milk.

In Austria, three plaques are used to indicate vehicles that have had their maximum weight modified under certain conditions:

- 'R' – for vehicles authorized for use only on special routes;
- 'H' – for vehicles that have had their maximum permissible weight increased;
- 'E' – for vehicles that have had their maximum permissible weight reduced.

Miscellaneous Requirements

Trailer Registration and Certification

UK international road hauliers travelling to the EU now need to ensure that commercial trailers over 750 kg and all trailers over 3,500 kg are registered with their own registration number plate consisting of one alpha and seven numeric figures if they are to travel to Europe and that a trailer 'MoT' type certificate is gained to prove the trailer has a valid annual test. This requirement enables the UK to comply with the Vienna Convention on Road Traffic 1968. Registration can be done online and the certificates confirming registration sent by post.

Registration details required will include the operators details, trailer manufacturer, VIN/chassis number, GVW and ULW and, once registered, any change in ownership will need to be declared.

Costs are £26.00 for first time registration, £21.00 for subsequent registrations and there is a £10.00 administration charge for a replacement certificate.

The physical plates must be displayed at the rear of the trailer, although they do not have to be lit. They do, however, need to be in a set format. This requires the plate to have one letter and seven figures (for example B2345678). In addition, the number plate of the drawing vehicle is also still required on the rear of the trailer and this must be lit.

Something that may be a problem is the fact that the paper registration document must travel with the trailer. This may certainly be a problem with unaccompanied trailers, not least because security and weather-proofing may both be issues.

The requirements for specific countries countries will almost certainly change over the coming 12 months but, as Brexit is still not confirmed in any formal format, actual changes are, as yet, unknown.

Austria

In 2017 Austria introduced a requirement for drivers carrying out cabotage operations within that country to produce proof that they are in receipt of wages at least equal to those set by the Austrian minimum wage levels. This requirement has now also become a frequent requirement in France and Germany (see below for both countries).

France

Speed-limit offenders in France face instant loss of their driving licence if they exceed statutory limits by more than 40 kph (ie approximately 25 mph). Heavy vehicles in France are restricted to 90 kph (ie approx 56 mph) on motorways, 80 kph (ie approx 50 mph) on dual carriageways, 80 kph on country roads (only 60 kph, ie 37 mph, for vehicles drawing trailers) and 50 kph (ie approx 31 mph) in built-up areas.

NB: Many péage systems in France and other EU member states actually time the vehicle between ticket issue and pay points and, where the vehicle arrives at a pay point and it must have exceeded the speed limit in order to arrive so quickly, on the spot fines can be levied.

Drivers travelling to or through France must carry either:

- a copy of their contract of employment with their current employer;
- a letter of engagement from their employer (attestation of employment); or
- a valid recent (ie their last) payslip.

Operators also need to provide details of the carbon used in the supply of the goods to their customers as part of the French 'Carbon Reporting Scheme'. In addition, the French authorities are trying to enforce proof of minimum wage requirements and are enforcing this by fines of up to €4,000 for drivers not able to produce the required evidence. Failure to pay these fines results in the driver being banned from driving in France. France is also enforcing a ban on drivers wearing any earpiece that is capable of emitting sound. There is also some concern as France is trying to stop foreign truck drivers from taking their weekly rest in the cab of the vehicle. This is supposedly being challenged but there are likely to be changes to weekly rest requirements throughout the EU in the near future.

Germany

The German authorities require the drivers of small goods vehicles between 2,800 and 3,500 kg to keep driver's record books. In addition, there is also a new requirement for all drivers delivering goods to Germany (not in transit through Germany) to carry evidence that they are being paid at least at the same rate as the German national minimum wage. Books are available through the UK trade associations, if required.

Netherlands

If the authorities in the Netherlands require proof that a UK driver's earnings exceed the Netherlands minimum wage level they contact the driver's employer for this information and do not ask the driver themselves for documentary evidence.

Impounding in Italy

The Italian authorities are strict on law compliance and increasingly use vehicle impounding as a means of penalty for infringements – sometimes holding vehicles for as long as three months even for relatively minor infringements, according to FTA reports.

Attestation of Activities

UK LGV drivers, particularly on international journeys, may be asked to provide evidence of their activities that are not covered by a valid tachograph record. For this purpose the EU has devised an official form of activity attestation (not to be confused with a driver's employment attestation – see below). However, this form was required under EEC Regulation 3821/85 which has now been superseded by Regulation EU 165/2014. In Regulation 165/2014 there is no requirement to use a letter of attestation for activities although drivers are still expected to produce records of their activities to the authorities. Until such time that the EU or D*f*T produces an acceptable replacement form it seems logical for UK operators to continue to use the old-style letters of attestation in order for the driver to be able to provide a record of the past 28 days of activity. A version of this form should be completed by the employer and issued to drivers on such journeys. A typical form is illustrated opposite and other copies can be downloaded from the United Road Transport Union (URTU)'s website at: www.urtu.com (archived at https://perma.cc/8P9E-VV6S).

Attestation (2)

LGV drivers who are non-EU nationals employed to drive EU-owned and EU-based vehicles are required to carry a letter of attestation affirming their employment status as required under EU Regulation 1072/2009/EC. The purpose of this document (commonly referred to as the 'third country' attestation) certifies that the driver of a

ATTESTATION OF ACTIVITIES UNDER REGULATION (EC) NO 561/2006
OR
THE EUROPEAN AGREEMENT CONCERNING THE WORK OF CREWS OF VEHICLES ENGAGED IN INTERNATIONAL ROAD TRANSPORT (AETR) (*)

To be filled in by typing and signed before a journey
To be kept with the original tachograph records wherever they are required to be kept
False attestations constitute an infringement

1 Name of the undertaking: ______

2 Street address, postal code, city, country: ______, ______, ______, ______

3 Telephone number (including international prefix): ______

4 Fax number (including international prefix): ______

5 Email address: ______

I, the undersigned

6 Name: ______________

7 Position in the undertaking: ______

declare that the driver

8 Name: ______________

9 Date of birth: ______

10 Driving licence number or identity card number or passport number: ____________

for the period

11 from (time-day-month-year) ______-______-______-______

12 to (time-day-month-year) ______-______-______-______

13 ☐ was on sick leave (**)

14 ☐ was on annual leave (**)

15 ☐ drove a vehicle exempted from the scope of Regulation (EC) No 561/2006 or AETR (**)

16 For the undertaking, place ______date ______signature ____________

17 I, the driver, confirm that I have not been driving a vehicle falling under the scope of Regulation (EC) No 561/2006 or AETR during the period mentioned above.

18 Place ______date ______Signature of the driver ______________

(*) This form is available in an electronic and printable version on the internet at ec.europa.eu.

(**) Only one of the boxes 13, 14 or 15 may be chosen.

vehicle carrying out road haulage operations between member states is either 'lawfully employed by the EU transport operator concerned in the member state in which the operator is established, or is lawfully placed at the disposal of that operator.' Normally, it should be accompanied by a valid and current work visa or permit for the individual driver.

Drink-Driving Limits

Drivers are warned that while the English and Welsh drink-driving (ie blood-alcohol level) limit at 80 mg per 100 ml of blood (ie 0.08 per cent breath alcohol content (BAC)) may appear to be strict, the limits in many other European countries are as strict or even stricter, as the following list for professional drivers indicates:

- 0 mg – Estonia, Lithuania, Romania, Slovakia, Czech Republic, Hungary (this means zero tolerance);
- 20 mg (0.02 per cent) – Croatia, Norway, Poland, Sweden;
- 50 mg (0.05 per cent) – Belgium, Bulgaria, Denmark, Germany (Germany is 30 mg (0.03 per cent) if you're in an accident), Finland, France, Greece, Italy, Scotland, Serbia/Montenegro, Latvia, Macedonia, Netherlands, Austria, Portugal, Slovenia, Spain, Turkey, Cyprus (North);
- 80 mg (0.08 per cent) – England, Ireland, Luxembourg, Malta, Switzerland, Wales;
- 90 mg (0.09 per cent) – Cyprus (South).

Under legislation introduced in the Scottish Parliament a reduced drink-drive limit came into effect in Scotland from 5 December 2014, bringing Scotland into line with most other European countries. The Northern Ireland Assembly was also considering reducing the blood alcohol limit in Northern Ireland to 50 mg in every 100 ml of blood as part of proposals contained in the Road Traffic (Amendment) Bill; subject to the legislative process and the Assembly being re-convened, this did not become law as planned and the blood alcohol limit remains at 80 mg per 100 ml of blood in the Province. The legal limit in the rest of England and Wales also remains 80 mg per 100 ml of blood.

NB: Lower limits apply in some countries to new drivers and those found well above the limits can expect to be dealt with very severely.

From 1 July 2012 it has been a legal requirement in France that drivers of all vehicles (except mopeds) carry an unused French-approved NF personal-use breathalyser kit which should be available for inspection at roadside checks by the gendarmerie – ideally drivers should carry two such kits in case one has to be used. However, although the legislation still exists there is now no fine if they are not carried. This anomalous situation came about following a change of government in France which saw the requirement remain but the fine disappear.

If these kits are carried out, they should be calibrated to read BAC of 0.02 per cent for professional drivers (ie of LGVs, PSVs and taxis) and 0.05 per cent for other drivers.

More information on safe driving in Europe can be found on the Safe Travel website at: http://www.safetravel.co.uk (archived at https://perma.cc/3856-JM2B).

Driver Health Cover Abroad

Drivers engaged on international journeys should carry their own personal European Health Insurance Card (EHIC) to provide cover for any medical treatment required as a result of accident or illness while in any European Economic Area country. The card (which replaced the former E111 document) is obtainable free of charge from the NHS and can be applied for on the internet – just enter EHIC in the Google search facility. The card enables holders to obtain some free emergency medical attention from state-run hospitals and medical centres on the same basis as the local populace. However, changes to the system introduced in 2014 mean that EHIC holders will now not be able to claim a full refund for services termed 'patient contributions' or 'co-payments'. These types of services include things like a consultation with a GP or dentist and stays in hospital. In these cases only a partial refund will now be made. In addition it should be noted that the EHIC does not cover:

- treatment in private medical facilities abroad;
- repatriation when the patient is well enough to travel;
- the cost of recovering the vehicle;
- the cost of hospital visits by relatives;
- the costs of funeral transport from abroad.

All these additional items, if required, should be covered by private medical insurance taken out by the driver or his employer.

The position of EHIC post-Brexit depends very much on the terms of Brexit. What is most likely is that if the UK leaves the EU with a deal then the UK EHIC will continue to be valid at least until 31 December 2020. If there is no deal then the UK EHIC 'could' be invalid right across the EU or it 'could' be accepted by some individual member states, from the date of our departure.

Single European Emergency (Phone) Number 112

Lorry and coach drivers on international journeys are advised that using this telephone number will provide them with a rapid and effective response in case of a road accident. In the UK either 999 or 112 will alert the emergency services.

The number can be dialled from fixed and mobile phones free of charge throughout the EU. Calls are answered by an operator who will handle the request either directly or by transferring it to the appropriate emergency service.

This 24 hour emergency number 112 is said to constitute a very efficient tool to further improve road safety, security and the efficiency of response in emergency cases.

Intermodal Freight Transport

27

Intermodal freighting is a form of transport operation in which two or more individual transport modes are used in combination (such as road and rail, or road and inland waterway) to form an integrated transport chain. Principally, the concept is intended to achieve more operationally efficient and cost-effective delivery of goods in an environmentally sustainable manner from their point of origin to their final destination.

In recent years, the concept of intermodal freight transport and, indeed, the wider concept of multi-modalism, have become of increasing interest to the UK road haulage industry and freight shippers in general. Some of this interest has been generated by the UK's decision to leave the EU and the subsequent issues surrounding permit application and permit allowances along with much heralded publicity and media activity (at times unjustified) aimed at emphasising potential delays at ports.

This interest is also being driven forward by a number of other key incentives as follows:

- government pressure to remove heavy freight traffic from the roads and onto rail and inland waterways;
- to effect a reduction in road traffic congestion and road accidents;
- to reduce the consumption of scarce fossil fuels;
- to reduce adverse environmental pollution caused by vehicle exhaust emissions and noise;
- to reduce the volume of dangerous and hazardous goods travelling by road;
- to counter growing resistance by local authorities and the general public aimed at reducing the numbers of goods vehicles, especially large goods vehicles, operating in the urban environment.

In addition, the D*f*T supports the shift away from road to rail and water transport through the Mode Shift Revenue Support (MSRS) scheme, which has now been approved to run until 2020 and provides a sliding scale of grants for moving containers around the UK, and the Waterborne Freight Grant (WFG) scheme which provides grants for using coastal and short-sea shipping where to do so is more expensive than using road. This scheme has also been extended to 2020. Details of these grants are available on the GOV.UK website. What is as yet unclear is whether or not these schemes will be extended due to the delayed implementation of Brexit.

It is worthy of note that goods in containers are currently outside of the road permit schemes and do not require permits. Moving goods in containers may well be an attractive option for organizations moving goods internationally to the EU in the future.

Intermodalism is far from a new idea; in fact, freight containers of wooden construction were being transferred to and from horse-drawn wagons onto rail as long ago as the late 1800s. However, the 1994 Report of the Royal Commission on Environmental Pollution, *Transport and the Environment*, determined that an important objective for a sustainable transport policy must be founded on the concept of increasing 'the proportions of... freight transport [carried] by environmentally less damaging modes and to make the best use of existing infrastructure'.

The Report effectively warned that the likely consequences of taking more and more land to provide new infrastructure to cope with the forecast massive growth in road use could not be sustainable, so alternatives had to be devised and developed. It highlighted the fact that the projected growth of heavy goods vehicle traffic between 1989 (when the National Road Traffic Forecasts were made) and 2025 was no less than 140 per cent and it concluded that even with a large-scale shift to rail, road transport would remain the dominant mode for freight transport and therefore it was important to explore all possible ways of limiting its adverse environmental impact.

In 1998 a 'new approach' was adopted with publication by the D*f*T of its White Paper *A New Deal for Transport: Better for Everyone*, signalling that the Government was looking for a radical change in transport – in particular, seeking to achieve a more integrated transport system to tackle the growing problems of congestion and pollution. Prior to publication of this White Paper, a number of other key documents set out the Government's strategies for overcoming the adverse effects of the motor vehicle – especially the heavy lorry – on our lives.

While some freight movements may use, and justify the use of, a number of different transport modes such as road and rail, or road and inland waterway or either short-sea or deep-sea shipping, thus making them multi-modal operations, in the majority of instances efficient movements are invariably achieved by the use of just two modes: most commonly road haulage collection and final delivery journeys combined with a rail freight trunk-haul journey in what is commonly known as a 'combined road–rail' operation, with the Channel Tunnel rail service carrying over 1,301,460 metric tonnes of freight in 2018. However, where operational circumstances dictate or a feasible alternative option is available, road haulage or rail freighting may be combined instead with an inland waterway journey via river or canal or with a short-sea shipping operation – typically a coastal or a cross-Channel sailing.

Combined transport operations involving either road haulage or rail freight in conjunction with deep-sea container services or with an airfreight operation also feature in intermodal and multi-modal scenarios. Whilst moving freight by air has been seen as a relatively small sector of the transport industry, it is expanding rapidly with the growth of regional airports, the need to move goods rapidly, the drive for retail chains to reduce level of inventory, more fuel-efficient aircraft and congestion on the road network.

Determining the choice of mode or modes to be used depends on circumstances; sometimes cost alone will be the deciding factor, but frequently other considerations are decisive. For instance, operational practicalities like frequency of service, speed of delivery, the availability of special handling facilities, the ability to meet particular packaging requirements, security considerations or the sheer volumes of freight to be moved may be a factor or indeed it may be that a number of these various service 'pluses', in combination, produce the ideal solution. But other less tangible issues may also enter the equation such as the need to follow corporate environmental policies, company image, carbon trading, or to assuage a shipper's social conscience.

Freighting by intermodal or multi-modal combinations is the alternative to consigning loads for the whole of their journey by a single mode – as is the case with some 78 per cent of domestic freight moved in Great Britain (according to the D*f*T's *Transport Statistics for Great Britain 2018*) being transported by road (with rail, air and sea freight figures falling). It is a fact that the haulage of goods by road from their source direct to their final destination remains the preferred method in the majority of cases, and it is this preference that individuals, corporate bodies and Government departments alike who champion the cause of intermodal transport are trying to break down. It must also be noted that the figure of 78 per cent does fluctuate and that the proportion moved by foreign vehicles continues to rise with Polish vehicles being the largest number of vehicles from an EU country entering the UK. However, Brexit is most likely to see some radical changes to the situation and it is expected that although road freight will dominate in the future the proportion moved by foreign vehicles will fall should cabotage become illegal.

It might also be noted that during the 20th century most long-distance road transport was nationalized to make it service the national railway system. However, this was not at all successful and within a few years it was 're-privatized' as the railways were simply too inefficient to cope with the levels of traffic and as a state-run enterprise, the then British Road Services were also inefficient and costly.

Since by far the largest proportion of freight traffic commences and ends its journey on the back of a lorry, intermodalism is principally understood to mean the use of an alternative mode to undertake the middle, long-haul or trunk leg of the journey. Typically this involves transhipping the unitized load from a lorry at a railhead or inland waterway terminal or at a seaport, for onward shipment by rail, inland waterway barge or sea-going ship, and then transhipping it back again onto a lorry for the final delivery leg to the customer – the consignee. This takes time and incurs cost and, in a relatively small country such as the UK, these disadvantages have led to a resistance to using road alternatives. In some instances it is not just the unitized load that is transhipped, but the whole road vehicle, or at least its semi-trailer, which is loaded aboard a rail freight wagon, an inland waterway barge, a short-sea vessel – invariably a roll-on/roll-off ferry ship – or an ocean-going ship for onward transportation.

No matter what the particular freighting arrangement, the essence of the whole operation is to utilize the key characteristics of each individual transport mode to its best advantage. The lorry has the benefits of a door-to-door capability, immediacy and flexibility in its favour plus the ability to effect collections and deliveries of goods from locations that have no rail sidings or waterway quays for loading. It is also better able than the other modes to cope with fluctuating demand and the need, particularly in the retail sector, to reduce the levels of inventory in the supply chain.

Whilst rail freighting offers a lower-cost alternative for multiple loads carried over longer transits and a much less polluting effect on the environment, as does barge traffic shipped on the navigable rivers and canals of inland waterway networks, the problems for small countries such as the UK are obvious. Thus road haulage in any combination with rail freighting, inland waterway, short-sea and coastal shipping may prove to be the most viable option, both economically and operationally. But in certain cases, particularly where no roll-on/roll-off vehicle ferry service or road or rail tunnel facility exists, shipping by container vessel may be necessary, and especially for trans-global freight movements.

It is useful to explain here the various constituent parts of a freight movement.

Unit Loads and Loading Units

A unit load is a consignment of freight – usually, but not always, comprising a combination of small consignments, as in a groupage load, which is unitized to save transhipment and repacking time and cost at each individual stage of the journey, and also for ease of handling. Such unitization involves units such as pallets, roll cages etc. Such loads are usually consolidated into an ISO shipping container or a swap body built to internationally recognized and accepted standards, or into an articulated lorry semi-trailer. Unitization and containerization are different in their nature, composition and use and this point is often overlooked by some non-transport professionals. Containerization of freight into standard loading units in this manner is a vital element of the intermodal transport concept, providing speed and efficiency in handling, security for the load in transit and reduced risk of damage. This type of transport continues to expand within the UK with 'Freightarranger' offering 'low carbon' online services to move containers by rail between all major UK cities and then by road to the final destination. They also offer container hire but declare that the journey needs to be in excess of 150 miles for them to accept the goods, but they do also offer deep water services and move containers between some UK ports. It should also be noted that as global trading expands and the use of container hub and spoke systems increases, so do the numbers of containers in use and the volume of container traffic. This is clearly evidenced by the expansion of the intermodal services offered by Eddie Stobart using skeletal trailers and rail containers on daily services from their depot at Daventry International Rail Freight Terminal (DIRFT).

Bimodal Systems

'RoadRailer' is a brand name for an interchangeable, bimodal road–rail trailer system conceived in the United States by Wabash National Inc of Indiana. It is based on the use of a road-going semi-trailer with a six-wheel undercarriage that is pneumatically raised, allowing the front and rear ends of the trailer to be mounted on rail bogies and formed into a train for rail transit. The RoadRailer system was trialled in the UK in the 1960s but failed to attract sufficient interest largely due to what was seen then as unacceptable weight penalties, the rail operation at the time, the relatively small distances involved and technical complexity. In more recent times Novatrans (see below) operates bimodal services throughout Europe and continues to expand its network. It could be that the distances able to be covered in Europe make bimodal transport a better option for larger land masses than that of the UK.

In March 2018, Roadrailer services were accepted as a new service to move automobiles and fast-moving consumer goods in India after three years of planning and negotiation.

Rolling Motorway Systems

A rolling motorway system is one where complete road vehicles are driven onto specially built rail wagons for the rail transit. The system gets its name because, in effect, vehicles are driven straight off the motorway onto the rail wagon at one end of the journey, then off again and onto the motorway at the other end of the trunk leg, the driver travelling on the train accompanying his vehicle. Hence the rail link is seen as a continuation of the motorway journey.

Eurotunnel's freight shuttle service through the Channel Tunnel between the UK and France is a rolling motorway system, having special transfer wagons enabling vehicles to be driven onto the train from the platform, and off again at the other end of the through-Tunnel journey. Novatrans (see below) also offers rolling motorway services on some of its routes. By this means loading and unloading is both easily and rapidly accomplished, reducing journey delays to an absolute minimum – one of its main advantages over roll-on/roll-off ferry ship operation where there are often delays in loading and unloading and adverse weather conditions can be a major problem.

Piggyback Transport

Unaccompanied articulated semi-trailers are carried on certain UK and European rail services by a method known as 'piggyback' transport. The largest operator is Novatrans who offers services in countries stretching from Norway to Greece, that can carry vehicles, trailers and containers right across Europe. Novatrans used to be partly owned by the French Railways SNCF but was bought privately in 2009, has expanded rapidly and continues to grow as many road haulage companies operating across Europe take advantage of the network for moving goods over long distances. In relation to the piggyback operation Novatrans also offers a range of services including groupage, packing and track and trace.

When moving semi-trailers, the semi-trailers are either:

- lifted onto special low-height rail wagons by container crane or by straddle carriers fitted with grapple arms which locate into strengthened pockets in the trailer under frame; or
- shunted, by a terminal tractor, onto special rail wagons with a swivelling, tilting load-bed, which rotates and lowers to form a ramp.

Piggyback was at one time seen to be one of the most promising methods of switching long-haul freight from road to rail, and a number of major studies have been carried out in connection with its potential development. For example, ECMT issued a report in 1992 on improvements in so-called piggyback links across Europe, while in the UK a consortium of consultants and operators, among others, studied and for a while vigorously promoted this particular concept of road–rail transport. However, for its development to progress in the UK, substantial and very costly infrastructure works were needed to increase the rail loading gauge to provide both top corner and platform clearance for the passage of normal height semi-trailers and 9 ft 6 in high ISO containers. At the time, these costs were deemed too high for the project to be economically viable.

Rail Freight

In the UK, the rail freight element – operated by companies such as Colas Rail, DB Schenker (formerly EWS), Freightliner, Direct Rail Services and GB Railfreight – relies heavily on the use of a variety of intermodal wagons specifically designed to carry ISO shipping containers, standard swap bodies or whole vehicle combinations (eg piggyback style). The former are usually skeletal-framed flat wagons, built to provide a low loading height to accommodate 9 ft 6in tall 'high-cube' ISO containers and are fitted with twist locks at 20 ft and 40 ft centres.

Other companies such as DHL and Eddie Stobart also use these types of trailers. Stobarts use them to move goods for Tesco between the rail/road terminal in Daventry (DIRFT) and Scotland. Stobarts also operate rail services between Tilbury and Daventry and to Cardiff and London and have some international rail freight operations to Spain. Schenkers have also established new 'high speed' services from Dagenham and Barking to and from Spain for the movement of perishable foodstuffs and automotive components.

Vehicular traffic (ie semi-trailers and whole-vehicle combinations) are carried on special pocket wagons or on spine wagons which provide safe and secure accommodation for vehicles in transit, their road wheels sitting low on the wagon to provide adequate overhead clearance for bridges and tunnels (known as 'loading gauge' clearance). Depending on the system being used, the vehicles are either lifted on or off the rail wagon or are driven on or off via special loading ramps built into the wagon. The Channel Tunnel freight shuttle also uses a direct drive-on system.

Inland Waterways

Intermodal freight traffic on the inland waterways is carried on barges equipped to accommodate either complete road vehicles, but more usually ISO containers stacked both in the cargo hold and on deck. Rarely are such vessels seen on UK inland waterways, but they are a common sight on major European rivers such as the Rhine, the Elbe and the Danube which, along with other inland navigations, carry a great deal of freight traffic, a fair proportion of which is intermodal traffic.

Short-Sea Shipping

Increasingly, short-sea shipping (SSS) is being seen as a key alternative to road freighting and a solution to the burdens caused by traffic congestion and air pollution across the whole of Europe (this is not just a UK problem). The use of SSS has been helped by the increase in containerized goods, because although they are not 'container ships' in the general sense of the term, containers unloaded by cranes, and such, do still allow much faster turnaround times for ships in port. The ships used in these types of operation are familiar enough to anybody making a port visit. They are generally small freighters (or coasters in common terminology to differentiate them from ocean-going vessels), typically of some 1,000–5,000 deadweight tonnes (dwt).

Containers

Freight containers, or shipping containers as they are usually termed, are generally constructed of steel for strength and to meet the requirements of legislation and to standard dimensions established by the International Organization for Standardization (ISO) – hence the term ISO container. They are capable of being lifted from the top corner twist-lock castings by purpose-built container cranes, straddle carriers or stackers, or from the bottom by heavy-duty forklift trucks, for which purpose many containers also have strengthened fork pockets in the underside. These containers are sufficiently rigid and strong to be stacked eight, or even in some cases nine or 10 units high in container terminals or within specially built cellular container ships where they are subjected to considerable stress. Standard ISO containers are 20 ft, 30 ft, 40 ft and 45 ft long by 8 ft wide (2.44 metres); and 8 ft 6 in and, increasingly, 9 ft 6 in height.

Container ship capacity is measured and container industry statistics are compiled in relation to a single 20 ft ISO container defined as 1 teu (ie a 20 ft equivalent unit). Thus a 40 ft container is counted as 2 teu. The largest of the current generation of sea-going container ships is the OOCL Hong Kong capable of carrying 21,413 containers, whilst MSC Oscar has a capacity of 19,224 containers. Other large container ships include the MSC Globe (19,100 containers), whilst Maersk have three ships that can carry 18,270 or more 20 ft equivalent containers (ie 18,270 teu). The first arrival of a 14,000 teu container ship into the Port of Felixstowe was reported early in 2009 and the Hong Kong visited in 2017 but it should be noted that the very largest ships require extremely deep water and deep water ports and so they are limited to the routes that they can ply. This in turn is driving the expansion of short-sea shipping services (see above) where the major container port (in the case of the EU this is Rotterdam) is used as a hub for the massive container ships and other, smaller ports, including minor ports, are used as 'spokes' and served by smaller short-sea service ships.

Twenty-foot and forty-foot ISO units are those most commonly used since they provide greater flexibility in loading and more effectively match the legal dimensions for road vehicles – 30-footers being an odd size and square-ended 45-footers being too long for legal carriage on European road vehicles. However, 45 ft containers with the Geest patented type of twist-lock corner casting are now becoming increasingly common and these overcome the difficulties of meeting the legally specified 'swept circle' dimension for maximum length semi-trailers thus allowing the 45-footer to be carried legally.

A variety of different container designs are used for special purposes including half-height types for carrying particularly heavy, low capacity freight such as machinery or sheet steel, refrigerated units with built-in 'reefer' units, and bulk liquid or powder tanks mounted within standard-dimension steel container frames.

All these containers are fitted with standard design corner castings that enable them to be quickly and safely secured and released from matching twist lock equipment mounted on road vehicle trailers, rail wagons, and lifting and loading equipment. Twist locks on vehicles and rail wagons may be recessed within load platforms to allow a clear deck for general freight carrying, or mounted on special purpose-built skeletal frames – hence the term skeletal trailer.

These can be used for no other purpose than container or swap body carrying, but by their nature they weigh less than a standard platform body and therefore provide a lower unladen vehicle weight which in turn allows a greater load-carrying capacity within legal gross weight limits. Other non-standard, non-stackable containers and demountable bodies used in domestic transport and builders' skips are not included in this definition, and are not found in intermodal transport operations.

A second generation of ISO pallet-wide containers is now in use, patented by GESeaCo and brand-named 'SeaCell'. These units have a revolutionary sidewall construction permitting sideways stowage of two, 1,200 mm, standard Euro-pallets within the standard ISO exterior dimensions (45 ft by 8 ft). This configuration increases load capacity from 27 Euro pallets (ie 1,200 mm by 800 mm) to 33 pallets.

It should be noted that ISO containers being moved by sea now need certified proof of weight before they will be loaded onto the ship. This rule does not apply to short sea crossings or ro-ro ferry movements of these containers.

Swap Bodies

Swap bodies (in French, *caisses mobiles* – a term frequently encountered) are loading units sufficiently strong for lifting, when loaded, to or from road vehicles and rail wagons with ease. Many of the shorter (ie 7.15 m and 7.45 m) units have fold-down legs so they can be free-standing. All swap bodies are equipped with specially strengthened lifting pockets, located at standard dimensions, in the underside of the base frame for lifting by stacker or by overhead crane with grapple arms. They are built to a lighter construction than an ISO container thus saving on tare weight and increasing payload potential, but in consequence they are not sufficiently strong for top lifting or stacking like a container, although some more recent versions allow for stacking when empty.

A variety of bodywork types are encountered: the solid closed type, or those with curtain sides, or open with drop-down sideboards and tailboard for ease of loading and unloading. When used exclusively in intermodal operations, they are built to standard dimensions of 7.15 m, 7.45 m, 7.82 m and 13.6 m lengths; 2.5 m, 2.55 m or 2.6 m wide; and up to 2.77 m high, allowing them to be carried within legal limits on European road vehicles and providing sufficient gauge (ie bridge and tunnel) clearance for rail freighting.

In Europe, intermodalism has grown significantly; typically with such operations as the road–rail systems like Novatrans which carries containers, swap bodies and road vehicles on long-haul, trans-European rail journeys.

Among the many catalysts which prompted such developments was the fact that (pre-SEM, 1 January 1993) international road hauliers wishing to cross France or Germany needed road haulage permits authorizing transit through these countries. These were available only on a very limited allocation basis, but hauliers willing to load their vehicles onto rail, piggyback-style (ie on the old 'Kangourou' system in France and the 'Kombi-Trans' system in Germany), from one side of the country to the other, were granted transit rights without the need for one of these scarce permits. Such permits are no longer required in the free market, but the need for them at the time certainly enabled the piggyback style services, mentioned above, to flourish.

This situation may be another option for some UK international operators struggling to obtain sufficient numbers of permits if transit permit schemes are introduced for UK vehicles transiting individual EU member states. It is unclear whether or not these schemes will be extended due to the delayed implementation of Brexit.

APPENDICES

APPENDIX I

Vehicle Operator Licensing System (VOL)

National number for all queries: The telephone contact number for all Traffic Area Offices is 0300 123 9000 (see below). This is the CLO national telephone number, which is manned by staff trained to deal with all general enquiries between the hours of 09.00–17.00 Monday to Friday. Other DVSA enquiry telephone numbers covering other areas are available on the GOV.UK website, as individual departments are responsible for individual areas of compliance, booking, amendments and specific enquiries.

Postal contact can be made to the following address:

Central Licensing Office
Hillcrest House
386 Harehills Lane
Leeds LS9 6NF
Tel: 0300 123 9000

Post for the public inquiry and regional intelligence units, and personal post for the TCs, should continue to be sent to local offices.

The Senior Traffic Commissioner (STC) is Richard Turfitt – appointed in April 2017 but still in post.

Traffic Area	Areas Covered
North-Eastern Hillcrest House 386 Harehills Lane Leeds LS9 6NF Email: enquiries@otc.gsi.gov.uk Tel: 0300 123 9000 Fax: 0113 240 3954 *Traffic Commissioner* *Tim Blackmore, OBE* Office hours: 9.30 am to 4.00 pm, Monday to Friday Telephone hours: 8.30 am to 5.00 pm, Monday to Friday	The metropolitan boroughs within South Yorkshire, Tyne and Wear and West Yorkshire; the counties of Durham, Northumberland, Nottinghamshire and North Yorkshire; the districts of Darlington, East Riding of Yorkshire, Hartlepool, Kingston upon Hull, Middlesbrough, North Lincolnshire, North East Lincolnshire, Nottingham, Redcar and Cleveland, Stockton on Tees and York.

North-Western Suite 4 Stone Cross Place Stone Cross Lane Golborne Warrington WA3 2SH Email: enquiries@otc.gsi.gov.uk Tel: 0300 123 9000 Fax: 01942 728 297 *Traffic Commissioner* *Simon Evans* Office hours: 9.30 am to 4.00 pm, Monday to Friday. Telephone hours: 8.30 am to 5.00 pm, Monday to Friday	The metropolitan boroughs within Greater Manchester and Merseyside; the counties of Cheshire, Cumbria, Derbyshire and Lancashire; the districts of Blackburn with Darwen, Blackpool, Derby City and Warrington.
West Midlands 38 George Road Edgbaston Birmingham B15 1PL Email: enquiries@otc.gsi.gov.uk Tel: 0300 123 9000 Fax: 0121 456 4250 *Traffic Commissioner* *Nick Denton* Office hours: 9.30 am to 4.00 pm, Monday to Friday Telephone hours: 8.30 am to 5.00 pm, Monday to Friday	The metropolitan boroughs within the West Midlands; the counties of Shropshire, Staffordshire, Warwickshire and Worcestershire; the districts of Herefordshire, Stoke on Trent and Telford and Wrekin.
East of England Eastbrook Shaftesbury Avenue Cambridge CB2 8DR Email: enquiries@otc.gsi.gov.uk Tel: 0300 123 9000 Fax: 01223 309 681 *Traffic Commissioner* *Richard Turfitt* Office and telephone hours: 9.30am to 4.00 pm, Monday to Thursday; 9.30am to 3.30 pm, Friday	The counties of Bedfordshire, Buckinghamshire, Cambridgeshire, Hertfordshire, Essex, Leicestershire, Lincolnshire (except the districts of North Lincolnshire and North East Lincolnshire), Norfolk, Northamptonshire and Suffolk; the Districts of Leicester, Luton, Milton Keynes, Peterborough, Rutland, Southend on Sea and Thurrock.

Wales 38 George Road Edgbaston Birmingham B15 1PL Tel: 0300 123 9000 Fax: 0121 456 4250 *Traffic Commissioner* *Nick Jones* Email: nick.jones@otc.gsi.co.uk	Counties of Clwyd, Dyfed, Gwent, Gwynedd, Mid Glamorgan, Powys, South Glamorgan and West Glamorgan. *NB: These details may change if the TC for Wales relocates to Cardiff.*
Western Jubilee House Croyden Street Bristol BS5 0DA Email: enquiries@otc.gsi.gov.uk Tel: 0300 123 9000 Fax: 0117 941 4983 *Traffic Commissioner* *Kevin Rooney* Office hours: 9.30 am to 4.00 pm, Monday to Friday Telephone hours: 8.30 am to 5.00 pm, Monday to Friday	The counties of Cornwall, Devon, Dorset, Gloucestershire, Hampshire, Oxfordshire, Somerset and Wiltshire; the districts of Bath and North East Somerset, Bournemouth, Bracknell Forest, Bristol, Isle of Wight, North Somerset, Plymouth, Poole, Portsmouth, Reading, Slough, Southampton, South Gloucestershire, Swindon, Torbay, West Berkshire, Windsor and Maidenhead, and Wokingham.
London and the South East Ivy House 3 Ivy Terrace Eastbourne BN21 4QT Email: enquiries@otc.gsi.gov.uk Tel: 0300 123 9000 Fax: 01323 739 037 *Traffic Commissioner* *Sarah Bell* Office hours: 9.30 am to 4.00 pm, Monday to Friday Telephone hours: 8.30 am to 5.00 pm, Monday to Thursday; 8.30 am to 4.30 pm, Friday	Greater London; the counties of Kent, Surrey, East Sussex and West Sussex; the districts of Brighton and Hove, the Medway Towns.

Scottish Level 6 The Stamp Office 10 Waterloo Place Edinburgh EH1 3EG Email: enquiries@otc.gsi.gov.uk Tel: 0300 123 9000 Fax: 0131 229 0682 *Traffic Commissioner* *Claire Gilmore* Office hours: 9.30 am to 4.00 pm, Monday to Friday Telephone hours: 8.30 am to 5.00 pm, Monday to Friday	Scotland.
Northern Ireland Department of the Environment Goodwood House 44–58 May Street, Town Parks Belfast BT1 4NN www.doeni.gov.uk(archived at https://perma.cc/3CFX-SSN8) Tel: 028 9054 0540	Northern Ireland.

International Road Freight Office

The issue of authorizations and permits for international road freight transport is dealt with by IRFO, which is a part of the DVSA in Cambridge at:

International Road Freight Office
City House
126–130 Hills Rd
Cambridge CB2 1NP
Tel: 01223 531030

APPENDIX II

Transport Trade Associations and Professional Bodies

Freight Transport Association Regional Offices

Head Office
Hermes House
157 St John's Road
Tunbridge Wells
Kent TN4 9UZ
Tel: 01892 526171
Fax: 01892 534989

London and South-Eastern
Hermes House
157 St John's Road
Tunbridge Wells
Kent TN4 9UZ
Tel: 01892 526171
Fax: 01892 534989

Midlands and West
Hermes House
20 Coventry Road
Cubbington
Leamington Spa
Warwickshire CU32 7JN
Tel: 01926 450020
Fax: 01926 452765

Northern
Hermes House
2 Manor Road
Horsforth
Leeds LS18 4DX
Tel: 0113 258 9861
Fax: 0113 258 6501

Scottish
Pavilion 1
Castlecraig Business Park
Players Road
Stirling
FK7 7SH
Tel: 01786 457500
Fax: 01786 450412

Northern Ireland
109 Airport Road West
Belfast
BT3 9ED
Tel: 028 9046 6699
Fax: 028 9046 6690

Brussels
14 Rue de la Science
1040 Brussels
Belgium
Tel: 00 322 231 0321
Fax: 00 322 230 4140

Member Advice Centre
Tel: 0370 605 0000

Member Service Centre
Tel: 0371 711 2222

Enquiries regarding management training should be made to:
Training and Personnel Services
Hermes House
Tunbridge Wells (see Head Office).

Road Haulage Association District Offices

Head Office
Roadway House
Bretton Way
Bretton
Peterborough
PE3 8DD
Tel: 01733 261131
Email: rhaheadoffice@rha.uk.net

Scotland and Northern Ireland
Kirkton House
Allen Road
Kirkton North
Livingston EH54 6TQ
Tel: 01506 414073
Email:
scotland-northernireland@rha.uk.net

Northern
Roadway House
Little Wood Drive
West 26 Industrial Estate
Cleckheaton
West Yorks BD19 4TQ
Tel: 01274 863100
Email: northern@rha.uk.net

London
22 Greencoat Place
Westminster
London SW1P 1PR
Tel: Chris Seaton 07979 531464
Email: london@rha.uk.net

Weybridge Office
Roadway House
The Old Forge
South Road
Weybridge
Surrey
KT13 9DZ
Tel: 01932 841515
Email: weybridge@rha.uk.net

RHA Shop
Unit 12
Stevern Way
Peterborough PE1 5EL
Tel: 01733 263434
Email: rhashop@rha.uk.net

Other Trade Associations

Local Government Association
18 Smith Square
Westminster
London SW1P 3HZ
Tel: 020 7664 3000
Email: info@local.gov.uk

Association of Lorry Loader Manufacturers and Importers (ALLMI)
Unit 7b
Cavalier Court
Bumpers Farm
Chippenham, Wilts
SN14 6LH
Tel: 0844 858 4334
www.allmi.com (archived at https://perma.cc/Y5XC-5F3G)

Association of Vehicle Recovery Operators (AVRO)
1 Bath Street
Rugby CV21 3JF
Tel: 01788 572850
Email: sara@avrouk.com

British Association of Removers (BAR)
Tangent House
62 Exchange Road
Watford, Herts
WD18 0TG
Tel: 01923 699480
www.bar.co.uk (archived at https://perma.cc/DDL5-MHFK)

British Industrial Truck Association
7 High Street
Sunninghill
Ascot
Berkshire SL5 9NQ
Tel: 01344 623800
Email: info@bita.org.uk

British International Freight Association (BIFA)
Redfern House
Browells Lane
Feltham
Middlesex TW13 7EP
Tel: 020 8844 2266
www.bifa.org (archived at https://perma.cc/7BCJ-EQKT)

British Vehicle Rental and Leasing Association (BVRLA)
Badminton Court
Church Street
Amersham
Bucks HP7 0DD
Tel: 01494 434747
www.bvrla.co.uk
(archived at https://perma.cc/SPV9-MKBY)

Chemical Industries Association
Kings Buildings
Smith Square
London SW1P 3JJ
Tel: 020 7834 3399
Email: enquiries@cia.org.uk

Environmental Services Association (ESA)
3rd Floor
154 Buckingham Palace Road
London SW1W 9TR
Tel: 020 7824 8882
Email: info@esauk.org

Food Storage and Distribution Federation (FSDF)
Diddenham Court
Lamb Wood Hill
Grazeley
Reading
Berks RG7 1JQ
Tel: 0118 988 4468
Email: info@fsdf.org.uk

Joint Approvals Unit for Periodic Training (JAUPT)
12 Warren Yard
Warren Park
Stratford Road
Milton Keynes MK12 5NW
Tel: 0844 800 4184
Email: enquiries@jaupt.org.uk

National Tyre Distributors Association (NTDA)
Above STS Tyre Pros
Park Street
Aylesbury, Bucks
HP20 1DX
Tel: 01296 482128
Email: info@ntda.co.uk

Retail Motor Industry Federation (RMI)
201 Great Portland Street
London W1W 5AB
Tel: 020 7580 9122
Email: enquiries@rmif.co.uk

Road Operators Safety Council (ROSCO)
Tel: 01557 500680
Email: admin@rosco-uk.org

Society of Motor Manufacturers and Traders (SMMT)
The Society of Motor Manufacturers and Traders Limited
71 Great Peter Street
London
SW1P 2BN
Tel: 020 7235 7000
Email: info@smmt.co.uk

Transport Association
PO Box 374
Leatherhead
Surrey KT22 2EY
Tel: 07507 785845
Email:
marion@transportassociation.org.uk

UK Warehousing Association (UKWA)
11 Gower Street
Fitzrovia
London WC1E 6HB
Tel: 020 7636 8856
Email (Chief Executive):
pward@ukwa.org.uk

Vehicle Builders and Repairers Association (VBRA)
22–23 Pullan Way
Morley
Leeds
LS27 0BZ
Tel: 0113 253 8333
www.vbra.co.uk (archived at https://perma.cc/VL8T-T3B6)

Professional Bodies in Transport

Institute of Advanced Motorists Roadsmart IAM
1 Albany Place
Hyde Way
Welwyn Garden City
AL7 3BT
Tel: 0300 303 1134
Email: support@iam.org.uk

Institute of Grocery Distribution
Grange Lane
Radlett
Watford
Hertfordshire WD25 8GD
Tel: 01932 857141
Email: igd@igd.com

Chartered Institute of Logistics and Transport (UK)
Earlstrees Court
Earlstrees Road
Corby
Northamptonshire NN17 4AX
Tel: 01536 740100
www.ciltuk.org.uk (archived at https://perma.cc/58MW-8LSA)

The Chartered Institute of Highways and Transportation (CIHT)
119 Brittania Walk
London N1 7JE
Tel: 020 7336 1555
Email: info@ciht.org.uk

Institute of the Motor Industry (IMI)
'Fanshaws'
Brickendon
Hertford SG13 8PQ
Tel: 01992 511521
Email: comms@theimi.org.uk

Institution of Mechanical Engineers (IMechE)
1 Birdcage Walk
London SW1H 9JJ
Tel: 020 7222 7899
Email: enquiries@imeche.org

Institute of Transport Administration (IoTA)
The Old Studio
25 Greenfield Road
Westoning
Beds MK45 5JD
Tel: 01525 634940
Email: director@iota.org.uk

Society of Operations Engineers
22 Greencoat Place
London SW1P 1PR
Tel: 020 7630 1111
Email: soe@soe.org.uk

APPENDIX III

Other Organizations Connected with Transport and Transport Journals

Automobile Association (AA)
Fanum House
Basing View
Basingstoke
RG21 4EA
Tel: 0370 544 8866
www.theaa.com (archived at https://perma.cc/D3CD-TLUV)

Brake (for safe road transport)
PO Box 548
Huddersfield HD1 2XZ
Tel: 01484 559909
Email: brake@brake.org.uk

British Standards Institution (BSI)
389 Chiswick High Road
London W4 4AL
Tel: 0345 086 9001
Website: www.bsigroup.com (archived at https://perma.cc/Y7DG-PYT4)

CENEX (Centre for Low Carbon and Fuel Technologies)
Holywell Building
Holywell Park
Ashby Road
Loughborough
LE11 3UZ
Tel: 01509 642 500
Email: info@cenex.co.uk

Department for Transport
Enquiry Helpline
Tel: 0300 330 3000
www.gov.uk/government/organisations/department-for-transport (archived at https://perma.cc/VB22-DU94)

Driver and Vehicle Licensing Agency (DVLA)
General Enquiries (Driver Licensing)
Tel: 0300 790 6801
General Enquiries (Vehicles)
Tel: 0300 790 6802

Driver and Vehicle Standards Agency (DVSA) (Vehicle Enquiries)
The Ellipse
Padley Road
Swansea SA1 8AN
Tel: 030 123 9000
Email: enquiries@dvsa.gov.uk

Driver and Vehicle Standards Agency (DVSA) (Driving Enquiries)
Eastgate House
Kings Manor Business Park
Newcastle-Upon-Tyne
NE1 6PB
Tel: 0300 200 1122
Email: customerservices@dvsa.gov.uk

Green Flag National Breakdown
The Wharf
Neville Street
Leeds LS1 4AZ
Tel: 0843 835 0019
www.greenflag.com (archived at https://perma.cc/9K6L-PY84)

International Road Freight Office
City House
126–128 Hills Road
Cambridge CB2 1NP
Tel: 01223 531030
www.gov.uk (archived at https://perma.cc/7S45-2BRS)

International Road Transport Union (IRU) Headquarters
La Voie-Creuse 16 (CP 44)
CH-1211 Genève 20
Switzerland
Tel: 0041 22 918 2700
Email: iru@iru.org

International Transport Workers Federation (ITF)
ITF House
49–60 Borough Road
London SE1 1DR
Tel: 020 7403 2733
Email: mail@itf.org.uk

OCR
Progress House
Westwood Way
Westwood Business Park
Coventry CV4 8JQ
For vocational examination enquiries
Tel: 02476 851509
Email: vocational.qualifications@ocr.org.uk

Recruitment and Employment Confederation (REC)
Dorset House
27–45 Stamford Street
South Bank
London SE1 9NT
Tel: 020 7009 2100
Email: info@rec.uk.com

Royal Automobile Club (RAC)
RAC Motoring Services
RAC House
Brockhurst Crescent
Walsall WS5 4AW
Tel: 0843 837 0526
www.rac.co.uk (archived at https://perma.cc/C88K-DQMF)

Royal Society for the Prevention of Accidents (RoSPA)
RoSPA Head Office
RoSPA House
28 Calthorpe Road
Edgbaston
Birmingham B15 1RP
Tel: 0121 248 2000
Email: help@rospa.com

RoSPA Scotland
43 Discovery Terrace
Heriot-Watt University Research Park
Edinburgh EH14 4AP
Tel: 0131 449 9379

RoSPA Wales
2nd Floor
2 Cwrt-y-Parc
Parc Ty Glas
Cardiff Business Park
Llanishen
Cardiff CF14 5GH
Tel: 02920 250600

RoSPA Northern Ireland
Karen McDonnell
Operations Division
Tel: 0131 449 9378
Email: kmcdonnell@rospa.com

JAUPT
9 Warren Yard
Warren Farm Office Village
Stratford Road
Milton Keynes
MK12 5NM
Tel: 0844 800 4184
Email: enquiries@jaupt.org.uk

Transport Journals

Commercial Motor (General Enquiries)
6th Floor
Chancery House
St Nicholas Way
Sutton
Surrey
SM1 1JB
Tel: 020 8912 2163
www.roadtransportmedia.co.uk
(archived at https://perma.cc/MJY6-23R8)

Export and Freight
The Old Coach House
12 Main Street
Hillsborough
Co. Down BT26 6AE
Northern Ireland
Tel: 028 9268 8888
Email: helen@4squaremedia.net

FTA Freight & Logistics (Journal of FTA)
Hermes House
St John's Road
Tunbridge Wells TN4 9UZ
Tel: 01892 552211
www.fta.co.uk (archived at https://perma.cc/FA3N-YN3T)

International Freighting Weekly (IFW)
Mead House
21 John Street
London
WC1N 2BP
Tel: 020 7505 3551
www.informa.com (archived at https://perma.cc/FDX7-TWJB)

Logistics and Transport Focus (Journal of the Chartered Institute of Logistics and Transport)
Earlstrees Court
Earlstrees Road
Corby
Northants NN17 4XQ
Tel: 01536 740100
www.ciltuk.org.uk (archived at https://perma.cc/58MW-8LSA)

Motor Transport (General Enquiries)
Road Transport Media Ltd
6th Floor
Chancery House
St Nicholas Way
Sutton
Surrey SM1 1JB
Tel: 020 8912 2163
www.roadtransportmedia.co.uk
(archived at https://perma.cc/MJY6-23R8)

NB: Both Commercial Motor *and* Motor Transport *are published by Road Transport Media Ltd. This company also publishes* Truck and Driver *magazine.*

Removals and Storage (Journal of British Association of Removers)
The British Association of Removers
Tangent House
62 Exchange Street
Watford
Herts WD18 0TG
Tel: 01923 699480
www.bar.co.uk (archived at https://perma.cc/DDL5-MHFK)

Roadway (Journal of RHA)
Road Haulage Association
35 Monument Hill
Weybridge
Surrey KT13 8RN
Tel: 01932 838913
Email: publications@rha.uk.net

Transport Engineer
MA Business Ltd
Hawley Mill
Hawley Road
Dartford DA2 7TJ
Tel: 0322 221144

Transport News
Wheatsheaf House
Montgomery Street
The Village
East Kilbride G74 4JS
Tel: 01355 279077
Email: info@transportnews.co.uk

Transport News Digest (TND)
1st Floor
26 Station Approach
Hinchley Wood
Esher
Surrey KT10 0SR
Tel: 0207 928 6464
www.transporttrust.com (archived at https://perma.cc/3AV5-8VH6)

Truck and Driver
See above for *Commercial Motor* and *Motor Transport* publishers.

Trucking Magazine
Kelsey Publishing Group
PO Box 978
Peterborough
PE1 9FL
Tel: 01733 347559
Email: trucking.ed@kelsey.co.uk

APPENDIX IV

Driver and Vehicle Standards Agency (DVSA) Weighbridges

The list this year shows the last geographical locations of DVSA dynamic axle weighbridges within Traffic Areas and is again dated as the DVSA no longer publishes comprehensive lists of weighbridges within the UK. They do operate a 'find your local weighbridge' facility on the GOV.UK website where an operator or driver types in their location and the nearest weighbridge is shown on the screen. This is ideal when an operator or driver needs the nearest weighbridge but does not help operators or drivers trying to locate a weighbridge in a different area.

With cut-backs in levels and frequency of roadside enforcement, using mobile weighing equipment, many of these weighbridges are now not open, or available for use every day of the week and operators may need to rely more heavily on the private sector for these facilities. This is why the YELL facility (see below) is so valuable.

In addition, we have to accept that this list is subject to change as the DVSA now makes more use of the 'Weigh in Motion' axle weighing technology that is found on major routes and which uses ANPR to record details of the vehicle being weighed as it travels over the sensor in the surface of the road. In addition, as we know, the DVSA has also closed, and is closing, a number of LGV test stations and has opened, and is opening, Approved Test Facilities (ATFs) which are often owned by large hauliers or dealerships who may or may not have a weighing facility. In addition roadwork and road improvement schemes also often lead to the temporary closure of weighbridges.

Although somewhat dated, the lists below are a true representation of the weighbridge network as it was before national records ceased.

What is important is that readers know to use the YELL website where they will be able to locate their nearest weighbridge by town, postcode or county. Simply go to: https://www.yell.com (archived at https://perma.cc/F62C-9JL2) to locate the weighbridges around the UK.

In the meantime the list below groups weighbridges into geographical regions and areas and provides at least some information on where they may be found.

Locations (Grouped into Geographical Areas/Regions)

A75 Castle Kennedy nr Stranraer
A90 Cramond nr Edinburgh
A74 Beattock Summit by Beattock
M9 Craigforth nr Stirling
Perth GVTS

A55 Dalar Hir, Anglesey
M62/A622 (J20) Thornham nr Rochdale
M65 Cuerden
A556 Rostherne (nr J19 M6)
M6 Sandbach
M6 Todhills
A55 Ewloe
M57 Switch Island

A1/A66 Scotch Corner
A19 Wellfield nr Stockton-on-Tees
A1/A659 Boston Spa nr Wetherby
M62 Ainley Top nr Huddersfield
M1/A61 Tankersley nr Rotherham
King George Dock, Hull
A46/A52 Saxondale nr Nottingham
Leeds GVTS
Newcastle GVTS

M6(J14) Doxey nr Stafford
M5(J3)/A456 Quinton nr Halesowen
A40/M50(J4) Ross-on-Wye
M4/A449 Coldra
Perry Barr M6 Birmingham

A17/A15 Holdingham
M1(J18)/A428 Crick
Felixstowe Docks
A45(East)/A142 Risby nr Newmarket
A1 (south) Sawtry (s of Peterborough)
M11(J7)/A414 Harlow
M1(J14)/A509 Newport Pagnell
M40(J1)/A412 Denham
Crimplesham GVTS, Kings Lynn
Norwich GVTS

M5(J27)/A373 Sampford Peverell
Poole Docks
M4(J18)/A46 Tormarton
A34 Abingdon (s of Oxford)
Portsmouth Docks
A31 Ashley Heath, Dorset
Plymouth GVTS
Badbury

M25(J9)/A243 Leatherhead
A23 Handcross
A2 Boughton
A27 Withy Patch nr Lancing
Newhaven
A13 Dagenham
Yeading GVTS
A26/A27 Beddingham
M25 Dartford Bridge
Dover Docks

APPENDIX V

Authorities and Police Forces (for Notification of Abnormal Load Movements)

The movement of AILs is controlled by the Electronic Service Delivery for Abnormal Loads (ESDAL) organization who have a helpdesk for problems, issues or questions. ESDAL recently announced that the helpdesk telephone number had changed to: 0300 470 3733 and that the Helpdesk details are: esdalenquiries@highwaysengland.co.uk. ESDAL itself has undergone some major improvements in order to make it more user-friendly and a lot quicker. This improved service is now referred to as ESDAL2.

Operators who do not register and so do not get a password to access ESDAL should note that they will need to contact all the authorities in all the areas that the movement concerned will load, pass through or unload and so ESDAL certainly saves operators a lot of time and effort as the ESDAL team do all the required notifications, once they have the intended movement and proposed route. This is particularly useful if operators need to use routes where bridge authorities or tunnel authorities need to be informed and special provisions made and/or where the route is over a long distance.

The alphabetical list below gives details of the roads and areas, the responsible authorities or organizations, and the points of contact for the movement of AILs within the UK. The list includes local authorities, metropolitan authorities, unitary authorities, road authorities, police forces, infrastructure partners, utility companies, bridge and tunnel authorities and port and airport operators.

Many of the areas listed are controlled by private organizations. These are also listed alphabetically, but with the area identified under the name of the organization responsible. This means that the actual areas are not in strict order and may appear later in the list of areas.

Since 2 November 2015, all AIL movements for the whole of Scotland have been handled by a single point of contact based in Glenrothes, Fife. However, in April 2016 the mailbox address was changed by Police Scotland. The ESDAL2 mailbox contact details for the Scottish point of contact can be found below under 'Police Scotland'.

Whilst the details below are available it should be noted that Highways England request that all AIL movements are registered through ESDAL as this ensures that all the relevant authorities will be contacted and that operators will not be subject to proceedings being taken against them should they fail to contact all the authorities required.

NB: Those marked with an asterisk are 'Design, Build, Finance and Operate' (DBFO) organizations.

TABLE A5.1

Road/area or authority, etc	Tel:	Fax:	Email:
*A1 Dishforth to Darrington	0191 224 6611	0191 224 6599	alan.brown@aecom.com
*A1(M) Alconbury to Peterborough	01733 245445	01733 244095	a1m@rmspeterborough.co.uk
*A168/A19 Dishforth to Tyne Tunnel	01642 567456	01642 561125	A19DBFOabnormalloads@sir-robert-mcalpine.com
*A30/A35 Exeter to Bere Regis	01404 823381	01404 823710	ConnectA30@balfourbeatty.com
*A417/419 Swindon to Gloucester	01285 840048	01285 651080	office@rmscirencester.co.uk
*A50/A564 Stoke to Derby	01283 585666	01283 585242	connectA50@bbcel.co.uk
A55 UK Highways	01407 721296	01407 720145	derrickwilliams@gwynedd.gov.uk
*A69 Carlisle to Newcastle		0191 2114843	a69abnormalloads@newcastle.gov.uk
Amey Infrastructure Services (Bedfordshire Highways)	0845 3656101	0845 3656375	abnormalloads.bedford@amey.co.uk
Amey (on behalf of Liverpool City Council)	0151728 1666 x67220	0151 2374000	liverpool.abloads@amey.co.uk
Isle and County of Anglesey	01248 752312	01248 724839	ertht@anglesey.gov.uk
Area 2 Skanska (Note – *Severn River Crossing)*	0845 600 9993	0117 9824998	area2.abloads@skanska.co.uk
Associated British Ports	01482 608540		pcatley@abports.co.uk
*Autolink M6ROM	01576 205200 x225	01576 204554	abnormal.loads@m6dbfo.co.uk

TABLE A5.1 *continued*

Road/area or authority, etc	Tel:	Fax:	Email:
Avon and Somerset Constabulary	01275 816885	01275 816884	abloads@avonandsomerset.police.uk
B2/M2MAC Area4 (A249 Stockbury to Sheerness) Abloads Service	01483 813202		area4abloads.com
Barking and Dagenham London Borough Council	020 8227 3419	020 8227 2608	john.walker@lbbd.gov.uk
Barnet London Borough Council	020 8359 7180		Kugan.sabanayagam@barnet.gov.uk
Barnsley Metropolitan Borough Council	01226 772123	01226 772125	abnormalloads@barnsley.gov.uk
Bath and North East Somerset Council	01225 477610	01225 394338	abnormal_loads@bathnes.gov.uk
Bedfordshire Police	01234 846854	01234 846424	Abloads@herts.pnn.police.uk
Bexley London Borough Council	0203 0453637		abnormalloads@bexley.gov.uk
Birmingham City Council	0121 212 5051	0121 333 4705	bhmabloads@amey.co.uk
Blackburn and Darwen Borough Council	01254 273531		danielle.curwen@capita.co.uk
Blackpool Borough Council	01253 476152	01253 476315	streetworksmanagement@blackpool.gov.uk
Bournemouth Borough Council	01202 451379	01202 451008	steve.wait@bournemouth.gov.uk
Bracknell Forest Borough Council	01454 662000 x2311	01454 663333	bracknell.abloads@atkinsglobal.com
Brent London Borough Council	0208 937 5162	0208 937 5092	abnormalloads@brent.gov.uk

TABLE A5.1 *continued*

Road/area or authority, etc	Tel:	Fax:	Email:
Bridgend County Borough Council	01656 642857	01656 642890	abloads@bridgend.gov.uk
Brighton and Hove City Council Unitary Authority	01273 292067	01273 292089	networkco-ordination@brighton-hove.gov.uk
Bristol City Council	0117 922 3188		abnormal.loads@bristol.gov.uk
Bromley London Borough Council	01727 535000 x5283	01727 535999	abloadsbromley.europe@aecom.com
BT (Utility Company)	0208 280 4049		highloadroutes@openreach.co.uk
Buckinghamshire County Council	01296 387149	01296 383189	abloads@buckscc.gov.uk
Cambridgeshire Constabulary	01234 846854	01234 846424	Abloads@herts.pnn.police.uk
Cambridgeshire County Council	01923 616264	0845 6017763	cambridgeshire.abloads@skanska.co.uk
Camden London Borough Council	0207 974 8739		abnormalloads@camden.gov.uk
Canal and River Trust (ex British Waterways, all areas England and Wales)	0303 0404040 x3		abnormal.loads@canalrivertrust.org.uk
Capita Symonds (Blaenau Gwent County) (includes Newport City Council and Caerphilly and Torfaen County Councils)	02920 803500 x3569	02920 803699	Loads.Abnormal@capita.co.uk
Cardiff City and County Council	02920 785462		abnormal.loads@cardiff.gov.uk
Cardiff Docks ABP	02920 835015	02920 495127	gperry@abports.co.uk

TABLE A5.1 *continued*

Road/area or authority, etc	Tel:	Fax:	Email:
Carmarthenshire County Council	01267 228037	01267 231007	abnormalloads@carmarthenshire.gov.uk
Ceredigion County Council	01545 572415	01545 572589	hpw@ceredigion.gov.uk
Cheshire Constabulary	01606 362215	0845 3595916	abnormal.loads@cheshire.pnn.police.uk
Cheshire East Council	01260 371056	01260 297396	AbnormalLoadsEast@cheshireeast.gov.uk
Cheshire West Council	01244 973683	01606 271879	abnormalloadswest@cheshirewestandchester.gov.uk
City and County of Swansea	01792 637447	01792 635270	Abnormal.Loads@swansea.gov.uk
City of London	0207 3323122		bridges@cityoflondon.gov.uk
City of London (Police)	020 7601 2190		trafficmanagement@city-of-london.police.uk
City of York	01904 551368	01904 551412	highway.regulation@york.gov.uk
Cleveland Police			abnormal.loads@cleveland.pnn.police.uk
Clifton Suspension Bridge Trust	01179 731579	01179 734152	bridgemaster@cliftonbridge.org.uk
Clydeport Operations Ltd			peter.little@clydeport.co.uk
Connect Plus M25	0203 386 8936	0203 386 8503	abloads@connectplusm25.co.uk
Connect Roads Balfour Beatty	01228 713 050	01228 713 051	connectpostbox@bbrcel.co.uk
Conwy County Borough Council	01492 575427	01492 575448	abnormalloads@conwy.gov.uk

TABLE A5.1 *continued*

Road/area or authority, etc	Tel:	Fax:	Email:
Cornwall Council	01872 327350	01872 327233	abloads@cornwall.gov.uk
Council of the Isles of Scilly	01720 424000 x4000	01720 424017	cdryden@scilly.gov.uk
Coventry City Council	02476 831352	02476 831324	diane.hernon@coventry.gov.uk
Croydon London Borough Council	020 8726 6000 x64058	020 8633 9575	indra.patel@croydon.gov.uk
Cumbria Constabulary	0845 3300 247		abnormalloads@cumbria.pnn.police.uk
Cumbria County Council	01228 221 393	01228 227658	christine.scott@cumbria.gov.uk
Darlington Borough Council	01325 406651	01325 388724	pam.goodwill@darlington.gov.uk
Dartford-Thurrock River Crossing (Connect Plus M25)	0203 386 8936	0203 386 8503	abloads@connectplusm25.co.uk
Denbighshire County Council	01824 706884	01824 706865	abnormal.loads@denbighshire.gov.uk
Derby City Council	01332 642507	01332 255959	engineering@derby.gov.uk
Derbyshire Constabulary		0870 7625618	abloads@derbyshire.pnn.police.uk
Derbyshire County Council	01629 538612	01629 538698	netmanadmin@derbyshire.gov.uk
Devon and Cornwall Police	01392 452268	01392 452426	abloads@ devonandcornwall.pnn.police.uk
Devon County Council	01392 380380	01392 382321	HOCC@devon.gov.uk
Doncaster Metropolitan Borough Council	01302 735263	01302 735038	abnormal_loads@doncaster.gov.uk
Dorset County Council	01305 225347	01305 225301	abloads@dorsetcc.gov.uk

TABLE A5.1 *continued*

Road/area or authority, etc	Tel:	Fax:	Email:
Dorset Police	01305 226329	01305 226335	abloads@doest.pnn.police.uk
Dudley Metropolitan Borough Council	01384 814469	01384 15400	abloads@dudley.gov.uk
Dunham Bridge Company	01777 228222		manager@dunhambridge.co.uk
Durham Constabulary		0191 375 2105	abloads@durham.pnn.police.uk
Durham County Council	0300 0267 102		abnormal_loads@durham.gov.uk
Dyfed-Powys Police	01267 226011		geraint.owen@ dyfed-powys.pnn.police.uk
Ealing London Borough Council			abnormalloads@ealing.gov.uk
East Riding of Yorkshire Council	01482 395596		abnormal.loads@eastriding.gov.uk
East Sussex County Council	07748 334997	01273 482955	structures@eastsussex.gov.uk
Electricity North West (Utility Company)	01772 848298	01772 848195	SystemOperations@enwl.co.uk
Enfield London Borough Council	0208 379 2127	0208 379 3494	nrswa@enfield.gov.uk
Eon (Utility Company)	02476 183875		adam.archer@eon-uk.com
ESDAL Helpdesk	01642 049 830	0844 7707892	
Essex County Council	01642 204 939		eccabloads@essexhighways.org
Essex Police	01245 240600	01245 235111	abloads@essex.pnn.police.uk
Flintshire County Council	01352 704805	01352 755024	abnormalloads@flintshire.gov.uk

TABLE A5.1 *continued*

Road/area or authority, etc	Tel:	Fax:	Email:
Gateshead Metropolitan Borough Council	0191 4333157	0191 4771170	abnormalloads@gateshead.gov.uk
Gloucestershire Constabulary	01242 247091	01242 224094	abloads@gloucestershire.police.uk
Gloucestershire County Council (inc Cheltenham Borough Council)	01452 583491	01452 530493	GCCAbloads@amey.co.uk
Great Central Railways (Nottingham) Ltd	0115 9405705	0115 9405905	
Great Yarmouth Port Company	01493 335516	01493 852659	sclark@eastportuk.co.uk
Greater Manchester Police	0161 872 5050 x68375	0161 855 2190	abnormal.loads@gmp.pnn.police.uk
Greenwich London Borough Council	0208 921 5457	0208 855 9324	emeka.oraelosi@royalgreenwich.gov.uk
Gwent Police	01633 642232	01633 642312	abnormal-loads@gwent.pnn.police.uk
Gwynedd County Council	01286 679434	01286 679299	LlwythAbnormal@gwynedd.gov.uk
HA ASC Area 3	01962 892313	0845 8734889	abloads.area3emhighways.co.uk
HA ASC Area 6	01223 205700		asc6abloads@amey.co.uk
HA ASC Area 8	01223 205700		asc8abloads@amey.co.uk
HA ASC Area 1	01392 312652	01392 312572	Area1roadspace@emhighways.co.uk
HA ASC Area 10	01483 811822	01483 811844	area10@abloads.com
HA ASC Area 12	01483 811822	01483 811844	area12@abloads.com
HA ASC Area 13	01768 860996	01768 861001	area13abloads@emhighways.co.uk
HA ASC Area 14	01325 341635	01325 385777	abnormalloads@aone.uk.com

TABLE A5.1 *continued*

Road/area or authority, etc	Tel:	Fax:	Email:
HA ASC Area 5 (now Connect Plus M25)	0203 386 8936	0203 386 8503	abloads@connectplusm25.co.uk
HA ASC Area 7	01623 886717		area7.abnormalload@aone.uk.com
HA ASC Area 9	01483 811822	0203 4370671	Area9@abloads.com
Hackney London Borough Council			mark.earle@hackney.gov.uk
Halton Borough Council Unitary Authority	0151 5117566	0151 5116348	abnormalloads@halton.gov.uk
Hammersmith and Fulham London Borough Council	0208 753 3033	0208 753 3048	anvar.alizadeh@lbhf.gov.uk
Hampshire Constabulary	023 8074 5535 x718202	0845 3015625	abnormal.loads@ hampshire.pnn.police.uk
Hampshire County Council	01962 832240	01962 854045	abnormal.loads@hants.gov.uk
Haringey London Borough Council	0208 489 5147	0208 489 5229	structures@haringey.gov.uk
Harrow London Borough Council	0208 416 8048		nrswa@harrow.gov.uk
Hartlepool Borough Council Unitary Authority	01429 523586		sam.caizley@hartlepool.gov.uk
Heathrow Airport Ltd	0208 757 4110	0208 757 4225	malcolm_strachan@bas.com
Herefordshire Council			HerefordshireABLoads@ bblivingplaces.com
Hertfordshire Constabulary	01234 846854	01234 846424	Abloads@herts.pnn.police.uk
Hertfordshire County Council	01992 658159	01992 658039	abnormal.loads@hertfordshire.gov.uk

TABLE A5.1 *continued*

Road/area or authority, etc	Tel:	Fax:	Email:
Hillingdon London Borough Council	01895 250442	01895 250676	abnormalloads@hillingdon.gov.uk
Hounslow London Borough Council	0208 538 5789		fazlul.huq@hounslowhighways.org
Humber Bridge Board	01482 647161	01482 640838	chris.day@humberbridge.co.uk
Humberside Police	01482 597683	01482 597645	AbnormalLoads@humberside.pnn.police.uk
Island Roads (Isle of Wight)	01983 828580		abnormalloads@islandroads.com
Jacobs UK Ltd (Berkshire, Havering London Borough and Windsor and Maidenhead Royal Borough Councils)	0118 946 7574		berks.abloads@jacobs.com
Kensington and Chelsea Royal London Borough Council	0207 341 5217	0207 370 5723	highways@rbkc.gov.uk
Kent County Council (inc Medway Unitary Council)	01622 695841		kcc@abloads.com
Kent Police	01622 798545	01622 798549	abloads@kent.pnn.police.uk
Kingston upon Hull City Council	01482 616545	01482 616567	abloads@hullcc.gov.uk
Kingston upon Thames, Royal Borough of			tracy.gossington@rbk.kingston.gov.uk
Knowsley Metropolitan Borough Council	0151 443 2226	0151 443 2335	abnormal.loads2@knowsley.gov.uk
Lambeth London Borough Council	0207 926 0680	0207 926 2357	jthillaivasan@lambeth.gov.uk

TABLE A5.1 *continued*

Road/area or authority, etc	Tel:	Fax:	Email:
Lancashire County Council	01772 534477		abloads@lancashire.gov.uk
Lancashire Police	01772 410787	01772 412481	AbnormalLoads@Lancashire.pnn.police.uk
Leeds City Council (inc Bradford City, Wakefield Metropolitan Council, Kirklees and Calderdale Councils)	0113 247 6174	0113 247 6357	abnormalloads@leeds.gov.uk
Leicester City Council	0116 223 2119	0116 229 4379	abloads@leicester.gov.uk
Leicestershire County Council	0116 305 7210	0116 305 7014	abloads@leics.gov.uk
Leicestershire Police	0116 248 2442	0870 7622925	ab.loads@leicestershire.pnn.police.uk
Lewisham London Borough Council	0208 314 2589	0208 690 4905	gill.redrup@lewisham.gov.uk
Lincolnshire County Council	01522 552379	01522 516716	ab_loads@lincolnshire.gov.uk
Lincolnshire Police	01522 558125	01522 558098	abnormalloads@lincs.pnn.police.uk
London Borough Council Unitary Authority	01582 546553	01582 547167	alan.pitkin@luton.gov.uk
London Borough of Islington	0207 527 2582	0207 527 2194	Barry.lucas@islington.gov.uk
London Tramlink (TfL)	07850 248425		darrensingh@tfl.gov.uk
London Underground Ltd	0207 027 8219	0207 918 3778	lulcedip@tube.tfl.gov.uk
*M1 – A1 Link (Lofthouse to Bramham)	0113 2814400	0113 2812238	christopher.haigh@balfourbeatty.com
*M40 (Denham to Warwick)	01707 608530	01707 608536	M40Abloads@carillionplc.com

TABLE A5.1 *continued*

Road/area or authority, etc	Tel:	Fax:	Email:
Merseyside Police	0151 777 3725		osu.abnormal.loads@merseyside.pnn.police.uk
Merseytravel	0151 330 4545		john.merrill@merseytravel.gov.uk
Merthyr Tydfil County and Borough Council	01685 726341	01443 693872	Carwyn.Morris@merthyr.gov.uk
Merton London Borough Council	0208 545 3106	0208 545 3038	trafficandhighways@merton.gov.uk
Metropolitan Police	0207 232 7486		abloads@met.police.uk
Middlesborough Council	01642 728644	01642 728969	abnormal_loads@middlesborough.gov.uk
Midland Expressway Ltd	01543 267000	01543 267005	control.room@m6toll.co.uk
Milton Keynes Unitary Authority	01908 252231	01908 252719	highwaystructures@milton-keynes.gov.uk
Monmouthshire Council	01633 644765	01633 644174	streetworks@monmouthshire.gov.uk
National Grid – Gas Distribution (Utility Company)	0800 688 588		plantprotection@nationalgrid.com
Neath Port Talbot County Borough Council	01639 686447	01639 686108	abloads@npt.gov.uk
Network Rail	01908 783 140		abnormalloadscontract@networkrail.co.uk
Network Rail LC and Rail over Road	01908 783 140		abnormal.loads@networkrail.co.uk
Newcastle City Council	0191 211 5966	0191 211 4843	abnormalloads@newcastle.gov.uk
Newham London Borough Council	0203 373 1841		Abloads.Notification@newham.gov.uk

TABLE A5.1 *continued*

Road/area or authority, etc	Tel:	Fax:	Email:
Norfolk Constabulary	01953 424672	01953 424656	Abnormalloads@norfolk.pnn.police.uk
Norfolk County Council	01603 223287	01603 627258	abnormalloads@norfolk.gov.uk
North and Mid Wales Trunk Road Agency	01286 685186		Enquiries@nmtra.org.uk
North East Lincolnshire Highways	01472 324539	01472 325657	abnormalloads@nelincs.gov.uk
North Lincolnshire Council Unitary Authority	01724 297520	01724 297880	highway.maintenance@ northlincs.gov.uk
North Somerset Council Unitary Authority	01275 884708	01934 426884	abnormal.loads@n-somerset.gov.uk
North Tyneside Metropolitan Borough Council	0191 643 6537	0191 643 2426	abloads@northtyneside.gov.uk
North Wales Police	01492 805407	01492 805409	abnormalloads@ nthwales.pnn.police.uk
North Yorkshire County Council	01609 785744	01609 781046	abnormalloads@jacobs.com
North Yorkshire Police	01904 618891	01904 618892	crsu@northyorkshire.pnn.police.uk
Northamptonshire County Council	01604 889985	01604 883456	northantsabloads@mgwsp.co.uk
Northamptonshire Police		01604 703417	abnormalloads@ northants.pnn.police.uk
Northern Gas Networks (Utility Company)	07721 648503		
Northern Power Grid (Utility Company)	0845 0707172		
Northumberland County Council	01670 624144	01670 625560	carolyn.woodhouse@ northumberland.gov.uk

TABLE A5.1 *continued*

Road/area or authority, etc	Tel:	Fax:	Email:
Northumbria Police	01661 869964	01661 868629	fru@northumbria.pnn.police.uk
Nottingham City Council	0115 8765405		abnormalloads@nottinghamcity.gov.uk
Nottinghamshire County Council	0115 9774490	0115 9772406	abnormalloads.EN@nottscc.gov.uk
Nottinghamshire Police	0115 9672143	0115 9672145	abloads@ nottinghamshire.pnn.police.uk
Oxfordshire County Council	01865 815741		bridges@oxfordshire.gov.uk
Pembrokeshire County Council	01437 776153	01437 775409	abloads@pembrokeshire.gov.uk
Philips 66	01469 555337		dan.smith2@p66.com
Plymouth City Council	01752 234400	01752 269327	plymouth.watchman@amey.co.uk
Police Scotland (all of Scotland)	101		abnormalloadsscotland@ scotland.pnn.police.uk
Poole Borough Council Unitary Authority	01202 262164	01202 262091	t.parfett@poole.gov.uk
Portsmouth City Council (Colas Ltd)	023 9231 0937	023 9231 0995	chris.dawkins@colas.co.uk
Powys County Council	01597 826619	01597 826628	highways.management@ powys.gov.uk
Reading Borough Council	0118 9500761 x460	0845 8620292	abnormalloadenquiries@ peterbrett.com
Redbridge London Borough Council	0208 708 3612	0208 708 3473	quyyom.ahmed@redbridge.gov.uk
Redcar and Cleveland Borough Council	01287 612543		engineering@redcar-cleveland.gov.uk

TABLE A5.1 *continued*

Road/area or authority, etc	Tel:	Fax:	Email:
Rhondda Cynon Taf County Borough Council	01443 494708		highwaysabnormalloads@rctcbc.gov.uk
Richmond upon Thames London Borough Council	0208 831 6033		HighwaysAndTransport@richmond.gov.uk
Road Management Services (RMS (A13) plc)	0207 510 9705	0207 987 2499	
Rotherham Metropolitan Borough Council	01709 822919	01709 372419	structures@rotherham.gov.uk
Rutland County Council Unitary Authority	01572 758285	01572 758307	gtoogood@rutland.gcsx.gov.uk
Sandwell Metropolitan Borough Council	0121 569 4726		ab_loads@sandwell.gov.uk
Sefton Metropolitan Borough Council	0151 934 4538	0151 934 4532	peter.mccabe@sefton.gov.uk
Serco Docklands	0207 363 9679	0207 363 9672	hayley.stock@sercodocklands.co.uk
Sheffield City Council			ssac.abloads@amey.co.uk
Shropshire Council	01743 254961	01743 254984	bridge.maintenance@shropshire.gov.uk
Skanska UK (Peterborough City Council)	01923 616264	0845 6017763	cambridgeshire.abloads@skanska.co.uk
Slough Borough Council	01454 662000 x2311	01454 663333	slough.abloads@atkinsglobal.com
Solihull Metropolitan Borough Council	0121 7046479		abnormalloads@solihull.gov.uk
Somerset County Council	01823 357562	01823 357551	somersetail@somerset.gov.uk

TABLE A5.1 *continued*

Road/area or authority, etc	Tel:	Fax:	Email:
South Gloucestershire Council	01454 868746		streetworks@southglos.gov.uk
South Ribble Borough Council	01772 625435	01772 622287	rhandscombe@southribble.gov.uk
South Tyneside Council	0191 4247621	0191 4549522	abloads@southtyneside.gov.uk
South Wales Police	01656 869379	01656 869397	abnormal.loads@ south-wales.pnn.police.uk
South Wales Trunk Road Agency	01792 325900	01792 325902	abnormalloads@southwales-tra.gov.uk
South Yorkshire Police	01142 202858	01142 523250	abnormal.loads@southyorks.pnn. police.uk
Southend on Sea Borough Council	01702 215719		richardatkins@southend.gov.uk
Southern Electric (Utility Company)	02392 624560	02392 624330	portsmouth.control.centre@sse.com
Southern Gas Networks (Scotia) (Utility Company)	0845 070 3497	0141 429 6432	plantlocation@sgn.co.uk
Southwark London Borough Council			leah.mellis@southwark.gov.uk
St Helens Metropolitan Borough Council	01744 676405		alanharrison@sthelens.gov.uk
Staffordshire County Council	01785 276721	01785 276712	abnormalloads@staffordshire.gov.uk
Staffordshire Police	01785 235025	01785 218714	tmu@staffordshire.pnn.police.uk
Stockton on Tees Borough Council	01642 526701	01642 526713	zoe.seaman@stockton.gov.uk
Stoke on Trent City Council	01782 231937	01782 232471	traffic.management@stoke.gov.uk

TABLE A5.1 *continued*

Road/area or authority, etc	Tel:	Fax:	Email:
Suffolk Constabulary	01953 424672	01953 424656	abnormalloads@norfolk.pnn.police.uk
Suffolk County Council	01473 264452	01473 216864	ail@suffolk.gov.uk
Sunderland City Council	0191 5617527	0191 5531464	networkoperations@ sunderland.gov.uk
Surrey County Council	0208 541 7450	0208 541 7377	abnormal.loads@surreycc.gov.uk
Surrey Police	0870 1224421	0870 1224420	Abloads@surrey.pnn.police.uk
Sussex Police	01273 404187	01273 404566	abloads.surrey-sussex.pnn.police.uk
Sutton London Borough Council	0208 770 6294		tamby.skanda@sutton.gov.uk
Swindon Borough Council	01793 445501	01793 466446	streetworks@swindon.gov.uk
Telford and Wrekin Borough Council	01952 384650	01952 384634	streetworks@telford.gov.uk
Thames Valley Police	01865 293422	01865 293726	abloads@thamesvalley.pnn.police.uk
The Highways Agency (Historical Railways Estate)	0118 946574		rsgbrb@jacobs.com
The Tamar Bridge	01752 361577	01752 360528	abnormalloads@tamarcrossings.org.uk
Thurrock District Council Unitary Authority	01279 507346	01279 758219	thurrock.routing@ pellfrischmann.com
Torbay Council	01803 207727	01803 207639	rob.ketch@torbay.gov.uk
Total Lindsey Oil Refinery	01469 563452	01469 563766	manuel.tortosa-perez@total.com
Tower Hamlets London Borough Council	0207 3646752		martin.waugh@towerhamlets.gov.uk

TABLE A5.1 *continued*

Road/area or authority, etc	Tel:	Fax:	Email:
Transport for Greater Manchester (inc Rochdale, Salford, Wigan, Trafford, Tameside, Stockport, Oldham, Bury and Bolton Metropolitan Borough Councils)			abnormal.loads@tfgm.com
Transport for London			abnormalloads@tfl.gov.uk
TT2 Ltd	0191 2598123	0191 2631031	s.sutton@tt2.co.uk
Tyne and Wear Metro (Nexus)	0191 2033367	0191 2033144	jonathan.watkins@nexus.org.uk
UK Power Networks (Utility Company)	0800 056 5866		
Vale of Glamorgan Council	02920 673105	02920 673114	cbright@valeofglamorgan.gov.uk
Wales & West Utilities (Utility Company)			plantprotectionenquiries@ wwutilities.co.uk
Walsall Council	01922 654645	01922 654800	griffithss@walsall.gov.uk
Waltham Forest London Borough Council	0208 496 2528	0208 496 2530	highways.admin@ walthamforest.gov.uk
Wandsworth London Borough Council	0208 871 8052	0208 871 0218	abloads@wandsworth.gov.uk
Warrington Borough Council	01925 442540	01925 443324	bridges@warrington.gov.uk
Warwickshire County Council	01926 412585 x2585	01926 412903	abnormalloads@warwickshire.gov.uk
Warwickshire Police	01926 415847	08702 413868	warwicks.abloads@btconnect.com
Welsh Assembly			Mark.Suller@Wales.GSI.gov.uk

TABLE A5.1 *continued*

Road/area or authority, etc	Tel:	Fax:	Email:
West Berkshire Council Unitary Authority	01635 519107 x2107	01635 519637	HTabloads@westberks.gov.uk
West Mercia Police	01905 727532	01386 565 878	abloads.hq@westmercia.pnn.police.uk
West Midlands Police	0121 3226018	0121 3226039	abnormal.loads@ west-midlands.pnn.police.uk
West Sussex County Council	0330 2226379	01243 777845	ENVAbloads@westsussex.gov.uk
West Yorkshire Police	01924 293138	01924 293123	abnloads@westyorkshire.pnn.police.uk
Western Power Distribution (S Wales) (Utility Company)	0845 601 2989		
Western Power Distribution (S Western) (Utility Company)	0845 601 3341		
Westminster City Council	0207 394 3879	0207 394 2638	abloads@fmconway.co.uk
Wiltshire Council	01225 713496	01225 713309	abnormalloads@wiltshire.gov.uk
Wiltshire Police	01380 731488	01380 738690	abnormal.loads@ wiltshire.pnn.police.uk
Wirral Council	0151 6062370	0151 6062405	traffic.co-ord@wirral.gov.uk
Wokingham Borough Council Unitary Authority	0118 974 6816	0118 974 6313	abnormalloads@wokingham.gov.uk
Wolverhampton City Council	01902 555432	01902 555796	keith.bradshaw@ wolverhampton.gov.uk
Worcestershire County Council	01905 361290	01905 361236	abloads@worcestershire.gov.uk
Wrexham County Borough Council	01978 729723	01978 729676	abnormal_loads@wrexham.gov.uk

If any operator has questions relating to the movement of AILs they should contact the telephone helpdesk operated by the Electronic Service Delivery for Abnormal Loads (ESDAL) organization on 0300 470 3733. The helpdesk is open from 8.00 am to 6.00 pm, Monday to Friday.
Details can also be found at:

ESDAL
Highways England
Great North House
20 Allington Way
Darlington
DL1 4QB
Tel: 0300 470 3733
Email: esdalenquiries@highwaysengland.co.uk.

APPENDIX VI

UK Bridge, Tunnel and Toll Road Tolls

Bridge tolls are no longer charged in Scotland although there are many minor tolls and charges placed on river crossings. These can range from a few pence to a fee based on a sliding scale dependant on the number of crossings. It is also worth noting that there are tunnel and motorway tolls throughout both Europe and the Republic of Ireland.

Dartford River Crossing

TABLE A6.1

Vehicle	Single journey	(2200–0600)
Motor car, including motor car with three wheels or taxi	£2.50	FREE
Light or medium goods vehicle, motor coach, omnibus or tractor, having no more than two axles	£3.00	FREE
Heavy goods vehicle, motor coach or omnibus having more than two axles	£6.00	FREE

Dart-Tag

Discount charges apply to account customers who are holders of Dart-Tags as follows:

TABLE A6.2

	Day	Night 2200–0600
Car	£1.67	FREE
Two-axle goods vehicles	£2.63	FREE
Multi-axle goods vehicles	£5.19	FREE

Towed trailers are now free.

Different height limits apply: vehicles of more than 4.8 metres height can only use the Eastern Tunnel whilst vehicles of more than 5.0 metres height cannot use the tunnels at all. There is an information line for assistance on 0300 123 5000.

Overheight or oversize vehicles and vehicles carrying dangerous goods are detected on their approach. Overheight and oversize vehicles are stopped and diverted away from the tunnels, whilst vehicles carrying dangerous goods are diverted to await an escort vehicle.

The tunnel authorities use traffic lights and barriers to stop oversize vehicles and this does cause delays to all traffic. Offenders can, if necessary, be prosecuted, fined and receive penalty points on their driving licences.

There are additional charges for AILs transiting the bridge and the tunnels. Operators need to contact the authorities on the website below.

Local residents are able to subscribe to an annual 'local residents scheme' where they can have an annual number (currently 50) of free crossings per year and then additional crossings at a much reduced fee. Details can be found on the Dart-Tag website.

Breakdown Recovery

Breakdown recovery of vehicles causing an obstruction on the carriageway within the Crossing area will be undertaken free of charge to the nearest place of safety at the Crossing.

Note: from October 2014 payment is not able to be made at the barriers. Drivers need to pay in advance, or before midnight the day after the crossing. To pay in advance, accounts can be set up or payment can be made online, by text, by telephone or by post. Payments can be made for several crossings or even single crossings. (Single crossing payments can also be paid by paying at one of several retail outlets or even using the 'pingit' app.). There are also local resident discount schemes and discounts for some disabled drivers. Further details can be found at the Dartford Crossing website: https://tfl.gov.uk/modes/driving/congestion-charge/dart-charge (archived at https://perma.cc/Z9WY-75UU).

Forth Road Bridge and Queensferry Crossing

Although bridge tolls are no longer charged in Scotland, at the time of writing there is a 193 tonne weight limit and a single axle weight limit of 16 tonnes being enforced on the Forth bridge. In addition, no more than two vehicles over 80 tonnes may use the bridge at the same time, and they are subject to a 15 mph speed limit whilst on the bridge. There are also restrictions on vehicle and load width (2.90 m) and length (18.65 m) where advanced notification to the bridge authorities is required.

The Queensferry Crossing opened in 2017 and is in effect a two-lane motorway crossing close to the older Forth Road Bridge. The new bridge required major alterations to the M9 motorway both north and south. However, at the time of writing there appears to be few restrictions as the bridge has already carried a vehicle weighing 180 tonnes. Further details can be found at forth-bridges.co.uk/queensferry-crossing/about (archived at https://perma.cc/C63G-GQQ4).

Humber Bridge

TABLE A6.3

	Single crossing	Discounted price per book of 20 tickets
Cars and goods vehicles having a maximum weight not exceeding 3.5 tonnes Motor caravans	£1.50	£27.00
Goods vehicles having a maximum gross vehicle weight exceeding 3.5 tonnes but not exceeding 7.5 tonnes Vehicles within Class 2 above, with trailers Small buses (with seating for 9–16 passengers)	£4.00	£72.00
Goods vehicles having a maximum gross vehicle weight exceeding 7.5 tonnes with two axles Large buses (with seating for 17 or more passengers)	£4.00	£72.00
Goods vehicles having a maximum gross vehicle weight exceeding 7.5 tonnes with three axles	£12.00	£216.00
Goods vehicles having a maximum gross vehicle weight exceeding 7.5 tonnes with four or more axles	£12.00	£216.00

The Humber Bridge now also operates an electronic TAG scheme which provides a 10 per cent discount on the prices above.

NB: The fees for crossing the Humber Bridge were frozen for five years in 2016.

Abnormal Loads

An additional scale of charges applies to abnormal load movements across the bridge. See www.humberbridge.co.uk (archived at https://perma.cc/G7JL-69A2).

Mersey Tunnel

TABLE A6.4

	Standard	Fast Tag
Private/light goods vehicle up to 3.5 tonnes (ie under 1.525 tonnes unladen)	£1.80	£1.20
Private/light goods vehicle up to 3.5 tonnes, with trailer	£3.60	£2.40
Heavy goods vehicle over 3.5 tonnes, with two axles	£3.60	£2.40
Heavy goods vehicle over 3.5 tonnes, with three axles	£5.40	£3.60
Heavy goods vehicle over 3.5 tonnes, with four or more axles	£7.20	£4.80

NB: Additional charges of £20.00–£45.00 are made for escorts and for breakdowns and a further surcharge of £16.00 is levied if these charges or the tolls above are not paid within 14 days.

Severn Crossings

The tolls for both of the Severn Crossings were abolished from 17 December 2018.

Skye Bridge

Bridge tolls are no longer charged in Scotland.

Tamar Bridge and Torpoint Ferry

TABLE A6.5

	Cash toll	Discount toll
Vehicles up to 3.5 tonnes mgw and up to eight seats Cars, vans, motorcycle combinations	£1.50	75p
Vehicles over 3.5 tonnes mgw and vehicles with more than eight seats according to axle count:		
two axles:	£3.70	£1.85
three axles:	£6.00	£3.00
four+ axles:	£8.20	£4.10
Vehicles towing trailers	charge is doubled	

Tolls, which were frozen from January 2015 for four years, are payable eastbound only. Tolls for drivers using the Tamar Tag system benefit from a 50 per cent discount in all charge bands. Vehicles towing trailers are subject to a 100 per cent surcharge and so pay a 'double charge' for crossing.

NB: Vehicles exceeding 18 tonnes mpw with more than 2 axles are not allowed to use the Torpoint Ferry.

Special toll rates apply to abnormal loads. See www.tamarcrossings.org.uk (archived at https://perma.cc/4HSC-R5TW).

NB: This website address also contains PDF files with detailed information relating to different types of abnormal loads hoping to use the crossings.

Tyne Tunnel

TABLE A6.6

	Standard	Permit holder
Car or light van (up to 3,500 kg gross weight with two axles)	£1.80	£1.62
Goods vehicle or passenger-carrying vehicle (over 3,500 kg gross weight with three or more axles)	£3.60	£3.24

M6 Toll Road

TABLE A6.7

Main Toll Plazas	Weeford Park (between T4 & T3 – southbound) or Great Wyrley (between T6 & T7 – northbound)
Junction Toll Plazas	Langley Mill (T3), Weeford Junction (T4), Shenstone (T5) or Burntwood (T6)

Tolls at the local toll plazas are less than those at the main toll plazas as the vehicle will only travel on part of the toll road and not the full route.

TABLE A6.8 Main Toll Plaza

Vehicle	Mon–Fri 0700–1900	TAG (5% discount)	Sat–Sun 0500–2300	TAG (5% discount)	Night 2300–0500	TAG (5% discount)
Van and Coach Class 4	£11.80	£11.21	£10.10	£9.60	£9.00	£8.55
HGV and Coach Class 5	£12.00	£11.40	£10.30	£9.79	£9.10	£8.65

Morning off peak (05.00–07.00) and evening off peak (19.00–23.00) attract a 10p or 20p discount.

NB: These prices are declared by the toll authorities as a 'guide' only as tolls do vary depending upon demand. Further details can be found on the website: www.m6toll.co.uk (archived at https://perma.cc/4DXW-4E6Q) *or by calling the toll road customer service team on 0330 660 0790.*

APPENDIX VII

Dimensions, Weights and Capacities for ISO Containers (Imperial and Metric Units)

The dimensions below are for the ISO dry steel containers because these are the most commonly used containers. Details of refrigerated containers, open top containers, flat rack containers, collapsible containers, hanger containers and aluminium containers etc can be found by visiting any of the container shipping company websites. These details are courtesy of the Mr Box Containers website: www.mrbox.co.uk (archived at https://perma.cc/M6CU-HFVN).

TABLE A7.1 20 ft steel dry container

Exterior			Interior		
Length	**Width**	**Height**	**Length**	**Width**	**Height**
19′10″	8′0″	8′6″	19′4″	7′8 19/32″	7′10″
6.06 m	2.44 m	2.6 m	5.9 m	2.35 m	2.39 m
Weight			**Door opening**		
MGW	**TARE**	**NET**		**Width**	**Height**
52,910 lb	5,140 lb	47,770 lb		7′8″	7′5″
67,200 lb	5,290 lb	61,910 lb		2.34 m	2.28 m
24,000 kg	2,330 kg	21,670 kg		**Cu. mtre**	**Cu. feet**
30,480 kg	2,240 kg	28,240 kg		33.1	1,170

TABLE A7.2 40 ft steel dry container

Exterior			Interior		
Length	Width	Height	Length	Width	Height
40′0″	8′0″	8′6″	39′5″	7′8″	7′10″
12.2 m	2.43 m	2.59 m	12.04 m	2.35 m	2.39 m
Weight			Door opening		
MGW	TARE	NET		Width	Height
67,200 lb	8,820 lb	58,380 lb		7′8″	7′5″
30,480 kg	4,000 kg	26,480 kg		2.34 m	2.24 m
				Cu. mtre	Cu. feet
				67.6	2,386

TABLE A7.3 40 ft high cube steel dry container

Exterior			Interior		
Length	Width	Height	Length	Width	Height
40′0″	8′0″	9′6″	39′5″	7′8″	8′10″
12.2 m	2.43 m	2.89 m	12.04 m	2.35 m	2.69 m
Weight			Door opening		
MGW	TARE	NET		Width	Height
67,200 lb	9,260 lb	57,940 lb		7′5″	8′5″
30,480 kg	4,200 kg	26,280 kg		2.34 m	2.58 m
				Cu. mtre	Cu. feet
				76.2	2,700

TABLE A7.4 45 ft high cube steel dry container

Exterior			Interior		
Length	Width	Height	Length	Width	Height
40′0″	8′0″	9′6″	39′5″	7′8″	8′10″
12.2 m	2.43 m	2.89 m	12.04 m	2.35 m	2.69 m
Weight			**Door opening**		
MGW	**TARE**	**NET**		**Width**	**Height**
67,200 lb	9,260 lb	57,940 lb		7′5″	8′5″
30,480 kg	4,200 kg	26,280 kg		2.34 m	2.58 m
				Cu. mtre	**Cu. feet**
				76.2	2,700

There are also 48 ft and 53 ft ISO containers but their use is limited in road transport.

Further information or details can be obtained from Mr Box; Tel: 0800 783 9885 or 01473 833775 or by emailing: sales@mrbox.co.uk.

APPENDIX VIII

Permissible Maximum Vehicle Dimensions in Europe

TABLE A8.1

Country	Height	Width	Length		
			Lorry or trailer	Road train	Articulated vehicle
Albania	4 m	2.55 m (3)	12 m	18.75 m	16.50 m
Armenia	4 m	2.55 m	12 m	20 m	20 m
Austria	4 m	2.55 m (3)	12 m	18.75 m	16.50 m
Azerbaijan	4 m	2.55 m	12 m	20 m	
Belarus	4 m	2.55 m (3)	12 m	20 m	24 m
Belgium	4 m	2.55 m (3)	12 m	18.75 m	16.50 m
Bosnia and Herzegovina	4 m	2.55 m (3)	12 m	18.75 m	16.50 m
Bulgaria	4 m	2.55 m	12 m	18.75 m	16.50 m
Croatia	4 m	2.55 m (3)	12 m	18.75 m (13)	16.50 m
Czech Republic (4)	4 m	2.55 m (3)	12 m	18.75 m	16.50 m
Denmark	4 m	2.55 m (3)	12 m	18.75 m	16.50 m
Estonia	4 m	2.55 m (3)	12 m	18.75 m	16.50 m
Finland (1)	4.40 m	2.60 m (6)	12 m	25.25 m	16.50 m
France	not defined	2.55 m (3)	12 m	18.75 m	16.50 m
FYROM	4 m (2a)	2.55 m (3)	12 m	18.75 m	16.50 m

TABLE A8.1 *continued*

Country	Height	Width	Length		
			Lorry or trailer	Road train	Articulated vehicle
Georgia	4 m (18)	2.55 m (3)	12 m	18.75/ 20 m (19)	16.50 m
Germany	4 m	2.55 m (3)	12 m	18.75 m	16.50 m
Greece	4 m	2.55 m	12 m	18.75 m	16.50 m
Hungary	4 m	2.55 m (3)	12 m	18.75 m (14)	16.50 m
Iceland	4.20 m	2.55 m (3)	12 m	22 m	18.75 m
Ireland	4.65 m	2.55 m (3)	12 m	18.75 m (7)	16.50 m
Italy (2)	4 m	2.55 m (3)	12 m	18.75 m	16.50 m
Latvia	4 m	2.55 m (3)	12 m	18.75 m	16.50 m
Liechtenstein	4 m	2.55 m (3)	12 m	18.75 m	16.50 m
Lithuania	4 m	2.55 m (3)	12 m	18.75 m (4)	16.50 m
Luxembourg	4 m	2.55 m (3)	12 m	18.75 m	16.50 m
Malta	4 m	2.55 m (3)	12 m	18.75 m	16.50 m
Moldova	4 m (9)	2.60 m	12 m	18.75 m	16.50 m
Netherlands (8)	4 m	2.55 m (3)	12 m	18.75 m	16.50 m
Norway	not defined	2.55 m (3)	12 m	19.50 m (10)	17.50 m
Poland	4 m	2.55 m (3)	12 m	18.75 m	16.50 m
Portugal (2)	4/4.15 m (2)	2.55 m (3)	12 m	18.75 m	16.50 m
Romania	4 m	2.55 m	12 m	18.75 m	16.50 m
Russia	4 m	2.55 m (3)	12 m	20 m	20 m
Serbia	4 m	2.55 m (3) 3.00 m (15)	12 m	18.75 m	16.50/ 21.00 m (16)
Slovakia	4 m	2.55 m (3)	12 m	18.75 m	16.50 m
Slovenia	4.2 m	2.55 m (3)	12 m	18.75 m (17)	16.50 m

TABLE A8.1 *continued*

Country	Height	Width	Length		
			Lorry or trailer	Road train	Articulated vehicle
Spain	4 m (11)	2.55 m (3)	12 m	18.75 m (12)	16.50 m
Sweden	not defined	2.60 m	24 m	25.25 m (5)	24 m
Switzerland	4 m	2.55 m (3)	12 m	18.75 m	16.50 m
Turkey	4 m	2.55 m (3)	12 m	18.75 m	16.50 m
Ukraine	4 m (9)	2.60 m	22 m	22 m	22 m
United Kingdom	not defined	2.55 m (3)	12 m	18.75 m	16.50 m

(Note the proposal relating to the fitting of aerodynamic kits to some goods vehicles, mentioned in Chapter 11.)

Notes

1 For vehicles registered in an EEA member country.

2 Increased values are applicable for certain types of transport (ie containers, motorcars, etc);

2a Increased value = 4.10 m.

3 Vehicles at controlled temperatures = 2.60 m.

4 Road train specialized in the carriage of cars: height = 4.20 m; length = 20.75 m.

6 Road train (total length over 22 m); width = 2.55 m as from 1 January 2010. Road train (>22 m) units and coaches fitted with a new vehicle body on 1 October 2004 or later; width = 2.55 m. Vehicles at controlled temperatures.

7 But may be allowed up to 22 m subject to certain restrictions.

8 Under specific conditions EMS (European Modular System) combinations may have a max length of 25.25 m and max weight of 60 tons. Domestic transport of 45 ft containers is accepted with combinations of vehicles (tractor – trailer – container) of max length of 17.27 m (B) or 17.30 m (NL). The maximum overhang of the container to the rear of the semi-trailer shall not exceed 0.77 m (B).The maximum overhang of the container to the (rear) underrun protection shall not exceed 0.40 m B) or 0.60 m (NL).

9 Container trucks = 4.35 m.

10 Heavy goods vehicles specially designed for the transport of timber = 24 m. EMS (European Modular System) combinations up to 25.25 m.

11 Auto-transport specialized in transporting vehicles, cranes for removal of vehicles, vehicles transporting containers approved for combined transport = 4.50 m.

12 Road train specialized in the carriage of cars (loaded) = 20.55 m.

13 Road train specialized in the carriage of cars (loaded) = 21 m.

14 Lorry with two trailers = 24 m.

15 Vehicle type N, which has removable devices for road maintenance.

16 Road train or articulated vehicle specialized in the carriage of containers or cars.

17 Specialized in transporting vehicles (only on motorways, dual carriageways and major roads) = 22.00 m.

18 Vehicles specialized in the carriage of cars and vehicles specialized in the carriage of containers: heights = 4.30 m.

19 Specialized road train.

These figures were correct at the time of writing but operators need to appreciate that figures can change with little or no notice.

APPENDIX IX

Permissible Maximum Vehicle Weights in Europe (Tonnes)

TABLE A9.1

Country	Weight per bearing axle	Weight per drive axle	Lorry 2 axles	Lorry 3 axles	Road train 4 axles	Road train 5 axles and +	Articulated vehicle 5 axles and +
Albania	10	11.5 (3)	18	26 (2)	36	40	44
Armenia	10	10	18	22	36 (19)	36 (19)	36 (19)
Austria	10	11.5	18	26	36	40/44 (10)	40/44 (10)
Azerbaijan	10	10	18	24	36	42	44
Belarus	10	10/11.5	18/20	25	38/40	40/42	42/44
Belgium	10	12	19	26	39	44	44 (1)
Bosnia and Herzegovina	10	11.5	19	26	38	40	40
Bulgaria	10	11.5	18	26 (2)	36	40	40
Croatia	10	11.5	18	26 (2)	36	40	40/44 (10)
Czech Republic	10	11.5	18	26 (2)	36	42/48 (2)	42/48
Denmark	10	11.5	18	26 (36)	38	42/56 (35)	42/56 (12, 35)
Estonia	10	11.5	18	26 (2, 34)	36 (4)	40 (5)	40/44 (5, 13)
Finland (6)	10	11.5	18	26 (2)	36	44/76 (7)	42/48

TABLE A9.1 *continued*

Country	Weight per bearing axle	Weight per drive axle	Lorry 2 axles	Lorry 3 axles	Road train 4 axles	Road train 5 axles and +	Articulated vehicle 5 axles and +
France	13/12 (31)	13/12 (31)	19	26	38	40/44 (32)	40/44 (32)
North Macedonia	10	11.5	18	25	36 (4)	40	40
Georgia	10	11.5	18	25/26 (46)	36	40	40/42 (50)/44 (51)
Germany	10	11.5	18	26 (2)	36	40	40
Greece	7/10	13	19	26	33 (20)/ 38 (21)	42	42/44 (13)
Hungary	10	11.5 (37)	18 (38)	25 (39)	36 (40)	40	40/44 (8)
Iceland	10	11.5	18	26 (2)	36	40	44
Ireland	10	11.5 (9)	18	26 (43)	36	44 (2)/46 (44)	44 (2)/46 (45)/44 (13)
Italy	12	12	18	26 (2)	40	44	44
Latvia	10	11.5	18	25/26 (46)	36	40	40/44 (13)
Liechtenstein	10	11.5	18	26 (2)	36	40	40
Lithuania	10	11.5	18	26 (2)	36	40	40/44 (10)
Luxembourg	10	12 (11)	19	26	44	44	44
Malta	10	11.5	18	25	36	40	40/44 (8)
Moldova	10	11.5	20	24	36	40	40/44 (8)
Netherlands (12)	10	11.5	21.5	21.5/ 30.5 (22)	40	50	50
Norway (12)	10	11.5	19	26	39	46/50 (23)	46/50 (24)

TABLE A9.1 *continued*

Country	Weight per bearing axle	Weight per drive axle	Lorry 2 axles	Lorry 3 axles	Road train 4 axles	Road train 5 axles and +	Articulated vehicle 5 axles and +
Poland	10	11.5	18	26 (2)	36	40	40
Portugal	10/12 (49)	12	19	26	37	40/44 (25)/60 (49)	40/44 (26)
Romania	10	11.5	18	25/26 (46)	36	40	40/44 (13)
Russia	10	10/11.5 (27)	18	25/28 (28)	36/32 (29)	40/44 (41)	40/44 (41)
Serbia	10	11.5	18	25/26 (34)	36/33 (33, 1)	40	40/44 (8, 25)
Slovakia	10	11.5	18	26 (2)	36	40	40
Slovenia	10	11.5	18	25/26 (34)	36	40	40/44 (47)
Spain	10	11.5	18	25/26 (34)	36 (33)	40	42 (14)/44 (13)
Sweden	10	11.5	18	26 (46)	38	48/64 (30)	48/64 (30)
Switzerland	10	11.5	18	26 (2)	36	40	40
Turkey	10	11.5	18	25/26 (16)	36/32 (29) 38 (48)	40	40/44 (10)
Ukraine	11	11	16 (17)	22 (17)	38 (17)	38 (17)	38 (17)
United Kingdom	10	11.5	18	26 (42)	38	40/44 (18)	40/44 (10,18)

Notes

1. 2 axles tractor + 3 axles semi-trailer: mechanical suspension = 43 t; pneumatic suspension = 44 t.
2. Only with air suspension or similar, and ABS (Anti-lock Braking System).
3. Weight per drive axle: national traffic = 10 t; international traffic = 11.5 t; lorry 3 axles: national traffic = 24 t; international traffic = 26 t.
4. 3 axle tractor + 1 axle trailer = 35 t.
5. 3 and + axles tractor + 3 and + axles trailer = 44 t.
6. For vehicles registered in an EEA member country.
7. 5 axles = 44 t; 6 axles = 56 t; 7 axles = 60 t, 8 axles 64–68 t (restrictions for ADR), 69–76 t (not for ADR).
8. 44 t is applicable for 40 feet long ISO containers.
9. Weight per drive axle: mechanical suspension (national traffic) = 10.5 t; road friendly suspension (national traffic) = 11.5 t; international traffic = 11.5 t.
10. For vehicles engaged in combined transport. In Austria – initial and final road hauls in combined transport to/from the nearest technically suitable terminal in Austria.
11. Weight per drive axle: mechanical suspension = 11.5 t.
12. Under specific conditions EMS (European Modular System) combinations may have a maximum length of 25.25 m and maximum mass of 60 t.
13. 3 axle motor vehicle with 2 or 3 axle semi-trailer carrying a 40 feet ISO container as a combined transport operation.
14. 2 axle motor vehicle with 3 axle semi-trailer carrying a 40 feet ISO container as a combined transport operation.
15. 5 axles = 48 t; 6 axles = 58 t; 7 axles = 60 t.
16. With the conditions laid down in Regulation for type approval.
17. Container trucks 2 axles = 18 t; 3 axles = 24 t; road train 4 axles, 5 axles and + and articulated vehicles 5 axles and + = 44 t; container trucks licensed by the state Motor Road service of Ukraine and State Traffic Inspection Department: road trains and articulated vehicle 5 axles and + = 46 t.
18. For general operation at 44 t, at least 6 axles are required. The drive axle(s) must not exceed 10.5 t and have twin tyres / road friendly suspension. Vehicles not having road friendly suspension on the drive axle(s) must have twin tyres and a maximum axle weight not exceeding 8.5 t. Each part of the combination must have at least 3 axles and the trailer must have road friendly suspension.
19. Above the authorized weight of 36 tonnes, each additional tone is subject to a fine of 55 AMD (1 USD = 364 AMD) per km.
20. 3 axle tractor + 1 axle trailer.

21 2 axle motor vehicle with 2 axle semi-trailer carrying a container = 40 t.

22 Depending on the distance between the axles, number of driven axles, type of suspension and single or double mounted tyres.

23 5 axles (3 + 2) = 46 t; 5 axles (2 + 3) = 47 t; 6 axles = 50 t; 60 t for timber transports between 19.50 and 24 meters with an overall wheelbase of at least 19 m.

24 5 axles [(2 + 3) fixed] = 43 t, 5 axles (2 + 3 [with a tandem axle with axle spacing 1.30 – 1.79 m followed by a positive steering axle at a distance of more than 1.79 m, where at least the fixed axles has twin wheels]) = 46 t; 5 axles (3 + 2 [axle spacing 1.30 – 1.79 m]) = 43 t; 5 axles (3 + 2 [axle spacing ≥ 1.80 m]) = 46 tonnes; 6 axles (3 + 3) = 50 t.

25 44 t is applicable for two 20′ ISO containers.

26 44 t is applicable for two 20′ or one 40′ ISO containers; 60 t under specific conditions: for the transportation of woody material, paper, wood paper and ceramic products.

27 11.5 t = only for the road sections constructed according to this norm.

28 28 t = only for 3 axle road train.

29 32 t = if 4 axle (single unit) lorry.

30 5 axles = 46 t, 6 axles = 64 t, 7 axles = 64 t.

31 13 t for trucks 1.8 m and the motor vehicle MMA is respected (18 t) and the MMA of the axle tandem of the semi-trailer (20 t).

32 When the semi-trailer (the wheelbase of the semitrailer is ≥ 1.8 m) is equipped with enhanced tipper body specifically for the use in construction or mining it will be 38 t, provided that the burden imposed on the coupling device is compatible with the maximum mass per axle.

33 For articulated vehicles with 4 axles = 38 t in the following cases: 1. When the driving axle is fitted with twin tyres and pneumatic suspension or recognized as equivalent to EU level, the wheelbase of the semitrailer is > 1.8 m and the motor vehicle MMA is respected (18 t) and the MMA of the axle tandem of the semitrailer (20 t). 2. When the semitrailer (the wheelbase of the semitrailer is > 1.8 m) is equipped with enhanced tipper body specifically for the use in construction or mining it will be 38 t, provided that the burden imposed on the coupling device is compatible with the maximum mass per axle.

34 When the driving axle is fitted and pneumatic suspension or recognized as equivalent to EU level, or where each driving axle is fitted with double tires and the MMA on each axle doesn't exceed 9.5 t = 26 t.

35 6 axles = 50 t; 7 axles = 56 t.

36 When the driving axle is fitted with double tires and pneumatic suspension 26 t, otherwise 24 t.

37 +20 per cent if the vehicle fitted on the same axle: a. with four or more wheels at least 0.65 meters distance from each other and two independent suspension, b. three or more wheels fitted with independent suspension.

38 20 t = only in national traffic.

39 26 t = road friendly suspension.

40 38 t = for a towing vehicle with a semi-trailer where the towing vehicle has a road friendly suspension and the wheelbase of the semi-trailer is ≥ 1.8 m.

41 6 axles and +.

42 Only with air suspension or similar.

43 Provided that the vehicle is equipped with twin tyres and an air suspension system or an equivalent system on each driving axle, OR is equipped with twin tyres and 2 driving axles neither of which transmits to the surface of a road a weight in excess of 9.5 tonnes.

44 6 or more axle rigid truck and drawbar trailer combinations may operate at 46 tonnes provided they are fitted with road friendly or equivalent suspension and electronic braking systems. Rigid trucks (with not more than 3 axles) first registered from 1st June 2015 must also be equipped with electronic stability control for 46 tonne operation, with drawbar trailers first licensed from 1st June 2015 requiring roll stability control. cf. http://www.rsa.ie/en/RSA/Your-Vehicle/Vehicle-Standards/Weights--Dimensions-/46-tonne-weight-limit-rigid-and-drawbar-trailer/ (archived at https://perma.cc/4BZQ-BYZS).

45 6 or more axle articulated vehicle combinations may operate at 46 tonnes provided they are fitted with road friendly or equivalent suspension and electronic braking systems. Tractor units first registered since 1st April 2013 must also be equipped with electronic stability control for 46 tonne operation, with semi-trailers first licensed since 1st April 2013 requiring roll stability control. cf. http://www.rsa.ie/en/RSA/YourVehicle/Vehicle-Standards/Weights--Dimensions-/46-tonne-weight-limit/ (archived at https://perma.cc/N3J5-GWNC).

46 For vehicles with three axles equipped with double mounted tires on running axle and with pneumatic suspension or an equivalent system to EU level, OR each running axle has double mounted tires and axle load less than 9, 5 t.

47 44 t is applicable for triaxial tractor with a two or triaxial trailer in combined transport transporting the container(s) or if the trailer has been strengthened for unattended transport service or if the trailer has been adapted for interchangeable load compartments, and on highway section A3 Terminal Sežana – Terminal Fernetiči, No. of section 0372.

48 Vehicles with 4 axles and axle group weight of 20 tonnes of the semi-trailers.

49 Increased values are applicable for certain types of transport. 3 August 2015.

50 Two-axle motor vehicle with three-axle semi-trailer carrying, in intermodal transport operations, one or more containers or swap bodies, up to a total maximum length of 45 feet.

51 Three-axle motor vehicle with two-or three-axle semi-trailer carrying, in intermodal transport operations, one or more containers or swap bodies, up to a total maximum length of 45 feet.

As in Appendix VIII the warning about any recent changes also applies to the data above.

APPENDIX X

Post-Brexit (General Requirements and Specific Options Summary)

This appendix is a summary of both deal and no-deal items that could not be included within the main text due to the great uncertainty as to the terms and conditions regarding the agreement (at the time of writing, yet to be reached) which will enable the UK to leave the EU. What could be included in relevant sections has been, but below are some issues for information and possible consideration by readers. These notes, by necessity, have been written as late as possible in 2019, as they were in 2018, but whilst they are based on GOV.UK releases there is no guarantee that the issues covered will be 100 per cent accurate.

It should be noted that in the event of a 'deal' being struck for the UK to leave the EU then there would be some changes from the way we operate today. Naturally, there are changes already mentioned in the text relating to the passport, driving licence format, GB plates, IDPs, trailer registration, etc, but many, many more changes will be required over the coming months and years once Brexit is agreed. If there is a no-deal Brexit then the UK effectively becomes a third-party country to the EU. In some respects, trade will be done in a way that is similar to how things were done before the UK joined the EU, but we will also need to adopt some completely new ways of trading and operating internationally, not least because of the march of technology and the need for international trade to be as seamless as possible.

Some of the changes in this appendix have been referred to in the various sections of the *Handbook*, but in order to be able to include the latest changes and proposals this appendix features recommendations and preferred actions contained within information releases made by HM Government.

In addition, it should be noted that, whilst some changes may be immediate, others will happen over declared transition and 'honeymoon' periods.

As a reminder, it may help to clarify some of the market issues that the UK will face. Firstly, in relation to Brexit, two trading areas and one other country will have an impact upon the UK's international freight industry trade post-Brexit:

- The European Union – The EU is an economic and political union of 27 countries. It operates as a 'single market' allowing goods, people and services to pass and operate freely between member states (Austria, Belgium, Bulgaria, Croatia, Republic of Cyprus, the Czech Republic, Denmark, Estonia, Finland, France, Germany, Greece, Hungary, Ireland, Italy, Latvia, Lithuania, Luxembourg, Malta, the Netherlands, Poland, Portugal, Romania, Slovakia, Slovenia, Spain, Sweden).

- The European Economic Area (EEA) – The EEA includes all the EU member states plus Iceland, Liechtenstein and Norway, which are also empowered to be a part of the EU's single market.
- Switzerland –Switzerland is not a member of either the EU or the EEA but is a part of the single market, and so its citizens and transport businesses broadly enjoy the same rights as EU/EEA citizens and transport businesses.

There will be no change to the rights and status of EU/EEA or Swiss citizens living in the UK until 2021. Those who choose to stay in the UK will simply need to apply for 'settled status' before June 2021.

We will now consider the actions that will need to be taken in order to trade with these areas and countries, before we look at some of the transport-specific issues.

NB: When we refer to the EU or EC in this appendix we include the EEA countries, as both areas are generally linked in the matters discussed below.

Trading with the EU

Below is an updated summary of the likely impact that both 'deal' and 'no-deal' situations would have on trade between the UK and the EU. Obviously, in the case of a deal then it is reasonable to assume that whatever is agreed will apply right across the EU. Unfortunately, in the event of a no-deal then each EU member state may be able to insist on individual rules, regulations and procedures, making the picture extremely confused in relation to the UK trading with Europe.

Basically, in the event of a no-deal, goods moving from the UK to the EU will become subject to the same customs and excise rules as current non-EU goods; goods moving from the EU to the UK may also become subject to import duty. This means that export and import declarations will need to be completed, as would safety and security declarations for goods from the EU to the UK and vice versa. Different rules will apply if moving excise goods.

Let us begin by looking at some basic trading rules. When trading either with or without a deal with the EU, the UK trader's Economic Operator Registration Identification (EORI) number will need to have a GB prefix. This changes if the UK trader needs to trade intra-EU, in which case they will require an EU-EORI number. This is important because if we need to comply with full Customs procedures it is absolutely vital to ascertain who actually needs the EORI number. It is also important due to the need to register for an EORI number, if one is required, as the status of 'exporter' or 'importer' must be met when applying and it is this that is important and not the actual ownership of the goods.

They will also need to decide how to classify the goods, using the Customs Tariff, and how to value them. It may be that many companies will choose to use the services of a Customs broker or agent.

When UK businesses import goods from the EU they will need their valid EORI number, to ensure that the carrier they use has submitted an Entry Summary Declaration (ENS) to HMRC, and to pay any VAT or import duty.

Businesses wishing to export goods to the EU will also need to register for a UK EORI number and to make sure that the terms of export are accurate and that they are registered as an exporter. They will also need to consider how to submit their export declarations and also possibly use the services of a Customs broker or agent.

When UK businesses export goods to the EU they will need the valid EORI number, to submit an Export Summary Declaration (EXS) to HMRC, and may need to apply for an export licence.

NB: Issues surrounding the movement of goods between Northern Ireland and the Republic of Ireland are, at the time of writing, not confirmed. One issue that does seem to have been resolved is that if goods are travelling from the mainland to Northern Ireland but it is 'possible/probable' that they may go to the Irish Republic then the EU rate of duty will need to be paid on the goods. Goods moving between Northern Ireland and the mainland, in either direction, will remain free from duty.

VAT is also an area where changes will be experienced if we leave with no deal. In short, trade with the EU will attract import duty and VAT but most World Trade Organization goods have been set at 0 per cent in order to mitigate this duty and the VAT. In addition, Inward Processing Relief is available on raw materials for processing and Outward Processing Relief is only paid on the increase in value of goods imported and then re-exported back to the EU. These are only two schemes aimed at enabling UK businesses to avoid some taxation and minimize other taxation, and UK businesses operating vehicles moving goods between the UK and Europe should seek advice on what schemes they may find beneficial.

In order to help businesses there will be a number of temporary offices set up at motorway and other service areas to offer advice and to offer to scrutinize paperwork for operators travelling to the channel ports in order to try to avoid problems at the embarkation point.

Whilst the changes are certainly a major issue there will be some sort of 'honeymoon' period, although how each EU member state will interpret this is unclear at the time of writing.

As a side issue, but one that may be of interest to some operators, on 1 January 2020 a new version of Incoterms will be available. In brief, Delivered at Terminal (DAT) becomes Delivered at Place Unloaded (DPU) but remains the same in all other respects as DAT. There are also minor changes to Carriage and Insurance Paid (CIP) and Cost Insurance and Freight (CIF), Free Carrier (FCA) and Free On Board (FOB). Whilst Incoterms 2020 can be used from 1 January, Incoterms 2010 may still be used providing that this is declared.

Having considered how import and export businesses may need to change following Brexit, we will now look at some transport-specific issues.

ECMT Permits

Because UK legislation will continue to comply with the requirements of the European Agreement Concerning the Work of Crews of Vehicles Engaged in International Road Transport (AETR), UK drivers will be able to operate in the EU when driving trucks covered by an ECMT permit or any newly agreed bilateral permit scheme, providing they meet licensing and other criteria.

If there is a no-deal EU exit, EU and EEA countries may not recognize UK-issued Community Licences/Licences for the Community (these are issued with the Standard International Operator's Licence), but a period of grace has been announced by the EU. That said, individual member states may decide to act unilaterally. Should this be the case, the UK would need to renegotiate new bilateral agreements or reinstate old bilateral agreements with individual EU and EEA countries in order to gain access for haulage operations.

Note that vehicles not exceeding 3.5 tonnes and those engaged in own-account operations are normally exempted from permit ECMT requirements, although France requires own-account operators to have permits for both delivery and transit. It should also be noted that ECMT permits do not allow cabotage operations; cabotage rules post-Brexit are outlined in Chapter 26.

The required bilateral permits are European Conference of Ministers of Transport (ECMT) permits, and are issued by the DVSA's International Road Freight Office (IRFO). They are currently limited in numbers under a quota system, although the numbers have been dramatically increased. ECMT permits allow haulage operations in the EU and EEA (except Cyprus) and 15 other countries. To apply for ECMT permits operators need to have a Vehicle Operator Licence (VOL) online account.

If you need an ECMT international road haulage permit to transport goods you will need to provide IRFO with the following information:

- Which of your current valid standard international or restricted goods operator licences do you want to use when you apply for an ECMT international road haulage permit?
- How many international trips did you make in the last 12 months using this goods operator licence? An outward and return trip counts as one journey (if you're an operator in Northern Ireland, licensed by the Department for Infrastructure, exclude journeys made from Northern Ireland to the Republic of Ireland).
- What percentage of your trips made in the last 12 months were international? You will need to provide a percentage bracket and will be given percentage bandings to make one choice.

When you apply, you will need to select which sector you mainly transport goods in. You'll have to select one category which represents the bulk of your international journeys from:

- chemicals;
- food products;
- furniture;
- metal;
- mail and parcels;
- raw materials and waste;
- refined fuels;
- transport and machinery;
- textiles;

- unrefined fuels;
- wood;
- other non-metallic mineral products;
- none of these sectors (you can select this if you don't transport goods mainly in one of the other categories).

You'll also need to consider the countries you intend to transport goods to over the next 12 months, as there are restrictions for some ECMT member countries.

There are also different types of ECMT permits. There are tightly controlled ECMT Multilateral Permits, which are quota permits. There are also ECMT International Removals Permits, which allow you to remove goods between or across ECMT member countries, and there are special permits for laden or empty transit journeys and third-country journeys between member countries.

The DVSA is concerned about the potential shortage of permits and expects demand to far outstrip its ability to supply the limited quantities it has. Because of this, permits will not be allocated on a 'first come, first served' basis, but rather according to criteria set out in regulations under the Haulage Permits and Trailer Registration Act 2018.

Hauliers should therefore consider how many permits they may require to operate internationally so they are ready to apply later in the year. Importantly, hauliers and businesses should consider what contingency plans they need to have in place for the movement of goods if they do not receive the number of permits they applied for (see below).

Hauliers and businesses will, of course, need to ensure the correct documentation and permissions are carried to be able to trade, including any permits, licences and proof of qualification. Businesses should also ensure they have the correct Customs documentation for the goods concerned.

Note 1: To apply for permits, hauliers will need a VOL online account.

Note 2: ECMT permits are valid up to one year but 'short-term' permits are available.

Note 3: ECMT permits are prioritized for regular international operations, and some ECMT permits are restricted to Euro VI vehicles.

Note 4: When operating under permits, a log book must be kept in the vehicle and completed, and a compliance certificate must also be kept in the vehicle along with the permit itself. Records from this log book are to be detached and sent to IRFO within two weeks of the end of each calendar month.

Further information can be obtained from:

DVSA International Road Freight Office
Hillcrest House
386 Harehills Lane
Leeds
LS9 6NF
Tel: 0300 123 9000/0113 202 6072

A list of the ECMT countries is below:

Albania
Armenia
Austria
Azerbaijan
Belarus
Belgium
Bosnia and Herzegovina
Bulgaria
Croatia
Czech-Republic
Denmark
Estonia
Finland
France
Georgia
Germany
Greece
Hungary
Ireland
Italy
Latvia
Liechtenstein
Lithuania
Luxembourg
FYR Macedonia
Malta
Moldova
Montenegro
Netherlands
Norway
Poland
Portugal
Romania
Russian Federation
Serbia
Slovak Republic
Slovenia
Spain
Sweden
Switzerland
Turkey
Ukraine
UK

NB: It is expected that operators with a Northern Ireland operator's licence will not be required to obtain an ECMT permit for a journey to the Republic of Ireland but other UK operators should apply for an ECMT permit if they intend to drive in the Republic of Ireland following Brexit, unless a deal is negotiated. Actual arrangements are unclear at the time of writing.

Borders and Traffic Management

A no-deal situation will almost certainly mean changes at border points. If nothing else, this will cause delays at ports and congestion on the routes to ports. Hauliers are being advised to consider using different (perhaps less congested) ports as alternatives and to consider alternative modes and procedures, such as containerization.

In particular, the DVSA suggests that hauliers and businesses should consider what contingency plans they need to have in place if there are delays at ports. These plans may include:

- planning alternative routes to move goods by roll-on/roll-off services;
- using alternative transport methods/modes, such as containerization or unaccompanied trailers;
- making appropriate arrangements to counter disruption to supply chains.

Hauliers, and businesses that use hauliers, should consider the implications of possible impacts on supply chains, including reduced capacity at ports, reduced reliability and potentially higher rates. There are also a host of other possible considerations, including changes to Movement Reference Number (MRN) requirements for France, (insofar that multiple MRNs on a consignment need to be scanned into the French 'smart' MRN website in order to produce a single MRN for scanning at check in), approval requirements for wooden pallets and changes to import and export procedures for Poland, planned for October 2020. The list goes on and on, but at the time of writing it is simply impossible to predict with any accuracy which of the planned changes will actually happen and, if they do, when that might be and the form they may take.

Where EU ports need to be used, traffic will be managed by the member state concerned and there will be changes. These include green lights for vehicles cleared on the ferry bound for France but an 'Orange Line' for vehicles disembarking but subject to French Customs scrutiny, where the driver will need to follow the orange arrows to a place of inspection. Although there are some different ways of working to come, the French and Belgian authorities have established check/information points on routes to the Channel ports where drivers can have their documentation checked prior to arrival at the ferry terminal.

In addition, there are issues such as phytosanitary checks which will be completed for traffic from the UK to the EU but are not, as yet, planned for traffic from the EU to the UK. Clearly, this will add delays and costs, as will any delay to the flow of goods, and it is also a fact that the volume of goods in the supply chain will have to rise dramatically in order to maintain adequate supply.

Note 1: In the event of delays at EU ports, the UK Government will implement contingency arrangements to manage the flow of traffic across the UK and plans known as Operation Brock and Operation Transition are in place to stack lorries, if required, for Dover and the Tunnel and Portsmouth respectively whilst 800 possible additional parking spaces have been made available for Holyhead. A major problem appears to be that, whilst there is space to stack lorries, there appear to be few driver facilities available (currently only at Manston, Kent) unless these are scheduled for later in the implementation procedures. The issue of drivers' hours also appears unclear should drivers be stacked for any considerable length of time.

Note 2: The DVSA also notes that agrifood goods may not be able to enter the EU except via a port with a Border Inspection Post (BIP). Certainly, Calais has already nominated areas of the port for the Customs processing of different types of goods such as temperature controlled and livestock, etc.

Vehicle Type Approval

This topic is only relevant in the event of a no-deal scenario. If this is the case, then UK type approval will not be valid for the EU market; and EC* type approval would not be valid for the UK market. This means that UK manufacturers of vehicles and components will need to get their products EC type approved for sales within the EU. This is not seen as a particular problem as the UK will continue to recognize UNECE type approvals. EU manufacturers would also need to ensure their goods met the UK type approval standards.

** The initials EC are used instead of EU due to EC type approval coming into effect before the term EU was used.*

In practice, it is proposed that the UK will accept the EC standards of type approval and so manufacturers with EC type approval will simply need to go through an administrative procedure to gain UK type approval. UK manufacturers will need to gain EC type approval from an EU type approval authority using the existing procedure for new products.

NB: Type approval applies to the following categories of goods vehicles: N1, N2 and N3, and trailers O1, O2, O3 and O4.

CO_2 Emissions

Currently, Regulation (EC) 443/2009 and Regulation (EU) 510/2011 are used by the UK to set CO_2 emission targets, and compliance, and information is sent to the European Commission. This will continue to be the case if a Brexit deal is struck. However, following a no-deal situation the DfT will bring the two regulations above into UK legislation, making adjustments as required to allow for a 'UK only' situation.

This means that adjustments (known as deficiencies) will be made to:

- the way CO_2 targets are set;
- derogation thresholds; and
- detailing how fines will be levied.

In effect, the DfT will take over the role of the European Environment Agency and set targets for UK manufacturers, monitor compliance and liaise with manufacturers, agree derogations and control CO_2 credits.

At the time of writing, Brexit negotiations and discussions are still ongoing. This appendix sketches out some of the 'most likely' outcomes based on current details and releases from HM Government; however, some of the detail we have outlined may not in fact come to fruition.

Preparation Overview

Clearly, there are several options still open to the Government as we approach Brexit. These include a hard Brexit, which means full Customs and border controls, and the soft Brexit option (the Norway model) with the UK remaining in the Customs Union and with few border checks.

Whichever option is decided upon, it is the professional operator that will need to manage any and all changes and in order to do that good planning and preparation are the key to reducing disruption as far as is reasonably possible. Various trade organizations also offer advice on the preparation that may be needed and most seem to agree that assessing the impact on the business should be the first step, followed by planning and associated training, resulting in the implementation of the required new ways of working.

To assess the impact, it's suggested that operators assess both the direct impact and the indirect impact of Brexit and that they work on a hard Brexit scenario in order to be able to plan for a Brexit that brings the most change.

In order to assess impact and to then try to minimize adverse effects, operators need to work with their suppliers, their customers and any service providers or partners they may have. This work to minimize adverse effects needs to cover all areas of the business, including supply chain operation, regulatory compliance, warehouse optimization, Customs procedures, taxation issues, human resources and systems compatibility. In addition, this work needs to look for the potential for new opportunities and ways of working that may enable operators to gain advantages from changed ways of working.

The DfT and DVSA are both working hard to produce advice and guidance on their websites, and the trade associations are also striving to encourage operators and members to plan for the changes that will undoubtedly result when we leave the EU. Operators are encouraged to sign up to receive the regular updates being produced by visiting www.gov.uk/help/update-email-notifications (archived at https://perma.cc/X2GT-SPFP).

A lot of the 'what if' circumstances and changes noted above are totally dependent upon the terms of the UK leaving the EU and so are liable to change, and it is also notable that most of the projected changes are based on a no-deal situation as the terms of any deal are simply impossible to predict.

Certainly by visiting the GOV.UK website regularly and/or registering on it in order to be kept informed of Brexit developments (both pre- and post-Brexit) operators will find masses of useful information and guidance to help them to manage the UK's transition to non-EU status.

More information in user-friendly format can be obtained from GOV.UK at:

www.gov.uk/brexit-haulage (archived at https://perma.cc/MZ3K-L894)
www.gov.uk/brexit-haulage-drivers (archived at https://perma.cc/N84M-9KBH)
www.gov.uk/brexit-haulage-vehicles (archived at https://perma.cc/J6EB-8643)

FURTHER INFORMATION

Driver and Vehicle Standards Agency (DVSA) Goods Vehicle Testing

Large goods vehicle testing continues to change. While testing continues in the public sector via the established network of D*f*T Goods Vehicle Testing Stations, public sector involvement is diminishing with more use being made of existing and new private sector testing stations to provide services at lower cost and at locations and times more convenient for the majority of customers. For example, LGV testing has been taking place for some time at non-DVSA sites called Authorized Testing Facilities (ATFs) where statutory LGV (and PSV) testing is carried out by DVSA staff using approved equipment. These facilities are authorized but not owned by the DVSA.

For further details of the new testing arrangements and links to LGV test booking facilities contact: https://www.gov.uk/government/organisations/vehicle-and-operator-services-agency (archived at https://perma.cc/W67S-899W) or www.dvsa.gov.uk (archived at https://perma.cc/RZU8-4MWM).

NB: Although VOSA no longer exists the acronym is still used on several Government websites.

Driver and Vehicle Standards Agency (DVSA) Area Offices and LGV Driving Test Centres

In July 2014, the DSA merged with VOSA to form the Driver and Vehicle Standards Agency (DVSA) which now controls information on all driving tests and facilities for booking driving tests. Further information can be found on the DVSA website www.dvsa.gov.uk (archived at https://perma.cc/RZU8-4MWM) or by contacting the DVSA Head Office at the address below:

DVSA
The Axis Building
112 Upper Parliament Street
Nottingham
NG1 6LP
Tel: 0300 200 1122 (Helpline)

Information relating to Periodic Driver CPC training, originally authorized by the then DSA, can be obtained by contacting The Joint Approvals Unit for Periodic Training (JAUPT): www.jaupt.org.uk (archived at https://perma.cc/2P2R-JZCX):

JAUPT,
9 Warren Yard,
Warren Park,
Stratford Road,
Milton Keynes,
MK12 5NW
enquiries@jaupt.org.uk
Tel: 0844 800 4184

Training Facilities for Dangerous Goods Drivers

A list of establishments, approved by the DVSA and SQA on behalf of the Department for Transport, provide training in the handling of various classes of dangerous goods for tanker vehicle drivers and for those drivers whose vehicles carry goods in packages – see Chapters 7 and 20 for full details of the relevant requirements.

NB: In England and Wales many private companies offer the DGSA and other DG training as do the CILT, RHA and FTA. The SQA have a list of Scottish providers which can be found on the SQA website at: www.sqa.org.uk (archived at https://perma.cc/P3LZ-7RGT). *Search for DGDT Approved Centre List. Permission has recently been given for ADR training to be incorporated into DCPC training. Candidates for training may be able to get further information from their training providers.*

Training Facilities for the Carriage of Livestock and Vehicle Certification

The training required by drivers in order to gain certification for some movements of livestock is offered by private organizations authorized to deliver the training by DEFRA. DEFRA have also authorized the FTA and some private companies to inspect and certify vehicles used to carry livestock. Details of these training and certification organizations can be found on the GOV.UK website under 'Animal Welfare'.

The organizations above and most of those mentioned in this book are all now contactable through the GOV.UK website, which contains information related to licensing, authorizations, legal positions and interpretations and the control and overseeing of most aspects of business and transport.

It should be noted that the international carriage of livestock and vehicle certification and specification could be areas where the UK's departure from the EU increases the compliance levels and requirements by individual European/EU countries for UK operators and those who may be affected when the UK leaves the EU and operators in this sector are advised to seek advice from DEFRA in order to avoid delays and problems when entering, transiting or leaving the EU.

General Training

As time progresses general training requirements become statutory obligations for many operators, drivers and employers. Training in MHE driving and operation, tail lift operation, mounted crane and double-deck operation along with hygiene, thermograph record keeping, Customs and border formalities, drivers' hours and tachographs, vehicle checking, security, etc is increasing in both volume and complexity and successful operators need to stay ahead of these changing requirements if they are to stay ahead of the competition.

The Government, the trade associations, the CILT and hundreds of private training providers can all provide training but it is largely the responsibility of the organization or employer to approach the training provider to try to develop training that is actually relevant and cost-effective and all operators and employers are advised to maintain close links with providers in order to ensure that any new requirements are not overlooked.

Given the UK's decision to leave the EU this must surely be a time when training needs will reach a peak as we need to change our old ways of working and develop new skills and techniques in order to maintain and grow our industry as the UK moves forward as a 'stand-alone' country. In reality, this is probably the greatest opportunity for business and for entrepreneurs to lay down the foundations on which the UK can build an ever stronger future transport industry.

INDEX

Note: page numbers in *italic* indicate figures or tables.